Aleksandr A. Svec

C000044329

STRATEGY

Edited by Kent D. Lee

Introductory essays by
Andrei A. Kokoshin
Valentin V. Larionov
Vladimir N. Lobov
Jacob W. Kipp

East View Publications
Minneapolis, Minnesota

PUBLICATIONS

3020 Harbor Lane N.
Minneapolis, Minnesota 55447 USA

Aleksandr Andreevich Svechin. Strategy.

A translation of: Strategiia. Moscow: Voennyi vestnik, 1927

Edited by Kent D. Lee.

Prefaces by Andrei A. Kokoshin, Valentin V. Larionov, Vladimir N Lobov, Jacob W. Kipp

ISBN 1-879944-33-2

First published in 1992. Third printing 1999.

Printed in Canada.

Library of Congress Cataloging-in-Publication Data:

CONTENTS

Appendices

FROM THE EDITOR

The intellectual rehabilitation of Aleksandr A. Svechin comes long overdue, correcting a historical injustice that has continued for nearly six decades. The publiciation of the premier work of his lifetime—the second edition of *Strategy*—in the English language now moves this rehabilitation effort into the international sphere, where historians and political scientists in many different lands will finally have an opportunity to judge him for his contributions. We think that this judgment will be quite favorable.

Svechin himself was tremendously influenced by the writings and analyses of the contemporary and classic European figures of his day. Struggling against the growing intellectual xenophobia and dogmatism that gradually dominated the Soviet military science establishment in the 1920s and 1930s, Svechin remained a cosmopolitan in the best sense of the word. To study war between states—an activity utterly antithetical to xenophobia—requires a deep understanding of other states' experiences and histories. Svechin's rich and integrated approach to this question put him head and shoulders above the rest of his colleagues. For this he paid dearly; first with his career, and ultimately with his life. It is a sad fate that he shares with far too many of Russia's best and brightest.

The publication of *Strategy* today, in the early 1990s, would be incomplete without some explanation of how it came about. Svechin's book, above all, represents his concept of the best approach to national security for the Soviet state. It is therefore quite logical that its rebirth should be linked to changes in current Soviet concepts of national security. Indeed it is.

Perhaps the most basic issue facing Mikhail Gorbachev upon his emergence as Soviet leader in early 1985 was the crushing Soviet defense burden, a gargantuan ball-and-chain on Soviet domestic and foreign policy development. New approaches to security were desperately required, approaches that would allow for resources to be shifted toward more productive ends. Foremost was required a change in the essence of Soviet military doctrine, which despite its claims to defensiveness was nonetheless based on an unambiguously offensive military strategy, which created and/or maintained enemies abroad (thus keeping the Soviets firmly in the grasp of the "security dilemma," which required ever-increasing defense expenditures) and well as bled the Soviet economy white as the technological imperatives of modern warfare in and of themselves demanded more resources.

Accordingly, the conceptual foundations had to be laid first. Such was the background to "new thinking" and "reasonable sufficiency," buzzwords that almost seem quaint now, in the aftermath of the monumental events of 1989 and 1990. Many commentators in the USSR weighed in with their contributions to these concepts, but a select few approached the issue in a unique way. Defensive thinking in the USSR, they argued, has important historical roots that cannot be ignored. Such thinking was legitimate back then (if wrongly and ultimately suppressed), and the very same geopolitical and economic factors make it legitimate today. Their line of argument was perhaps Byzantine, but the USSR is nothing if not a 20th century Byzantium. As Western observers we cannot forget that much of the Soviet national security elite even in the late 1980s still spoke a language of Lenin, justifying current actions and policy prescriptions in terms of chosen Lenin quotes. Svechin, Lenin's historical contemporary, not only provided the "new-thinkers" a source of useful quotes and arguments by themselves, but also proved to be a source of genuine intellectual stimulation as his fascinating legacy began to be uncovered and appreciated.

In the struggle with "old-thinkers" adamantly opposed to direct challenges (such as those made by Alexei Arbatov) in national security policymaking, the Svechin experience offered a way to deliver the same arguments through the back door. The use of Svechin—especially in 1988 and 1989—was one of the few ways for challengers to establish a dialogue in place of the two monologues. By citing Svechin, challengers to the status quo paid homage to Soviet military history, which helped them penetrate the rigid nature of Soviet military science, the no-man's land (for "incompetent civilians," at least) in which the requirements for national defense are set and budgetary issues established.

It would be wrong, however, to create the impression that Aleksandr Svechin was simply a convenient Trojan horse for those who would radically change Soviet national security policy. In fact, as his long-suppressed writings began to be rediscovered, a growing number of Soviet analysts and officers began to find inherent worth in much of their content. Most important was Svechin's intellectual approach, or method. As the introductory essays below state, and as the text of *Strategy* itself shows, Svechin's method was underlined by a spirit of critical inquiry, pluralism and civility of dialogue, elements often lacking in Soviet society and culture. So even if his particular insights are not remembered (which, the reader may conclude, are intriguing and ought well be), his method should. This method alone compels us to read Svechin, and keep him on our shelf next to Clausewitz and the other classics for many years to come.

With this background in mind, the reader may have a bit clearer notion of the assemblage of this book. Dr. Andrei Kokoshin, who writes jointly the first preface with Professor General-Major (ret.) Valentin Larionov, was the first and most important participant in the Soviet security debate to use Svechin, first gradually by means of citation,[1] and then later by several biographical and analytical articles. General Larionov, who comes to us already distinguished as perhaps the most outstanding Soviet military intellectual of the postwar period,[2] was one of the first Soviet military men to recognize Svechin's legacy favorably in the postwar period. General of the Army Vladimir N. Lobov, who wrote his essay just prior to being elevated to the supreme position of Chief of the General Staff of the USSR Armed Forces, has been the most influential active-duty Soviet military leader responsible for Svechin's renaissance within the Soviet military. His articles on the relevance

---

[1] See especially his article with Larionov "Kurskaia bitva v svete sovremennoi oboronitel'noi doktriny" [The Battle of Kursk in light of modern defensive doctrine], *Mezhdunarodnye otnosheniia i mirovaia ekonomika*, no. 8 (August 1987), pp. 32-40.

[2] In particular as one of the fundamental forces behind Sokolovskii's *Voennaia strategiia* [Military Strategy] (Moscow: Voenizdat, 1962 (1st edition), 1963 (2nd edition) and 1968 (3rd edition)), as well as the only author to win the coveted Frunze Prize (given annually for the best military book) for his works *Iadernaia strategiia* [Nuclear Strategy] (Moscow: 1965) and *Problemy koalitsionnoi voiny* [Problems of Coalition Warfare] (Moscow: 1970). Unfortunately these latter books remain classified and off limits to Western researchers.

of the debates and actors of the 1920s for the current Soviet debate, as well as his biographical essays on Svechin written with Kokoshin, have cast a bright spotlight on Svechin, his method and his ideas. In doing so, he has provided Svechin with the kind of vindication that only a Soviet state figure can offer, since it was the Soviet military and state establishment of the 1920s and 1930s that destroyed Svechin intellectually and physically.

Dr. Jacob Kipp of the U.S. Army's Foreign Military Studies Office, a highly respected historian of Soviet military and security affairs, rounds out the prefaces with an incisive assessment of Svechin's intellectual development and legacy. In addition to catholic interests and expertise that Svechin himself would have admired, Dr. Kipp brings to the book the necessary perspective of a Western scholar intimately familiar with Russian and Soviet history as well as with the classics of Western military-historical thought.

In addition to the introductory essays by these appropriate commentators, the book also offers the reader a notion of how Svechin's work was accepted by his own contemporaries. Accordingly, we have included three book reviews in the appendix. All of them appeared in the journal *Voina i revoliutsiia* [War and Revolution], the Red Army's premier military-theoretical journal of the time (succeeded today by the respected *Voennaia mysl'* [Military Thought]). In reading them one must keep in mind the atmosphere of the time. Svechin and his ideas were clearly under attack by the military establishment—most importantly Mikhail Tukhachevskii—which was solidly behind the Stalinist rush to quickly industrialize the USSR, and in addition was enthralled with the notion of the militant expansion of communism, perhaps even with the help of the Red Army. So compelling was Svechin's book that the foremost Soviet military journal chose to review it not once, but twice, the only book ever given such treatment in the military press of the USSR. This, moreover, came within just months of a massive, four-author review of the first edition of *Strategy*. The attention alone Svechin garnished is worthy of note, and helps give those unfamiliar with him some idea of his import in the eyes of his colleagues. He was not an obscure professor writing books that no one cared about.

Our book also includes a bibliography of Svechin's published works, which we have tried to make as comprehensive as possible. Any omissions are solely the fault of the editor.

Throughout the book we have adhered to the transliteration style of the U.S. Library of Congress; in a few cases (Trotsky rather that Trotskii, Yudenich rather than Iudenich) we have deviated to reflect more traditonal spellings. The editor has endeavored to represent the correct spelling and diacritical marks of foreign

---

[3] See General-Major A. Prokhorov and Lieutenant-Colonel V. Larionov, "Protiv rashiritel'nogo tolkovaniia predmeta i soderzhaniia sovetskoi voennoi nauki" [Against an expanded interpretation of the subject and content of Sovet military science], *Voennaia mysl'*, no. 12 (December 1959), pp. 56-65.

[4] See Colonel-General V. N. Lobov, "Aktual'nye voprosy razvitiia teorii sovetskoi voennoi strategii 20-kh-serediny 30-kh godov" [Urgent question in the development of Soviet military strategy in the 1920s and mid-1930s], *Voenno-istoricheskii zhurnal*, no. 2 (February 1989), pp. 41-50; also Kokoshin, A. A. and V. N. Lobov, "Predvidenie (General Svechin ob evoliutsii voennogo iskusstva)" [Foresight (General Svechin on the evolution of military art)], *Znamia*, no. 2 (February 1990), pp. 170-182.

(especially French and German) proper names. We beg forgiveness if and where we have failed.

Finally, enormous thanks are due to a number of key individuals. We begin with acknowledging our deep debt to the responsible U.S. government officials who initiated in the late 1980s a major effort to translate a number of Soviet military-theoretical classics from the 1920s in a rare, historically-based attempt to understand current Soviet policy. Such foresight in our government is all too rare, and we applaud it. The first draft of this book came from that series; we hope other manuscripts will be published soon.

Mary Albon, now of the Charter 77 Foundation, brought coherence to the entire manuscript and most of the prefaces and essays. It was a great pleasure to work with her, and she raised numerous critical and substantive points that would have otherwise eluded the editor. To the extent that the editor has not managed to obfuscate passages originally made clear by Mary, the reader will also thank her greatly.

A number of translators deserve acknowledgement for their role in bringing two of the prefaces and all of the book reviews into the English language. They are: Harry Orenstein, Jack Anderson, Sergei Mikheev and V. Blokhin.

Much of the work regarding the prefaces, bibliography and the greater effort of East View Publications to assemble the complete collected works of Svechin was conducted in Moscow. Accordingly, enormous credit goes to Vladimir Frangulov and Yuri Usachev of East View's Moscow office. Similar credit goes to Major-General (ret.) Yuri Kirshin and Aleksandr Kavtaradze.

Typesetting, proofing, printing and advertising services were provided by the highly qualified staff at Kocina Communications, including especially Don and Damon Kocina. With their help we hope to put Minneapolis on the map as a center for high-quality publishing in the area of international affairs.

The editor also wishes to thank Dr. Ted Warner of the RAND Corporation, who in his capacity as adjunct professor of political science at Columbia University's Graduate School of Arts and Sciences provided an opportunity for the editor to examine in a seminar paper the importance of the role of historical interpretation in the formulation of current Soviet military policy, and thus make an acquaintence with Svechin.

A final thank-you also needs to be given to Professor Marshall Shulman, former director of the W. Averell Harriman Institute for the Advanced Study of the USSR, for his role in encouraging his students to pay attention to and follow up on events that make one's nose twitch. For the editor, such a "nose-twitching" event was the footnoted and somewhat cryptic references to Svechin in the aformetioned article by Kokoshin and Larionov some four years ago. This book is a consequence of that effort to follow up, and we hope that the reader will not be disappointed that we did.

Kent D. Lee
November 1, 1991

PREFACE

Origins of the Intellectual Rehabilitation of A. A. Svechin
by A. A. Kokoshin and V. V. Larionov

Sixty-five years separate us from the year of the first edition of the book, *Strategy*, the most significant of the works by the Russian and Soviet military historian and theorist, Aleksandr Andreevich Svechin.

Despite such a great period of time and the many changes in the life of nations and in military affairs, many truths formulated by this leading author of military-philosophical thought have not lost their freshness or significance.

Moreover, many elements of the Svechin school of strategic thought concerning rationalization of distribution of the nation's resources to defensive goals in peacetime and wartime, principles of mobilization and strategic planning, the combination of defense and offense, and military-political and military control, which in their time were subjected to sharp and undeserved criticism in the Soviet press and at conferences, are only today being recognized as worthy not only of study, but also of practical consideration in military development.

Svechin taught: "Each segment of the past is rich in large events and shifts, is linked one way or another with tasks standing before us, and, therefore, is in no way only of academic interest to us."[1]

Svechin's works shared the fate of the books of many personalities who were repressed at the end of the 1930s. Today his works have become a great bibliographical rarity, which is at variance with the increasing interest in them. The personality of the author himself is of no less interest.

Born into the family of a tsarist general who took part in the Russo-Turkish War, A. A. Svechin followed in the footsteps of his father. He graduated from an artillery school and commanded an artillery company. As an artillery corps staff officer he entered the General Staff Academy in 1903. In 1904-1905 he took part in the Russo-Japanese War as a staff officer of the commander in chief. Then, until 1914, he served on the General Staff. During World War I for some time he was an officer assigned to the chief of staff of the supreme commander in chief; he then commanded a regiment and a division. In 1916, as chief of staff of the Fifth Army, he attained the rank of major general. In September 1917 Svechin became chief of staff of the Northern Front.

After the October Revolution, beginning in March 1918, General Svechin served as military leader of the Smolensk Region (military district, in modern parlance). In August 1918 Svechin became chief of the republic field staff (*Vseroglavshtab*).

Several months later Svechin was forced to leave this post and transfer to instructional work at the Military Academy of the Workers' and Peasants' Red Army (*RKKA*). At the same time he headed the military-historical commission for investigating the experience of World War I.

---

[1] *Strategiia XX veka v pervom etape* [Strategy of the 20th century at the first stage] (Moscow: Akademiia General'nogo shtaba, 1937), p. 5.

Thus, as Svechin himself afterwards ironically spoke about the similar fates of military men, already in 1919 he "shared the lot of all objectionable but qualified workers—he was thrown into military-historical work."

In 1924, in a testimonial to Svechin, the leading professor of the department of history and strategy, R. A. Muklevich, commissar of the Military Academy of the *RKKA* and well-known party and state personality, wrote:

> A thoroughly educated military specialist. He has enormous experience [in the Japanese and imperialist wars]. A very talented man and quick-witted professor. Svechin is one of the most valuable professors in the Military Academy. His classes in strategy, thanks to his unfailing originality of thought, are always simple and clever and are...one of the great achievements in the old course...
>
> Paradoxically his nature is extremely malicious in the dormitory; he does not miss an opportunity to get his digs in at any time.
>
> However, his work is very fruitful.
>
> ...Being a sensible politician, he took the situation into account and adapted to it. But not as clumsily as Zaionchkovskii ("sympathetic to the Communist Party"), and not as "sugary" as Verkhovskii, but with dignity and with a sense of critical attitude toward political issues.... He is especially valued as a fighter against the routine and conservatism of his comrades from the old army, the weak aspects of whom he knows better than anyone.
>
> Svechin is the most distinguished professor of the academy.[2]

But Svechin's biographers will be mistaken if they think that their hero, being an academy professor, completely withdrew from dynamic operational and reform activities in the Red Army. In the first place, in 1927 Svechin became the deputy chief leader of the military academies of the *RKKA* for strategy (the leader was M. N. Tukhachevskii). In 1935 he was given the military rank of division commander (*komdiv*), the equivalent of lieutenant general. In 1936 he became assistant chief of the department of military history of the General Staff Academy. In 1938 Svechin was discharged from the *RKKA* and arrested, and soon perished. Information concerning the circumstances of his death is contradictory.

In 1923-1924, Svechin's three-volume work, *Istoriia voennogo iskusstva* [History of military art] was published. Later this opus was reworked into the two-volume *Evoliutsiia voennogo iskusstva* [Evolution of military art]. In 1926 and 1927, Svechin's magnum opus, *Strategiia* [Strategy] was published in two editions; in 1935 his book Clausewitz was published, and in 1937 *Strategiia XX veka na pervom etape* [Strategy of the 20th century at the first stage] was published. Svechin was not only a thorough analyst of the military and military-political sphere, but also a brilliant stylist (his book *Clausewitz*, which was published in a large quantity in the series *The Life of Remarkable Men*, is especially distinguished in this respect).

Several articles and analytical notes focused on, among other things, the higher military command of the country have issued from Svechin's pen. In one

---

[2]   *Voenno-istoricheskii zhurnal*, no. 9 (September 1966), pp. 117-118.

of these articles in particular he initiated a public discussion on Soviet military doctrine, which in the final analysis led to the formation in subsequent years of such a doctrine, the form of which, we believe, has no analogues in Western countries.

Since A. A. Svechin was for many years (until 1935, inclusive) the Soviet Union's undisputed authority in the field of military history and strategy, had trained a whole galaxy of pupils to become military leaders and like-minded military scholars, and had created many works with substantiated views on matters which did not coincide with what was generally accepted, the leadership of the communist party at that time and the leadership of the military department (Voroshilov, Bubnov, Tukhachevskii, et al.) considered it appropriate to discuss the appearance of Professor Svechin's school of strategic and military-historical thought.

In fact, many components of Svechin's works did not have a narrow military focus, but had a military-political nature. Thus to a significant degree Svechin's works can be considered the forerunners of the formation of military-political research as a new branch of knowledge, the development of which is necessary under modern conditions.[3]

A number of postulates stated by the father of this school did not subscribe to views which were dominant at that time. As a result, the school was labeled reactionary.

In April 1931 a special meeting in the section for problems of war of the Communist Academy, an adjunct to the USSR Central Executive Committee, was organized with the agenda, "Criticism of Professor Svechin's Strategic and Military-Historical Views."[4]

According to the standards of "scientific conferences" at that time, and with such an agenda, the discussion was far from objective. Unfortunately, Tukhachevskii, who was striving to become the leading military theorist of the Red Army (and having no little success in this), set the dominant tone in the rout of Svechin's school.

What, then, were the basic postulates of Svechin's theory ("school"), and of what did his critics accuse him?

The first group of accusations concerned Svechin's methodology.

The entire essence of the scholar's methodological approach consisted of not recognizing the monopoly of the ideology of a revolutionary proletariat, although the author considered himself a dialectician and materialist in the broad sense of the word. At the same time, Svechin could not acknowledge the proletarian ideology of a revolutionary rupture of power as the only true one among other teachings. As he himself said, he did not wish to fit into classical "restricted," "narrow-minded" and "one-sided" thinking.

---

3   For more details about the subject of military-political research as a new scientific discipline, see A. A. Kokoshin, *V poiskakh vykhoda. Voenno-politicheskie aspekty mezhdunarodnoi bezopasnosti* [In search of a way out. Military-political aspects of international security] (Moscow: Politizdat, 1989), pp. 4-5.

4   *Protiv reaktsionnykh teorii na voenno-nauchnom fronte* [Against reactionary theories on the military-scientific front] (Moscow: Gosvoenizdat, 1931).

Svechin wrote, "Theory is capable of benefitting only those who have raised themselves above the fray and have become completely dispassionate... A narrow doctrine would probably confuse us more than guide us."[5]

Critics called this position "scientific objectivism" and ascribed to the author an "expert mastery of the bourgeois weapon of class struggle" and "a clever camouflage of anti-proletarian positions."[6]

It should be noted that Svechin was never an enemy of the ideology of the proletariat and did not consider himself as such. But he fought his entire life against routine, one-sidedness and preconception in scientific research. He was accused of a non-party bent for this.

Svechin expressed common sense about the necessity of studying history before a person took on the study of the theory of strategy, and he was accused of empiricism and metaphysics for this.

Svechin wrote, for example, "If we do not furnish our thought with a number of military-historical facts, we will be subject to the danger of getting lost in the abstract tenets of the theory of strategic art."[7]

It particularly fell to the theorist to specify the degree of precision of military theory and objectiveness of the laws of armed struggle. Svechin was completely justified when he wrote:

> The conclusions of military theory are not indisputably exact.... We are inclined to call any system of knowledge which facilitates our understanding of life and experience a science. The theory of all military art, including strategy, undoubtedly fits into this broad definition.[8]

In other words, in the opinion of the theorist, the theory of strategy cannot be based on precise determined and objective laws, for, in the strict sense of the word, they do not exist in nature. In military affairs and in the leadership of wars, operations and battle, there is present a subjective human impulse in a commander of any rank, but there are also specific principles and rules. Svechin considered military science to fall between natural and social sciences, and labeled such sciences "second-class."

This definition was enough to categorize the scholar as a formal objectivist, eclectic and empiricist.

Svechin's *Strategy* is a major work which incorporated the best of military thought from Russia, the young Soviet power, Germany, France and other foreign countries. This work was the result of Svechin's two years (1923-1924) of teaching a strategy course at the Military Academy of the *RKKA*. No other works on this theme were published in the USSR until 1962, when *Voennaia strategiia* [Military

---

[5]   A. A. Svechin, *Strategiia* [Strategy], 2nd edition (Moscow: Voennyi Vestnik, 1927), pp. 8-9.

[6]   *Protiv reaktsionnykh teorii...*, p. 45.

[7]   Ibid., p. 49.

[8]   Svechin, *Strategiia*, 2nd edition, pp. 16-17.

[9]   Editor's note: V. V. Larionov is one of the primary authors of the collective work *Voennaia strategiia* [Military strategy], published in three editions in Moscow by Voenizdat in 1962, 1963 and 1968

strategy] was published under the editorship of Marshal of the Soviet Union V. D. Sokolovskii.[9]

Above all we will turn our attention to how Svechin pictured, respectively, the function of *Strategy*:

> This book has been written for a rather modest purpose. namely to be a guideline for independent work on strategy and to help the reader get a start and give him several broad perspectives in order to make it possible for strategic think-ing to get out of back alleys and dead ends and onto the main road as quickly as possible.[10]

Svechin constantly emphasized his negative attitude toward rigid schemes in scientific research and the statement of its results and toward didacticism. He emphasized that strategy, according to Clausewitz's testament, should avoid "shifting from a form of reflection to a rigid channeling of precisely stated doctrine from rules, deductions, and conclusions."

Svechin wrote:

> I criticize many of my colleagues in the study of prob-lems of military history and tsarist Russia, in that they usually strove, immediately following a factual statement of events, to develop their deductions and conclusions, which often had rather limited scope and depth.

He wrote with justification that a truly scientific approach consists of, once the facts have been stated, shifting to a reflection of them. "The difference between the terms, conclusion [*vyvod*], on the one hand, and contemplation [*razmyshlenie*], on the other, reflects different understandings of the relationships between theory and real life."[11]

Such an understanding of the tasks of scientific research and statements of the problems of strategy contrasted with the style and spirit of work in the field of social sciences, asserted in the 1930s, in which there was practically no place at all for deliberation.

All of Svechin's work is penetrated by the idea of the necessity of the strategist's continuous deliberation on history: "Isolation from an historical basis is dangerous for both the strategist and the politician."

Emphasizing the significance of political history for an understanding of strategic issues, Svechin wrote that "readers interested in strategy will find more thought-provoking observations in the political history of past wars rather than in military treatises, particularly so-called 'strategic essays.'"[12]

According to Svechin's definition, "strategy is the art of combining prepara-tions for war and the grouping of operations for achieving the goal set by the war for the armed forces."[13]

---

[10] Svechin, *Strategiia*, 2nd edition, p. 23.

[11] Ibid.

[12] Ibid.

[13] Ibid., p. 15.

[14] Ibid., p. 16.

[15] Ibid., p. 19.

He came out against using such terms as strategy of the air fleet, naval strategy, colonial strategy, etc., asserting that they were based on a "misunderstanding."[14] He considered that one could speak openly about naval operational art, since the armed forces at sea have an independent operational goal. The same could be said, in his opinion, about the air fleet, with even greater reservations.

According to Svechin, strategy is the art of the entire command personnel of the armed forces, not only of general headquarters [*stavka*] or *front* and army commanders. In his opinion, even a corps commander cannot cope with his operational missions if he does not have clear strategic thinking.

> Any time an operational artist must make a choice between two alternatives he will be unable to justify a particular operational method if he stays solely within the realm of operational art, and he will have to rise to a strategic level of thinking.[15]

Svechin considered an understanding and knowledge of strategy necessary not only for command personnel of the armed forces, but also for political state leaders:

> Responsible politicians should be familiar with strategy...
> Bismarck would not have been able to guide Prussian politics so authoritatively if he had not had such a profound understanding of the situation in the theater of war.[16]

Emphasizing that the dominance of politics over strategy is "universal in nature," Svechin at the same time repeated several times that political decisions also should conform with strategy and should take into account military capabilities; i.e., a politician must most attentively listen to the opinions of the military command and military experts and know how the military organism operates, what the military-mobilization capabilities of the state are, etc.

Svechin's digressions into examining issues of the correlation between politics and strategy were by no means purely academic in the 1920s. The views of a number of Western (above all, German) military leaders and military theorists, who stood for definite autonomy of strategy from politics, thus modifying in their own way Clausewitz's famous formula, were well known in the ranks of the *RKKA*. These views were by no means simply adopted by the ranks of the prominent Red Army commanders, including Tukhachevskii. Meanwhile, the higher political leadership of the country, above all Stalin, barely delved into the issues of military strategy, and often ignored the opinion of military professionals. Later such a state of affairs was manifested in the large-scale military-strategic errors in the war against Finland in 1939-1940, and in the initial period of the Great Patriotic War of 1941-1945.

Svechin's methodology was especially criticized because, operating from a position of "pure military science," he classified all wars, former and future, only according to two forms: destruction or attrition, short-term or protracted, wars with decisive or limited goals. In connection with this it was argued that he mechanically applied this division to policy being implemented and to the behavior of the state leadership in one or another large-scale undertaking.

---

[16] Ibid., p. 18

Svechin's Strategic Views

This basic part of Svechin's work was subjected to the greatest criticism and attacks.

The spectrum of the scholar's strategic predilections was quite broad. But the principal differences of opinion centered around several fundamental points of strategic thinking. Among these the following should be particularly singled out:

- The mutual relationship between politics and strategy.
- The interconnection between defense and offense on a strategic scale.
- The nature of the preparation of the country and the armed forces for war.
- Strategic deployment of the armed forces.

On all these issues Svechin had his own original views, based on an analysis of military history, the geostrategic and economic position of the USSR and the global level of military-technological development.

If one summed up Svechin's various works, the essence of his judgements on these issues would be as follows: Svechin proceeded from the possibility of conflict between the USSR and its probable enemies in the immediate future, i.e., at the beginning of the 1930s. He forecasted the correlation of forces in these years as a superiority of moral spirit on the side of the Red Army and its ideological supporters abroad, with a technical and economic superiority for the joint forces of capitalist encirclement of the USSR. From this it followed that the best strategy for the USSR should be a course aimed at a protracted, defensive war in the first stage. Svechin doubted the grounds for the Red Army's dynamic offensive doctrine, a doctrine of "destruction" and transfer of the "fire of revolution" abroad.

But we will examine everything in order. Svechin undoubtedly recognized the superiority of politics over strategy, saying that the goal and methods of resolving a political problem could not help but affect the nature and forms of conducting war. The theorist considered that this was especially true when the creator of policy is a "young class" advancing "toward a broad future," the "historical health" of which is reflected in its policies. But when an outmoded class or an unhealthy social group stands at the head of the government, then their policies will inevitably continue an unhealthy and detrimental strategy.

Svechin held that strategy naturally strives to be emancipated from poor policies. He wrote, "Mistaken policies will also bear the same pitiful fruit in war as they do in any other field."[17]

But at the same time, Svechin repeated many times that a political decision must be weighed with strategy, especially in wartime. In his thinking, a politician must be clearly aware of what can be achieved through strategy and what lies beyond the limits of its capabilities, and how one can politically influence change for the best in a strategic situation.

The next important aspect of Svechin's strategic theory is the defense and offense, attrition and destruction, and the interrelationship between these concepts in politics and strategy.

Svechin viewed offense and defense broadly, on a historical scale, extending these two concepts to politics. He considered that the art of directing society—i.e., politics—and the art of directing war—i.e., strategy—are grouped according to

---

[17]   Ibid., p. 31.

two trends: destruction (offensive, onslaught, routing) and attrition (defense, disquieting actions, achievement of success by means of winning a number of small successes in order to combine them in the long run into a general overall victory). In our opinion, this schematic, dualistic approach was at the basis of Svechin's analysis of politics and strategy for all times and nations.

In criticizing Svechin, M. N. Tukhachevskii apparently had justification for not accepting such an approach, which replaced the gamut of political and strategic nuances of various epochs, nations and classes.

Nevertheless, Svechin maintained that immobility, a state of equilibrium in the system of human relations, was an illusion disseminated by pacifists and outdated specialists in state affairs.

All nations and peoples are in dynamic motion and interaction. Svechin concluded from this that the different tempo and the direction of development provide some governments and nations with superiority over others. This superiority is expressed in everything, including the ability to maintain a larger and technically better-equipped armed force. Svechin saw this as the reason for the historical advance of German tribes west of the Elbe in the thirteenth through the eighteenth centuries, the advance of Slavic tribes from the Volga east in the sixteenth through nineteenth centuries, and the advance of the Anglo-Saxons against all lines of weak resistance on the globe.

In the eighteenth century, an acceleration of the tempo of the advance of the bourgeoisie was observed; in the twentieth century there was an acceleration of the tempo of the advance of the proletariat. Time will pass, and the poorest proletariat will cede its position to the technically-armed working intelligentsia. This was already a class explanation of social processes.

According to Svechin, in a strategy depending on politics, a division of army activity into capability and inclination for offense or defense, for destruction or attrition, was also observed.

Svechin also divided wars into two types: wars of destruction and wars of attrition. Svechin considered that for the Soviet republic at the end of the 1920s, a war of attrition or a war with limited goals was still practicable. He said that the time for a proletarian war of destruction had still not arrived.

This assertion resulted in the most vehement attacks on the professor. Critics tried to prove that the Soviet Union, "with its colossally growing industrialization, with the enormous growth of the positions of socialism in the country...not only could, but should prepare for destruction."[18]

As for the military-technical backwardness of the Red Army compared to bourgeois armies of the 1920s, Svechin considered that enthusiasm and a revolutionary lifting of the masses could not compensate for this. But his opponents counted precisely on these features.

A discussion of this problem is very instructive for today in many respects, both from a theoretical and a practical point of view.

In practice, the study of Svechin's views on the nature of preparing the country and the armed forces for resolving military problems which stand before them is very important. Svechin tried to demonstrate the necessity of permanent mobilization. In other words, he came out against putting large assets into the military

---

[18] M. N. Tukhachevskii, "O strategicheskikh vzgliadakh prof. Svechina" [On Professor Svechin's strategic views], *Protiv reaktsionnykh teorii...*, pp. 15-16.

budget in the hope of assuring full prewar readiness of the country in the present, while undermining its capabilities for the future.

We will return to this later. Here we will add that under conditions of a war of attrition and the possibility of withdrawal, what Svechin forecasted has turned out to be prophetic.

Svechin as a Military Historian

A. A. Svechin's military-historical views are of interest today in two respects. First, it is worth studying him as a military historian for an objective illumination, unbiased and not narrowly confined to party interpretation, of historical events and decisions of the military and political leadership of the Soviet Union. Second, today, when passions have more or less flared up concerning an answer to the question of who is to blame for the failures of the initial period of the Great Patriotic War, we can objectively assess his insight and the cost of neglecting those warnings which were made (and not only by Svechin) in 1935-1937.

For the USSR, this is a chronicle of bitter mistakes and costs resulting from incompetence and political crimes.

Svechin both led the course of study of strategy and military history at the Academy of the RKKA and gave lectures on the full course of study of the history of military art in senior courses. With the publication in 1923-1924 of *Istoriia voennogo iskusstva* in three volumes, Svechin became the first in the Soviet era to publish on this subject. In 1927-1928 this was reworked and published in two volumes entitled *Evoliutsiia voennogo iskusstva*.

In 1931, when Svechin's theoretical views were subjected to criticism in the Communist Academy's section on problems of war, special attention was focused on his military-historical views. From the very beginning it was emphasized that his errors were especially dangerous because he was a generally accepted authority in the USSR on the history of military art.

It is sufficient to cite the following evaluations of that time: "Russia's military society can congratulate itself for this major and clear product of military thought"; "We will have to wait many years before someone will be able to approach this issue as seriously and conscientiously as Svechin"; "We have no one in the Soviet Union...who can replace Svechin, and he will remain unsurpassed for a long time in the field of military history."[19]

All these assessments, which were made by leading professors of military history at the Academy of the *RKKA* and the Military-Political Academy, were subsequently confirmed. The first Soviet work after Svechin's on the history of military art, *Istoriia voennogo iskusstva s drevneishikh vremen do pervoi mirovoi imperialisticheskoi voiny 1914-1918 gg.* [The history of military art from ancient times to the first imperialist world war, 1914-1918] by Colonel E. Razin, a professor in the Frunze Academy, was published in the USSR only in 1939. This work included abundant citations from Stalin, Engels, Marx and Lenin, and was beautifully illustrated, but it represented a step not forward, but backward in comparison with the works of Svechin as well as of Delbrueck. It presented a quite simplified account of wars of the period of slave-owning society, but the thorough critical analysis of ancient Greek and ancient Roman sources and literature done by

---

[19]   All these are cited from the collection *Protiv reaktsionnykh teorii....*

Delbrueck, and on which Svechin based much of his own work, was not at all taken into consideration.

Svechin was criticized mainly because he used the views of the German military writer Hans Delbrueck, and not those of Frunze or Bubnov, as the basis of his *Weltanschauung*. Second, he did not disseminate Marxist views or the foundations of historical materialism in his writing, but observed "scientific objectivism." In other words, critics perceived, and perhaps not without justification, Svechin's inclination toward the "truth of fact" rather than the "truth of history."

Today we do not see this as a great crime since we have already learned to relate to a pluralism of scientific views with sufficient sangfroid. But at the time when Svechin was writing, ignoring the authorities and the "classics of historical materialism" was considered nothing less than the creation of a school of reactionary thought.

It is true that critics often recognized that following the truth of historical facts, and not their deliberate distortion for the sake of class interests, often led the scholar to the correct conclusions. But at that time they solidly stood for the point of view of the superiority of the truth of history when assessing the place and role of events in the historical process of social development. Whatever views were held, one cannot help but agree with the following declaration from Professor Svechin: "No one method of studying military art, taken by itself, makes it possible to grasp it as a whole. It is necessary to use the achievements of all methods in order to investigate this as widely as possible."[20]

Another aspect of Svechin's military-historical legacy is not, strictly speaking, associated with his historical works. His surprisingly insightful prognoses of events of the forthcoming war in several general aspects and even in details are a worthy subject for a special detailed work. Although several efforts in this direction have already been undertaken, a work of this type still awaits its authors.[21]

We will note only briefly some of A. A. Svechin's prognoses. For instance, already in 1927 Svechin prophetically warned that the first victim in a future large-scale war in Europe would be Poland, which would be subjected to a German strike.

As for the nature of a war in which the USSR would have to take part, in Svechin's opinion this would be of a protracted nature, and would require enormous mobilization efforts. He considered that it was necessary to prepare most seriously for a long period of defensive actions and correspondingly prepare rear defensive lines. Svechin cautioned against placing all new large industrial objectives in the vicinity of the USSR's western border, considering that they could be lost as a result of defensive engagements in the initial period of war. In this connection he came out against "superconcentration" of industry and population in Leningrad, calling this "the Sevastopol of a future war," since during the Crimean War in the nineteenth century Sevastopol was relatively isolated from

---

[20] Protiv reaktsionnykh teorii..., p. 23.

[21] See A. A. Kokoshin and V. N. Lobov, "*Predvidenie (General Svechin ob evoliutsii voennogo iskusstva)*" [Foresight (General Svechin on the evolution of military art)], Znamia, No. 2 (February 1990), pp. 170-182.

the primary territory of the Russian empire, and its defense against Anglo-Franco-Turkish forces was implemented with great difficulty and great sacrifices for the Russian army and populace.

At that time, a clearly offensive attitude predominated in the Red Army, dictated by, among other things, offensive motives. Many military commanders and political workers of the *RKKA* asserted that an offensive strategy of destruction was, above all, inherent to the "government of the leading revolutionary class" by its very nature.

As a result, before the Great Patriotic War the idea of the primacy of offensive strategic operations, a kind of "meeting strategic blow" according to the well-turned expression of Soviet military theorist Lieutenant General E. D. Grebish, prevailed in the Red Army. Correspondingly, as the analysis of various archival documents and memoirs by authors shows, operational-strategic planning was also implemented on the eve of the war. For example, large shock groupings were created on the Lvov and Bialystok axes, and were called up immediately following the unleashing of war by the Germans to execute powerful strikes into the depth of their territory. The General Staff of the *RKKA* planned to concentrate *front* efforts above all in first-echelon armies for the purpose of providing a powerful initial strike in response to the aggression. In its turn, such a configuration of our forces in the West made them very vulnerable to a deep envelopment by enemy groupings, which the Germans basically succeeded in doing after their invasion of USSR territory on June 22, 1941. Essentially, in 1941 the Soviet armed forces were not ready for either offense or defense.[22]

Unfortunately, for many years the experience of the initial period of the Great Patriotic War was not duly taken into consideration in Soviet military-historical and military-political thought, despite attempts by individual authors. The events of this period of the war clearly showed the higher government-political and military leadership in an unfavorable light. A clear distortion was made in favor of using the experience of the successful strategic offensive operations of 1943–1945, which took place after the course of the war had changed. What occurred was, in fact, what Svechin in his time had warned against when he came out against overstating the experience of only the successful offensive operations of the 1918-1922 Civil War in Russia. To a significant degree, this conditioned the dominance of the offensive on a strategic scale in Soviet military thought right up to the second half of the 1980s despite the declared defensive nature of Soviet military doctrine.

At the end of the 1920s, just as he had made forecasts of a military-political and military-strategic nature, Svechin also made military-economic predictions in *Strategy*.

In the 1930s the economic geography of the USSR had changed considerably. A Ural metallurgical base and fuel bases in the Far East and eastern Siberia had been created, and industrial centers had been created in Central Asia. But industry was also growing rapidly in the western regions of the country. As a result, in 1941 when German forces swiftly advanced into the depth of the Soviet Union, country, it was necessary to relocate an enormous number of industrial enterprises,

---

[22] For more details, see A. Kokoshin and V. Larionov, "Voennaia doktrina na sluzhbe mira" [Military doctrine in the service of peace], *Kommunist*, no. 15 (October 1990), pp. 101-102.

equipment and raw materials to the far reaches of the country, and to evacuate production personnel in the shortest possible period of time and with considerable losses. What could not be carried away was blown up and destroyed.

One can determine, to a certain degree, the quantitative cost of not having taken into consideration and duly adopting Svechin's forecasts: as a result, above all, of the evacuation of industrial enterprises from the western USSR to the eastern parts of the country and losses of a considerable portion of them, the USSR's gross industrial production fell from June through November 1941 by 2.1 times. Production of rolled steel diminished by 3.1 times, rolled nonferrous metals by 430 times, and ball bearings, without which it was impossible to produce airplanes, tanks and artillery, by 21 times.[23]

During World War II, this severe shortfall in industrial output persisted for two years in the Soviet Union.[24] Only by the end of the initial period of the Great Patriotic War, more specifically by the beginning of the summer-autumn campaign of 1943, did the Soviet strategic leadership acquire the necessary experience and demonstrate the ability for the first time in the war to plan an entire campaign and simultaneously coordinate the actions of several *fronts* (from five at the beginning to eight at the end of the campaign) on various strategic axes.

Here, the fact that a large portion of experienced cadres at the strategic level of leadership had been victims of Stalin's repressions at the end of the 1930s undoubtedly played an adverse role. Only by the summer of 1943 did the *Stavka* and the General Staff somehow succeed in filling this gap.

The Theory of Gradual Mobilization

We would like to linger on this theory more extensively. What is its essence, and what lessons can be extracted today from Svechin's views on this problem and from the heated discussions of the 1930s?

Above all, it must be said that Svechin's views on this issue, unlike the views of other theorists, were partially realized. The essence of the theory consisted of the following: Svechin reduced everything to the question, What kind of a war awaited us and, depending on this, how could we prepare for it economically? In other words, what percentage of assets should be allocated for prewar preparation of the country and the armed forces, what requirements would have to be reckoned with in the course of the war, and in what period of time.

Svechin forecasted a protracted war entailing a large expenditure of resources, financial assets, equipment and ammunition, and the inevitability of prolonged defensive engagements and withdrawals on a number of axes for the sake of a future offensive and victory. Svechin's opponents basically counted on a swift and easy victory, a shift of the war to foreign territory and the achievement of victory "with little blood and a powerful blow." The principal differences of opinion in the *RKKA* leadership stemmed from this divergence. Svechin wrote,

---

[23] N. Voznesenskii, *Voennaia ekonomiia SSSR v period Otechestvennoi voiny* [The War Economy of the USSR during the Patriotic War] (Moscow: Gosudarstvennoe izdatel'stvo politicheskoi literatury, 1948), pp. 42-43.

[24] World War II began for the Soviet Union on June 22, 1941, with the mass invasion by the forces of Hitler's Wehrmacht and of Nazi Germany's satellites.

[25] Svechin, *Strategiia*, 2nd edition, p. 106.

"We indicate the need to extend several aspects of preparation far into the war (for example, the need to mobilize in phases)."[25]

This recommendation was based on Svechin's assessment that the war's culmination or highest period of tension would occur not at the beginning, but several months after the primary mass of forces had been drawn into battle (as is known, the actual beginning of the turning point of the Great Patriotic War was autumn 1942). The beginning of the war was envisioned as a time for conducting covering operations.

From this in turn, according to Svechin, the growth of military production had to be determined by the requirements of the most intensive operations of the "peak of the war," and not conversely—i.e., the intensity of military actions should not be dictated by military-economic "surplus."

Svechin asserted that before a war it is not necessary to implement a military "assimilation" of civilian industry. As might be said now, a broad conversion of enterprises with a military profile is needed. However, it is necessary to constantly maintain a small portion of professional military factories and to transfer civilian factories to military production in the course of the war—but only in accordance with the actual requirements of the war: what and how much is necessary.

The theory of permanent, or three-echelon, mobilization in its generalized form envisioned the following:

- minimum mobilization reserves gathered by the beginning of the war—the first echelon of material support of the army;
- second echelon—special military industry capable of supporting the army until the final mobilization of all remaining industry; and
- third mobilization echelon—civilian industry supporting the army and the country until the end of the war, after exhausting mobilization reserves.

All this, naturally, was not suggested separately, but as a cumulative whole.

These are the fundamental views of Professor Aleksandr Andreevich Svechin, major general of the Russian army and division commander of the Red Army, which are displayed in his numerous works.

PREFACE

The Significance of Svechin's Military-Theoretical Legacy Today
by V. N. Lobov

We rightly consider Professor A. A. Svechin our prominent contemporary. If his works had only a purely historical value, then however brilliant they might be in form and content, interest in them would not be so considerable as it is today.

Nevertheless, we cannot unconditionally accept all his legacy, and not all of it is uniformly relevant in our time.

To search for an analogy and for commentaries, I selected from the richest legacy of the scholar only those premises of his strategic school which can be of help in making responsible decisions in military development at the present time, and which, most of all, personally impress me.

Among those premises I refer to the following:

- the interrelationship of politics and strategy and personalities personifying one and the other in the government;
- the basis of the development of the armed forces (principles of outfitting, correlation of men and military equipment, determination of criteria of sufficiency for defense, rational distribution of the military budget); and
- military doctrine: correlation of defense and offense, combination of ground and naval strategy, and principles of military leadership and troop control.

I propose to examine all these premises in the plan "Svechin and Contemporaneity."

On the Interrelationship of Politics and Strategy

In all his works, Professor Svechin came out as a consistent advocate of the primacy of politics over strategy, but at the same time he advocated the idea of the reasonable sovereignty of each in the sphere of their competency.

He subjected to devastating criticism the views of those military leaders and military theorists who advocated the independence of military strategy from politics. He wrote that from this resulted all the "bitter misfortunes" of those who view war "as a gigantic duel between two nations." The theorist noted that it was necessary to distinguish the spheres: rulers should specialize in politics, generals in strategy.

In this respect he supported Bismarck's point of view:

> The purpose of the high command is to destroy hostile military forces, while the purpose of war is to win a peace which meets the political conditions set forth by the state. The establishment and delineation of the goals to be achieved by the war and the provision of advice to the monarch in this regard during the course of the war is a political task, and the methods of accomplishing this political task cannot help but affect the conduct of a war.[1]

---

[1] A. Svechin, *Strategiia* [Strategy], 2nd edition (Moscow: Voennyi Vestnik, 1927), p. 30, n. 3.

Svechin did not simply refute the views of those who did not acknowledge the superiority of politics over strategy; he explained the reasons according to which strategy could strive to come out from under the subordination of politics and even turn politics into its own servant.

> In our opinion, the claim that politics is superior to strategy is universal in nature... It is natural for strategy to try to gain emancipation from bad politics, but strategy cannot exist in a vacuum without politics and is condemned to pay for all the sins of politics.[2]

But here, "one should not confuse protests against political errors with refusal to acknowledge the right and obligation of politics to determine the basic directions of a war."[3]

Thus wrote a military theorist who was not a communist and not a Marxist, convinced of what we today are convinced. In reality, political solutions require strict accord with strategy and with military capabilities. The politician is simply obliged to listen attentively to the opinion of military professionals, to know how the military machine operates, what is within its powers and what lies beyond the limits of its capabilities, what is the military-mobilization mechanism of the state, etc.

We will cite one more excerpt which hits the mark:

> Responsible politicians should be familiar with strategy... [T]he politician who sets a political goal for military operations must have an idea of what is feasible for strategy given the resources available and how politics may affect the situation for better or worse. Strategy is one of the most important tools of politics, and even in peacetime political calculations must to a great degree be based on the military capabilities of friendly and hostile nations.[4]

We recall the strategic lessons of the war between the USSR and Finland in 1939-1940, and of the initial period of the Great Patriotic War. The fact that Stalin and his close, incompetent circle (Beria, Voroshilov, Budennyi, Mekhlis) inadequately understood new (for that time) military-strategic and operational issues significantly exacerbated the difficult position of the Red Army in 1941 and 1942. Stalin did not duly use the General Staff and military professionals to work out and make decisions in the first months of the war.

Under contemporary conditions, when the thesis that war cannot serve as a rational means of politics (at least in its most radical form—general nuclear war), it is recognized that the higher government and political leadership must be familiar with the theory and practice of military strategy, and the forms and methods of implementing political decisions by means of a military mechanism. It seems that politicians must especially be familiar with the actual capabilities of systems and means of control, both their own and those of their opponent, communications and intelligence, and systems which warn of a rocket attack. The general public should also understand basic military-strategic categories, so that

---

[2] Ibid., p. 31.

[3] Ibid.

[4] Ibid., p. 18.

openness [*glasnost*] is necessary here and now. Otherwise politics will not be able to implement real, rather than merely declared, control over military strategy, and there will be no correspondence between the political and military-technological components of a state's military doctrine. It seems to me that it is namely a deficit of such knowledge that the Soviet political leadership and parliamentary figures who are in charge of or members of commissions and committees associated with resolving issues of defense and security are experiencing.

This is why the study of the works of Professor Svechin concerning the interrelationship of politics and strategy makes one think.

Svechin's Opinions on the Foundations of Development of the Armed Forces and Contemporaneity

A. A. Svechin placed at the foundation of the development of the armed forces a definition of the nature of future war based on a thorough knowledge and understanding of the history and prospects of military affairs. One also cannot silently bypass the theorist's requirement to take into account the "nature of the historical moment" and economic potentials of the country at each individual moment.

In 1924-1925, when the Red Army was experiencing an era of military reforms under conditions of stabilization of capitalism, Svechin demonstrated models of analyzing principles of outfitting the army and wrote a number of articles on the combination of the militia and cadre system.

Even today his conclusions still sound topical.

Of course, times have changed. Weapons and equipment have become so complex and expensive that even conscript soldiers, not to mention militia reservists, cannot exploit them effectively.

It is still necessary to take into account that in the future there will be a reduction in the duration of the period of service in the Soviet army and navy.

How, then, are we to fulfill the requirement of improving the quality of personnel under these conditions?

In my opinion, there can be only one solution: staffing primary specialties such as commanders of crews, teams and combat posts, mechanic-drivers of combat vehicles and weapons systems adjuster-operators on the basis of a contract system.

With the general trend of personnel reductions and a qualitative development of weapons and military equipment, not only equality with a probable enemy, but also superiority over him must be assured.

Here it is appropriate to remember the words of the Military Commissar of the Tank Industry during the war, V. A. Malyshev: "It is impossible to make military equipment to last forever. These are not tractors. And one cannot 'take a count' and rely on quantitative superiority. The resources of the country are not limitless."[5]

This well-aimed statement has a direct relationship to the subject of our discussion on the legacy of A. A. Svechin. As is known, Svechin in his time underestimated the prospects of the development of technology; because of this, he argued for the predominance of "close battle" for Red Army tactics. Life and

---

[5]   V. A. Chakmaev, *Malyshev*, 2nd edition (Moscow: Molodaia Gvardiia, 1981), p. 106.

World War II disproved these views of the scholar. But this did not make some of his other penetrating forecasts any less significant. In particular, Svechin's ideas about the rationalism of distributing resources for peaceful and military development are of great value. Today we associate this with determining sufficiency in allotting resources to resolving issues of guaranteeing the USSR's military security.

But what does rationalism mean in this matter, and how is it determined?

In my opinion, the problem of establishing quantitative criteria of sufficiency for defense advances to the foreground here. This is necessary for the reason that determining the optimum composition of armed forces only for defense will be unrealistic if this is implemented, as we have accepted, by a simple arithmetic comparison of the tanks, artillery and airplanes of the two sides. What is needed here is a comparison of combat capabilities of the force groupings of both sides.

In contemporary times, defense must, under conditions of wide use of radioelectronic warfare assets, be capable of repelling an unexpected attack from the air by aviation and rockets, and to counter a ground forces strike, particularly one by tanks and mechanized formations and units.

It is also still necessary to take into account the possible nature and methods of actions of the navy in a war. It is not at all the same if a navy will be operating on the ocean and conducting dynamic operations in fighting against enemy naval forces, if it will be fighting against lines of communication, or if it will be restricted to actions within the limits of an economic zone in support of ground forces conducting an anti-assault defense.

The effectiveness of the functioning of the control system and the anticipated degree of its disruption and regeneration capabilities must be added to all this in the criteria of sufficiency.

In all his fundamental works, Svechin called on not only government and political leaders, but also military leaders to consider carefully economic factors and the industrial-economic resources of the country, emphasizing here the importance of optimal distribution of the nation's resources. In particular, he questioned the expediency of creating a large surface fleet in the USSR. Structures of a line fleet under conditions of an extremely disadvantageous distribution of Russian ports in the depth of, as Svechin wrote, "the operational back seat of the seas," bereft of an appropriate foundation, would be doomed to inaction.

Svechin understood that the construction of the newest battleships for the Baltic and Black Sea fleets was being determined, to a considerable degree, by the desire to reestablish the naval prestige of the Russian Empire, lost after the Russo-Japanese War, and not by thorough operational-strategic considerations.

Svechin evaluated the "blue-water navy" concept similarly, with which Germany, under the Kaiser, challenged the naval might of Great Britain after such a fleet had been created. He wrote that the German army was very negatively affected by the attempt on the part of the country's political leadership to prepare the grounds for a fight against England for domination of the seas: from the sums allotted by the budget for military purposes, the ground forces received two-thirds and one-third went for the creation of a navy.

Here Svechin's views coincided with the views of People's Commissar of the Navy M. V. Frunze, who was for the reestablishment of the navy, but who stressed that the scale of its construction had to be strictly regulated "by budgetary limitations and a program of small ships of a defensive nature." Frunze's conclusion was supported by the following considerations: first, "the navy is a very expensive weapon," and under conditions of a general insufficiency of assets, they would be better used for keener and more immediate needs having specific significance for the country's defense; second, the fate of a future war would be decided in continental theaters of military actions, and the main mission of the navy would be to support actions of ground forces groupings on maritime directions; and third, Russian fleets did not have a direct outlet to large water expanses.

Frunze's line with respect to the Red Fleet was not held for long. Already in 1937 an extensive shipbuilding program was undertaken, envisioning the creation of expensive, metal-consuming battleships and heavy cruisers. The planning and making of ships was done on an ever increasing scale at an extremely rapid tempo, especially after Hitler's attack on Poland in September 1939. This required colossal expenditures for the creation of naval bases, docks, factories, etc. The production of all types of ground weapons—cannons, tanks, etc.—intensified in this period. There was not enough metal or power.

The program for building large ships began to be curtailed in the spring of 1940, and it was reviewed in October. Now they began to build only submarines and small surface ships—destroyers, mine sweepers, etc.—and the battleships which had not been fully built remained on the stocks. At the beginning of the war an acute lack of minesweepers, sweeping assets and special assault-landing assets was noticed; ship assets of air defense were very poor, and ships were inadequately equipped with radar and hydroacoustic instruments. All this resulted in great losses from mines and enemy aviation. During the war there were no combat engagements between our battleships and cruisers and the enemy's large surface ships. Such was the bitter result of incompetency and vainly spent resources, which could have gone to strengthen the ground forces or for more optimally developing the navy itself. Frunze's and Svechin's ideas on the place and functions of the navy in supporting the interests of the state are very current today as well, taking into account, of course, all new realities and the growing role of a number of ocean areas for the USSR's national security.

Much of what Svechin wrote in noting the weakness of technical outfitting of the Red Army for a future war turned out to be substantiated, despite the fact that scales of industrialization were much more considerable than he speculated. At the beginning of the Great Patriotic War the Red Army was inadequately provided with the most important assets for a maneuver war and offensive operations, i.e., motor vehicle transport, light automatic weapons, artillery on mechanical traction and radio communications. Even the latest assets such as the T-34 medium tank and the KV heavy tank, the Il-2 low-flying aircraft, and Pe-2 dive bombers, which at that time had no equal in the world, were very poorly equipped with radio stations, just as were headquarters at all levels. The network of highways and railroad lines in the border regions were poorly developed. And although at the commencement of Hitler's aggression there were more airplanes and tanks in the armaments of the Workers' and Peasants' Red Army than, apparently, Svechin could have imagined, the quality and material-technical support of a considerable portion of this equipment did not correspond to the demands made by the military-political situation.

Correlation Between Offense and Defense

The theoretical considerations and conclusions of A. A. Svechin on the correlation between the offense and defense on a strategic scale derive from his views on future war, the material capabilities of the USSR, and the external political course of the Soviet Union. The majority of his contemporaries focused their primary attention on strategic offensive actions. Svechin was an advocate of combining defense and offense. And he gave preference to defense in the first stage of the war.

He wrote that in the first stage, defense has the possibility of using the lines and depth of the theater, which compels the attacking side to expend forces and time to fortify an expanse and to pass through it; and gaining any amount of time is a new plus for the defense. The defense reaps where it sows, since the offensive often is stopped by false reconnaissance data, false fears and inertness.

Regardless of accusations, which in his time were plentiful, of his putting unwarranted reliance on the defense, Svechin examined it in a dialectical unity with the offense—as a means for providing conditions for going over to an effective counteroffensive, leading to the defeat of an enemy.

Svechin's conclusions were confirmed in many operations of World War II, and have not lost their significance even under contemporary conditions (of course, with all corrections for the development of military technology and new tactical and operational forms of conducting military actions). Svechin's statements to the effect that the defense is the strongest form of combat actions are relevant as well, in light of the concept of reasonable (defensive) sufficiency for the USSR. It is noteworthy that well-known military specialists and political and social figures in the West, who are attempting to respond to the ideas of new thinking advanced by the Soviet Union on issues of strengthening international security, are turning more and more to these statements.

Attempting to thoroughly examine the sources of the unpopularity of strategic defense, Svechin wrote about a stable category of military art such as dynamism.

Using events of World War I, he convincingly demonstrated that in the name of dynamism and seizing and holding the initiative, the most prominent military figures made mistakes which, in the final analysis, led to defeat. In works on military history and military strategy, and in service memoirs, Svechin, using historical examples, illustrated how strategic defense, while being the only true method for defeating an enemy, was unjustly rejected by both the political leadership and the military command, and was not supported by the public.

Svechin in no way suggested that the size of the USSR, the lack of roads and the severe winters supported a strategic defense, as was ascribed to him. He saw strategic defense as, above all, the totality of operations, including counterstrikes and counterattacks on various lines which had been prepared beforehand. He warned against relying on the possibilities which the territory and climate presented to the USSR. His foresight was completely confirmed on all fronts of World War II. Moreover, it is correct under contemporary conditions, when transport assets and assets for delivering ammunition to targets have rapidly developed.

Works by the General Staff Academy on the theme "The Army and Defense," implemented in 1938 (for the first time in the history of such academies), have remained practically unnoticed. The thesis on the supremacy of the offense over the defense, advocated by both the political leadership and the leadership of the People's Commissariat of Defense, was an obstacle to the understanding of these works. The dialectic of the correlation of the defense and offense was not taken into account. Ideas concerning shifting the war without fail at its very beginning to enemy territory took root with the state leaders of the USSR.

Groupings of Soviet forces, oriented on a swift counteroffensive turning into a general offensive, and not covered by a deeply echeloned defense, were themselves very vulnerable to powerful sudden strikes. The control and communications system, the disruption of which was almost the primary factor which sharply changed the correlation of real combat capabilities to the aggressor's advantage, especially suffered. It is thought that this factor, even today, is not sufficiently taken into account [in Soviet military science—Ed.].

With a bitter feeling of resentment in the soul, it must be mentioned that in Soviet works on strategy and operational art of the Great Patriotic War, until recently it was predominantly the experience of successful strategic offensive operations, beginning with the second half of 1943, which were examined. It was often not mentioned that they were possible only after a series of strategic defensive operations, and that the strategic initiative was torn away from a most dangerous enemy at a cost of enormous sacrifices.

Only recently, especially after the proclamation of the strictly defensive nature of the USSR's military doctrine, has the situation begun to change.

Significant changes have been introduced into the content of the military-technical aspect of Soviet military doctrine (in strategy, operational art and tactics). Since summer 1987 a position was announced that the primary method of action of the armed forces of the USSR in repelling aggression would not be offensive but defensive operations and combat actions, as well as the counteroffensive.

One of the main principles of the development of the Soviet armed forces under contemporary conditions was the principle of reasonable defensive sufficiency. Practically speaking, this means imparting to them a nonoffensive structure, maximally restricting strike systems in their overall composition, changing deployment with a view to carrying out strictly defensive missions and reducing parameters of mobilization deployment of the armed forces and the volume of military production.

Of course, with this we have not exhausted all major problems which A. A. Svechin's military-theoretical legacy has stimulated us to consider.

Now, when these problems of the theory of strategy and military art as a whole and of restriction and reduction of armed forces and armaments are being widely discussed and implemented, it is important in practice to examine them in a historical context and to turn to forgotten or semi-forgotten works of Soviet political and military theorists of the 1920s and early 1930s, among whom a significant place belongs to A. A. Svechin.

PREFACE

General-Major A. A. Svechin and Modern Warfare: Military History and Military Theory*

by Jacob W. Kipp

Peter dines. Proud and lucid,
And glories fill his gaze,
His royal banquet is excellent.
To the cheers of his troops,
In his own tent he hosts
his own leaders, foreign ones,
And flatters his glorious prisoners,
To his teachers, his cup,
in toast he raises.

But where is our first, invited guest?
Where is our first, dread teacher,
whose lasting fury,
Poltava's victor has subdued?[1]

While in the process of preparing this essay for publication, especially when "Operation Desert Storm" had culminated in a decisive victory, the author discussed the influence of Soviet military theory on U.S. Army "AirLand Battle" doctrine. These lines from Pushkin's poem "Poltava" kept returning. In the aftermath of the Cold War it seems not at all strange to seek this linkage between a Russian "teacher-theorist" and an American practitioner-victor of modern war. When General H. Norman Schwarzkopf in his post-campaign briefing spoke of "operational art" the very term he chose to use made that tie more explicit, for it was General-Major Alexander Andreevich Svechin (1878-1938), who first applied the term "operational art" [operativnoe iskusstvo] to refer to a third category of military art between strategy and tactics.[2] The very nature of the Coalition's campaign, its limited political objectives and the strict congruence between these objectives and the military means chosen, the initial defensive posture, economic sanctions, the gradual buildup of forces in theater, the subsequent initial air campaign aimed at the attrition of Iraqi military potential, and, finally, the decisive blow aimed at achieving the destruction of the enemy forces in theater and the termination of the war with limited political gains, the liberation of Kuwait, fit the strategic model which Svechin described as attrition. Therefore, it is altogether fitting and proper that Svechin's major study, *Strategy*, be made accessible to Western military analysts, officer-students and military historians.

---

* The views expressed here are those of the author and should not be construed to represent those of the Department of Defense or the Department of the Army.

[1] Alexander Pushkin, "Poltava," *Sochineniia* [Works] (Moscow: Izdatel'stvo "Khudozhestvennaia Literatura," 1964), vol. I, pp. 199-200.

[2] On the details of this relationship see: James J. Schneider, "Introduction" in: V. K. Triandafillov, *The Nature of the Operations of Modern Armies*, edited by Jacob W. Kipp (London: Frank Cass, forthcoming). On General Schwarzkopf's use of the term "operational art" see: General H. Norman Schwarzkopf, "CENTCOM News Briefing" (Riyadh, Saudi Arabia, February 27, 1991), p. 10.

As the other introductory essays to this volume suggest, the legacy of General-Major Svechin has become a topic of much debate in the Soviet Union. Civil analysts, military theorists and officers of the General Staff have found much of merit in Svechin's views on alternative strategies. These have been well presented by my colleagues, A. A. Kokoshin, V. V. Larionov and V. N. Lobov in their essays. The focus of this essay will be Svechin's views on the relationship between military history and military theory. Svechin's contributions to these fields are best understood in the context of his times and the challenges facing military art and science in the early twentieth century. Many of Svechin's insights are, however, still relevant to those who must deal with the problem of finding a place for military history in officer education.

Svechin served, fought, studied and wrote in a time of momentous changes in the nature of war. His career as an officer of the Imperial General Staff [*genshtabist*] and military specialist in service of Soviet power [*voenspets*] underscores the themes of continuity and change in the Russian/Soviet military. If there is one theme that unites all of his studies, it is imperative to understand those trends which were guiding the evolution of military art under the impact of the industrialization of warfare.

> The great commanders, as with all successful practioners, were first of all sons of their age. In the epoch of Napoleon the techniques of Frederick the Great were utterly defeated and now the application of the techniques for the Napoleonic epoch lead only to failure. Successful action most of all must be proper to its place and time, and therefore it must agree with the contemporary situation.[3]

His own approach to military art and theory could be described in the same fashion as he characterized that of the German military historian Hans Delbrueck: a combination of the Hegelian dialectic and historical materialism.[4] Introducing such a dialectical approach to an evolving military art had the same impact on military theory that Einstein had on Newtonian physics. In place of certainty and eternal laws in military affairs there appeared the principle of "relativity" [*otnositel'nost'*] negating the very "decisiveness, absence of vacillation, and goal-directedness," which had so much importance.[5] Svechin emphasized the evolution of military art and warned against any effort to create closed systems on the basis of past combat experience. The proper topic of military history was the study of those tendencies shaping future war.[6]

In 1903 when Svechin entered the Nikolaevsk Academy of the General Staff, the Napoleonic paradigm of strategic deployment, march-maneuver and tactical engagement in a grand battle still dominated military thought. Evidence to the

---

[3] Aleksandr Svechin, *Predrazsudki i boevaia deistvitel'nost'* [Prejudices and Combat Reality] (St. Petersburg: Komissioner Voenno-uchebnykh zavedeniia, 1907), p. 1.

[4] A. A. Svechin, "Del'briuk — istorik izmora i sokrusheniia" [Delbrueck—historian of attrition and destruction] in: A. A. Svechin, ed., *Strategiia v trudakh voennykh klassikov* [Strategy in the Works of the Military Classics], two volumes (Moscow: Gosvoenizdat, 1926), vol. II, pp. 233-235.

[5] Ibid., p. 235.

[6] A. Svechin, *Evoliutsiia voennogo iskusstva* [The Evolution of Military Art], two volumes (Moscow: Gosvoenizdat, 1927-1928), vol. II, pp. 537 ff.

contrary, such as Moltke's campaigns or the American Civil War, were either cut to fit the existing theory or ignored. The lessons of Russia's own experience in the Russo-Turkish War of 1877-1878 were still unassimilated. The Imperial Russian Army lacked the leadership and mechanisms to grasp the central lessons of the Russo-Turkish War. On the one hand, this was the result of court-command politics, involving members of the imperial family, who did not want their reputations sullied.[7] In such a climate the myth of General Mikhail Dmitrievich Skobelev on his white stallion at Sheinovo cast aside any concern over the implications of Plevna first, second and third.[8] On the other hand, it was also a result of a particular mindset among the army's most important military thinkers, especially General H. A. Leer (1829-1904) who taught strategy at the Nikolaevsk Academy of the General Staff. Leer believed in eternal principles and laws, interpreted Moltke as a mid-century Napoleon, and had a disdain for the recent unpleasantness in the Balkans. Neither his book on strategy, which dominated the field until his death, nor the guide to his lectures at the Academy, which was published in 1887, addressed the lessons of 1877-1878. Some civilian critics, notably the Warsaw financier and railroad magnate Jan Bloch, had already concluded that a future war would be shaped by the destructive power of new weapons, by million-man armies, and by the economic mobilization of society by the belligerent states.[9] Leer and his generation of officers looked for didactic tools rather than evolutionary concepts. In a time of radical change in the instruments of war they sought a firm doctrine. Leer emphasized and reemphasized the role and function of the operational line in determining the strategic direction of a campaign which would culminate in a decisive engagement.[10] Technological change might reshape tactics, an applied art, but they could not negate strategic principles, which were unchanging. Strategy presented in this manner slowly ossified into dogma. Such was Svechin's critical judgment of the army's theory on the eve of the Russo-Japanese War.

Svechin and the Russo-Japanese War: The Impulse for Reform

When Russia went to war in 1904, Svechin went too. By the summer of 1904 he was commanding an infantry company in the mountains of Manchuria. Later, he served as a staff officer in General Kuropatkin's headquarters. In Manchuria he got a first-hand appreciation of the problems of industrial war, which haunted General Kuropatkin and his staff. Much later, he would write that the central problem for Kuropatkin was his failure to understand that in a given theater of war there could only be one military strategy. While Japanese strategy had subordinated continental and maritime operations to a single strategic vision,

---

[7] P. A. Zaionchkovskii, *Samoderzhavie i russkaia armiia na rubezhe XIX-XX stoletii* [Autocracy and the Russian Army at the Turn of the Nineteenth-Twentieth Century] (Moscow: Mysl', 1973), p. 322. See also: A. K. Gerua, *Posle voiny, o nashei armii* [After the War, On Our Army] (St. Petersburg: Tipografiia A. S. Suvorova, 1907), pp. 30-32.

[8] A. Svechin and Iu. D. Romanovskii, *Russko-iaponskaia voina*, 1904-1905 gg. [The Russo-Japanese War, 1904-1905] (Oranienbaum: Izdanie Ofitserskoi Strelkovoi Shkoly, 1910), p. vii.

[9] I. Bliokh [Jan Bloch], "Budushchaia voina, eia ekonomicheskiia prichiny i posledstviia" [The future war, its economic causes and consequences], *Voennyi sbornik*, no. 224 (April 1893), pp. 181-217.

[10] Svechin, *Strategiia v trudakh voennykh klassikov*, vol. II, pp. 272-273.

Kuropatkin ignored the maritime dimension of warfare.[11] In the war's aftermath Svechin authored a major strategic survey of the Manchurian campaign with the intention of addressing the central lessons that the Russian army should master to avoid another such defeat. And for Svechin the key strategic issue was the fact that while the Japanese had concentrated their military power to achieve victory in the theater, for Russia war in Manchuria began as and remained a war of an advanced guard against the enemy's main force. His second focus was the art of conducting operations in theater.[12]

Two decades before the term operational art was coined reform-minded tsarist officers had noted that modern war had destroyed the symmetry of the Napoleonic paradigm in which tactics were the management of forces on the field of battle and strategy the maneuver of forces to the field of battle. For these officers of the Imperial General Staff Manchuria had been the classroom and the Japanese army the harsh teacher. The Battle of Mukden in January 1905 dwarfed Borodino in firepower, area and time and posed a host of new problems relating to the control of troops. At Mukden in 1905 three Russian armies, numbering 300,000 men, 1,475 field guns and 56 machine guns, faced five Japanese armies, numbering 270,000 men, 1,063 guns and about 200 machine guns. The fighting lasted for six days and covered a front of 155 km and a depth of 80 km.[13] The battlefield had become more vast, less dense, but more lethal. Railroads could move greater masses of troops over greater distances and sustain the flow of men and materiel into the theater. Troop control on this expanded battlefield had become far more difficult as multiple armies operated over broader frontages, raising a host of issues associated with the evolving nature of the application of combined arms to achieve success. The magazine rifle, quick-firing field gun and the machine gun had altered the relationship between offense and defense and called into question the means by which commanders sought to onduct maneuver, fire and shock. Mass armies, industrialization of society and the acquisition of new weapons had brought these changes in the scale, physical dimensions and temporal character of modern combat, replacing the great culminating battle with a series of tactical engagements united by a commander's concept to form a single operation. Successive operations in a theater according to a unified theater conception became a campaign strategy. Successive operations recast the problem of logistical support in the theater of military actions and raised but did not resolve the problem of pursuit and exhaustion.

Colonel Svechin's interest in the conduct of operations evolved out of a systematic critique of the failure of tactics to address the problem of troop control in modern theater warfare, first observed during the Russo-Japanese War. This

[11] A. Svechin, "Osnovy sovremennoi iaponskoi strategii i taktiki [Principles of Modern Japanese Strategy and Tactics], *Voennaia mysl'*, no. 1 (January 1937), pp. 141-142.

[12] A. Svechin, "Strategicheskii ocherk Russko-iaponskoi voiny ot nachala kampanii do srazheniia pod Liaoianom vkliuchitel'no" [A strategic outline of the Russo-Japanese War from beginning of the campaign to the engagement at Liaoyuan inclusively], *Voennyi sbornik*, no. 3 (March 1907), pp. 47-69; no. 4 (April 1907), pp. 47-63; and no. 5 (May 1907), pp. 47-69.

[13] Svechin and Romanovskii, *Russko-iaponskaia voina, 1904-1905 gg.*, pp. 337-381. See also: *Voennaia entsiklopediia* [Military Encyclopedia] (St. Petersburg: I. D. Sytin, 1914), vol. 14, pp. 474 ff.

operational focus became a means of drawing the attention of senior officers to the need to provide effective leadership over a battlefield, which had been recast in terms of time, space and scale of combat assets engaged. This battlefield required that control be exercised through a modern headquarters and staff, linked with the front and rear by telegraphic and telephonic ties. Effective troop control called for an effort to link together a succession of tactical bounds under a unified campaign plan designed to achieve strategic success in a theater.

Svechin's analysis addressed those problems which went beyond the "genius" or lack of genius of a particular commander, in this case the defeated Russian commander, General Aleksei Nikolaevich Kuropatkin. Kuropatkin had been an excellent chief of staff to General Skobelev in the Balkans, had written extensively on that experience and had later campaigned effectively in Central Asia.[14] As minister of war he had directed Russia's rearmament in the years before the outbreak of war and proved a talented logistician. Russia mobilized a half million men and sent them over 5,000 miles by rail.

Kuropatkin was also a devoted disciple of Leer. His initial deployments and the slow buildup of his operations on the Mukden-Port Arthur axis were clear proof that he understood and was applying the concept of the operational line. What he and his staff could not do was provide effective command and control of his forces in the field. The Russian High Command spent the entire war in Manchuria seeking the single set-piece battle which would decide the campaign. Its elaborate march-maneuvers to position forces favorably for a general engagement were frustrated by Japanese preemptive meeting engagement. Svechin warned against any cavalier assessment of the lessons of the war

> in which the failures are explained exclusively either by the inabilities of individual commanders or the super-natural combat capabilities of the enemy, or illiteracy of the Russian peoples, or the unrest within the state. We do not need criminals or idols; they only interfere with the assessment of our mistakes and a rational correction of them.[15]

The Japanese, using the German mission-oriented tactics of Sigismund von Schlichting, seized the initiative, threatened Kuropatkin's flanks and repeatedly forced him to abandon the field after a spirited but inconclusive defense. The Japanese commander, rather than waiting to deploy his forces and then enter into a general engagement, allowed his troops to engage the enemy from the march, thereby seizing the initiative and frustrating Kuropatkin's elaborate plans.[16] Japanese junior officers understood their commander's intent, responded to unexpected developments by exercising their own initiative and accomplished their tactical missions. That spirit was too often lacking in Russian officers, including officers of the General Staff, who fell back upon school solutions and became "operational lawyers" and bureaucrats, not soldiers. Their first concern was to make sure that no one could question their decisions.[17]

---

[14] A. N. Kuropatkin, *Deistviia otriadov generala Skobeleva v russko-turetskuiu voinu 1877-1878 godov* [Actions of the General Skobelev's Detachments in the Russo-Turkish War of 1877-1878] (St. Petersburg: Voennaia tipografiia, 1885), vol. II, pp. 674-678.

[15] Svechin, *Russko-iaponskaia voina, 1904-1905 gg.*, p. 387.

In Manchuria the battlefield had assumed a breadth and depth that were unthinkable only a half century before. It required a new sort of commander who could conquer space and time to bring about concentration of combat power at the decisive point and time to press the combat to culmination. Repeatedly, Japanese commanders achieved such results against numerically superior Russian forces. At Mukden Russian reserves found themselves marching from one side of the battlefield to the other and either taking no decisive part in the action or being so exhausted by the process that they had lost their effectiveness. Having lost the initiative to the Japanese, Kuropatkin repeatedly found himself on the tactical defense and forced to withdrawal under strong enemy pressure.

Critics, such as Svechin, concluded that the impact of technology on the scale of battle was in the process of working a radical change in the conduct of war. Russian officers began to speak of a new focal point in military art between strategy and tactics, war and battle. They sought a new terminology to give expression to this intermediary level of combat and employed engagement [*srazhenie*] to define the scale of combat above battle, and operation [*operatsiia*], to describe the linking together of maneuver and combat into a series of "individual bounds of the attacker forward and the defender backward."[18] For Lieutenant Colonel A. Neznamov, the Russian defeats in the Far East had one basic cause: "We did not understand modern war."[19] Already in 1909 Neznamov had used a public lecture to identify the central changes in the art of military leadership which were arising from the demands of mass, industrial war. Much of what Neznamov said was taken from German writings, especially Schlichting, but they were presented within a very Russian context. Neznamov redefined control [*upravlenie*] and initiative [*pochin*] so as to stress the role of the commander in imposing order from above in the form of his plan of action. Initiative among junior commanders became subject to the limits imposed by their understanding of each of their units' role in that plan and the subordination of their actions to its needs. Initiative no longer meant shouting hurrah and leading the troops forward into battle but the application of professional skills to the persistent development of the attack in the necessary direction. Control embraced a feedback loop as well, for the commander could only develop his operational plan on the basis of timely intelligence and situation reports.[20] The available technical means of control and communication were not, however, equal to the demands of time and space that the new weapons imposed.

This attention to the operation as the keystone of modern war stirred considerable controversy within Russian military circles and within the imperial govern-

---

[16] Svechin, "Strategicheskii ocherk...," *Voennyi sbornik*, no. 4 (April 1907), pp. 68-69.

[17] A. Svechin, "Otvetstvennost' i takticheskie zadachi" [Responsibility and tactical missions], *Voennaia nauka i revoliutsiia*, no. 2 (December 1921), pp. 177-180.

[18] A. Neznamov, *Sovremennaia voina: Deistviia polevoi armii* [Modern War: Field Army Actions], 2nd edition (Moscow: 1912), pp. 13-17.

[19] Ibid., p. vi.

[20] A. Neznamov, *Konspekt lektsii podpolkovnika Neznamova* (26-go marta 1909 g.): *Trebovaniia, kotorye pred'iavliaet sovremennyi boi k podgotovke nachal'nikov i mass* [Synopsis of Lecture of Lieutenant Colonel Neznamov (26 March 1909): Requirements Posed by Modern Battle to the Preparation of Senior Officers and the Masses] (St. Petersburg: Tipografiia Gr. Skachkova, 1909), pp. 21-37.

ment. On the one hand, critics were accused of presenting foreign, i.e., German or French, military theory without regard for Russian traditions.   B.   M. Shaposhnikov, then a student at the Academy of the General Staff, reports in his memoirs that when a Russian translation of Schlichting's work became available in 1910 it was apparent that his professor, Lieutenant Colonel Neznamov, "had been bringing us German views on operational art."[21] Much later A. Svechin openly acknowledged the influence that Schlichting had on his wn concepts of strategy. A close reading of Svechin's presentation suggests that the German's ideas also influenced the views of I. I. Mikhnevich, the officer who succeeded Leer in the chair of Strategy at the Academy.[22]

Some senior faculty members were particularly concerned that such foreign ideas would evolve into an undigested dogma, stifling critical thought and promoting stereotyped solutions among junior officers.[23] On the other hand, the competing conceptions quickly degenerated into intrigue and back-stabbing among the teaching staff of the General Staff Academy. B. A. Gerua, who taught there during that period, reports in his memoirs that he and his fellow "Young Turks" associated with the Francophile approach to the teaching of applied tactics which N. N. Golovin championed were removed thanks to the denunciations carried to the suspicious V. A. Sukhomlinov, then the minister of war. The "informer," according to Gerua, was Colonel M. D. Bonch-Bruevich, an intimate of Sukhomlinov's during the later's tenure in the Kiev Military District as Chief of Staff.24   At the same time Shaposhnikov, then a student at the Academy, complained about the total domination of French ideas and concepts at the institution.   For that reason the war game [Kriegspiel] did not figure in the educational program.[25] The subtext to much of this intrigue and animosity at the Academy was the hostility between the professional officers, drawn from the poor nobility and service estates of the empire, and the higher aristocracy with its access to the Court, the Corps of Pages and the Guard.

Colonel Neznamov's advocacy of a unified military doctrine to prepare the entire state for the conduct of modern war brought the young professor into conflict with Nicholas II himself, who ordered the colonel to cease his writings on that topic.[26] Neznamov's views were in no way radical or subversive of the autocracy. As General Mikhnevich stated in his book on strategy, Russian military theorists had concluded that modern war required a centralized, coordinated

[21] B. M. Shaposhnikov, *Vospominaniia. Voenno-nauchnye trudy* [Memoirs. Military-Scientific Works] (Moscow: Voenizdat, 1974), p. 144.

[22] A. A. Svechin, "Evoliutsiia strategicheskikh teorii" [The evolution of strategic theory], in: B. Gorev, ed., *Voina i voennoe iskusstvo v svete istoricheskogo materializma* [War and Military Art in the Light of Historical Materialism] (Moscow: Gosizdat, Otdel voenlit, 1927), pp. 88-100.

[23] P. A. Zhilin, *Problemy voennoi istorii* [Problems of Militaruy History] (Moscow: Voenizdat, 1975), pp. 135-140. General Zaionchkovskii, himself an honored professor at the General Staff Academy, argued that the young Turks within the Academy of the General Staff proved better critics than builders. See: A. Zaionchkovskii, *Mirovaia voina 1914-1918 gg.: Obshchii strategicheskii ocherk* [The World War of 1914-1918: A General Strategic Outline] (Moscow: Gosvoenizdat, 1924), pp. 22-23.

[24] Boris Vladimirovich Gerua, *Vospominaniia o moei zhizni* [My Life's Memoirs], two volumes (Paris: Tanais, 1969), vol. I, pp. 250-261.

[25] Shaposhnikov, *Vospominaniia. Voenno-nauchnye trudy*, pp. 164-165.

effort that would mobilize the nation's total resources for war. The ideal state structure for such an effort was, according to Mikhnevich, *"a powerful monarchy"* which could maintain internal political unity and sustain the war effort to make maximum use of time and space in the conduct of the struggle.[27] The fumbling, disjointed and ineffective national leadership provided by Nicholas II's government during the war years hardly fit what Mikhnevich or Neznamov had in mind. The polemics over unified military doctrine was renewed a decade later in the Trotsky-Frunze debates of the early 1920s. By this time, however, they had a new ideological content, militant Marxism, and a new venue, the communist party. But it was the same debate.[28]

These interwar debates did, however, have some impact upon the way in which Russia went to war in 1914. On the one hand, the critics were able to get the concept of a unified supreme headquarters [*Stavka*] accepted and were able to introduce the intermediary command instance of *front* to control the operations of a group of armies in a given sector of the theater. New Russian field regulations placed greater emphasis upon effective combined arms, and the meeting engagement replaced the march-maneuver. In addition, thanks in part to changing diplomatic circumstances and bureaucratic politics, Russian war plans shifted from General Mikhnevich's covering force strategy to one of initial offensive action, a position in keeping with the requirements of the Franco-Russian military alliance. Some reform-minded officers accepted the need for initial offensive operations as the only way in which decisive victory could rapidly be achieved. Others were concerned with the fact that a Russian offensive against Germany in East Prussia would have to be mounted before the Russian armies could complete their mobilization.[29]

Such a course of action was dictated by French strategic assumptions, which required an immediate Russian offensive to tie down German forces in the East and thereby provide a more favorable balance of forces to assure the success of the French offensive. Already in August 1913 Svechin doubted the wisdom of tying Russian war plans and allied strategy to the success of the initial French offensive. The French army was gambling on "an extraordinarily short and decisive campaign."[30]

Writing at the time when the Russian armament program of 1912 was beginning to impact upon the strategic calculus of Europe, Svechin proposed that the allies shift their offensive priorities and have Russia launch the first allied offensive, while France stood on the defensive. In this fashion the Russian army could attack when it had completed mobilization and not before. France, with the opportunity to stand on the defense, could avoid heavy losses in the initial period

---

[26] Zhilin, *Problemy voennoi istorii*, pp. 140-141.

[27] N. I. Mikhnevich, *Strategiia* [Strategy], 3rd edition (St. Petersburg: Beregovskii, 1911), pp. 106-107.

[28] D. Petrovskii, "Edinaia voennaia doktrina i A. G. Sh." [A Unified Military Doctrine and the Academy of the General Staff] *Voennoe znanie*, nos. 14-15 (August 1921), pp. 11-14.

[29] I. I. Rostunov, *Russkii front pervoi mirovoi voiny* [The Russian Front of the First World War], pp. 93-95; Zaionchkovskii, *Mirovaia voina 1914-1918 gg.*, pp. 50-53; and A. Zaionchkovskii, *Podgotovka Rossii k mirovoi voine* [Russia's Preparation for the World War] (Moscow: Shtab RKKA, 1926), pp. 141-154.

and thereby sustain its war effort. Svechin argued that these implications of Russia's armament program were connected to France's increased vulnerability in case of the failure of France's initial offensive. Svechin stated that Russia would have to mount and conduct decisive offensive operations within two months of the outbreak of hostilities, and linked this delayed Russian offensive to a French shift from an immediate offensive to the strategic defense. His rationale was that "the Russian front has for Germany become the most important theater of operations. And first-class theater of operations refers to the Russian preparations for war which are on a completely unique scale."[31]

Evident in Svechin's proposal were two features of his strategic thought which were shaped by Manchuria and would remain cornerstones of his analysis. A major war would be protracted, and gambling on initial successes to bring about war termination ran the risk of undermining the ability to sustain combat actions. Svechin believed that the study of military history could be fruitfully applied to the solution of current military problems. One cardinal lesson was that commanders started each war with plans for the decisive destruction of the enemy, but that most wars did not end that way. The most pressing problem for modern strategy and operations had become the control of troops in large-scale operations.

Applied Military History

During World War I Svechin served at Stavka, then commanded a regiment and division, and from September 1917 was chief of staff of the Northern Front. Following the October Revolution and the disbandment of the Imperial army Svechin joined the Workers' and Peasants' Red Army [RKKA] in March 1918 and held a series of posts connected with the defensive "screens" which the Soviet regime attempted to maintain along the front while it negotiated peace with the Central Powers. In August 1918, as the Civil War was intensifying, Svechin was appointed chief of the All-Russian Main Staff and held that post until October of that year. Thereafter, he took up his teaching duties in the newly established Academy of the General Staff of the RKKA.

Intellectual speculation about the nature of operations took second place to the praxis of war for Svechin, like most other Russian officers, over the next few years. World war and civil war tore apart the fabric of Russian society and with it the old army. Russian officers had, however, built up a rich fund of experience in modern war, and some of these officers, especially those who joined the Red Army as military specialists [voenspetsy], had an opportunity to develop a theory of operational art on the basis of the prewar speculations and experience in World War I and the Civil War. This opportunity was to some measure the product of the Bolsheviks' and Lenin's attitude toward the expertise of the professional soldier.[32] In part, it was a product of ideological commitment to a transcendent Russian nationalism of the type which moved General Brusilov to offer his services to the Soviet state during the Polish attack in the spring of 1920. Finally, it was partly a matter of chance and luck.

---

[30] A. Svechin, "Bol'shaia voennaia programma" [The Grand War Program], *Russkaia mysl'*, god 34, kn. 8 (August 1913), pp. 19-20.

[31] Ibid., p. 23.

However, as the war dragged·on and the need to train more general staff officers became evident, the Academy was reopened in late 1916. During the next turbulent year the Academy resumed its mission under the most difficult circumstances.[33] Following the October Revolution and the German advance on Pskov toward Petrograd, the commandant of the Academy ordered most of the faculty and students and the library moved to safety. In this case safety was Kazan, where most of those who went joined Kolchak. The minority of faculty and students moved to Moscow, where the Soviet government set about organizing its own Academy of the General Staff.[34] As I. A. Korotkov has acknowledged, the first steps taken by Soviet military science during the Civil War were carried out by *voenspetsy* associated with the tsarist general staff and its academy. The first Soviet professional military journal, *Voennoe delo*, carried articles on military doctrine by Neznamov, Svechin and P. I. Izmest'ev—the last being the author of a major, wartime study on the significance of the estimate in the working out and conduct of military operations.[35]

Lenin's government found the tsarist General Staff's post-1905 approach to the study and use of military history worthy of emulation. One of the first acts of the Soviet Republic in 1918 was the creation of the Commission for the Study and Use of the Experience of the War, 1914-1918.[36] This effort drew upon the talents of many former officers of the Russian General Staff, including Svechin, who headed

[32]   Jacob W. Kipp, "Lenin and Clausewitz: The Militarization of Marxism," *Military Affairs*, vol. 49 (October 1985), pp. 184-191.

[33]   Gerua, *Vospominaniia o moei zhizni*, vol. I, pp. 273-275.

[34]   S. A. Fediukin, *Sovetskaia vlast' i burzhuaznye spetsialisty* [Soviet Power and the Bourgeois Specialists] (Moscow: Mysl', 1965), pp. 71-72.

[35]   I. A. Korotkov, *Istoriia sovetskoi voennoi mysli* [The History of Soviet Military Thought] (Moscow: Voenizdat, 1980), pp. 27-28. Izmest'ev's study titled "Znachenie rascheta pri razrabotke i vedenii voennykh operatsii" [The significance of estimation in the development and conduct of military operations] was serialized in *Voennyi sbornik* from March 1915 to June 1916. Basing his study on a historical analysis of military operations and the writings of Clausewitz, Schlichting and Jomini, Ismest'ev concluded his study with a plea for the need to see the working out and conduct of military operations as one of the most complex and demanding of human activities. Modern war would not tolerate an eyeball estimate [*glazomer*] of the situation. Only the intellect [*um*] could deal with the complexity of modern operations. In a critique of Europe's war planners before 1914, Izmest'ev noted the tendency to suppose that the war plan and the plan of initial operations were the end of the estimate process. This estimate process began with the war plan and moved to the campaign plan, which he defined as the preparation and execution of the plan of war in a given theater of military action but also included the plans of individual operations which could not be worked out in advance in such detail. Izmest'ev firmly believed that the estimates on which the war plan was based should for the most part be "a mathematically absolutely exact estimate." Such calculations should carry over to the first operations of the initial phase of the war. After that the commander and his staff would have to engage in their calculations based on their assessment of the mission, theater, enemy, their own forces and time. He wrote: "Only an amateur [*profan*]·can think that the entire campaign will unfold according to the prearranged plan without a deviation and that the original plan could be maintained up to the end in all its features. Of course, the military commander never lets his main objective pass from view and is not distracted by accidents or changes in events but he can not predetermine beforehand with confidence the path by which to achieve this goal."[*Voennyi sbornik*, no. 4 (April 1916), pp. 29-30.]

[36]   Korotkov, *Istoriia sovetskoi voennoi mysli*, p. 28.

and provided editorial direction to the project. Svechin used the introduction to the first volume of essays published by the Commission to call for further study of changes in strategy and tactics made evident by the World War.[37] Regarding the deeper political and socioeconomic changes wrought by World War I, Svechin consigned their study to the realm of the Socialist Academy and identified the Commission's work as narrowly military and immediately practical. He recognized the twin problems of masses of information and the need for an operational focus.[38]

Svechin's treatment of the war was noteworthy for the absence of a Marxist analytical framework and the presence of an integral Russian nationalism, which even in 1919 linked together the past accomplishments of Russian arms and national military valor, which Svechin described as "a cement, uniting us into one whole."[39] At the same time Svechin promised an objectivity which transcended even that of Moltke the Elder's injunction to his General Staff in writing up the history of the Franco-Prussian War: "the truth, only the truth, but not all the truth." Instead, Svechin said that the Commission's motto would be Clausewitz's: "the truth, only the truth, the whole truth." The reputations of commanders from an army overthrown by social revolution did not need the same special care as those linked to an ancient dynasty.[40] Later when the Commission's task was extended to the study and use of Civil War experience it proved difficult for Soviet military authors to live up to this standard when studying the *RKKA*'s own experience. A little over a decade later Stalinism made a mockery of even Moltke's formula by substituting outright lies for historical judgment to create its own mythical past and by applying terror to transform historical actors into non-persons and historical events into non-events. Nonetheless, for a decade Svechin's standard did remain the criteria for judgment of *RKKA* studies over a wide range of topics. Their high caliber and professional quality owed very much to the example which he set.

Svechin's approach to military history was anything but dogmatic. He understood that his views had been shaped by the experiences of his own generation of General Staff officers. He was sympathetic to the young Red commanders, who upon arriving from the fronts of the Civil War, questioned the applicability of school solutions and textbook military science to their war. Svechin noted that these students were soldier-revolutionaries and not traditional student-officers. These young men were already hardened veterans, having seen combat in World War I and the bloody and bitter Civil War. Full of enthusiasm for a cause but distrustful of the professors from the tsarist Nikolaevsk Academy of the General Staff, who were suspected as "class enemies," they refused to be intimidated by classical authorities or to accept the "school" solutions. Their test of instruction was its relevance to their own practical experience in the field. Svechin could see in the face of each man " . . . an idea which is blasphemous to the temple of science, i.e., to bring in something of his own—to criticize

---

[37] A. Svechin, "Trudy Komissii po issledovaniiu i ispol'zovaniia opyta voiny 1914-1918 gg." [Works of the Commission on the Study and Use of the Experience of the War of 1914-1918], *Voenno-istoricheskii sbornik*, vol. I (1919), pp. 3-8.

[38] Ibid., pp. 4-5.

[39] Ibid., p. 6.

[40] Ibid., p. 9.

thoroughly the ideas presented to them. Their enthusiasm merged with a scorn for the old forms of military science."[41]

These extraordinary circumstances created a unique climate for the serious study of military art. Vigorous debate and sharp polemics were the order of the day. According to Marshal M. V. Zakharov, who was one of Svechin's students, "They [his lectures] inculcated a love for military history, widened the scale of their knowledge, raised the level of general culture, and what is especially important, stimulated students to think creatively and to approach historical phenomena critically."[42]

Svechin's colleague, General A. I. Verkhovskii (1886-1938), Professor of Tactics at the Military Academy and former Minister of War of the provisional government, saw the *voenspets*-professors, such as Svechin and himself, as military "realists," engaged in "a war on two fronts." The realists had to contend with conservatives, on the one hand, who wanted to maintain past views because they were sanctioned by history and the unchanging laws of military science, and the futurists, on the other, who, on the basis of their experience in the Revolution and Civil War, put their faith in crude military means and political agitation and trusted in class struggle to ignite revolution behind the enemy's lines. On occasion the conservatives and futurists made common cause against the realists. In assessing this struggle during the Academy's first decade, 1918-1928, Verkhovskii concluded that it had been one full of vitality. The Red Army had made significant progress in the study of military science and military art.[43]

In such heady times a rough-and-tumble theory conditioned by practical experience and guided by a militant ideology became the basis for a new military science. Its demand for a unity of theory and praxis was fulfilled in the "scientific" analysis of the new Soviet state's own combat experience as reflected in the activities of the Military Academy's Military-Scientific-Society.[44] Svechin played a prominent role in promoting the study of military classics and in digesting the core of military strategy for the students of the Military Academy of the *RKKA*. His goal was to make accessible to his students his own teachers—i.e., the military theorists who had contributed most to military science—and thereby provide the students with some context in which to study the evolution of military art and to place in context the salient features of the World War and Civil War, which would shape its further evolution. This included a major translation program of classic foreign military works, such as Clausewitz's recently published letters on *Prin-*

---

[41]   A. I. Reznichenko, ed., *Akademiia imeni M. V. Frunze: Istoriia Voennoi ordena Lenina, Krasnoznamennoi ordena Suvorova Akademii* [History of the Red Banner, Order of Lenin, Order of Suvorov M. V. Frunze Military Academy] (Moscow: Voenizdat, 1972), p. 40.

[42]   M. V. Zakharov, *General'nyi shtab v predvoennye gody* [The General Staff in the Prewar Years] (Moscow: Voenizdat, 1989), p. 59.

[43]   A. Verkhovskii, "Evoliutsiia prepodavaniia taktiki v 1918-1928 gg." [The evolution of the teaching of tactics, 1918-1928], *Voina i revoliutsiia*, no. 11 (November 1928), pp. 50-52. On Verkhovskii's background and career see: *Voennyi entsiklopedicheskii slovar'* [The Military-Encyclopedic Dictionary] (Moscow: Voenizdat, 1983), p. 126.

[44]   *Voennaia akademiia imeni M. V. Frunze: Istoriia voennoi ordenov Lenina i Oktiabr'skoi Revoliutsii Krasnoznamennoi Ordena Suvorova Akademii* [The M.V. Frunze Military Academy: A History of the Military Orders of Lenin and the October Revolution Red Banner Order of Suvorov Academy] (Moscow: Voenizdat, 1980), p. 41. citing *Voennaia akademiia za piat' let* [The Military Academy After Five Years], p. 168.

ciples of Strategic Decision, memoirs of senior commanders from World War I (i.e., Ludendorff, Conrad and Falkenhayn) and theoretical works, such as von Schlieffen's *Cannae*. Svechin's own contributions to this endeavor were broad and profound and included editing and providing commentary on the selected essays on strategy by leading military theorists from the eighteenth through the twentieth centuries.[45]

A professional soldier, Svechin appreciated the need for a rigorous and structured approach to the study of combat experience. The key to success in military-historical study lay not in the number of primary sources used or the time spent in archives but in the application of a professional soldier's insights to sound methodology in the examination of issues of current military importance. Svechin was very dubious about any attempt to get past events to fit current military or political dogma. In a review of General A. Zaionchkovskii's *Russia's Preparation for War* Svechin critiqued the author for failing to appreciate the real problems associated with Russian war plans and deployments on the eve of World War I. Zaionchkovskii blamed the initial failures of Russian strategic deployment on the decision to redeploy many units in the Polish salient deep within Russia. In the introduction to Zaionchkovskii's volume M. N. Tukhachevskii had speculated that this redeployment had been the result of conservative fears of social revolution, i.e., a need to reposition units to deal with armed rebellion rather than the external threat. Svechin rejected both interpretations, pointing out that reform-minded officers, and not conservatives, had pushed the redeployment to escape the dilemma of placing too many units forward where they would be vulnerable to an initial German offensive before mobilization had been completed. Military prudence, as Svechin had pointed out before the war, imposed the conclusion that Germany would win any mobilization race because of significant advantages in rail networks and transport capacity. The evolution of operational deployment under modern conditions demanded dispositions that would minimize enemy opportunities to disrupt deployment. Moreover, the problem for tsarist Russia had been premature offensive operations in the initial period of war when mobilization had not yet been completed. That had been the primary cause of disaster in East Prussia.[46]

Military history was

> not lifeless monuments but a weapon for struggle in the present, the key to understanding. Each generation must itself forge a new historical weapon no matter how difficult that might be and master it in order to have the possibility of freely setting off on its own road and not be stuck at the tail of the column behind others."[47]

---

[45] I. Marievskii, "Stanovlenie i razvitie teorii operativnogo iskusstva" [The establishment and development of the theory of operational art], *Voenno-istoricheskii zhurnal*, no. 3 (March 1962), pp. 27-28. K. Klausevits, *Osnovy strategicheskogo resheniia* [Principles of Strategic Decision], translated from the German and edited by A. Svechin (Moscow: Gosizdat, 1924).

[46] A. Kolenkovskii, *Manevrennyi period pervoi mirovoi imperialisticheskoi voiny, 1914 g.* [The Maneuver Period of the First World Imperialist War, 1914] (Moscow: Gosvoenizdat, 1940), pp. 175-217, 348-349.

[47] A. Svechin, "Izuchenie voennoi istorii" [The study of military history], *Voina i revolutsiia*, no. 4 (April 1927), p. 66.

Svechin stressed the role of a general staff in cultivating applied historical studies to the problems of operational art. Such studies were one foundation for mastery of troop control of large formations.[48] Military history was the solid foundation for theoretic speculation on strategy:

> The history of military art is the absolutely necessary introduction to the present work [*Strategy*]. Without it we risk making ourselves quite unintelligible. Not keeping our attention focused on the most important military phenomena of history and not furnishing our reflections with a series of military-historical facts, we run the risk of drifting into confusion in abstract propositions from the theory of strategic art. The benefit we derive from it will be proportionate to the experience and military-historical baggage we have at our disposal upon beginning our study of strategy.[49]

Svechin warned in his introduction to *Strategy*, that the brain itself had to be educated to grasp the connections between the theory and practice of strategy; no amount of tactical experience would ever suffice to prepare commanders to conduct operations using large formations in keeping with strategic requirements. Modern war required of statesmen and soldiers a common appreciation of the complex relationship between war and the economy, war and society.[50] Svechin claimed no special political expertise, no profound knowledge of Marxism, but he did assert that the military specialist was the best source of information on military-technical issues.

One of the gravest problems confronting military education was the dangerous tendency for senior military schools to stifle original thought and promote dogma as doctrine. Writing about Sigismund von Schlichting's contribution to military strategy, Svechin noted that Schlichting represented a new breed of military theorist. Having received a fine university education and then serving with the General Staff during the Franco-Prussian War, Schlichting learned about strategy and the conduct of war by reading Moltke's reports. Whereas the General Staff Academy sought to turn Moltke into an epigone of Napoleon, Schlichting studied the Napoleonic art of war not as dogma taught at the Academy but as an intellectual measure against which to judge Moltkian practice. In this fashion Schlichting added a new term, "contemporary," to military art. The study of military history became one means of guaging the impact of changes in civil and military affairs on military art.[51]

Svechin wanted the education of senior officers to be structured so that their critical skills would be developed. In the strategic dialogue between senior officers and civilian statesmen, Svechin stressed the need for the soldiers to be conversant with diplomatic, political and economic realities shaping strategy. At the same time the military officers also had to master their own craft, the military-technical questions associated with the conduct of war (i.e., operational art) and be able to convey its realities to the civilian leadership.[52]

---

[48] Ibid., pp. 59-60.

[49] A. Svechin, *Strategiia* [Strategy], 1st edition (Moscow: Gosvoenizdat, 1926), p. 31.

[50] Ibid., pp. 5-6.

[51] Svechin, "Evoliutsiia strategicheskikh teorii," pp. 88-99.

For advocating such a role for a general staff in preparing for war and planning operations, Svechin was attacked by a host of politically-minded opponents, who accused him of promoting a "narrow-cast group," the class essence of which was hostile to socialism. V. Levichev saw a distinct challenge to the young Red commanders' authority in Svechin's claims for operational art:

> The knowledge of the "General Staff" invested it with a special privileged trust in operational art and the knowledge of the secrets of victories. This special position of officers of the General Staff in the army created much internal hatred and open hostility from the side of rank-and-file commanders, who because of a lack of family connections (and this was the main line of promotion to general in the old army) and the titles of officers of the General Staff, had no advantages in promotion.[53]

According to Levichev, the Soviet state had the party to guide its preparations for war and thus had no requirement for such a narrow cast of specialists. Instead, it needed commander-generalists, who were trained to lead regiments and above, not a "narrow group of red military specialists" calling themselves the General Staff.[54]

Yet the issue was not simply one of an old cast institution being inevitably hostile to a workers' state or even party guidance. A general staff was critical to the further development of operational art in practice since it would possess those skills necessary to answer the most pressing military-technical questions associated with planning and preparing for war. Using Conrad von Hotzendorf's memoirs as a vehicle to explore the role of the general staff in modern war and preparations for war, the *voenspets-genshtabist* Boris Mikhailovich Shaposhnikov characterized that role as "the brain of the army."[55] Shaposhnikov acknowledged his debt to Svechin and stressed the linkages between the political and military sides of doctrine in the process of war planning. Central to this point was Svechin's invocation of Clausewitz to stress the concept of "war as a continuation of politics by other means" and to assert the centrality of fitting war plans and mobilization to political requirements and not the reverse, as had happened in 1914. Indeed, mobilization was a political act, the very gateway to war. For Shaposhnikov, politics embraced the international class struggle as well as the class struggle within each belligerent. Whereas Svechin clung to the idea of the general staff as the apolitical agents of a supra-class state, Shaposhnikov, himself a *voenspets* and still not a member of the communist party, embraced the idea of a politically-literate general staff, operating under the party's guidance.[56]

Operational Art

Only in 1923-1924 did Svechin tackle the problem of redefining the content of military art. In a cycle of lectures on strategy given at the Military Academy of the

---

[52] Svechin, *Strategiia*, 1st edition, pp. 354-380.

[53] V. Levichev, "'Genshtab i voennaia akademiia RKKA" [The General Staff and the military akademy of the RKKA], *Voina i revoliutsiia*, no. 7 (July 1928), p. 75.

[54] Ibid., p. 77.

[55] B. M. Shaposhnikov, *Mozg armii* [The Brain of the Army] (Moscow: Voennyi Vestnik, 1927), vol. I, pp. 112 ff.

RKKA, Svechin introduced the term "operational art" as the bridge between tactics and strategy, i.e., the means by which the senior commander transformed a series of tactical successes into operational "bounds" linked together by the commander's intent and plan and contributing to strategic success in a given theater of military actions.[57] In his lectures Svechin defined operational art as the "totality of maneuvers and battles in a given part of a theater of military action directed toward the achievement of the common goal, set as final in the given period of the campaign."[58] Svechin's rationale for this redefinition was based on his observation that the former division had been based on the integral concept of "the general engagement" which had disappeared in practice. In its place had emerged a series of successive operations.[59] These lectures served as the basis for Svechin's *Strategiia*, which appeared in 1926. Here Svechin for the first time wrote about the nature of "operational art" and its relationship to strategy and tactics:

> We define an operation as such as an act of war in the course
> of which, without any pauses, the efforts of the forces in a
> particular area of a theater of military actions are directed
> toward the achievement of a specific, intermediary goal.[60]

As Svechin formulated their relationship, politics shaped strategy in all its dimensions, strategy set the parameters of operational art, and operational art shaped tactics to the demands of the theater campaign. Varfolomeev presented the same relationship in terms of means and ends:

> Thus, combat is the means of the operation. Tactics are the
> material of operational art. The operation is the means of
> strategy, and operational art is the material of strategy. Such
> is the essence of this three-part formula.[61]

Svechin's conceptualization of operational art coincided with Mikhail Frunze's appointment as chief of staff of the *RKKA* and chief of the Military Academy. The Red Army, in the aftermath of a rapid demobilization following the Civil War, was in the process of enacting major reforms and adapting itself to the requirements of Lenin's New Economic Policy (NEP). At Frunze's initiative, a Chair of Army Operations was established at the Academy of the *RKKA* in 1924, but it did not survive for long.[62] The content of that part of the Academy's curriculum was directed at the techniques required to conduct operations. Herein was the art or "know-how" [*umenie*]. Initially, however, emphasis was placed more upon general commentary than practical preparation of staff officers for conducting operations. Typical of this literature was M. Bonch-Bruevich's essay on principles of operational leadership in modern war which laid out the content of an operational plan, outlining its features: mission statement, intelligence on enemy forces and their probable courses of action, information on the status of one's own forces, the specific missions of subordinated units, the structure of rear services,

---

[56] Shaposhnikov, *Mozg armii in: Vospominaniia. Voenno-nauchnye trudy*, pp. 425-429.

[57] A. A. Svechin, *Strategiia*, 2nd edition (Moscow: Voennyi Vestnik, 1927), pp. 14 ff.

[58] N. Varfolomeev, "Strategiia v akademicheskoi postanovke" [Strategy in an academic setting], *Voina i revoliutsiia*, no. 11 (November 1928), pp. 83-84.

[59] *Krasnye zori*, no. 11(22), (November 1924), p. 23.

[60] Svechin, *Strategiia*, 1st edition, pp. 18.

[61] Varfolomeev, "Strategiia v akademicheskoi postanovke," p. 84.

the organization of supply and the support of the operation. Bonch-Bruevich emphasized the role of the organs of troop control in turning the commander's intent to an operational plan and outlined the various areas where the staff had to conduct its estimates of the situation. His list of such activities was extensive and encompassed all aspects of operational planning. Bonch-Bruevich emphasized the art of troop control as critical to operational leadership and pointed out the role of the struggle for time in "all preparatory actions and during execution."[63]

N. Varfolomeev, the deputy head of the Department of Strategy during the same period, noted the fact that objective changes in the nature of warfare associated with the appearance of million-man armies and technological innovations had recast the face of battle, increased its spacial and temporal dimensions, broken down the conventional forms of combined arms, forced a rethinking of problems of command and control and laid the foundation for the emergence of the operation as the bridge between strategy and tactics. Tactics became the conduct of battle/combat [*boi*]; the engagement [*srazhenie*], which in the Napoleonic era had been conducted as a series of combats on a single battlefield under the observation of the commander, now took place over a much broader front and at much greater depths well beyond the ability of any commander to exercise direct control. In this manner the operation emerged as the bridge to strategy. Varfolomeev described the modern operation as:

the totality of maneuvers and battles in a given sector of a
theater of military actions [*TVD*] which are directed toward
the achievement of a common objective, which has been set as
final in a given period of the campaign. The conduct of an
operation is not a matter of tactics. It has become the lot of
operational art.[64]

Under Svechin's leadership the Commission for the Study and Use of War Experience had been particularly critical of the prewar tsarist war games, which had downplayed logistics and failed to provide effective guidance for the reformulation of war plans.[65] Military education for senior commanders and staff had to combine military science and military art, "knowledge" [*znanie*] with "knowhow" [*umenie*], to be effective.[66] In 1923 Svechin recommended that wargaming take on the task of assessing operational and tactical concepts under active, informed exercise directors. Participants should not feel that they are being judged. Rather, the focus should be on testing the applicability and effectiveness of various concepts and ideas.[67]

Frunze played a leading role in promoting such an approach by invigorating the Military Academy's Higher Military-Academic Courses [*VVAK*] or senior Red Army commanders, which focused on the further education of brigade and higher commanders.[68] Frunze's commitment to this program brought more attention to

[62]   *Akademiia im. M. V. Frunze*, p. 98.

[63]   M. Bonch-Bruevich, "Nekotorye osnovy operativnogo rukovodstva v sovremennoi voine" [Certain principles of operational leadership in modern war], *Voina i revoliutsiia*, no. 12 (December 1927), pp. 46-63.

[64]   Varfolomeev, "Strategiia v akademicheskoi postanovke," pp. 83-84

[65]   A. N. Suvorov, "*Voennaia igra starshikh voiskovykh nachal'nikov v aprele 1914 goda*" [War game of the senior command in April 1914], *Voenno-istoricheskii sbornik*, vol. I (1919), pp. 9-22.

the Chair of Strategy and its further development. He emphasized the need to change the content of the course on the conduct of operations by shifting from general observations to working out the practical details and techniques for the conduct of operations.[69] Over the next several years this led to the development of a program of operational war-gaming in which students were expected to do the necessary calculations and estimates necessary to prepare for an army operation. This "applied" approach to training future commanders and staff officers was a major break with past Russian tradition and placed primary stress on finding means in the educational process of unifying theory and practice. The leaders in the development of operational war-gaming at the Academy were V. K. Triandafillov, K. Berends and Varfolomeev.[70] The summer campaign of 1920 against Pilsudski's Poland served as both a model and a case-study for such operational gaming since it embraced a major operational axis in a war against one of the most probable future opponents of the Soviet state.

Svechin's Strategic Paradigm

The core of Svechin's *Strategy* and its most controversial element to both his contemporaries and present-day analysts was a dualistic strategic paradigm, which Svechin borrowed from Hans Delbrueck, the eminent German military historian and theorist. The two poles of this paradigm, attrition (Delbrueck's *Ermattungsstrategie,* or Svechin's *izmor* ["starvation"] in Russian) and destruction (Delbrueck's *Niederwerfungsstrategie,* or Svechin's *sokrushenie* in Russian), were conditioned by the circumstances of war itself. A belligerent power, depending on its war aims, the military potential of its society and economy, its military capabilities, the nature of the theater and the nature of its opponent, could employ either model. Like Delbrueck, Svechin thought that soldiers were all too eager to take the strategy of destruction as the only appropriate course to seize and exploit the initiative and bring about a decision in a one-sided reading of Clausewitz's assessment of the legacy of Napoleon.[71]

As had also happened with Delbrueck, whose comparison of Frederick the Great and Napoleon as examples of two different strategic models had sparked intense polemics between the author and the German General Staff, Svechin's

---

[66] E. Smyslovskii, "Voennaia nauka i voennoe iskusstvo" [Military science and Military Art] *Voennaia mysl' i revoliutsiia,* no. 3 (1922), pp. 11-20.

[67] A. Svechin, "Voennaia igra" [The war game], *Voennaia mysl' i revoliutsiia,* no. 3 (July 1923), pp. 76-80.

[68] *Akademiia General'nogo Shtaba: Istoriia Voennoi ordenov Lenina i Suvorova I stepeni akademii General'nogo shtaba Vooruzhennykh Sil SSSR imeni K. E. Voroshilova* [The Academy of the General Staff: A History of the Military Orders of Lenin and Suvorov First Degree K. E. Voroshilov Academy of the General Staff of the USSR Armed Forces], 2nd edition (Moscow: Voenizdat, 1987), p. 22-24.

[69] Mikhail Frunze, *Izbrannye proizvedenniya* [Selected Works] (Moscow: Voenizdat, 1957), vol. II, p. 35.

[70] Varfolomeev, "Strategiia v akademicheskoi postanovke," pp. 92-93; Varfolomeev, "Operativnaia voennaia igra" [The Operational war game], *Voina i revoliutsiia,* no. 6 (1928), pp. 18-35; K. Berends, "Shtabnye voyennye igry" [Staff war games], *Voina i revoliutsiia,* no. 6 (June 1928), pp. 36-55; and V. Triandafillov, "Materialy dlia zadachi na shtabnuiu voennuiu igru" [Materials for holding a staff war game], *Voina i revoliutsiia,* no. 12 (December 1927), pp. 31-45.

presentation set off an intense debate within the Red Army. In keeping with the economic realities of the NEP, the social character of the Soviet regime, the geostrategic features of the probable main theater of a future war and the nature of the forces of probable opponents, Svechin advocated a strategy of attrition for Soviet Russia.[72] The NEP as the political-economic framework of Soviet strategy represented a welcome departure from what Svechin called "dangerous illusions:"

> One must welcome the rejection by Soviet power of any
> sort of chauvinism, from the pressure to use the Red Army
> for promoting revolution by force of arms. But should such
> manifestations of chauvinism appear, then look at a map,
> reflect on modern technology and give up any sort of pleas-
> ant but even more so dangerous illusions."[73]

In advocating a strategy of attrition Svechin could invoke the support of many prominent figures in the Red Army, including Mikhail Frunze, who until his death in October 1925 advocated preparations for protracted war. Svechin's most vehement opponents were those who viewed class war and a strategy of destruction as the only appropriate course of action for the Red Army. Most vocal in promoting a strategy of destruction was M. N. Tukhachevskii, a young Red commander, hero of the Civil War and the advocate of using the Red Army as an instrument of "revolution from without" [revoliutsiia izvne].

In early 1926 at a special conference held to debate the merits of strategies of attrition [izmor] and destruction [sokrushenie] faculty members from the Military Academy and officers of the Main Staff of the RKKA took opposing sides. The intensity of the debate over the issue of the advantages of a strategy of attrition influenced Svechin to recast the second edition of Strategy, which appeared in 1927. In the introduction to the second edition he acknowledged his debt to Delbrueck's concepts and defended them as "tools of historical research needed to give meaning to the military-historical past." He concluded: "For us these phenomena are alive in the present and have come together in a single era, and we would consider it impossible to construct any theory of strategy without appropriate concepts and terms."[74]

In his section devoted to a typology of operations in the first edition of Strategy and in subsequent defense of a strategy of attrition it is apparent that Svechin's views on the advantages of a strategy of attrition were much influenced by his assumptions about the protracted nature of a future war and the relative inability of Soviet Russia to mount a decisive initial blow against a major opponent. Moreover, Soviet Russia, like tsarist Russia, was not vulnerable to the sort of lightning blow which could annihilate a smaller state. A strategy of attrition was not to be favored at all times.[75] In the second edition, Svechin did note that specific

---

[71]   Svechin, *Strategiia*, 2nd edition, pp. 12-14.

[72]   Ibid., pp. 250-251. For work on Delbrueck and his strategic paradigm see: Gordon Craig, "Delbrueck: The Military Historian," in: Edward Mead Earle, *Makers of Modern Strategy*, 1st edition (Princeton: Princeton University Press, 1943), pp. 260-286; and Arden Bucholz, *Hans Delbrueck and the German Military Establishment* (Iowa City: Iowa University Press, 1985), pp. 52 ff.

[73]   A. Svechin, "Opasnye illiuzii" [Dangerous illusions], *Voennaia mysl' i revoliutsiia*, no. 2 (March 1924), pp. 49-50.

conditions could create opportunities for the application of a strategy of destruction. These conditions he identified as a national military posture ensuring maximum military preparedness to such a degree that a state could commit the maximum amount of its military potential as fielded capabilities in the initial period of war; a theater dominated by a land frontier served by a dense rail and road network; a significant superiority of combat power over the opponent; and a weak state and social system wracked by conflict and vulnerable to an external blow.[76] Neither the Soviet state nor its probable opponents in a coalition war in Eastern Europe fit such a situation.

This focus on attrition strategy led Svechin to turn his attention to the problem of linking national strategy to the problem of prewar preparation for war. Here he emphasized the need to address the political and economic preparation of the nation for war. In his formulation of the alternative strategic concepts, i.e., destruction [sokrushenie] and attrition [izmor], a host of issues regarding the relationship between operational art and the paradigm of future war quickly emerged as topics for debate. Drawing upon the work of Delbrueck, Svechin was critical of the German General Staff's one-sided emphasis on the conduct of decisive operations in the initial period of war.[77] Svechin recognized the seeds of disaster in such short-war illusions. He stressed the need to prepare for a long war, given the geostrategic and political situation confronting the USSR. For Svechin, modern war was by definition total war, a drama in three acts: prologue, initial period, and second part. The second part was, in its essence, a people's war. Svechin identified several classic models of the second act, including Napoleon's Russian campaign after the capture of Moscow, the guerilla war in Spain and the German national insurrection of 1813. Finally, Svechin agreed with Clausewitz that the objective in this act of war was the destabilization of the enemy government.[78] Gambling on decisive victory in the first act and ignoring the second was an invitation to disaster. Hubris invited nemesis.

Svechin emphasized political and economic objectives for strategy at the expense of any immediate attempt to annihilate the enemy's armed forces. He defended the Russian General Staff's assessment in 1912-1914 of the problems of deploying its fronts and armies in the initial period of war against Germany and Austria-Hungary. Where it had gone wrong was in tying Russian war plans to French requirements for immediate offensive operations, even if mobilization, concentration and deployment of forces could not be completed in a timely manner. Svechin noted that the Russian reformers of 1908-1909 had been intent upon moving the weight of the army away from the frontier to provide greater depth of deployment. For him the most central and conspicuous problem was the commitment to the initial forward deployment of Russian forces in Poland. With the center of gravity away from the frontier, the Russian army ceased to be vulnerable to an initial German offensive intent upon annihilating its first strategic

---

[74] Svechin, *Strategiia*, 2nd edition, p. 11.

[75] Svechin, *Strategiia*, 1st edition, pp. 250-265.

[76] Svechin, *Strategiia*, 2nd edition, p. 43.

[77] Svechin, *Strategiia* 2nd edition, pp. 12-26.

[78] A. Svechin, "Vtoraia chast' mirovoi voiny" [The second part of the World War], *Voennaia mysl' i revoliutsiia*, no. 5 (September-October 1923), pp. 23-29.

echelon in Poland. France's requirement for an immediate Russian offensive against Germany was not dictated by defensive considerations but by French offensive requirements. With such deeper deployments and a complete mobilization, the German High Command might, at best, achieve some success against covering forces, but hardly force a strategic decision. Svechin concluded that the second act of the war with Germany had just begun with the French occupation of the Ruhr. The political content of that act would be a German national resistance to Versailles.

The proper response to the Schlieffen Plan was neither plan "A" nor plan "G" with their immediate offensive objectives in East Prussia or Galicia. A "Russian Schlieffen Plan" was an invitation to disaster:

> Plans of deployment are two-sided affairs, affecting each side. This the author seems to forget. The Russian General Staff was not running away from an "apparition" but provoked the transformation of German power along the Russian border into an apparition. By doing that, did it betray Russian interests?[79]

For Svechin the answer to this dilemma was to pull the forward armies' points of concentration back from the border, trading time for space in order to complete deployments. In the end, he maintained, the very nature of the Russian state suited it for a strategy of protracted war and attrition.

> The development of the Russian state, as of other states, moved in the direction of preparing it for a protracted war, for attrition, and not destruction. This process took place unnoticed even by the very leaders of reform in the army... But a cruel evolution led change of preparation of Russian deployment toward attrition. Russia's force for destruction had not increased during those 14 years [1900-1914]. In this direction, which the evolution of Russian military power took, the single correct decision would be not an immediate campaign against Berlin, but a struggle for a further stage of deployment on the Danzig-Peremyshl' front.[80]

This focus led Svechin and others into a consideration of the problem of the relationship between the civilian and military leadership in the conduct of war and preparations for war. He argued that Russia traditionally and the Soviet Union then faced special conditions that made a strategy of attrition particularly attractive.[81] At the same time, however, Russia's military experience had concealed that fact. Svechin argued that one of the legacies of Russia's heritage of frontier warfare was the tendency of military commanders to turn their own rear areas into satrapies, where immediate supply requirements of front commands took precedence over a rational mobilization of the entire state economy. He criticized such a narrow perception of military logistics and emphasized the need for a unification of front and rear through the planned mobilization of the entire "state rear," by which he meant the national economy, for the purpose of supporting front operations. The state rear in this context defined the strategic and

---

[79] A. Svechin, "Evoliutsiia operativnogo razvertyvania" [The evolution of operational deployment], *Voina i revoliutsiia*, no. 5 (May 1926), p. 20.

[80] Ibid., p. 24.

operational capabilities of Soviet forces in a given theater and set limits on what was militarily feasible.[82] The strategic realities of Soviet Russia's state rear were determined by its territorial extent, population size, agrarian base, NEP economy and political order (i.e., a party-dominated system based upon an alliance between workers and peasants). National strategy could not be recut to fit revolutionary romanticism and a cult of the offensive.

Svechin's argument for a national strategy based on attrition had its roots in his own vision of Russian society and the historical experience of the World War. His fellow professor and colleague A. Verkhovskii, in defending an "attrition" strategy, enraged the offensive-minded young Red commanders when he asserted that it might be better in the initial period of a future Polish-Soviet war "to give up Minsk and Kiev than to take Bialystok and Brest." To those who identified Marxism-Leninism with a strictly offensive style of war, such retreats were quite unthinkable.[83]

As the Red Army's leading author on tactics, Verkhovskii championed preparing the Red Army for battle with a concrete enemy in specific circumstances. The features which marked this "new school" of tactics from the old were:

- the features of one's own weapons;
- the influence of class and national conflict within which a future war would be fought;
- the quantity of troops available to the enemy and the Red Army, the size of the theater, density of forces and depth of deployments;
- how the opponents will act "not with our weapons but with his and according to his own regulations which are in keeping with his weapons and his troops";
- the decisive influence of locality in the sense of both theater of war and within the confines of the field of battle; and finally
- the closest and most intense scrutiny had to be given to calculating the influence of the element of time on the forms of struggle and on the degree of its organization, not only on the enemy side but also on the Soviet side, i.e., a search for an advantage in staff procedures which would permit one army to decide, plan and execute more rapidly than the opponent.[84]

All these points, while touching on strategic topics in one way or another, addressed operational issues. Density and depth of forces expressed as number of troops and guns on a given front could be reduced to calculations of density of forces per kilometer of front. "Without calculations all these forms lack content. Furthermore, it is very important to know the density of forces in a given front at which the saturation point is reached in those cases when we wish to set the form of a march-maneuver in a future war."[85]

Svechin had observed that war plans and operational considerations regarding future war were exercises in foresight. He was uncomfortable with any claim

---

81 Svechin, *Strategiia*, 2nd edition, pp. 56-59.

82 A. Svechin, "Gosudarstvennyi i frontovoi tyl" [The state and front rear], *Voina i revoliutsiia*, no. 11 (November 1928), pp. 94-108.

83 A. Svechin, *Klauzevits* [Clausewitz] (Moscow: Zhurnal'no-Gazetnoe Ob'edinenie, 1935), p. 19.

that foresight involved prediction, a guide to a commander in a real war in all its complexity. Instead he discussed the problem of articulating a general strategic line of conduct, i.e., a broad design for successive operations leading to victory. Such a design would provide the "key" to the interpretation of the demands of constantly changing conditions and permit the commander to adjust to new circumstances. Great commanders were not "prophets."

> In strategy prophecy may only be charlatanism, and even a genius is incapable of seeing how a war will unfold. But he must put together a perspective in which he will evaluate the phenomena of war. A military leader needs a working hypothesis.[86]

The wrong hypothesis, a set of incorrect assumptions about political ends and military means or about combat capabilities and logistical support, could and would lead to disaster. Thus, in criticizing Tukhachevskii's "March Beyond the Vistula" in 1920, V. Melikov noted the asymmetry between the commander's operational concepts and his logistics. The risks of a strategy of destruction under such circumstances were great.[87]

A much more narrow critique of attrition strategy built on Svechin's own observation that in the initial period of war the attacker—i.e., the side adapted to decisive initial operations—could impose its style of warfare on the defender. Vasilii Novitskii noted that a strategy based on attrition stood on totally different principles than one based upon destruction. Destruction required the ability to conduct large-scale, immediate, decisive, lightning operations. In place of mobilizing the civilian economy for war, a strategy of destruction required an in-place war industry which would in peacetime provide all the weapons and materiel necessary to conduct decisive operations. Svechin had assumed that the side which adopted a strategy of destruction would be able to impose its war on the other side by seizing the initiative and mounting initial offensive operations. Counting on victory in a short war, the side adopting a strategy of destruction could avoid a host of difficult peacetime sacrifices necessary to create a unity of front and rear in a protracted war. However, failure in those initial operations would expose the adventurism at the heart of such a policy by underscoring the disconnection between military strategy and political-economic preparations. Novitskii reformulated Svechin's assumption that the initiative always goes to the side following a strategy of destruction by focusing on the problem of the struggle for mobilization and deployment. In the age of air power, he emphasized the possibility of a covering force army conducting initial operations so as to disrupt enemy mobilization and deployment and thereby to win the "struggle for the nature of future war."[88] Novitskii's work on this aspect of future war contributed to the development of a specific line of Soviet military writings devoted to the

---

[84] A. Verkhovskii, "Novaia i staraia shkola" [The new and old school], *Voina i revoliutsiia*, no. 4 (April 1928), pp. 100-101.

[85] Ibid., p. 109.

[86] Svechin, *Strategiia*, 2nd edition, pp. 235-236.

[87] V. Melikov, *Marna, Visla, Smirna* [The Marne, the Vistula, the Smirna] (Moscow: *Voennyi vestnik*, 1928), p. 198.

nature, form, content and law-governed patterns [*zakonnomernosti*] of the development of the "initial period of war."[89]

As V. K. Triandafillov would point out in 1929, the pace of economic and technological change in Europe was creating two different military worlds. In Western Europe and America economic development had created the preconditions for he mechanization of warfare. When they went to war those states would draw upon the full potential of an industrial rear. In Eastern Europe, including the Soviet Union, the economic and technological bases of military power were a peasant rear [*krest'ianskii tyl*]. Large-scale mechanization was beyond any possibility.[90]

By the time Svechin had revised *Strategy* Soviet Russia was already moving into crisis because of a breakdown of the NEP. The outcome of that crisis was Stalin's revolution from above: industrialization, collectivization, totalitarian controls and militarization of Soviet society. If *izmor* was the expression of the NEP in strategic terms, then *sokrushenie* would become the expression of Stalin's revolution. In their advocacy of a strategy of destruction, Tukhachevskii and his supporters combined revolutionary enthusiasm with a technological determinism, which Svechin rejected on both counts. Regarding the impact of technology, he warned against any attempt to achieve technological surprise on an operational scale. The historical record suggested that the development of advanced technology, its mass production, integration into the armed forces and articulation of new combat forms which would optimize its advantages were, in fact, protracted processes. Prudent state policy sought to seize and maintain the technological initiative, which could be exploited tactically and have operational consequences. The key to maintaining the technological initiative was the systematic study of the scientific and technological achievements of other powers while concealing one's own efforts.[91]

---

[88] Vasilii Novitskii, "Bor'ba za kharakter budushchei voiny" [Struggle for the character of the future war], *Voina i revoliutsiia* no. 5 (May 1929), pp. 1-13.

[89] A. Lapchinskii, "Deistvie aviatsii v nachal'nom periode voiny" [Actions of aviation in the initial period of war], *Voina i revoliutsiia*, no. 6 (June 1929), pp. 55-66; Ia. Ia. Alksnis, "Nachal'nyi period voiny" [The initial period of war], *Voina i revoliutsiia*, no. 9 (September 1929), pp. 3-22 and no. 10 (October 1929), pp. 3-15; V. Novitskii, "Deistviia aviatsii v nachal'nom periode voiny" [Actions of aviation in the initial period of war], *Voina i revoliutsiia*, no. 9 (September 1929), pp. 23-31; R. P. Eideman, "K *voprosu o kharaktere nachal'nogo perioda voiny*" [Toward the question of the character of the initial period of war], *Voina i revoliutsiia*, no. 8 (August 1931), pp. 3-12; E. Shilovskii, "*Nachal'nyi period voiny*" [The initial period of war], *Voina i revoliutsiia*, no. 9-10, (September-October 1933), pp. 3-11; M. N. Tukhachevskii, "Kharakter pogranichnykh operatsii" [The character of border operations], in: *Izbrannye proizvedeniia* [Selected Works] (Moscow: Voenizdat, 1964), vol. II, pp. 212-221; S. N. Krasil'nikov, "*Nachal'nyi period budushchei voiny*" [The initial period of a future war], Pravda (May 20, 1936), p. 2; G. Isserson, *Novye formy bor'by* [New Forms of Struggle] (Moscow: Voenizdat, 1940); A. I. Starunin, "Operativnaia vnezapnost'" [Operational Surprise], *Voennaia mysl'*, no. 3 (March 1941), pp. 27-35.

[90] V. K. Triandafillov, *Kharakter operatsii sovremennykh armii* [The Character of the Operations of Modern Armies], 1st edition (Moscow: Gosizdat, Otdel Voennoi Literatury, 1929), pp. 70-72.

Tukhachevskii and the Strategy of Destruction

Svechin's opponents had argued that technological developments and the nature of the external threat made it absolutely essential to carry out a total "machinization" of the Red Army and Soviet rear. One of the leading proponents of such views was M. V. Tukhachevskii, who served as Chief of the *RKKA* Staff from 1925 to 1928. Tukhachevskii argued that what was required to make the new operational art into a sound strategic posture was nothing less than "complete militarization" of the national economy to provide the new instruments of mechanized warfare. Committed to an operational art that would end in the total destruction of the enemy, Tukhachevskii crossed pens with Svechin, whom he accused of being an advocate of attrition.[92] According to G. S. Isserson, one of Tukhachevskii's closest collaborators in the 1930s, during the war scare of 1927 when the party leadership feared conflict with Great Britain, Tukhachevskii came forward with a master plan for the mechanization of the Red Army in December 1927, only to have it turned down by the party leadership under Stalin.[93]

Tukhachevskii's views won favor several years later in 1930, after Stalin had broken with Bukharin's thesis on the stabilization of capitalism and began to associate the Depression with a rising threat of war to the Soviet Union. The party leadership openly used this threat to justify the brutal processes of industrialization and forced collectivization by linking them with an improvement in the level of national defense. In 1931 Stalin employed a basic calculus to justify the drive for modernization in which he linked backwardness and defeat:

> Those who fall behind, get beaten. . . . Such is jungle law of capitalism. You are backward, you are weak—therefore, you are wrong. Hence you can be beaten and enslaved. You are mighty; therefore, you are right. Hence, we must be wary of you....
>
> We are 50 to 100 years behind the leading countries. We must make up this distance in ten years. Either we do that or they will suppress us.[94]

During the intervening two years Tukhachevskii had left the *RKKA* Staff to take over as commander of the Leningrad Military District, where he conducted a number of experiments relating to mechanization. These experiments came at a time when motorization versus mechanization had emerged in Western Europe as alternative solutions to the problem of integrating the internal combustion engine into the armed forces. The former implied grafting automobile transport on to existing combat arms, while the latter called for the creation of "self-propelled combat means" with an emphasis on armor, especially tanks, armored cars and self-propelled artillery. Soviet officers who followed developments in France, England and the United States noted that all armies were exploring both

[91] Svechin, *Strategiia*, 2nd edition, pp. 69-71.

[92] M. N. Tukhachevskii, "K voprosu o sovremennoi strategii" [Toward the question of modern strategy], in: *Voina i voennoe isskustvo v svete istoricheskogo materializma* (Moscow: Gosizdat, 1927), p. 127-133.

[93] G. Isserson, "Zapiski sovremennika o M. N. Tukhachevskom" [A contemporary's notes on M. N. Tukhachevskii], *Voenno-istoricheskii zhurnal*, no. 4 (April 1964), pp. 65-67.

[94] I. V. Stalin, "O zadachakh khoziaistvennikov" [On the tasks of the economic managers], in: *Sochineniia* [Essays], (Moscow: *Gosizdat politicheskoi literatury*, 1951), vol. 13, p. 39.

paths but that, owing to strategic, operational, tactical, political and financial circumstances, the French army was more sympathetic to motorization and the British to mechanization.[95] In his comments on the training exercises of the troops of the Leningrad Military District Tukhachevskii emphasized the need to increase their mobility as a combined-arms force which could engage in a multi-echeloned offensive. His interest in the development of tank, aviation and airborne forces during this period marked him as an advocate of mechanization.[96]

At the 16th Party Congress and 9th Congress of the Komsomol in 1930-1931 K. E. Voroshilov, the Commissar of War and Stalin's closest collaborator, spoke out regarding the mechanization of warfare as bringing about a qualitative change in the nature of future wars. But in Voroshilov's case mechanization would in the future bring about the possibility of a short, bloodless war, carried quickly on to the territory of the attacking enemy.[97] Such views emerged at a time when it appeared that world capitalism had gone back into a profound political-economic crisis which was creating greater instability and increased risks of war. This in turn, it was feared, had created the bases for the formation of a broad anti-Soviet alliance, which threatened war on every frontier. At home the strains of the first five-year plan were also underscoring the possibilities of an alliance etween the external threat and the so-called internal enemy, i.e. the forces of counterrevolution.

Stalin himself had put that face on the so-called "Shakhty Affair," already at the April plenum of the Central Committee of the party in 1928. His "facts" were that there was an "economic counterrevolution," led by *"spetsy"* and funded by capitalist organizations in the West to sabotage the Soviet coal industry. Stalin linked this "economic intervention of West European, anti-Soviet capitalist organizations" with the earlier military-political intervention of the Civil War. In both cases the appropriate answer was to liquidate the threat, and in both cases the threat came from class enemies, i.e., bourgeois specialists, who put their talents in the service of the encircling capitalist powers. Stalin warned: "We have internal enemies. We have external enemies. Comrades, we cannot forget about this for even one minute." From *spetsy* to kulaks, to wreckers within the very highest reaches of the party itself—that was the terrible logic of Stalin's campaign against wreckers and enemies of the people.[98]

In 1930 Tukhachevskii presented his own powerful arguments for a mass, mechanized army as the means to execute the new operational art. He used many forums to present this argument. One was the foreword to the Russian translation of Hans Delbrueck's *Geschichte der Kriegskunst im Rahmen der politischen Geschichte*, which provided a forum in which to attack Svechin's concept of attrition as the appropriate strategy for the USSR.[99] This work was conspicuous for the tenor of

---

[95] "Motorizatsiia i mekhanizatsiia inostrannykh armii (k nachalu 1929 g.)" [Motorization and mechanization of foreign armies (as of early 1929)], *Informatsionnyi sbornik*, no. 12 (December 1928), pp. 145-157.

[96] Tukhachevskii, "Na baze dostignutogo — k novym zadacham" [On the basis of the achieved—toward new tasks], *Izbrannye proizvedeniia*, vol. II, pp. 67-68; and D. N. Nikishev, "Chelovek dela" [A man of deed], in: N. I. Koritskii, et al., eds., *Marshal Tukhachevskii: Vospominaniia druzei i soratnikov* [Marshal Tukhachevskii: Memoirs of Friends and Compatriots] (Moscow: Voenizdat, 1965), pp. 199-202.

[97] *Sovetskaia voennaia entsiklopediia* [The Soviet Military Encyclopedia] (Moscow: Sovetskaia entsiklopediia, 1933), vol. II, pp. 842-843.

the political-ideological assault mounted by Tukhachevskii against the old *genshtabist*. In a time of heightened suspicions toward all specialists as wreckers, Tukhachevskii called his colleague an "idealist" in Marxist dress.

Worse attacks followed within the confines of the Section for the Study of the Problems of War in the Communist Academy, which was organized in 1929 as part of an effort to infuse Marxism-Leninism into military science. Within the Section, as within the Communist Academy, the notion of a struggle between an old, bourgeois past and a young, dynamic, communist future was given free rein. The Trotsky-Frunze debates of 1921-1922 over "unified military doctrine" were recalled but now within the context of a struggle over the issue of where the center for the study of military problems in the USSR should be. The leaders of the Section were promoting their institution as a rival to the Military Academy and hoped to enhance their position through Party ties and by building "strong ties with the Institute of Red Professorship and those young Marxist-Leninist forces which now move our Bolshevik science."[100]

There, armed with the appropriate citations from Lenin, Stalin and Voroshilov, Tukhachevskii attacked Professors Svechin and Verkhovskii. He described their writings as infested with bourgeois ideology. In Svechin's case, the fault was that he did not believe in the possibility of decisive operations but defended the idea of limited war. Verkhovskii was charged with favoring a professional army at the expense of mass. Tukhachevskii spoke positively of Triandafillov's book, which had critiqued Verkhovskii's concept of cadre-mechanized forces, but noted some shortcomings.[101] His line of criticism fit that offered in a review of Triandafillov's book, published in the spring of 1930, in which the reviewer took the author to task for talking of a peasant rear without noting the possibility of transforming that rear through industrialization. That industrialization, the reviewer pointed out, would make it possible to speed up the massing of forces and their maneuver, creating opportunities for decisive operations, if the political—i.e., revolutionary—possibilities were exploited.[102]

Tukhachevskii not only endorsed the Stalinist program of industrialization and collectivization as the necessary prerequisite for a strategy of "destruction," but sought to stigmatize those favoring a strategy of "attrition" as class enemies, bourgeois theorists and idealists. In seeking to establish his own credibility by invoking ideological purity and party loyalty, Tukhachevskii contributed to the end of professional debate within the Red Army. In his attack on a strategy of

---

[98] I. Stalin, "O rabotakh aprel'skogo ob'edineinnogo plenuma TsK i TsKK" [On the Works of the Joint April Plenum of the Central Commiootee and the Central Control Committee] in: *Sochineniia*, vol. 11, pp. 53-63.

[99] M. N. Tukhachevskii, "Predislovie k knige G. Del'briuka *Istoriia voennogo iskusstva v ramkakh politicheskoi istorii*" [Preface to Hans Delbrueck's book *The History of Military Art in the Framework of Political History*], in: *Izbrannye proizvedeniia*, vol. II, pp. 116-146.

[100] A. S. Bubnov, "Voennaia sektsiia i ee blizhaishie zadachi" [The military section and its immediate tasks], in: *Kommunisticheskaia Akademiia, Sektsiia po izucheniiu problem voiny, Zapiski* [Notes], vol. I, (1930), p. 5.

[101] M. N. Tukhachevskii, "O kharaktere sovremennykh voin v svete reshenii VI kongressa Kominterna" [On the character of modern wars in light of the decisions of the 6th Congress of the Comintern], in: Kommunisticheskaia Akademiia, Sektsiia po izucheniiu problem voiny, *Zapiski*, vol. 1, pp. 21-29.

attrition he marshalled a Clausewitz strikingly similar to that invoked by the German General Staff against Delbrueck, i.e., one in keeping with total war.[103]

That same year Tukhachevskii became deputy commissar of military and naval affairs, a member of the *Revvoensovet*, and director of armaments for the *RKKA*. Over the next six years he directed the mechanization of the Red Army, laying the foundations for the creation of mass, mechanized forces designed to conduct successive deep operations in a war of destruction. The Stalinist industrialization did make the USSR into a major industrial power with the capacity to mechanize its armed forces to an extent undreamed of by Triandafillov. During that same period the nature of the military threat confronting the USSR became more complex and serious. To his credit Tukhachevskii never fell into the trap of assuming that mechanization would negate mass war. He was an informed critic of "blitzkrieg theory," and his criticism of the works of Fuller, Liddell Hart and others deserves serious attention as it contains good clues to the emerging Soviet way of war. In 1931 Tukhachevskii wrote regarding the professional mechanized army:

> Let's imagine a war between Great Britain and the USA, a war, for example, which breaks out along the Canadian border. Both armies are mechanized, but the English have, let's say Fuller's cadres of 18 divisions, and the US Army has 180 divisions. The first has 5,000 tanks and 3,000 aircraft, but the second has 50,000 tanks and 30,000 planes. The small English army would be simply crushed. Is it not already clear that talk about small, but mobile, mechanized armies in major wars is a cock-and-bull story. Only frivolous people can take them seriously.[104]

Thus, in Tukhachevskii's writings, Soviet military theory, building on the work of the tsarist general staff and the combat experience of four industrial wars (the Russo-Turkish, Russo-Japanese, World War I and the Civil War), focused on the mechanization of the mass army as the means to conduct decisive operations in a total war. For Tukhachevskii, independent tank and mechanized formations were the keystone to such deep operations. The "long-range tanks," which would make up such mobile groups, had to be high-speed, rugged, reliable and, most important, armed with a heavy cannon to fight and defeat enemy tanks.[105]

The *Vremennyi polevoi ustav RKKA 1936* [Provisional Field Regulations of the Red Army, 1936], with its emphasis on the "decisive offensive on the main axis, completed by relentless pursuit" as the only means to bring about the total destruction of the enemy's men and equipment, underscored Tukhachevskii's twin themes of combined arms and mechanized forces. Tanks were to be used in mass, and mechanized formations, composed of tank, motorized infantry, and self-propelled guns, were expected to strike deep into the enemy's rear, using their

---

[102] *Voina i revoliutsiia*, no. 3 (March 1930), pp. 140-147.

[103] Tukhachevskii, "Predislovie k knige Del'briuka `Istoriia voennogo iskusstva v ramkakh politicheskoi istorii'," pp. 116-146.

[104] M. N. Tukhachevskii, "Predislovie k knige Dzh. Fullera *Reformatsiia voiny*" [Preface to J. Fuller's book *The Reformation of War*], *Izbrannye proizvedeniia*, vol. II, p. 152.

[105] Tukhachevskii, "Novye voprosy voiny" [New questions of war], in: *Izbrannye proizvedeniia*, vol. II, pp. 184-187.

mobility to outflank and encircle enemy forces. Aviation formations, apart from independent air operations, were expected to act in close operational-tactical cooperation with combined-arms formations. At the same time, airborne units were to be used to disorganize enemy command and control and rear services.[106]

Epilogue

Tukhachevskii won the strategic debate of the late 1920s and early 1930s. The Red Army adopted the strategy of destruction as it set out to create a mass, mechanized army. Svechin continued to write but his voice did not have the weight that it had enjoyed in the preceding decade. In 1934 he completed the editing of the first complete and accurate Russian translation of Clausewitz's *On War*.[107] Shortly thereafter, he published an interesting biography of Clausewitz. Svechin set out to place Clausewitz within the intellectual, political and military context of his times, and demonstrated his skills as a writer who could combine narrative with analysis.

As befitting the Stalinist intellectual climate, this work was published with an introduction outlining the mistaken notions of Delbrueck and Svechin and promoting Comrade Stalin as the architect of the Red Army's strategy of destruction. Attrition was a strategy imposed by an unfavorable correlation of forces, nothing more or less. If it embraced limited war aims, the occupation of a part of enemy territory, this had nothing to do with a "moderate mission." It came about because the military instrument was unequal to the task of striking "at the center of gravity of the enemy state."[108]

In the text, however, Svechin found ways to present his interpretation of Clausewitz and to defend a strategy of attrition from his critics. His biography, which demonstrated both his knowledge of German military history and Napoleonic warfare and displayed his skills as a writer of talent, contained a fine review of *On War*.[109] Moreover, in that review he called attention to the implicit tactical focus of the preference for strategies of destruction as embodied in the example of Cannae, the decisive general engagement leading to the encirclement and destruction of the opposing army. This was for Svechin the domain of operational art and not strategy proper. Indeed, Svechin asserted: "This area of strategy does not lie at the center of Clausewitz's attention and does not represent the strongest part of his work."[110] Svechin implied that the alternative strategic form, what Delbrueck had called "attrition," was connected with the political aims

---

[106] Narodnyi Komissariat Oborony SSSR, *Vremennyi polevoi ustav RKKA 1936* (PU 36) [1936 RKKA Provisional Field Regulations (PU-36)], (Moscow: Gosvoenizdat, 1937), pp. 9-16.

[107] Carl von Clausewitz, *O voine* [On War] (Moscow: Gosvoenizdat, 1934). On the significance of this translation see: A. Svechin, *Klausevits*, pp. 277-278. Clausewitz's *On War*, which was only published in a poor Russian translation as excerpts in *Voennyi sbornik* in the first decade of the twentieth century, did not get a truly first-class translation in 1934. Leer, himself a Baltic German, based his strategic views on Jomini and rejected Clausewitz's dialectics. Other Russian officers, relying on a bad translation, simply found Clausewitz too dense and difficult to read. Lenin, the professional revolutionary, had the language skills, philosophical basis and practical experience to appreciate the significance of Clausewitz's classic work and to build on it. See: Jacob W. Kipp, "Lenin and Clausewitz: The Militarization of Marxism," *Military Affairs*, vol. 49, No. 4 (December 1985), pp. 181-194.

[108] S. R. Budkevich, "Ot redaktora" [From the editor], in: Svechin, *Klausevits*, pp. 16-17.

of war itself, which, in turn, was connected to "the creation of the means by which to conduct war."[111] Moreover, Svechin noted that Clausewitz himself considered the sixth section of *On War* devoted to defense as a promising "experiment" which required revision. Here Svechin noted what Clausewitz termed the twin aspects of defense, "awaiting and action" in slightly different form to replace "action" i.e., timely offensive action by the defender, with counter-blow [*kontrudar*]. "The idea of retribution as the means of an answering blow lies at the basis of every defense; the way of waiting—this is the road of a more secure victory over the enemy, but only the answering blow establishes equality in the dynamic of offense and defense."[112]

Svechin noted that although *On War* itself contained "no concrete plan of a defensive war," Clausewitz did develop such ideas in connection with the defense of the revolutionary government of Naples in 1821. In that plan Clausewitz proposed that the defenders avoid a battle on the frontier against the Austrian army sent to put down the revolt. Instead, relying on the Apennine Mountains to force the Austrians to divide their forces into isolated columns, Clausewitz proposed the use of partisan detachments to attack Austrian communications to lead to the attrition of the attacking force, and then "the concentrated revolutionary army should suddenly fall upon the most important of the Austrian columns, destroy it and mount a pursuit with maximum energy." This was no matter of playing for time and hoping for opportunities but a campaign plan in which a powerful counterblow could decide the entire campaign.[113] The Neapolitan commander had thrown away such advantages by trying to invade the Papal states, failing, and then accepting an engagement at the Neapolitan frontier, where he suffered a major defeat which decided the fate of the revolution. The implications of this lesson for Soviet Russia remained implicit.

Svechin's last published work, which appeared in early 1937, marked a return to old themes in a very new context. His topic, "Principles of Modern Japanese Strategy and Tactics," linked together his own experiences in warfare against Japan in the Far East with a brilliant analysis of contemporary Japanese military capabilities and intentions. Svechin set out to demonstrate that national strategy, in this case Japanese strategy, operates under a set of constraints that dictate the nature of the forces created, the strategy chosen, the development of operational art and even the details of tactics.[114] Japanese military art was not a stereotypical copy of European military art, but a national art adapted to Japanese conditions.

Svechin identified the Japanese navy as the dominant arm of the Japanese military. Its requirements for oceanic warfare took first priority for the island empire. The navy was a small, elite, volunteer force. Its primary focus was on the threat posed by the U.S. Navy. In seeking external models and training the

---

[109] This chapter compares well with Bernard Brodie's "A Guide to the Reading of On War," in: Carl von Clausewitz, *On War*, Edited and Translated by Michael Howard and Peter Paret (Princeton: Princeton University Press, 1976), pp. 641-711.

[110] Svechin, *Klauzevits*, p. 256.

[111] Ibid., p. 258.

[112] Ibid., p. 260.

[113] Ibid., p. 263.

[114] Svechin, "Osnovy sovremennoi iaponskoi strategii i taktiki", pp. 141-165.

Japanese navy had looked and still looked to the Royal Navy. The army, in contrast, was much more deeply involved in domestic politics. It depended on peasant recruits to fill its ranks as conscripts and was thus connected with the social crisis of rural Japan, which created the preconditions for Japanese fascism and contributed to the leading role of junior military officers in such events as the February 1936 "Putsch." In seeking foreign advice the Japanese army had looked to Germany before World War I and in the interwar period had turned to France.[115]

Svechin analyzed the rivalry between the two services, which led to a navy with its own amphibious assault divisions, equipped with tanks and artillery, and the army's control of its own naval transports and the authority to mobilize the Japanese merchant marine during wartime. Both navy and army had their own air forces. This rivalry, however, did not preclude cooperation on key issues. Svechin argued that Japan's expansion in Asia was conditioned by maritime concerns, which shaped strategy and operational art in theater. Strategic impact could be seen in the importance which Japan attached to control of ports during the Sino-Japanese War of 1894-1895, the Russo-Japanese War of 1904-1905 and the Siberian intervention. Operational impact could be seen in the priority given to the capture of Port Arthur during the Russo-Japanese War even at the expense of reducing the size of the field army in Manchuria.[116]

The army's strategic orientation was continental, with the focus being on control of Manchuria. However, the realities of strategic logistics has placed the Japanese army in the position of being dependent upon available maritime transport to bring troops and reinforcements to the Asian theater of military actions. Thus Japan had a relatively small army. Svechin noted the failure of various Japanese efforts to employ local populations to provide supplemental forces in Korea, Manchuria and Outer Mongolia. Attempts to encourage the immigration of Japanese peasants to Manchuria had also failed and led to "disillusionment" regarding the possibility of creating a continental base for the Japanese army.[117]

These circumstances created the conditions under which the Japanese military had to address the issues of force posture and force modernization. Svechin noted the strength of Japanese infantry, the recent modernization of their weaponry and their tactical virtues, especially their endurance and mobility. At the same time he pointed out that their focus on the Manchuria led to an emphasis on forces adapted to warfare in an underdeveloped [*malokul'turnyi*] theater of military actions. The ruggedness of the terrain and an underdeveloped communications network led the Japanese army to emphasize direct-support artillery at the regimental and divisional levels and a disregard for corps and army artillery.[118]

In other areas of technological modernization Japan's level of economic development and its strategic position as a maritime power greatly circumscribed the motorization and mechanization. In the first case, a weak Japanese automobile industry precluded motorization of the infantry and artillery. In the latter case, a weak Japanese steel industry, confronted by the serious potential demands for

---

[115] Ibid., pp. 141-143.

[116] Ibid., p. 143.

[117] Ibid., pp. 143-146.

[118] Ibid., pp. 146-147.

replacement of merchant ships in case of unrestricted submarine warfare, precluded the development of substantial armored forces.[119] The one area of technology that both the army and navy had made a substantial investment in modernizing was tactical aviation, which recommended itself as a highly flexible resource which could be shifted from continental to oceanic theater and back.[120]

Turning to the Japanese assessment of the initial period of war, Svechin noted that in Japan's case it would be a matter of months, not weeks, as was the case in Europe. The Japanese military leadership sought by various means to overcome this situation. One way to maintain a high degree of combat readiness was with first echelon forces. Svechin focused on continental warfare and saw the navy's role in such a struggle limited to demonstrations and secondary objectives. He did note, however, that the Navy could attempt to use a surprise attack before an official declaration of war, à la Port Arthur, to change the correlation of forces in the oceanic theater.[121]

Finally, Svechin examined Japanese military art and doctrine in the context of the Manchurian TVD and concluded that operational art, i.e., maneuver warfare in theater, took precedence over tactical considerations. In the absence of superior numbers and technological superiority, Japanese ground forces depended on a developed rear to support their maneuver capabilities. In comparison with the West European TVD, strategic mobility was, however, considerably smaller in Manchuria.[122] The tendency to maintain a relatively even combat density across the entire front gave Japanese encirclement operations a single-echelon character. "Success of the manuever can be achieved only by especially energetic conduct of the frontal battle by Japanese troops." In this fashion enemy reserves must be drawn into action so that they cannot regroup to counter the Japanese envelopment. Pressure all along the front must rob the enemy of the initiative. Even in the face of an opponent with greater numbers and superior weapons Japanese military art calls for pressing the offensive.[123] The key to success in such operations lies in a superior infantry conducting numerous attacks across an entire front, relying on small unit tactics to achieve numerous penetrations of the defense. Striving to achieve encirclements, Japanese military art put very little emphasis upon pursuit.[124] Addressing the further development of Japanese military art in the face of the challenges of motorization and mechanization, Svechin concluded that the Japanese would give preference to the motorization of their artillery. This would, however, take its own particular form in keeping with the special features of the Far Eastern theater of military actions.

Svechin's observations on Japanese military art were, of course, timely. Within six months of the appearance of this article, Japan attacked China, beginning a protracted war of attrition, in which repeated operational successes failed to bring about war termination. As the Soviet Union clandestinely offered military assistance to China, Soviet-Japanese relations deteriorated over the next

---

[119] Ibid., pp. 147-148.

[120] Ibid., pp. 148-149.

[121] Ibid., pp. 150-151.

[122] Ibid., pp. 153-154.

[123] Ibid., pp. 158-159.

[124] Ibid., pp. 159-162.

several years, leading to a border confrontation at Lake Khasan in 1938 and large-scale fighting at Khalkhin-Gol in the summer of 1939. Svechin would have approved of this campaign on several grounds. The willingness to delay counter-offensive operations until a buildup in theater had been completed; the nature of Zhukov's mechanized counter-attack which leveraged the Japanese deployment in a single echelon to create opportunities for envelopment; and the congruence of limited political objectives within limited military means to bring about war termination on favorable terms in theater.

By that time, however, Svechin was dead, a victim, along with his rival, M. N. Tukhachevskii, of Stalin's blood purge of the Soviet military. Tukhachevskii did not live to see the fate of his mass mechanized army during the initial period of war, when it was all but annihilated. Following those initial defeats, another Soviet army, as was befitting Svechin's "second act," arose. This people's army lost battle after battle, was surrounded, smashed, and phoenix-like arose from its own ashes to confound the architects of blitzkrieg. With its blood, the blood of millions, it bought time for a new generation of military leaders to master operational art and for the nation to forge the new weapons of war. This was the army of attrition, the army of *izmor*, the army of people's war, the army of Russia, the army of Svechin. Moscow and Stalingrad were its victories.

Conclusion

Svechin's major contributions to military theory can be summarized as an explicit attack on the old strategy-tactics dichotomy and the articulation of a new and very different approach in which operational art assumed central importance. His historical insights were drawn from practical experience and emphasized the need to understand contemporary military art, i.e., those trends which were in the process of reshaping warfare. The key elements of the system he elaborated in *Strategy* can be enumerated as the following:

- the establishment of a political-economic foundation beneath strategy;
- a division of strategy into two ideal types: attrition [*izmor*] and destruction [*sokrushenie*];
- the delineation of operational art and the assertion of a radically new understanding of the concept of operations;
- a reduction of the role of tactical combat in shaping force structure;
- denial of the importance of the single decisive engagement and the transformation of combat into an ongoing, episodic process;
- radical reduction of the role of march-maneuver as a major strategic factor and the emerging importance of the meeting engagement;
- emphasizing the role of transportation and communications in strategy and the significance of military-technical superiority; and
- the emphasis on theater-specific conditions in shaping the appropriate strategy and operational art.

This system itself is much less important than Svechin's method. Svechin was a firm opponent of military dogmatism. He championed open debate over key issues of military art and theory. If Lenin adapted Clausewitz to the needs of revolutionary Marxism, then Svechin deserves credit as the most important popularizer and adapter of Clausewitz for the Red Army. Finally, his strategic system emphasized the enduring features of national military strategy. Because of such features, soldiers and statesmen operated in a world of necessity, limiting their strategic choices and shaping their military system. Trying to understand Russian/Soviet military thought in the first half of the twentieth century without reference to Svechin leads to a bifurcated approach in which the tsarist and Soviet military experiences are seen as simply the latter being a negation of the former. Nevertheless, as Svechin's career and thought confirm the need to examine the continuities as well.

Following his death, Svechin became a non-person. His books and articles were placed in closed collections available only to those with special access. Outside the Soviet Union he was all but unknown to Western military historians and analysts until the recent revival of interest in the Soviet Union.[125] This status is proof of both the terrible power of modern totalitarianism, which not only can terminate potential enemies physically but also has the tools to create its own mythic past, turning historical figures into non-persons, and inducing a party-fostered amnesia. The fact that *glasnost'* and *perestroika* have sparked a revival of interest in Svechin and his ideas is one more testimony to the power of the word once it has been nailed to the page. At the present time, when it is very fashionable in Soviet military circles to call into question the analysis of civilian scholars on defense and security questions because they lack competence, one would do well to remember Svechin's defense of the inclusion of Delbrueck among the classical military thinkers as both an eminent military historian and military thinker with a "dialectical-evolutionary point of view."

---

[125] The exception here is, of course, John Erickson, who discussed Svechin's thought and career in the Red Army within the context of the party politics of the Soviet High Command. See: John Erickson, *The Soviet High Command: A Military-Political History, 1918-1941* (London: Macmillan & Co., 1962), passim.

А. СВЕЧИН

СТРАТЕГИЯ

ВТОРОЕ ИЗДАНИЕ

ВОЕННЫЙ ВЕСТНИК

1927

Aleksandr A. Svechin

STRATEGY

SECOND EDITION

VOENNYI VESTNIK

1927

PREFACE TO THE FIRST EDITION

The last practical example of Moltke's strategy, namely the Franco-Prussian War, and Napoleon's last operation, which was decided near Waterloo, were 55 years apart. And there are 55 years between us and the Sedan operation.

There is no way that we can say that the evolution of the art of war has slowed down. While Moltke had reasons to revise the strategic and operational thinking he inherited from Napoleon, we have even more reasons to revise the strategic thinking we inherited from Moltke. We could refer to a number of new material factors which have compelled us to take a new look at the art of strategy. For example, we could talk about railroads, which in Moltke's day played an essential role only in initial operational deployment, while at present railroad maneuvers are involved in every operation and constitute an essential part of them; we could point out the greater significance of logistics, economics and politics in warfare, and the permanence of mobilization for war, which has moved the moment of greatest strategic intensity from the twentieth day of a war to several months ahead, and so forth.

A whole series of truths which were still valid in Moltke's day have now become outworn.

To a large extent, Napoleon's splendid military art made Jomini and Clausewitz's theoretical work on strategy much easier: Jomini's works are merely a theoretical codification of Napoleon's practice. Moltke left his junior Schlichting no less a wealth of material, with a number of masterly solutions, albeit not as complete. The contemporary student of strategy, relying on the experience of the World War and Civil War, of course could not complain of a lack of new historical material, but his tasks are much more difficult than the tasks that befell Jomini and Schlichting, because neither the World War nor the Civil War had practitioners who were fully up to all the requirements presented by the new conditions and who could have confirmed a new strategic theory by the authority of their masterful solutions crowned by victory. Neither Ludendorff, Foch nor the military men of the civil war dominated events, but were rather carried away by the maelstrom.

This is where the greater freedom of the modern strategic writer comes from, but he has to pay for his freedom with a great deal of hard work and perhaps even greater difficulty in getting his views acknowledged. We attack a large number of strategic prejudices, which, perhaps, in the eyes of many, have not yet suffered a final defeat in life and the theater of war. New phenomena have compelled us to make new definitions and establish new terminology;[1] we have tried to avoid abusing novelties, and given this cautious approach, no matter how confused the obsolete terms are, they will find their defenders. Marshall de Marmont, who was scolded for the fact that he used the terms "operational line" instead of "defensive line," which had a completely different meaning, was nevertheless discombobulated enough to call people who tried to get military terminology in agreement with military reality "charlatans"!

---

[1]   This is the inalienable right of any author. In mathematics numbers and formulas have a very exact meaning, while in strategy the terms represent the same kind of formulas, which, however, often have completely different contents.

The nature of our work makes it impossible for us to cite authorities to confirm our views. When strategists are reproached for "mere military politeness," which conceals emptiness, in the old barracks saying, a major role in discrediting strategy has been played by pure compilations, which contain a wealth of aphorisms borrowed from great men and writers of different eras. We don't rely on any authorities; we have tried to encourage critical thought, and our references refer to either a source of factual material which we have used or cite the primary source of certain well-worn ideas which have taken root in our theory. Our initial plan was to write a treatise on strategy without any citations; that's how hateful these collections of aphorisms had become. We have tried to doubt everything and construct a theory of war solely on the basis of the reality of modern wars, but we have not succeeded in doing it. We also did not want to get into polemics, and that is why we did not emphasize the contradictions between the definitions and explanations which are ours and the opinions of very many remarkable writers. To our disappointment, our work contains many more contradictions than would be required to consider it original. This is unfortunate, because this could make the book difficult to understand if one were just to skim through it.

We hope that these difficulties will be partially alleviated by the reader's familiarity with our work on the history of the art of war and several courses of lectures on strategy which we have delivered in the last two years and which have somewhat popularized our views on several topics.

We are looking at modern war with all its possibilities, and we have not tried to narrow our theory to an outline of Soviet strategic doctrine. It is extremely difficult to predict a war situation in which the Soviet Union could become involved, and we must handle any restrictions on the overall science of war with extreme caution. A particular strategic policy must be devised for every war; each war is a special case, which requires its own particular logic rather than any kind of stereotype or pattern, no matter how splendid it may be. The more our theory encompasses the entire content of modern war, the quicker it will assist us in analyzing a given situation. A narrow doctrine would probably confuse us more than guide us. And we must not forget that only maneuvers are one-sided, while wars are always two-sided. We must be able to get a grasp of war as it is perceived by the opposing side and clarify the other side's desires and goals. Theory is capable of benefitting only those who have raised themselves above the fray and have become completely dispassionate; we have chosen this path, despite the dissatisfaction with which several of our young critics have encountered the excess of objectivity, "the posture of an American observer," in military questions. Any change in scientific objectivity will at the same time be a change in the dialectic method to which we have firmly decided to adhere. Within the broad framework of the overall science of modern war, dialectics allow a much more vivid characterization of the strategic line of conduct which must be chosen for a given case than could be done by means of a theory, even one which only has this particular case in mind. Knowledge is made possible only by distinction.

But we had no intention of writing something like a strategic Baedeker which would cover all the finest details of strategy. We do not deny the utility of putting such a guidebook together, which at best would probably be some kind of strategic explanatory dictionary that would elaborate all strategic concepts with logical consistency. Our treatise is a more practical attempt. We have only covered about 190 topics and grouped them into 18 chapters. Our exposition, which at times is more profound and well thought out, may at times be incomplete and superficial and at times seem to be a defense and advocation of a certain understanding of war and a guideline to preparations for war and military operations and methods of strategic command. Our treatise is far from encyclopedic in nature.

Our exposition of political topics, which are covered quite frequently and play a major role in this treatise, may seem to be particularly one-sided. A more profound study would probably have led us to a weak and banal repetition of the strong and vivid ideas developed very authoritatively and persuasively in Lenin and Radek's writings devoted to war and imperialism. Unfortunately our authority in the contemporary interpretation of Marxism is so negligible and so dubious that it would be useless to attempt such an interpretation. Hence, in analyzing the relationship between the superstructure of war and its economic basis, we have decided to examine political topics solely from the vantage point of the military expert; on one hand, we have reminded ourselves and warned the reader that our conclusions on political topics such as the price of grain, the city and countryside, covering the expenses of warfare and so forth are only some of the many guidelines a politician should follow in resolving these questions. It is no mistake if a cobbler criticizes the painting of a famous artist from the point of view of the shoe drawn in it. This kind of criticism may be instructive even for the artist.

We have succeeded in keeping our treatise comparatively short by avoiding a detailed presentation of military history. We have no intention of having the reader accept our conclusions on blind faith: let the reader get familiar with them and perhaps make certain corrections after analyzing it himself. We could get a true laboratory study of strategic theory if a circle of readers were to take on the job of repeating our work, dividing the references to different operations among themselves, and after pondering them, compare their thoughts and conclusions with those given in this book. A theoretical treatise on strategy should merely provide the framework for the independent work of the person studying it. History should be material for independent study rather than a set of illustrative, often garbled examples to be learned by rote.

It is likely that many people will not approve of the book's lack of any agitation in favor of the offensive or even a victory by destruction. This book approaches the subjects of the offensive and defensive, victory by destruction and victory by attrition, maneuver warfare and positional warfare quite objectively because its purpose is to pick the fruit from the tree of knowledge of good and evil and to broaden the reader's view as much as possible rather than train him to think in any particular direction. This book does not advocate some kind of strategic heaven. At one time Victor Cousin advocated the subordination of philosophical truth to moral utility. Many strategic doctrinaires, who have formed a sort of cult of the offensive, have avoided an objective approach to the phenomena of war, and have believed this point of view and have even garbled the facts in order to get their views across. But we are quite remote from these views. We do not think that strategic theory is responsible in the slightest for the offensive impulse of an army. This offensive impulse originates from completely different sources.

Clausewitz, who considered defense the most powerful form of warfare, did not pervert the German army.

We have avoided chasing details and giving rules. The study of details is the task of disciplines related to strategy which dwell on the details of characteristics of particular countries. Rules are inappropriate in strategy. It is true that the Chinese proverb said that wisdom was created for wise men and laws were created for fools. However, strategic theory has tried in vain to create rules and has tried to popularize its thinking in the form of rules for people who are unable to immerse themselves in the study of strategic topics and get to the heart of the matter. Theory is incapable of making a hard and fast decision in any question of strategy and should appeal to the wisdom of the person making the decision.

From the above the reader should avoid the conclusion that the author sees the peak of perfection in his work. The author could have worked on these topics for decades more. That is the way it was with Clausewitz, who never managed to complete his study of war and only made a final edition of the first chapter, but nevertheless managed to write a book which is still significant in part in the second century of its existence. This kind of overarching fundamental analysis is inappropriate for our time. Ideas are evolving at such a pace that if one were to work on making a book more profound for decades and decades he would be more likely to lag behind developments rather than catch up to them. It seems to us that this book meets current requirements for strategic generalization of a certain extent and that even with all its imperfections it may still prove useful in explaining the contemporary features of warfare and be suitable to persons preparing for practical work in the field of strategy.

These were the only considerations which impelled the author to publish this book. Of course, far from all of it is original. In many places the reader will encounter ideas which he knows from the works of Clausewitz, von der Goltz, Blume, Delbrueck, Ragueneau and a number of the most recent military and political thinkers. The author believed that it would be useless to fill the book with endless references to the primary sources of the ideas which are at the root of this book and are a part of it as a logical whole.

PREFACE TO THE SECOND EDITION

In 1923 and 1924 the author was given the assignment of teaching a course on strategy. This book was the result of these two years of work. The author was faced with two tasks. The first, which was the book's center of gravity, was to make a careful study of recent wars and observe the way in which strategic art has evolved in the last 65 years and study the material preconditions which have determined this evolution. The second task was to fit the reality of our time into a certain theoretical framework and make a number of generalizations which would help make practical strategic questions more profound and meaningful.

In this second edition the author has elaborated many points and has developed the military historical bases of his conclusions to a certain extent. He has conscientiously reviewed all the numerous critical comments he has received either in published form or in letters written by certain obscure military men and politicians. Because he was able to understand and grasp the point of view of the critics, he made use of these criticisms and is grateful for the attention which has been given to this book. In general, the author's ideas on the evolution of strategy encountered practically no argument at all, but his terminology, particularly his definition of the categories of a victory by destruction and victory by attrition, have encountered different interpretations and counterdefinitions.

In this edition the author has developed and supplemented his previous thinking on topics of dispute. He cannot agree with other boundaries between a victory by destruction and victory by attrition: the most highly developed critical view is that a war is a war of attrition if its center of gravity lies on the economic and political fronts, while a war becomes a war of victory by destruction if its center of gravity lies on the military front. This is false, because one should look for the boundary between a victory by destruction and a victory by attrition within rather than outside the military front. The concepts of a victory by destruction and a victory by attrition apply not only to strategy, but to politics, economics and boxing, to any form of conflict, and should be explained in terms of the dynamics of the conflict themselves.

Several difficulties have arisen from the fact that we did not invent these terms. Professor Delbrueck, who developed the concepts behind them, saw in them a tool of historical research needed to give meaning to the military historical past, which cannot be understood in a single cross section but requires the application of the scale of destruction or the scale of attrition in evaluating the facts of war, depending on the era. For us these phenomena are alive in the present and have come together in a single era, and we would consider it impossible to construct any theory of strategy without appropriate concepts and terms. We are not responsible for someone else's interpretation of a victory by destruction and victory by attrition.

We consider ourselves bound to Clausewitz's splendid definition of destruction, and it would be pitiful to attempt to replace his vivid, rich definition of destruction with some watered down concept of a half-destruction or an attritional destruction, which yields no corollaries or inferences, under the pretext that destruction in pure form is inapplicable today. We are more eager to go in the opposite direction and take the concept of destruction to the limit, which would hardly be fulfilled even by a real Napoleonic strategy, but rather is its idealization.

The thinking of previous strategic theoreticians was almost exclusively tied to the idea of maximum destruction, and in order to adhere to the logic of destruction they set forth the principle of a partial victory, looked for turning points, denied the existence of strategic reserves, ignored the resurrection of military power in the course of a war and so forth. This has made the strategy of destruction seem to be a strategy of the past, and because of the contrast has made the author, who has striven for objectivity but has made an abrupt break with his predecessors, seem like some kind of lover of attrition. In our opinion, this division into destruction and attrition is not a tool for classifying wars. This topic has been debated in different ways for three millennia. These abstract concepts lie outside the realm of evolution. The colors of the spectrum have not evolved, but the colors of objects have faded and changed. And it is reasonable for us to leave certain general concepts outside the realm of evolution itself. We do not see the slightest sense in making war by destruction evolve into war by attrition instead of recognizing that the evolution has been running from destruction to attrition.

INTRODUCTION

STRATEGY IN A NUMBER OF
MILITARY DISCIPLINES

A Classification of Military Disciplines

The art of war, in the broad sense, encompasses all aspects of the military profession, including: 1) studying weapons and other equipment used in warfare and studying defensive fortifications; 2) studying military geography and evaluating the resources at the disposal of different countries for waging war, studying social tendencies and analyzing possible theaters of military operations; 3) studying of military administration, which analyzes aspects of the organization of the armed forces, their administration and logistics, and finally 4) studying of the conduct of military operations.

As late as the era of the great French Revolution the military technical topics included in the first category represented the basic content of the concept of the art of war. The art of conducting military operations was a field which only a few military historians had studied, primarily concerning themselves with formal and elementary topics such as formations, reformations and battle formations, and was analyzed in courses on tactics as a subject of daily military exercises.

Recently topics related to the conduct of military operations have become much more complex and profound. Now it would be impossible to count on waging any kind of successful war against a prepared enemy if one's commanders were not prepared ahead of time to solve the problems which would face them once military operations began. This aspect of the art of war has now become so broad and so significant that currently we consider the conduct of military operations to be the art of war in the narrow sense of the word.

The art of conducting military operations cannot be divided by any clear boundaries into completely independent and delineated sections. It is a single whole which includes the assignment of missions to fronts and armies and leading a small reconnaissance patrol. However, it is very difficult to study it as a whole. This kind of study would run the risk of not giving all topics the appropriate attention: on one hand, we could approach the fundamental issues of warfare from the point of view of trivial requirements, or on the other hand, we could approach the study of small unit operations in an excessively generalized manner and ignore very essential details. Hence it would be quite reasonable to divide the art of conducting military operations into several individual parts on the condition that we do not ignore the close relationship between them and do not forget the arbitrary nature of this division. We should make this division in order to avoid fragmenting the issues which must be resolved on the basis of similar conditions among the different sections. We should mention that is is most natural to divide the art of conducting military operations into the art of waging war, the art of conducting an operation and the art of conducting combat operations. The requirements of the modern battle, the modern operation and warfare as a whole constitute three comparatively definite stages, which form the most natural basis for classifying military disciplines.

Tactics

Tactical art is more closely related to battle requirements than the other components of military art. Battle requirements, given a specific kind of equipment, specific national cultural conditions, and a specific theater of military operations and a specific intensity of the war, constitute a certain entity; on the basis of the reality of the modern battlefield, tactics orchestrate specific technical operations into an integrated kind of battle, and tactics try to rationalize all military equipment, establish criteria for organizing, arming and indoctrinating troops, for troop movements and for rest, reconnaissance and security in accordance with combat requirements. Tactical theory is nothing more than technical topics (meaning troop movement techniques and so forth) which are examined together rather than separately from the perspective of the modern battle conditions they engender as a whole.[1]

If we define the essence of tactics as adapting equipment to battle conditions, we greatly narrow the limits of tactics by comparison with previous definitions. The old definitions of tactics were based on the notion of the major battle, and the art of waging such a battle was classified as tactics. But now there are practically no major battles: combat operations are fragmented in time and space into a number of separate battles which constitute an operation, which cannot be a subject of study for tactics. Tactics should focus their attention solely on an individual battle which follows from the deployment of troops moving on the same road, and thus tactics cannot focus on the study of organized formations larger than a division. Nevertheless it is necessary to study operations within a division, because the division is the smallest organization formation in which the different branches of the armed services and equipment are fully represented. In studying the operations of smaller units such as infantry regiments, we are still concerned with tactics because we should not forget that a battle is not single combat between infantry units but the combined operation of all our men and equipment against all the enemy's.

Operational Art

In turn, tactical creativity is governed by operational art. Combat operations are not self-contained, they are only the basic material from which an operation is formed. Only in very infrequent cases can one rely on achieving the ultimate goal of combat operations in a single battle. Normally this path to the ultimate goal is

---

[1] While strategy pursues goals, tactics solve problems. A goal means a comparatively major objective from which we are separated by a certain distance; the achievement of one goal requires the solution of several problems; the problems facing us grow in immediate proximity to us and become very urgent in nature. By this we would like to emphasize that strategy is essentially future-oriented, while tactics are practically immeasurable in time: while tactics may divide the conduct of a battle into certain phases, these phases are very close to one another and follow one another very quickly.

broken down into a series of operations separated by more or less lengthy pauses, which take place in different areas in a theater and differ significantly from one another due to the differences between the immediate goals one's forces temporarily strive for. We call an operation an act of war if the efforts of troops are directed toward the achievement of a certain intermediate goal in a certain theater of military operations without any interruptions. An operation is a conglomerate of quite different actions: namely, drawing up the plan of the operation; logistical preparations; concentrating one's forces at the starting position; building defensive fortifications; marching; fighting battles which lead to the encirclement or destruction of a portion of the hostile forces and the forced withdrawal of other hostile forces, either as a result of a direct envelopment or as a result of a preliminary breakthrough, and to the capture or holding of a certain line or geographical area. Tactics and administration are the material of operational art and the success of the development of an operation depends on both the successful solution of individual tactical problems by the forces and the provision of all the material they need to conduct an operation without interruption until the ultimate goal is achieved. On the basis of the goal of an operation, operational art sets forth a whole series of tactical missions and a number of logistical requirements. Operational art also dictates the basic line of conduct of an operation, depending on the material available, the time which may be allotted to the handling of different tactical missions, the forces which may be deployed for battle on a certain front, and finally on the nature of the operation itself. We cannot acknowledge the full superiority of objective battlefield conditions over our will. Combat operations are only one aspect of the greater whole represented by an operation, and the nature of the planned operation. Nivelle in April 1917 and Ludendorff in March 1918, who had decided to make a breakthrough on the Western Front in order to rout the enemy's positional front, tried to vary the tactics of their forces quite drastically in accordance with he nature of the planned operations.

Strategy as an Art

The success of an individual operation is not the ultimate goal pursued in conducting military operations however. The Germans won many operations in the World War but lost the last one, and with it the entire war. Ludendorff, who had made outstanding achievements in operational art, was unable to combine a series of operational successes to gain even the slightest advantages when Germany concluded peace, and ultimately all his successes did not do Germany the slightest bit of good.

Strategy is the art of combining preparations for war and the grouping of operations for achieving the goal set by the war for the armed forces. Strategy decides issues associated with the employment of the armed forces and all the resources of a country for achieving ultimate war aims. While operational art must take into account the possibilities presented by the immediate rear (front logistics), the strategist must take into account the entire rear, both his own and the enemy's, represented by the state with all its economic and political capabilities. A strategist will be successful if he correctly evaluates the nature of a war, which depends on different economic, social, geographic, administrative and technical factors.

Strategy cannot be indifferent to operational art. The nature of the war with which a strategist deals should not be an abstract concept separate from military activity. The strategist should subordinate the actual kinds of operations undertaken, their scale and intensity, their sequence and the relative importance assigned to them to his understanding of the possible nature of the war. This makes it necessary for the strategist to dictate basic policies to operational art and, if a particular operation is extremely important, even concentrate the direct leadership of the operation in his own hands.

However, like the tactician and operations specialist, a strategist is not completely independent in his field. Just as tactics is an extension of operational art and operational art is an extension of strategy, strategy is an extension of politics. A special portion of our study is devoted to the relationships between politics and strategy which follow from this.

Quite often we encounter the terms naval strategy, air force strategy, colonial war strategy and so forth. This terminology is obviously based on a misunderstanding. We can only speak of naval operational art when naval forces are given separate operational goals, and we could speak of air force operational art, but with even greater hedging. Because of the close relationship between the operations of air forces, land armies and navies, air force operational art is solely concerned with the separate bombing operations the air force may undertake, but because such operations are still not significant in and of themselves but are only one, albeit quite important, component of an overall operation, we should examine the bombing, reconnaissance and combat operations of the air force as only a part of overall operational art. There is no need to speak of strategy in this case at all, because it would be a clear misuse of the term. In the same way, there could never be a strategy of colonial warfare, because we can only talk about the aspects of strategic art in the war of an imperialist state against an inferior, technically and culturally backward enemy in a colonial theater of war.

Strategy as a Theory of Art

Strategy as a practical art, which is a very important component of military leadership, has existed since prehistoric times when human societies began to wage war. But a theory of strategy began to develop only 150 years ago, at the same time when political economy became scientific in nature. On the basis of the Seven Years' War, a contemporary of Adam Smith, the Englishman Lloyd, who received the same education as Adam Smith and who served in the Austrian, Prussian and Russian armies, began to work on topics which were far beyond the realm of ordinary military tactics. His work inaugurated the modern era of the development of military thought, which had already yielded a number of profound studies of strategy, which were, however, either incomplete or one-sided. A great deal of time and effort was wasted on the subject of whether strategy was a science or theory of art. The answer is highly dependent on the extent of the requirements of science which characterize one's notion of a science. Clausewitz, Willisen and Blume, who considered strategy an art, proceeded from the requirement of adopictic (indisputable) exactness which Kant had made of "science proper." However, the conclusions of military theory are not indisputably exact. But Kant had already allowed for the possibility of calling any systematic theory encompassing a particular field whose knowledge is ordered on the basis of certain fundamentals and principles a science. These theories were supposedly sciences of the second rank. In order to count strategy as a science of the second rank, many outstanding writers on strategy gave particular attention to demonstrating the presence of eternal and unshakable strategic principles on which they constructed their theories. But now our views on science have become much broader. We are inclined to call any system of knowledge which facilitates our understanding of life and experience a science. The theory of all military art, including strategy, undoubtedly fits into this broad definition.

The Relationship of Theory to Practice

There is no doubt that strategic practice is not a branch of scientific activity but is a field of application of an art. Strategic theory should consist of systematized knowledge which makes it easier for us to understand the phenomena of war.

But while human societies were able to implement strategic art in practice without any conception of strategic theory and strategic science for millennia, doesn't this indicate that strategic science is superfluous, artificial and fruitless ballast, the fruit of the intellectual pastimes of our era? We do not think so. If in general being determines consciousness, then in several complex practical fields consciousness has lagged entire centuries behind practical accomplishments. There are rules and laws of speech from which the science of grammar has taken shape, there are certain economic relationships from which the science of political economy has taken shape, a sort of economic grammar, and finally there are certain laws of thinking from which its grammar, namely logic, has taken shape. But can't we see that correct speech preceded the study of grammar, can't we see economic policies in the historical past which corresponded to certain economic interests long before the birth of political economy, and haven't we encountered good thinkers who never took a course in logic? The same applies to warfare — not only in the remote past, but in the very recent times of the civil war we could observe solutions of very difficult problems of strategic art having no connection with any preliminary study of the theory of strategy. But from this we do not conclude that it is desirable to leave grammar out of a program of general education. We find that every responsible statesman should at least have a rudimentary knowledge of political economy. Without denying the right of persons who have not studied logic to think on their own, we invariably include logic in educational programs for persons attempting to make an independent criticism of philosophical and economic doctrines. Familiarity with grammar, political economy, logic and strategy may protect us from many errors in working in any of these fields and make it possible for us to get a quick grasp of relationships whose understanding would otherwise require a great deal of effort from us or perhaps even be impossible.

It would be wrong to interpret these ideas as a comparison of strategy with something like a theory of eloquence about which even the most eloquent orators do not have the slightest idea. True knowledge cannot be neutral: if it is incapable of changing anything in our system of actions, then it is deprived of any content whatsoever. If when we go to practice we must forget about theory in order to make a practical decision rather than a decision by the book, then this kind of thinking is fruitful only by virtue of points of view assimilated by preceding reflections and theoretical studies.

Already in the era of Napoleon we could see that his marshals were inadequately prepared from a theoretical point of view, particularly given the scale which the war took on in 1813. Napoleon's marshals, who were often of humble origins, had not all received an adequate education, but, as they moved from one battlefield to another for 20 years, they had received splendid tactical training. They skillfully got their bearing in difficult situations, were able to think under hostile fire and knew how to organize the efforts of 20,000 to 30,000 soldiers to achieve the goals set forth by Napoleon. However, in the same way that political wisdom is not studied by a bureaucrat working for decades in the same department from 9:00 to 5:00, strategic art is not mastered either by taking part in many campaigns or looking at a lot of battle pictures. When Napoleon's marshals had to act as independent leaders of operations, with a few exceptions they seemed like persons wandering around in the dark who had no clear understanding of their mission and possible ways of accomplishing it, and therefore they acted indecisively. The better educated generals of the coalition fighting Napoleon, who were greatly inferior to Napoleon's marshals in tactics, were superior to them in strategy. One of the most talented revolutionary generals, Clebert, whom Napoleon considered the most naturally talented, predicted the collapse of many revolutionary careers, saying, "It's harder to keep a military reputation than to earn it, and theory, which always wants to go hand in hand with experience, will sooner or later take its revenge if it is not given the proper attention."[2]

Waging war has become much more complicated in the last century, and the effects of inadequate theoretical training will now be much more perceptible. The example of the most outstanding strategist of the post-Napoleonic era, Moltke, is very instructive. He received a very miserly primary education in the Danish Corps of Cadets which barely gave him any more knowledge than a first grader now receives. After serving as a company commander he never served in the rank and file again. His curiosity, it seemed, was totally directed away from issues directly related to war. When Moltke was appointed the chief of the Prussian general staff, he was an officer who was quite distant from military life but was a true scholar, who was very competent in geography, the history of ancient Rome, philosophy and politics and was familiar with the cultural and economic evolution of Europe. Even though he was practically a civilian, once he was placed at the head of the Prussian general staff, he was able to figure out the spirit of a new strategy. Of course it was not Moltke who started a revolution in the art of war; his creativity was limited to recognizing the requirements of the evolution of the art of war which had developed despite the will of individuals and to comprehending the resources required at a given moment. But it was Moltke's new approach to strategic problems that constituted a major step toward the victories of 1866 and 1870. If you study the career of the elder Moltke you get the idea that his position as an observer of the army from off to the side, which made it possible for him to delve into many issues and grow mentally, opportunities which overworked practical men are often deprived of, also was the reason for his superior thinking once he reached the age of 60. It is true that Moltke was an exceptional man. In 1866 Dragomirov characterized him as follows: "General Moltke is one of those strong and exceptional people for which theoretical study of the military profession has almost completely replaced practice."[3]

---

[2] *Revue d'Histoire*, vol. 8, no. 1 (1911), p. 197.

We have referred to M. I. Dragomirov because he was far from being a particular proponent of theory to the detriment of practice. Dragomirov's view of theory is even clearer in his characterization of Benedek, an outstanding practitioner:

> His personal energy is unmistakable; he is an indispensable man for getting men into battle for the purpose of accomplishing their mission, *but he is hardly capable of stating it himself.* In short, while he is a remarkable tactician, Benedek is in no way a strategist. He went off to Bohemia involuntarily, because he had no idea, as he said, of the theater of war or the enemy he would have to fight. This makes me think that Benedek had hardly received any theoretical training for the military preparation at all, and his strength lay in the practical training which he acquired in the Italian theater. He had probably proven himself in this campaign also. Inadequate theoretical training most probably explains his indecisiveness and weakness in strategic combinations, because in practical knowledge of his business and personal resoluteness he had no shortcomings.[4]

Strategy is the Art of Military Leaders

Strategy is the art of military leaders, primarily the art of those persons called on to resolve the basic problems set forth by a wartime situation and to transmit their strategic decisions for execution by operational artists. Strategy is the art of the entire high command of an army, because not only front commanders and army commanders, but also corp commanders, would be incapable of accomplishing their operational missions if they are incapable of clear strategic thinking. Any time an operational artist must make a choice between two alternatives he will be unable to justify a particular operational method if he stays solely within the realm of operational art, and he will have to rise to a strategic level of thinking.

While tactics live by decisions required by the moment, and all tactical work is extremely urgent, strategy begins when we see a series of successive goals, or stages, toward the achievement of the ultimate goal of the war. Strategy must look forward and take the very long term into consideration. The strategist advances by operations, and these strategic steps extend several weeks or even months in time. The strategist must make a profound accounting of the situation and possible changes in it in order to avoid changing the fundamentals of its directives when an operation is merely beginning to unfold. The strategist must be farsighted in order for operational and tactical art to operate smoothly. Prior to the World War the Germans believed that, thanks to Clausewitz, who was still not understood by the other armies, they possessed a monopoly on strategic foresight. But farsightedness is possible only with a broad ideological view; it is easy to point out a large number of tacticians who were mentally limited people, but we cannot

---

3   M. Dragomirov, *Ocherki Austro-Prusskoi voiny* v 1866 g. [Essays on the Austro-Prussian War of 1866] Saint Petersburg: 1867), p. 67.

4   Ibid., p. 86.

find any outstanding strategists among such people. Each leader who points the way is at least some kind of prophet.

The importance of a correctly indicated and clearly outlined goal for the activity of human masses is immeasurable. The chaos of uncoordinated actions, the general confusion which results from incoherence, intentions working at cross purposes and goals which cancel one another out will all disappear once a general slant is given to the goal indicated by the leader. Actions will become ordered and coalesce into small streams flowing down to the goal and will form one broad stream as a result, and the efforts of each and every one in all questions will automatically and naturally run in the same direction. Indicating a proper goal will lead to a feverish stream of ideas and will.

Responsible Politicians Should Be Familiar with Strategy

Not only the high command of an army must study strategy. A strategist issuing directives to the echelons which are the direct leaders of operations should have a clear idea of the limits which are feasible for operational art with the available resources and have a keen operational and tactical eye in order for his forces to operate under the most favorable possible conditions. In exactly the same way a politician who sets a political goal for military operations must have an idea of what is feasible for strategy given the resources available and how politics may affect the situation for better or for worse. Strategy is one of the most important tools of politics, and even in peacetime political calculations must to a great extent be based on the military capabilities of friendly and hostile nations. Bismarck would not have been able to guide Prussian politics so authoritatively if he had not had such a profound understanding of the situation in the theater of war.[5]

All Commanders Must Be Familiar with Strategy

Individual leaders must receive serious strategic training to enable the coop-eration of large masses of men on fronts stretching hundreds of miles. This truth was somewhat forgotten during the positional period of the World War, which favored the extreme centralization of command. In a war of maneuver, corps commanders always have to make critical decisions that will give an operation one strategic slant or another.

On August 16, 1870, the Third Prussian Corps commanded by General d'Alvensleben reached the Metz-Verdun Highway, and the army command directing the Third Corps had assumed that it would reach the road after Bazaine's army had withdrawn to Verdun from Metz and would follow its tail. In reality, General d'Alvensleben was in front of the head of the French army rather than behind its tail and had blocked off the road. Despite the fact that during the day he could only get support from corps (the Tenth), d'Alvensleben decided to engage the entire French army (which included five strong corps) at Mars-la-Tour. This critical decision, which subsequently resulted in the capture of Bazaine's army at Metz, could have been made only on the basis of a strategic evaluation of the situation.

Let us give an even more convincing example. In the interval between the border battle and the operation on the Marne, a strong detachment headed by

---

[5] For example, in the peace negotiations with Austria in August 1866, when there was the danger that France would enter the war.

Captain Lepic was moved forward from the combined cavalry division of Manoury's army and gradually withdrew in front of the attacking right flank columns of Kluck's German army. At 11:30 on August 31, 1914, Captain Lepic, who was northwest of Compiègne, observed with surprise that large German columns, instead of continuing to move south toward Estre-St.-Denis, were turning toward Compiègne. This surprise apparently was not reflected in the nature of his report or in his fate: the report was transmitted through normal channels and was included in the scouting reports. Incidentally, if we ascribe a strategic meaning to what the captain observed in very simple terms, it becomes quite clear that the Germans had avoided including Paris in their envelopment and were rushing with all their forces to the Verdun-Paris gap, exposing their right flank to attacks from Paris. However, the French high command realized this truth only after 80 hours, by the evening of September 2, but it was of colossal importance, engendering all the preconditions for victory at the Marne. If Captain Lepic and all the echelons through which his report was transmitted had been better prepared strategically, then the French command could possibly have begun to make systematic preparations for an operation on the Marne two days earlier, on the evening of September 1, for after all, the loss of ten hours of valuable time is not always without consequence. Just think of all the valuable reports by aviators and patrols we did not take advantage of during the World War because of the strategic stupidity of our commanders and staffs! Just remember the wealth of reconnaissance information we had at our disposal during the Samsonov Operation, if only on the concentration of the German First Corps, which was not taken into consideration either by the army or front command.

In the Civil War, sometimes when means of communication were inadequate, and often when the authority of command was inadequate, the decisions of individual leaders could play a major role in strategy. A lack of strategic ability played a major role in the failure of the Warsaw Operation of 1920. Strategic errors were evident in the work of all echelons of command. All we have to do is compare the actions of the 16th Red Army on August 15-18, 1920, with the actions of Kluck's Germany army on September 5-7, 1914, to establish the clear strategic inferiority of the Red command as opposed to the Germans. Kluck's actions were far from perfect, but we can see two armies threatened by flank attacks, and Kluck's vast and massive army took a big step backward, even with a bit too much delicacy, turned all its forces and repelled the French attack, while our 16th Army watched passively as one division after another taken by the flank was destroyed by the enemy, whose actions could have been predicted quite clearly as early as August 13, 1920.

We will still have occasion to emphasize that the Red Army needs to devote serious attention to strategic questions more than any other army. Meanwhile, foreign armies have recognized the need to publicize good strategic ideas widely among their men. As early as 1805 Viscount Charles considered it necessary to publish a strategic manual for Austrian generals.[6] Moltke followed his example in 1869. Before the World War the German and French armies had manuals for high commanders, and in 1920 the British published Part II of a Field Manual for the same purpose, and at present similar work is underway in the Red Army. It is true

---

[6]   *Strategiia v trudakh voennykh klassikov* [Strategy in the Works of the Military Classics] (Moscow: Gosvoenizdat, 1926), vol. 2, pp. 69-84.

that these manuals are primarily operational rather than strategic in nature and that strategy, by its very nature resists codification in field manuals. But the need for efforts to raise the level of strategic thinking is recognized everywhere.

The study of strategy by just a small circle of commanders, such as the general staff, leads to the creation of a "strategic caste," and when strategy is isolated, it becomes scholarly pedantry, divorced from practice, and it creates an undesirable gap between strategists and tacticians among commanders and destroys mutual understanding between staffs and line units. Strategy should not become a kind of Latin which separates the believers and the nonbelievers!

Strategy should Be Studied at the Beginning of Serious Study on the Art of War

The need for all commanders to study strategy follows from the fact that it should not be put off until the time a person is assigned to a critical leadership position. Strategy is a discipline in which success depends very little on the memorization of precepts issued by a school or the assimilation of logical constructs contained in textbooks on strategy. A unity of doctrine based on the unity of strategic guidelines is illusory. In strategy the center of gravity lies in developing an independent point of view which primarily requires careful homework. Familiarization with strategic topics must begin at the start of military service, and one must study the military historical past from the vantage point of these topics, evaluate the military events one has personally experienced and examine the current evolution of the military profession.[7] Significant efforts must be made in military history in order to move from so-called "strategic essays," which are very broad descriptions of the external course of events, to truly profound criticisms of the most important decisions made in a war.

The Purpose of a Course on Strategy

The purpose of a course on strategy is not to exhaust the unlimited scope of this discipline but to lay the groundwork for subsequent independent thought, indicate the directions in which it should be developed and engender the conditions for coordinating individual efforts. Instruction on strategy at military higher educational institutions has become particularly important in our transitional era, in which not only Europe but the entire globe is becoming a completely strategic

---

[7] Fashions come from Paris, and that is why practically everywhere, particularly after France's ultimate success, there are adherents of the French system of higher military education and the programs of the Parisian Military Academy, in which strategy is practically absent. We recommend that anyone who is interested become familiar with Cordonnier's work *La méthode dans l'étude de stratégie*, and in particular, Ragueneau's *Les études militaires en France* (1913). Ragueneau considers the French Academy to be an elementary school because of its inadequate strategic preparation. In 1910 Foch made a fruitless attempt to change it by introducing, following the Russian pattern, a third additional year specially devoted to strategy. Ragueneau eloquently demonstrates the impossibility of developing strategic training solely on the basis of advanced officer's training. Bonnal (*Méthodes de commandement, d'éducation et d'instruction*) also demonstrates the impossibility of providing completely different training for midlevel and high commanders. The study of strategy should be the task of everyone planning on playing a critical part in a war. An army trying to overcome its characteristic inflexibility should not make the study of strategy a matter for a few military thinkers. Strategic thinking should be given major attention at field exercises, in military literature and in the reports of military science societies.

landscape and in which the art of war is in many respects switching to new methods and techniques of waging war and is acquiring new forms in a situation of increasing social upheaval.

This book has been written for a rather modest purpose, namely to be a guideline for independent work on strategy and to help the reader get a start and give him several broad perspectives in order to make it possible for strategic thinking to get out of back alleys and dead ends and onto the main road as quickly as possible. We have tried to point out the basic landmarks of the strategic present and we have assumed that the reader is familiar with the past evolution of the art of war.

Military History

The history of the art of war is a completely necessary introduction to this book, because without it we would risk becoming completely incomprehensible. Without first dwelling on the most important military historical facts, we run the risk of getting lost in the abstract theoretical principles of strategic art, and the benefits we derive from it will be proportional to the experience and military historical baggage we possess as we begin to study strategy.

Criticism and experience should go hand in hand. The study of strategy is of little use without military historical knowledge, but in turn conscientious thinking on military history is possible only on the basis of a certain strategic view. After all, in military history, simply memorizing facts is capable at best of giving us an idea only of known patterns which existed at one time in the conduct of military operations. And in military history independent work is most valuable. No matter how difficult it is to make a serious independent strategic evaluation of any important moment in military history which would encompass reality as a whole, this is easier to do in the historical past than it is in wartime, in present conditions. In essence, all of strategy is basically a contemplation of military history. And strategy, according to Clausewitz, should avoid going from a form of contemplation to the hard and fast doctrine of rules, inferences and conclusions. Russian military historians have usually tried to develop inferences and conclusions of a quite limited depth and scope after a factual accounting of events. A Clausewitzian historian, after presenting a fact, proceeds to contemplate it (*Betrachtung*). The difference between the terms, conclusions, on the one hand, and contemplation, on the other, reflects different understandings of the relationships between theory and real life.

Issues of military history are particularly pertinent to persons involved in the study of strategy, because by its very methods strategy is merely a systematic contemplation of military history. A divorce from history is just as dangerous for the strategist as it is for the politician, because in view of the multiplicity of factors and the complexity of the relationships between them, a theoretical, speculative approach which does not grasp all the information necessary for a correct decision may often lead to very gross errors. In strategy, as in politics, hens often hatch ducklings and consequences may prove to be quite unlike to the causes which gave rise to them. For example, all strategic writers before the World War believed that railroads were a factor that would accelerate the development of military operations, make them decisive in nature from the very beginning and lead to the exclusive use of strategy of destruction. In practice everyone ignored the equalizing effect of railroads, which help the defenses delay an attacker moving away from them, make it possible to plug breakthroughs on the front and make it easier to use all the nation's manpower on the front. As a result, quicker movements on railroads laid a duckling, namely a stationary positional front and a strategy of attrition.

Unfortunately, the current state of military history does not satisfy the most modest desires of strategy. The disproportionately strong development of the first part of this book, namely the part on the relationship between politics and strategy, is due to the scientific prostration of our military history.[8] Since military history was divided into the history of the art of war and the history of wars, the broad view became the merit of the first, while the second became more trivial, ignoring the role of politics and merely studying the course of operations. The causal connection of military conditions is only sought in terms of purely military considerations, which is undoubtedly mistaken. Instructional value has been lost, and a great many illusions have taken root: strategy has suffered from the distortion of the logic of events by military historians and not only cannot rely on their works but is forced to expend excessive efforts on dispelling the prejudices they have sown. Readers interested in strategy will find more thought-provoking observations in the political histories of past wars rather than in military treatises, particularly so-called "strategic essays."

Maneuvers

But the study of strategy should also include contemplation of the present. Any experience in the field of human relationships applies to the past, but strategy must make a comprehensive effort to predict the future. Many of the conditions which determined the strategic course of events in past wars have now disappeared and their place has been taken by new conditions. Only in rare instances can we conduct an experiment in order to establish their reality before a war breaks out. For example, the French General Laval experimentally demonstrated the possibility of a strategic concentration of up to 15,000 to 20,000 soldiers per kilometer of front on the German border, which required the movement of all infantry, cavalry and field artillery without roads and in columns so as to leave the roads for supplies and the delivery of heavy artillery. For operational art large-scale maneuvers may play the role, in a highly imperfect form, of an experiment. They may be used to study the movement of large units with modern equipment and the organization of communications and command over wide fronts, but it is impossible to use maneuvers to make a complete test of logistics and aerial reconnaissance because of the impossibility of setting up in peacetime the complete logistical system which would operate in wartime. Even very important operational issues related to combat operations such as frontages, the durations of

---

8   Military historians often have not moved very far away from Napoleon III, who did not understand the causes of the shattering defeats suffered by the French armies of the Second Empire: he was not stupid, but he was ill, with reduced strength of will and wit. Napoleon III travelled in the rear of the French armies moving toward Sedan and observed soldiers straggling, numerous carts slowing up the columns and a certain air of disorder and slackness in the rear. Hence when on September 2, 1870 the King of Prussia asked Napoleon III, who had been taken prisoner, what he thought the cause of the defeat was, he answered: "a lack of discipline, a lack of cooperation, a lack of order, overburdened soldiers, officer trains too large" (M. Welschinger, *La guerre de 1870. Causes et responsabilités*, vol. 1, p. 315). It's hard to see the forest for the trees.

battles, munitions expenditure rates and numerical superiority on attack sectors cannot be taken into consideration in any way even by means of the most extensive and expensive peacetime experiments. Our opinion of strategic maneuvers is even lower. Large-scale maneuvers, which at one time were given a great deal of importance in training the armed forces, are now increasingly becoming a kind of gigantic tactical parade and demonstration of the coordination and combat-readiness of an army.

The War Game

If the simulation of combat operations in maneuvers is too remote from the reality of war, we could try to move our exercises from the ground to a map. The method of solving tactical problems on a map is the basic method used in tactics. It is equally useful for studying operational art. However, the main value of this method does not lie in studying new topics but in enabling the transmission of practical skills from a teacher to a student, because the problems basically make it possible to study the purely technical aspect of art, leaving the fundamental questions in the background. That is why the value of solving problems on a map is quite relative, because strategic techniques are not very complicated.

In order to make fundamental questions more important, war games are employed, meaning conducting two-sided exercises on a map. In this case techniques become less important, and the entire exercise should be considered to be the choice of a certain amount of material in interesting geographical conditions with contemporary organizational and technical information for a final discussion. The value of this discussion is exclusively determined by the competence of the leadership, and the war game is a powerful tool for publicizing certain strategic and operational views but is doubtful as a method of analyzing a problem. The leaders of war games only play their roles when the assignment itself and the scenarios they give stack the deck for the final discussion. Fair war games with dispassionate umpires are incapable of producing any results.

In essence, field exercises and field excursions are essentially the same as map problems and war games[9] and are merely transferred to more instructive venues. If field excursions are organized with sufficient communications equipment, they are capable of providing good practice for staff officers and familiarizing the participants with important areas of a theater of operations. But for strategy, they only make it possible to organize a discussion whose significance is proportional to the similarity between the assignment for the excursion and the actual assumptions of our operational deployment.

Thus, the applied method in strategy may primarily be significant for popularizing certain strategic ideas among commanders and clarifying existing views of burning strategic issues.

Studying the Classics

If one has received adequate general military training, contemplating classical treatises on strategy is a way of obtaining a more profound understanding of modern strategic reality. No matter how strong the thinking of their outstanding

---

[9] The war game, or *Kriegespiel*, considered as a tool of positive analysis, is in fact deserving of the ironic sense given to the term by French writers, who always put it in quotation marks.

authors was and no matter how strong the history of strategic theory has been (only a century and a half), strategic evolution has proceeded at such a pace that all these treatises are now a part of history and mark the stages through which human thought has passed. Even Clausewitz, for whom the duration of a battle was only a strategic instant and the extent of a battlefront was only a strategic point, has undoubtedly become obsolete in many respects. He had no knowledge of operational art, because for him an operation did not present either spatial or temporal dimensions. Hence studying the classics will be of value if we focus our attention not only on the principles that are still completely relevant but also on the principles that do not totally satisfy us, which have either become completely obsolete or should be subjected to extensive modifications. If we measure our experience of the civil and imperialist wars against the principles of the most important writers on strategy who wrote before these wars, we will be able to perceive the new principles which characterize contemporary strategy.

We recommend approaching the authorities of the past and avoid memorizing as many quotes and aphorisms as possible, but with a critical attitude. We will be able to get a great deal from the great strategic thinkers only after we discard false modesty and adopt the apparent shamelessness of a student of the truth. We must not only read them, we must make serious critical studies of them, which could probably be better made by means of group seminars or discussions than by independent studies.

By their very nature strategic decisions are radical, and strategic evaluations should get to the heart of an issue, and there is nowhere else where one's thinking must be more independent, consistent, and free than in strategy or where pedantic thinking will yield more pitiful results. And it seems to us that the piety of the dogmatists, who see strategic scriptures in Napoleon's heritage, the ideal of the strategic bureaucrats, is a cruel mockery of strategic wisdom.

STRATEGY AND POLITICS

1. POLITICS AND ECONOMICS

Offense and Defense on a Historical Scale

Immobility and a state of equilibrium in a system of human factions seem to be an illusion which is shared only by pacifists and backward political scientists. The different paces and trends in the development of economic life give some nations and states an advantage over others. This advantage can be expressed in very different ways, including: an expansion of economic activity; the accumulation of material resources; more rapid population growth; better infrastructure; the capability of maintaining larger and better equipped military forces; the organization of a stronger central authority and greater national unity; the broadening of the dependence of other states on a given state; and the increase in the number of ideological adherents or a kind of citizen with dual loyalties abroad. This advantage is expressed in a process of a historical advance by those factions which are gradually conquering the future, and in a process of historical defense by other factions forced to defend their positions under conditions of an increasingly unfavorable balance of forces. For example, we could mention the historical advance of the German tribes west of the Elbe River from the 8th to the 17th centuries, the advance of the Russian tribe east of the Volga River from the 17th to the 19th centuries, and the advance of the Anglo-Saxon race, which is still going on, on all lines of weak resistance on the globe. In the 18th century we witnessed a faster rate of advance by the bourgeoisie, which led to the great French Revolution. In the early 19th century a historical advance of nations developed which took on the nature of a struggle for the establishment of integrated nation-states such as Germany and Italy, while a similar process among the Slavs forced the Turks to renounce gradually all their conquests on the European continent and forced Austria to go on the historical defensive, which it did not abandon until it disintegrated in 1918.

Against the background of this political and economic process different factions have acquired their own class, national, local and colonial interests and have found it necessary to struggle for the purpose of defending them. The ruling class in a state is inclined to regard its own interests as state interests and resorts to the aid of the state apparatus to defend them.

The Art of Politics

Any struggle for one's interests can only become sufficiently conscious and consistent when its goals have been clarified. Once they have been systematized, these goals form the program or idea of a given faction. These programs can sometimes be reconstructed only by a historian, while sometimes they exist in written form but are never proclaimed openly. Often they are proclaimed in an intentionally distorted form in order to make it possible to draw as many people as possible into a faction.

Organizations of individual factions for the purpose of struggling for a particular program are called political parties, because politics is the art of orienting a struggle for the purpose of carrying out the program of a certain faction. Because every program is based on economic interests and economics is the basis for a developing historical advance, we can see politics as a "concentrated expression of economics." Only movements which are based on real interests can acquire a major significance. Even such a nationalistic writer as General von der Goltz has admitted that pure patriotism is wet powder which is incapable of igniting the masses.

But politics is also the art of manipulating millions of people, and in fact, in a situation of opposition by other factions, politics will get the opportunity to take a direct route to its goal only under exceptionally favorable conditions, and quite often politics must wait it out, retreat and take roundabout paths and lead the masses in the process. The art of politics, which operates on the basis of a program which has already been developed, lies in pointing out immediate goals for specific work. Any politics which ignored these immediate goals and focused all its attention on the ultimate idea would be a pitiful degeneration of practical art into a sociology or philosophy of history. The imaginary logical line which connects the successive stages we are trying to reach and is oriented toward the ideal of the program is called a political line of conduct.

The ruling class in a state not only is required to struggle within the state for a particular program, that is, carry out a domestic policy determined by its interests, but is also required to defend its interests in relations with other states, that is, carry out a foreign policy. The latter is obviously determined by the domestic interests of the ruling class and is a logical extension of domestic policy. But it also depends on the directions of the policies of other states. The domination of a ruling class is strong only when it does not interpret its interests too narrowly: the hegemony which guides foreign policy cannot sacrifice the interests of the common historical whole without causing a fatal crisis.

Politics, both foreign and domestic, constitute the guiding reasons for historical decisions.

Violence

The political conflict that pervades all human existence is usually conducted within the framework of conditions set by ruling classes, that is, within a legal framework. However, there are times when a situation is created in which this conflict turns into violence.

If we are discussing foreign policy, this means that standards of international law have been violated, and the offended party, if it possesses sufficient strength, is not always limited to a mere protest, and political conflict takes the form of war. If we are discussing domestic politics, then the resort to violence by a nonruling class or nonruling nationality becomes a civil war. We are not talking about the violence of the ruling class, because it takes place every minute of the existence of a state and constitutes the essence of its existence.

The pacifist slant of 18th-century philosophy, because of its lack of comprehension of the historical process, led to a situation in which wars were examined within a legal framework where they were considered the unjustifiable attack of the strong on the weak, and the ideal of the 18th century lay in maintaining the existing political balance.[1]

Today, however, peace itself is primarily the result of violence and is maintained by violence. Every state border is the result of a war, the outlines of states on the map make us familiar with the strategic and political thinking of the victories, and political geography and peace treaties constitute a lesson in strategy. In every corner of Central Europe there are irredentas, that is, conquered territories which have not been returned to their rightful owners and contradict the desires of nations for self-determination.

In the 20th century, even the hypocritical League of Nations has been unable to maintain the point of view of preserving the existing equilibrium and has been compelled to acknowledge the need for evolution: Paragraph 19 of its Charter gives a plenary session of the League the right to invite members of the League's council to review treaties which cannot be carried out and to review international relations which constitute a threat to peace. It would be wrong to ascribe the origins of war to the shortcomings of different governments, be they monarchies or republics. The causes of war lie in economic inequality, in the contradictions between the interests of individual factions, in all the conditions of the historical process and primarily in private property in the means of production. And both civil and foreign wars are still the inevitable costs of history.[2]

War is a Component of Political Conflict

Thus foreign and civil wars are not self-contained but form only a portion of the continuous political interaction among human factions. During a war the political life of the countries waging it continues rather than grinds to a halt.

War is only a part of political conflict. The art of politics lies in defending the interests of a certain faction among all other factions. It operates in an atmosphere of the clash of many forces, and although economics primarily determines

---

[1] However, Montesquieu, in his *Dukh zakonov* [The Spirit of Laws], also examined the progressive significance of violence, which was the subject of chapter 4, book 10, entitled "O nekotorykh vyvodakh pobezhdennykh harodov" [On Several Advantages of Conquered Nations].

[2] Moltke's opinion that property rather than the kind of political regime is the source of war is set forth in his speech before the Reichstag in 1890. See *Strategia v trudakh voennykh klassikov*, vol. 2, pp. 179-181. And from the experience of the millennia even Montesquieu concluded that the triumphs of democracies are always more costly to the defeated than the triumphs of monarchies, and that the fate of those defeated by a democracy is harsher (*Dukh zakonov*, book 10, chapter 7). The creators of the Peace of Versailles have taken on the task of confirming this truth one more time.

whether they are hostile, cooperative or neutral, at different times not only the intensity of opposition or cooperation may change, but an ally may become an enemy, and vice versa. In principle, the art of war has recognized only two sides at the barricades raised by the war, namely our side and the enemy. But during military operations one must seriously consider the interests of third political factions which have not yet taken definite positions on our side or that of the enemy, and make sure that unity is maintained in one's camp and that the enemy camp disintegrates. These are purely political tasks and must be handled by politics and because the leaders of military operations are responsible for only a part, albeit an essential part, of this political solution, they must be subordinate to political requirements.

War is waged not only on an armed front; it is also waged on the class and economic fronts. Operations on all fronts must be coordinated by politics. In the process, of course, one must consider the characteristics of the resources which must be employed on each front and not switch operational methods from one front to another without considering these characteristics. For example, the concentration of efforts is very important on the armed front. Because of this, political agitators employ similar techniques in their work; namely, if they have 10,000 propaganda leaflets, they will distribute 9,000 at the point to be attacked and the other 1,000 elsewhere. But after all, the characteristics of the leaflets on which we are concentrating are quite different from the characteristics of shells and bullets. Propaganda leaflets make no impression at all on a class enemy and a very weak impression on enemy soldiers who are not prepared to heed their call to intensify class conflict. The fruits are far from proportional to the seeds we sow. Good farmers sow fewer seeds than bad ones.

It is obvious that political agitation cannot be random but should be carried out where the groundwork has been laid. Any political agitator who would follow on the heels of tacticians rather than determine his own line of least resistance would be making a mistake. It would be just as mistaken to require from strategy actions which would conflict with the characteristics of the resources at its disposal.

Strategists should not complain about political interference in the leadership of military operations because strategy itself is a projection of politics,[3] and it stands to reason that mistaken policies will also bear the same pitiful fruit in war as they do in any other field, but one should not confuse protests against political

---

[3] Bismarck (*Erinnerungen*, vol. 2, pp. 94-95) defends the right of politics to interfere in strategy in the following, quite moderate terms: "The purpose of the high command is to destroy hostile military forces, while the purpose of war is to win a peace which meets the political conditions set forth by the state. The establishment and delineation of the goals to be achieved by the war and the provision of advice to the monarch in this regard during the course of the war is a political task, and the methods of accomplishing this political task cannot help but affect the conduct of a war. The ways and means of waging war will always depend on the greater or lesser results which are trying to be achieved, on whether we must annex territory or not, and on whether we wish to capture a certain objective as a bargaining chip, and on how much time we have available." Germany's lack of political direction in the 20th century has in part been characterized by the emancipation of German strategy from political directives. The triumph of strategy over politics can be partially explained by the weakness of the German bourgeoisie and the triumph of the Junkers over it.

errors with refusal to acknowledge the right and obligation of politics to determine the basic direction of a war.[4]

In our opinion, the claim that politics is superior to strategy is universal in nature. There is no doubt that it is true when the creators of policy constitute a young class advancing to a bright future and whose historical health is reflected in the form of a sound policy. But it always leads to doubts in states which represent the organized dominance of an obsolete class, which are on the historical defensive and whose regimes have become decadent and have been compelled to follow unsound policies and sacrifice the interests of the whole to maintain their domination. And in this case, unsound politics are inevitably followed by unsound strategy. This is why the protests of bourgeoisie military writers, particularly the French writers impressed by the fatal effects of the rotten politics of the Second Empire on strategy, are quite understandable. It is natural for strategy to try to gain emancipation from bad politics, but strategy cannot exist in a vacuum without politics and is condemned to pay for all the sins of politics. Only the September Revolution which toppled the Second Empire was capable of saving French strategy in 1870 from the fatal continuation of the political line of the government of the Second Empire.

The Struggle for Economic Readiness for War

The above means that all international life in peacetime is a continuous clash of interests among individual states conducting a continuous economic struggle.

---

[4]   The elder Moltke, Ludendorff and Laval are the most important authorities who have refused to acknowledge fully the principle established by Buelow and Clausewitz that strategy is subordinate to politics. A protest against the supremacy of politics permeates Moltke's article "On Strategy" (*Strategiia v trudakh voennykh klassikov*, vol. 2, pp. 176-179). Moltke finds that primarily military considerations are decisive for the course of a war (which he toned down in the 1882 edition): that strategy is independent of politics in resolving its problems. In trying to achieve better results with the resources at its disposal, strategy is best able to fulfill the hopes placed on it. Hindenburg held the same view. Ludendorff made a similar protest in his not too successful book *Kriegsfuehrung und Politik*. Ludendorff arrived at the conclusion that war is an extension of (only) foreign policy by other means, while all other policies should be subordinate to war. Laval, who was affected by the intervention of the "rotten" regime of the Second Empire in leading the French armies in 1870, was the most vivid in objecting to political intervention in strategy. In his introduction to positive strategy Laval stated the following: Clausewitz, in analyzing only the monarch military leaders, Frederick the Great and Napoleon, confused the political and strategic aspects of their activity. A war should be examined in isolation as a gigantic duel between two nations. Rulers should specialize in politics while generals should specialize in strategy. Politics is related to war only to the extent it determines the extent of the sacrifices made by the nation in peacetime to organize the armed forces. In wartime politics continues to operate without regard to military plans. Once war is declared everyone should shut up. Strategy requires secrecy and unanimity. Discussions with politicians lead to anemia and a loss of will and energy. Politics is an opium for strategy and leads to weakness. All power to the chosen military leader! A politician who understands anything about the military profession is a chimera. One should not distract a military leader from his main business with politics. A general should answer a politician who wishes to interfere in his business in the same way that Pelissier, who besieged Sevastopol, answered the French Minister of War: "If you want to command the Army, take my place." We have cited Laval's statements because they still represent the views of many French generals and it would be useful to get acquainted with them in order to clarify the train of thought of many leaders of the bourgeois armies.

We are interested in that aspect of the struggle which has in mind military interests. Strategy is quite concerned with different solutions to economic problems. The current political wisdom is "If you want peace, prepare for war." Every state, in order to avoid being caught unawares, tries to establish a certain correspondence between its economic development and the economic conditions for successfully waging war in peacetime. This leads to a situation in which an economy, as it develops, is consistently adapted to the tasks it will have to face once a war begins. The mere anticipation of war and preparations for it deforms an economy, changes the balance between individual components of the economy and forces the use of different methods. This tendency of a peacetime economy to approach wartime forms is a general and inevitable law, but the overenergetic distortion of the natural form of economic development has a quite negative effect and hinders the overall economic success of a country.

A strategic approach to economic phenomena should establish a point of view on the economic foundations of a state's military might and yield an assessment which would make it possible to judge the actual forces and nature of a future war. This is the goal we pursue over the entire course of our work.

Foreign Trade

Small states, because of the comparative lack of diversity of the goods they produce, are highly dependent on foreign markets. During the World War, Romania suffered from surpluses of oil and wheat and was forced to get military equipment from France by way of Arkhangelsk. The size of small countries makes it impossible for them to find areas where military industry could operate unhindered during wartime. In most cases this compels them to avoid attempts to prepare for waging war on their own by means of setting up an independent military industry and keep to more natural paths of economic development. That is why the economies of small countries outdistance the economies of large continental powers who have already made major advances in developing war economies.

A large continental state is much less dependent on foreign markets because its industry primarily utilizes domestic raw materials and mainly produces for the domestic market. However, the trend toward specialization into a separate economic entity quite often leads to a rise in production costs because many industrial sectors must be organized under economic conditions which are less favorable than at other spots on the globe. These sectors must be protected by tariffs and freight subsidies.

A protective tariff policy is desirable from the vantage point of the war economy for any country which would be incapable of guaranteeing freedom of the seas during wartime, because it prepares the state for any forthcoming blockade. Until recently only Great Britain has been able to maintain the principle of free trade, but this was a result of its domination of the seas and the possibility of maintaining free access to its ports during wartime. By the second half of the war the submarine blockade had compelled Britain to switch to a temporary policy of subsidies and protective tariffs for agriculture (guaranteeing high grain prices to farmers, buying 5,000 tractors and so forth). If Britain's extremely favorable situation with respect to freedom of the seas had been disrupted by the successes of the U-boats and the air force, then Great Britain would also have been compelled to radically restructure its economic system.

In 1902 Germany implemented a policy of high grain subsidies. The German farmers had argued that high grain prices, by satisfying their class interests, would also significantly improve the country's economic capacity for war. Perhaps the statistics[5] they cited were not completely objective, but nevertheless they do give evidence of a relationship between grain prices and yields. In 12 years (1895-1907), due to higher prices, the number of cattle in Germany had increase to 3 million head, the number of pigs had increased to 5.3 million head, the rye harvest had increased from 6.6 million tons to 12.2 million tons, the wheat harvest had increased from 2.8 million to 4.65 million tons, the barley harvest had increased from 2.4 million tons to 2.67 million tons, the oats harvest had increased from 5.2 million tons to 9.7 million and the potato harvest had increased form 31.7 million to 54.1 million tons. Despite the rapid growth of the urban population, in 1900 Germany imported 16 percent of its total food needs, while in 1906 this figure had dropped to 10 percent. Ultimately the blockade broke Germany in the World War, but if the tariff policy had not doubled its agricultural output, Germany would have been forced to surrender before the harvest of 1915.

The Development of Industry

The mobilization of industry is greatly facilitated by preliminary economic preparations.[6] Any state going to war with Great Britain will be cut off from the Chilean and Indian saltpeter needed to make powder and any sort of explosives. This is the reason for the enormous significance of the production of nitrogen from air for any state conducting an independent policy.

The dye industry has also become more important, because its equipment and semifinished products are quite suitable for making chemical weapons. Of course, all states in the world are now trying to produce aniline dyes at home and are more or less following the example Great Britain set in 1920 (the Dyestuffs Act), which requires special authorization for any dye imports. War swallows up enormous amounts of copper, which is why one should not examine copper production at copper smelting plants solely from the perspective of simple economic gain or loss.

---

[5]   We have taken these statistics from Fuerst Buelow, *Deutsche Politik* (Berlin: 1916), p. 269. We should keep in mind that German agriculture had developed on a footing which was not completely sound: while the average wage of an unskilled industrial worker had reached 1 mark for a 10-hour day in 1921, agriculture was based primarily on millions of seasonal workers from Russian Poland and Austria rather than on expensive German labor, and because war had been declared in the summer, the Russian Poles could be detained and made serfs by the landowners for the entire war, while some of the remaining requirements for manpower could be met by prisoners of war.

Here we should mention a basic contradiction of German policy: its construction of a large battleship fleet expressed Germany's desire to compete with Britain for domination of the seas and for free trade, while the grain tariffs marked a continental trend in German policy and its preparations for war with Russia. This lack of consistency in German policy made it easier for Great Britain to encircle Germany politically and ultimately led to Germany's defeat. Germany could fight a war with Great Britain only if it had Russian grain at its disposal, while in a continental war the presence of a large navy, which scared Great Britain, could only have been a hindrance. Alexander the Great, in planning to conquer Persia did not fragment his resources by building a navy and organizing a land army.

We shall not dwell on the completely obvious issue of the significance of military exports in peacetime, which makes it possible to keep major industrial facilities going.

Timely stockpiling of foreign raw materials (if one does not have one's own) presents major difficulties because of the need to tie up a great deal of capital, which presents difficulties to even the wealthiest country. However, sometimes one can avoid the difficulties by subsidizing private imports and storage of particular materials. For example, before the World War Germany set up a project for building huge elevators for subsidized import and storage of Russian grain in the anticipation of good prices at Koenigsberg and Danzig. This project could have somewhat alleviated Germany's food situation in the war, but it was never carried out because of the resistance of German farmers, who were worried by the constant pressure on prices of large visible supplies of grain. In the future the idea of free ports may do a great deal to alleviate commodity shortages.

Economic Positions Abroad

In the era of imperialism capitalist relations have outgrown the boundaries of individual states and capital has captured positions far from the borders of its own country. Economic activity is a characteristic of economic prosperity. The exploitation of colonies, steamship lines between foreign ports, participation in profitable foreign enterprises such as railroads, banks, industry and plantations, the organization of large stores of commodities on foreign soil and the investment of capital in foreign loans are all typical manifestations of imperialism.

Economic activity helps a state greatly extend its political influence in peacetime and even make economically weak states its vassals (e.g., Great Britain and Portugal). But extensive economic positions abroad have their flip side, because they cannot be defended by military force and undermine a state's economic readiness for war.

The Geographical Distribution of Industry

Essentially we are now faced with the same question we would be faced with if we were to go from the legal concept of a border between two countries to the military notion of a line which more or less reliably protects the territory behind it with the armed forces available in the country and its distance from the enemy protects it from bombings and other hostile attacks.

It is important to try to locate all military industry and develop industrial centers in areas which are well protected by their geographical locations and which are as close as possible to sources of fuel and raw materials. Threatened border areas with high industrial concentrations make it extremely difficult to maneuver, require the allocation of major forces and expensive permanent forti-

---

[6] We shall not dwell on the obvious question of the strengthening of the economic readiness of a state for war in connection with the overall health of its industrial development. A. Gulevich's treatise, *Voina i narodnoe khoziaistvo* [War and the Economy] (1898), which compares the Russian economy and the main European economies from the military perspective, is full of falsehoods: the author, clearly possessed by a chauvinistic servility, attempted to prove Russia's superiority over Germany by supposedly demonstrating the greater adaptability of peasant farming to wartime as opposed to commercial farming. Gulevich borrowed this ridiculous idea from I. S. Bliukh's (J. S. Bloch) five-volume work, *Budushchaia voina* [The Future War].

fications to defend them, and despite this will often fall into enemy hands. The concentration of French industry, particularly the metallurgical industry, in the north of France, had an extremely unfavorable effect on the French conduct of the war. Fortunately for France its most important war plants, namely the Schneider plants, were located in the center of the country (Creseau) outside the area occupied by the Germans, and the large appetite for steel was met by imports from the United States. Perhaps it was the presence of the Saar coal field that inclined the Germans to reject the elder Moltke's reasonable plan of limiting themselves to a defense against France in fighting on two fronts.

Concentrating an entire industry at one point is just as dangerous.

The entire French aviation industry, the entire optical industry, all the precision mechanics shops and practically three fourths of the automotive industry were concentrated in Paris. A certain amount of dispersal would have improved France's defensive capabilities. The threat posed to the Silesian industrial region by the Russians in early November 1914 compelled Ludendorff to begin the Lodz Operation two weeks early, prior to the arrival of major reinforcements from the Western Front, which perhaps saved two or three Russian armies from total disaster. The concentration of industry in the western provinces (Lodz, Warsaw, Bialystok, Szawli, Riga) presented the same disadvantage for tsarist Russia: some plants had to be surrendered to the enemy; some were evacuated on time, but this tied up freight cars at a time when they were particularly important for military purposes. The fact that before the war Petrograd was supplied with coal from Great Britain while the western provinces were supplied with coal from the Dombrowo pits, which were located at the Silesian border and were lost on the very first day of the war, was also very disadvantageous. The Donetsk coal fields were not prepared to handle this and it also placed additional burdens on transportation.

Now Leningrad's industry has raised certain doubts. The tsarist government decided to crowd many plants into Leningrad without being bothered by the fact that it conflicted with nature. In 1925 Leningrad had 11.6 percent of all Soviet industry, including 56 percent of the rubber industry, 48 percent of the electrical industry and more than 13 percent of the metal industry, which is so important for building engines, machine tools and equipment.

Leningrad is now the same kind of border city that Nancy was in prewar France. The location of this ancient capital of Lorraine greatly hindered the freedom of action of the French armies in August and September 1914. The disadvantages of Leningrad's strategic location are made even greater by its distance from sources of fuel, grain and raw materials. In peacetime this distance is reflected only in the higher costs of Leningrad's products, which are partially cancelled out by its good factory equipment, industrial traditions, skilled workers and housing. But in wartime we would not only have to deal with overhead, we would also have to deal with the disruption of transportation by long-distance deliveries of raw materials, fuel and food which will create very undesirable complications in the war economy.

Radical changes in economic policies entail grave and painful consequences. But a wise economic policy consistently carried out over a number of decades could gradually shift the center of gravity of industry to areas which are better located in terms of the economic conditions of waging war. However, extreme caution in altering the natural course of economic development is not equivalent to giving it the opportunity to grow in stages. A policy of setting prices and freight rates, the allocation of orders and credit and the construction of new lines of communication, housing and factories should gradually but steadily lead to the aforementioned goal.

Oil from Baku and Grozny could be refined locally, which would fully meet strategic requirements, but economically it would seem advantageous to ship a large amount of this oil to Black Sea ports by pipeline and refine it there. However, the production of such militarily vital products as gasoline, semifinished products for explosives and so forth would be threatened by hostile naval forces. Obviously, the issue of the most suitable sites for petroleum refineries can be resolved only by means of a careful accounting of both economic and military pluses and minuses.

In the same way the construction of powerful sources of electrical power, such as the Dneprostroi and Svirstroi, which in the future will be used to industrialize entire regions, will also require competent strategic analysis as well as technical and economic analysis.

2. THE POLITICAL GOAL OF WARFARE

Economic War Aims

The World War was a vast and complex collision of economic interests. While the direct pretext for it was provided by the collision of Austro-Hungary and Serbia, in which economic motives were not so clear, the entire nature and scope of the war were closely tied to the fact that in the 25 years before the war Germany had increased its exports 228 percent and was thus catching up to Great Britain, which had only succeeded in increasing its exports by 87 percent. War has economic causes, it is conducted on a certain economic base, it is a feverish economic process which sometimes turns into an economic revolution and it leads to certain economic results. "The Entente's military victory must be complemented by an economic victory, because if not it will soon become a glorious but vain memory," proclaimed one of the bulletins of French headquarters.

We should recognize the legitimacy of economic aims even in a war involving a power representing the interests of the international workers' movement against the bourgeois world. The need to pursue negative economic goals in a conflict could only be denied by Tolstoyans. But this is not enough. As a matter of fact, any phase of the conflict for world revolution that did not involve the achievement of certain economic goals accompanied by the expansion of the economic basis of the side opposing the bourgeoisie and weakening the economic position of capitalism could not be considered a major success.

War is not only an arena for the armed forces. The economic aims of a war are achieved at the same time that the armed forces fight for their military goals and in conjunction with fierce fighting on the political front. If the enemy offers stiff resistance, victory will require efforts on all three fronts to destroy the very material conditions which make it possible for him to resist.

The political goal of a war,[1] which guides the struggle on the armed, class (and in economically backward countries, national) and economic fronts, is determined on the basis of the interests affected by the war, the anticipated enemy resistance, the participation of unarmed forces in the conflict and one's conception of the nature of the coming war and military capabilities.

Formulation of the Political Goal

The first duty of the art of politics with respect to strategy is to formulate the political goal of a war. Any goal should be strictly coordinated with the resources available to achieve it. The political goal should be appropriate to one's war-waging capabilities.

---

[1] We must clearly differentiate between the causes of a war and its political aims. The causes follow from an ongoing political and economic process, while the political goal constitutes the basis for the directives of the supreme authority concerning the conduct of the war, and may be altered, depending on the course of military events. While it governs the preparations for war, the political goal in turn must be appropriate to the level achieved by this preparation on the armed, class and economic fronts at any given moment.

To meet this requirement, a politician must have a correct conception of the relations of friendly to hostile forces, which requires extremely mature and profound judgment; a knowledge of the history, politics and statistics of both hostile states; and a certain amount of competence in basic military matters.[2] The final statement of the goal would be made by the politician after an appropriate exchange of views with strategists, and it should help rather than hinder strategic decisions.

The Political Base

In a civil war the political goal of the side starting a rebellion will involve the creation of an inadequate political base, that is, in seizing power in the capital or a particularly important provincial center. Julius Caesar did not aim his first attacks at Pompey's legions in Spain; leaving the manpower of the Senate and Pompey off to the side, he crossed the Rubicon and captured Rome with negligible forces. Gaul, where his legions were and whence he drew the necessary resources for the civil war, was his economic base, but he needed the political support Rome could give him. After capturing Rome, Julius Caesar was already acting as the defender of national interests rather than factional interests. The Senate had lost its political base, because after it fled from Rome it had already lost its state authority and became a private collection of emigres.

The Political Offensive and Defensive

The statement of a political goal should include an indication of whether a war is pursued for politically offensive or defensive purposes. As early as the 14th century the feudal lord de Coucy reported to the French King Charles V that "The English are weakest at home, and there is no easier place to beat them than in their homeland." Montesquieu agreed with this[3] and acknowledged that imperialist nations such as the Carthaginians, Romans and English deployed all their might in offensive undertakings, where their forces are unified by martial authority and discipline, while at home these forces are divided by political and social interests. Napoleon shared these illusions and claimed that the world would sometimes be very astonished after finding out how easy England could be defeated by an army landing on its shores. This is where many people have gotten the notion of the saving grace of the political offensive which would cover up one's own internal disputes and make it possible to deal with individual political parties rather than a hostile state as a whole. To us this view of war as a mold into which a political offensive is cast seems to be fundamentally incorrect. One cannot overestimate the purely external effect of the cessation of strikes and attacks by the opposition and the apparent unanimity which is established once a war begins. War is not a medicine to cure the internal illnesses of a state; rather, it is a very serious test of the health of domestic politics. Only the firm domination of certain classes within

---

[2]   Buelow ascribed such importance to military competence that he demanded that diplomats primarily be soldiers. This is wrong, because military knowledge should only constitute a part of the mental baggage required of a politician. Familiarity with the class factions of one's own side and the enemy side carried to exhaustive depth and to familiarity with class tendencies, tendencies which are fully manifested only in a crisis, constitute the politician's obligatory speciality.

[3]   Montesquieu, *L'espirit des lois*, book 2, chapter 8.

a country makes it possible to carry out prolonged political and strategic offensives. Coucy, Montesquieu and Napoleon were all mistaken concerning the resistance that would be encountered by a landing party on English shores. A political offensive flows out of a historical offensive, it is a consequence of a complex political and economic process and cannot merely be considered a more advanced technique of political conflict. The internal weakness of a state is evident more quickly in an offensive than a defensive. The tragedy of the Germans' conduct of the war from 1914 to 1918 lies in the fact that under the conditions Germany could have won this war only as a politically defensive war. Incidentally, the Germans realized this only in August 1918 after all their forces had been exhausted and they were faced with capitulation. German strategy had gone beyond the bounds of the political defensive when they violated Belgian neutrality in August 1914; when they penetrated too deep into Russia in 1915 (Ludendorff's dreams of capturing the Baltic states); when they declared a submarine blockade of Britain in early 1917 (bringing the United States into the war); when they took an insufficiently conciliatory position toward the Russian Revolution (the offensive of the summer of 1917, the Brest-Litovsk Treaty); when their stubbornness made it difficult to negotiate; and when they turned to a strategy of total victory in March-July 1918.[4] Because they were inappropriate for a political defensive, Ludendorff's partial successes were only a step toward ultimate defeat. With respect to the advantage the Germans gained from waging the war by occupying new territories and moving the action away from the German fatherland, we must look at this quite skeptically. Long ago Rousseau observed: "'I have broken the Romans,' Hannibal wrote, 'Send me men; I have extracted tribute throughout all of Italy....Send me money.' That's what all the Te Deums, fireworks, and delight of the nation means when its rulers triumph."[5]

The Development of the Idea of the Political Offensive

The mission of a political offensive should be outlined in as great detail as possible in the political goal. A strategist must know whether he will have to uproot a hostile regime and shed the last drop of enemy blood (saigner au blanc [bleed him white], in Bismarck's expression) or whether a compromise is possible.

The statement of an offensive political goal should assist the strategist faced with operating against a large state or a large coalition of small states. If an enemy of this kind stays unified, he is practically impossible to defeat overwhelmingly. But if a very close examination is made one can always find political weak points in the enemy which make it easier to triumph over him. Sometimes these are political boundaries: an attack on the political boundary between the Savoyan and Austrian armies inaugurated Bonaparte's brilliant career in 1796. Napoleon I, Napoleon III and Foch all planned to attack the boundary between southern and northern Germany, which had grown up under different historical, political and economic conditions.

---

[4]   "You will have many other reasons to count on victory if in this war you do not attempt to gain new acquisitions and do not voluntarily create other dangers for yourselves... [Y]our own mistakes are more terrifying than your enemy's plans." *Fukidid* [Thucydides], vol. 1, p. 144.

[5]   Jean Jacques Rousseau, *Politique* (1790), partie 1, p. 404.

This political goal, namely splitting a hostile state into individual political fragments, involves a study of the domestic political situation.[6] On the other hand, sometimes the political goal will involve the political encirclement of the foe, to which the efforts of the British government were obviously leading with respect to Germany after the Russo-Japanese War.

If the enemy constitutes a unified state entity, such as France, its capital is of major significance as a political base where all the political life and conflicting political factions are concentrated. Paris is such a place. All the political will of the French state is concentrated in Paris. And Paris has always been the goal of invasions of France, because the capture of Paris has emasculated the ruling class and opened up space for the forces operating against it. Power over Paris has made it possible to conclude a peace with a France rendered unable to resist any further. A period of intensified political conflict greatly enhances the political and thus the military significance of a capital.

Victory by Destruction and Attrition

We shall subsequently give a detailed characterization of these categories of military operations in our chapter on the forms of conducting military operations. But we should already mention that these categories are not simply characteristic of armed struggle or of our era alone. Attrition and destruction flow directly from the dynamics of any conflict, because we can observe them in boxing just as we can in the very complicated conditions of national and class struggle. The thinking of outstanding politicians has undoubtedly had these categories in mind. Didn't Karl Marx have destruction in mind in his speech of November 29, 1847 on the Polish question when he examined it as part of a theater of the overall struggle for liberation, albeit a secondary one?

> The contradictions between the proletariat and the bour-
> geoisie are more highly developed in England than in any
> other country. herefore the victory of the English proletariat
> over the English bourgeoisie is of decisive importance for the
> victory of all the oppressed over their oppressors. Because of
> this Poland will be liberated in England, not in Poland.[7]

---

[6]   The old formula of political imperialism, namely divide and rule, lies at the heart of political maneuvering and in our time has begun to converge with the concept of the interior strategic position. Operations on interior lines will now be employed primarily on two fronts. The armed front will set up a screen against one faction and attack another. In order to achieve success we must coordinate operations and politics. In the World War Germany was in an interior political position with respect to Russia and France, but the Germans failed to coordinate their military and political operations.

[7]   We are quoting from D. Riazanov's *Ocherki po istorii marksizma* [Essays on the History of Marxism] (Moscow: 1923), p. 611. The reader will undoubtedly see the similarity between Marx's logic in this respect and Schlieffen's claim that Serbia would be defeated not on the Save River but on the Russian front and that the war would be won for Austria not on the Russian border but by a decisive success in France and so forth. In 1847 in *The Principles of Communism*, Friedrich Engels answered the remarkable question of whether a proletarian revolution could occur in a single country in the negative on the basis of the logic of destruction; while Lenin in his theory on the possibility of the victory of socialism in one country began to go over to the logic of attrition in 1915 and gave the intensification of the internal contradictions of imperialism as his reason for his break with the strategy of victory by destruction and his acknowledgement of the possibility of victory by attrition.

Therefore there is no reason for you Chartists to express your honorable wishes for the liberation of oppressed nations. Destroy your own domestic enemies, and you will then be proud to know that in the process you have defeated all of the old society.

In different periods of Lenin's career we can find different kinds of political maneuvering depending on the requirements of the situation. In the spring of 1920 Lenin advocated a policy of attrition and in his brochure entitled *The Infantile Disorder of Leftism in Communism* he attacked the doctrinaires who blindly insisted on political destruction. He characterized this leftist dogmatism as an attempt to ignore limited intermediate goals and achieve the ultimate goal in a single bound and as the naive desire to turn their own impatience into a theoretical argument that if we have the desire to skip the intermediate stages, this means that the cat is in the bag. The slogan "Forward, without compromises, straight ahead" is a blind, imitative, uncritical application of one kind of experience to different conditions and a different situation: namely they wanted to make a difficult climb up an unexplored mountain with everything planned beforehand, never zigzag, never turn back, once you have chosen one direction don't try another; it means falling in love with one particular form, turning it into a panacea, failing to understand its one-sidedness, fearing to see the drastic turn which has become inevitable due to objective conditions and repeating simple schoolboy adages such as "three is greater than two." This is the infantile fear of the slightest difficulty facing us today and the failure to comprehend the immeasurably greater difficulties which we will have to overcome tomorrow; this is an unprepared attack.

Lenin contrasted the "battering ram" policy of his opponents to a clear statement of the ultimate goal and constant efforts to solve limited practical problems; to conquer one industry, one region after another; to maintain maximum flexibility in selecting a path to our ultimate destination; compromises, conciliation, zigzags, concessions and avoiding fighting under unfavorable conditions. Lenin proceeded from a recognition of the impossibility of defeating the bourgeoisie without a long, stubborn, desperate war to the death, a war which would require restraint, discipline, firmness and unwavering willpower. Political activity is not a sidewalk on Nevsky Prospect, general prescriptions are ridiculous, we must think for ourselves in order to understand any specific case, and we must master all the ways and means of struggle which the enemy has or could have at his disposal. Lenin foresaw not only the last decisive battle, he also shifted the center of gravity of politics to the struggle for the most advantageous balance of all class forces and to occupy a good position for the final attack.

We think that this characterization[8] is sufficient to illustrate the significance of the questions of victory by destruction and attrition in evaluating a phase of a political struggle. These issues constitute an essential component of the ideas which guide political leaders.

It would be mistaken to understand victory by destruction and victory by attrition as moments which can exist in a struggle simultaneously, in the way that

---

[8] We have not quoted Lenin directly in order to avoid cluttering our book with hundreds of quotations on a topic which is quite clear. We think that the subject of "the questions of victory by destruction and victory by attrition in Lenin's works" merit a detailed study which would make it possible for us to get a much better understanding of political theory.

one side is on the offensive and the other side is on the defensive. If a destructive strike is feasible and is attempted by one side, the opposing side is compelled to organize his counteractions in accordance with the logic of destruction. If destruction is not feasible, then, even if both sides were to swear by Napoleon and draw up only destruction plans, the struggle will fall into the rut of attrition, despite the mass of efforts wasted in vain. That's the way it was in the World War, in which all the general staffs, who thought solely in terms of destruction, suffered a cruel fiasco.

But armed struggle is only a part of the overall political struggle. Politics and strategy must be strictly coordinated. This was not the case in 1920, when Lenin made a drastic shift to a policy of attrition, while we strategists continued to develop the very same leftist doctrinaire slants which Lenin had attacked on the diplomatic, trade union, party and economic fronts.

Thus the task of politics is to define a future war not only as a defensive war or an offensive war but as a war of attrition or a war of victory by destruction.

In 1870 Bismarck was quite afraid that other powers would intervene in the Franco-Prussian War, and believing that the favorable political conditions Prussia was in would only be temporary, he advocated a quick destructive strike to France by an attack on Paris rather than a blockade.

Strategists of the old school usually said that any delay in war would be to the detriment of the attacker. This is valid if we have in mind only the strategy of destruction and limit the concept of an offensive only to the military front. However, if an offensive means the pursuit of positive goals in contrast to a defensive, which pursues negative goals, we can see the possibility of a political and economic offensive which would require a long time to have an effect on the enemy and for which prolonging a war could be beneficial. All the attempts of the Russians to inflict a destructive strike blow on Dagestan were unsuccessful, but once the Russians organized a systematic war of attrition and cut off Chechenia, which supplied Dagestan with grain, Shamil was defeated, and Dagestan was conquered. During the World War the Entente pursued very active goals against Germany, trying to disarm Germany completely in the military and economic sense, but employed methods of attrition, and time worked in favor of the Entente's political offensive rather than in favor of Germany.

The fact that a war of attrition may lead to the achievement of the most decisive ultimate goals and to the complete physical exhaustion of the enemy never makes

---

9   We completely disagree with Blume's generally accepted terminology (W. Blume, *Stratégie* (1912), pp. 24-27). Blume, who denies the division into destruction and attrition, classifies wars, in terms of intensity, as wars to the last man (*Vollkrieg*), such as the war of Prussia against Napoleon in 1806 and 1807 or the Boer Wars (1900-1903); as shortened wars (*abgekuerzter Vollkrieg*), which begin with the same energy but are interrupted before all resources are exhausted due to the hopelessness of resistance and the sufferings of the people; and as wars with limited aims, in which armed conflict does not develop at full speed. Wars with limited aims (which Blume would like to call wars of attrition) are merely low-intensity wars for modest goals. Such wars were typical of the 18th century, but it would be difficult to expect a replay in the 20th century, while wars of attrition could easily take place. The first such war in history was the Peloponnesian War at the end of the 5th Century B.C. described so vividly by Thucydides, while more recent wars of attrition were the Crimean War (1853-1856), the American Civil War, the Russo-Japanese War and the World War.

it possible for us to agree with the term "a war with limited aims." As a matter of fact, the strategy of attrition, in contrast to a strategy of destruction, involves operations with limited goals up to the moment of the final crisis, but the goals of the war itself may be far from modest.[9]

Elaborating one's choice of destruction or attrition in stating the political goal is of huge importance for guiding all military activity, but it is even more important for the correct choice of a political line of conduct and organizing economic preparations, because the latter may be directed in completely opposite ways depending on whether we are preparing for quick developments of maximum intensity or the development of prolonged, successive operations. A war of destruction may be conducted primarily by means of supplies stockpiled in peacetime, and foreign purchases made prior to the war may be extremely appropriate in this case. A large state can base a war of attrition exclusively on the work of its own industry during the war: because a military industry may develop exclusively by means of military procurements and keeping it idle during peacetime while making procurements abroad is more a crime than a mistake. Preparations for a war of attrition should primarily demonstrate concern for the overall proportional development and health of the nation's economy, because naturally a sick economy will not be able to withstand the severe tests of attrition.

Although the statement of a political goal may not seem so tricky at first glance, in fact it constitutes a very difficult test of a politician's thinking. The gravest mistakes are possible. Just remember Napoleon's statement of an offensive goal for the Franco-Prussian War or the destruction goals formulated by all the general staff at the beginning of the World War. The choice between destruction and attrition is particularly difficult. The overwhelming majority of military men and economists before the World War were sadly mistaken when they assumed that it would last about three and no more than twelve months, and only the elder Moltke and Kitchener did not make this mistake. Their mistake lay in their application of formal logic, namely that an exceptionally expensive and destructive war should end quickly. However, historical dialectics teaches us that if a war is destructive and consumes a great deal of resources, then after a certain duration one side will be destroyed while the other will remain standing, and the last sack of grain is the means of victory, and it is the costliness of war and its disintegrating effect on governments that makes a war of attrition sensible. That is the way it was in the early 16th century, when mercenaries and artillery made war much more expensive, and that is the way it was in the second half of the 19th century, when weapons again became much more complicated, and the number of men involved grew rapidly. In practice, the difficulty of clarifying the nature of a coming war will probably lead to a compromise between a quick destructive strike and a prolonged war of attrition in the political statement establishing the political goal of the war, and the preparations for war will also contain a compromise between preparations for quick operations by a portion of one's forces and the opposite tendency to enable prolonged conflict.

The nature and duration of a war are a result of the conditions on all three fronts of the war. An enemy suffering from major class contradictions could be defeated by destroying his armed forces, but perhaps the line of least resistance runs through prolonging the war, which would cause the enemy to collapse politically. A large enemy not characterized by significant class conflicts could hardly be defeated by a destructive strike without prolonged preparations for a war of attrition. When a state is poorly prepared for land war (Great Britain, the United States), its peak of strategic intensity obviously could not coincide with the first weeks of the war but would rather be postponed one, two or three years. States which have weak armies in peacetime wage long wars. Shifting the center of gravity to mobilizing military industry leads to the same situation. The military dissimilarity of two opponents, namely sea and land powers, leads to wars of attrition (Great Britain and Russia), while the distance between two states which may enter into a conflict only in a remote theater of war separated by seas or distance from the most important centers of the hostile states (Japan and Russia) would obviously prevent a war of destruction. Military parity also leads to the renunciation of a destructive strike.

Military preparations made for the purpose of maximizing strategic intensity as quickly as possible and extensive land boundaries crossed by good lines of communication, a significant superiority in forces and a hostile state whose political structure resembles a giant with feet of clay are conditions which favor a destructive strike and make it possible to end a war very quickly with minimal expenditures of material and human lives. Inasmuch as military budgets, despite their growth, have lagged behind economic growth, and maximum strategic intensity is feasible only half a year after the end of economic mobilization, that is, no earlier than the second year of the war, the wars of the future will probably be prolonged.

If one's policy were to avoid calling for any kind of destructive strike, then economic preparations, which are primarily determined by considerations of the economic front of the conflict, would naturally tend toward a war of attrition. But this omission would be incorrect, despite the high probability of a prolonged conflict in the future. Perhaps preparing an economy for a war of attrition would not be completely appropriate for purely military preparations and would probably make it necessary to renounce the opportunity to resolve the conflict with a single strike and take the shortest path to the ultimate goal, following the example of the great military leaders. Decisions that do not consider the conditions of a given war are unacceptable. What is the point of preparing for a ten-year war if the preparations are so detrimental to our initial military efforts that an enemy employing destruction techniques is able to achieve his political aims in two or three months? If politics should require a lightning attack on one's neighbor, then the appropriate economic decisions should be made.

The Political Goal and the Peace Program

War is not an end in itself but is waged for the purpose of concluding a peace on certain terms. In determining the political goal of a war, a politician should keep in mind the positions on the military, social and economic fronts whose capture would put him in a favorable position for conducting peace talks. At peace talks it is extremely important to try to avoid gaining any new advantages; one should act like the side which already has what it needs or has a valuable pawn which may be traded for what it needs. If the World War had ended without a catastrophe for Germany, Germany could have counted on getting all or part of its colonies in exchange for German-occupied Belgium.

The practical importance of the program of accomplishments required from a war is very great in the case of a war of attrition. In the World War Great Britain expended hundreds of thousands of soldiers and vast material resources on the direct conquest of all the German colonies. This decision was more appropriate to purely British interests than if it had avoided expenditures of billions on colonial wars and directed the same resources to the European theaters thinking that the fate of the colonies would be resolved by victory over the German metropolis and that the colonies could have been obtained without any effort, like a ripe fruit from a tree. The Russian imperialists, who dreamed of the Bosporus, were hardly on the right track when they assumed that the keys to the Bosporus were in Berlin, when they were satisfied with the promises of their allies and when they avoided undertaking direct operations against the Bosporus. Every time the forces allocated for this operation were thrown into the common kitty of the Entente and sent to the German-Austrian front. One could only agree with the logic of Russia's actions if the war was heading for destruction. However in the actual conditions of the World War this logic merely indicated that the Russians did not have a sufficiently clear idea of the goals they were pursuing and lacked the will to pursue them, which was characteristic of Russia's dependent political posture in the World War.

Preventive War

Preventive wars have played a major role in history. Preventive wars are wars provoked by one state because it fears that the growing strength of its neighbor will threaten it in a future war which would have to be conducted under more adverse conditions than those of the present. Thus a preventive war is character-ized by a situation of political defense and strategic offense. The weakening Austrian state entity waged a preventive war against the Piedmont in 1859 in order to interfere with the unification of Italy, and in 1911 against Serbia in order to overcome the disintegrative force of the Great Serbian movement. After the defeat of France in 1870 the Prussian general staff proposed attacking France more than once (in the mid-1870s and 1880s) in order to keep France from getting back on its feet. In 1905 Count von Schlieffen insisted on such a preventive war in order to defeat France and take advantage of the weakness of Russia, which was tied down by the war in the Far East and the revolutionary movement. Thus the roots of war lie not only in the strengthening of some political factions, but also in the lack of growth or weakening of other factions. The growing strength of the workers' movement, and in particular, the Union of Soviet Socialist Republics, could easily make the bourgeoisie consider a preventive war.

Preventive wars are particularly significant for the strategy of destruction, whose lightning attacks make it possible to change the situation quickly before other states have a chance to intervene. In 1756 Frederick the Great began the Seven Years' War as a preventive war because of the information he had received on the formation of a large coalition. But by using a strategy of attrition he was only able to occupy Saxony and destroy the Saxon army. If he could have employed a strategy of destruction, he would have been able to deal a fatal blow to his main enemy, Austria, before Russia and France could have intervened.

Politics Determine the Most Important Theater of a War

Political goals are not some kind of abstract digression for the strategist; they defined the main directions of the war. Everyone knows, for example, that in the Soviet-Polish War, the center of gravity of the operations in the west could have been shifted from Belorussia to the Ukraine, or vice versa, depending on political aims. In this respect political considerations are incomparably more important than military-technical ones.

The statement of a definite political goal not only constitutes a mission for the armed forces but a directive for political preparations for a war, preparations which cover broad issues of domestic and foreign policy.

The Integral Military Leader

War is waged by the supreme authorities of a state, because the decisions which must be made by the leaders of a war are too important and critical to be entrusted to any agent of executive authority.

Our notions of leadership have been perverted by the use of the term "supreme commander in chief," because we associate it with a person to whom the active armies and navy are subordinate and who has supreme authority in a theater of operations. In fact, this kind of commander in chief is not supreme, because he does not direct foreign and domestic policy or the entire rear of the active armies, because he does not have all power over the entire state. A strategist and commander in chief is only part of the leadership of a war, and sometimes decisions are made without his knowledge and sometimes completely against his will. Giving full power to a chosen military leader is an obsolete formula which never reflected any kind of reality. It was never possible to subordinate the minister of war and high civilian authorities to the commanding general in a theater of operations if the general himself was not a monarch.

Leadership on the political, economic and military fronts must be integrated. Preparations for war on all these fronts must be coordinated. Only the ruling head of the ruling class who personifies the highest political competence in the state and who exercises supreme power and draws on the most professionally and politically trustworthy strategists is up to this task. The collective of this head constitutes an integral military leader. Under the current conditions of increasingly complex military leadership it would be difficult to think of combining the required political, economic and strategic competence in a single person. Hence even in monarchies the integral military leader is a collective rather than just the monarch himself.

In 1870 this integral military leader was a triumvirate consisting of a monarch, Kaiser Wilhelm, a politician, Bismarck, and a strategist, Moltke.[10] In the World War, the French Cabinet took on the task of deciding the basic questions of the war, and the commanders in chief had to ask their approval for basic strategic policies. Issues of allied support were more the business of politicians than strategists. In 1919, as we can see from Stalin's article on Leninism and Trotskyism, the Central Committee of the Communist Party considered and resolved such issues as the scope and time of troop movements from the Eastern Front (the Urals) to the

---

10 Schlieffen's article "Polkovodets" [The Military Leader], in *Strategiia v trudakh voennykh klassikov* [Strategy in the Works of the Military Classics] (Moscow: Vysshei voennyi redaktsionnyi sovet, 1924), vol. 1.

Southern Front, because in essence the question of the necessary extent of taking advantage of the victory over Kolchak and the possibilities of waiting a while before stopping Denikin's offensive on Kharkov concerned vital political interests and could not be resolved within the framework of strategy alone. The transfer of responsibility for resolving vital war issues to the leadership of the dictatorship was completely natural.

At present this statement of the issue is generally accepted. In the USSR, the military is part of the Council of Labor and Defense while other states have national defense councils or skeleton staffs preparing for their formation.

The Joint Work of Politicians and Military Men

Dupuis, a major assigned to the French general staff, has arrived at a daring conclusion[11] from an analysis of how democracies organize the leadership of a war: it is beneficial to assign persons delegated by the political authorities to military headquarters so that they may live in direct contact with officers and men. This is what the Jacobin revolutionary government did, and they had no reason to regret it. It is most likely that a great many unfortunate disagreements could have been avoided in 1870 and 1871 if the civilian members of the Turkish delegation had spent a bit more time among the senior generals and observed the latest troubles of the war side by side with them. Dupuis has found that because Napoleon I's talents are encountered only as a rare exception, cooperation is better than undivided command in the high command. The lessons of the past have indicated that if a truly outstanding military leader turns up among the generals, he will rapidly acquire the deciding vote and become the heart of the undertaking.

This conclusion, which this leading military theoretician arrived at in 1912, was in general completely confirmed by the course of events of the Soviet Civil War of 1918-1920. The authorities should not only stay close to the masses, they should also stay close to the commanders. Undivided command, which is so appropriate at lower and midlevel echelons of command, is now impractical at the higher levels. The command procedures followed in the Civil War not only represent the successful solution of a particular problem but also contain something fundamentally positive.

Of course we should not specify some ideal form of organization of the political leadership of a war; we must look for some specific optimal compromise in every particular instance. The, experience of the past has taught us that it is not every easy to construct a politically and militarily satisfactory command organization in a revolutionary situation and that we should be satisfied with at least bearable conditions for cooperation.

---

[11] Commandant bréveté V. Dupuis, *La direction de la guerre. La liberté d'action des généraux en chef* (1912), p. 363.

3. PLANS FOR SAFEGUARDING DOMESTIC SECURITY

Immediate Safeguards for Domestic Security

"War may be waged only by the will of a united people. Hence the purpose of a state which has taken up arms is to exert pressure on the consciousness of a hostile people so that the people would compel their government to sue for peace.[1] Modern war, which captures the interests of broad masses of hostile states, has an energetic effect on the consciousness of certain classes and strives to cause a struggle for peace in the rear of every warring party.

Since the French Revolution, issues of domestic policy have played a significant role in war preparations. Only to a limited extent can the state count on its armed forces to maintain order and ensure that taxes are paid and that the masses of people perform their obligations in the deep rear. The element of compulsion and the presence of a certain amount of force in the hands of the state authorities, the firm organization of supervision and the use of punitive measures against saboteurs, traitors and rebels naturally remain in full force in wartime. Domestic agencies should have their own mobilization plans, which should include all the measures needed to maintain firm order in the country at a time when large masses of people are torn away from work in the countryside, go to assembly points to join the army and double the population of cities to meet the needs of military industry. The crisis caused by these population shifts is made even worse by enemy propaganda and is made more acute by the activities of enemies of the existing social structure and the hopes which certain national and class factions may have for the recognition of their interests at a time when the ruling class is fainting under the burden of war. All measures to maintain order along lines of communication, to account for all doubtful elements, to combat desertion, to combat enemy counterintelligence and propaganda, to conduct censorship and so forth, and, if necessary, to substitute special forces of reliable elements for military units sent to the front[2] or by strengthening the militia must be carefully thought out.

Domestic Politics

At the same time preparations for struggle on the domestic front are made, the domestic security plan should include an extensive program of political propaganda. However, political agitation will never be effective unless it is based on sound domestic policies which do not isolate the ruling class (in the Soviet system)

---

[1] *Angliiskii polevyi ustav* [British Field Regulations], Part 2, Chapter 2, Section 2, Paragraph 4.

[2] This was the reason for the formation of a militia from Catholic elements in 1688: Louis XIV's Minister of War Louvois anticipated a Huguenot uprising at the time war broke out between France and the Protestant alliance after the revocation of the Edict of Nantes, and he took measures to guarantee the domestic security of France. See A. A. Svechin, *Istoriia voennogo iskusstva* [The History of Military Art] (Moscow: Vysshei voennyi redaktsionnyi sovet, 1922), vol. 2, p. 41.

from the peasantry, but rather open up the possibilities for close relationships with the peasants.

The importance of sound domestic policy for waging war was recognized in ancient times. We see a great thinker in the historian Polybius because in his history of Rome he relates the writing of the Roman Constitution to a very major military crisis suffered by the Roman Republic placing the Constitution within the framework of the Second Punic War and he discusses this right after the chapter on Cannae, which was a very serious military blow suffered by the Romans. But in fact, isn't it in light of the experience of the Cannae disaster and Hannibal's energetic actions aimed at breaking down the Roman state that the internal soundness of the Roman political structure becomes most clear? While the purpose of certain economic measures is to create a battle-ready economic entity in a state, the task of domestic policy as a whole is to create a political entity that could withstand hard tests on the class and national fronts of the war.

The significance of domestic policy is especially clear at moments of military failures when military operations go deep into our own territory. In the event of major failures, strategy clearly becomes a derivative of politics. That is why we shall also focus our attention on Napoleon's deep incursions into Prussia and Russia.

The Peasant Issue in Prussia and Russia in the Early 19th Century

After the defeat at Jena the politician Stein emancipated the Junker peasantry from serfdom as a first step toward preparing a new war between Prussia and Napoleon. In fact, if Prussia had maintained serfdom, it would have been powerless against Napoleon, because in a new war Napoleon could have called for extending the conquests of the French Revolution to Prussia and it would have been difficult to compel the Prussian peasants to sacrifice their lives for the preservation of serfdom.

Similar conditions existed in Russia in 1812. Of all the wars waged by old Russia, this war "for the fatherland" differed greatly in terms of the ruling class' fears of a new Pugachev revolt which could have broken out if Napoleon had included revolutionary slogans in his program for the war. The Russian nobility came to hate Napoleon because of their fears that he would appeal to the Russian peasantry. However, the aging Napoleon had already lost his political talents by 1812 and let this major opportunity pass on account of his personal reactionary attitudes and his unjustified hopes of handling the tasks of the war exclusively with his armed forces.[3]

The Significance of the Rear

At present the rear, as well as domestic policy, have become much more important than in the past: its influence has increased, and the misfortunes suffered during wartime by those in the rear have multiplied. Currently the rear

---

[3] He was probably also restrained by his ideas of how his allies, namely Poland and Austria, would respond to a Russian peasant uprising provoked by him. Jomini and other writers after 1812 had a lively discussion of the effect of Napoleon's refusal to employ revolutionary slogans in 1812 on the outcome of the war. See Jomini's treatise in *Strategiia v trudakh voennykh klassikov*, vol. 2; and Amfiteatrov's *Iz istorii russkogo patriotizma, 1812 god* [From the History of Russian Patriotism: 1812].

is often the first to break down. Poor lines of communications, consisting exclusively of dirt roads, once limited the destruction of war to the immediate vicinity of the fighting. Now railroads deliver all a country's resources to the front and have extended the area of high prices and hunger from the theater of war to the country as a whole. Aviation, radio, telegraphs, the need to provide continuous supplies of manpower for the front, the conditions for supplying them with military equipment and getting them home from the active army, conditions which were previously unknown, have now moved the front closer to the rear. Success in war is now possible only with a high level of discipline in the rear. Currently, armies, like sensitive seismographs, react to the slightest economic, social or political movements in the rear. Maintaining discipline in an army, in addition to the conscientiousness of the rank and file, is primarily the responsibility of the cadres of the army, namely its commanders. Maintaining discipline in the rear is the responsibility of the cadres of the nation, namely its agencies of civil authority.

Vera Zasulich and the Triple Alliance

In recent Russian history domestic policy has had a fatal effect on foreign demonstrations of Russian force. On April 11, 1878, the bourgeois jurors trying Vera Zasulich for her attempt on the mayor of St. Petersburg acquitted her. This meant that the authorities of tsarist Russia could not even rely on the support of the bourgeoisie in their struggle with the revolutionary movement. Under these conditions there was no need to measure the military might of old Russia by the number of bayonets in the army. Bismarck, at the Congress of Berlin, was the first to take into consideration this symptom of Russia's weakness, which became even more striking when we consider that Lord Beaconsfield, who represented the opposite side, was supported at that time by the acute chauvinism of broad sectors of the English population: this was the time of the jingoists, or real Englishmen. Russia's internal weakness as evidenced by the acquittal of Vera Zasulich was the final straw which compelled Bismarck to avoid unconditional support for Russia and forced the Russians to yield to England on very vital issues. Bismarck, although he did not have a high regard for the strength of the Austro-Hungarian empire, nevertheless gave it higher marks than the decadent Russian system and preferred to switch to a policy based on an alliance with Austro-Hungary from the traditional policy of friendship with Russia. The founding of the Triple Alliance was directly related to the attitude of the Russian bourgeoisie toward the revolutionary movement.[4]

The Adventure of the Russo-Japanese War

Many writers call a war in which a strategist does not demonstrate sufficient concern for the security of his lines of communication with the base and thus places the army at great risk an adventure. We consider an adventure a war which is inadequately prepared for politically, is not based on the consciousness of the

---

[4]   Emil Daniels, "Benjamin Disraeli, Earl of Beaconsfield," in *Pr. Jahrbuecher*, vol. 1, p. 194. The ideas cited above do not contradict our belief that economics lies at the root of the most important political decisions. However, in this case we do not consider it necessary to go to the economic roots of the matter to look for the motives behind the attitudes of the Russian bourgeoisie.

masses and is a kind of Blanquism (in the simplified sense of the concept) in foreign policy. While Alexander III's peaceful inclinations can be explained in the same way as those of Bismarck as based on an assessment of Russia's domestic situation, Nicholas II was not sufficiently conscious of this. The Russo-Japanese War of 1901-1905 was completely unprepared for in the political sense and could only have led to the Sviatopolk Mirskii spring and then to the first Russian revolution. Political errors also extended to strategy. Tsushima was the same kind of adventure as Sedan-namely a last ditch effort to overcome domestic difficulties. We are probably too harsh in condemning Kuropatkin as a strategist because we forget about the rotten political foundations on which he had to conduct war.[5]

Durnovo's Note

Before the World War the well known leader of the right wing in the Council of State, Durnovo, analyzed the class factions of old Russia and arrived at the completely correct conclusion that considerations of domestic policy should keep Russia out of the war, because war could only result in the triumph of the most extreme currents and revolution carried to its logical conclusion. Our diplomatic preparations for the war were superior, our financial and military preparation were quite adequate, but with respect to domestic policy we were completely unprepared, and the revolution of 1917 itself was no surprise, the surprise was the fact that it came two years late.

Preparations of a State for War in Terms of Domestic Policy

The domestic political preparations of a state should enable it to go through the entire war without significant shifts. If one can anticipate the need to make certain concessions to certain classes or factions in the event of a prolonged war, · it is much better to make these concessions beforehand.

Franz Josef, in preparing to take revenge on Prussia after the defeat of 1866, primarily focused his attention on the danger a Hungarian Revolution would pose to the monarchy at a critical moment in the theater of military operations. The dualistic constitution approved by Franz Josef which gave the Hungarians sovereignty in a territory in which an equal number of Slavs and Romanians lived was not the consequence of a lost war but rather preparation for a new war which would secure his political rear. This disarmed the national intransigence of the Hungarians at a major cost to Austrian sovereignty. However, Koeniggraetz was

---

[5] Prussia started a war with Austria in 1866, despite the opinion of the majority of the Prussian political parties, and won this war, for which it was completely unprepared in domestic policy. However, we must keep in mind the firm policy of the government and Prussia's strong standing army, its superior weaponry and the continuous series of victories which rapidly changed the attitudes of the Prussian public. Failures would have isolated Prussia in 1866. Given the current importance of the war, it seems to us that it would be impossible to duplicate the politically unprepared Prussian successes of 1866.

[6] The Hungarians had a clear understanding of the motives behind Franz Josef's sudden concern for them and were concerned about the durability of this constitution and the reaction to it which would be evoked in the event of a victory by Austria-Hungary allied with France against Germany. That is why their traditional policy was to maintain a friendly attitude toward Germany and an inclination toward a Triple Alliance, which greatly blunted the effect of Franz Josef's act. Michael Graf Karolyi, *Gegen eine ganze Welt* (1924), pp. 42-49.

born out by Sedan and there was no need to take immediate advantage of the state's domestic political preparations.[6]

The Offensive Front of Domestic Policy

We must not be guided by exclusively defensive considerations: domestic policy has its own active, offensive front, particularly in a revolutionary era. The revolutionary organization of an irredenta, the use of slogans inside a country which could evoke a broad response abroad, an appropriate class policy and a high level of economic prosperity are some of the most important conditions for waging war and create powerful levers for manipulating the consciousness of the populations of hostile states. The domestic policy of every state should also be considered from the perspective of creating a sound basis in the state for agitation and propaganda abroad. Only this basis will make the "paper war" which has always accompanied armed operations strong and significant.

Wars pose a number of problems for domestic policy which, if not resolved, could undermine the possibility of military success.[7] Food, housing fuel and transportation issues become much more pressing. The eight-hour work day and labor codes will have to be temporarily suspended. The work day will have to be made longer and harder and wages will have to be cut. Making demands on the masses, condemning them to forced labor and depriving them of bearable living conditions will have to go hand in hand with the struggle for the same masses, for their consciousness and for their faith in the slogans of the struggle. And there is no doubt that this struggle for the masses in the rear of every state will be two-sided rather than one-sided in nature. Hunger due to reduced rations will be made more acute by the whispering of hostile agitation.[8]

Future wars will undoubtedly be waged in an atmosphere of intense class struggle which will create more or less strong hostile factions in every state taking part in the conflict. Hence domestic policy will become even more important.[9]

---

[7]   For example, the Hungarian Revolution of 1919 was defeated primarily as a result of the unsuccessful agrarian policy of the Central Committee of the Hungarian Communist Party, which had decided not to turn over the estates of the Hungarian magnates to the peasants but rather convert them into state farms. For more details, see Wilhelm Boehm, *Im Kreuzfeuer zweier Revolutionen* (Munich: 1924).

[8]   The agitation organized by Stein in 1812 at the behest of the Prussian government in Napoleon's German rear was quite interesting because of its scope: in several respects the extent of this agitation has not yet been exceeded even today. For a detailed description see: Max Lehmann, *Freiherr von Stein* (Leipzig: 1921).

[9]   Here we do not touch on the very important issue of the relationship between domestic policy and the construction of armed forces, because it will be discussed in a separate chapter.

4. THE ECONOMIC PLAN OF THE WAR

The Scope of the Economic Struggle

The economic goals of a war concern efforts on all fronts of conflict. In this section we shall only discuss the economic front and its missions. They invariably include defensive elements, namely the satisfaction of needs generated by the conduct of military operations to the greatest extent possible and maintaining the capacity for work of the rear, which, with the exception of the armed forces, is the entire country; but the missions of the economic front may also include offensive elements which are developed to different extents and are aimed at attacking the enemy's economy.

Economic swords are double-edged and often inflict the same wounds on those who wield them as they do on the enemy. We do not mean this in a broad economic sense, for example, in the sense that by defeating Germany its competitors lost one of their best customers.

On every occasion we must carefully weigh which losses due to hostile actions will be more serious and have a more decisive effect on the outcome of a war. In the World War Germany prohibited the export of aniline dyes and medicines to hostile countries via neutral countries. Of course, the Entente's textile industry experienced certain difficulties: for a time English calicos became surprisingly faded, and doctors experienced certain difficulties in writing prescriptions, but on the whole, didn't Germany's measures inflict more damage on Germany itself by undermining its monopoly in these industries and depriving it of export markets during the war?

Every economic offensive brings conflicting forces to life. We cannot deny the inspiration with which different classes of the Russian people greeted the beginning of war with Germany in 1914. Incidentally, the war had been preceded by one and a half centuries of peaceful, neighborly relations. We can ascribe this inspiration to the fact that since the 18th century, Russia had been the object of an offensive by German capital, labor and culture. The Russian bourgeoisie harbored a hatred for the more businesslike German bourgeoisie and for the successful German manufacturer or baker in Russia. The gentry complained about the high tariffs on grain imposed by the German farmers, while the peasants thought of dividing up the land of the German gentry and settlers. Germanophobic feelings even prevailed among a large portion of the intelligentsia. Before the war one of Delbrueck's students[1] told his mentor about the Germanophobic attitudes of the petty bourgeoisie prevailing in the Russian provinces. And wasn't the motherland of Slavophilic chauvinism, Czechia, full of hostility toward the Germans as early as the 15th century because of attempts to colonize it with Germans?

In order to interfere with American deliveries of military equipment to the Entente, Germany attempted to organize large-scale sabotage in the United States: it arranged for accidents at war plants, outbid the war plants for the raw materials they needed, arranged for the intentional production of shoddy goods and

---

[1] Hans Delbrueck, *Krieg und Politik*, vol 1, pp. 5-19.

conducted agitation among the workers. Germany established ties with the United States' closest enemy, namely weak Mexico. This stupid policy led to a situation in which Germany compromised 20 million U.S. citizens of German origin who had to prove that they were Americans, not Germans, and despised the Germans' methods. This resulted in a situation in which 20 million Germans lost the opportunity to be politically active and could not raise their voices against America's entry into the war against Germany. German economic activity merely gave its enemies an extra weapon. Wilson could state in his declaration of war on April 2, 1917, that "the Prussian autocracy has engaged in criminal intrigues against our industry and our trade. Its intrigues have almost spread discord in our country."

It is quite possible that economic offensives would not be advantageous for any side and that military operations could develop without parallel engagements of the economic front. This was the case in 1870: very economically weak Prussia limited itself to operations on the military front, while wealthy France was incapable of intensifying the economic conflict but its military affairs were going poorly and the Germans possessed valuable pawns.

In the exact same way, it was reasonable for economically weak Russian and Italy to avoid intensifying the economic conflict with Germany during the World War. In this case an economic front broke out long after the beginning of the war. As late as the fall of 1915 there were 250,000 Germans residing peacefully in Petrograd, half of them German citizens, and they continued their commercial and industrial activities, and Russia continued to trade with Germany via Scandinavia on an unofficial basis. It was politically disadvantageous for the tsarist government to begin persecuting Germans inside Russia. But both the Entente and the Moscow bourgeoisie, who saw competition from German contraband and German businessmen inside Russia, tried to get the government to do this. It began with a pogrom against German shops in Moscow in the spring of 1915, and then the government started to ban German goods, deport persons of German nationality, confiscate their property and so forth. All these steps greatly sped up the demise of the old regime.

On May 23, 1915, Italy declared war on Austria-Hungary, but not on Germany; it maintained trade relations with Germany because it needed rolling stock for its railroads and the coal with which Germany supplied it. Only 15 months later, under stiff pressure from the Entente and in hopes of a quick end to the war (the time when Romania entered the war), and in order to obtain the right to get part of the reparations which Germany would pay, did Italy enter the war against Germany on the economic front after declaring war on it. Thus the economic conflict may not coincide with the armed conflict either in time or in space.

However, we must remember that we will not always be able to avoid operations on the economic front, because enemy attacks must be answered by appropriate measures. The economic weapon is particularly important in a war of attrition. The strong capitalist Anglo-Saxon states are always particularly eager to resort to it. A future war will apparently be accompanied by terrible economic conflicts such as the war of Napoleon against England (the continental system) or the war between the North and the South in the United States (starving the South) or the last world war. The weaker a state is economically, the more attention must be paid to the economic front in order to prevent a breakthrough.

The Economic Plan of War

The old strategic wisdom limited the extent of the plans of a campaign to the moment of the decisive collision. Any detailed planning of subsequent operations was considered pure prejudice, because, as they explained it, one would have to operate in a completely new situation the next day after a decisive collision. Thus only preparatory operations and the occupation of an initial position for decisive operations were planned in detail.

An economic plan should be even more limited and concern itself more with preparations because the economic front of a war is not self-contained, and any turn in military operations may completely change the requirements made of the economy and the situation in which it will have to meet them.

However, the economic plan should be a mere list of goals of economic preparation; while one cannot prophesy the course of events or pile premises on premises (ifs on ifs), the economic plan should nevertheless set forth a line of economic conduct that would not lead us into a blind alley in any probable situation.

The plan should be based exclusively on reality. Its writing should be preceded by a comprehensive analysis of one's own and the enemy's economic strengths. There should be a businesslike presentation of economic statistics and additional studies of economic capabilities and economic intelligence. Economic intelligence should not only encompass possible enemies but also all economically advanced countries, because the conditions of the global economy should be clear to the writer of an economic plan for a war. Economic intelligence is a normal responsibility of agents of a state's consular service or trade representatives. The consuls of the United States are famous for their inclination to employ espionage techniques. It is remarkable that the chairman of ARA* was a person who occupied a prominent position in American counterintelligence.

In light of the information at one's disposal on the political goal of the war, assessments of friendly and hostile economic strengths should lead to the formulation of definite missions for the economic front, a statement of the resources for accomplishing these missions and a calculation of the minimal economic base needed for waging war.

From this will follow all guidelines for 1) regulating the development of the economy to achieve the required results, and the implementation of these guidelines constitutes the basic purpose of economic policy; 2) preparing transportation; and 3) preparing financial and economic mobilization.

In order to plan the military dimension of a war plan, it is highly desirable that the economic plan contain ideas on questions such as the time that will be required to mobilize the country economically; the limits planned for the capacity of military industry; and how long industry can work at full speed until there is an inevitable loss of capacity due to the overall economic exhaustion of the country. Even the roughest, most approximate judgments on these issues are of great value for clarifying the nature of a coming war for us and our possible enemies.

We have already touched on the problems of developing a combat-ready economy in our chapter on politics and now we shall dwell on transportation and preparation for mobilization.

---

* Editor's note: American Relief Agency.

Transport

Estonia could deploy operationally before we could without resorting to railroads, because one can easily walk from one end of Estonia to the other in a week. While a small country can wage war without being too dependent on the condition of its transportation system, the transportation capabilities of a large country are extremely important for its defensive capabilities. And, because resources for waging war must be drawn from the entire country, it is important not to limit preparations of railroads and the highways exclusively to the routes for moving troops to the deployment area. Before the World War the French insisted that the Russians build the four-track Orel-to-Sedlets trunk line, because they were interested in speeding up Russian concentration as much as possible, and the conditions for Russia waging a major war required the establishment of solid railroad communications with Arctic ports, namely the construction of the Murmansk Railway and changing the Arkhangelsk Railway to broad gauge. While the development of lines of communication at the theater of war is primarily appropriate for a strategy of destruction, the overall improvement of transportation is particularly important for a prolonged conflict, or war of attrition.

The economic powerlessness of a country that results from a lack of roads is evident from the following examples taken from the experience of the French colonies in the World War. The French procured 4,200 tons of cereal on the Ivory Coast. Moving them to the coast required the mobilization of 125,000 Negro porters who spent a total of 2.5 million working days. On account of the damp climate, the lack of storage facilities and delays in loading the ships, most of the cereal rotted. The French Sudan could easily have supplied 60,000 tons of grain. The plan for transporting the grain was as follows: building 30 drying kilns and 20 intermediate storage facilities, acquiring one million sacks and a large number of winnowers, hiring 50 weighers, making 60,000 goatskin sacks for transporting grain in shuttles, building 300 shuttles with a capacity of four to eight tons for picking up grain from the bank of the Niger. One third of the grain would have to be delivered from the procurement points to the river by bearers, on the average over a distance of 200 kilometers, which would have required four million work days from the Negro porters. And this figure does not include the work of Negroes in carrying grain to the procurement centers and delivering grain on shuttles to the railroad.[2] It is clear that any state not dying of starvation would avoid this kind of painstaking and expensive grain procurement.

The fact that the French colonies gave France only 600,000 soldiers and 200,000 workers in the World War and the percentage of French colonials who participated in combat operations was ten to 20 times lower than the percentage of citizens of the metropolis cannot be explained by the desire of the French government to avoid more extensive exploitation of the colored population of the colonies or by a lack of opportunity to exert greater pressure on them. The only explanation is the lack of means of communication and transportation, that the natives lived many hundreds of kilometers from reception points, the fact that reception points were separated by the same distances from ports or rail stations and that in many instances it was extremely difficult to transport natives by them.

Even the transportation system of France itself, which had been so carefully developed for centuries, was incapable of taking care of the front. In order to

---

[2]   Albert Sarrant, ministre des colonies, *La mise en valeur des colonies françaises* (1923).

deliver supplies to the British army (which in certain months were as high as 333,000 tons) 49,000 cars, an appropriate number of locomotives with men and one railroad division had to be borrowed from England. While moving the American army from the Atlantic coast to Lorraine required tremendous efforts to expand French ports, build gigantic barracks and depots for the men and cargo, expand stations, build new lines and develop existing ones; in the fall of 1918 approximately 250,000 men and 41,000 tons of freight arrived every month, and by 1919 the supplies of the U.S. army were to double and require 100,000 railroad technicians, who were not available in France but the Americans promised to provide (only 30,000 technicians got there). Rolling stock was to be supplied by the Americans in monthly allotments of 268 locomotives and 7,550 30-ton cars. The allies were to expand the capacity of French stations by laying 6,000 kilometers of track at them. During the four years of the war the French themselves had to lay 8,420 kilometers of new track, that is, lay as much track as they would normally lay in ten years. Not only Russia but wealthy France, which had foreign trade capabilities, had to resort to cannibalism and take apart 1,500 kilometers of track and 670 switches from existing railroads in order to build new ones, because of a lack of transportation and the involvement of heavy industry in armaments production. The percentage of ailing locomotives rose 50 by percent.

At present a large state needs 100 to 200 trains to supply a front every day, while in 1870 three German armies could be supplied by one or two trains a day each, and only the movement of siege guns required greater efforts from the railroads.

Currently the weight of a four-day supply of munitions for an army attacking a fortified front with a wealth of heavy artillery requires the capacity of 60 to 80 trains. Even when artillery expenditure rates are low, up to 30 trains are required. If battles acquire a material character their development on the front of a single army would require seven to ten trains with munitions every day. When the front is quiet it would require up to one and a half trains per division every day, while during battles it would require up to four trains per division.

But at present, maneuvers are also the job of rail lines: operational redeployments are made several times during a war with up to 300 or more trains required every day to move 30 to 40 divisions in an important direction in three to four days. To a great extent, the inability of Russian troops and railroads to carry out these rapid redeployments explains the failure of our defensive operations in the spring and summer of 1915.

One can speed up movements made by a road formation by driving men and horses to exhaustion. But speeding up a railroad maneuver has very narrow limits according to the conditions of the rail system. Reinforcements for Samsonov were moved on a single-track railroad to Mlava with traffic in one direction and the derailment of part of the rolling stock that encumbered the railhead. The disorder and losses were significant, while the gains were negligible.

But this gigantic effort by the railways to maintain the front is far from everything. Previously many people imagined war as a vision of general unemployment in the rear awaiting the end of the war and a halt to all commercial and industrial activity. But in fact the picture is completely opposite: in order to maintain the front, the rear must engage in intense industrial activity.

The urban population is not only not without work, but it almost doubles it. Much has to be built and created anew. A great deal has to be carried over much greater distances, because the closest sources of grain, raw materials or goods are exhausted. Coastal shipping must be replaced by rail transportation. The exploitation of remote sources must be organized which resources in peacetime are held back for economic reasons. As a result, the number of passengers and the amount of freight and the distance they travel on railroads increase significantly. While for France, which had highly developed prewar rail traffic, the World War increased the load of railroads by 40 percent not counting front traffic, in the USSR we could expect that the requirements for rail shipments would increase by at least 60 percent with the beginning of a war.

No matter how great the advantage of truck traffic on highways is over animal cartage on tracks, it is incomparably less efficient than a broad-gauge railroad. Simply maintaining a highway on which heavy trucks travel requires almost as much manpower as building a large two-track railway and as much material as it takes to build a railroad. At Verdun the maintenance of the "sacred" highway used to supply the front required 8,400 workers and 2,300 cubic meters of stone per day, while 6,400 workers plus eight railroad companies build a 60-kilometer railroad with two wide tracks designed to carry 24 pairs of trains in three months. A railroad built beforehand would have made the "sacred" highway superfluous.

Regarding personnel, rail transportation is ten times more economical than truck transportation. This figure is valid for short trips of no more than 60 to 80 kilometers, and subsequently it becomes even less advantageous for the trucks, because on any trips of more than 150 kilometers the truck is very uneconomical. All of the 120,000 trucks with their army of 250,000 drivers that supplied the Entente's western front over a distance of 300 kilometers could have been replaced by a single rail trunk line.

Because a wide gauge railroad is four times more economical than a narrow gauge in terms of human labor, it is particularly important for organizing transportation on the vast territory of an economically poor state.

The economics of war require the maximum development of railroads. The European scale, not just our Soviet scale, no longer meets the requirements for warfare; we must follow the example of the United States with its 30-ton freight cars, longer trains, twice as fast freight traffic and the lowest rates in the world.[3]

Inland waterways constitute a powerful reserve; we need to organzie then in a way that would allow their extensive use in wartime to assist the railroads in resolving problems which the latter are incapable of handling. The Danube and the network of German and French canals played a very important role in the economy of the World War. They made it possible to relieve railroads of many tasks in the rear (in Germany they were used to move farm products from the east to the west, they were used to carry a large amount of bituminous coal and the Danube was used to carry oil and grain from Romania), but they were also used

---

[3] As we know, American railroads are often criticized for making hundreds of millions of dollars by exploiting farmers for transporting agricultural freight; however, exploitation is possible only because of the high level of organization of the American railroads, which charge rates which are one and a half to two times lower than those of Russian railroads and two to three times lower than the most expensive railroads, the British ones. The European railroads would go bankrupt if they attempted to "exploit" the public in this way.

to deliver cement, stone, wood and fuel to the front lines, and while locomotives were shot up in delivering supplies, small barge tugs were also knocked out in performing their duties.

The organization of animal and automotive transportation in a country is very important.

Mobilization will remove thousands of motor vehicles and one and a half million of the best horses from public use,[4] leaving the public to do all agricultural work and doubling the demand of the cities and industry. A country's economy will be in particular danger if animals are not given sufficient care at the front and drop after working for a very short time. The record was set by the British army operating in East Africa against Lettow-Vorbeck. During the offensive the British army had anywhere from 12,000 to 20,000 draught animals at different times. Of them, 3,000 horses and 3,000 mules dropped on average every month, while bulls dropped more frequently: once 4,500 bulls dropped in three weeks; and bulls lasted no more than six weeks, mules lasted no more than two months, while donkeys, which were harnessed to carts in teams of 16, lasted somewhat longer. A total of more than 100,000 animals had died in the 14 months before May 1917, that is, six times more than the number of men that died. Trucks lasted an average of six months, swallowing up 100 percent of the spare parts, instead of ten percent of the European standard, and 600 percent of the springs, and were then junked.[5] The reasons were the tse-tse fly, predators, the rough African hay, bad roads, but primarily the poor care given to the animals and the bad driving of Chinese and Negro drivers. In 1917, although there were no tse-tse flies in Russia, many times more horses died on the front than normal. If statistics had been kept for the Civil War, they would have indicated extreme carelessness with respect to the country's supply of horses.

The resulting difficulties can be over come only by means of very strict discipline and extreme economy in providing transportation of the army and in terms of authorized baggage; we must renounce our habit of having vehicles for "just in case" and mercilessly combat the encumbrance of our men with unauthorized baggage. At the same time we must give the public and the army a sense

---

[4] In May 1918 the German army had 956,856 horses (Wrisberg, *Heer und Heimat 1914-1918*, p. 76), and to this we must add hundreds of thousands of horses which died during the war. It is true that the German army was very large, but first of all, this was the fourth year of trench warfare, and second the Germans made very extensive use of narrow-gauge railways to deliver supplies, some of their guns were not hauled by horses at all, caissons were hauled by four instead of six horses, the German cavalry had been practically disbanded, some divisions had practically no cars and maximum economy had been introduced practically everywhere. The percentage of horses in the Soviet army will be much, much larger. Right now we have more horses in an army corps than we do soldiers. In a front organization we need up to 1,400 horses per 1,000 men; we are having to pay for the underdevelopment of our rail system.

[5] Commandant breveté J. Buhrer, *L'Afrique orientale Allemande et la guerre de 1914-1918* (Paris), pp. 376, 377, 406, 407. This treatise will be of great interest to students of colonial wars.

[6] During the World War the French expended more than 26 million tons of material, primarily stone, on maintaining roads in the theater of war, and more than 6.5 million tons were transported by rail to areas where stone was in short supply. The French used up to 80,000 workers to repair the roads. Under these conditions the French were able to save several million noncombatants as compared with the Russian army.

of responsibility and make them understand the benefits of repairing bridges and roads on a regular basis, which will yield very great saving of animal drawn vehicles.[6]

Of course under Russian conditions one must completely avoid truck maneuvers. As many as 600 trucks and a very good highway are needed to transport a non-combat-ready division without baggage and horses. 1,100 trucks would be needed to transport the most important baggage, if only several caissons and a very limited number of horses, four per gun and two per caisson. Counting 30 meters per truck, we would get a convoy 33 kilometers long, and the slightest misunderstanding on the highway could stop and disrupt its movement. There is no doubt that we cannot permit ourselves the luxury of transporting horses by truck; even in the West maneuvering on trucks would be important not as a condition of comfort but rather as a means of warfare only if mechanical traction replaced horse traction in the artillery and mounted machine guns. Of course the above does not rule out the possibility of using trucks for small detachments used to maintain order in occupied areas and fight small partisan units.[7]

The conditions of transportation, as an element of economic preparations for war, seems to us to be much more important for a large state such as the USSR than any sort of financial successes, all the way up to the achievement of a sound monetary system. Frederick the Great paid a great deal of attention to building canals, while Napoleon focused his attention on building roads and Moltke concentrated on organizing the rail system. In our era questions of transportation are no less urgent in view of the extraordinary amount of resources required by war. Perhaps we should base our economic plan on a calculation of the capacity of our transportation system; and on one hand we will have to concentrate major efforts on the further development of transportation, and on the other hand we shall have to clarify the limit of economic mobilization which could not be crossed given the current condition of transportation.

The Cost of War and the Military

The cost of war although it has had a clear tendency to increase as military equipment has become more complex, undergoes extreme fluctuations. Twenty gold francs per day constitutes the current minimum level of military expenditures for a bourgeois state, If war has to be waged a long distance away (the siege of Sevastopol), its cost has a tendency to increase 50 percent due to high transportation costs and the need to set up a new base. For such a large state as Russia military expenditures have always been higher than normal due to the need to gather manpower and resources from a vast territory and the losses of productivity associated with it. If a war becomes positional in nature, direct expenditures

---

[7] We consider the extensive use of trucks to deliver suplies to the army when good roads are available to be a powerful means of reducing the number of noncombatants in the army. In fact, a three-ton truck does 200 to 250 ton-kilometers of work per day, while a two-horse cart dies 15 to 20 times less, only 12 to 13 ton-kilometers. Even if we figure three noncombatants per truck, we save five to seven times more noncombatants, and every truck saves the govenment the labor of 12 to 17 workers and a herd of 40 horses. The two-wheeled cart, which doubles the number of noncombatants by comparison with the two-horse cart but is so beloved by many commanders for its mobility, is a true sign of poverty and a drop in the productivity of human labor.

will double due to the less extensive use of local resources and the material nature acquired by the armed conflict.

But military expenditures increase particularly significantly when peacetime preparations are inadequate, The United States, which up to the First World War maintained a very small standing army, has always waged war uneconomically. Both in 1861-1865 and 1917-1918 the United States had to immediately order and produce all its military equipment, including rifles, cartridges, overcoats, camps, regulations and tactical manuals, command schools, carts and horses riding schools, and firing ranges. Orders, procurements, and construction had to be organized in an atmosphere of extreme prices. The government had to call on suppliers, who after they got an order still had to build plants and hire workers to fill the orders. A hastily improvised and inexperienced administrative staff which has the same vague idea as the suppliers did of the specifications which the equipment had to meet had to do business with these suppliers. And because the military authorities had no stockpiles and their need for them was so acute, they were unable to refuse unsound proposals or protect the interests of the treasury. And there were no guidelines to correct prices which could have been used to restrain predatory appetites. That is why in the World War it cost 50 times more per day to keep an American soldier at the front than it did to keep a European soldier there. Of course the Americans had made capital investments and fought for a very short time, and only half of their soldiers were sent to France, but nevertheless it is clear that any state has to pay tenfold in wartime for all its skimping on the military in peacetime.

When defense work is done by industry in peacetime, there are detailed blueprints and completed models, templates, molds, industrial traditions, and definite peacetime prices, which means that equipment can be made much faster, on a greater scale, with better quality, and at lower cost during the war itself. To the military authorities, procurement becomes a matter of course rather than an adventure.

The military budget should be a means not only of preparing a powerful army but of lowering the costs of a future war. It should provide the state with the capital equipment for a war, mobilization stockpiles, and large masses of trained people in order to reduce expenditures for training in reserve units, which keeps millions of working hands away from both the front and work in the rear at the hottest time of the war

Of course mobilization stockpiles of equipment cannot fully meet current war requirements as they did 50 years ago; production during the World War itself was tens of times higher than what was produced before the war. However the military authorities' depots must not be empty before the beginning of the war and military industry must be encouraged to replenish stockpiles in order to gain time for mobilization and getting up to full capacity. If necessary, stockpiles should be sufficient for a victory by destruction. Without stockpiles, we would have to take very slippery steps including procuring expensive and dubious foreign contraband.

A military budget should be characterized by the percentage of it devoted to procuring mobilization stockpiles and capital equipment (weapons, fortifications, communications, and so forth). This percentage of the budget may vary from 10 percent (peacetime expenditures for stockpiles of uniforms, ammunition, and so forth) to 70 percent. In Czarist Russia it was as high as 37 percent. The productivity of the rest of the budget should be measured by the number of trained Red Army men transferred to reserve duty during the year (men who have gone through training at regional training facilities) and the quality of training. A modern army is a school and should be judged by the quality of its graduates.

A military budget may be properly balanced only if it is large enough, because a miserly budget will be completely swallowed up by the cadres without anything left over. Proper allocation of the military budget will mean incomparably better economic prospects for war.[8]

Resources for War

Frederick the Great kept 333,000 tons of grain in his fortress in peacetime, which was enough to keep his 200,000 man army in bread and oats for three years and kept a stockpile of silver sufficient to pay his men for three years, which is why he could consider himself economically prepared for war.

War is waged partially at the expense of the stockpiles allotted to it and partially at the expense of resources taken from the economy over the course of the war itself. Stockpiles may be allocated to both military and other authorities (for example, a two month mobilization stockpile of fuel for the railroads, stockpiles of foreign raw materials, and equipment in industry.) As productive forces have developed and equipment has become more complex there has been a tendency for prepared stockpiles to become more important and for the significance of economic efforts made in the course of the war itself to become more evident.

The first month of the war cost Germany, France, and Russia 800 to 1500 million gold rubles. The resources needed for a war may be extracted from the economy in different ways: 1) by means of avoiding investing national income in new capital outlays such as building housing, new factories, new roads, and electrical power plants or organizing new undertakings or making foreign investments; 2) by means of selling stockpiles of gold and currency abroad or taking out foreign loans; 3) by means of gradual confiscation of capital invested in the economy by means of economizing on building and equipment repairs and reducing liquid capital; 4) by means of reducing real wages while raising labor productivity and making extensive use of women's and children's labor and reducing outlays on education, public health, welfare, and so forth. War takes resources away from the future and the past, has an adverse effect on the productivity of labor and does not compensate it in full, and squanders the health of future generations.

A large annual surplus in national income is expressed in energetic capitalistic or socialistic accumulation. It usually involves major expenditures on new facilities with the investment of new capital in the state's industrial plant. In turn, in a large state, the latter usually involves a prospering heavy industry. In this case, the state is best prepared for war in an economic sense, and in fact, the United

---

8 "The merits of the military economy lie not in maintaining forces, they lie in giving the state the capability of having all the resources for war (material and financial) at a critical moment." L. Shtein, *Uchenie o voennom byte, kak chast' nauki o gosudarstve* [The Study of Military Life as a Part of the Science of Government] (St. Petersburg: 1875). See also M. Sindeev, "Osnovy nauchnoi voenno-ekonomicheskoi podgotovki" [The fundamentals of scientific military economic preparations] in *Voennaia mysl' i revoliutsiia*, no. 4 (August 1923).

States, which sets aside 12 to 15 billion rubles from an annual labor productivity as high as 135 billion rubles, in essence must only refrain from economic progress in the event of a war and direct heavy industry away from the production of rails, beams, and machinery towards the production of military equipment.[9] The weakness of socialist accumulation in the Soviet Union and the halting successes in reconstructing our heavy industry constitute major obstacles to be overcome in order to create a fully combat ready economic system. Raising socialist accumulation to a level of at least 10 percent of all labor productivity, as is the case in the United States, would constitute a major budgetary success which would be of colossal significance for war readiness.

The second source, namely selling gold or currency abroad or taking out loans, is of importance only for bourgeoisie states which have good sea lines of communication with foreign markets.

The third source, namely confiscating a portion of liquid capital, is very important for softening the crises and jolts engendered by wars. This is the fat of an economic organism which it consumes when it hasn't had any dinner. But in our current economic situation this source is extremely limited.

We will have to resort to the fourth source, namely reducing the personal expenditures of the public, reducing their standard of living, and speeding up work at lower pay. Instead of any cost of living allowances, we have to think about lengthening the work day, reducing wages, putting school age children to work, and raising the tax burden on the peasants, bourgeoisie and state trusts. Now war is waged by the people and all their resources. And waging war not only means protesting and stating one's feelings towards a hostile regime and violating the civil rights of the populations of occupied territories. Waging war means fighting, going hungry, suffering, bearing deprivations, and obeying orders, both at the front and in the deep rear.[10] Lowering wages in the rear is also justified by the fact that in economic terms workers in the rear are comparable to combatants on the front.

Of course, the greater public prosperity is in peacetime, the greater the resources yielded by this source are. But the ability of human needs to stretch and contract is surprising: the experience of 1919-1920 makes it possible to predict that if the level of enthusiasm of the class waging the war is high, a state with a gross national product of 10 billion rubles per year could wage a war which would otherwise cost 15 billion rubles per year.

Financial might is far from military might. Only when highly civilized nations wage war against nations at a very low level of economic development without slogans around which they could unite can war be considered an undertaking whose success is guaranteed by technological superiority and adequate monetary

---

[9] Great Britain, which has still not fully recovered from the World War, set aside 2.5 billion gold rubles in 1924.

[10] Our statement contradicts the old wisdom hat "People do not act with the same conviction in wartime as they do when they start a war; they change their attitudes with the twists and turns of the war... Wars are waged not so much by payments extracted by force as they are by the resources at hand. People who live by the work of their hands are more eager to sacrifice their lives for a war than their money... A very important hindrance for them will be a shortage of money, because money will always be slow in coming, but the events of war will not wait." (*Fukidid* [Thucydides], vol. I, pp.140-142).

allocations. Caesar who relied on superior Roman technology and economic power, experienced quit a few difficulties in Gaul. Italy in Abyssinia and Spain in Morocco squandered thousands of lives and vast resources without getting anywhere. In his strategy Buelow emphasized the lack of a direct correspondence between the amount of monetary resources at a state' disposal and the amount of material resources (including manpower, in Buelow's terms) deployed in a border mobilization. In August, 1870 Prussia, which had deployed superior forces on the Rhine was at a financial dead end, because the Prussian bourgeoisie wasn't buying war bonds. Only a series of victories on the front, which dispelled any doubt as to the outcome of the war, opened up the pursestrings for the Prussian Minister of Finance. On the other hand, France, whose army had immediately gotten into a catastrophic situation and had suffered defeats everywhere and which was experiencing a revolution at home, was financially sound. If the outcome of the war had been dictated by bankers, Prussia would have undoubtedly been defeated by the French in 1870. The national wealth of the United States, which has been estimated at 635 billion dollars, is an extremely important statistic which defines the economic front. But there is still the class front and the armed front. There is no doubt that bankers are capable of igniting a war, but wars are decided by other forces.[11]

War Communism

If the cost of a war is equal to the entire gross national product of a state, then war can only be waged with additional labor by the population accompanied by a systematic transition to a diet of black bread and potatoes in limited amounts. If the public is sufficiently conscientious, this transition may be effected by energetic means of covering the costs of a war. However if we should refuse to look the economic problem facing us squarely in the eye and act indecisively, then rampant inflation and extremely high prices will force us to resort to a less advantageous solution, namely "war communism" which involves putting the entire population on rations and potatoes.

Economic Mobilization

The tasks of economic mobilization encompass all aspects of economic activity. A proper assessment of economic capabilities is very important, because the

---

[11] We shall take advantage of this opportunity to focus the reader's attention on the frequent abuse of a quote from Montecuccoli's work: "War requires money, money, money." Montecuccoli also concentrated on the fact that money alone is not enough, that extensive preparations are required, that the troops should not be disbanded after a war and should be kept intact, and that immediately after a peace treaty is concluded one must begin preparing for the next war. He said that war requires money, money and more money merely for the purpose of characterizing the notions of limited and narrow-minded people concerning the requirements of war. And by the scandelous idiocy of the same writer, this popular nonsense, which Montecuccoli ridiculed, is now ascribed to Montecuccoli himself!

[12] We must consider the law of February 17, 1915, which gave commanders the right to requisition and prohibit the export of supplies from their districts and gave them the right to fix prices, an economic shock treatment. Because of the economic illiteracy of the enforcers of this law, Russia was immediately divided into several satrapies where every satrap prohibited the export of local products from his satrapy in order to procure these products more cheaply. Thousands of local customs stations were set up. The resultant economic chaos proved to be so threatening that the law had to be repealed.

readiness for war of a state may be undermined by asking too much of the economy. The excess zeal manifested in Czarist Russia in 1916, particularly by Vankov, did more harm than the insufficient energy characteristic of 1914 and early 1915. Between the development of an appropriate economic base for waging a prolonged war of attrition and economic shock treatments[12] such as modifying railroad shops for war needs there is the same contradiction that characterizes the statement of all strategic problems. The resolution of this contradiction will only be correct if it is appropriate for the nature of a given war.

Problems of economic mobilization cannot be worked out before hand with the same clarity and exhaustive completeness as problems of purely military mobilization. Resolving problems of economic mobilization involves organizing the war and adapting the life of the entire country to wartime conditions. This problem cannot be resolved completely by purely bureaucratic means. Every person in his place must make every effort to adapt his work to the conditions of a war economy. Success is achieved by the conscientious work of the masses under firm and farsighted leadership from above.

The Permanence of Economic Mobilization

One would be quite mistaken in picturing economic mobilization as the transition of industry from peacetime military production quotas to rigid, tens of times higher, wartime quotas over the course of five to eight to twelve months in a single step. This is contradicted by the experience of the World War, which indicated that industrial quotas are raised in a number of phases. Industry went from producing tens of thousands of rounds per month to producing hundreds of thousands of rounds per month and then went from producing hundreds of thousands to producing millions per month. Italy, which managed to effect a partial economic mobilization prior to its delayed entry into the war nevertheless boosted its production of rounds by a factor of 9 (from 5 to 15 thousand rounds per day), its production of rifles by a factor of 5.5 (from 600 to 3,300 per day), and its production of machine guns by a factor of 40 (from 1 to 40 per day) over the course of the war. As late as 1917 Italy was only producing 358 guns per month, but the catastrophe at Caporetto in the fall of 1917, when Italy lost half of its artillery (3,152 guns out of a total of 7,138), compelled Italy to boost its quotas, and in May of 1918 Italian industry produced a record 1,338 guns, with a monthly average of 852 guns in 1918.

The phasing of quotas naturally proceeds from the immediate requirements of the war: one must not set out to maximize it but rather boost it quickly. When a critical shortage of supplies set in on the Russian front in February, it was natural to direct that their production should be boosted by a factor of 10 rather than 25, if the former could be accomplished in 7 months while the latter would take 27 months.[13]

---

[13] In January 1915 Russia produced 60 tons of explosives. The February quota was to boost production to 600 tons per month (100 percent). This quota was met seven months later, in August 1915, in the 13th month of the war. It is obvious that preparations had been made to expand production in the initial months of the war. In June 1915 the quota was raised an additional 266 percent to 2196 tons per month. It took more than 19 months to meet this requirement (output in 1917 was 2130 tons) and it was obvious that the plants needed to effect this had to be built from scratch.

That's why it seems to us that attempts to achieve maximum results from economic mobilization immediately are completely futile. If necessary, the ultimate goal will be achieved in several phases. Major wars usually break out at the beginning of harvest time in the south. Eight months later, in the spring, a new act of war or new campaign will begin and will be carried out almost exclusively with material which has been produced during the war itself. All preparations for economic mobilization should be aimed at organizing the use of these eight months. Peacetime plans should keep subsequent advances in mind only to the extent that the steps planned for the first eight months do not constitute an obstacle to further military industrial growth.

During these first eight months the armed forces mobilized at the start of the war may be strengthened by 50, 100 or 300 percent with new forces. The issue of the time and number of new corps can be resolved only in connection with the issue of the time required to manufacture equipment for them. Economic mobilization is closely related to military mobilization, which is currently as we shall say, permanent. It is very important to divide these eight months into two or three phases of quota boosting. Only then will issues of economic mobilization stand on completely firm ground. We must plan in detail two to three phases of economic mobilization, each lasting no more than two to three months. The first phase will coincide with the depletion of some peacetime stockpiles, the second phase will provide weapons to new forces and the third phase will involve preparations for a new campaign.

The Organizational Issue

Economic mobilization encompasses organizational, transportation, financial and manpower issues and the issues of the relationship of the city to the country and industrial mobilization. We shall dwell in more detail only on the last three issues. The organizational issue in the Soviet Union is made much less difficult by the fact that all of our peacetime economy as military agencies, namely the Council of Labor and Defense, the Supreme Council of the Economy, and the State Trade Agency, and our mobilization does not require any kind of organizational break, while the bourgeois states will have to improvise, that is; create and expand a supreme leadership of the economic effort. Our advantage in mobilizing the economy is the same advantage Frederick the Great's army had, which went into war at full peacetime strength, over contemporary half a million man armies. To a significant extent our economy is operating according to a general plan in peacetime. Once war is declared managerial agencies will stay in place and only the economic program they carry out will change. They must be well prepared for this change in their activity by working out mobilization plans.

Transportation and financial mobilization has already had a 60 year history and it should be quite systematic. We have already spoken of the tasks of transportation for which it must be prepared and our notions of the ways of covering the costs of a war. The latter constitutes the essence of financial

---

[14] For material on the financial aspects of war see A. Svechin, *Istoriia voennogo iskusstva* [The History of Military Art], vol. 3 (Moscow: Vysshei voennyi redaktsionnyi sovet, 1923), p. 30. One can find valuable supplements to the history of the World War in the book of the former German finance minister, Helferich (*Der Weltkreig* (1919), vol. 2, pp. 111-282). For material on the financial aspects of the Entente's war see the book of the former French finance minister, I.I. Klutz, *De la guerre à la paix* (1923).

mobilization, which otherwise merely involves having a sufficient mobilization. Financial techniques were highly refined in all countries by the World War.[14]

The Allocation of Manpower

The allocation of manpower which accompanies mobilization is an extensive and complex economic operation in which we have a rather advantageous situation. No matter how strong an army we field, if we avoid squandering manpower in the rear, then with our population we will be able to take a lower percentage of workers away from productive labor than other countries. The Soviet countryside, which will account for more than 90 percent of the mobilizees, is far from utilizing all its manpower completely in peacetime. We will apparently be able to limit ourselves to giving peasants the economic incentive to work their land carefully and organizing public assistance for the farms of mobilized combatants and noncombatants.

The desire to keep as many workers as possible in the ranks of the Red Army during wartime is completely understandable. However we must be extremely cautions in order to avoid the adverse consequences observed in the World War, which all the warring countries entered without a well planned system of draft deferments. The World War presented a picture of mass confusion in which workers were drafted into active armies and were than sent back to their factories as skilled specialists without which industry would not have been able to handle its assigned tasks. The military authorities, who expended a great deal of effort in vain, and transportation, and industry, which was gravely affected by the departures of workers to reserve units and the front lines, all suffered from this. In France, the number of persons called back from the front was high as 700,000 men by the fall of 1917, and by the end of the war this number was over a million.[15] This kind of home leave could only create a negative impression among the tired warriors in the trenches. In the fall of 1916, in order to get over a coal crisis, Ludendorff sent 50,000 miners from the front to the mines on one fell swoop. This wavering continued in Germany until the end of the war: the military authorities saw persons with military obligations in industry who could be replaced with women or the disabled, while industry tried to get particularly valuable workers (who often had connections) back from the army: as late as September, 1918, when the German army was suffering from a severe manpower crisis, industry took 34,769 workers away from the army and gave it 24,175 men.[16] Industrial requirements accounted for up to 20 percent of the German army's total losses. At the end of the war when the German army was melting away due to insufficient manpower, a total of 2,434,000 persons with military obligations, including 1,888,000 persons who were physically fit for active duty, were working in industry.

---

[15] Of these, by the end of the war only 500,000 worked in military industry; the rest, no doubt, became "needed" administrative workers. If we observe the incomparably smaller swallowing of the qualified male workforce by industry in France in comparison with Germany, then this is explained first of all by the fact that France—having lost together with its north its mines, pits, blast and open-hearth furnaces—survived the entire war primarily on American steel; in Germany, however, the mining industry swallowed a mass of draft-age men.

[16] These statistics on the German army were taken from Wrisberg, *Heer und Heimat, 1914-1918*, pp. 100, 292. Figures on the French army were borrowed from Painlev, *Comment j'ai nommé Foch et Pétain*.

The army must be relieved of such 20 percent excess losses by any means possible. We must think carefully of what categories of workers could be drafted for the front because their work is not essential to the interests of the war or could be replaced by the labor of unskilled workers or women and children or men who are physically unfit for service.[17] In the process we must be very strict and particularly so as to keep the Red Army from turning into a 100 percent peasant army. But where skilled labor is required, workers should immediately be exempted for the draft in a mobilization. While we cannot recommend giving deferments to all such workers in peacetime, we can express our doubts as to the advisability of the proposal made by certain persons to assign the first territorial divisions to industrial regions. A division of Donetsk miners or a division of Moscow division railway workers would be militarily worthless because it could not be mobilized. As indicated by Germany's experience, 50 percent of all deferments must be given to the mining industry, 25 percent must be given to transportation, and only 25 percent must be given to all other industry and "indispensable" white collar workers.

Of course the issue of manpower mobilization has many other aspects, but they are of less interest to the strategist.

The City and the Countryside

In economic mobilization we must maintain the existing economic balance between the city and the countryside and the workers and the peasants. The white collar and blue collar workers living in the cities do not directly meet their personal needs by their own production and are much more dependent on the marketplace than the peasants, who get their food and fuel from their farms, repair their own homes, and often make their own clothes. Wars, which empty the marketplace and disrupt the monetary system, have a tendency to disturb this balance by putting the urban population into an incomparably more difficult situation than the rural population, which survives to a great extent by means of a natural economy. Once a war starts there is a rapid reduction in the supply of farm products, producers cease to compete, and food prices rise. Industry, which has focused its effort on war production, is incapable of supplying rural markets with consumer goods.

A sound economic policy should maintain this balance by any means possible, and shortages of goods for the countryside should be replaced with appropriate tax pressures. Economic mobilization should foresee the kinds of war taxes imposed on the peasants which will be proportional to the reduction in real wages in the cities. We must not permit even the slightest symptom of profit off the social misery of war. The war is already lost once large numbers of people get the urge to profit off it.

Economic mobilization should incorporate a number of energetic steps to keep bread prices low, although there may be differences of opinion on the advisability of these steps prior to the beginning of a war. The mobilization of an army leads to a significant rise in the demand for oats, because horses drafted into the army are given five to six kilograms per day instead of the two kilograms per

---

[17] By the end of the World War there were 1,700,000 workers at 15,000 factories and shops in the French war industry, one third of whom were women and children (430,000 women and 130,000 minors).

day they are normally given on a peasant farm. The overall demand for food will not rise, for all intents and purposes, because the public will eat less to compensate for the greater consumption of the front line soldier. But while before this forage and food was gathered bit by bit on different farms, now the demand for it is immediately evident as an overall total. We need a high level of organization in order to resolve the difficulties which will arise.[18] The task would be much easier if we were exporting the usual amount of grain in peacetime. But because the USSR is gradually becoming a country which is no longer a major grain exporter and is trying to replace these exports with exports of more valuable farm products, we might have to think about organizing large stockpiles of grain in order to overcome the anarchy of the peasant market.[19]

Germany had to resort to a massive and compulsory slaughter of pigs in order to supply the cities with at least potatoes.

Industrial Mobilization

Industry has still never been mobilized systematically if we ignore Italy's rather dubious preparations in the first ten months of the World War, when it still wasn't a direct participant in military operations; historical experience has merely indicated the need for industrial mobilization and provided information on the anarchic process of converting industry to war production in the World War. Accounting for all the necessary raw materials and allocating them, accounting for and rationalizing the use of factory equipment, reassigning technical supervisors and workers, making full use of the unemployed, getting new manpower from the countryside, and setting quotas which are appropriate for the capabilities of available resources and the needs of the war, constitute the essence of this mobilization. Perhaps the experience of managing the economic life of the Soviet Union in peacetime is the best school for the planners of industrial mobilization.

The harmony of an industrial mobilization plan is particularly important. The growth of military production must be even: if artillery ordnance production is stepped up but there is not enough steel or the transportation system cannot handle coal shipments, the process will grind to a half. But the rounds would be

---

[18] Czarist Russia had about 300,000 tons of food, including more than 100,000 tons of oats, at its military depots and fortressed in the western border districts. This kind of stockpile is very important for gaining time for organizational measures. Putting it into the hands of the military authorities makes it possible to relieve the transportation system of the burden of shipping this stockpile in the first two months of a war, which are particularly stressful for transportation.

[19] What we said above about the need to maintain a balance between the city and the country is equally applicable to the balance between the different states and regions of the federation. Economic policy should strive for an even distribution of the burdens and deprivations of the war. The behavior of Hungary in the World War provides an extremely instructive bad example. Hungary did not want to part with its privileges as a producer and set up a domestic custom border separating it from Austria. Agriculturally Hungary remained comparatively prosperous while Austria, which was involved in war production, was at times literally without a crust of bread. It seems to me that these domestic customs houses were reflected in the different levels of persistence with which the Austrians and Hungarians fought on the front. Hungary's egoism was particularly evident in the railway issue: Hungary tried to avoid undermining the importance of the railroad outlets to the Adriatic, which were in Hungarian hands, and even interfered with the construction of a railway on the Austro-Italian border during the war. Kraus, *Die Ursachen unserer Niederlage* (1920), pp. 28, 62-66, 174.

completely useless if there were not enough powder, cartridge cases, or tubes. The number of rounds fired should be fully coordinated with the production of gun barrels to replace worn or destroyed guns. One-sided development of the production of hand grenades or rifles or soldiers' boots and uniforms will have a grave effect on the state's material resources and will not give the army any real benefits. No matter how extensive the demand for military equipment is in a war, there are not always people in war who consume this military equipment and therefore military equipment overproduction crises are possible in a war. If we consider the Hindenburg Program undertaken by German industry at the end of 1916 as a program for a new economic mobilization in the middle of the war, we can derive a number of indicators of the danger of overemphasizing the military aspect of the program for mobilizing the economy. In 1916 Ludendorff set a monthly quota of 3000 field guns for German industry, which was much higher than the actual demand: new plants had to be built, new machine tools had to be produced, steel production has to be stepped up, coal had to be diverted for this purpose, and army reserves had to be weakened in order to get the large amount of manpower needed to extract raw materials, operate the transportation system, build the plants, and make the guns. In May 1917 Ludendorff acknowledged the error in his program and issued directives to produce no more than 1500 guns per month; in September, 1917 he reduced the quota to 1,100 and in March, 1918 to 725 guns per month. However industrial production is characterized by a large amount of inertia supported by the persons interested in it; at times production got as high as three monthly quotas per month and it took a great deal of effort by logistical agencies to reduce this output. As late as June 1918 monthly output equalled 2,498 field guns. As a result the German rear was swamped with brand new field guns; in Cologne alone there was a stockpile of 3,500 new field guns, and 2,500 new field howitzers. Only Foch provided a certain amount of relief: desiring to disarm Germany with his armistice conditions, after calculating the amount of German artillery which should be on hand in active German army, he demanded that the Germans turn over 2,500 field guns and 2,500 heavy guns. His demand concerning the field guns was met by giving him brand new field guns from the depots without taking any guns which had been delivered to the field away. The Entente inspection commissions involved in destroying German weapons were subsequently swamped by the tens of thousands of German guns turned over to them to be scraped.[20]

We must clearly realize that the effort a state is capable of making on the front and the rear constitutes a single entity, and that overstressing the rear leads to the weakening of the front. When the German army began to melt away in the summer of 1918, it would have been natural to reduce the amount of war work in the rear in order to keep the front ready for battle. What was the point of making enough munitions in one year to fill up a train stretching from Hamburg to Constantinople if there weren't enough hands on the front to fire them? We can see the illogic of Ludendorff, who allowed Germany to get into the November crisis of 1918 with no one at the front and with a war industry in the rear which operated at full capacity. The fact that Russia produced excesses of tens of millions

---

[20] Ludwig Wurtzbacher, "Die Versorgung des Heeres mit Waffen und Munition," in M. Schwarte, *Der grosse Krieg 1914-1918*, vol. 9, part 1, pp. 131-134; Wrisberg, *Wehr und Waffen 1914-1918*, pp. 18, 19, 57.

of rounds by 1917 pales before this fact. The production of military equipment requires intelligence, not the desire to break world records.

Military industry must be technically prepared for mobilization. In peacetime the tendency to maximize product quality and shelf life is natural. In wartime there is no sense in producing expensive powder with a shelf life of 15 years if it will be expended in several months, and one can avoid being particularly picky about quality if there is nothing to shoot with. However the development of less rigid specifications is a procedure which requires a great deal of attention and time, and this procedure should be carried out in peacetime.

At the same time we must have simplified models of equipment on hand in the event that refined models cannot be produced in the necessary quantities. Mechanically strong explosives may replace TNT in shells, and if necessary cast iron grenades may replace steel ones, and the lack of completely safe fuses should not make the artillery fall silent, because very simple fuses which are not quite as safe can be used to fire guns, and even the traditional brass may be replaced with a cheaper material for cartridge cases. We should never allow technology to be subject to a bureaucratic attitude in the determination of the requirements of war, as was the case in the old Russian army, where the attitude was if we have it, that's good, but if we don't, we can do without it. Technology should be applied to the conditions of war and be subordinate to them and its flexibility should be ensured by mobilization preparations. In order to enable a factory not engaged in military production in peacetime to make a transition to mass military production in wartime, it must be supplied with enough copies of the blueprints and specifications, the necessary molds and templates, and the necessary stockpile of raw materials, and constant replacements, and a work force must be put together and trained to produce the new product. Mass production of blueprints and templates requires a great deal of time, but this could be done or prepared for in peacetime at low cost. Problems with raw materials and equipment can be resolved much more quickly if they are pondered in peacetime. It takes up to two months to train a work force for production. In the World War it often took more than one year to mobilize a metallurgical plant.[21] We believe that even the slightest attention towards this question in peacetime should make mobilization twice as successful.

Technical Surprise

As early as the Civil War the United States made major advances in quite different fields of military technology, producing mines, ironclad vessels, 12-inch guns, repeating rifles, machine guns, and so forth. In the war of 1870 Napoleon III secretly prepared to arm the French army with 200 machine guns and was quite confident of achieving technical surprise. However the use of machine guns was not carefully considered in a tactical sense and was not coordinated with the tactics of the French forces; the firing range artillery mathematicians assigned to prepare the machine guns only managed to think of reequipping some of their batteries with machine guns and organized machine gun batteries primarily for long range combat. This lack of tactical understanding not only negated technical

---

[21] Such a simple operation as mobilizing an equipment shop which had a cadre of 10 percent of the required number of workers and all of the required machinery in peacetime is nevertheless delayed in the World War. It took at least three to four weeks to begin full scale production with the full complement of 450 workers.

surprise It also delayed the introduction of machine guns in Europe for thirty years.

In the World War the Germans partially achieved technical surprise with the 42 centimeter howitzer despite the fact that the Russians for their own tests had ordered a sample of this howitzer in France before the war, that everything was clear theoretically and the new Russian permanent fortifications were designed for 11-16 inch siege artillery rather than 6-8 inch guns, and that we had conducted extensive experiments with the 11-inch gun. Nevertheless, all the fortresses in the world were terribly confused when they observed the effect of the German Berthas, which had been inflated to fantastic dimensions by skillful advertising. Other major advances in German technical thought were not implemented so intelligently: Falkenhayn approved the use of poison gases on the front only in the form of a test, and the extra long range artillery fired only sporadically: the bombardment of Paris from a distance of over 100 kilometers became a kind of sporting exercise for the Krupp artillery but never a serious undertaking (303 rounds, in 44 days, 183 of which fell in the city). The Entente took the technical initiative only in the development of tanks: in 1916 it began experiments on the front which were quite unsuccessful, and although tanks were employed success-fully in 1918,[22] it was not because the Germans hadn't had time to prepare for them and repulse them and acquire their own tanks: the German command's overesti-mation of their success over the first tanks, a lack of attention and contempt for the Entente's technical efforts, and their own equipment, were the conditions which created suitable conditions for the Entente's tank attacks in the summer of 1918 along with the beginning of the disintegration of the German Army.

In a future war technical initiative will be over-whelmingly important. But the general staff must take a favorable attitude towards technical innovations and conduct the first steps in the deep rear in complete secrecy. New weapons suitable for combat may be developed in secret if the technicians and tacticians involved are highly skilled and if military academic committees, which by their very essence and organization are strongholds of technical reaction and a graveyard for new ideas, are kept out of the operation. And the top leadership must be confident enough to begin mass production without first trying out the equipment in battle. Of course there is the grave danger that if tactical and technical thinking is not up to part, vast resources will be expended for nothing. But this risk must be consciously taken. A truly intelligent man such as General Staff Colonel Bauer in Germany is invaluable in this respect. A new weapon must be introduced in large quantities immediately because it is also a reserve which must not be expended drop by drop, because there is no need for gradualists, and experiment on the battlefield!

The Economic General Staff

The economic general staff is a reflection of the current broader notion of the leadership of a war. If a war involves armed, class and economic fronts, military agencies responsible for directing preparations and preparing themselves to lead

---

[22] We completely disagree with Field Marshal Haig, who credits himself with the first combat use of tanks as of 1916, which led to improvements in their design and use. All this had to be carried out in the rear.

these fronts must be organized ahead of time. The organization of a military economic staff is an urgent measure.

The experience of the past has demonstrated that without a special military agency the activity of different extradepartmental agencies involved in overall preparations for war may die (The National Defense Council organized in France 20 years ago) or be concentrated exclusively on resolving current problems of peacetime (the Council of Labor and Defense in past years in the Soviet Union) The extraordinary complex interrelatedness of all economic issues rules out any possibility of success for sporadic interventions of military authorities and attacks on individual economic issues. All major economic measures, even those such as the Volkhov Project, the problem of electrification as a whole, or simply setting prices for peasants' rye may seem to have no direct relation to preparations for war but in fact lead to economic changes which may have a positive or negative effect on preparations for war and therefore must be critically evaluated from the point of view of military economics. Of course, the overriding importance of the overall development and improvement of the economy may quite frequently compel us to ignore the interests of war preparations temporarily, but consciousness of the latter should permeate all economic life.

An economic general staff may be small, but its members should be very highly qualified. We believe that some of its members should be persons closely linked to the Red Army by their training and service who have graduated from military higher educational schools and have experience in industry and have done individual work on military economics, while some of its members should be outstanding economists and technicians with broad views who have specialized in war-related economic issues and have spent the time to become familiar with the history of several recent wars, strategy, and administration. In Germany the issue of the economic general staff came up prior to the World War but was never resolved, while France is now in the first stage of organizing such an agency.

5. THE DIPLOMATIC PLAN

The Tasks of Diplomacy

The relationship between the military and economic conditions in which a foreign war has to be waged and foreign policy is obvious.

In an offensive diplomacy must give us the advantages of political surprise, and limit our disadvantages on the defensive. Diplomats are faced with the task of making it possible for a state to avoid armed conflicts with its neighbors at undesirable times, and, on the other hand, if the historical goals a state has set for itself cannot be achieved without the use of armed force, diplomacy must start a war at the most convenient time in terms of purely military and economic conditions with the most favorable international conditions.

These favorable international conditions include: isolating a hostile state from possible allies; providing active allies for oneself; engendering hostile attitudes on the part of neutral countries toward the enemy and sympathetic attitudes toward oneself; depriving the enemy of the possibility of getting loans and acquiring the raw materials and weapons he needs to wage war; and opening up foreign sources of economic cooperation for oneself. The odium of declaring war must be directed away from oneself and toward the enemy if possible.

The Slogans of War

Dynastic wars are now a thing of the past. At present foreign policy increasingly reflects economic and class motives rather than national motives. The art of diplomacy must cause a break with the enemy by employing slogans which will have broad appeal in foreign countries and will be understood by broad masses of the population.

Great Britian, which entered the World War in order to destroy its economic competitor Germany, was able to strike the knightly pose of the defender of international law and small countries in particular, namely Belgium, from the violence of large countries. The clear hypocrisy of this pose and the nauseating idealization of a "small heroic nation" subjected to an attack by the "contemporary Huns" made it possible for the British point of view to penetrate all the countries of the world during the World War.

The Dependence of Foreign Policy on Domestic Policy

Foreign policy is an extension of domestic policy, and is therefore far from free in its maneuvers. "Order requires the separation of the department of foreign affairs from the department of domestic affairs," wrote Adam Mueller, a political scientist of the early 19th century, while at the same time developing the opinion that foreign and domestic affairs should constitute a single entity in the minds of the government and the nation.

In 1870 the domestic policy of Bonapartism was based on very close unity with the Catholic elements in France, where a strong liberal movement which threatened the government of the Second Empire had taken root. The ruling class, which united around Empress Eugenie, was inclined to abolish the Constitution and deal a destructive strike to the opposition. But this domestic victory would require a preliminary military victory, which would make the dynasty more popular in France. Thus the reactionary elements of the Second Empire gave rise to a war party, which was a quite desirable partner for Bismarck, who also needed a war with France in order to complete the unification of Germany.

French foreign policy needed an alliance with Austria for a joint conflict with Prussia. But Austria, which remembered 1866 when it had to wage a war on two fronts at the same time against Prussia and Italy, demanded that Italy be included in the alliance as a precondition for its participation. The Italian government, which was very close to Napoleon III, would have gladly entered into an alliance with France and Austria but demanded that it be given the authorization to occupy Rome and deprive the pope of secular authority as a precondition for its participation, and if this authorization were not granted, the Italian government would not be able to withstand pressure from Italian patriots and revolutionaries who had demanded that the unification of Italy be completed and had obtained promises of money and arms from Bismarck. However, because of domestic political considerations, the Second Empire could not leave the pope without support, and thus diplomacy was incapable of achieving good results. The issue of forming an alliance had not gone beyond the stage of negotiation when the cannon fire at Woerth and Spicheren forced all talk of it to cease.

Neutral States

The diplomatic plan must take into account international relations on a global scale rather than concentrating all its attention on probable enemies. Now it is easier than ever for a conflict between two states to turn into a global conflagration, because economic interests now constitute an integrated global network. The vital interests of neutral states are affected by wars. The world economy is a single entity, no matter how hard certain states may try to become self-sufficient economic entities. A major war is a colossal economic undertaking which sweeps up a vast amount of manpower, raw materials, manufactured goods and vehicles and which totally alters the entire situation of the world economy. Prices, suppliers and credit, production, exchange, relations, and demand conditions also change.

Sometimes neutrals fall into a blockade and are capable of maintaining foreign trade solely by the permission of foreign states. In Switzerland the joint company S.S.S. (Société Suisse de Surveillance) was formed under Entente supervision, while a similar company was formed in Holland and was known as the N.O.T. trust (Nederlansche Overzu-Trust); These societies regulated all the foreign trade of these countries. The Scandinavian countries particularly Norway, were bossed by diplomatic representatives of the Entente.[1] But this pressure on neutral countries was only possible once the neutrals recognized the overwhelming superiority of the Entente's forces.

In general one must look after neutrals and carefully watch over their economic interests, remembering that from their point of view, everything that

---

[1] M.W.W.P. Consett. *The Triumph of Unarmed Forces 1914-1918* (London: 1923). The author claims that Great Britian wasted the first two years in unsuccessful attempts to create a blockade against Germany on the Scandinavian Peninsula.

happens during a war should be done in their interest and that they should make a profit at the expense of the warring parties.

Diplomatic Preparations for War

Japan's diplomatic preparations for war with Russia in 1904 were exemplary. After the Japanese victory over China in 1895 Japanese diplomats were faced with a united front of the white race, namely Russia, France and Germany. First of all Japan had to make sure that this front was never formed. That is why Japan included an insurance treaty with Great Britain which obligated the latter to render military aid to Japan if Japan were involved in a war with more than one country. Britain took on the duties of a second who made sure that nobody could help Russia in its duel with Japan. The Japanese acted as protectors of the Far East from Russian imperialism and as the paladins of all the other imperialists wishing to protect their interests in China. Japanese diplomats also managed to establish friendly relations with the Chinese, which was very important in view of the fact that military operations were conducted on Chinese territory, and was not very easy after the defeat and violence China suffered in 1895. It wasn't easy for the representatives of the yellow race to break through the white front and make it possible to get loans and military supplies from the United States and Western Europe. As we know, during the war itself Japan was even able to purchase Hotchkiss machineguns from Russia's ally, France.

Such major accomplishments were the result of a foreign policy which set itself a definite goal and systematically worked toward it. The World War for Germany in 1914 was far from being the same kind of goal as the war with Russia in 1904 was for the Japanese. That is why we can only see the uncoordinated actions of German diplomats, which were frequently contradictory from the perspective of the war. The construction of a large navy was only a threat to Great Britain which was compelled to join the Franco-Russian coalition. German diplomacy made it much easier for Britain to effect a diplomatic encirclement of Germany. Regarding Russia, France, Great Britain and Japan, Wilhelm II occupied the worst possible political position, a sheep in a wolf's clothing.[2]

In this ring of hostile states German foreign policy could only have taken a position of extreme peaceableness and appeasement in order to improve the situation regarding France, Great Britain and Russia and await the disintegration of the Entente, or selected a certain time for a preventive war under especially favorable political, economic and international conditions. Germany took the fatal third road, the middle road, believing that its desire for peace would make war impossible while at the same time believing that it would have to make no concessions and would be able to improve its military and political situation.[3]

The Crusade

The errors of German foreign policy had a grave effect on German strategy. The diplomats needed to have a clear idea of the strategic tail which was an extension of the foreign policy they created. The nature and shortcomings of

---

[2]   That is, a position which seemed like an offensive position when Germany was actually on the political defensive. The threat of a campaign against India was also a wolf's skin on the shoulders of the tsarist government of Russia.

[3]   B. W. von Buelow, *Die Krisis*, 3rd edition (Berlin: 1922), pp. 176-177.

foreign policy are naturally transmitted to strategy. The irrational, mystical nature of politics, which led to the first crusades at the beginning of our millennium, engendered the irrational, antipositive strategy of the crusades. Ranke was sad that Frederick Barbarossa did not first seize the Balkan Peninsula for a German operational base before going into Asia. But this kind of movement forward, from phase to phase, expending the lives of entire generations and systematically broadening one's cultural, economic and operational base, is quite the opposite of what we understand a crusade to be. The fate of the crusaders was to have their tracks lost in the ocean of ground they covered in the same way that all traces of a ship are lost at sea...

The thinking of a true politician,[4] like a strategist, not only avoids any mysticism but it is firmly rooted in reality; from this his fantasy grows, and his creation is determined solely by the building material provided by reality. A certain amount of mysticism was characteristic of the German leadership in the World War. In early 1915, in German political circles there were lively discussions of the desirable "orientation" of German attacks—i.e. against "democratic" France or tsarist Russia. Ludendorff supported the Russian orientation and received energetic support from the Social Democrats. Falkenhayn supported a Western orientation, allowing for an offensive against Russia with only limited aims. In fact, the more setbacks the tsarist government suffered, the more impossible it was for Russsia to conclude a separate peace. Ultimately the anti-Russian orientation triumphed because of the unpopularity of tsarist Russia among the Social Democrats and left-wing bourgeoisie. The German campaign on the Russian front in 1915 resembled Don Quixote's actions and was moreover politically criminal because it placed the life of the German nation at risk. A contrast to this antipolitical approach of the German Social Democrats, who classified their enemies on the basis of their sympathies rather than their implacability, is offered by the policies of the Fascist Mussolini, who established diplomatic and trade relations with the Soviet Union, actions far from any kind of mysticism and guided by actual benefits without mixing sympathies and business.

The League of Nations

The League of Nations, which is a sort of stock exchange for diplomats and government officials and is under the strong influence of Britain which with its dominions has six votes in the General Assembly, and France, has hypocritically pursued the goal of a general peace. There is no doubt that its meetings offer opportunities for agreements among groups of bourgeois states; moreover, in view of the fact that in principle the League looks for practical political routes to

---

[4] Jomini wrote about "dogmatic wars" ("Les guerres d'opinions," in Jomini, *Precis de l'art de la guerre* (1837), vol. 1, pp. 54-61), pointing out their special nature and the possibilities they offer for creating discord in a hostile state. In these cases the strategist should avoid what could be interpreted as the pursuit of national or imperial goals merely camouflaged by lofty slogans. That is why it is necessary to avoid seizing fortresses and occupying a province for the purpose of setting up a base of operation and why one must preserve the local administration in occupied areas and avoid any kind of requisitions and look like unpaid allies to the like thinkers among the population. This is the style with which the French army under the mandate of the Holy Alliance conducted the Spanish campaign of 1823 and was able to suppress the radical revolutionary movement on the entire peninsula in three months.

agreements and does not stand on juridical or legal grounds. The founders of the League have consciously strived not to create any kind of supergovernment, federation or superstate which would restrict the liberty of its members. All obligations have been minimized; any kind of clear statements have been eliminated from the charter, leaving the states belonging to the League free to form hostile factions and join military conventions; and League arbitration in the event of a crisis is facultative rather than binding in nature. Although it appears to give broad freedom to the small countries, in fact the League is the tool of British and French hegemony and has facilitated the creation of an anti-Soviet bloc. Powerless in major matters, the League tries to exercise a certain amount of authority in minor matters, such as sanitation, land, postal, telegraph and other international agreements. The League's lack of sincerity is at least evident from its resolution prohibiting the use of toxic substances in wartime, which in no way prevents its members from actively preparing for chemical warfare under the pretext that poison gases would be necessary if an enemy feels like ignoring the League's resolution and begins to use them. The weapon of the economic boycott, which basically involves an embargo (Paragraph 16) and would most probably be the height of the League's activity, and then a three-month postponement of the initiation of military activities (Paragraph 12) in the case of League mediation draw attention to themselves: the countries that won the World War and adopted the charter were apparently interested in lengthening the premobilization period in order to prepare their own military industries for war. While it is possible to speak of the League of Nations as an institution which to a certain extent makes it possible to gain time for mobilization, it is completely impossible to consider it an agency that guarantees peace.

Coalitions

In the 18th century, alliances, as Clausewitz observed were a kind of trade company with limited liability: every state in an alliance bought shares in the form of 30,000 to 40,000 soldiers; and the amount of the investment depended on the danger a given state was in and the benefits it planned to reap. These alliances were clearly affected by "natural human weaknesses and limitations." As early as the beginning of the 19th century, when wars had become national wars rather than cabinet wars, alliances were quite fragile structures. As Clausewitz suggested, "The defeat of Europe in Napoleon's era depended much more on political errors than military errors."

The Difficulties of a Separate Peace

Now alliances are less fragile. Currently allies are often indoctrinated and cultivated long before a war begins. The alliance sometimes seems to be a unique form of vassaldom of the era of imperialistic development. Portugal's participation in the World War can only be explained by its vassal relations to Great Britain. All the small and medium-sized countries on the Soviet Union's western border are trying to get themselves sugar daddies. But large countries are also bound into alliances by firm capitalistic relations. Modern warfare requires the interest not only of a government but of major political parties which reflect the desires of certain classes. Thus, currently alliance obligations are not merely pieces of paper, they have powerful segments of the population behind them, and governments cannot leave an alliance and conclude a separate peace with the same freedom as they did earlier. Today such a decision may often be made only at the cost of a civil war on class or national grounds inside the country concluding the separate peace. In the World War, Count Czernin, who was a prominent Austro-Hungarian politician, observed how the prolonged war was exhausting all the strength of the Austrian government and would inevitably lead to its collapse, and on many occasions brought up the issue of concluding a separate peace but each time concluded that it was physically impossible; because the most valuable national element for Austrian sovereignty, namely ethnic Germans, would have supported the German point of view, and the Germans would not think twice about overthrowing the Austrian government with German troops stationed on the Austrian front.[5] Likewise we have unverified allegations that the French government, in the period between the border conflict and the Marne operation, was discussing concluding a separate peace but that Great Britain told France that its only choice was war with Germany or war with Britain and that the latter would entail the loss of all France's colonies. Several French politicians who had previously supported unconditional continuation of the war, such as Painlevé, were already trying to set themselves apart from this and take an independent stance as early as September 1914, when the French government moved from Paris to Bordeaux.

For its part Russia could not be subjected to the direct pressure of its former allies in concluding a separate peace as Austria-Hungary or France were. However, the mere suggestion that the tsarist government was secretly preparing to conclude a separate peace led to an outbreak of public dissatisfaction stirred up by diplomatic representatives of the Entente, who despite all their disclaimers, thus played a direct role in creating attitudes that accelerated the onset of the Russian Revolution. October and the subsequent civil war were required to allow Russia's exit from the war.

Bulgaria, Turkey and Austria-Hungary all left the World War separately, but in a situation in which the defeat of the Central Powers was already recognized and under conditions of collapse and revolutionary upheavals.[6]

State Egoism

Despite the enhanced political strength of modern coalitions, their strengths are less than the sum of their parts. Even when the governments in an alliance are completely sincere, any of them may renege without severe detriment to their own sovereignty. A coalition is always a wagon to which a stallion and a trembling doe are harnessed. An honest agreement is incapable of making us forget about our healthy national egoism. That is partly the reason why the tsarist government could not stay in the war with the Entente to the end because it was too selfless in contributing to the World War and did not take Russian national interests into

---

[5]   Czernin, *Im Weltkrieg*, p. 29.

[6]   It is true that Italy betrayed the Triple Alliance and did not carry out the obligations of its military pact with Germany. However, this betrayal took place before Italy had bound itself to Germany and Austria-Hungary by a declaration of war. In addition, the ease with which Italy abrogated the treaty can be explained by the fact that Britain's influence and Italy's economic and military dependence (its long coastline) on Britain were greater than its dependence on Germany.

account. As a general conclusion from the World War, Marshall Haig has prescribed the requirement that a coalition should not only establish a joint command for all the armed forces but should appoint a single politician to direct the political affairs of the coalition. In our opinion this is a chimera. The preconditions for such a coalition are lacking in the same way that the preconditions for a United States of Europe are. By its very essence a coalition is still not a federation.

Vassals of the Era of Imperialism

Of course, a modern coalition is not just a military alliance. Now we cannot limit our discussion of alliance warfare to the coordination of military efforts. Financial and economic aid must be granted to the weaker members of the alliance; the ships at the alliance's disposal must be integrated and allocated as necessary; neutral markets for procuring military equipment and raw materials must be allocated among the allies; general principles must be established for agitation and propaganda; and certain areas of activity must be assigned to individual states. There is no doubt that war must be waged by cartels. This cartelization explains the strength of modern alliances. Economically weaker states are dependent on the capital of the other allies. In 1915, long before Soviet power established a monopoly on foreign trade, Kitchener established such a monopoly for Russia inside out by instituting allied control over all Russian orders and purchases on foreign markets. We were compelled to give reports on our needs and requirements for hard currency and we were to appeal to Kitchener as an intermediary for placing our orders in Great Britain and the United States (J. P. Morgan); our inspectors were easily compromised and eliminated; we did not get what we wanted and received shoddy goods; and we were unable to refuse to purchase rounds for our field guns abroad when our own industry was satisfying our needs under the threat of suspicion of unwillingness to wage an energetic war.[7] The divisive effect of foreign military missions, namely strategic and technical controllers, was evident in Russia both before and after the revolution of February 1917.

The loss of economic independence naturally entails a loss of strategic independence. As we know, our allies had been waging a war of attrition since October 1914 without letting Russia know it, and they encouraged Russia to wage an energetic and active war against Germany with promises of a quick transition to a decisive offensive. That is why when an allied conference met in Petrograd on February 1, 1917, the Russian chairman, General Gurko, posed the question: "Should the campaign of 1917 be decisive in nature? Or should we avoid trying to achieve our ultimate aims this year?" This natural question of the chairman, which expressed his desire to place Russia on an equal footing with France and Great Britain in the activity of the war, evoked surprise and dissatisfaction from the representatives of Entente. The Russians have allowed themselves to express

---

[7]   Russia had already lost a certain amount of independence in the Franco-Russian alliance in 1907, when France provided loans to enable the tsarist government to get out of the difficulties caused by the war and the first revolution. Before that time Russia had energetically defended its interests in the alliance.

[8]   Maurice Paléologue, *Tsarskaia Rossiia nakanune revoliutsii* [Tsarist Russia on the Eve of the Revolution], p. 314.

an opinion! One has to read about this agitation in the memoirs of Maurice Paléologue[8] in order to get an idea of the situation of the "Strategic Negroes."

An economically weak country must be wary of attempts by economically strong allies to enslave it. Incidentally, contemporary forms of economic aid favor these attempts. There is no doubt that the success of a coalition requires the fullest possible use of all strengths, including economic strengths, and the latter requires the generalization of an alliance's economic base and throwing all the money into a common pot.

A wealthier state must support a poorer ally. The greater economic sacrifices made by a wealthy state are justified in most cases by the fact that it has a greater economic interest in the outcome of the war. As early as the Napoleonic era Austria, Russia, Prussia and Sweden traded with England, promising to put up a certain number of soldiers against Napoleon and demanding a certain subsidy for every month of the war. The size of the payment made by England for every soldier depended on the particular country's possibilities of bowing out of the war. In 1813, Sweden, and then Russia, received the largest subsidies, while Prussia received the smallest. These kinds of subsidies, which were established at the dawn of capitalism, became inconvenient after the introduction of universal military obligations, and contemporary ideology opposes open traffic in the blood of its citizens. That is why instead of subsidies we now have loans with very easy payment terms. However, debts in the hands of an economically strong ally, even if they can never be paid back, constitute a means of pressure, enslavement and so forth. The old way was better and more honest. This category of loan subsidies includes both Russia's war debts and some of the loans it took out before the war in connection with its treaty obligations and used in the preparations for war required by the treaty.

Now our closest neighbors are extensively resorting to the help of foreign military missions and apparently do not notice their adverse effects. Incidentally, a ruling class cannot demonstrate its servility to foreigners without inflicting severe damage on its own authority. Isn't that why Poland died as a state at the end of the 18th century? Ludendorff, who tried to subordinate the Austrian army to German command, did not understand this. Despite all the advantages of putting the Austrian forces under German command, we recognize that is was truth, and not simply egoism that lay at the root of the objections made by Konrad, the chief of the Austrian general staff. Konrad believed that the loss of any remnant of independence by the Austrian armies and explicit recognition of German hegemony would be a new phase in the sickness of Austrian sovereignty on the way to a fatal end, and that it would serve as a new stimulus for the development of centrifugal tendencies within the state and would weaken morale on the front lines. Nothing came of Ludendorff's attempt to retrain Austrian soldiers under the command of German officers. Suvorov's attempt in 1799 to retrain Austrian troops who had come under his command using Russian officers in two or three days, which was clearly offensive to the Austrians, in our opinion was also dubious. But Suvorov was only concerned with tactical issues, while Ludendorff delved into the conditions of unit life. It is remarkable that despite the very careful selection of the officers and men in the Russian forces sent to France and despite all the punitive possibilities on the French front, in the summer of 1917

Russian forces on the Western front disintegrated more rapidly than they did on the Eastern front.

Unwilling Allies

We must make a clear distinction between allies by interest and allies by duty. Napoleon forced Austria and Prussia to take part in the war against Russia in 1812. In drawing them into the war against their will, Napoleon was essentially deceiving himself; the secret agreements made the hostile actions of the forces of these German states illusory, and this deceptive appearance of cooperation could not avoid turning the failure of the campaign into a catastrophe. Jomini was quite right in reproaching Napoleon because in getting into this major war with Russia he did not guarantee himself effective, not just formal, support from one of these great powers with their old military traditions by luring one of them into this war with major concessions and conquests, but rather preferred to rely on the illusory state of Poland, which he himself had created.

Under the intense political stress of modern war, however, violence will often be employed to turn neutral countries into unwilling allies. Greece was compelled by force of arms to join the Entente. In the winter of 1915-1916 the Central Powers discussed whether they should compel Romania to join them by force of arms using their troops concentrated in the Balkans after the defeat of Serbia; the Romanian government entered into talks with the Russian command about obtaining aid if this should occur. Of course, it is incomparably more advantageous if compulsion is carved out by bribing the press and leading politicians, concluding agreements with political factions, exerting economic pressure and so forth rather than by the threat of war. Neutral states are objects of intensive pressure. In this diplomatic war the Entente was defeated in Turkey and Bulgaria and triumphed in Italy and Romania. Cartelized warfare makes it possible to make states drawn into a bad deal quite faithful, albeit at times capricious, allies.

Great Powers and Small Allies

The ideas below seeming to indicate the desirability of extreme peaceableness for small states whose fate during wartime is to renounce their interests and all ndependence and follow the path of the great powers and take on the ungrateful role of their obedient tools. A small state is of value for waging war only when it unconditionally subordinates its army to the command of a great power.[9] The only exception is the need for the territory of a small state on which the great power can maneuver its armed forces or the need for the use of its ports, particularly in colonies, for basing the great power's navy. But in general a small ally operating on its own and pursuing its own particular goals with its own army has more negatives than positives. By taking on the leadership of its armed forces, the command of a great power is obligated to consider the small ally's interests its own and not make any distinctions between defending its own territory and its

---

[9] We are, however, far from advocating great power arrogance toward small powers. In 1706 Savoy was the banana peel on which Louis XIV's plans of conquest slipped. It is impossible to deny the military importance of Serbia in 1914 for the Russian front. But if Russia was drawn into the World War on account of its small ally, didn't Russia have the right to control its politics and strategy? And while the pressure of the Russian high command on Serbian strategy was at times unreasonable and mistaken, these errors, like any other error, cannot be opposed to the principle itself.

ally's territory. If a small ally tries to pursue its own goals in a war and keeps the leadership of its army in its own hands, then this state should be considered a fellow traveler to whom one is not militarily obligated at all rather than an ally. Hanover, Bavaria, Hesse, Baden, Württemburg and the other German allies of Austria in 1866 did not do Austria any good and distracted a mere three Prussian divisions, because they waged a cautious, parallel war on their own. On the other hand, the Saxon army, which abandoned its own country to Prussian occupation and linked up with the Austrian main forces, gave Austria perceptible support, and in concluding peace, Austria rightly placed Saxon interests on an equal footing with its own and did not give up one inch of Saxon territory, while letting its other allies fend for themselves. Before the war of 1870 Moltke convinced the Southern German contingents to become fully subordinate to Prussian command. In 1916 Alekseev held Moltke's views and was skeptical about Romania's entry into the war as an independent military power capable of wavering and making certain requirements for Russian aid. In 1916 Romania acted like a fellow traveler, to whom we stupidly obligated ourselves with our promises of support. Only when Valakhin was lost did Romania acknowledge the need to join forces with the Russians and agree to form a Russian-Romanian front only under the nominal command of the Romanian king. The adventure of the old Romanian alliance and its failures proved to be a severe blow to the old Russian state. Our actions in this matter were compelled by the Entente powers, who had a poor idea of strategic requirements and were not not concerned with putting Romania's entry into the war in the best possible framework but rather were primarily comncerned with involving a new country in the war against the Central Powers and giving the Germans new cause for worry.

Military Conventions

Treaties of alliance leave the issues of the form and nature of armed support for allied states unclarified. An alliance acquires practical value only when it is complemented by a military convention. The latter must clearly formulate in advance the resolution of all the basic questions related to waging war common to the armed forces of both allies insofar as these issues can be predicted. The convention should clearly establish the conditions that obligate one state to take part in an armed conflict into which the other ally could be drawn; the minimum number of troops and the period of time, starting with the first day of mobilization, in which each ally is obligated to undertake operations on the front, insofar as these operations are offensive in nature; the conditions of the integration and liaison of the allied command; the obligation to refrain from concluding a separate peace; and the conditions for roviding material and men and exchanging technical information and intelligence.

The peculiarly military nature of military conventions requires a direct agreement between representatives of the military high commands of both sides to conclude them, and then this agreement must be examined by diplomats and ratified by the supreme state authorities. Because the essence of military conventions is closely related to preparations for war and the operational plans of both sides, conventions must be revised as these plans and preparations are updated and changed, and this makes it necessary for the chiefs of the general staffs to meet on a periodic basis. Trips by chiefs of general staffs to friendly countries, albeit under the pretext of a vacation, are events which require attentive surveillance.

It is doubtful whether military obligations which are not governed by any military convention, such as the obligations which in certain cases follow from Paragraph 16 of the Charter of the League of Nations and concern military action against a state that has violated the peace, are of any practical value, because they give no indication as to when and with what number of men each state is obligated to take part in the operation; and naturally any state will undertake to meet this obligation only if it plans to derive special advantages for itself in the process.

The Franco-Russian military convention, which was concluded in 1892, came seven years before the conclusion of a formal alliance between France and Russia.[10]

No military convention concerning joint operations on the Russian front was concluded between Germany and Austria-Hungary before the World War. Beginning in 1909 General Konrad, the chief of the Austrian General Staff, tried to get Germany to take on specific obligations. Austria-Hungary, which was forced to conduct its main operation on the Russian front with 40 to 48 divisions, was interested in regulating the cooperation of forces beforehand. Germany, which preferred to leave only 13 divisions at most against Russia, avoided taking on specific obligations. In fact, given this balance of forces, the integration of command could only extend to subordinating the 8th German Army to the Austrian commander in chief, and the integration of efforts would have involved sacrificing the local interests of East Prussia in favor of the power of a joint attack made with the Austrians. However, it was disadvantageous for the Germans to refuse categorically to make an agreement with the Austrians, because it would have meant that the Austrians would begin immediate preparations for a defense beyond the San and the Carpathians, sacrificing Eastern Galicia, which would have deprived Germany of the opportunity to defend East Prussia. Thus the younger Moltke tried to get the Austro-Hungarians to go on the offensive between the Bug and the Vistula and on his part promised to keep at least 13 divisions in the 8th Army.[11] During the Galician operation Konrad energetically insisted, particularly after the Samsonov operation, on the promised movement of the 8th Army across the Narev to Sedlets. The dispatching of two corps from the French front to East Prussia after the German failure at Gumbinnen could be considered as bringing the 8th Army up to the stipulated number of field and reserve divisions (which was initially nine instead of 13). However, after the operation against Samsonov the Germans began their operations against Rennenkampf. The only help the Germans provided in the decisive sector of the Russian front, Galicia, was Woyrsch's Landwehr corps. On the whole, by taking advantage of the lack of a military convention, the Germans provoked Konrad into an offensive operation which drew Russian forces away from East Prussia and made it possible

---

[10] N. Valentinov, "Voennye soglasheniia Rossii s innostrannymi gosudarstvami" [Russia's military agreements with foreign states] in *Voenno-istoricheskii sbornik. Trudy Komissii po issledovaniiu i ispol'zovaniiu opyta voiny 1914-1918* [Military History Collection. Works of the Commission on the Study and Use of the Experience of the War of 1914-1918], vol. 2 (Moscow: 1919), pp. 104-128.

[11] Reichsarchiv, *Der Weltkrieg 1914-1918*, pp. 3-14.

[12] In January 1915 in a conversation with Count Stuergkh, Konrad qualified the Germans as "our domestic enemy." Stuergkh, *Im deutschen Hauptquartier* (Leipzig).

for Germans to win a number of victories at the expense of the loss of the nucleus of the Austrian Army. The Germans acted to defend their local interests—i.e., East Prussia. Ultimately the collapse of Austria-Hungary was the price the Germans paid for this provocation.[12]

Political Boundaries

Previously the political boundary between two armies played a major role in fighting a coalition. Napoleon's career got off to a splendid start in 1769 with his breakthrough of the political boundary between the Savoyan and Austrian armies at Montenot. The diverging interests of the allies forced them to withdraw in different directions, to Turin and Milan, which made it easy for Napoleon to get the Savoyans to leave the war and force the Austrians to withdraw to the Tyrol. He had captured Italy with a minimum of effort by ripping enemy resistance at the political seam. Now the cartelized nature of war has made political boundaries more solid, but they are still important. In March 1918 Ludendorff's attack on the boundary of the Anglo-French front came close to compelling the French to regroup to defend Paris and the British to regroup to defend the northern coast of France, which would cause the allies to lose direct contact. In general, the importance of political boundaries is particularly evident at critical moments when things are going poorly on the front. But even when there is no crisis in defending their interests allies may ignore the most important direction in favor of secondary directions, and a coalition war always has a certain tendency to become a war of attrition.

The art of strategy in fighting a coalition will only be manifested when the vital interests of each state forming a hostile coalition are clarified; in wartime these interests are expressed in differences in the allies' understanding of their missions and interests and in their pursuit of different political and military goals. One must be able to predict and be prepared to take advantage of differences between allies. Certain undertakings, such as demonstrative warfare on one front, which would be a mistake in a war against a single state, could be optimal in a war against a coalition if they are appropriate to the differences in the political interests represented by the coalition.

A Coordinated Coalition Strategy

The different political orientations of allies are evident not only in failures but also in offensive operations. In Prussia, Russia, England and Austria pursued different political goals in 1813 and 1814; it is extremely instructive to examine how these differences were expressed in a discussion of strategy by the allied command. Each side, without revealing its political game, supported its views with the strangest strategic theories, which were then taken seriously by some students of strategy.[13]

The difficulties of strategically coordinating the operations of the armed forces of equal members of a coalition lie, in addition to differences in political goals, in the fact that the armed forces of each country are unique with respect to the time it takes them to get ready for decisive operations, their ability to withstand prolonged stress, their offensive capabilities and so forth. The size and structure

---

[13] For a very interesting book see: Gustav Roloff, *Politik und Kriegsfuehrung waehrend des Feldzuges von 1814* (Berlin: 1891).

of the territory, the level of economic and cultural development of a state and the class system all affect the character of a given army and determine special strategic methods which are suitable for this army and this army alone. In coalition operations the strategy of each ally should take into consideration the characteristics of one's own country and the coalition as a whole, and the army is deprived of the opportunity to demonstrate its strong points. The harmony of its preparation and strategic capabilities is disrupted. The Franco-Russian alliance compelled Russia to go on the offensive on the 15th day after war had been declared, which was completely unnatural under Russian conditions and could be accomplished only by an intentional break in the development of the Russian army and expending colossal resources on preparations for war which would make it possible to support France, albeit with half of its forces, in the third week of the war. There are certain limits beyond which this kind of break and sacrifice in favor of one's allies is detrimental to the common cause of the coalition. The Samsonov operation indicated that Russia had gone beyond rational limits in subordinating its interests to France. The same was true of the Serbian offensive across the Sava into Austrian territory in the fall of 1914 at the insistence of the Russian high command, because of the purely defensive qualities of the Serbian Army, which was only a good militia at the beginning of the World War. Such offensives can only lead to defeat.

6. POLITICAL POLICY DURING WARTIME

Political Maneuvering

Only the surprising capacity of human intelligence for error can explain the opinion of prominent military authorities who, although they acknowledge the role of politics in preparing for war and drafting the initial plan, rule out the possibility that politics can affect strategy once a war has started. The plan is not a decree whose execution is assigned to bureaucrats. The plan requires creativity in its execution which depends on changes in the political situation. Political and military staffs are called on to execute it, not bureaucrats, as they are sometimes called due to philological ignorance. Political preparations must be complemented by appropriate political maneuvers during a war.

A politics that would renounce the retention of its authority over the leadership of a war and acknowledge the primacy of military specialists and silently conform to their requirements would itself acknowledge its own bankruptcy. In the eyes of a politician even strategy should be military technology, and the technical leadership of a war should be subordinate to the political leadership, because war is a part of politics. Strategy may be understood as coordinating military operations with the requirements of politics.

Domestic politics should strive to maximize the use of a state's strengths to achieve the aims of the war. Domestic politics must weigh the relations between the front and the rear and decide which efforts can be required from the population for the war, the limits that must be established for mobilizations and compulsory supplies of horses and carts and how to regulate the tax burden and wages and prices.

Politicians must eliminate anything that could turn the masses against the war and maintain their will for conflict, which is the foundation of success. The leadership must be sensitive and insightful and carefully study the course of political life at home and throughout the world to keep from drifting or taking a number of palliative measures and exercise effective political leadership in the course of a war. Energetic economic measures to regulate the hunger, need and deprivations of the population are conceivable only if the masses have a conscientious attitude toward them. Economic policy should be intelligently interpreted and explained to the population.

Occupation Policy

Occupation policy, as a direct extension of domestic policy, should be carefully thought out in order to avoid complications for the conduct of military operations. The Russian army's occupation of territory in 1813-1814 is quite instructive. All issues of occupation were decided by a special high administrative council headed by Stein, an outstanding Prussian politician and reformer who had been appointed by Alexander I and had directed our agitation in the German rear in 1812. The relationship between agitation in hostile areas and their occupation is obvious: the latter is an extension of the former when our forces occupy enemy territory. The purpose of the administrative council was to gather resources in the occupied territory to continue the war against Napoleon and form new military units in German regions to reinforce our army. Stein could have achieved even greater results if he had definitely proclaimed the slogan of fighting for German unity and expelling Napoleon's German class vassals, but in this case certain limits had been drawn in connection with the general tendencies of Russian foreign policy. In several German principalities, such as Saxony, governor-generalships headed by Russian aristocrats with leading Germans devoted to Stein as advisers were organized. Where Metternich had attempted to preserve a German ruler who had switched from Napoleon's Reich Alliance to the coalition, Stein placed his own agent with plenary commissioner powers next to the sovereign. In the reception room of the administrative council, handfuls if not crowds of German sovereigns waited for hours to see Stein.

In 1814, before Napoleon's attack, Russian forces had occupied French territory with a population of 12 million. Swarms of French noble emigres offered their services to Alexander I in administering occupied France. If their requests had been met, this would have strengthened Napoleon's hand, because the French would have immediately realized the need to band together to defend the gains of the revolution. It is probable that resorting to aristocratic emigres would have soon led to major uprisings in the rear of the Russian army. Therefore, despite the clear desire to assist the Russians against Napoleon, despite their knowledge of the language and the country, and despite the presence of certain elements in the population such as the clergy who would have supported the emigres, their offers were refused; and Stein received a directive to use only Russian and German officials to organize the occupation in France.

In 1914, in the occupation of Galicia, artificial russification had a harmful effect on relations between the authorities and the population and was in general a setback to the Russian cause in Galicia. Involving unqualified bureaucrats in the process turned russification into caricature and bribery.

During a war it is not always advantageous to intensify the class struggle in occupied areas with a particular balance of forces; one must get an influx of forces rather than driving large segments of the population into the enemy camp by means of crude techniques. One must also set limits on the use of local resources in order to avoid the complete ruin of the population and the creation of material for bandits and partisain forces in our rear.

As early as the 18th century, when Russian troops occupied East Prussia, we assumed that the fact that actual power had passed into our hands was equivalent to our accession to supreme power and that the Prussian population had come under the rule of Tsarina Elizabeth. Modern international law as governed by the Hague Conventions of 1899 and 1907 holds a different point of view and requires (Article 43) "respect for the laws in force in a given territory unless it is absolutely impossible." Thus the decree of December 17, 1792, by which the National Convention ordered the generals of the republic to proclaim the supreme power of the people in the era preceding the World War was considered a violation of international law. However, international law was evidently written by jurists especially to be broken; as early as 1863 Lincoln took the opposite point of view, and his ideological position is still of interest to Soviet jurists and diplomats. The drama lies in the fact that international law stands on a principled position which rejects any intervention in foreign domestic affairs and condemns any intervention. But because the wars of the near future, at least in part, will inevitably involve intervention in one's neighbors' affairs, all the decrees of international law have proven to be unacceptable. Germany was in violation of international law in November 1916 when it proclaimed the independence of Poland[1]

Broadening the Base of the War

Issues of occupation have received special attention in the Red Army. If war is waged under normal European conditions and does not involve energetic activity on the purely political front, with strong classes or national movements, moving forward will become very costly; in an attack on a vast area the attacking side loses more men and resources than the men and resources it could extract from occupied territories and appropriate for its own use. Hence the very prominent strategic writers raised on European bourgeois thought, namely Buelow and Jomini, both indicate the difficulties of long-range invasions and are very modest in evaluating the benefits that can be extracted from occupied territory.[2] Clausewitz even included the principle of the culminating point of an offensive after which the forces of the offender would diminish in the very essence of his theory. European strategic thought has considered the erritory of a hostile state as a source of weakness for the attacker.

This point of view has been opposed as early as the Middle Ages by the Asiatic perspective based on the success of Genghis Khan and Tamerlane. If the enemy, in terms of his sovereignty, culture and economy, stands on the lower rungs of development, and if, in particular, he has not yet abandoned a nomadic way of life, we have a situation in which moving forward will expend fewer men and resources than "exploiting" occupied territory: herds will change owners without resistance and will continue to remain on the same pastures, the population is partially put to the sword and partially incorporated into the ranks of the attacking army. Clausewitz's principle is radically overturned: an army becomes stronger the more occupied territory it manages to capture. This is a very real phenomenon. No more than one-twentieth of the men in Baty's hordes who defeated Kievan Rus' were ethnic Mongols, and two-thirds of the hordes consisted of tribes who had lived in the Urals and on the Volga and had just been conquered by Baty

---

[1] Germany has always left room for guidelines concerning the existing standards of international law in an occupation in its field regulations. In the introduction (p. 84) to the German field regulations concerning the leadership and combat of combined armed forces (1924) it is stated that "after the dishonorable and illegal behavior of the French in occupying the Ruhr in peacetime, it would be 'strange' to mention the Hague Convention in German field regulations."

[2] On issues of occupation, see: Raymond Robin, *Des occupations militaires en dehors des occupations de guerre* (1913); V. Bernier, *De l'occupation militaire en temps de guerre* (1881); Lorriot, *De la nature de l'occupation de guerre* (1906); as well as all major treatises on international law. Stein's work as the director of the Russian occupation in 1813-1814 is examined in Max Lehmann's monograph devoted to it. There is a great deal of literature on individual cases of occupation (such as the Ruhr occupation). The techniques of organizing military service in a hostile occupied country are examined in the somewhat outdated but splendid treatise by Cardinal von Widdern, *Der Kleine Krieg und der Etappendienst* (1894). Concerning British methods of administering occupied colonial regions, the "political service" and the work of political officers who are uniformed civilian agents in the history of colonial campaigns see, for example, Buhrer, *L'Afrique Orientale allemande et al guerre de 1914-1918* (1922), pp. 414-415.

on the way to the Dnepr. Although subsequently many of the surviving Russians formed special detachments in Baty's army, apparently this influx of forces from occupied territory was incapable of compensating for the losses of the offender in agricultural Europe, and in Hungary the Asian avalanche was held up because the Clausewitz doctrine was true of Europe.

We have allowed ourselves to dwell on this Asiatic strategy because in times of revolution conditions are also created in Europe in which conquering territory becomes less expensive and the opportunity to exploit the men and resources of occupied territories is greater. The class stratification of the population of the occupied provinces may prove to be so significant that an attacking army will encounter segments of the population which greet it with delight and which provide an influx of volunteers, maintain order in the rear, rebuild the economy and gather the resources the army needs. During the French Revolution the capture of territory on the Rhine and in Italy was a real rather than imaginary augmentation of French might. The wisdom of the Chinese philosopher who inspired Genghis Khan and defined the qualifications of a military leader on the basis of his ability to make a hostile state pay for a war comes to life again in a revolutionary situation.

There is no doubt that in future wars, with the intense class struggles associated with them, there will also be more favorable conditions for exploiting occupied territories than there were in the World War. The experience of 1920 indicated the need to prepare carefully to take advantage of the existing situation. A great deal of room is opening up for dreams of making Tamerlane-like thrusts over thousands of kilometers. But in our era dreams are more dangerous than they have ever been before. Overestimation of the possibilities of utilizing the manpower and resources of occupied territory may distort one's perspective and lead to a view of war as an expansion of the overall base. This kind of doctrine would be dangerous because of its one-sidedness, its characterization of the capture of territory by any means possible as the basic tasks of the armed front, its tendency to measure victories by the number of captured kilometers outside the boundaries of the state, its underestimation of the importance of the bird in the hand represented by the existing rear and its lines of communication, and its chase after the bird in the bush of "the forward base."

The economy of modern Europe is extremely complex and had a hard time coping with changes in borders, let alone changes in the front lines of hostile countries. The new borders (as determined by the Treaty of Versailles) have led to general economic disruption in Europe. The factories of Vienna, Lodz and Riga have not yet managed to fit into their procrustean beds ten years after the establishment of the new borders. This economy is completely different from the one on which Genghis Khan based his conquests. Intelligent, not predatory, use of the resources of an occupied area requires economic organization of the area, which in turn takes months rather than days. One can raid the inventory of a factory and plunder the finished goods there, but this will not do much good and will alienate the workers from the conqueror; but supplying fuel, raw materials and food, maintaining productive capacity and guiding it in the necessary direction are tasks that require systematic, long-term efforts. Before an occupied area can yield a noticeable increment of resources, the attacker himself would have to expend major and highly qualified manpower on administering the area left behind his front lines.

The manpower and resources of captured territory may be utilized much more successfully if there is a preliminary plan of occupation and if a cadre of political and economic officials has been trained. However, administrative and economic programs develop at a much slower pace than military operations and a certain amount of time is needed for the new authorities to gain the population's belief in their strength, and only if there is a long pause between operations (such as during the winter), can one expect a significant augmentation of our might by territory captured in one operation for the next operation. If military operations develop according to a strategy of destruction and operations continuously come one after the other and coalesce into a single operation, there is no need to count on an influx of new manpower and resources from occupied territory with the exception of food, fodder, housing and large visible stockpiles of goods directly used by the troops.

Evacuation and Refugees

With the introduction of universal military service and given the intensity the World War acquired, the entire employable adult population of an enemy country had to be considered an element of the enemy's strength, had to be accounted for during an occupation and in evacuating a country had to be considered prisoners of war and removed. This is how the Germans acted in France during the World War. In the areas they abandoned they left only extra mouths to feed, but no working hands. The Russians neglected to do this in East Prussia. It stands to reason that in the conditions of the current class struggle attitudes toward the population will be based on other principles, and the boundary between friends and enemies will be marked not by borders but by social divisions. However, there is no doubt that in certain areas we will have to deal with dominant national movements.

Sometimes evacuation is understood as the Scythians and Huns understood it. There is the tendency to turn abandoned territory into a desert, burn villages, destroy the harvest and carry away the population and its livestock. The natural movement of refugees not only is not restrained, but it is caused artificially and is even compelled by force.

We must keep in mind that massive punishment of a territory, such as Pfalz, which was rendered completely desolate by French troops on the orders of Louis XIV, survive in the memory of the population for many decades, if not for centuries, and will subsequently make any political work on this territory extremely difficult. In addition, refugee traffic weakens rather than strengthens a country waging a war because it is completely unprepared to take on a massive influx of refugees given the conditions of the housing, transportation and food crises which always accompany a war. In August 1914 a wave of 800,000 German refugees[3] caused by the Russian invasion of several districts in East Prussia greatly hindered German troop maneuvers. While 100,000 refugees with their possessions, carts and livestock were blocking up the East Prussian roads, 400,000 refugees had already crossed the Vistula, and the head of the column had reached Berlin, jamming the railroad stations and creating a very grave impression. If the

---

[3]   Reichsarchiv, *Der Weltkrieg 1914-1918*, vol. 2, p. 329.

Russian offensive had progressed a little bit further, the fold of refugees would have threatened to break down all of Germany's organization and render Germany defenseless.

In June and July 1915, when the Russian armies retreated from Poland, the purpose of evacuation was understood by many as leaving behind a desert for the Germans. But the existing network of lines of communication, especially during wartime, was completely unadapted to mass migration of the population, particularly given its density at the time. Fortunately the Russian forces were soon given the order to leave the population where it was, because otherwise our forces would have been completely unable to maneuver, since the population would have clogged up all the junctions and roads in the immediate rear. As late as 1919 there were up to three million refugees in the Soviet Union who had abandoned their homeland when the Russians withdrew in 1915.

An improper refugee policy may speed up the loss of a war. In 1878 after the Russians crossed the Balkans, the Turks were compelled to make a hasty retreat to Constantinople. Partly because they feared reprisals by the Christian population against Moslems to settle old scores and partly because they wanted to render the territory in front of the Russians desolate, the Turks organized extensive refugee traffic among the Moslems. The Turkish forces, who were deprived of the opportunity to make a quick retreat, suffered excessive casualties, and the flood of refugees overwhelmed Constantinople. Disease and hunger among the refugees in the capital made the Turks incapable of any resistance and forced them to agree to any Russian terms.

A class war in the future will also lead to a flood of refugees, namely the bourgeoisie, from one side and workers and communists from the other side.

In 1919 the refugee problem was already critical for both the Reds and the Whites. It had to be resolved with extreme caution, and the politicians had to make a good accounting of the possibilities of transporting and taking care of the refugees.

One must approach economic evacuation with extreme caution to avoid causing panicky refugee traffic. It requires attentive and thoughtful preparation to keep from clogging and crippling the transportation system and prevent valuable freight from rotting on the way (such as leather in the tanning stage in the evacuation of tanneries in 1915). It would seem that livestock is easier than anything else to evacuate. The Germans had this mind in the two Russian invasions of East Prussia in 1914, but they managed to evacuate only 20,000 horses and 80,000 head of cattle (3.5 percent and 5.5 percent respectively of the total number of horses and cattle on the right bank of the Vistula). German agricultural losses suffered as a result of the Russian invasion of East Prussia have been calculated as 135,000 horses, 250,000 head of cattle and 200,000 pigs. Apparently, in a war of maneuver economic evacuation is incapable of producing any noticeable results.

Changes in the Political Goal of a War

Foreign policy cannot rest on the laurels of successes achieved before the beginning of a war. The political goals established during preparations for a war can in no way be considered unalterable. On the contrary, these goals may be narrowed, widened or completely altered, depending on the course of the war. If a war is waged by a coalition, it is very difficult to change political means in the neutral countries and in the enemy's rear and in this case we also need to put all the particular private goals we are striving for into a definite logical order; we need a common line of political conduct that follows from an analysis of the overall political situation.

Both failures and major successes may sometimes serve as the reason for reviewing our political goals. For example, in 1870, after the initial Prussian successes and Bazaine's army had surrounded Metz, there was no longer any doubt that a revolution would occur in France that would topple the Second Empire. The basic question facing the leaders of the war was whether the Germans should stop in Lorraine and let the French stew in their own juices. Should we advance on Paris, which will now be revolutionary? Any answer to this question would either change or preserve the political goal; the relationship between strategic goals and the resolution of this question is clear, and the latter depended on an extensive evaluation of the domestic political situations in France and Germany, the positions of other powers and the degree of desire to annex French territory. This desire was decisive in Prussia's preserving its former political goals and continuing its advance on Paris.

If a war proves to be clearly contradictory to the conceptions that guided the planners of the war in their initial directives, it may require a radical revision of the very fundamentals of political conduct. The American Civil War was started by the leader of the North, President Abraham Lincoln, as a war whose political goal was to force the seceding Southern states to return to the federation by force of arms and establish customs houses on their shores which would make it possible for Northern industry to retain an extraordinarily valuable domestic market and source of raw materials; initially there was no plan to interfere in the internal social structure of the Southern slaveowning states, because the Constitution left social order up to each state. Lincoln, having set forth a modest political goal, could remain on firm legal ground and guarantee the support of many Northern Democrats, which was particularly important because practically all the military and administrative apparatus was in their hands.

The modest political goal was to be achieved by a quick destruction, because only 150 kilometers separated Washington from Richmond, the Southern capital. No appeal for sacrifices was to be made to the broad masses. The army was to be formed solely by volunteers, and the forthcoming conflict would supposedly be so short that the volunteers were initially called on to enlist for only three months.

By the end of the second year of the war it finally became clear to Lincoln that the cohesive resistance of the Southern gentry could not be overcome by destruction techniques and that a prolonged, fierce struggle and the destruction of all the South's sources of livelihood would be required to achieve victory. The volunteers did not produce a sufficiently strong component of manpower and their numbers had become insufficient. Because of war expenditures the buying power of the dollar had decreased significantly and inflation had risen. The Northern Democratic party, which represented the intelligentsia, or the ruling classes in general, was becoming increasingly less reliable as the conflict and its associated social contradictions became wider and deeper, was opposing energetic operations and was calling for negotiations with the South.

The transition to a war of attrition made it necessary to review the political fundamentals that had been established on the basis of a quick victory of destruction. With his previous political goals Lincoln was unable to institute a draft in the Northern states, which was so important for military victory, and he was unable to demand further sacrifices from the broad masses. Under these conditions Lincoln decided to break with the Democrats, give the war an extremely classist, antigentry character, declare the emancipation of all the Negroes, provoke them to attack the gentry holdings in the South and rely on the antigentry feelings of Northern farmers and workers. All aspects of the war became quite different. If on the armed front the situation had gotten to a point where it was necessary to put the entire Southern population in concentration camps and destroy all the economic capabilities of the Southern states, and if water mains were destroyed and ublic buildings were burned in the important cities of the South that the Northerners could not count on holding, what was the point in holding on to the political slogan of nonintervention in the internal affairs of the South? Of particular interest in this example is the fact that a transition from a strategy of destruction to attrition on the armed front in no way means a reduction in the political goals of the war. The coordination of politics and strategy is a complicated matter and cannot be resolved by establishing proportions between political and operational scales.

Sheridan, returning from his attack on the Shenandoah Valley in the fourth year of the war, reported that he had destroyed $37 million worth of gentry property. At the beginning of the war this kind of activity would have been completely unacceptable and regarded as barbarism, but in the fourth year of the war it was a major feat which brought the war closer to a decisive end. Lincoln's political line of conduct had been intelligently applied to the objectively altered conditions of warfare. Humble Lincoln, with his narrow petit bourgeois ideology, completely changed during the course of the war, and moving as far to the left as necessary, he strengthened his dictatorship and by the end of the third year of the war resorted to terror in the Northern states and exchanged greetings with Karl Marx at the First International. His policy was flexible enough to win the war because his political goals had been revised in a timely manner. The new direction of his policy, which was welcomed by the British working class, protected him from imminent intervention by the British on the Southern side.

Any attempt to go deeper into the issues of foreign and domestic policy that follow from warfare would lead us off on a tangent and distract us from our main purpose. We have even avoided listing these issues and have turned to the most interesting point: how politics affects the leadership of military operations during the course of a war. This point has two aspects to it: the directives issued by politics and the orientation that a strategist tries to get from politics for making his own decisions. In this case we are primarily concerned with the first aspect; the second aspect permeates all our work, which considers all military operations to derive from the political base constituted by both parties to a conflict.

Politics and the Freedom of Withdrawal Maneuver

Each moment of a war represents a wide range of political interests and every basic decision is made under pressure from a number of political demands. War is not waged in a vacuum. The suggestion that war is a free conflict between two armies understands nothing about the nature of warfare.[4] Let us compare Kutuzov's actions in 1805 and 1812. In both instances the Russian army was vastly inferior to Napoleon's, and one could have predicted an unfavorable outcome to the tactical decisions in both cases. But in 1812 Kutuzov gave us the battle of Borodino, while in 1805 he made a quick retreat from the Bavarian border to Moravia. "It is always easy to play the role of Fabius in an allied country where there is no need to concern oneself with the capital or with threatened provinces and where one can be guided solely by military considerations." Don't these words of Jomini acknowledge the importance of the atmosphere of political pressure which essentially determines strategic decisions? French, who withdrew the British army in the period between the border battle and the Marne operation in 1914, beating the French armies by one or two days' march, was no more cowardly than the French generals and no stupider in his analysis of the war with Germany. Their different decisions can be explained by differences in the evaluation of the strategic situation which followed from the different attitudes of the British and French generals toward the political act of sacrificing French territory.

Borodino

Borodino was an act of domestic politics. The replacement of Barclay with Kutuzov, who was greatly inferior to the former in military terms and was not valued very highly by Alexander I, was the result of the pressure of the ruling class, who did not trust Barclay and could not imagine the risk under which Barclay retreated, and demanded that Napoleon's invasion be halted. Political conditions required a major battle from the strategy. This political order to the army from the court and the entire nation acted as a law for strategy and was the reason for the advisability of the battle of Borodino. Kutuzov came to the army with this political order although he was counting on a tactical victory over Napoleon even less than Barclay had. He organized Borodino not as a fight for victory but as a great bloodletting required by politics. After making this sacrifice, Kutuzov tried to take maximum political advantage of the battle. He did everything possible, even to the extent of using forged orders from Napoleon, to portray Borodino as a victory or at least not as a total disaster. Kutuzov maintained the people's confidence in victory despite the abandonment of Moscow:

> With unmitigated gall he posed as the victor after Borodino, took every opportunity to announce the imminent demise of the enemy's army, to the last minute acted like he was ready to fight a second battle to save Moscow, and never hesitated to boast. That is how he encouraged a sense of pride among the army and the people and tried to boost

---

[4]   This is the basic principle of Clausewitz's doctrine and the leitmotiv of all his treatises. Clausewitz's work has made it possible for us to avoid spending a great deal of time on explaining the political nature of war which determines its basic lines of development. Of great interest is a brochure by Clausewitz, *Osnovy strategicheskogo resheniia* [Principles of Strategic Decision] (Moscow: Vysshei voennyi redaktsionnyi sovet, 1924), p. 31.

[5]   Clausewitz, *Hinterlassene Werke*, 2nd edition, vol. 7, p. 117.

confidence, albeit artificial, but it was based on true circumstances, namely the poor condition of the French army. And
this flippancy and this false advertising of the old fox were
more useful to the cause than Barclay's honesty.[5]

Kutuzov was a politician and he splendidly guided the military operations in 1812
in the most favorable and appropriate direction for Russsia's war aims and
resources.

Military operations involve resolving basic historical issues with weapons in
hand. The historical process is governed by economic considerations and the
balance of forces of nations and classes, but under certain conditions, at a certain
stage, these economic forces do not operate directly but are measured by the
accurate yardstick of the battlefield; in the same way that the entire universe is
reflected in a drop of water, all politics are ultimately reflected in an operation. In
the battle of Waterloo, Napoleon continued to insist on frontal attacks on
Wellington's troops despite the fact that Bluecher's Prussians had already reached
the flank and part of the rear of the French army. Was Napoleon's action a gross
error which caused the French failure to turn into a disaster? No, because
Napoleon's political situation, after he had returned from Elba and driven out the
Bourbons, during the 100 days of his second reign was such that only a series of
victories would make it possible for him to hold on to power. A minor failure
against Wellington would also have compelled him to abdicate the throne and
prepare for a trip to St. Helena. At Borodino he did not send the old guard, his
political support and most devoted troops into battle, but at Waterloo he threw his
old guard into a final, desperate, almost hopeless attack, because he either had to
conquer or close all accounts.[6]

The Sedan Operation

Sedan, this strategic madness of the Second Empire, was Napoleon's III's
Waterloo, can only be understood as the final steps of logically bankrupt
Bonapartism and its rotten edifice.[7] In the very last moments of the death of the
French army we can see the personification of Bonapartist politics at Sedan in
General Vimpheme, who had been given his mandate to command the army and
had eliminated Ducrot with his attempt to save the army by retreating to Mézieres
and attempted to organize a breakthrough not toward Paris but toward Metz. He
did not even manage to persuade the ill Napoleon to stand next to him at the head
of the final attempt at a breakthrough, because Bonapartism was only concerned
that a stray bullet not kill Napoleon III in an attack in order to protect dynastic
interests in the future after the inevitable revolution in Paris.

The Schlieffen Plan

The plan of a wide turn through Belgium, to which Germany basically
adhered during the World War, was perhaps justified by the political situation at

---

6   It seens that Napoleon refused to meet his allies' conditions as early as 1813 when he
    said to Metternich, "Your legitimate monarchies are in a different situation. They can
    lose battles and entire campaigns. A 'parvenu' cannot permit himself this luxury." A.
    von Boguslavski, *Betrachtungen ueber Heerwesen und Kriegsfuehrung*, p. 9.

7   See A. Svechin, *Istoriia voennogo iskusstva*, vol. 3, pp. 154-164; also Ibid., pp. 97-101 on
    Clausewitz's views and the conflict between Moltke and Bismarck.

the time it was conceived (the time of the Russo-Japanese War and the first Russian Revolution). But by 1914 the Schlieffen plan was based solely on military-technical considerations, namely strengthening the French border, the current frontages and Russian deployments for a withdrawal from Poland. The plan was not discussed politically, and the politicians were barely familiar with it. All the destructivenes of the elder Moltke's thought (1871-1882), that primarily military considerations constituted the guidelines for the course of a war (the elder Moltke himself always proceeded from political considerations in his plans), was evident in the execution of Schlieffen's very technically sound plan for a strategy of destruction. Politics, which had been left out of the plan, could not help but affect the course of military operations.

The Basic Line of Conduct of Germany and Great Britain in the World War

German strategy never had a clear political line at any point in the war. Germany's major political blunder lay in regarding the main enemy, namely Great Britain, as an auxiliary force of France. We can observe many inconsistencies in the development of operations in both sectors which the Germans could have attempted to break Britain's will to continue the war. In the Baghdad sector this included the temporary halt to tunnel construction on the Baghdad Railway, the more than idiotic raid on the Suez Canal, the failure to take Salonica in the Serbian campaign of the fall of 1915[8] and the secondary importance assigned to this sector, which incidentally cut off 85 percent of Russia's capacity for foreign dealings. In the other sector, namely the submarine blockade of Great Britain, we can see that the Germans had every opportunity to capture the northwest coast of France at the beginning of the war, an opportunity which they let slip away, and when they subsequently, undertook operations for this purpose (for example, the battle of the Isre in October, 1914), they were sporadic and unsystematic, and there was so much wavering and indecisiveness before they decided to undertake submarine warfare that England managed to be fully prepared for it. The lack of political clarity led to a situation in which German pressure on India and the hunger blockade of Britain were rigid operations similar to the raids of the German zeppelins on London: the fervor and energy of the British were aroused to the limit, and British combat-readiness increased rather than decreased.

On the other hand, in the case of the British we sometimes find pitiful tactical solutions to the problems facing them but a very clear political line: an extensive economic offensive involving the capture of all German colonies and strong points

---

[8]   The German strategists' ideas that the Central Powers should not attempt to defeat the Entente forces in the Balkans because the Entente's retention of Salonica would leave a military objective for the Bulgarian army were quite dubious. They believed that if the Anglo-French forces had sailed away from the Balkan Peninsula, the Bulgarian army, which did not wish to operate in other theaters of the war, would have stopped fighting, and the Central Powers would have been compelled to drop two dozen from their ledger. However, there is no doubt that the political, economic and strategic situation of the Central Powers would have been greatly improved if they had successfully captured the Balkans. Such ideas—avoiding final victory in order to leave one's ally something to do—have been encountered in history. This was the French position in the American war for independence from Great Britain in 1775-1783: France assisted the United States but was interested in keeping them from utterly defeating the English, because if this had occurred, England would have stopped fighting the Americans and would have been able to direct all its resources against the French.

on the globe for the purpose of destroying a competitor; the hunger blockade of Germany; the formation of Kitchener's army, designed to last three or four years; the battle for the coast of northern France and Belgium, which was the most threatening strategic position for the British; and the war in the Baghdad sector in Mesopotamia, Syria, the Dardanelles and Salonica. One would have to be very naive to assume that Churchill sacrificed 300,000 English soldiers, primarily colonial subjects in the Dardanelles, to turn Constantinople over to Russia.

The Marne Operation

Let us dwell on the French maneuver at the Marne in September 1914; we can characterize it as: 1) the starting of a decisive conflict with the Germans, particularly on the very important French left flank inside France; and 2) an attempt to envelop the German right flank. Domestic political considerations, which were basically true but whose importance was overexaggerated, forced Joffre to make every effort to move the center of gravity of the operation to the frontier battle and oppose the retreat to the Marne; whereas General Lanrezac, the initiator of the withdrawal, was even stripped of his command. German assistance in the form of strong frontal assaults helped Joffre get over this mistaken interpretation of political requirements. As early as August 25, ten days after the Marne operation had been planned, Minister of War Messimy issued an order to Joffre: "if the efforts of our forces are not crowned with victory and the army is compelled to withdraw, you are to detach an army consisting of at lease three field army corps which must be dispatched to the fortified camp of Paris to provide it with security. As a result of this order, which was completely the consequence of domestic political requirements, Manoury's army did not move back with the rest of the front, but was held up at Paris and wound up on the German flank. Thus we can clearly discern political lines in the Marne maneuver.

Nivelle's Strategy of Destruction

Foreign politics determine the development of strategy just as domestic politics do. The weakening of Russia by early 1917 and the possibility that it would leave the war was the reason for France's change to a strategy of destruction, which was represented by Nivelle's strategy and ended in defeat on April 16, 1917; and the United States' entry into the war determined Foch and Pétain's decision to go on the defensive for 14 months until July 1918 and determined Ludendorff's decision to put an end to the Western front in the first half of 1918.[9]

The Assistance of Politics in Ending a War

The close relationship between foreign policy and strategy also stems from the fact that in most cases strategy is incapable of bringing a war to an end solely by military means. Even the greatest representative of the strategy of destruction, Napoleon, was incapable of ending his most successful wars solely by means of armed violence and was compelled to make extensive use of political means to conclude a favorable peace. Napoleon's popularity among the French peasantry was primarily due to his reputation as a peacemaker. Only Napoleon has been able to conclude revolutionary wars with peace treaties, the first time in 1797 and the second time in 1800. Such techniques as conceding Venetia to defeated Austria

---

[9]   A. Svechin, "Integral'noe ponimanie voennogo iskusstva" [An Integral Understanding of the Art of War], *Krasnye Zori*, no. 11 (November 1924).

in 1797, creating the Rhine Alliance, making advances to Austria before Austerlitz and dividing rule in Europe with Alexander I, who had been severely beaten at Friedland, are Napoleon's splendid political achievements which got his strategy out of difficult situations at moments when waging war threatened to carry him beyond the culminating point of his success. When Napoleon lost his political talents, his military undertakings began to end in catastrophes—namely the Spanish, Russian and German disasters.

Bismarck also kept several political tricks on hand for getting his strategy out of trouble and make an enemy more agreeable to peace. For example, in 1866, when he arranged for a national revolution in Hungary in the event that Austria remained implacable and concluded an alliance with France, he would not start it off unless he needed to because he relied on the Junker (Agrarian) Party and wanted to keep the war dynastic in nature.[10] Bismarck maintained ties with Italian revolutionaries to be able to foil the hostile actions of the Italian king in 1870. And in 1870 when Moltke believed that the war was almost over after Sedan, Bismarck was seriously concerned because he was afraid of becoming politically defenseless against the French Revolution.

The World War also demonstrated that one has to know with whom to make peace, and in this respect strategy must blindly follow the dictates of politics and prepare the ground for it. Bethmann-Hollweg, the German chancellor, made a political blunder when looking for a partner for peace talks. He tried to make peace with Great Britain at Russia's expense without understanding that Britain was Germany's most implacable enemy, which was why the German efforts were unsuccessful. In 1916 he responded very unenthusiastically to proposals to attempt to conclude a separate peace with Russia. When he made this attempt, then, placing his trust in an expert on the Russian issue, the Bulgarian emissary Rizov, and the consul Marks, he decided not to rely on the reactionary Russian parties, who were truly afraid of continuing the war and were therefore ready for peace, but on the left-wing liberals, who were wholeheartedly on the side of the Entente. This explains the political blunders of late 1916 and early 1917, the stupidity of his approach to a separate peace, the newspaper campaigns against the Russian political die-hards who were prepared to extend their hands to the Germans, the proclamation of Polish independence and similar stupid application of Bismarck's tricks.

Politics and the Choice of an Operational Direction

In the 18th century, in the era of recruited armies, which had a strong inclination to desert, the choice of an operational direction had to take into account considerations such as the forest cover along the army's route. An army remained more intact on open terrain, while on wooded terrain the number of deserters increased significantly.

In modern civil wars the territory on which combat operations develop is also very important. In a civil war, the disorganized and often weak logistical system makes local resources very important for meeting the needs of an army. In a civil war, it is quite often the case that the area of military operations not only feeds an

---

[10] On July 11, 1866 Bismarck reported that a Hungarian legion had been formed under the command of the best revolutionary general, the Hungarian Klapka. As an result of the peace treaty the legion was unable to take part in military operations.

army but clothes it and even provides its weapons, and in particular, it is a very important source of manpower. The class structure of a population is clearly reflected in the desertion rate and the influx of new men into an army. The strength of an army that has moved into a "dying" area melts away quickly, while the might of an army that has moved into an area with a favorable class structure rapidly increases; such an army not only can get by without assistance from its economically weak center but can often send it valuable presents from the front. The offensive against Kolchak was essentially carried out by the forces and resources of Siberia alone which had rallied around cadres sent from Russia. Lugansk and the entire Donbass were quite valuable for the Soviet armies.

This is the reason for the great temptation of selecting primary directions for offensives solely on the basis of political considerations. But we must mention that the more powerful the center is and the more orderly the provision of supplies from the rear and the firmer the discipline and morale of the troops is, the less dependent attacking armies are on the political coloration of the territory they are passing through. The importance of manpower and resources provided by the locale is lower in comparison with the major support provided by the rear. Several tens of thousands of volunteers, who still have to be provided with officers, uniforms, weapons and training, may be of decisive significance in a civil war if the entire strength of the front does not exceed the number of volunteers, but may be comparatively insignificant when the front swallows up 150,000 well-trained and disciplined soldiers dispatched as reinforcements from the center on a monthly basis.

The element of political geography, insofar as it is not an important component of the ultimate political goal, should be evaluated by military commanders in the same way as any other geographical element. This is merely one condition of the overall situation. Overestimation of the geographical element always results in strategic monograms, in this case, political monograms.

The Geographical Objective of Operations
The conduct of a conflict on the economic or class front may often be made much easier by capturing certain geographical points, or, on the other hand, may be made much more difficult by their loss. The Turkish and German logjam in the Dardanelles made it much more difficult for Russia to take part in the World War. It is probable that Count von Schlieffen, who moved the direction of the main thrust toward the French front through Belgium, was not completely free of economic motives, because there was nothing to take from Russia, whereas the French had capital and colonies and the capture of Belgium and the north of France with their industrial wealth was both a valuable prize for waging war and a valuable pawn for concluding peace. Wealth always draws lightning. But the very question of the best way to win a war always puts us in an ultraoffensive frame of mind, and it would have been more logical for the Germans to concentrate on how to avoid losing it. Galicia was more enticing to the Russian command than the incomparably wealthier East Prussia for political reasons. In 1917 the Germans launched a successful operation against the grain and oil wealthy Romanians.

In the Civil War, when Soviet Russia felt the "bony hand of hunger" strangling it, the struggle for the Ukraine with its grain, for Don Coal and Baku oil and for the entire Volga, which at one time had led Muscovy out of its historical isolation into the broader world arena, was a very urgent matter. Urgent economic necessity guided the flight of the Red Army. The importance of geographical goals increase to the extent that one's economic base is destroyed. The capture of Warsaw in 1920 would have brought hundreds of thousands of proletarians into the ranks of the revolution.

Politics is usually the handmaiden of economic and class geographical interests. From this, however, it does not follow that geographical objectives should invariably take precedence over the objective toward which a strategist's attention is particularly drawn, the enemy's manpower. If politics establishes a destructive strike as the goal of the war, then it probably will only provide a very general indication of the geographic goal, perhaps in terms of countries of the world if we are encircled by enemies, or in terms of states if they form a single solid fence, in terms of the boundaries between them, or in terms of their capitals. If the political goal is oriented toward attrition in a theater, it may include geographic objectives for individual operations. That which politics includes in the political goal of the war is a hard and fast law for strategy. With respect to other issues of importance for the economic and class fronts, the strategist is no longer a subordinate but a representative of the armed front, possessing equal rights, and he must become involved in evaluating political and economic ideas insofar as they are possible and advisable in terms of our line of strategic conduct, which is oriented toward the most important political goal of the war.

A strategist will be implacable in pursuing destruction. If a destructive strike is planned, then his concern for the overall base should recede far into the background. Schlieffen was completely logical in assigning only negligible forces to defend major German economic interests in Lorraine, Alsace and East Prussia. The basic mistake made by the younger Moltke, who tried to retain the idea of a destructive strike, was to pay too much attention to protecting the economic interests of these regions.

The desire to defend one's overall base and hurt the enemy economically is natural in a war of attrition. One has to look for a compromise and make the war against the enemy's manpower and the defense of geographical interests compatible.

A geographical point that is important to the enemy is particularly suitable for an offensive if our purpose is to engage the enemy, force him to do battle and make him fight a material battle in unfavorable conditions (e.g., Verdun). This was the Russians' problem with Sevastopol in the Crimean War: it would have been much better for the Russians to fight the Anglo-French, who were afraid to penetrate Russian territory not so close to the shoreline, but the importance of Sevastopol, the base of the Black Sea fleet, compelled us to engage in battle at the very edge of the water where the enemy had most advantageous lines of communication and we had the worst. Leningrad could play the same role in the future. The abundance of vital geographic points in the west, such as large cities and industrial centers, makes strategy inflexible to the extreme. On the other hand, the lack of vital geographic points on the Polish-Belorussian front makes strategy very flexible there. In this locale the freedom of withdrawal could be hampered only by the encumbrance of military equipment. A large cluster of military depots also constitutes a geographic objective. If it were not for the tens of thousands of trains of military supplies which had to be moved from the Germam rear and whose traffic jams often got out of the control of the German staff, Ludendorff would have had much greater freedom of withdrawal in September and October of 1918 and could have avoided the fierce and disadvantageous battles of retreat he had to fight.

A wise policy would be very cautious in defending geographical interests, particularly those of a local, parochial nature. Frequently it will limit itself to indicating a strategy for accounting purposes without any emphasis on the need to defend them. Of course, politics cannot view strategy as a universal instrument for satisfying everyone. The words written by Peter the Great in his manual on the role of the quartermaster general in quartering troops are particularly applicable to the strategist: "There's never been a man who could make everybody happy." This is why we need to keep strategy independent of local authorities and bring it into direct contact with the supreme authority of the state. Both politics and strategy will stay on the right track only if they set forth common goals and interests which are purely national in scope and reject private solicitations inasmuch as they threaten to distract us from our ultimate goal.

Independent Naval and Air Operations

In their independent operations the navy and air force are primarily weapons of economic pressure. Naval superiority places very important maritime trade routes off limits. Military operations at sea are especially important in a prolonged war, particularly when the war is for global superiority (e.g., Carthage and Rome; England and Spain; England and Holland; England and France of Louis XIV and Napoleon I). The battleship fleet merely covers the economic operations of more lightly armed vessels by blockades and laying mines and by monitoring commercial navigation and cooperates with them in bombarding coastal objectives. Air forces are capable of carrying out increasingly energetic bombing raids on important geographical points at ever increasing distances from the land front. Systematic air raids are capable of greatly reducing the effectiveness of important transportation arteries and partially paralyzing the production of industrial centers that are not too far away.

Bombardments are irritating but not always effective. The city of Dar es Salaam, the capital of German East Africa, was subjected to English naval bombardments 27 times at the beginning of the World War, but because the population took shelter and the navy had no high trajectory guns, only one white person was killed. Aerial bombardments will be somewhat more effective. However, we must weigh their strategic advisability, because they could have negative consequences. The bombing of Paris and London destroyed scores of houses and crippled several hundred residents. The economic expenditures on the bombing raids (in particular, building the zeppelins) probably exceeded the losses inflicted on the enemy, and hundreds of brave aviators died. And for the Entente, given its strong will for victory, these bombing raids were only pin pricks which led to outbreaks of furor and made it easier for the hostile governments to acquire the resources they needed to wage the war more energetically. This game also can not be justified by the German idea that their raids tied down large air defense forces in the enemy capitals. The losses were clearly greater than the possible gains.

A side suffering setbacks at the front will avoid bombing out of the fear of raising the price it will have to pay. Ludendorff ordered a bombing halt in the last three months of the war.

If the struggle on the political front becomes especially intense, one must be particularly cautious in using bombing. Several toxic bombs from an airplane could completely ruin the ground for political agitation by filling the infirmaries with victims. Political consultation is required any time this weapon is employed. The importance of bombing is highly dependent on the intensity of the war: the punitive results of British raids in Iraq, given the low intensity of the war there, were quite significant, while the bombs dropped by the Spanish and French, which were just as lethal and just as toxic as the British bombs, proved to be ineffective because of the high level of enthusiasm of the Moroccans.

Military operations that pursue economic goals must be carefully thought out, but at times their planning is an economic problem of great complexity. The submarine blockade of Great Britain was a problem of this kind. The German naval general staff and the economic experts they called on arrived at the conclusion that at the rate the German U-boats were sinking ships delivering supplies to Great Britain (500,000 tons per month), a half year later there would not be enough ships left in the world to meet British needs, and, threatened by famine and economically shaken Great Britain would have to make peace.

Because the declaration of submarine warfare could not help but lead to U.S. intervention in the war, the decision to engage in this type of warfare was extremely important. The decision-maker had to consider the stress placed on world shipping by the World War; the ability of the world's shipyards to replace sunken ships; the possibility that the oceangoing fleet servicing Great Britain could be strengthened by taking ships from secondary lines, using obsolete ships, and chartering neutral vessels and finally by reducing the need for ocean transportation by limiting consumption and switching to an economic system in which foreign trade would be drastically curtailed and every state would try to cover most of its needs with its own products. The Germans were mistaken: the United States embarked on a vast merchant marine construction program; neutral states greatly curtailed their demands; and Great Britain, using American tractors, began a major program of agricultural expansion, and at the same time, by switching to a rationing system, greatly curtailed its own consumption. Despite the fact that the the British had taken a large number of well-planned countermeasures, the German U-boats justified the military component of the plan: in eleven months in 1917 they sunk 9,125,000 tons, that is, 66 percent more tonnage than the theoretically calculated average, and even in 1918, when the submarine war was winding down, they sank 5,198,000 tons in nine months. Apparently the Germans erred in their calculations of the effectiveness of U-boat operations by more than double. The singlemindedness with which the Germans pursued their goal can be judged by the fact that they assigned all their U-boats to accomplish it despite Austrian indications of the desirability of sinking American troop transports. The Americans vainly strutted the successful organization of their security, in fact nobody was hunting them. In the same way the Germans, in order to strengthen their blockade of Great Britain, avoided sending submarines to the Mediterranean, which made the Entente's efforts to supply the Salonica front much easier.

The Influence of Foreign Policy at the Beginning and End of War

Special diplomatic considerations must be taken into account primarily at the beginning and end of a war. On August 6, 1870, at the very beginning of the Franco-Prussian war, vanguard units of the 5th Prussian and 2nd Bavarian Corps engaged the French in battle at Woerth. Because a general attack had been planned for August 7, the Prussian crown prince commanding the 3rd Army gave the order to disengage. General Kirchbach received this order only when the battle had really gotten hot. Keeping in mind that the disengagement of the 5th Prussian Corps could give the French grounds to claim the first victory, and considering the impression a French victory bulletin could make on wavering Austria and Italy, General Kirchbach decided to ignore the order: the battle continued and ended in a French defeat. Bismarck's energetic politics were incarnated in tactics.

Sometimes a neutral state may be restrained from joining our enemies only by a major success, which forces us to put a half-bared sword in our scabbard. In a case such as this we have to take a risk that we otherwise would have avoided. But one must know where to stop.

Whereas General Kirchbach oriented his tactical operations at Worth toward the impression they would make on wavering neutral states, in the spring of 1915 all operations on the Russian front were oriented toward Italy's forthcoming entry into the war. General Falkenhayn decided to avoid continuing his offensive in France in 1915 and shifted the center of gravity of his efforts to the Russian front in the hope of using a major success in Galicia to keep Italy out of the war, having demonstrated the total illusoriness of the hope that the Russian armies would reach the Hungarian plain.[11] A correct assessment of Italy's war preparations should have indicated to the Russian command that in the near future the French theater would become secondary and that they should conserve their strength, because Italy's entry into the war would draw lightning toward the Russian front rather than away from it. However, we had an oversimplified, nearsighted understanding of the relationships between politics and strategy. The Southwestern front, after finding out that Italy, counting on the imminent collapse of the Austro-Hungarian front, was ready to sign treaties of alliance and proceed to mobilize, undertook the Carpathian adventure, which was supposed to maintain the illusion that the Russians were making active preparations for a campaign against Hungary until Italy finally committed itself.

The staff, which comprehended all the military undesirability of this operation and the shortage of material for it (weapons, ammunition), overestimated the provocative importance of this Carpathian offensive to Italy, did not understand the significance of Italy's entry into the war for the Russian front and did not take drastic steps to halt General Ivanov's initiative. As a result, we paid a much higher price for Italy's entry into the war (by a breakthrough on the Danube at Gorlice) than Italy's participation in the war was worth.

On July 10, 1866, the Commander of the Prussian Main Army Falkenstein routed the Bavarians at Kissingen. It would have been natural to pursue the enemy. But Bismarck had reason to believe that military operations would be concluded a few days later and that the Prussians could not count on making any

---

[11] Falkenhayn, *Verkhovnoe komandovanie* [The High Command], p. 84.

acquisitions in Bavaria. Thus instead of pursuing the Bavarians toward Werzburg, at Bismarck's direct request Falkenstein moved in the opposite direction toward Frankfurt in order to capture this wealthy city, the cradle of the Rothschilds, until an armistice was signed. This kind of fighting for the "front-line map" is typical of the end of a war. The failure of certain Red Army officers to give adequate consideration to this led to our abandonment of certain points, including Lunints, on the eve of the conclusion of a truce with the Poles in 1920 and was obviously reflected in the Treaty of Riga.

Sometimes diplomacy is capable of keeping a third party neutral only if we respect his interests in conducting military operations, —e.g., by keeping military operations out of certain territories. For example, in 1912 Great Britain took on the obligation of defending French interests in the Atlantic Ocean and thus, even without engaging in war, it was restraining the German navy from undertaking hostile actions against France.[12] At the beginning of the war Italy demanded and received a guarantee of neutrality for the Suez Canal from the Central Powers and Turkey in exchange for its neutrality (with Great Britain standing behind it). The Turks attacked the canal only after Italy entered the war. While it was a neutral the United States greatly hampered the freedom of operation of the German U-boats and thus gained time for Great Britain to prepare for submarine warfare.

---

[12] At the beginning of the war in 1914 Great Britain demanded that Germany respect the neutrality of Belgium. The Prussian General Staff did not listen, because it believed that Belgium was just a pretext and that Britain would be drawn into the war no matter what. Nevertheless, the violation of Belgian neutrality was one of Germany's biggest political mistakes, a mistake which tied the hands of its friends and untied the hands of its enemies all over the world. Belgium owed its existence as a state to the consistent eight-century-old British policy of safeguarding the independence of the territory on the lower Schelde from any great power.

PREPARING THE ARMED FRONT

1. INITIAL PRINCIPLES

The Significance of the Armed Front

Mistaken views often lead to incorrect evaluations of individual fronts—economic, class and armed—of a war in such a way that the significance of different results of military operations is completely disregarded. The results of armed conflicts are assumed to be negligible a priori. We cannot help but consider this ideology fatal and hazardous, because it leads to indifference in military preparations and undermines moral flexibility in battle. It is on the armed front that history makes its evaluations of class consciousness and economic advances. The slightest consideration of dialectics will persuade us that in a war, events on the political and economic fronts do not develop in isolation but rather in close conjunction with the twists and turns of the armed conflict. We cannot help but emphasize French setbacks in the Seven Years' War as one of the causes of the French Revolution. In the eyes of the French bourgeoisie, these setbacks were evidence of the feudal nobility's failure in a historical test, a failure that put the issue of eliminating the hegemony of this class, which was unfit to rule, on the agenda. The Russo-Japanese War and Russian setbacks in the World War were the prologues to the two Russian revolutions. Likewise, the victory of 1871 and the catastrophe of 1918 were reflected on the German economic front in completely different ways.

One would have to be blind to deny that military operations constitute a naked form of violence and an appeal to force. The most immutable law of nature is the law of the powerful. There are no laws of constitutions that could grant exemptions from this law. "All human artifice cannot interfere with the violence of the strong against the weak."[1] The same philosopher added that "war is only the embodiment of events which have been predetermined by moral [we would say class or economic] causes, which are rarely noticed by historians.[2] The insignificance of military operations does not follow from this predetermination,

---

[1] Rousseau, *Politique* (1790 edition), vol. 8, pp. 396, 408.

[2] Ibid. (1793 edition), vol. 36, p. 382.

but just the opposite; for example, in a future war the Red Army will be tested not only on its own account but on behalf of the entire new social structure of the Soviet Union, the Russian Revolution and the self-consciousness of the working class.

Determining the relative significance of the armed front as opposed to the class and economic fronts and determining war preparation budgets accordingly are matters for the supreme authorities in a state. "Policy determines the strength of the armed forces, which must be maintained in peacetime or mobilized for war, and responsibility for this policy falls on the government."[3]

The War Plan and the Operational Plan

One essential characteristic of civil wars is the lack of systematic preparations for large-scale operations on the armed front. We cannot completely deny the existence of such preparations. The Poles, in preparing for an armed uprising against Russia in the 1860s, had schools to provide military training for command cadres in the Romance countries and published field service regulations in Polish. In 1923 the German working class organized the red hundreds, who tried to improve their combat readiness through regular military exercises.

Fascist organizations are also elements of military preparation for a civil war.

In the American Civil War we observe a unique situation in the winter of 1860-1861: the side preparing to rebel (the South) was in power for four months and would then have to turn it over to the already elected leader of the Northern Republicans, Abraham Lincoln, in 1861. In these conditions preparations for an armed rebellion became somewhat more systematic in nature: Minister of War Floyd transferred stockpiles of rifles from the North to the South, sold supposedly surplus rifles in Southern markets for arming Southern fighting squads, and because the class composition of the federal army made it inaccessible to Southern propaganda, Floyd ordered the withdrawal of garrisons from Southern coastal fortifications, leaving only a handful of guards there. Floyd sent most of the army to the Far West to fight Indians and to the desert, but the depots that had supplied these forces were located on Southern territory and their chiefs were loyal Southern agents, and when the uprising began these military units were powerless and were compelled to lay down their arms. By the time Abraham Lincoln took office Washington, the capital, had no military security whatsoever.

Right after the war began, the state of Kentucky tried to stay neutral. However, partisans on both sides immediately began making preparations just in case. The Southerners, who had the state government on their side, began to work on the organized militia. The supporters of the North, fearing a sudden St. Bartholomew's Night, began to gather in two camps far from the state capital and started getting arms from Northern states that had already entered the war. These developments made it impossible to stay neutral, and Kentucky was divided between the hostile sides.

In studying the Civil War in Russia, of course we will find elements of military preparation in an analysis of the October Revolution and in an analysis of the actions of Krasnov's, Kornilov's and the Czechs. However, despite a certain tendency for preparations to become more extensive, the preparations of an armed

---

[3] *Angliiskii polevoi ustav 1920* [British Field Regulations 1920], Part 2, section 4, paragraph 3.

front in a civil war are sporadic in nature by necessity, particularly in comparison with the scale of the political preparations for a civil war. In principle civil wars are waged on the ruins of national military preparations: weapons, communications equipment, arsenals, depots, fortresses, barracks, defense plants, regulations and military skills are all borrowed from the results of preceding military preparations, and only gradually, in the course of the civil war itself, do the armed forces of the sides take root and the sides begin to take steps to build an army of a given class. Initially, despite the new principles on which the army is built, the new spirit and the completely different slogans, we must resort to someone else's forms, and years will pass before we can replace them with our own which we have developed for the conditions.

This characteristic of a civil war leads to a situation in which the capability of armed forces for strategic efforts builds up only gradually, and the peak of strategic intensity, despite any desire to employ a strategy of destruction, comes long after an uprising has begun. The combat-readiness of the Red Army was much higher in 1919 than it was in 1918 and continued to improve subsequently.

If we have to wage war against a foreign enemy prepared to make a major strategic effort several weeks after a break, it would be extremely irrational to count on being able to organize a defense in the process of the war itself.

In order to win victory with a minimum of national manpower and resources, we must rationalize the use of all the military opportunities that turn up. A framework must be created in which the energy of the ruling class and all the resources of the state could quickly and appropriately go to the armed front. An extensive system of steps is required to prepare the state for armed conflict. In addition to political and economic war plans, we need a purely military plan tied by many threads to politics and economics.

Until the 19th century war plans and specific military preparations commenced only when politics presented a state with a specific hostile faction. But it was the 17th century that led to the creation of standing armies, and left us Montecuccoli's precept that the conclusion of peace should not mean the liquidation of the military organization but should constitute merely the beginning of preparations for a new war. But these preparations only involved maintaining a standing army and certain stockpiles and building fortresses on threatened borders and were quite general in nature. Following Louis XIV's example, the German princes tried to build six-inch guns, not considering the fact that they would not have to lay siege to fortresses and they did not have the paved roads and canals which covered Northern France and the Netherlands. Preparations for war were not governed by clear operational thinking, they were abstract in nature, and did not reckon with the requirements of a future war.

In 1802 a colonel on the Russian general staff, one Massenbach, proposed that, regardless of our good or poor political relations with our neighbors, we should have annual campaign plans in the event of a conflict with any one of them. His proposal, which was initially rejected, was implemented after Napoleon was toppled. At its congresses the Holy Alliance devised intervention plans in the event of a new outbreak of revolution in France, and the Prussian general staff included French, Austrian and Russian departments, military agents were appointed, and statistical, intelligence and reconnaissance activities commenced.

Railroads, which greatly accelerated the development of the initial phase of military operations, made it necessary for all states to work on issues related to the commencement of operations in peacetime and to orient their peacetime preparations accordingly.

Whereas the dawn of capitalism witnessed the inauguration of standing armies which were not fully disbanded after peace had been concluded, the flowering of imperialism has extended the requirement of war preparation to all sectors of state activity. Now we must draw a clear line between the war plan, which governs the military preparations of the entire state as a whole for creating an armed front, and the operational plan, or as it is frequently called, the campaign plan, which is the plan for preceding to initial military operations. Whereas a war plan is primarily a program for the development of the armed forces and resources of a state over several years, the operational plan is only a small but very important part of the war plan which indicates how we must operate at any given moment in the event of war with the actual forces and resources at our disposal. From the operational plan follows the missions assigned to the armed forces during a war. Analysis of the missions indicates the discrepancy between them and the war preparations that have already been made, and thus the operational plan to a significant extent gives meaning to subsequent preparations and the content of the entire war plan. From the operational plan we can arrive at conclusions concerning the required amount of armed forces and the nature of their organization, weapons and training to achieve our war aims quickly; the needed improvements in the organization of the theater of war with respect to lines of communication and the construction of permanent fortifications; the necessary changes in mobilization orders; the stockpiles which are particularly important; and the intelligence data which are of particular interest.

Working on the operational plan and war plan and carrying out the directives which follow from them are of great importance to the outcome of foreign wars and constitute the mission of the general staff in peacetime. If we have allies, this work is complemented by work on the intelligent coordination of war plans and, in particular, the operational plans of allied states (see the section on Military Conventions in Chapter 5 above). However, a war plan as a whole covers such extensive areas that only the supreme authorities can take responsibility for it. A general staff is only a tool that presents its ideas to the supreme authorities.[4]

Several writers, following Sérigny, have attempted to differentiate between strategic work on the war plan and work on conducting military operations, calling the former a science and the latter an art. Whereas in waging a war one must make decisions in far from clear situations, in the dark, hastily and in a nervous atmosphere, in their opinion, work on the war plan is comparatively calm and based on relatively hard facts, the analysis it contains makes it scientific in nature and it tries to predict and cover everything and in principle avoids any improvisation. That is why the writers of treatises on strategy who have appeared in the last decade have shifted the center of gravity of their treatises to so-called

---

[4] "Responsibility for the war plan (adoption, modification, revision) lies with the government, which approves it and in principle takes on the responsibility of providing the necessary forces and resources for its execution." Ibid., Part 2, chapter 2, section 4, paragraph 6.

preparatory operations and have only very superficially analyzed the issues of waging war itself.

Of course we will admit that work prior to the declaration of war is done in a more academic atmosphere than when the guns start going off. But we deny that there is any fundamental difference. Both kinds of work are not based on any principle; they are based on our conceptions of the nature of a future war and the appropriate harmonization of all the preparations and operations of the armed front. A mistaken conception of a future war will put both preparations and execution on the wrong track. In addition, as the reader will see, we, on one hand, indicate the need to extend several aspects of preparation far into the war (for example, the need to mobilize in phases) and, on the other hand, we give maneuvering a wide berth as early as the period of operational deployment. The boundaries between preparations and execution have a tendency to become blurred. A war of attrition introduces into the conduct of war the same elements of long-term calculation which should penetrate the entire war plan.

The success of warfare depends to an equal extent on careful and attentive development of a plan of mobilization, concentration, manpower and logistics and the art of conducting operations.

Militarization

Political and economic plans are not limited to any single agency, and the political and economic directives that follow from them should permeate all governmental activity and be primarily compulsory for the military authorities. In the exact same way the war plan should never be limited to the army and the navy, because now the entire country takes part in a war, and military directives must be taken into consideration on a very broad front of state activity. For example, command schools will have to graduate hundreds of thousands of Red commanders in the course of a war, while the military authorities will only have a very few months to train them. Naturally the command schools will have to be attended by youngsters who have completed secondary school or even students in higher educational institutions. The educations the youths receive in the Commissariat of Public Education's schools will be greatly reflected in the qualities of the junior commanders the Red Army gets during the course of a war. Hence the country's war preparation plan cannot be indifferent to the activity of the Commissariat of Public Education. Thus it its necessary to study how we could improve the graduates of its schools in terms of military qualifications without distracting the commissariat from its main purposes by developing physical training, combatting pacifistic thinking, providing elementary military information, rifle training, if only under the banner of athletic clubs, indoctrinating them in the spirit of the Red Army and so forth.

Commanding the armed forces during a war and mobilization itself are very closely related to the development of a permanent telegraph system. The men of many military signal units will only be up to par if the People's Commissariat of Postal and Telegraph Services shares its proven and well-trained employees with the military and also provides material assistance, such as teletypes, in a mobilization and if in developing the peacetime telegraph system it keeps the requirements of war in mind.

Every offensive requires the repair of hundreds of railroad bridges and the linkage and organization of the operation of several thousand miles of track, tens of thousands of railroad agents, maintenance train, and a large number of rail cars. The very process of concentrating troops at borders once a war starts will require thousands of trains, and the delivery of rolling stock and the organization of traffic must be prepared in all details. This is made possible only through close coordination of the work of the military high command and the People's Commissariat of Railways.

All mobilization issues are closely related to the People's Commissariat of Internal Affairs because they require the energetic cooperation of the local administration. The question of draft deferments for essential employees affects the interests of all people's commissariats and so forth.

Given the gigantic scale of armed conflict, the military authorities cannot even think of making due with their own little People's Commissariat of Education in the form of a military school administration,[5] with their own communications administration, their own railroad troops and their own judicial system; they cannot organize themselves into a special state within a state, or rely on their own specialists and own supplies; they must prepare the entire country and all government agencies with their wealth of manpower for war. This is why the military high command must have permanent liaisons with the civil authorities for the purpose of advising them on military requirements.[6] And every higher civilian agency must have a department that represents military interests and makes preparations to get the agency on a war footing in order for it to meet the requirements made by a war.

The switch to territorial formations is a measure that primarily relies on the use of the manpower, resources, skills, specialties, knowledge and energy of the entire nation. The standing army can be reduced while building up the territorial units only if there is a simultaneous rise in the interest of the entire governing apparatus and the masses or workers and peasants in the military profession and national defense. Now, to a great extent, the plan of preparing a state for war is a plan for militarizing the state. We use the term despite its opprobrious connotations. Sometimes it is understood as the domination of military directives over the peaceful development of society and the concomitant hegemony of a military caste in a country. However, nothing could be further from the truth: the

---

[5] On the shield of Athena-Pallas the brilliant Thydius drew Pericles fighting the Amazons with a sword and himself in sculptor's clothes hurling pieces of marble at the attackers. Art joining its efforts to assist the civilian militiaman is an emblem of militarization that has existed for 2,360 years. Unfortunately in our time some cultural figures and artists have gone over to the Amazon camp rather than against them, calling all military men professional murderers.

[6] The list of issues which must be resolved by civil authorities in preparations for war is given quite completely in P. P. Lebedev's brochure entitled *Gosudarstvennaia oborona* [National Defense] (Moscow: Gosvoenizdat, 1924). The author also describes a system by which the war work of all civilian agencies could be organized: the Council of Labor and Defense, and the Secretariat of Defense of the Union as a whole, the Mobilization Committee, the mobilization agencies at central departments, local mobilization agencies and cells. However, we cannot agree with the organization suggested by the respected author. We do not need a sort of parliament of agencies which reflect all centrifugal tendencies like the Mobilization Committee does; we need a General Staff.

scope of activity of military specialists and standing armies can only be reduced by setting up military departments at universities, creating the hearts and minds of platoon leaders in persons studying accounting and other peaceful occupations and giving the entire population a taste for the military. That fervent hater of standing armies, Rousseau,[7] who called them "the pestilence and depopulation of Europe," focused our attention on the extraordinarily strong spirit of militarism in the only country in Europe that did not have a standing army—Switzerland— and considered it normal, and did not approve of the attempts of the federal government to dampen the martial ardor of its civilian militiamen.

The extensive militarization of all aspects of state and public activity is a law of modern war preparations. Woe to him to whom militarization is merely metaphysics.

However, some critics may find our definition of militarization too narrow. The center of gravity of our understanding lies in the militarization of civil agencies and the public and the greater ease of utilizing existing railways, telegraph systems and so forth associated with militarization. Others would like to put what we understand as forms of the war economy in the framework of militarization, namely the militarization of agriculture and the militarization of certain industrial sectors. We shall retain our narrower definition, because we also see the possibility of abusing this concept. In fact, the very concept of militarization grew out of the inability of one military authority to prepare for war in the 20th Century. In a certain interpretation, militarization may be understood as the bankruptcy of military authority, bankruptcy which has become a doctrine, which takes responsibility away from military men, makes it possible to substitute the paper obligations of different trusts for stockpiles and makes it possible to substitute paperwork for authentic material war preparations. The understanding of militarization as the bankruptcy of the military authority is even more dangerous because an economy drive can go too far, and the military budget could practically disappear and almost be totally swallowed up in maintaining military personnel. It seems to us that this would be a fatal interpretation of the experience of recent wars.

Intelligence

By their very essence, the war plan and campaign plan should not merely call for the absolute growth of the armed forces but should prepare them for the missions the army and navy will have to carry out once a war begins. Hence work on the war plan should be based on clarifying the nature of a forthcoming war and the characteristics of the enemy, which is why intelligence is so significant. It is quite important to gather information that characterizes the enemy's political situation, his relations with other states, the tendencies of certain classes and the intensity of the struggle between them, the enemy's overall economic situation and the special economic measures he has taken to prepare for war, and this information, supplemented by a study of the personalities of leading politicians, the history of the hostile state and the most authoritative opinions expressed in the press, make it possible to get an idea of the current economic and political policies of a state with whom war is possible and of how its ruling class pictures the

---

[7] Rousseau, *Politique* (1790 edition), vol. 8, Part 2, p. 397.

continuation of these policies once a war begins. Only on the basis of this general study will a study of the enemy's military capabilities be fruitful, and the latter should not be limited to getting an idea of the current strength of his armed forces and the accomplishments of his military preparations; it should also encompass the history of the growth of his army and the different phases of his resolution of war preparation issues. This study will allow a clearer view of the tendencies of his military development, the nature of his general staff's conceptions of a future war and recent assumptions concerning initial operations. For example, a study of the condition of German railways on the left bank of the Rhine at a certain moment down to the smallest details was still incapable of revealing the Schlieffen Plan before the World War. But study of the systematic development of the German railway system would have led to the discovery that most of the railroad platforms on the French border were built in the 1870s and 1880s, whereas at the beginning of the 20th century all of Germany's efforts were directed toward obtaining new outlets to the Belgian border and a large number of military platforms there and toward opening up new points for linking German railroads to Belgian railroads. If the data for the last 20 years before the war were juxtaposed with the fact that railroad construction on the French border had come to a halt during this period but the Germans had built up a large number of fortifications there, one could have already arrived at the conclusion that the Germans were planning an enveloping maneuver through Belgium. Any war plan is evident in certain aspects, but if we ignore the evolution of the preparations, we are faced with a jumbled mass of measures applying to different periods and reflecting different operational plans.

Particular attention must be given to the study of the military budget and the priceless commentaries on it provided by budget talks in parliamentary commissions and full sessions n parliamentary countries. A critical comparison of a number of budgets will make it possible, despite all efforts to conceal secret measures, to make a number of important inferences and evaluate the tendencies of military preparations.

A characteristic error of general staffs before the World War was to study the enemy on an excessively narrow, purely military basis. They studied the smallest details pertaining to the forces of the state that had already been organized for the war and completely ignored latent forces. Sufficient attention was not paid to the enemy's economic capabilities and the configuration of his industrial centers. The history of the state in question was completely ignored. Notions of political factions were limited to conversations on the growth of the German Social Democratic Party. These excessively narrow views, this lack of education and the resultant tendentiousness was clearly evident in the work of intelligence agencies. As early as the end of 1914 the French general staff announced that the Germans had exhausted their manpower because they overestimated German casualties by a factor greater than two.

A lack of education leads to the overestimation of Pinkerton intelligence techniques. While a great deal of very important data published in the press (in the USSR, for example, many articles in *Ekonomicheskaia zhizn'* [Economic Affairs]) are not given proper attention, every piece of paper marked "Secret" obtained by secret agents in a hostile state is considered an important intelligence coup, although it may be a mere circular with good intentions which is completely divorced from reality. Before the World War the Russian general staff was highly successful at acquiring the contents of the safes at German provincial headquarters, and in Vienna they succeeded in penetrating the central secret treasurehouse. The basic documents of the Austrian plan of deployment fell into the hands of Russian photographers. But because Konrad changed this plan before the war, the intelligence data confused the Russian command more than helped it. At the same time the scores of Russian agents caught by the Germans every year had a perceptibly negative effect on diplomatic relations.

Experience teaches that we must be extremely careful in the classification process in order to provide effective security for important military secrets. Russian two-kilometer secret maps were purchased by the Germans for the modest price of 35 marks, while the Russian general staff knew of the German collection plans with a list of the sheets which they still needed. At present all our neighbors are fully aware of this secret and it is completely worthless on the espionage market, but our maps are still secret...

We repeat: intelligence primarily requires persons of the highest qualifications in the economic, political, historical and strategic sense, truly refined scholars who have immersed themselves in the study of a certain state. All the prewar general staffs suffered from a lack of such people. Without them intelligence work on a war plan is reduced to a kind of Pinkerton joke.

A state which cannot rely on the use of allied intelligence and is condemned to live by its own wits must focus particular attention on gathering intelligence.

2. BUILDING THE ARMED FORCES

The Political Basis of an Army

"The mission of the army is lofty and noble; an army should not stoop to the level of political parties." This idealistic formula was generated by French hypocrisy in 1872 and owes its origin to the creativity of the old Bonapartist Chaslou-Leba, who reported the basic law on the French Republican Army in parliament. The French Third Republic inherited an army whose cadres consisted of monarchist and Bonapartist elements. The reactionary elements were firmly counting on the army to attempt a coup at an appropriate time and found a fig leaf in this formula in order to justify anti-Republican commanders at the head of a Republican Army.[1] General Boulanger, who had been appointed the minister of war, devoted his first speech in parliament to the apolitical character of the army and immediately proceeded to prepare a coup.

Apoliticism[2] is difficult to imagine even among mercenaries tied to the state solely by monetary interests: even declasse soldiers are compelled by the course of events to become representatives of certain interests. An army cannot help but be a reflection of the class factions existing in a country, and elementary logic demands that the ruling class guide the thinking of the army in accordance with the requirements of its policies. The living conditions of standing armies offer extensive opportunities to do this. In Switzerland, England and the United States even the militia is far from apolitical and constitutes an energetic reflection of the class views of the bourgeoisie.

There is no doubt that the morale of an army is based on economics, and the political ideology of an army should have a certain relationship to the economic base. In the era of the natural economy the predominance of and hierarchically ordered land ownership, the knights were united solely by a spirit of feudal loyalism. A vassal was obligated by loyalty to his lord and did not know what a fatherland was. As late as 1549 a French writer stated, *qui a pays, n'a que faire de patrie* (he who has a native land needs no fatherland).[3] The province is juxtaposed to the rest of the world. During the World War we heard an echo of this world view: "We are Kalugans."

The capitalist era introduced the concept of patriotism to replace feudal loyalty. *Patrios* means both paternal and fatherland. The concepts of fatherland and inherited property form a single patriotic sense in bourgeois ideology which

---

[1]   V. Dupuis, *La direction de la guerre* (Paris: 1912), pp. 345-351.

[2]   In ancient Greece the word *Idiotes* meant an inhabitant who was ignorant of and not interested in state affairs (see, for example, Heise, *Fremdwoerterbuch*, 16th edition (1879), p. 446) and also a lower class person deprived of political rights. In view of the high level of political consciousness and the intensity of the political struggle in Athens, the word *idiot*, instead of its initial meaning of apoliticism, came to mean a stupid person, because, in the Greeks' opinion, one has to have a radical shortage of brainpower not to be interested in politics.

[3]   The citation belongs to Charlieu Fontaine. See Alphonse Aulard, *Le patriotisme français de la Renaissance á la Révolution* (Paris: 1921).

demands the defense of the position of the ruling classes in a state. Patriotism is related to a certain territory bounded by the borders of a state, and is intensified by nationalism, which is based on the notion of the unity of a certain segment of the population speaking the same language; nationalism is opposed to the concept of world citizenship and humanism and involves a chauvinistic faith in the superiority of one's own culture, one own material strengths, intelligence and character. The growth of local capital is often a precondition for nationalism. This is possibly the basis for the current wave of nationalism in Asia.

Patriotism is still the foundation on which national armies are constructed. But in other armies, particularly in civil wars, when the class struggle takes on acute forms, ideology is based on class feelings rather than patriotism.

It is impossible to provide any hard and fast prescription for selecting the foundations on which to build one's armed forces. The army should grow completely out of a given state. Of eternal value is the advice given 150 years ago to the Poles, who were facing the threat of partition:

> By its nature, administration, laws and language the Polish nation not only differs from its neighbors but from all other European nations. We would also like it to differ in terms of its military structure, tactics and disciplines and like it to be itself rather than something else. Only then will it become everything it can be and extract all the resources which it can possess from itself.[4]

Building an army in any other way would be a mistake.

In the bourgeoisie armies in the World War the struggle for political enlightenment of the army was quite halfhearted; relying on the strength of military traditions and the political orientation given to youngsters in schools, the military limited itself to ineffective instruction in "military philology." The experience of the war and the intensity of the class struggle demonstrated that this decision was wrong. In 1917 Ludendorff[5] introduced classes on "patriotic education" in the German army at the front and in the rear. The commanders were poorly prepared to hold political talks with their soldiers, and after the war the Germans planned to introduce a compulsory nine-month course for young officers at universities at which they would become familiar with political, social and economic issues.[6] The Red Army is fully justified in paying a great deal of attention to the political training of its commanders and soldiers.

The policies pursued by a state require giving its armed forces an appropriate political physiognomy. There is no such thing as an army in general, but there are armies of certain states, certain eras and certain classes organized for certain missions.

A special form of subordinating the organization of armies to political requirements is the formation of military units of citizens of an enemy state on the basis of national traits, partly from political emigres, partly from politically indoctri-

---

[4] Rousseau, *Politique*, vol. 8, p. 396.

[5] Ludendorff, *Moi vospominaniia o voine 1914-1918* [My Memoirs on the War, 1914-1918], vol. 2 (Moscow: Vysshei voennyi redaktsionnyi sovet, 1924), pp. 48-52.

[6] Freitag-Loringofen, *Vyvody iz mirovoi voiny* [Conclusions from the World War], pp. 77-78.

nated prisoners of war and partly from irredentists. The best enemy forces Alexander the Great had to fight were the detachments of Greek Republicans who entered the Persian service when the Macedonians subjugated the Greek republics. In 1812-1813, at Stein's insistence, the Russian government was quite successful in organizing a German legion from defectors under the slogan of liberating Germany from the French yoke.

In the World War we encounter the formation of Czechoslovakian units on the Russian front out of Austrian prisoners of war and the disintegration of Austrian sovereignty made it possible for the Entente to reinforce the Serbian army with prisoners of war from the southern Slavic regions of Austria. Austria-Hungary, which had begun to form Polish legions with Pilsudski's assistance, from the very beginning of the war took the same path regarding tsarist Russia. This beginning was not too successful, because Pilsudski's legions were primarily formed by transferring Poles from other Austrian regiments and persons with Austrian military obligations, while the profound contradictions between the interests of the Polish and German bourgeoisie and Russian promises of autonomy kept Poles who were Russian subjects from joining Pilsudski's legions en masse.

Morale

The basic source of a soldier's morale is the conscientious attitude toward war of the class to which he belongs, or the alteration of his consciousness by the state, insofar as the latter is able to accomplish this. A standing army, with its traditions and its firm barracks discipline, is a powerful tool for altering human consciousness. However, this alteration requires a lot of time and is possible only on a limited scale. Modern warfare, which requires millions of men for mobilization and for reinforcing the armed front, cannot rely solely on the consciousness artificially created in the barracks, and only if the purposes of a war are clearly understood and close to broad segments of the public can we count on the armed forces fighting for long periods of time with a great deal of enthusiasm and pertinacity. If this is not the case, we would observe phenomena similar to those which took place in the Austrian infantry: Austrian infantry units fought quite well in the first battles, but as soon as combat operations wiped off the barracks greasepaint, as soon as the cadres fell, as soon as the units were diluted with new men and as soon as the armed nation began to appear on the front, the combat-readiness of the Austrian infantry dropped quickly and abruptly and it members began surrendering en masse. We observed the same phenomenon, albeit on a smaller scale, in the old Russian army.

Despite the anarchy of this phenomenon, the outstanding qualities of the commanders, firm discipline in units, the organization evident in all actions, the successful progress of military operations and the obvious advisability of orders issued by the chiefs are greatly responsible for the authority of command and can not only maintain but raise the level of morale. The extreme diversity of commanders in the old Russian army also led to extreme differences in the morale of different regiments: next to the units who were just waiting in line to surrender or run off, there were units who were capable of operating well in a situation of maximum tactical stress. Intelligence in supply and distribution, material satisfaction, concern for the preservation of human lives, putting the common good ahead of personal egoism and the explicit recognition of the negligibility of all personal attitudes as opposed to the requirements of the nation generate a high level of moral stability in wartime. In its own order and particularly in the self-sacrifice of its commanders, an army is capable of generating a powerful moral momentum. In modern times the issue of command cadres and their reinforcements is extremely important.

Modern military technology, which requires working around different kinds of long-range and close-range military equipment, is also a source for the consolidation of order, and a certain amount of morale is generated in the process of the labor it mechanizes.

However, this idea should not be developed to the extent of a unique military Fordism which puts organization and equipment ahead of the people in the organization who operate this equipment. War is not simply the mass production of automobiles. The dream of a technology that would dominate the battlefield and crowd out the person was born in the brain of a bourgeois philosopher of a nation deprived of the "gift of women," namely numerous births, at the time of the commencement of the revolutionary upheavals caused by the World War:

> now weaponry is attempting to replace combatant, and we could predict a time when a dying machine will replace a warrior in the same way that coal replaced the slave. On this day the current million-man armies will be replaced by small teams of specialists trained to control gigantic machines of destruction.[7]

In evaluating the relationship between man and technology, we must take into consideration our experience of the Russo-Japanese War, in which victory was achieved by our opponent, who was no wealthier or more technologically developed than we were. Strategic thinking can only go along with the opinion of a financier who studied the Russo-Japanese War:

> We should not think that the significance of the human being and everything directly associated with him has diminished as a result of massive technological development Such a notion would be even more mistaken than the notion that the economic evolution of handicrafts into mass production involved the crowding out of people by machinery. The multiplicity of human material, human physical capacity for work and training, human morale, organization, discipline and leadership are all factors that cannot be replaced by any technical equipment, whether it be machinery in industry or battleships and guns in war. The sense of technology lies in enhancing and multiplying the effectiveness of these factors rather than in eliminating them.[8]

We should not always seek the causes of lowered morale outside the activity of the armed front itself and ascribe it, for example, solely to enemy agitation. A number of stupid steps taken by Nivelle and the poor organization of the April offensive in 1917, which was obvious to everybody, led to a loss of command authority in the French army and revolutionary outbreaks. The latter were ascribed to the hostile agitation of German agents. But the German command not

---

[7]   Gustave Le Bon, *Premieres conséquences de la guerre* (Paris: 1917).

[8]   Karl Helferich, *Das Geld im russisch-japanischen Kriege* (Berlin: 1906).

only found out about this ferment much later, and Ludendorff used this as a justification for not going on the offensive on the French front in May 1917 and not taking advantage of the enemy's temporary weakness.

Quantity and Quality

A state may have a smaller army which is better supplied and trained or a larger army of inferior quality. If the draft is in effect, the resources allocated by the state may be expended on a larger or smaller mass. Some states (e.g., France) use all of their combat capable population, while other states are faced with the issue of quantity and quality.

It is hardly true that there is such a thing as too many troops or troops who are too good. There is no such thing as too many crack troops. Charles XII, who invaded Russia, sank in the ocean of Russian land. His small crack army lost its lines of communication and perished at Poltava because of its inability to resist numbers. On the other hand, Napoleon, who organized the invasion of Russia by an army numbering 500,000, erred in the opposite direction. Many elements of this horde were completely unreliable; ten percent of his regiments consisted wholly of deserters and convicts; Napoleon was guided by a limitless contempt for human morals because he believed that anyone could be made into a hero. And this horde was much too large for the scant resources of Lithuania and Belorussia, the area of the Smolensk Highway. The enemy, the Russian army, numbered only 150,000 and did not require the concentration of such vast forces, which could not be supplied from 800 kilometers away. A Napoleonic army half the size using the same local resources would have suffered much less deprivation. But the other half should not have been totally discarded: it could have been used to form second-echelon and reserve units and to occupy the rear and reinforce the first-echelon units. Napoleon's human material could have been used much more economically.

In 1812 Napoleon suffered from a shortage of replacements and rear units. The occupation of large areas required an appropriate number of men. After three and a half months of war, when Napoleon reached Moscow, he had travelled 800 kilometers from the Neman at Kovno, occupied 235,000 square kilometers, the total strength of his forces had decreased to 213,000 and there were 0.9 soldiers per kilometer of occupied territory. In 1870 Moltke began his operations with fewer troops than Napoleon had, 450,000, but despite the fierce battles, after three and a half months, when the Germans reached the banks of the Loire, his army had only decreased to 425,000, thanks to his good system of replacements; he only penetrated 235 kilometers into France, occupied a territory of 72,000 kilometers and had six German soldiers per kilometer of occupied territory, that is, almost seven times more than Napoleon had and twelve times more than Tukhachevskii had in 1920 on the Vistula (an advance of 550 kilometers, 190,000 square kilometers of occupied territory and no more than 95,000 Red Army soldiers there).[9] This explains the strength of Moltke's position near Paris in 1870 and Napoleon's weakness.

Reality provides a very firm answer to the question: one should not sacrifice quality or quantity too much. The operations of a large state against Moscow or

[9] Jork von Wartenburg, *Napoleon I, als Feldherr*, vol.I, pp. 160-161; von der Golz, *Krieg und Heerfuehrung*, p.60; A. Svechin, "Opasnye illiuzii," [Dangerous Illusions] *Voennaia Mysl' i Revoliutsiia*, no. 2 (March 1924), p. 51.

Warsaw would require penetrating 550 to 750 kilometers into the enemy country and occupying 200 to 300 thousand square kilometers of territory. This is a mission that an army of closer to a million than a half million men could accomplish,[10] and even if destruction techniques were employed, it would take at least ten to 12 weeks during which appropriate reinforcements would have to be dispatched. Quality also must not be lowered below a certain limit of combat readiness, and any troops below this level would be mere ballast and would resemble the long-gone Chinese horde of the "green flag."

In the 18th century, which was characterized by high quality marching, everyone preferred quality over quantity. As late as 1877 the Russian command made a gross error by beginning military operations with insufficient forces. The setbacks at Plevna compelled the Russians to triple the size of their army in four months, from eight divisions to 25. From 1878 to 1901 the Russian army conducted an equally unjustifiable drive for quantity. The experience of Manchuria, which gave evidence of a lack of quality, compelled them to think a bit. From 1905 to 1913 the size of the Russian army remained the same, although military expenditures were increased significantly. In the World War we allowed poorly trained and equipped units without adequate cadres to go to the front. Ludendorff's attempts in 1917 to increase the number of divisions in the German army were also unjustified.

At the height of the Civil War, in the first half of 1919, the central logistics agency raised the issue of reducing the Red Army, it seems, from 56 to 27 divisions, in view of the need to bring the regular complement of the army and the possibilities for their provision in line with each other. It seems to us that the size of the divisions should have been cut in half. The somewhat careless dismissal of this proposal led to a situation in which the strength of the army decreased anarchically rather than systematically in line with its economic basis, and this anarchic reduction extended to the most precious working elements of the army, the line infantry, while the swollen rear was untouched.

We should keep in mind that current tactical tendencies associated with the refinement of weapons and a change to group procedures require a special emphasis on quality. A well trained soldier with good weapons has enormous advantages over a poorly trained and equipped soldier. General Langula even formulated the superiority of quality over quantity as a law of historical development after the Russo-Japanese War. It is particularly important for an economically poor state to avoid pursuing quantity at the expense of quality. A bad soldier has the same stomach, takes up just as much room in a railcar and requires the same number of noncombatants as a good soldier. But he is much more expensive when a war begins because he expends ammunition much less economically, and an automatic weapon in his hands is a terrible tool of extravagance. All items of supply are destroyed with surprising mercilessness in a bad company, because a bad company is a leaky sieve which is always ragged and weaponless because it sells its equipment and loses overcoats and shoes, leaves weapons and telephones in the battlefield, and it is more gluttonous, because it falsifies its strength and demands excess rations. It expends just as much effort as a good company in

---

[10] Of course, by counting on sympathetic attitude on the part of certain classes of the population in the occupied regions one may significantly effect a reduction of this number.

kicking up mud on the roads or shivering in the rain but fills the hospitals with many more wounded, completely exhausts local resources, disgusts the local population and suffers heavy casualties in battle (including self-inflicted casualties). A bad company can melt away like ice in the summer, and while it expends a vast amount of lives, health and efforts, it does very little useful work. Everything is spent on overcoming internal frictions and fighting figments of a sick imagination rather than the actual enemy. It takes a very wealthy country to fight a modern war with bad troops. What are troops who have bad attitudes and are poorly trained worth in war?

Nevertheless, armies have gotten larger. In the war of 1870 Germany mobilized 3.5 percent of its population, while in the World War Germany, France and Austria mobilized 20 percent of their populations. The answer to our question should be stated as follows: warfare requires an adequate number of high-quality troops. Relying exclusively on quality is hazardous to the extent that over the course of a prolonged war the combat value of the combatants has a tendency to even out, because inferior troops gradually become battle hardened and learn the enemy's tricks, while the better troops are gradually diluted with increasingly inferior replacements. That is why the better armies are drawn to a strategy of destruction in order to take advantage of their qualitative superiority.

Small States

Because they naturally desire to be compared with large states, achieving more appearances than results, small states always tend to organize armies whose numbers are greater than the economic capabilities of their rears. In no way do their armies meet the requirements of a major war. All of their munitions, equipment and uniforms could be swallowed up by a single major operation. Replacements dry up very quickly. In the Balkan war of 1912 the Serbs were left without rifles and the Bulgarians were left without overcoats, and Russia provided extensive aid to both of them at different times. The fate of the armies of small states in the World War was to shrivel up and be swallowed up by large allies. Serbia dried up by early 1915. The Romanian army had to be reduced by more than half after three months of war because in some divisions only the headquarters were left. The division of Europe into a number of small states and its Balkanization by the Versailles Treaty naturally led to an increase in the total strength of the armed forces maintained in peacetime and deployable in wartime and an increase in military expenditures. But it would be a mistake to calculate the forces of an alliance of small states by adding up the figures indicating the strengths of their armies. In the flame of war small states burn up very quickly. Their armies, which are only capable of staying in the field for several weeks, are merely vanguards which can gain time for the intervention of the great powers. For them a half a year of war is conceivable only with abundant economic support from abroad. Their offensive capabilities are especially low. Their attention is absorbed by the unresolvable problem of defending themselves on their own, and their parochial interests are incompatible with offensive preparations. The Sava River constituted an insurmountable obstacle for Serbia in the World War. In the spring of 1915 when Italy entered the war, Austria-Hungray moved five divisions from the Serbian front to Izontso. In order to cover Austria-Hungary on the Sava and the Danube, Germany transferred a formation of three new German divisions to this region adjacent to Serbia. This pitiful force proved to be effective. In the process we must keep in mind that the Serbians in and of themselves were splendid soldier material. Austria-Hungary covered its Black Mountain border with a number of blockhouses, which would have been ridiculous against any other enemy and merely reinforced its border guard to a certain extent.

The Regular Army and Partisans

In terms of their relation to the executive authorities of a state, armed forces are clearly divided into two categories. Regular forces[11] are unwavering executors of the orders of the executive authorities. Guerrillas may be characterized as fellow travellers.

The French Revolution, which moved the masses to the forefront of the historical arena, opened up a great deal of room for the participation of partisans in warfare. Napoleon eliminated the Spanish regular army with one stroke of his pen, but was not able to handle the popular movement and the partisans. In the Tyrol a popular uprising gave him a great deal of trouble. In 1812 Russian partisans turned the failure of Napoleon's campaign into a disaster. In 1813 extensive partisan activity developed in Germany.

Over the last century the role of partisans has decreased to very modest dimensions. The most important reason for this is universal military service which drew in to the ranks of the regular army an increasingly larger percentage of young men, and thus left worthless material for the recruitment of partisan detachments. On the other hand, in the conditions of current economic development, partisan operations closely tied to the sympathies of the peasant masses could easily become a kind of class warfare, which both hostile sides feared equally. There were a great many young Frenchmen left in the departments captured by the Germans in 1870 because far from all the population was liable for military service, and these young men formed *franc-tireur* (free riflemen) detachments which were quite worrisome to the German command but also caused panic among the French petit bourgeoisie because their actions were sometimes directed not only against the Germans but also against the kulaks. At the beginning of the World War Belgium used only a small portion of the population for its armed forces, and in the earliest moments of the German occupation there were extensive armed attacks on German logistics and individual German soldiers which compelled the Germans to take severe reprisals, all the way up to burning down entire villages; the Germans coped with the movement, but at the price of measures which gave the Entente a great deal of material for agitation against "German barbarism."

---

[11] We can include in their numbers militias, although in the past, and in several states still today, militias have been chartered by the executive authorities: for example, in many instances militias according to their charters may be employed only for defensive warfare within a state or even within the limits of their own province. Legally militias should have been classified as an intermediate category between regular units and partisans. However, all state authorities have become so strong that in the event of war they completely disregard the prerogatives of militias, and on the basis of public opinion they can compel the militias themselves to request the temporary suspension of their privileges. The British militias even travelled to South Africa to the Boer War. During the World War the Germans made no distinction between reservists, *Landwehr* forces, and *Landsturm* forces.

Currently, in several states (e.g., Germany) military service has been violently abolished and we can envision a rebirth of the basic conditions for the extensive development of partisan movements. The underground organizations which now exist in peacetime constitute splendid cadres for partisan detachments. On the other hand, the naked class character of future wars will undoubtedly intensify partisan actions as exemplified by the experience of the Civil War of 1918-1920 (in the Ukraine, Siberia, Belorussia, and so forth).

A future war will cause acute class conflicts in all hostile states and will undoubtedly be waged not only by regular units but by a large number of partisan fellow travellers. However, it would be a gross error to overestimate the possibility and importance of the latter and slacken our efforts to prepare regular armed forces. The 20th century has paved the way for organization, discipline and cohesion and for fighters who are under firm guidance and obediently direct their efforts toward a goal rather than for fellow travellers, be they whimsical, impressionable or accidental, but always untrained, unequipped and understanding their missions in different ways.

Partisans, as fellow travellers, are generally useful in the strategic underground, i.e., the enemy's rear. In the same territory, if it is seized by our forces, they could do more harm than good and become dangerous; and everything that is valuable within their ranks should be incorporated in a regular organization as quickly as possible.

Recruitment

The nature and forms of recruitment are extremely important for strategy. In medieval days the most important part of the army, the heavy cavalry, was manned primarily by the ruling class, the feudal elite. Therefore, although victory was not always followed up by pursuit and both the victors and vanquished went home after a battle, battles were nevertheless politically important. In Russian history the bourgeoisie has almost never joined the army, which undoubtedly had to be reflected in the less businesslike formulation of the art of war in Russia. The gray peasant hordes of the Russian regiments were reflected in the less economical expenditure of human material.

We have already discussed the necessary limitations of the use of the working class for manning the army. But in the same way that the old Russian army could have used "broken horses"[12] and sons of the bourgeoisie in the ranks of a peasant army, which would have improved its tactical characteristics, made it more flexible and enhanced the sense of responsibility of the commanders, the Red Army needs a certain percentage of workers. In discussing an economic mobilization plan, we must reach an agreement concerning the sacrifices of skilled manpower that industry will have to make. There is no doubt that we will have to be quite economical with it.

We shall only dwell on the quantitative aspect of this issue, which has a significant effect on strategy.

---

[12]   In the 16th century this was the name given to poor French knights who on orders from the king took off their armor, abandoned their horses and went to serve as privates in an infantry assembled from adventurers and professionals in order to tie these bands to the consciousness of the ruling class and make them a more obedient tool. At that time discipline and appointed commanders were still foreign concepts for the infantry.

Gustavus Adolphus had 10,000 new recruits a year, primarily provided by the Swedish peasantry, and other monarches, who were completely dependent on the supply of recruits in the marketplace, were quite envious of him. Frederick the Great, who had organized an energetic and diversified network of *agents provocateurs* (the official French title of recruiters) and took advantage of canton obligations, could count on 15,000 recruits per year, not counting prisoners of war. Because of the lack of reserve units, the recruits were trained by the regiments themselves at winter quarters. Incidentally, the battle at Zorndorf against the Russians took 18,000 from Frederick's army, while the battle at Kunersdorf took 25,000. If a battle lasting several hours could swallow up a half a year's supply of manpower, this should have led strategy to greater caution in resorting to battle and a preference for maneuver as a means of achieving the aim of the war.

The French Revolution put a vast amount of human material at the disposal of the state for waging war and made it possible to move battles to the forefront and pursue a strategy of destruction. Napoleon was called a general who swallowed up 3,000 men a day by the people who hated and envied him.

In 1870 the Germans had 25 percent at full strength trained in the rear for the active army. Despite the fact that the experience of the war soon revealed the inadequacy of this figure, by the early 20th century the generally accepted standard was the formation of reserve infantry units with a strength 25 percent of that of the active army.

The importance of this issue was underestimated in the Russian army. In particular, major reductions were allowed to occur in the Far East, where the plan called for a mere 11 reserve battalions plus the eight battalions of the Siberian Military District. This standard was not met either by the addition of third battalions to Siberian infantry regiments or by the reinforcement of local forces with new units (brigades of the 10th and 17th Corps). There was only one battalion per division. Transports, hospitals and bakeries, in other words, the entire logistical system, had to be manned at the expense of this paltry manpower. Some of the reserve battalions had to be brought up to a strength of 14 companies, which was clearly reflected in their training. An additional six battalions had to be formed in August 1904, 27 battalions had to be formed in October and 96 had to be formed in December. As a result, our infantry units were far under strength at very important moments: after Liaoyuan the army was 48,000 men short, and it only got 4,000 new men plus 5,000 recovered wounded; after the battle on the Sha Ho River 86,000 men were lacking and after Mukden this figure rose to 146,000, and only by the time peace had been concluded had this manpower shortage been practically eliminated (reduced to 8,000). The entire issue of manpower was resolved by groping in the dark, and before the war began nobody imagined that the war budget in Manchuria would require 30,000 men a month. A total of 158,000 replacements had to be sent to Manchuria, 5 percent of whom never got there and 6.5 percent of whom were swallowed up by the rear. The misunderstandings caused by an incorrect accounting of the need for reserve units would have led to even graver results if there had not been the possibility of getting help from the idle part of the army in European Russia: only 59 percent were in reserve units, 11 percent were draftees in European regiments and 30 percent were new recruits trained by the European regiments.[13]

The Russian army went into the World War without enough reserve units: it planned on having no more than 190 reserve battalions. In this respect the Russian general staff had committed a gross error and for some reason never even considered the lessons of the Russo-Japanese War. Only one- fifth of the entire Russian army took part in the Russo-Japanese War, while in a general mobilization they should have counted on a number five times greater than that required in that war. At the very beginning of the war they had to increase the number of reserve battalions by 160.[14]

The manning of the German army in the World War is very instructive. We have already discussed one aspect of this issue, namely the mistaken conscription of workers and the need to release them from the front gradually. Reserve units in the rear amounted to a single battalion per active regiment, and in view of the formation of new forces improvised during the war, the number of reserve units had to be doubled. In addition, field recruit depots that included 2,000 men each were formed for the first line corps on the Western Front. These reserve units proved to be very convenient, not only because they enabled immediate replacement of a corps' losses but also because they were run by commanders taken from active units and thus their training could be tailored to meet the requirements of the war. In the rear reserve units the cadres were very ignorant of the new tactical conditions, and while they attempted to teach combat operations involving the use of certain groups and techniques used in crack storm troops, this training, which was based on a lack of experience, led to a caricature of tactics and to the development of a false conception of battle among the reservists, causing them to pick up improper fighting techniques. In the fall of 1917 Ludendorff was compelled to prohibit these useless attempts on the part of rear reserve units and limit their program to elementary rifle training and instruction in the principles of military service. The strength of the corps depots was increased to 4,000, tank depots were organized for all corps and separate divisions and, in addition, large front depots were organized at camps near Warsaw and Benerloo (in Belgium), which received about 25,000 men per month from rear corps districts. Four weeks of training in rear reserve units befire transfering the conscripts to front-line reserve units was considered sufficient.

---

[13] Voenno-istoricheskaia komissiia [The Military History Commission], *Russko-iapanskaia voina 1904-1905* gg. [The Russo-Japanese War of 1904-1905], vol. 7, Part 1, pp. 25-101.

[14] Miscalculation of the number of reserve battalions was based on the miscalculation of mobilization stockpiles. One of our reserve battalions was supposed to have twice the ordinary number of rifles, because replacements would have to take some of the weapons with them to the front. If the aforementioned 160 battalions had been taken into account in the plan, we would have had 350,000 extra rifles, which would have come in very handy in 1915. We are inclined to ascribe the poor handling of the issue of reserve units in the Russian army to the vastness of our territory which compels us to imagine every war more or less as waging war on one front, which involves only a part of our forces, while the other part is able to take on part of the functions of reserve units. We didn't even think of the World War. Because the interconnectedness of all interests in the era of imperialism will also make us prepare for global wars in the future, we should rule out the possibility of keeping some of the Red Army idle while others are fighting in our plans. But we can already discern an element of gross error in preparations for the World War from the fact that in mobilization order No. 6, which mobilized the Russian army for war with the Turks in 1877 (37 years before the World War), called for 199 reserve battalions, i.e., a score and a half more!

Despite the fact that reserve units had to provide more manpower in Germany than in Russia and that Prussia alone provided an average of 180,000 men a month in 1915 and 1916, 204,000 men a month in 1917 and 133,000 men a month in 1918, the comparatively moderate strength of reserve units, which fluctuated over the course of the war around 500-600,000 (a minimum of 388,000 in 1915 and a maximum of 720,000 in January 1916), draws attention to itself; this kind of moderate strength made it possible to train energetically and avoid taking excess manpower away from productive labor, while in Russia the millions of reservists in the rear highlighted the complete lack of flexibility on the part of the ministry of war. In Germany the strength of reserve units increased only by the time of the revolution, in November 1918, when the flow of reinforcements to the front had practically stopped and there were 1,044,000 men in reserve units, but only 75,000 of them were trained and physically fit for service on the front. Most of the reserve units were fit only for service in the rear or in work details (624,000), and only 32,000 of them were fit for dispatch. The reserve units were manned by cadres, the ill, persons temporarily assigned to war industry and new recruits born in 1900 who were conscripted in June. The reserve mechanism had ceased functioning.

If a good accounting of the wounded is made, one-third of the new men required by the front can be provided by recovered wounded, and this figure may go as high as half for the infantry, which suffers the greatest casualties, if military operations on the front do not (as took place in Germany in 1918) take a catastrophic turn.

Before the World War an agrarian perspective concerning manpower was predominant; not only was the birth rate lower in the large cities than in the country (117 births per 1,000 women as opposed to 168), but the city dwellers were less physically fit (before the war only 32 percent of the city dwellers were considered physically fit as opposed to 67 percent of the peasants). Given the rapid change in the percentages of urban and rural inhabitants in Germany (the peasantry accounted for 65 percent of the population in 1850 and only 28.6 percent in 1907), One should have expected a significant drop in the quality of manpower. However, reality proved otherwise. The agrarians had used these statistics to justify high grain tariffs in order to save the countryside from abandonment. Apparently peacetime standards for accepting workers in the army were overly strict.[15] With the lower physical requirements of wartime approximately 70 percent of the conscripts proved to be fit for service, including 60 percent for service in the active army, but because these figures included 30-to-40 year-old draftees, who accounted for most of the rejects, the fitness of 20-year-olds was even higher. German statistics on the war reveal no significant difference between the fitness of the urban population and the fitness of the rural population. If the urban population was weaker than the rural population, it was not by much; this can be judged by statistics on the physically weakest segment of the urban population, namely the Jews: of a total of 600,000 German Jews, 74,323 had been drafted by October 1916, only 17 percent were considered unfit for service, 50 percent were considered fit for service in the active army and 33 percent were considered fit for rear service.

---

[15]   These statistics were taken from Fuerst Buelow, *Deutsche Politik* (1916).

During each year of the war Germans drafted two age groups: one age group yielded 350,000 soldiers, that is, one-sixth of the yearly requirements for new men; and the draft age had already been lowered to 18 by 1917 and could not be lowered any more. In the last 16 months of the war the German army had to be satisfied with one year, which made the problem of manpower get much worse. Such steps as pardoning 1,500 men who had been deprived of their civil rights (apparently out of 300,000 criminals) and wanted to leave prison to go fight were of course incapable of helping.

The flexibility of German organization and the lack of stress on reserve units can be explained by the rights of corps districts to conscript on their own: initially depending on their requirements, they drafted entire classes, and only subsequently did the central authorities begin to equalize the conscription burden in different parts of Germany.

The strategic importance of a well-developed manpower system is obvious from the following data. In the Ivangorod-Warsaw operation the Russians succeeded in inflicting heavy casualties on Ludendorff's army, the Germans commenced a general retreat on October 27, 1914. and crossed the Silesian border on November 5, 1914. In the interval between November 5 and 10 the German corps were moved from Silesia to Hohensalz to a front between Torun and the Varta River, and five corps received 40,000 reinforcements,[16] i.e., German infantry units received reinforcements that accounted for practically 40 percent of their strength. On November 1, the German army, which was fresh and at full strength and did not seem like it had just been soundly thrashed, began the Lodz operation against the Russian armies, who were still not at full strength.

A smoothly functioning manpower system is largely responsible for the current difficulty of employing a strategy of destruction, because the rapid resurrection of the strength of an army after it has suffered casualties completely alters the significance of the battles of an operation. People die, are wounded, and are taken prisoner, but their units continue to live and receive fresh blood, and neither machine guns nor cannons are effective against them as long as the rear is not completely exhausted, on the condition that one avoids a repetition of an operation on the front like that at Cannae.

The experience of the Civil War has confirmed the conclusions of the World War concerning the advantages of frontline reserve units and has indicated the importance of volunteers in the theater of operations itself.

Large numbers of volunteers (in their own territory, of course) mainly indicate that universal military service does not provide adequate coverage of the population, and the large number of volunteers in Germany in the fall of 1914 primarily pointed out that inadequate war preparations, which covered only 70 percent of those fit for military service and did not exhaust all the draft-age men.

It was thoughtless of the German ministry of war to accept large numbers of volunteers below draft age (18 and 19 years old). In the battle on the Isère[17] and

---

[16] Wrisberg, *Heer und Heimat, 1914-1918*, p. 21.

[17] That is why Isère is called "the battle of the children," because a major role in this battle was played by new corps formed primarily from university students, gymnasium pupils and other volunteers. There were also a great many volunteers among the 40,000 recruits gathered from all over Germany for Ludendorff's army before the Lodz operation.

in the Lodz operation this flower of German youth was mowed down for no particular reason, and only a few of these underage bodies could withstand the severe conditions of the fall campaign, and future drafts were greatly weakened both quantitatively and, in particular, qualitatively.

It is clear that calculations of the enemy's reinforcement capabilities must have the same importance in our considerations as the forces he can immediately dispatch to the front. The use of automatic weapons gives rise to the need for automatic replacements.[18]

Organization

People who are inclined toward patterns try to bring their favorite theoretical constructs to life. But life has demonstrated that there are no ideal organizational schemes although there are schemes which more or less meet the requirements of a given case. There is no one definite answer even to the question of whether the number three or one is better in determining the hierarchical organization of the infantry. The need for infantry will undoubtedly be greater before the completion of economic mobilization than after it is completed when the front will receive more wire, ammunition and submachine guns.

Thus perhaps initially four battalions in regiments or four companies in battalions would be good, but by the end of the war they would probably become superfluous and it would be better to use them to form new divisions.

The organization of the Russian army in 1914 was based on the requirements of the Franco-Russian alliance, namely the requirement of being ready to cross the German border on the 15th day of the war. This was the reason for the increase in the standing army and its cadres, the complete disregard for the possibility of subsequent formations during the course of the war and the relative lack of concern for increasing reserves of trained men.

We in turn were concerned with the internal weakness of the French army, but Poincaré and Joffre promised and actually returned France from two years of compulsory service to three years.[19]

In all work related to the war plan most important is harmony among all measures: even the best ideas, if they are not in harmony with the situation, will do only harm. And the same harmony is required of organizational measures. Among other items, short terms of service require water mains, bathhouses and wood-cutting machinery. But if water has to be carried and wood has to be cut by hand and if a regiment has its own garden, longer terms of service are needed. The militia principle requires significant credits for training in order to make the army like a school. The purpose of the plan is to orchestrate and coordinate efforts.

Extensive adjustments have to be made because the gears of the mechanism must mesh. An abrupt break in any direction, for example, in the direction of developing exclusively territorial divisions while maintaining the same economy; the illiteracy of the countryside; the lack of culture; bad roads and so forth is an unstable and unharmonious organizational creation. And organizational har-

---

[18] In Germany the number killed in the World War amounted to 4.9 percent of the entire working-age population and the number maimed came to 3.7 percent. For France these figures are even higher: 5.3 percent killed and 5.6 percent maimed if we count women as part of the working-age population.

[19] Sukhomlinov's memoirs, p. 171.

mony must be linked to our general conceptions concerning the nature of a future war.

Current conditions of conducting an operation quite often require the formation of composite units. In battle reserves are improvised from certain sectors of the front where they are in excess. This stems from the duration of modern armed clashes. In the battle on the Sha Ho River General Kuropatkin was able to improvise a new reserve of 40 battalions, and not only did this help in taking Putilov Hill and turning a battle that had already been lost into a toss up, it also opened a new operational page.

A distinctive feature of the Germans in the World War was that the composite divisions and corps they formed by taking a battalion here and a battalion there from the entire front held their ground on the defensive almost as stubbornly as normally organized units. In September 1915 the Germans stopped a breakthrough in Champagne with a corps of 20 battalions belonging to ten different divisions. Their battalions, like building blocks, could be assembled in different ways. This required a high level of acumen on the part of the troops and their confidence that in any leader they would find a man to whom the interests of another German battalion were just as dear as the interests of his own battalion.

The French, and particularly the old Russian army, were much worse at improvising. In detaching one of his own units, a leader, guided by his egoism, would always select the weakest unit. This unit, sensing that it would not get any sympathy or win any medals in someone else's group, tended more to feign zeal than to prove it. Leaders who were able to handle someone else's troops were in short supply. The understanding of duty was usually limited to a narrow organizational framework.[20]

Territorial units, particularly in the initial phase of a war, require a careful attitude toward preserving their still fragile organizational skelton and by their very nature are inappropriate for this way of assembling a reserve.

The specific political goals that are kept in mind in preparing for war should naturally be pondered deeply and stated precisely: if these political goals are thoughtlessly stated, they will lead to unnecessary problems in the war plan and construction of the army. For example, the Slavophile dream of capturing Constantinople led to a situation in which for over two decades we expended significant but insufficient resources on preparing to move a landing force to the banks of the Bosporus. Up until the Russo-Japanese War the intellectual work of the Odessa Military District was focused on this landing force: landing maneuvers were made; special large landing craft were produced; and the normal devices for

---

[20] In Ye. N. Sergeev's book *Ot Dviny k Visle* [From the Dvina to the Vistula] (pp. 7, 8, 26–29) there are a number of statistics that make it possible to think that the aforementioned shortcomings of the old Russian army have not completely disappeared from Soviet territory. In the spring of 1920 the interior districts, dispatching divisions to fight the Poles, had the attitude of a "self-supporting person" [*otrezannyi lomot*]. The Belomorskii District took British uniforms and boots, carts and some horses away from the 18th Division before being dispatched, while the 7th Army in the Petrograd District comandeered a division's mobile field kitchen unit on the way. The Urals District gave approximately the same treatment to the 10th Cavalry Division before its trip to the front, and the 2nd Labor Army (building the Embinsk Railroad) seized some of the equipment that was supposed to go toward the formation of 4th Army headquarters, and so forth. In a situation of extreme economic disorder it is hardly possible to ask that persons refrain from pursuing parochial interests.

raising the boats on the ships of the Russian Shipping and Trade Society were replaced with stronger devices because they were too weak for these boats; and a special landing battalion with a great deal of material was formed in Odessa. Of course, any serious attempt to achieve this goal should have involved a number of very extensive economic, political and military measures, without which the work of the Odessa Military District would have been worth very little. And Sukhomlinov was quite right when he insisted on eliminating these landing preparations as "an expensive toy" which, "moreover," could become a dangerous pastime."[21]

The Ratio of Noncombatants to Combatants

One example of irrational organization is the way in which the Red infantry was organized in the Civil War. The basic desire to reduce the percentage of noncombatants led the first organizers to reject the corps as an organizational unit, which was undoubtedly correct in the conditions of the Civil War. But subsequently the size of a division rose to 50,000. The author of these lines reported in 1918 when he was on duty that, given the economic disorder and poor rail transportation at the time, small divisions would be the best for a civil war and should consist of eight battalions or even four battalions and three batteries, following the model of the prewar Transcaspian brigades, and that divisions with a strength of 5,000 to 6,000 would be most appropriate for the conditions of the Civil War. However, the opposing view, namely increasing the size of divisions from 18 to 27 battalions, prevailed. The 18 battalions in a division, given the economic conditions at the time, could only be very weak and the divisions could be no larger than several thousand; the desire to have more infantry led the high command to increase the number of battalions, but because the economy remained the same, the battalions became even weaker, and the number of combatants in a division did not increase. However, then the rears increased for all 27 battalions, and as a result we had to pay for the discrepancy between organization and the requirements of the war with an unbelievable increase in the number of noncombatants over combatants. A ratio of 12 noncombatants to one combatant was considered good, and this ratio was often much higher.[22] A division fought at the same strength of 2,000 to 6,000 the strength which the all-Russian main staff had planned. The extensive rears devoured the scraggly supplies that the center had dispatched to its heroic front, jammed up the railroads in the rear and hindered maneuvers. The war became incomparably more expensive.

In the World War the French, who were frightfully short of human material (because of their low birth rate —the lack of "the woman's gift"), had a very low ratio and even talked of a 0.5:1 ratio of noncombatants to combatants. In Germany in October 1916 there were 4,585,000 men in the field armies and 3,337,000 on the transports and in the rear; if we assume that 20 percent of the noncombatants were in the active army and that about 20 percent performed combat service in the rear, there were only 0.85 noncombatants for every German combatant.

In fact, however, the percentage of noncombatants in Germany was twice as high, because the delay in the growth of transport formations was too great and

---

[21]   Sukhomlinov's memoirs, p. 168.

[22]   In the Polish army of 1920 this ratio was apparently 7:1.

was compensated for by an abundance of persons commandeered from the ranks, in particular in the winter and in the period of positional calm; often the number of persons commandeered was as high as 400 per battalion, and a company which was supposed to have 150 men had no more than 60 or 70 men. Here is a list of reasons for absences: sick, arrested, on leave, in machine gun schools, in construction companies, in signal units, laying mines, guard duty, medics, litter bearers, grooms, orderlies, couriers, clerks, cartmen, employees of military cooperatives, officers' clubs, gunsmiths, mechanics, paymasters, the heads of ad hoc logistical teams. Special assembly points were indicated for these commandeered persons in the event of an enemy offensive, and sometimes large reserves were assembled in this way.

In the old Russian army the ratio of noncombatants to combatants was equal to two men in the rear for one combatant as early as the first mobilization in the World War, and ultimately it was greater than 3:1. In general this ratio is very indicative.[23] It reflects the size of the territory which led to an increase in the number of combatants on account of the distance between the front and supply and manpower areas, the greater or lesser wealth of the overall base, the procedure for mobilizing reserves and the extent to which the economic units of a given unit differed from the common interest. If regiments do not trust army supplies and try to produce everything they need on their own, including shovels, shields, flour and so forth, transport will immediately double: the amount of human material, the competence of the leaders, the level of discipline, the morale of the reinforcements, the density of the railway system[24] and the regularity of its operation, the quality of roads for horse traction and the proportions of drivers, two-horse carriages and two-wheelers in a convoy. After all a two-wheeler caravan requires twice as many drivers as one made up of two-horse carriages, and the persons who favor light two-wheelers will unknowingly assist in doubling the number of noncombatants.

The current extensive rears to a great extent developed as a result of the desire of modern armies to make the soldier as comfortable as possible and improve sanitation. Switching from dried crusts to fresh bread, which is extremely important for keeping the soldiers healthy, meant that the regimental and divisional transport for a three-division Russian corps in the 20th century had to have 324 more vehicles. Transport grew much larger with the introduction of field kitchens, which are very important for keeping soldiers strong. But in order to avoid a rear which is so large as to be unmanageable, one must carefully ponder the necessity of each extra vehicle. One of the essential weaknesses of the Northern forces in the American Civil War was the luxurious and very heavy ration provided to each pampered soldier, which made the Northern army absolutely dependent on railroads and waterways given the bad dirt roads of the time and deprived them of the freedom of maneuver which the half-starving Southern armies had. In order to achieve victory, the Northern armies were compelled to forgo many comforts and switch to a full but moderate ration which weighed 33 percent less than the original one.

---

[23] During the French Revolution, in 1794 of the 1.1 million draftees at least 400,000 were on very dubious assignments in the deep rear.

[24] Building another spur may cut the need for army transports in half.

Another reason for larger convoys and a larger number of noncombatants is the fragmentation of transport among supply sectors. Everyone knows the savings of vehicles that are effected when different forms of transportation are combined into powerful organizations in the cities. Major savings may also be effected in the rears of an active army by providing general-purpose transportation capable of satisfying all the army's needs. In this case we mean the elimination of artillery vehicle establishments, which now have no reason to exist. A simple cart using horse traction is 50 percent more economical than a caisson and travels better on bad roads or over furrowed fields. Special artillery vehicles are worthless when heavy fighting is under way and they lay idle for years when meanwhile there are not enough ordinary vehicles for delivering building materials for fortifications.

A division should have a certain quantity of transports to meet all its needs. It would be good to avoid linking these transports organizationally to the division. The need for them may vary significantly depending on the division's operational role. In addition, when a division is moved there is no need to haul all its transports behind it. While military units may not always operate successfully as part of other divisions, we can require transportation units to service forces that are completely unfamiliar to them.

The problem of reducing the percentage of noncombatants is also a problem of increasing the useful work of an army. If the planned strength of an army is greater than the economical capabilities of the state, we will encounter the unrestrained growth of the rear. Military laundries and theaters will sprout up and front workshops will appear which will grow to the size of factories, but the number of combatants will decrease rather than increase. A state such as the USSR, which can make war expenditures only with extreme effort, should be completely merciless and decisive in approaching the problem of reducing the number of noncombatants. And if, given our backward economy, we do not succeed in achieving the noncombatant-to combatant-ratios of the French and German armies and if we are condemned to wage war more expensively and expend human material more extensively, we must nevertheless set a limit to this. Victory will be won not by unlimited mobilizations of senior citizens but by a very strict accounting of every man drafted into the Red Army.

The Ratio Between Branches of the Armed Services

If a theater of military operations is located in high, rugged mountains, which turn the spaces accessible to cavalry into narrow defiles and its flatter part is covered with vineyards, gardens and large fences, an army preparing to operate on this kind of terrain will naturally have only a small cavalry. It was quite reasonable for the Italian army to have a smaller cavalry than other armies because cavalry operations could not be very extensive in the Alps, the Tyrol, the Hartz Mountains or Lombardy.

But it would be mistaken to limit our dialectic approach to resolving the issue of the proportions of the branches of the armed services solely to terrain conditions. It is quite clear that depending on the strengths of the armed forces of both sides one may either expect a solid, saturated front stretching through the entire theater of military operations or an intermittent and fluid front. In the latter instance the cavalry will have a great deal of room for quick maneuvers. We should assume that the lower the strength of the armed forces is in comparison to the area of operations, the greater will be the opportunities opened up for the cavalry, and consequently cavalry should make up a high percentage of a small army.

But the enemy's quality is more important than his strength. The golden age of the cavalry has always coincided with periods when the infantry was weak, incohesive and inclined to disintegrate and desert. This was the nature of Seydlitz's successes in the era of Frederick the Great. The laurels of the Red Cavalry can be ascribed not only to its bravery but to the disintegration of White and Polish infantry units. The cavalry of the Civil War consisted entirely of volunteers, while the infantry, with the exception of firm cadres who were assigned the most difficult missions, consisted primarily of forcibly mobilized peasants.

There is no doubt that in the World War certain cavalry commanders in all the armies left a lot to be desired. But in general the cavalry faded into the background not because it was bad but because the conditions of the war ruled out the possibility of achieving major successes with it. On the other hand, the economic disintegration of the Civil War years put the cavalry at the forefront, and its leaders proved to have the talents they needed.

Thus, cavalry, like any other branche of service, is of value not in and of itself but rather in connection with the room that the nature of a war provides for its activity. What percentage of cavalry should one have in an army? An answer may be given only on the basis of our evaluation of the future conditions of a conflict, the nature of the masses and their discipline, the extent to which we can count on disintegration in the enemy ranks as a result of the development of a class struggle and the areas in which we will have to fight.

The same applies to other other branches of service. The organizer of an army can neither be guided by patterns (four guns per 1,000 bayonets, supposedly following Napoleon's example) nor respond to fashions like an Aeolian harp responds to the blowing of the wind.

We must remember that in terms of the number of riflemen in it (4,000) a modern division is equivalent to an infantry regiment at the beginning of the World War, and, given today's extended fronts, the requirements for security, manpower, the depth of battle formations and the duration of intensity have increased. The mechanized company was born at the end of the World War in conditions of an acute shortage of replacements; a severe reduction of the offensive spirit of the infantry; combat operations which could be clearly defined as trampling over the same little piece of ground over and over again; complete industrial mobilization and an abundance of automatic weapons; solid barbed wire in front of the infantry and a solid line of batteries in back of it; a large number of tanks, which took on an important role in offensives; and splendid lines of communication in the rear. Nevertheless, the Germans noted that the American infantry, which was very poorly trained in tactics and had very weak skills and inexperienced commanders, gained more ground and inflicted heavier casualties by their masss attacks in the last major battles from September 26 to October 4, 1918, than did the experienced French infantry with their group tactics.

Incidentally, the French used infantry weapons extremely sparingly at the end of the World War. Close battle vehicles were more often present in battle than active in it. The French began their love affair with infantry fire after the war had ended. Infantry firepower is now some kind of absolute. In 1914 a French battalion had 12 kilograms of weaponry per soldier, whereas in 1921 it had 44 kilograms per soldier. The amount of ammunition a battalion could expend increased, in terms of the number of troops, by a factor of 7.1. This was obviously figured on the assumption of positional warfare and a dense network of railroads and highways. This indicates that the French are not planning on sending their infantry to areas similar to the Soviet theater but are probably planning on operating in a coastal area at the water's edge. This indicates that the French, who have grabbed vast chunks of German territory, have gone on the historical defensive. These figures are in no way a law. The actual firepower of a front is a derivative of many variables, including the road system.

The mechanized company also requires a dialectical approach. In some cases one level of mechanization is appropriate, while in other cases another level is appropriate. French heavy machine gun battalions are incapable of securing their own front and are completely helpless without solid barbed wire. But they may be appropriate if they occupy prefortified positions and make it possible to concentrate a battering ram assault in advantageous directions.

The experience of the Civil War has not yet been weighed. There were many cases in which regiments, whose strength had gotten down to the company level and had one machine gun for every 20 riflemen, were able to hold extensive sectors, while inexperienced massive divisions which had just been mobilized suffered setbacks in which the abundance of people just made things worse.

However, in discussing the proportions of infantry and other branches we should not forget that the pace at which the infantry moves in a battle is undoubtedly faster than the pace at which the combat-readiness of other branches of service melt away, particularly the artillery, and therefore we need more infantry than would be required by the best tactical proportions. In positional warfare there is an acute need for new infantry to replace infantry units taken from the front and let them rest. An even larger infantry is required in maneuver warfare with no barbed wire. All of Ludendorff's breakthroughs in 1918 were unsuccessful because the German armies were afraid of "baking a wedding cake" (which was how Kuropatkin expressed his misgivings in 1904) and they tried to maintain a solid front and rebuild a wire fence along the entire front as quickly as possible after a breakthrough; didn't this inability of the German forces to switch to maneuver warfare stem from the weakness of their infantry divisions and the excessive stress placed on their materiel?

Determining the percentage of infantry and its organization and tactics depends on the overall conditions of a war. In any case, group tactics requires trained group leaders and may develop only in accordance with their training, whereas defensive tendencies lead to a major concentration of equipment in the infantry.

Mechanization of the infantry should also be closely related to the growth of artillery fire. The nature of the artillery also depends on the situation. The energetic work done on fortifying French and Russian border regions impelled the Germans to organize a powerful heavy artillery. If the enemy has no concrete, there is no reason to burden oneself with very large guns. A poor country must make more extensive use of the least expensive form of artillery, the howitzer. In

Asian theaters, with their poor lines of communication, the percentage of artillery should be much lower and the guns much smaller. However, disregarding the need for powerful artillery in European theaters would lead to a situation in which the infantry would suffer heavy casualties and would quickly become inferior to the enemy with superior artillery in terms of fighting spirit and tactical training. And we must avoid being too inferior in quality: the range of field guns in the West is 12 kilometers and the range of six-inch guns is 30 kilometers.

The greater or lesser importance of the air force and its composition follow from the nature of a war. Aerial combat is natural when air space is limited, as was the case in the aerial battles that took place between Liège and Belfort, which can be covered in two hours of flight. In this case there will be more work for fighters, and "aces" will easily set records that the best aerial warriors would have a hard time setting on the extended Russian front. The development of an enemy country increases the number of bombing targets and requires a greater number of bombers. Aerial reconnaissance will yield the same results in wooded Belorussia as it will in the black earth steppes of the south. We should also not forget that aviation, which requires good airfields, is the least mobile branch of service.

We must get a clear conception of the nature of future operations and be able to determine the requirements they will make of tactics, and only then will it be possible to provide a proper solution for problems of organizing branches of service in the proportions that are actually necessary. The correct solution could lead to significant savings, but success will come only to an organizer who is a master in strategy, operational art and tactics.

Railroad Maneuvers

Previously all attention was focused on a logistical organization which would make it possible to reduce the depth of campaign columns and thus facilitate maneuvers carried out in campaign formations on dirt roads. At present railroad maneuvers are of major significance, and the speed of troop movements on rail is often decisive in nature. It would be mistaken to assume that this speed depends exclusively on railroad equipment and the ability of troops to get into and out of the cars quickly. In the World War a Russian division required almost 60 trains, whereas a German division only required 30. A German division took up half as much depth on the rails and could concentrate twice as fast under equal railroad conditions. The explanation lies not in the fact that a German division had three regiments while a Russian division had four. The organization of logistics was essential.

Forces must have a certain amount of supplies and a certain amount of transportation to carry these supplies and replace what has been expended. This supply organization must be assigned to certain hierarchical echelons. Although the function of supply allocator raises the authority of a command echelon to a certain extent, there is no need for every commander to have his own quartermaster section on the scale of the unit he commands.

In principle it is advantageous to concentrate supplies and supply functions in a few echelons. The concentration of supplies makes it possible to get by with fewer supplies than when they are dispersed and makes it possible to use them more efficiently: ammunition is delivered to people who are fighting and food is delivered to people who canot get it where they are. However, it would be unreasonable to centralize all the supplies of a front in the front echelon, because it is naturally unable to follow all the needs of different military units. A certain portion of mobile supplies and cartage should be included in the regular complement of individual units in order to give them the possibility of satisfying the needs that arise during combat. But the size of a division train is quite relative: a German division was relieved of practically all economic functions, which were turned over to the corps. This organizational lightness of a division is particularly appropriate for modern warfare. If a division has become frayed and worn out in the course of two-week battles and has withdrawn, what is the point of putting logistical agencies, which can operate regularly from day to day for many months, in reserve? Consequently there is an excess of these agencies. If we need to reinforce one sector of a front at the expense of another, in most cases we will only have to reinforce combatants rather than logistics. Thus the Germans viewed the corps as an economic entity and did not move corps unless it was particularly necessary, whereas divisions were moved from one front to another hundreds of times; divisions changed on a regular basis at hot spots on the Western Front. The German corps was a sort of hotel where a division could show up without its own teapot, dishes and linen, while the Russian division, like the gentry in old times, carried its whole household with it and of course was regularly late.

This tardiness increased with the size of the division's economic component. The Russian Guards needed 120 trains per division, because there was a particular abundance of all the agencies of the rural and city councils, including dentists' offices, field baths, detachments for digging artesian wells, campaign detachments of the officers' credit union and an endless number of medical detachments. The winter battle at the Masurian Lakes (February 1915) was to be a kind of encounter battle, but we were late in getting there: it took an infinite amount of time for the Guards to get from the Southwest Front to Lomzha, because they had sent agencies which were particularly useless for the battle ahead of time because the Guards Corps feared that higher headquarters would stop sending trains and cut them off from them. Even after hundreds of trains had arrived at Lomzha, the Guard was still not any kind of fighting force.

We could say that in the Civil War the number of trains a division required was sometimes inappropriate for the number of troops represented by the latter. Frequent interruptions in central supplies compelled the divisions to run their own economies and keep a two-month or more supply of flour on hand.

We must instill confidence in supplies from higher headquarters in our commanders and put an end to the gentry division. Everyone must understand what a crime it is to delay an operational maneuver on the rails by requiring an extra train. And by examples we must demonstrate that operational crimes, like felonies, will not go unpunished. We need an organizational break.

In peacetime strategists should pay sufficient attention to organizational matters, because in the future the organization that has been created will affect strategic decisions in a certain way.

3. MILITARY MOBILIZATION

The Permanence of Mobilization

Military mobilization is a test of the health of the entire state entity. After the Prussian success in 1870 sufficient attention was given to the art of mobilization everywhere, and every state had cadres of experienced mobilization technicians. However the theory of strategy cannot ignore issues of mobilization that are closely related to the combat-readiness of the armed forces and should approach them critically from the perspective of recent wars.

In 1870, during the course of the first month of military operations, the Prussians succeeded in locking in and surrounding at Metz the best French army commanded by Bazaine and taking the next army, de MacMahon's, prisoner at Sedan. Negligible remnants of French cadres, sailors, firemen and units still in the process of formation were assembled in Paris and were surrounded there by the Prussians. The French provinces seemed completely defenseless, but Gambetta, relying on the economic might of France and open sea lanes, was able to effect an extensive mobilization in all of France: in four and a half months of work he mobilized an average of 6,000 infantrymen and two batteries per day. Moltke was impressed by the speed at which new enemy forces grew up, and in December 1870 he wrote a letter to General Stile in which he said,

> In operations crowned by unparalleled successes the German army has been able to take prisoner all the forces the enemy deployed at the beginning of the war. Nevertheless, in just three months time France has been able to create a new army superior in numbers to the army that perished. The resources of the enemy country appear to be practically inexhaustible and can place in doubt the rapid and decisive success of our arms unless our fatherland responds with an equal effort.

Subsequently Moltke said on several occasions that "this conflict has surprised us from a military point of view to the extent that the question it has posed will have to be studied during the long years of peace."[1]

After weighing all the aforementioned circumstances, the elder Moltke came to the conclusion that in a conflict on two fronts one could not count on destroying either France or Russia in the course of a year and settled on a plan for a war of attrition involving going on the defensive against France and going on a limited offensive against Russia in the direction of Sedlets. But the question Moltke posed was not theoretically analyzed, because this analysis is possible only if one makes a radical break with strategic traditions.

In fact, if Gambetta was able to achieve impressive results after being compelled to improvise new formations in all their details, with a certain amount of preparation the mobilization of new forces of the state could have created an even more impressive and strong armed force.

---

[1]   Paul Deschanel, *Gambetta* (Paris: 1919), p. 112.

The evolution of human societies over the last hundred years has been characterized by an awesome rise in labor productivity, an accumulation of material goods, a powerful transportation system, speedy communications and the spread of organizational skills. Problems that previously could be resolved only over the course of many years can now be solved in several months. These circumstances are also the premises on which the successful formation of new units in a very short time is based, which no state now ever refrains from in the event of war. Quite recently mobilization seemed to be a moment; mobilization agencies mined the peacetime structure of the state in order to set off a one-time explosion and gather the human masses and materiel with which the war would begin to be waged, and be concluded in the course of two to three weeks. The communmication of the chief of the artillery administration before the World War that he would need 420 days to mobilize ammunition and ordnance evoked both grief and laughter. We tried to complete the strategic deployment of our forces and resources in the first month of the war.

Humanity's new economic might has given mobilization a temporal dimension, has extended it to the entire war and has made it permanent. It was undoubtedly a mistake that preparations for the World War were in essence preparations for a small war and had essentially small mobilizations in mind. In peacetime only 70 percent of the physically strongest segment of the German population was liable for military service; only a portion of this 70 percent was mobilized immediately when war was declared, while the other portion was to be reinforcements for them; and this 70 percent was provided mobilization stockpiles of equipment. But because the war placed an extreme strain on manpower, the other 30 percent of the human material could not be left unused; they could be used to form new units after they had been trained, cadres had been organized and the necessary equipment had been ordered and, of course, in the process the equipment left over from the units that had been mobilized first could be extensively used for the new units.

As in fact, two weeks after war had been declared, on August 16, 1914, as soon as mobilization was in full swing, the minister of war, General Falkenhayn issued an order to form six and a half new corps (the 12th-27th reserve corps, and a 6th bavarian reserve division). Fifty-five days were allotted for their formation (they were to be ready by October 10). The soldiers in these new corps, which were half volunteers, were superior, but the commanders left a lot to be desired, because no cadres for these units were taken from units in the field, and their commanders were retired and Landsturm officers. Because industry had only begun mobilizing, the equipment had to be gathered piecemeal; for example, the units were given helmets that had been taken from the police.

As soon as the military industry was going strong, an order concerning a third echelon was issued on November 13: four and a half new corps were mobilized (the 28th-41st) reserve corps and the 8th Bavarian reserve division). They were given 68 days to get ready (by January 20, 1915). The field artillery for these corps were obtained by borrowing it from the front lines, where the batteries were changed from a strength of six guns to a strength of four guns. Reliable infantry cadres and staffs were obtained by means of appointing energetic commanders from the front lines.

At the same time railroad, telegraph, truck, and aviation units with a total of 150,000 men had to be formed.

In 1915 50 divisions were formed by changing divisions to a strength of three regiments and adding new formations.

In 1916 fourteen new corps headquarters (Nos. 51-64) and 48 new divisions were formed, in part by reducing the strength of existing divisions. In 1917 ten new divisions were formed (Nos. 231-240), the order had been given on November 6, 1916, and was carried out by March 1917. The ten new divisions were followed by 14 new divisions and four new corps headquarters and eight new divisions were obtained by reducing the strength of old divisions.

At the same time the rear energetically organized machinegun units and increased the number of units by many times as opposed to the number of units called for by the initial mobilization plan; the number of light and mountain batteries was increased from 1,141 to 2,821; air defense artillery was increased from 18 to 2,558 guns; and heavy artillery grew from a strength of 35,000 men, 3,400 horses and 576 guns to a strength of 419,000 men, 202,000 horses and 6,500 guns.

Other technical units grew to the same extent. Great Britain is just as instructive an example of permanent mobilization. In peacetime the British army consisted of six field and 14 territorial divisions. As early as September a Canadian division had arrived to assist the field divisions on the French front, in November Indian divisions began to arrive and in December the first two territorial divisions had arrived from England. Kitchener put together a plan for doubling the field and territorial divisions and organizing 30 new (Kitchener) divisions, and this plan was carried out. In 1916, 20 months after the war had begun, England agreed to widen its front in France; all the divisions were ready in 1917, but the command was still unsure and the divisions would have been quite unsuitable for a war of maneuver. British intensity culminated in 1918. An even more striking example of permanent mobilization is the formation of the U.S. Army in 1917-1918; during this period the United States did not have to hold any front and could carry on its work quite calmly.

We have dwelled on examples from the World War. The American Civil War is also quite interesting.

The experience of our civil war also indicates the permanence of mobilization over the entire course of the war, because the entire Red Army arose in the process of formations carried out in wartime.

At present France resolves the mobilization issue in echelons. "The cover army," 32 divisions with strong cadres, forms the first echelon. The second echelon consists of new formations for which there are two million reservists, but a great deal is lacking, including 90 percent of the cadres and some needed equipment. Months rather than days will be required to mobilize the second echelon. And there will be completely separate mobilizations in the colonies to add black troops. Only the readiness of the cover army is completely independent of the success of industrial mobilization.

From this we should primarily conclude that the role of the rear in the war is far from limited to the first mobilization and the subsequent provision of reinforcements. Even if industrial mobilization were delayed and economic considerations compelled the authorities to avoid expanding the armed forces, there is no doubt that one would have to form many new technical units, because no matter how much peacetime plans strive to meet the requirements of a future war, its nature will in many respects be unknown to us, and we cannot avoid reckoning with the need to make major modifications of our existing organization.

Modern echelon mobilization compels us to remember the distant past. In the summer of 1813, during a truce, the Russian active army in Prussia was strengthened from 90,000 to 170,000 men; and at the same time in Poland Benigsen's so-called Polish reserve army was formed and dispatched to the battle of Leipzig; and the Russians proceeded to form the next echelon, Lobanov-Rostovskii's reserve army, in the interior provinces of Russia. Then, like now, the government was incapable of completing all its preparations by the beginning of the war and beginning the war at maximum intensity.

The Need for Flexibility

The need for mobilization plans to be flexible stems from the need to of subordinate mobilization to the political situation at the time of the mobilization. In 1914 Russia had a general mobilization plan, but the political situation required only a mobilization directed against Austria. The mobilization of the Petrograd and Vilna Districts and part of the Warsaw District was a measure clearly aimed at Germany, and it would have been desirable to avoid it in order to deflect the odium of a direct challenge to Germany for war. Incidentally, the mobilization of some military districts proved to be technically careless: the districts were tied together by extensive transfers of reserves and so forth, and the avoidance of a general mobilization planned out in all its details forced the Russian army to improvise. Hence the military command used all means possible to obtain an order for a general mobilization, which they succeeded in getting. Politics was subordinated to a clumsy inflexible mobilization. The means triumphed over the end.

Of course, mobilization puts a state into a situation similar to a raging torrent, and in order to avoid getting carried away, it is easiest to assign everyone a clearly defined role. But mobilization must be as flexible and as decentralized as possible, and an army should be able to mobilize any number of any divisions without disrupting the mobilization-readiness of the other divisions in the process. The mobilization of an entire army should be merely the sum of the mobilizations of all its units and not constitute a self-contained entity.

Because we now see mobilization as a continuous process rather than a single event, we can in no way consider the concept of a general mobilization as corresponding to reality. Not every mobilization is a partial mobilization, and even the mobilization of the entire Red Army at the beginning of the war can only be considered the first echelon of a mobilization.

In the historical period we are now entering we must anticipate a return to the prolonged preparations for war which predominated in the pre-Moltke era. Paragraph 12 of the League of Nations Charter, the desire to use the resources of one's dominions (England) and the black African colonies (France), the need to arm (Germany) and the low level of peacetime readiness (the United States) have convinced us of this. We can draw ourselves a picture of a declaration of economic mobilization in two hostile states while their armed forces remain on a peacetime footing.

The principle of economy of force should predominate decisively in all cases. This principle would be violated if we were to allocate a greater number of forces than the state is capable of providing. Russia had overmobilized by the beginning of 1917. It would also be violated if more forces were allocated for a war than required to accomplish the missions of the war with confidence.

The Premobilization Period

The table given below for the initial period of the World War convinces us that prior to the war all states focussed their attention on the use of the premobilization period. "Warning telegrams" in England, a situation of threatening danger in Germany and the seven steps of the period of tension and premobilization schedule B in France generally corresponded to Russian measures planned for the premobilization period. It is desirable for any army to proceed to mobilize after preparing everything that can be done without calling up the reserves and requisitioning horses. In the future we should anticipate an even greater level of activity in the premobilization period, Training or test assemblies of reserves, calling up territorial divisions for exercises. and primarily extensive economic measures will complement the premobilization period in the future. The afore-mentioned measures are clues which diplomatic and military agents must follow vigilantly in the same way that they follow diplomatic trips and bellicose positions taken in leading journals.[2]

Mobilization and the Plan of Operational Deployment

It is quite desirable to make mobilization measures and measures to utilize mobilized units for operational purposes completely independent of one another. Only with this kind of independence can one meet the requirements of flexibility for mobilization and operational plans. However, these measures are closely interrelated in border corps that will have to serve in combat time as soon as they are mobilized. If there are important objectives or large man-made structures (e.g., the railroad bridge across the Western Dvina) or a defensive position coincides with a borderline in a frontier sector (e.g., the Dnestr), the battle missions that must be accomplished may become very large in scale. These missions are usually handled by drawing on forces that can be mobilized as quickly as possible (the cavalry) or are capable of mobilization and fighting at the same time (aviation), and likewise in the formation of a composite infantry brigade with several batteries in each corps not too distant from the border; this composite brigade will operate with a peacetime strength and is reinforced with forces through procure-ments or at the expense of other military units and is mobilized either in a preliminary basis by calling up reserves individually or on the front by means of delivering reinforcements, caissons and carts to it, or in a second echelon that returns to its base as soon as it is relieved by units that have completed mobiliza-tion. There is the custom of maintaining border corps at high strength in order to make mobilization easier. In light of this technique, it would seem advantageous to make the peacetime strength of several regiments designed to cover the mobilization particularly great. Because of the need for covering forces, in France the law gave the minister of war the right to call up reserves individually without

---

[2]   The question of the significance to the Austrians of the first day of mobilzation against Russia will be illuminated in the discussion of the plan of operations.

Table 1. The Initial Period of the World War in Europe.

Date	Russia and Serbia	France
July 24		
July 25	*Mobilization in Serbia.* Nighttime: Return of Russian troops to their permanent duty stations.	Change in mobilization plan for French forces in Morocco for purpose of using them in Europe. Railway alert. Return of railroad agents from vacation.
July 26	Fortresses on war footing. Beginning of premobilization period in all of European Russia.	Cancellation of leaves. Everyone on leave called back. Railroad security provided by civilian elements.
July 27		Return of all military units to their permanent duty stations. Military security for railroads.
July 28		7 *Mesures du temps de tension.* Railway stations transferred to disposal of military.
July 29	Daytime: *Partial mobilization.*	
July 30	18:00: Order for general mobilization.	Order to establish border security (mobilization of 11 infantry divisions and 10 cavalry divisions).
July 31	First day of mobilization.	Fulfillment of measures as per mobilization schedule (Carnet B). Establishment of a second line of border security. Railroad mobilization. Beginning of covering transports.
August 1		16:40: Mobilization of army and navy.
August 2	Russian cavalry (4th Cavalry Division) crosses the German border.	First day of mobilization.
August 3		Morning: cover transports completed.
August 4		End of most mobilization transports.
August 5		Beginning of concentration transports.
August 6	First hostile actions on the Austrian border.	

England	Germany	Austria-Hungary
Order from the First Lord of the Admiralty: Navy to remain mobilized after maneuvers.		
Change of naval command.	Battleship squadron called back from Norway.	21:30: *Partial mobilization* against Serbia.
End of maneuvers; navy remains mobilized.		Corps on Serbian border put on war footing.
Replenishment of navy's stockpiles.	Local orders for XVI Army Corps to cancel leaves to Bavaria. Soldiers given leaves for the harvest go back to Metz.	
	Railroad employees provide security for railroads. Certain units return to permanent duty stations.	First day of mobilization against Serbia.
First line fleet moves to Scapa-Flow base. "Warning telegrams" sent to army and navy signaling threat of war.	Night: all units return to their permanent duty stations. All persons return from leave. Order to provide security for manmade structures and build positions for the mobilization period.	Evening: Four B corps start moving to Serbian front plus three border corps.
	Partial border security introduced in east at local discretion. Order to mobilize fortresses on the eastern border; Navy put on a war footing.	
	13:00: War threat issued. 15:00: Rail links and telegraph wire cut on French border.	War footing on the Russian front. 11:30: *General mobilization*.
14:15: Mobilization of the navy.	17:00: Mobilization of army and navy. Declaration of war against Russia. Capture of Kalisz.	First day of war footing against Russia.
02:15: Order to mobilize the reserve navy.	First day of mobilization.	
12:00: Mobilization of ground forces. August 5 designated first day of mobilization.	Declaration of war against France. German cavalry crosses Belgian border.	Units start arriving to reinforce cover of Galicia.
	Emich's six infantry brigades cross the Belgian border opposite Liège.	First day of mobilization against Russia.
	General assault on Liège begins in evening.	
		Austria-Hungary declares war on Russia.

declaring a general or partial mobilization. In this way the minister of war reinforced five border corps two days before the declaration of a general mobiliization without attracting the attention of legal agencies. Thus, individual call-ups made it possible to avoid major expenditures on maintaining the units at high strength.

Age Classifications

Mobilization should make rational use of human material numbering in the millions to bring the armed forces up to strength. In old Russia we only paid attention to their skills and disregarded the age of the draftees. In the home guards one could often encounter splendid 20-year-olds, remarkable physical specimens manning horse transports whereas in the infantry field units as early as August 1914 there were 40-year old-graybeards and very many 30-year-olds.

A company composed of both strong and weak troops should, in both a campaign and in battle, be considered equivalent to its weaker members. It cannot be led at a fast pace but must accommodate the slower pace of its older members. Discipline itself and training techniques also vary with age. We cannot handle the fathers of families in the same way as rascally, exuberant schoolboys. The Russian mobilization did not reckon with this and tried to man infantry companies with people who were closer at hand. This helped make the Russian infantry heavy. An infantry unit could move no faster than four kilometers per hour, and every 50 minutes it had to take a ten-minute break. There were inevitably a large number of stragglers in major movements.

At the beginning of the war the German infantry could travel ten kilometers in two hours and after taking a short break only after two hours could make long trips with practically no stragglers. In the field units at the beginning of the war 26 was the maximum age, 54 percent of the men were regular soldiers while 45 percent were reserves who had left active duty no more than two years before. It stands to reason that they had not had enough time to forget their training like the old Russian reserves had. The maximum age of the German reserves was 30 (1 percent regular army, 44 percent reservists, 55 percent Landwehr members). Even in the Landwehr infantry the maximum age was 36 (62 percent Landwehr in the first draft, 38 percent Landwehr in the second draft). During the war with its high manpower requirements the Germans had to renounce these standards, but every draftee was examined view in terms of his physical fitness and received an appropriate assignment.

We must put an end to the inefficient methods of Russian mobilization. We must firmly prohibit the assignment of healthy young men to noncombatant positions in the rear. We must introduce several classifications of military fitness (fit for service in the active army, in logistic units, in noncombatants units; and in work teams) and the Red infantry must be a young infantry.

The Mobilization Plan

Cannot encompass, as previously, the mobilization of only the first echelon. In our situation we perhaps should consider some of the territorial divisions a second echelon of mobilization.

We must avoid trying to set records for mobilization speed. If the 13th Corps of Samsonov's army proved unready for battle, this can partially be explained by the fact that it got its reserves just before boarding the rail cars and did not manage to become cohesive. The reinforcements remained nameless and unknown to their company commanders. The 15th Corps, which mobilized under better conditions, accomplished more in battle. The corps of Samsonov's army did not receive their cavalries or their carts; the army's staff had just come together from different parts of the country, and the communications system had just been put together. A postponement of even two or three days would have led to significant improvements.

From the above table it is evident that all countries perceived that their mobilization plans were too hasty. On July 25 Austria-Hungary decided to mobilize against Serbia, but decided to designate July 28 rather than July 26 as the first day. Great Britain decided to mobilize on August 3, but designated August 5 as the first day. A delay of three to five days in determining the 1st day of mobilization is normal if a major threat is not hanging over our heads (e.g., Austria-Hungary in its war against Serbia, or England). More work was required before mobilization could begin. It would have been more apropriate to construct mobilization plans to reflect a calmer pace of human activity.

Given inadequate training and inadequate supplies, it will often be more advantageous to keep several divisions and corps in the rear as a strategic reserve that will get ready and wait for a more suitable moment for going to the front. In particular frontline operations, especially if they involve retreat marches, are better carried out by the prepared component of an army.

A state will not be able to use its forces intelligently if there is such a sharp division of authority between the commanders in chief of the active armies and navy and the minister of war, who was responsible for the rear, as was the case with Russia in the World War. Authority over the rear and the front should be unified and should be placed in the hands of the military command. If the minister of war is a civilian, then there should be an authoritative specialist under him, namely the chief of the general staff, in order to unify the front and the rear. France reached this point because of its bitter experience in 1917, when General Pétain was the first chief of the general staff and Foch was the second. These names highlight the importance that must be assigned to the strategic leadership of the rear.

The success of subsequent formations in the rear is comprehensively related to the energy of operations on the front. Russia set itself modest goals in the fall of 1914: the organization of two corps in the rear, the 13th and the 15th, to replace the corps which had died with Samsonov. However, the front operated so energetically and uneconomically that it swallowed up all the human and material resources the ministry of war could gather. The front covered certain losses even through cannibalism so that three of the most damaged second-line divisions in Rennenkampf's army were disbanded in order to repair this army after its first defeat at the Masurian Lakes. The army was probably ready for offensive operations ten days earlier. Only in 1918 were the Germans compelled to disband existing divisions to cover battle casualties. The two corps which our ministry of war had worked on rebuilding were ready only in February 1915, that is, by the time that Germany had managed to form 11 new corps. These figures, two rebuilt and 11 new corps, do not express the relationship between the power of the German rear and the Russian rear at that time, because the extravagant nature of Russian operations provides a better explanation. Once a period of positional calm began in the fall of 1915, coinciding with recent successes in industrial mobilization, the Russian rear was able to form new divisions and technical units at a much faster pace.

Until now mobilization plans almost exclusively take into consideration reserves which have already been trained and actually existing supplies and they have dwelled exclusively on the mobilization of the first echelon. Of course, this part of the mobilization must be retained with corrections for flexibility, but it also should include a second part, the mobilization of new formations.

The latter will undoubtedly be more successful if the new formations are planned ahead of time and favorable methods and conditions are created for them. These formations should be tied to the program of economic mobilization and perhaps even be conditioned by behavior on the front. Experienced commanders and a system of courses for junior commanders must be prepared for them. We must ponder the use of supplies left in the country, even if they are only second-hand, and distribute all equipment among them and the reserve units preparing to act as reinforcements. We must avoid weakening the front in favor of them, particularly when we employ techniques of destruction, and we must not allow ourselves to reduce the overall skills of the army by an obsession with quantity.

We must have a plan ready for new formations and take into account the need for them and the amount and times of delivery of supplies in our industrial mobilization plan.

Once a war begins the practically ungovernable tendency for the best men to go to the front, particularly the general staff, also begins. In the World War on the Russian front the junior officers at division headquarters were often more qualified than persons occupying extremely high posts in the rear because of their unsuitability for the war. We must note ahead of time and retain the most outstanding and reliable officers for directing the rear during a war.

Deployment

We must prepare to set up mobilization centers in particular for machine gun, artillery, aviation and other technical units that require special training. It is most convenient to combine these mobilization centers with existing ranges, infantry schools, airfields and so forth. In the World War the officer infantry school played the role of a machine gun center and graduated hundreds of Colt machine gun teams. This important process should be systematic, not anarchic. Is our most important artillery training center, the Luga Range, in the right place for handling the mobilization missions assigned to it? Does our program of barracks construction meet mobilization requirements? After all, the USSR has winter barracks, where soldiers can be taught to shoot, fly and maneuver. We must build and equip these mobilization centers ahead of time, which merely requires the coordination of the peacetime training facilities of the army with mobilization requirements.

All peacetime force deployments must satisfy not only the convenience of the units but the requirements of war. In this case we are not talking about such digressions from strategic requirements as the transpolar deployment of elements of two different corps or of territorial units which have been mobilized for long periods of time near the border itself. The most important and threatened areas near the border must be sufficiently saturated with forces in peacetime in order to make it easier to cover and to speed up deployment.

But we must not move our forces any closer to the border than strictly necessary in operational terms. Mobilization can be flexible only insofar as the deployment of forces in peacetime gets them closer to sources of replacement when a war is declared. The territorial principle is the foundation of an armed nation, and excessively gross violation of this principle has major adverse effects. We should also remember that border regions are not strategically reliable sources of reinforcements and manpower.

From this perspective we must decisively condemn the deployment of the Russian army from 1890 to 1910. Under the pressure of the Franco-Russian alliance Obruchev tried to speed up the commitment of Russian forces against the Triple Alliance as much as possible to avoid giving the Germans the opportunity to destroy isolated France in the first weeks of the war. Because the capacity of the Russian railroads was vastly inferior to that of the German rails, Obruchev decided to deploy a large number of field units, particularly the cavalry, in the western border areas in peacetime. The deployment of the Russian army created a vast flux in the area of the Vistula. Before the Russo-Japanese War 16 corps were deployed in the western districts, four corps covered St. Petersburg and the Baltic coast and only seven corps, predominantly under strength, remained in the interior of the country and on other borders. The main body of the Russian interior, the Moscow and Kazan Districts, contained no more than 10 percent of the army's strength; this number of troops was barely sufficient for guard duty and maintaining the mobilization stockpiles for the reserve units which would have to be deployed here. Instruction and combat training in the interior districts were at an extremely low level.

This deployment proved to be completely useless during the Russo-Japanese War, which had to be begun with predominantly second-line weak forces, with the exception of the Siberian riflemen. The one-sidedness of the flux was fully evident. But this deployment was also poorly suited for a conflict with Germany. Only one-eighth of the new recruits served in their own districts, while seven-eighths were assigned to serve in areas remote from their homes; in these conditions the reserves not only had to join where they had not served before but under completely new circumstances. The national issue made the situation caused by the deployment even more difficult. In the event of a mobilization, all the Poles were supposed to be drafted into units which would reinforce the Warsaw Military District, but in order to give these forces a Russian cast in peacetime all the Poles were sent far to the east for their service and the Warsaw military district got all its new men from other districts. Despite the fact that in the mobilization 43-year-old-graybeards were immediately called up in the border districts and could not help but greatly reduce the quality of our infantry, there were not enough reserves in the area and hundreds of thousands of troops had to be transferred from district to district. And after 1910, when 128 battalions with corresponding artillery and cavalry, approximately 12 percent of the entire Russian army, were withdrawn from the Warsaw and Vilna Districts and stationed in the interior of the country, near sources of manpower, 223,000 reserves

---

[3]   Zaionchkovskii, *Podgotovka Rossii k mirovoi voine* [Russia's Preparation for the World War] (Moscow: Gosvoenizdat, 1926), p. 87.

had to be transferred from district to district in the event of a mobilization, including 82,000 to the Warsaw District.[3]

The mere additional construction of barracks in the border sector necessitated by Obruchev's deployment cost approximately 100,000 rubles. And these barracks in the Polish provinces could not be used for training reinforcements during the war, because the reserve units of the Warsaw District were systematically withdrawn to the interior of Russia once the war began.

Incidentally, the success of reserve reinforcements and forming new units are closely related to the legacy, namely the traditions, housing space, aiming rests, firing ranges and so forth—left behind by an army which has gone to war. In the second half of the war of 1870 one could see a significant difference in the success of new formations in the North of France, where many troops had been stationed in peacetime (Federbe's army) and in the interior (the Loire army), and the north was not only able to handle formations more quickly but also provided more battle-ready units. Of course the strong fighting spirit of the northern population, which had experienced many wars, had a large number of old well-equipped fortresses in its territory and had more industry than the agricultural south of France, was certainly significant. The central interior regions that will have the gigantic task of providing 100,000 to 150,000 soldiers every month once a war begins should be prepared for this task by peacetime deployments. Of course the latter should be coordinated with the rail system.

Districts or Corps?

The location of mobilization stockpiles will be optimized if every corps possesses all the materiel it needs for mobilization within the territory it occupies. The Austrians resolved this question in the worst way possible in the first half of the 19th century by building a gigantic national arsenal in Vienna.

In the west corps, districts play the role of our military districts. The corps district provides greater decentralization and better adaptation to local conditions. And the center will find more obedient agencies in corps districts than it will in military districts, which each take on their own cast and disrupt the uniformity of military training. In addition, working as the head of an interior military district has very little in common with the command of an army: it is a school for administrators and managers rather than strategists. An interior district is also a very poor echelon for combat training. The Russian army became fully convinced of this in 1914. From the point of view of war preparations it would be incomparably more advantageous to replace district commands with inspectorates that integrate several corps and are relieved of any administrative and managerial duties and constitute the concealed operational head of the army staff. Only several border districts make a certain amount of sense as a ready skeleton of front command in particularly important sectors.

Mobilization and Railroads

Railroads have a very difficult task in mobilization. They themselves have to be mobilized, that is, prepared for concentration transports. But at the same time they have to do a great deal of work on mobilization transports: that is, moving hundreds of thousands called-up reserves and requisitioned horses, delivering military freight quickly and at the same time providing covering transports, i.e., transports for the purpose of strengthening the defense of important sectors in border areas.[4] At the same time the civilian life of a country places extraordinary demands on the railroads: citizens try to return to their places of permanent residence by any means possible, or, once economic mobilization begins to get to their new work places. Cars and platforms must be relieved of freight to make it possible to begin handling troops; empties must be concentrated in areas from which concentration traffic will begin flowing toward the borders; personnel must be sent to the lines leading to the border to reinforce them; and the railways must do triple the amount of work that they do in peacetime. It is extremely important to warn the railways in advance of a forthcoming mobilization and it is very important to devise a railroad mobilization plan in all details. And it is particularly important to take into consideration the amount of work that the military can possibly require of the railroads. We must avoid attempts to ignore completely the civilian need for railroads once a war begins. Once a mobilization is under way the economic life of the country is clogged up. The stations are jammed with people waiting for an opportunity to get into cars, the roofs of the cars are filled with persons who have broken through security at minor stops and discipline in all aspects of life is affected. All one has to do is triple the fares, and at least a modest traffic should be maintained in order to meet the essential needs of the public.

The proper deployment of troops and supplies in peacetime is the best way to reduce mobilization transport, but if this is not done, mobilization transports will blow up to gigantic dimensions.

It took the Germans' three days to mobilize their railroads before the Would War, whereas it took the Russians four to eight days. The trouble this long delay caused the Russians is evident from the following calculations based on data from 1908 for several score of Russian railways: before the completion of mobilization they could carry 15.7 troop trains per day, that is their troop train capacity was 250 percent higher.

The poorer the railroads are, the more resources must be borrowed by the lines on which concentration transports are made from other rail lines and the longer it will take to mobilize the former. Every extra locomotive and every extra car manufactured in peacetime will speed up the mobilization process. Of particular importance is the availability of a two-to-three-month supply of fuel for the railroads, which would make it possible to relieve them of the burden of transporting heavy shipments of fuel during mobilization and deployment. This is particularly important for railroads that are far from fuel supplies, particularly if

---

[4] The mobilization in Germany required 20,800 trains, including 17,991 trains in the interval between the third and seventh days of the mobilization. The number of trains was larger than for the concentration transports, but the trains were shorter, and the work was evenly divided among the entire rail system. The presence of extensive agricultural regions in the east and highly industrialized areas in the west and in the center was unfavorable for the Germans, because first of all they had to move people from the west and horses from the east. The dense troop concentrations on the left bank of the Rhine required moving people and horses from the right bank of the Rhine. In eastern Germany the rail system was weak and had to be strengthened with 530 locomotives and 173 trains made up of 50 cars each from the industrialized west. Up to 400,000 tons of military freight was transported for the mobilization needs of deployment, fortresses and the navy.

the direction in which the fuel is shipped is the same as that of the troop movement. Before the World War the Siberian Railway was capable of handling 20 to 27 pairs of troop trains, but only until its mobilization stockpiles of coal were exhausted, and then troop traffic on it had to be reduced to 12 pairs.

4. PREPARING BORDER THEATERS

Organizational Preparations

During peacetime there is a certain military organization in border regions, including headquarters, stores and depots, which provide various supplies to the troops, maintenance ships, barracks, camps and rifle ranges. Peacetime needs are met by permanent lines of communication. In the border sector there are also border guard detachments who also have their own equipment.

A short time after a war begins border equipment must be replaced with frontline equipment. A great deal will have to be expanded and done anew. But this problem of creating a fighting organization will be greatly simplified if peacetime fortifications can be utilized fully and if a large portion of the border equipment is included in the front organization. At the same time, as is always the case in confusion, when thousands of commanders who are unfamiliar with the situation at the border arrive with their units and agencies from afar with the invariable order to clean up the railheads, immediately any stationary element of the overall apparatus that has been set up beforehand and has already begun to function at a permanent site is of colossal oreganizational importance. But there is a difference between setting up front and army headquarters at unimproved points or setting them up at the former locations of district and corps headquarters. It is much easier to expand a modest food store to the required size than to build a new one from scratch. An engineering equipment depot at a point where the construction of roads and fortifications will have to start immediately once mobilization begins will be a great deal of help. On the other hand, if everything has to be moved and evacuated and if mobilization is equivalent to mass migrations of people, the period of time in which everything can be set up and coordinated will be greatly prolonged, a great deal of additional work is required and the period of inevitable mass confusion will not increase confidence in the leadership of the war.

This makes it necessary to examine every organizational measure in border districts in terms of the frontline mission to be accomplished.

Road Preparations

Special measures to prepare the theater of a conflict should primarily involve the development and maintenance of the network of lines of communication. An army's productivity is directly proportional to the quality of the roads in its rear. Bad roads weaken the front and multiply the rear.

The tendency to build good roads in an area where the direction of our offensive is planned and let the roads go in an area where we plan to stay passive and fear an enemy attack is natural. However, we must deeply ponder the operational situation before we set up road traps. Before the World War we considered it advantageous to prepare for an invasion of East Prussia from the Neman River and an invasion of Galicia from the Kiev Military District, and we built a network of highways in these areas to the border itself. We considered the following directions threatening to us: to the Warsaw Military District bypassing the Vistula; from the north from eastern Prussia to the line of the Narev; and from the south from Galicia to the Lublin-Cholm line. In these areas there were practically no railways or paved roads, and the dirt roads ran through sand or marshes. However, the situation compelled us to operate very actively and use routes from the Narev (Samsonov's 2nd Army) for our invasion of East Prussia and routes from the Lublin-Cholm line (9th, 4th and 5th Armies) to invade Galicia, and thus we fell into our own trap. Samsonov's army, after travelling without roads, was in a very difficult situation. It was cut off, and its only line of communication, the Mlava Railway, ran from its left flank and was covered by the 1st Army Corps, and an attack on this corps would have compelled him to retreat along the railroad and thus expose the flank and rear of other corps. The entire operation would have turned out quite differently if there had been a railroad and several good highways to the north from Ostrolenka. Ultimately the 4th and 9th Armies handled the Austrians, but what a graveyard of trucks and carts the vicinity of the mangled highway south of Lublin was![1] The olumns had to go around it through the fields, and a very high percentage of the horses dropped from exhaustion on these Lublin fields. When Ludendorff's maneuver was discovered and the 4th, 5th and 9th Armies had to be moved to the New Alexandria-Warsaw front, the rear once again fell apart, the batteries lost a large number of horses, we were late in taking crossings on the Vistula and the Ivangorod-Warsaw operation was greatly prolonged.

We had Novogeorgievsk fortress on which we lavished large sums of money. This fortress acted as a triple bridgehead at the confluence of the Bug-Narev and Vistula. However, in order to make it difficult for the Germans to approach it from the left bank of the Vistula, not one decent road was built to the fortress at this spot. The loose sand on the left bank of the Vistula blocked the fortress in peacetime. Hence during the Warsaw operation (October 1914) when pressure had to be exerted on the left bank of the Vistula from the fortress, this pressure could only be very weak.

But we should not think only of offensives and build roads only in the immediate vicinities of disembarkation stations in the direction of the border. This was the basic tendency in our construction of military roads prior to 1901.[2] A narrow sector with good roads extending along the border could be turned against us if the enemy manages to knock us off it into the marshy forests lying beyond it. Road preparations should cover an adequate depth.

---

[1] Given the availability of this very important highway, we should have prepared millions of tons of stone and delivered it to use for round-the-clock-repairs.

[2] In the 20 years prior to the Russo-Japanese War Russia, in preparing border theaters of deployment, built an average of 160 kilometers of roads per year using the military budget and spent about 15,000 rubles per kilometer of road. In 1909, when the rears had become more cumbersome and we had to include trucks in our plans, road construction was to be expanded to 700 kilometers per year. Keeping in mind the fact that we had 50 to 200 times fewer paved roads in our border regions than Western Europe did and our rears were quite cumbersome, it would have been quite reasonable to resume an extensive highway rebuilding program. Because of the need to adapt the roadbed to two-way heavy truck traffic, highways would have to be widened and thickened, which would have more than doubled the cost per kilometer. But highway expenditures contribute to improving the ratio of combatants to noncombatants and waging war more economically and successfully.

There is no particular need to fear that the enemy will use the roads we build for an invasion. Military freight traffic is highly destructive even of highways, and what is not destroyed by hooves and wheels can be destroyed by explosions if appropriate preparations are not made. Setting up a number of deep furrows in hard-to-bypass places will hinder any traffic for long periods of time. In March 1917 Ludendorff did such great damage to the roads in the 40-kilometer sector in front of the Siegfried line (the Alberich Works) that despite the fact that the British and French spent a year repairing these roads, they experienced a great deal of difficulties in their offensive of March 1918. The "massive" destruction of roads is one of the innovations of the World War.

Equipping a war theater with railroads is of great strategic importance. We built at least 4,000 kilometers of railroads before the World War in the west for exclusively military purposes and, given the vast extent of our western border, no fewer kilometers of track should be included in our plan for strengthening our western border theaters. The existing system of track has gaps in several places that would make it extremely risky to occupy several important sectors of the front because there are no decent dirt roads in the rear. Reason dictates building these roads if it is decided to deploy in front of inaccessible places. And highways should be built everywhere that extensive cart and truck traffic is planned.

In the siege of Sevastopol in the Crimean War of 1853-1856, military operations acquired the character of a materiel competition and we had to haul massive freight to Sevastopol. Our rear made 132,000 deliveries, most of which were handled by a dirt road 200 kilometers long running from Kakhovka to Simferopol to Sevastopol. Because of the excessive stress placed on this road and exhaustion, fodder horses and oxen dropped by the thousands. Sometimes transports were as slow as four kilometers per day. Supplies were moved to Sevastopol in small amounts and with a great deal of delay. It is most likely that half the deliveries would have done just as much good. It would be a big mistake to assume that we can achieve good results by increasing the number of carts and ignoring the road system. In this case we have the discrepancy between the one-sided swelling of the Red Army's rear and the condition of our road system. What could one say about a People's Commissariat of Railways that would unilaterally increase the amount of rolling stock without any concern for the condition of the track or the amount of track?

If we are planning to make an attack from several sectors and peacetime experience indicates that at one point we will have to haul trucks by hand across stretches of sand laying down boards, then concern for the success of the attack will be expressed by building a good road ahead. The development of the road system should conform to the requirements of the deployment and the planned maneuver.

What we have said about the roads also applies to the telegraph system.

Of course, like all other issues of the war plan, issues of road preparations do not have a hard and fast answer for all cases and must be evaluated dialectically through the prism of our conceptions of the nature of a future war. What was more important for tsarist Russia, building the Orel-Sedlets four-track railway, upon which the French insisted on or building the Murmansk Railway? If we pursue a strategy of destruction, then a superroad that would make it possible to throw up to 150 extra trains a day into the concentration area would be incomparably more important, but in the strategy of attrition characteristic of the World War, the Murmansk Railway, which provided Russia with economic breathing room, was much more suitable.

Preparing Fortifications

In a natural economy the motto is the individual defense of each village; but as the capitalist economy has grown, the economic basis has been strengthened; and the weapons of attack have been built up, the possibilities of defending a point isolated from the territory of a large state are increasingly limited. Just as the closed redoubt is tactically obsolete, the closed fortress with a line of forts has become a thing of the strategic past. Any attempt to build such a fortress would necessitate increasing its girth to 100 kilometers, its artillery to 4,000 guns and the amount of ordnance to tens of millions of rounds. It would take more than a billion rubles to build such a fortress and its defense would require a garrison of 300,000 to 400,000 soldiers. Nevertheless, such a fortress could be captured in two to three weeks at a cost equal to 5 percent of the cost of building it with a force 20 to 30 percent the size of its garrison.

Fortresses of the old type may still be important in wars against an uncivilized and technically underdeveloped enemy if there is no decent system of lines of communication. Of course, every European army should be materially and mentally prepared to attack such a fortress, and it is only the lack of this training on the part of the Russian army that explains its long delay against Przemysl. The main requirement is to have a sufficiently mobile and organized heavy artillery and familiarize commanders and men with the techniques of a quick attack on permanent fortifications.

Denying the importance of fortresses is not equivalent to deny the importance of permanent fortifications. However, the latter must discard the now impossible goal of creating a self-contained fortification entity capable of offering resistance to the enemy without the close cooperation of maneuvering friendly forces. The fact of the matter is that the existence of long-term defensive fortifications is only meaningful in close cooperation with these maneuvers by reinforcing certain important lines in a war theater.

The need for fortifications in modern warfare stems primarily from the need to vary the density of occupation of a front significantly. To form a fist or battering ram in one sector, one must spread one's forces very thin in other sectors. In the last third of May 1916, the 32nd Corps was ordered to use half its forces in the Lutsk breakthrough, forming its extreme left sector; the corps concentrated its 101st division for the attack on a front two kilometers wide, and brought up elements of the 2nd Finnish infantry division as the army reserve behind the attack sector. The density of deployment on the active sector was 28 times greater than the density on the passive sector. It is true that in this case concentration was partially facilitated by the Ikva River, which reinforced most of the front of the 105th division, but even if such local advantages had not been there, the corps could have spread its forces thin on the passive sector by the intelligent use of fortifications.

If no fortifications have been built beforehand, energetic work will have to be done to prepare fortified positions once mobilization begins. The success of these operations, despite the preparation of drawings, shovels and wire and the organization of work teams and transports will nevertheless be doubtful, because this work must extend over a vast front, enemy raids may interfere with it and the first week after war is declared will have to be spent on organizational preparations, while in the third week, in some instances, the fortified sectors will already have to fulfill their purposes. This kind of feverish mobilization activity in building fortifications is always inevitable. However, if a certain prepared fortification skeleton is available, this work will go much better.

It is natural that forces will concentrate for attacks in areas that have more lines of communication, whereas passive sectors of the front will primarily consist of remote, roadless sectors. But from a comparison of this comment and previous remarks it would be mistaken to infer that one should set up a fortification fence on secondary sectors while leaving exposed the road junctions where "battering rams" will be assembled. A fortified position is a gateway as well as a barrier. Road junctions should primarily be secured by covering forces and the presence of permanent fortifications is particularly important for these forces. This is where the main forces will concentrate, and a permanent fortification will cover their concentration and play a major organizing role, and its presence will make it possible to gather a certain percentage of heavy artillery and equipment near a border and establish a permanent communications system. It is better to leave dead spots dead; covering them with a solid front may be postponed until later in the war; and if enemy hordes should break through them, we will not be in a bad situation, because with our secured road junctions we can make flank attacks under the most favorable possible conditions.

A line prepared in advance must be ready for this role as a shield to cover the development of a flank attack. We must avoid dispersing our resources on individual small positions which are incapable of supporting such a maneuver. If there is a solid local position, it also becomes possible to set up such lines in three to five days' march along the front. Good roads, fortifications in great depth on the flanks and careful placement of positional fortifications will have to ensure the success of future maneuvers. We must keep in mind positional preparations for an entire army rather than just the individual company or battalion.

The experience of the World War clearly demonstrated the unsuitability of positions in front of bridges. The best way to put one's forces in a position to be destroyed is to position them in front of bridges. But on our western border, where rivers form very important lines, there are great temptations to concentrate all of our fortification preparations on positions in front of bridges. However, sound strategic thinking should resolutely combat this tendency. It would be much cheaper to build a backup railroad bridge in the rear and prepare for quick repairs of demolished trusses rather than try to defend a bridge in an enemy attack by taking up positions in front of it. In modern conditions, the latter has to be moved a whole day's march from the river and the bridge, and fighting for it will always be carried out in unfavorable conditions.

River lines will, of course, have to be used on the defensive so that our forces will gain rather than lose from the river. Long-term fortification should try to reinforce the river line by forming a defensive or offensive flank, and it will often be possible to use the valleys of tributaries for this purpose. If the French were to cross the lower Rhine, then the Germans, in Willisen's thinking, would have to occupy the line of the Main River with a front to the north and the Mainz fortress on their left flank, which would have compelled the French to engage in a decisive battle under the worst possible conditions, with their rear to the North Sea, their left flank to the interior of Germany, and with the Rhine and the Dutch border hanging on their right flank and overextended lines of communication. An example of an active flank is the deployment of the 3rd German Army in front of the Rhine in August 1870; this deployment formed an active flank position and defended the entire watercourse of the river. In the World War a long-term position that blocked off the Alsace Valley at the height of Strasbourg covered the entire upper Rhine. Of course, setting up these kinds of offensive and defensive bends could be combined with the direct passive reinforcement of the obstacle of a river line. Sometimes it will be necessary to advance to the enemy's bank in order to secure important junctions lying directly in a valley but these kinds of operations should be considered definitely excessive and one must study whether it would be better to construct rail spurs and roads that would make it possible for us to manage without the threatened road junction. If necessary, it would be easy for our forces to cross to the enemy's bank without bridgeheads. The need for the bridgeheads as initial areas for reconnaissance has now diminished with the development of aviation.

It would be wasteful to spend a large portion of the military budget on building fortifications, but 1-2 percent of the budget systematically expended from year to year on improving the defenses of border theaters would undoubtedly pay for itself by making it possible for our vanguard strategic deployment units to stand on firm ground immediately.

We have not dwelled on the issues of preparing a theater of war for naval and air operations, because in general this would lead to an extensive discussion of operational art. With respect to naval bases we shall limit ourselves to saying that the closer a base lies to an ocean and the more secure its lines of communication to the overall base, namely the interior of the country, the greater its strategic value. All we have to do is compare the eastern base of the Russian squadron in 1904, Port Arthur, which lay deep in the Pechiliiskii Gulf and the base of the German Far East cruisers on the Shantung Peninsula, and remember the fate of the Russian fleet, which was tied down at Port Arthur, and the breakthrough of the German squadron, to which the British managed to catch up only at the coast of South America, in order to agree with this statement. If we consider the coastline of the Baltic and North Seas from Kronshtadt to Scapa Flow (on the Scottish coast), we must acknowledge the perfectly awful strategic location of Kronstadt as a naval base deep in the Marquis Pool and notice the gradual improvement of the strategic position of other harbors the farther west one goes from Kronstadt. Basing issues will play an even more decisive role in sea battles.

5. THE OPERATIONAL PLAN

The Content and Scope of the Operational Plan

The operational plan should include: a plan for initial operations, and a plan for all auxiliary transports, for the creation and operational deployment itself, and a supply plan.[1]

As we shall clarify below in our section on combining operations, the ultimate war aim has a programmatic, orienting significance, but the desire to work out in advance the entire path toward this goal even in general rather than calendar terms will only lead to an accumulation of preconditions, prejudices and conditionalities, and the task will invariably become utopian. We must establish two periods of prediction, the period before a conflict with the enemy's main forces and the period afterwards, and as much as possible we must work out in detail everything preceding an anticipated crisis however, just as the subsequent future of military operations seems to be shrouded by a barely permeable veil, certain statistical and operational efforts are desirable in order to prepare the thinking of the high command and general staff for opportunities to take advantage of a victory or alleviate the consequences of a defeat; however these efforts can only be purely theoretical. This is especially valid if a war is pursued for a destructive strike and an armed conflict with an enemy is formulated as a war to the bitter end. In a war planned for attrition, in certain respects planning predictions become more long term in nature, because we primarily define attrition as the rejection of the importance of a single and all-deciding means in the main operation; hence other means whose effect can be taken into consideration ahead of time may in some ways assist us in a war of attrition in planning a number of military measures that last longer than the anticipated first collision.

The ultimate war aim ties the strategist down in the same way that the politician is tied down by his party program. Strategists and politicians who consider the ultimate ideal while ignoring the realities of the day will wind up in the same situation as Krylov's metaphysician. Concern for immediate goals characterizes strategy as a practical art.

The Degree of Variability of the Operational Plan

The operational plan is based on existing information on the political and economic situation and on our conceptions of the enemy's and our own armed forces, the enemy's probable deployment and the strength and configuration of our railroad system, the conditions of our mobilization and the preparation of our border areas. All work on the war plan consists of a number of actions that determine the initial data for writing the operational plan. At the same time, the operational plan clearly indicates where the flaws in our preparations lie and what efforts must be made to improve them. Thus an analysis of the operational plan leads to directives for the war plan.

---

[1] We have already discussed evacuation policy in our chapter on politics and will not go back to the issues of evacuation or the evacuation plan in this chapter.

Work on the war plan must be done over a number of years in one and the same direction in order to produce perceptible results. Incidentally, the premises of the operational plan are quite variable data, e.g., the political momentum and strengths of the enemy; the views of hostile leaders and their plans; our variable situation, such as a crop failure or a conflict in some remote or secondary theater which has drawn off some of our armed forces, and these variable data may be assessed in quite different ways depending on the persons heading the high command. Naturally these conditions mean that operational plans may change greatly from year to year and even that several variations can and should exist at the same time as the primary operational plan. We may ask whether a flexible and variable operational plan can serve as a guideline for all the long years of work involved in preparation.

Experience has shown that it can. First of all, the significance of information on military geography changes very, very slowly. Gradually expanding networks of lines of communications are also subordinate to it. Minsk, Molodechno, Borisov, Bobruisk, Orsha, Smolensk, Vitebsk, Polotsk, Drissa, Berezina, the Dnepr, the Dvina and Ulla were of major importance in the Belorussian theater of 1812 and are still significant today. Routes across Belgium have always been the most convenient for an invasion of France. The Tatar raids from the Crimea in the 16th century were aimed at the water divide between the Don and the Dnepr, and Denikin chose the same direction for his offensive on Moscow in 1919. Kakhovka fed Sevastopol in 1855 and served as an important starting point for the operation against Wrangel in 1920. Minikh bypassed the Perekop fortifications via the Sivash 183 years before Frunze.[2] In general, the balance of our forces and those of the enemy changes quite gradually. In most cases an operational plan is not written completely anew but is merely updated every one or two years by making certain revisions in the preceding plan. Thus the stages of preparation that have already been achieved by the war plan do not entail a great deal of work that has been done in vain, and to a certain extent they may be utilized in a new operational plan since they stand on the path of historical succession.

When the mission is to inflict a destructive strike and the main forces are to be employed, the operational plan is less subject to radical change. After 1870 on the French front the Germans initially prepared for a predominantly defensive deployment on the Saar River, but in the last 15 years before the war they prepared for an offensive through Belgium and built up the scale of this offensive in 1905. On the Russian front the Germans planned to deploy first against the Narev, next against the Bobr, and then in Silesia (with small forces). And in every case there were clues to the deployment plans left in the scores of railheads and other structures. This work extended along the entire Russian border and was not done in vain, enabling the Germans to make rapid movements along the border.

In Russia deployment at Neman and in the Kiev Military District was firmly established during the 25 years preceding the war, only the Russians' view of their missions in the Warsaw Military District changed radically. Of course, drastic

---

[2]   Of course, there is nothing remarkable about this historical repetitiveness. The water divide between the Dnepr and the Don bypasses all river obstacles on the way to Moscow as far as the Oka. Kakhova is the point at which the Dnepr gets closest to the Crimea. The Sivash, which is dried by the west wind, is very deceptive security for the right flank of the Perekop isthmus.

changes in the high command had an adverse effect on war preparations. In Russia this change occurred in 1904 when Kuropatkin resigned as minister of war. In 1908, when the Russians returned to their preparations for war against Germany which had been interrupted by the Russo-Japanese War, there was a drastic change: many troops were withdrawn from the provinces near the Vistula to interior provinces, army fortresses were disarmed reserve brigades were disbanded, and so forth. But this change was based on the desire to take advantage of the experience of the Russo-Japanese War, primarily a more modest evaluation of the capabilities of Russian soldiers and commanders.

We must above all ensure the stability of the military high command and the continuity of the work of the agency responsible for the operational plan, the general staff. A great deal of attention and profound consideration of strategic issues are needed in order to avoid drifting aimlessly. We need leadership with proven views on the art of war. Of course, routine, conservatism and traditions are a great hazard in working on an operational plan (they were evident, for example, in the work of the French Plan 17). Assertions that are not firmly grounded but are repeated again and again in time turn into a kind of sacred truth and acquire a kind of absolute value, particularly when their content is a major secret and only a narrow circle of augurs is allowed to criticize them. But we do need wisdom to allow a certain steadiness of behavior and an understanding of the requirements of evolution and persistence rather than an idiotic conformity to fads. Revolutionary changes in operational views are hazardous and detrimental.

The Flexibility of an Operational Plan

We must not, for technical considerations, make decisions that would radically contradict the requirement of politics. Therefore an operational plan must be flexible and have several versions, which would make it possible to choose between war of destruction and a war of attrition, between the defensive and the offensive and between attacking one nation or another in a hostile alliance, depending on political guidelines.

The political goal of a war may be finally stated by responsible persons only at the last minute before a declaration of war, and the ultimate war aim of armed conflict may be precisely determined on the basis of it the political goal. However, certain political goals of a war with different enemies may by predicted far in advance and in working on an operational plan we already need to proceed from a certain political orientation. This orientation may be sufficient to make it possible to formulate a primary goal in operational plans, i.e.,a first stage toward the achievement of which our operational efforts must be primarily directed once a war begins. If the existing orientation is not clear enough and we cannot state a single primary goal, we must state two or even more and draw up a separate version of the operational plan for each of them. For example, one version may have an offensive primary goal, namely moving into enemy territory toward an important position ready to attack enemy armies who have assembled close to the border, whereas another version may have a defensive goal, defending a very important position on one's own border territory.

It is very important to determine the steps that must be taken in all cases and put them outside of the individual versions in order to make preparations for war more definitive. For example, it is extremely desirable to keep mobilization the same in all versions of an operational plan. Perhaps we could also retain the same front organization in different versions with the same command, boundaries and rears with only the numbers of armies or troops included in the varying, depending on the version. Perhaps we would be able to resolve questions of covering concentration in the same way; but if there are proposals to carry out a cavalry raid once mobilization begins (these raids played important roles in the Russian plans of the early 20th century), capture an important point on enemy territory (e.g., Liège) or carry out air raids, then, if primarily defensive operations have been selected, we must have another version of covering the concentration. In the concentration itself it is extremely important to determine the armies and corps to be deployed in all versions in the same areas. Regarding other corps dispatched to different areas depending on the version, we would perhaps be able to employ the same procedures for getting them into trains and use the same initial routes so that variations would begin only after the head echelon of a corps had reached the railroad junction that would send the transports right or left.

The operational plan of the Russian general staff was the most flexible one in the World War. Flexibility was extremely necessary for the Russians, because their deployment front was extraordinarily broad and the situation on their front could be quite different, depending on whether the Germans sent their main forces against France or against Russia. The deployment plan of 1912, Plan A, called for concentrating the main forces (744 battalions) against Austria-Hungary and smaller forces (480 battalions) against Germany with explicit offensive missions. In the second plan, Plan D, the center of gravity was shifted to East Prussia (672 battalions against Germany and 552 battalions against Austria-Hungary). Whereas most units were definitely assigned to one front or the other, the 4th Army would deploy at Lublin in one plan and in the area of Riga and Szawli in the other plan: a total of 192 battalions, 126 regular and Cossack squadrons and 708 guns, approximately 15 percent of all the forces to be deployed, which were to be dispatched in one direction or the other, completely altered the versions. The strengths of other armies were subjected to certain alterations in order to facilitate and reduce the number of transports. In the first days of the war everything followed both plans, and only on the eighth day of mobilization was the high command forced to choose Plan A or Plan D.[3]

However, in this plan the desire to meet the requirements of flexibility is still not emphatic. We even suspect that perhaps Plan D was written solely for the purpose of comforting the French, who had the right to demand, on the basis of the military convention, that we send 900,000 men against the Germans. We can at least see the flexibility of such a diplomatic procedure in the German operational plan carried out in 1914: five good reserve divisions, called ersatz divisions for purposes of concealment, wert to stay on the Russian front until the 11th day of the mobilization and could then be transferred to the French front (which is what actually happened). Here they were intentionally deceiving the Austrians: these five divisions, which were included in the plan for a wide turn through Belgium, were at the same time also included in the strength of the 13 to 14 active

---

[3] In order to make a correct choice, the Russian general staff had special agents in the areas of the German 2nd, 5th and 6th Corps who sent coded telegrams indicating that these corps had left for the west. This technique is extremely important when fighting an enemy who is fighting on two fronts.

divisions promised to the Austrian and left in East Prussia supposedly for an offensive across the Narev River toward Sedlets.

The requirements of flexibility are more evident in the Russian plan of 1914. First of all, the seven second-line divisions, which would take a longer time to mobilize and would arrive at the deployment area after the 26th day of mobilization, were not assigned ahead of time to armies but were put at the direct disposal of the supreme commander in chief. We cannot help but consider this intelligent. In fact, after the 20th day of mobilization one could have anticipated the development of fierce fighting on all fronts; one to two weeks later the situation could have changed drastically, and what would be the point of tying down new reinforcements to specific armies when the railroad system in the area of deployment made it possible to dispatch them to any sector of our extensive front?

There were no A and D versions in the Russian plan of 1914, but there were plans to deploy the Guards and 8th Corps on the northwestern front and the 1st, 16th and 24th and 25th Armies and the 3rd Caucasian Corps on the southwestern front, a total of seven corps for which different versions of transports were written, either to the Neman, or against Galicia. We could say that the Russian general staff, which was firm in its commitment of the forces of the Vilna and Kiev Military Districts and elements of the Moscow and Odessa Districts, left itself the freedom to deploy the corps of Petrograd, Kazan, and Caucasian Military Districts. Headquarters was also free to maneuver 168 battalions, initially prepared by the Asian districts for transports to the first line, which were to arrive at the rear of the deployment area between the 26th and 41st days of mobilization.

In the final analysis, 51.6 percent of the armed forces constituted a hard core (950 battalions) of operational deployment in the plan of 1914; 12.2 percent made up a group of seven corps whose locations at the front could vary on the basis of preliminary transport plans; 21.2 percent were the reserve of the commander in chief, which he could deploy at his discretion in the fifth, sixth and seventh weeks of mobilization (a group of late arriving second-line divisions, coastal surveillance units, the first echelon of the Asian corps); and 15 percent constituted the remainder of the Russian forces, primarily the second Asian echelon.[4] For the 1914 period we must acknowledge the major improvement in flexibility achieved by this plan.[5] Currently we are making even greater requirements for flexibility in deployment. The numerous modifications made in the plan of 1912 in the actual deployment of 1914 indicate that our railroad system, despite its major shortcomings still made it possible to alter plan proposals without any major complications.

These requirements were met to a much lesser extent in Austria-Hungary, because the conditions of concentrating in two opposite directions, namely against Serbia on the southwest toward the Sava River and against Russia in Galicia on the northeast were difficult. The deployment plan called for assigning the A units

---

[4]   A detailed exposition of Russian operational deployment plans in the 30 years prior to the World War analyzed from the perspective of the strategic thinking of the old generation and containing a wealth of archival material can be found in Zaionchkovskii, *Podgotovka Rossii k mirovoi voine.*

[5]   This means taking advantage of a "second hand," namely delays in deployment. It was not by accident that the Russian command set a record for flexibility in preparing for the World War. Because the operational deployment of forces scattered over the "ocean" of Russian land will always have a tendency to be prolonged, our situation places a particular emphasis on flexibility in operational deployment.

permanently to the Russian and Serbian fronts, while the B units, namely the 4th and 7th Corps and both Czech (8th and 13th) corps, could, depending on the circumstance, be deployed on the Russian or Serbian fronts. July 28 was the first day of mobilization against Serbia. The Austro-Hungarian command tried to inflict a destructive strike on the Serbians. Three A units, the 13th, 15th and 16th corps, reinforced by four B corps were assigned to fight Serbia; the forces on the Serbian front included 19 infantry divisions and one cavalry division. Because the Czech corps were not particularly reliable in fighting Slavs, the chief of the Austro-Hungarian general staff, General Konrad, decided to reinforce the Serbian front with the 3rd Corps and two divisions taken from the A units, i.e.,divisions, that had been permanently based on the Russian front according to the operational plan.

On the night of July 30 the Austro-Hungarians began moving troops to the Danube on four railroads. Personnel and rolling stock were extensively borrowed from other rail lines to mobilize the Danube system. The movement against Serbia required a total of 2,064 troop trains with 50 cars each (512,000 men, 64,000 horses, 19,300 carts and 60,000 tons of materiel). The transport was in full swing: because of a number of misunderstandings Vienna found out about the general mobilization in Russia only on the morning of August 1, 24 hours after Berlin did. The German general staff, in a telegram sent by Wilhelm (4:40 pm on July 31) demanded that Austria-Hungary put its main forces up against Russia and not get distracted by a campaign against Serbia. General Konrad wanted to stop the concentration against Serbia and send the B corps and the A units borrowed from the Russian front to Galicia. However, the chief of military communication, Colonel Straub, demonstrated the impossibility of changing the direction of 2,000 trains and receiving them in Galicia, where the railroads had not been mobilized. Only a single cavalry division (the 2nd) had not begun moving to the Danube. Colonel Straub agreed to send the 1st cavalry division, which was already on the way to the Danube, to Galicia. The other units on the way were conscientiously delivered to the Danube, disembarked and were then transferred to Galicia as second-line units.

Austria-Hungary had declared a general mobilization on July 31, but the first day of mobilization was to fall on August 4, because four days were required to put the conditions for a general mobilization in order after the uproar produced by the partial mobilization against Serbia. Only on the morning of August 6 did transports against Russia begin, a total of 3,998 trains on seven lines to Galicia, and only on August 6 did Austria-Hungary (which until then was unarmed) decide to declare war on Russia (five days after Germany did) and commence hostile operations on the border. The corps dispatched to the Danube (the 4th and 7th Corps, the 20th and 23d divisions) began to move only on August 18, and as we know, they were late in getting to the first half of the Battle of Galicia.[6]

---

[6]   General Konrad had foreseen these misunderstandings as early as 1901, as is evident from his memoirs and correspondence with Moltke concerning an agreement on the conduct of military operations on the Russian front. Konrad also allowed for the worst, that is, that the Russians would give the Austrians time to get into a war with Serbia and act only with delay. If they had sacrificed the Serbians in this way, the Russians only would have had 30 Austrian divisions facing them in Galicia for three months. Reichsarchiv, *Der Weltkrieg*, vol. 2, pp. 3-14.

In general, we must believe that Austria-Hungary paid for its attempt to start an adventure against Serbia with a five-day delay in deploying the A units in Galicia and a seven-day delay in deploying the B units because of its lack of flexibility. If the Austrians had acted consistently, they would have been able to begin the Galician operation five days earlier and double the strength of the screen they set up against the Kiev Military District. We believe that this would have led to an extremely severe crisis on the Lublin-Cholm line by August 29, the time of the Samsonov catastrophe and the quite probable withdrawal of Russian forces from the Vistula to the middle Bug.

Poland, in the event of a war on two fronts, would have difficulty finding the time to resolve the question of where the main attack would come because its directions of concentration were completely opposite. The German front is incomparably more important to Poland than the Russian front, because it is crossed by three times as many railroads tracks and economically important regions are near it. The worst scenario for Poland would be a war with Russia followed by German intervention after Poland began moving its forces to the east.

The lack of flexibility in operational plans before the World War can partially be ascribed to negative attitudes toward the concepts of strategic and operational reserves on the part of all general staffs;[7] strategic reserves usually included only future formations and units that had to come from another continent; (the Siberian corps and the British and French colonial divisions). All the men they had at hand they immediately tried to assign to armies and fronts. A different attitude toward a strategic reserve, the necessity of which we will justify in the future, would make it possible to make initial operational plans incomparably more flexible and avoid those misunderstandings from which the Austro-Hungarian deployment of 1914 suffered so.

Operational Deployment

The initial operations of a war are conducted in the same way as subsequent operations. The strategic approach is the same, and therefore we shall make a fundamental analysis of them in the next section of our treatise, which is devoted to the issue of combining operations to achieve the goal of a war. Here we must speak of them only because all preparations for initial operations should be made on the basis of the goals set for them. If in fact the initial operations follow from the deployment, then from the perspective of writing a plan, the deployment follows from the first planned operations. Deployment is a means that is subordinate to our end.[8]

---

[7] According to Plan 17 the French concentration in 1914 was extremely inflexible and allowed only for the possibility of changing the areas of disembarkation of two corps of the 4th Army, namely on different sides of the Ardennes; this inflexibility of the transport plan was explained by the fact that all of the ten available trunk lines leading to the area of concentration were fully occupied by transports (58 pairs per day per line). The desire to maximize saving time for the purpose of seizing the initiative made it necessary to avoid the opportunity for any kind of railroad maneuver. If the French had decided beforehand to organize an operational reserve of traffic by 20 to 30 percent, things would have turned out much better for them. Just the same, on the 15th day of mobilization (August 16), the French had to resort to a railway maneuver before all transports had ended in order to reinforce their left flank, but this maneuver was made under in extremely difficult conditions and reserves had to be taken from the right wing instead of dispatching them directly from Paris.

The same deployment, in general terms, will often be able to meet defensive and offensive needs and may often require changes in deployments only within armies and in extreme cases within a front.

However, the variations between a war of destruction and a war of attrition compel us to have different versions, because geographical objectives and generally secondary areas may force us to commit major forces to them in a war of attrition. Thus the strategic line of conduct we formulate will already be evident in the deployment plan.

The basic requirements for the planning of initial operations include foreseeing the nature of a war, considering our forces and enemy resistance, and setting goals that are appropriate for the available resources and are therefore feasible but avoid squandering precious time for taking advantage of the opportunities presented to us.

The correct choice of a position for assembling transported troops is very important for all organizational measures; this position, which is the starting point for an offensive, should at the same time be advantageous for the defensive, because initially covering forces should be kept there, and then if the enemy keeps us from concentrating there, it will perhaps be necessary to commit one part of our army to battle to make it possible for the other part to concentrate. If the enemy's mobilization-readiness and railroads are superior to ours, this position should be far enough away from the border for us to gain the time we need. The presence of permanent fortifications, strong local obstacles and the wealth of border regions form the basis for selecting a particular position near a border so as to minimize the loss of territory. In view of the possibility of getting involved in extremely intense and large battles in a deployment area, it is quite important to make extremely accurate calculations of the time the enemy needs to mobilize, concentrate and march from his area of deployment to ours. It is very desirable for us to have sufficient forces for resistance in the area of deployment by the time of a battle. Having one-third of the corps in the rear and on the rails cannot serve as an argument in favor of the need to move the deployment line deeper. This third, if an operation is conducted skillfully, will be in the advantageous situation of an operational reserve that will be able to go into battle at a decisive moment because currently major battles drag on for many days.

If the enemy's deployment is extremely uncertain, we may have versions of two deployments planned so that, if necessary, we can systematically put railheads in the depth of a country two to four days march away (Moltke in 1870).

We are not afraid of the criticism that we have deviated too far from Moltke's doctrine, because the 50 years that have elapsed and the appearance of a new factor, the railroad maneuver, explain our deviations. We consider Moltke's well-known idea obsolete:

---

[8]   In fact, as in the French Plan 17, operations may be written down only in the form of a very short list of missions assigned to armies, and the center of gravity of all preparatory work may lie in a movement and concentration plan developed in detail. However, the mental center of gravity should not lie in occupying an initial position but in operations, if only on paper. It is bad for the commander in chief to keep them a secret; we assign major importance to their development, if only in the form of different war games and field trips by the general staff; there may be no finally approved official decisions at all.

the primary task of strategy is to prepare materiel and the first deployment of the armies. In the process strategy must take into consideration multifaceted political, geographical and state considerations. A mistake made in the initial concentration of an army can hardly be corrected over the course of an entire campaign. But plans for it may be pondered beforehand, and if mobilization is timely and the transports are well organized, the plans should without fail lead to the anticipated results.[9]

At present operational deployment is not the primary task of strategy, and railroad maneuvers and the availability of an operational reserve can rectify deployment errors; during a deployment strategic work is not reduced to the automatic execution of a plan made in peacetime but involves the energetic adjustment of the deployment on the basis of new information received on the enemy, and work on operational deployments is of the same intensity as work on conducting an operation.

The Organization of Fronts

The determination of the amount of forces and their starting position follow from our conceptions of forthcoming operations. These forces must be organized into armies that occupy certain sectors. Several armies conducting a joint operation or deployed in a particular theater of operations make up a front. If it is possible to limit oneself to forces not exceeding six army corps with several cavalry divisions in a particular theater of operations, it is desirable to organize only a separate army.

After outlining a front, a campaign plan should also cover its organization, i.e., its command and its boundaries with adjacent fronts and the interior of the country. Boundaries should in no way limit the extent of the maneuver required by a planned operation. The rear boundary will be drawn depending on the probability of offensive and defensive changes on a front. If we are convinced that an offensive will be developed, then it would be better to give a front less room in depth, which would move all rears closer to the vanguard units, whereas if a major withdrawal is likely, it is better to make the front deeper in order to make it possible for it to echelon its logistical units adequately. Richer and more densely populated terrain makes it possible to limit the depth of a front, whereas on sparsely populated territory fronts must be deeper in order to obtain sufficient acomodations and space for its units and agencies. Many of these are closely linked to railroads, and they should only be put in populated areas close to railroad stations.

The number of rear agencies for a front and their size cannot be determined by a pattern, depending on the number of combatants; rather it should be based on the requirements made of the rear agencies by the planned operations and on the degree of ease, speed and security of delivering all the necessary items from the interior. Thus we need to make accurate calculations and make significant corrections for communications with the interior.

---

[9]   Moltke, *Militaerische Werke*, vol. 2, section 2, p. 287. This is an extract from the official history of the Franco-Prussian War published in 1872.

Sometimes there is a tendency to organize a front's rear as a self-contained, powerful economic entity. Insofar as the interior runs smoothly and railway communications with the interior are very secure, it would appear to be undesirable to expand the economic activity of a front. From the point of view of economic requirements, a front area should be limited as much as possible because it lies completely outside the realm of the country's normal economic life and thus increases the economic burden on the interior. Regarding the economic achievements of the front itself, they ordinarily involve extreme expenditures of mobilized human material, and the issue of their economic advisability can only be raised if a front develops its economy on occupied enemy territory rather than on friendly territory.

The Base of Operations

The forces of a front are concentrated at the position selected for deployment; at the same spot there are usually vanguard units which cover the assembly of the forces and try to hold up the enemy's offensive. In essence, this position is the true strategic boundary of a state. In Russia in 1914 the strategic boundary facing Germany was formed by the Neman, Bohr and Vistula rivers. Everything to the west and north of this line was a sort of forward strategic field; the Russian government was incapable of functioning reliably in this area once the war began; economically the area was beneficial to any enemy who happened to maneuver there; and these areas should be systematically evacuated once mobilization begins if one does not plan on going on the offensive.

The part of the front area between the aforementioned line and its rear boundary must be considered a base of operations. This base of operations should be provided with supplies which in combination with ocal resources would meet the needs of the concentrating troops until the railroads are operating at full capacity in transporting troops; moreover, there should be supplies which would make it possible to begin initial operations without delay. However, if supplies are in general inadequate, it would be mistaken to strip them from the interior and concentrate everything on the borders. One should adhere to the principle of echeloning supplies. In exactly the same way a lack of permanent fortifications and the instability of our situation on any borders may lead to a reduction in the amount of supplies stored at a base of operations.

It is quite desirable that a base of operations within a front be divided so that in relation to the rail system it is an independent entity and has at least one or two lateral rail lines.

Concentration Transports

During the World War the German army required 11,100 trains for its concentration transports.[10] These latter in turn required 165,000 boxcars and 60,000 flatcars, and the stock was turned around two to three times during the deployment. A maximum of 660 trains, including 550 beyond the Rhine, traveled on 13 trunk lines to the Western front every day. The two-track lines handled up to 72 pairs a day, while the single-track lines handled 24 or even 30 pairs, and 2,150 trains crossed the bridge at Cologne from August 2 to August 18. It is doubtful that in future wars concentration traffic will be so heavy: in Germany in 1914 the

---

[10] Reichsarchiv, *Der Weltkrieg*, vol. 1, pp. 144-145.

first echelon of the mobilization consisted of 3,120,000 men and 860,000 horses, whereas now all the European states, including France, mobilize much smaller forces in the first echelon. Thus it is doubtful that we will need the maximum of 30,000 cars arriving in the deployment sector as was achieved in 1914.

Concentration was very slow in the Soviet-Polish war. In March 1920 only 83 troop trains went to the western front, whereas in April 203 trains arrived. It took the railroads a month to do a day's work.

At present we are witnessing a gradual rise in Soviet rail traffic. Our railroads already handle more than 15,000 cars per day.[11] Our railroads have come a long way from the disastrous period of 1919-1920, when it was impossible to count on more than four pairs on a single track (eight pairs for a two-track line): given this two-thirds reduction in rail capacity, a corps, which requires 120 trains to move it 600 kilometers, can concentrate on foot just as fast as it can by a single track, and it would take an army, which requires 750 trains, two months to march 1,000 kilometers at a normal pace, while it would take it ten weeks to get there on three tracks.

We are also very optimistic about the near future in terms of concentration, of course, under the condition that persistent work on the rail system continues, because concentration transports are now becoming more limited and less complicated due to the overall improvement in the rail system. We have the opportunity to prepare for these transports in a leisurely manner, determine the requirements for every line, and account for shortages of locomotives and telegraph operators and borrow them in a mobilization from less burdened directions. The task of initial concentration is incomparably simpler for railroads then subsequent concentrations, when railroad maneuvers, or sudden movements of several hundred trains in a direction completely unprepared beforehand for a movement will be needed to plug a gap or make an attack on the enemy's flank. While previously strategists gave special weight to railroad lines running to the border with the idea of speeding up deployment in mind, they now consider this a problem which is more or less resolved[12] and are inclined to devote more attention to railroads running parallel to the border, which make it possible to move laterally and make extensive use of strategic and operational reserves.

Contemporary concentration techniques are determined by the current vast lengths of deployment fronts and the dependence of the combat-readiness of troops on the proper functioning of their rears. It would be very careless to set up a continuous front along an entire border immediately. One must try to become capable of fighting and maneuvering in important sectors as quickly as possible. Weakly screened covering forces and unoccupied gaps between them do not constitute a particular threat when large numbers of armed men are on the rails

---

[11] With satisfaction we retain this figure from the first edition, noting that in the second edition, one and a half years later, we must double this figure to 30,000 cars.

[12] We would not at all wish to be understood as advocating indifference toward the very important question of preparation for war: we fully share the opinion that the success of military actions depends in equal measure on the art of conducting operations and on the national preparation for mobilization, concentration transport and organization of recruitment and supply, and that for all these isues it is necessary to devote equal attention and to subject tham to the same thorough study. "Plany voiny" [The war plan], in *Angliiskii polevoi ustav 1920*, paragraph 5.

behind them and within two or three days the men in several hundred troop trains can be thrown into battle against enemy units breaking through.

Germany, which was in a good enough position to open the war on the French front with a major offensive and had firmly decided to employ Schlieffen's plan of destruction, could still allow itself the luxury of a rigid concentration plan in 1914. After the covering units were brought up to strength, on the second and third days of mobilization the Germans moved the men from the line-of-communication bakeries and "squadrons," the personnel for the line-of-communication transports, which were formed on the spot from local carts, into the deployment area; thus under the screen of a strong covering force the deployment area was logistically prepared for the time troop transports would begin; and this was important, because only field carts traveled with the troops, and the divisions and corps were moved out with no logistical equipment at all. Units of two corps were transported simultaneously on one trunk line; primarily infantry came on the first transports, then the artillery, and after a certain amount of time they we sometimes joined by an appropriate reserve corps; only after all the front-line troops had been transported did the Germans begin to transport the division and corps logistical units which took longer to mobilize. Normally units of four divisions of two corps were transported alternately, which, when each division disembarked at a special station, made it possible to operate embarkation and disembarkation stations simultaneously rather than in succession. The flexibility of the German concentration in 1870 was evident in the ability to move disembarkation stations several days back toward the Rhine; in 1914 there was no such flexibility; only four major lateral trunk lines crossing the deployment area at right angles constituted a powerful resource for regrouping in the hands of the high command.

After the World War, under no circumstances should divisions and corps be deprived of their logistical agencies, particularly when army and front logistics have not been organized. In Moltke's era one could still engage in fierce battles with supplies of ammunition and ordnance handcarried and transported by small units, but now this is impossible. The units moved to a deployment area should have the opportunity to maneuver rather than be tied to the railroads.

From the perspective of our conception of a flexible deployment system involving the possibility of railroad maneuvers, whether we move eight corps in 12 days on four trunk lines or move these corps in two lines, one six days after the other, or even have them concentrate two by two in three days, is very important. In the first instance, we will not have fully maneuverable units until the very end of the movement (Samsonov's corps did not receive their corps transports before they died); second it would be impossible to undertake any railroad maneuver over the course of all twelve days without extreme organizational confusion, because interrupting a transport and pointing the tails of the corps in a different direction than their heads is a measure which dire need may compel us to take but hich can in no way be recommended. Incidentally, in the second case, a corps not committed by disembarking its head unit can easily be switched to a new direction and transferred from one army to another.

For the purpose of putting their concentration transports into order, in 1914 the French divided them into two lines: on the 11th day of mobilization there was a 12-hour halt in order to give the railroads a breather and allow stragglers to catch up, of which there in fact were only 20 trains out of a total of 2,534 in the first line.

All the field corps and some reserve divisions were included in the first line of transports, whereas logistical and several technical units were included in the second line. We believe that the division of transports into several lines should be maintained, but that every line should represent not only a separate railroad operation but a separate operational entity. The next line of transports could be made in different way, in accordance with new maneuver requirements.

We understand that the echelon transports we have recommended could encounter a large number of difficulties: different transports would have to be determined for different corps, and it is trickier to deliver rolling stock and have a corps embark at a single point in a single area in three days than it is to disperse these operations. It will also be very difficult to speed up the mobilization of the divisional and corps rears of the first echelon corps. Disembarkation stations give us the least cause for concern, because if the disembarkation area is large enough, with a three-day-march diameter, then special equipment may not be required for this echelon transport. However, we must radically change our views on rail transports; in Moltke's day this was considered a period when troops were defenseless and strategists tried to secure it with covering forces or fortresses or make the deployment deeper; the troops in the cars were still passengers deferring to the will of the railroad authorities just as a traveler stepping on board a ship trusts the captain; but now they are not passengers but an operational reserve, and the transport itself should be understood as a maneuver on rails. Hundreds of trains make up an operational maneuver formation[13] Railroads have come such a long way since 1870 that, as it seems to us, they will be fully capable of meeting these new requirements. At the same time, in preparing concentration transports, in this way railroad men are also preparing for the railroad maneuvers that will repeatedly be required of them as the war goes on.

Rail transports must be extensively combined with marches. If an army is initially deployed in separate sectors rather than as a solid front, to maximize rail utilization the railhead stations can be selected on a broader sector extending one to two days' march beyond the ends of the selected deployment front so that the concentration can be acomplished by marching and movement toward the front. This is a normal railway maneuver technique for forming a "battering ram."

That our conceptions of railroad maneuvers are not fantasies but are appropriate for actual current real capabilities is at least demonstrated by the example of the Russian deployment in August 1914, when elements of railroad maneuvering were carried out by the 9th and 10th Russian armies. Initially the 9th Army was to play the role of a strategic reserve in the Warsaw vicinity and was to go on the offensive on the left bank of the Vistula and assist the 1st and 2nd Armies crossing the lower Vistula. After the unfortunate turn of events on the front the 9th Army, which had deployed southwest of Lublin, along with the 4th Army, corrected the primary flaw in the operational deployment of the southwestern front against Austria-Hungary, namely the extreme weakness of the right wing of the front, which had been assigned the most critical offensive missions. In general, the 9th

---

[13] It is completely reasonable for the Germans to organize transports in accordance with operational requirements: at the head is air defense artillery for securing the railhead; behind it are reconnaissance and signal units; then come engineer units and infantry with artillery and the vehicles needed for a fierce battle. The art of organizing a march must also be applied to railroads.

Army's maneuver was quite successful. The 10th Army, after the unfortunate turn of events in the 2nd Army, was to deploy between the 1st and 2nd Armies; it is true that the 10th Army was late and did not manage to play its role, but this delay was due to various miscues and a failure to comprehend the need to move the 1st army to the right to cover the disembarkation of the 10th Army and secure communications with it. However, the failure of the 10th Army's maneuver in no way casts doubt on the idea of railroad maneuvering and from the errors that were committed one can make a number of valuable operational conclusions concerning the methods of carrying out such a maneuver.

Despite the general disorder of the railways and their slowness during the Civil War, we could point out a number of successful railroad maneuvers in deployment: for example, in August and September of 1919 the concentration of a strike force in the 13th Army in going on a decisive offensive against Denikin, the concentration in repelling Yudenich's offensive against Petrograd and so forth.

France and Germany reaped major benefits because their railroads were largely standardized: the ten French trunk lines used for concentration transports were all designed to handle 57 pairs of troop trains, whereas in Germany the two-track lines were designed to handle 48 pairs and the single-track lines 24 pairs. If a rail system is standardized, then it is very easy to switch traffic from one two track line to another or to two single track links, and the opportunities for railroad maneuvering are greatly enhanced. In Russia every railroad was of its own special type; the military's sole concern was to maximize the success of transports on the basis of a rigidly established deployment and to remove blockage on every deployment artery; was completely unconcerned with standardization, and the military requirements themselves were evoked by the lack of coordination: for example, various sectors of the St. Petersburg-Warsaw line were to handle concentration traffic of different intensities, but its carrying capacity differed from sector to sector, from 30 to 65 pairs of troop trains. This kind of one-sided railroad preparations poses a major hazard to the success of railroad maneuvers by reducing the possibilities for changing the plan and it is completely inappropriate for the requirements of subsequent regroupings. Devising a railroad standard, if only a very broad standard, such as 12, 24, 48 and 60 pairs of troop trains, and adjusting the existing system to it would have greatly enhanced the opportunities for railroad maneuvers. At present our railroads are in a medieval kind of situation in which every gun and every rifle has its own special caliber and every pike has its own special length.

We would consider the preparations of railroads for deployments to be ideal when the chief railroad specialists, knowing the times of mobilization-readiness of corps at their stations and having studied all the characteristics of the rail system in great detail, would be able to put together a valid transport plan in three hours according to a completely improvised deployment plan and begin to carry it out in three days, taking into account the possibility of several major changes in the deployment plan during the transports themselves. Specialists who need to make up piles of lists and tables and require months of time do not meet the requirements of modern warfare.

Covering the Deployment

Obviously we need to devote a great deal of attention to avoiding slipups in the first steps of a war; if the enemy, having broken into the area we had planned for deployment, were to compromise troop concentrations and force us to abandon railheads in different directions, this would be a major setback for us. Beginnings have always been particularly important in warfare. But it would be mistaken to overestimate the importance of this and consider the beginning a self-contained phenomenon. That is what the French do when they relate all aspects of a battle to the vanguard. In strategy units that cover concentrations play a strategic security role in certain respects; the French overestimate this role to he such an extent that they call their existing standing army a "covering army," reasoning that its role is that of a strategic vanguard covering the second echelon of a mobilization.

The front, until deployment is complete, will be in a state of crisis and the situation on the border in the first week will be particularly doubtful as mobilization is still under way in the country and concentration transports concern only several units (cavalry units which are almost at wartime strength will mobilize in the first two days). During the course of this week small semimobilized units, some kind of brigade or border corps, will have to do critical work virtually without carts, reinforced only by a border guard and separated from their closest neighbors and logistical support by several days of marching. However such a crisis will also be occurring on the enemy's side of the border too.

If a deployment front is closer to the border and the terrain offers many valuable geographical objectives, frontier corps will be incapable of handling the covering mission and it will be necessary to utilize the forces of other corps and have a kind of first-echelon concentration of semimobilized units. In France, despite the shortness of its border with Germany and the dense deployment of troops in the border areas, it became necessary to send approximately 385 trains with covering units and a second series of 349 trains with individually called up reserves to form a covering force. The covering force grew as large as five corps and ten cavalry divisions. Covering transports began two days before the first day of mobilization and were completed on the morning of the second day. In terms of their scale these transports were somewhat greater than 10 percent of all concentration transports.

---

[14] Offensive undertakings in the first days of mobilization carried out with the goal of improving the conditions of operational deployment place huge demands on the readiness of forces and railroads. The siege of Liège and the occupation of Luxembourg demanded the strengthening of cover in Germany and the assignment of 1,440 trains, 340 of which were needed in the first and second days of mobilization. Since the Lige operation took shape in total secrecy, the railroads were not even notified in advance about half the covering transports connected with it.

At 12:45 a.m. on the first day of mobilization the 16th infantry division received an order to occupy Luxembourg. Immediately two regiments of the peacetime structure were loaded into an armoured train, regular trains, automobiles and even put on bicycles—and by morning the Grand Duchy of Luxembourg with all its important railroads was occupied. The remaining two regiments of the division appeared at 7:00 a.m. on the first day of mobilization. The division entrenched itself opposite the French border, and during the second through ourth days of mobilization it received reserves. The brigades that attacked Liège received reserves during the operation itself.

It is quite probable that in a future war we will not encounter such a drastic division: 15 days of calm assembly of forces on both sides of the border interrupted only by light cavalry raids or isolated separate attacks (e.g., Liège),[14] followed by a fierce encounter battle involving millions of men. The secondary goals set by a strategy of attrition will perhaps force us to begin a war with a number of secondary operations; we could foresee a series of hot clashes and the possibility of a major operation developing from increasingly stronger covering support. However, our western border does not have enough geographical value everywhere to justify this kind of activity in the period preceding the completion of concentration. In many sectors the terrain on both sides of the border is so poor that withdrawal maneuvers by covering units would seem to be justified and two days of forward marches would do nothing except endanger our lines of communication.

It would be mistaken to envision the purpose of covering as establishing some kind of cordon along the border. Covering units must be concentrated in the most important sectors, while less important sectors could be placed under the surveillance of border guards and separate squadrons. It would be advantageous if the population of a border sector were amenable to the organization of a special border militia which could prevent the infiltration of small enemy units into its territory and provide security for the most important man-made structures, and could fade into the underground in the event of an enemy offensive and provide a ready-made cadre for organizing partisan detachments in the enemy's rear.

Covering must not be merely linear and must be sufficiently deep, and reserves are necessary. At the most important junctions of a border area we must have ready trains and locomotives under steam and two or three companies with a pair of guns for immediately repelling enemy cavalry raids. This is particularly important for those sectors of the border which have high railroad concentrations; rivers running parallel to the border with a railroad on our bank also favor the use of this tactic. Once the transports begin to move, these railroad reserves are already unnecessary and in general all covering may be handled by the fronts, because the reserve role is passed to the troops on the rails.

The first French incursion into the Alsace at the beginning of the World War was repelled by German forces transported for concentration in Lorraine; after defeating the French they got back into their trains and headed toward their destination.

Mobile troops such as cavalry, self-propelled artillery units, armored cars, armored trains and separate companies travelling on carts provided by the local population are especially valuable for covering. If peacetime airfields are located at a distance that would enable air support for the covering operation from peacetime moorage, the air forces should immediately allocate sufficient forces for this purpose. In any case, temporary airfields will have to be set up in the concentration area. The air defense artillery will have to be ready to open fire in the entire border sector. It is particularly important for fighter planes to be active in the first days of war. The first air battles will be particularly fierce and will determine the capabilities and reputations of the air forces for a long time to come.

Covering should be based on a carefully worked out plan. The deployment of separate detachments, their missions, the mobilization of existing permanent fortifications, work on building new airfields and camouflage should be planned out by border corps for each particular area they occupy. All the commanders should be acquainted with their sectors and trained through appropriate tactical problems, reports, war games and field trips for their duties.

Particular attention must be paid to communications problems, because the distances our troops will have to handle are much greater than normal. The extensive development of a system of permanent telegraph and telephone cables in the deployment area will make covering much easier. But this system will be beneficial only if it is analyzed beforehand and its utilization is carefully pondered.

From the very first day covering must begin to fortify its front using local manpower as much as possible. In principle, a covering position is a point where a concentrated army will also have to fight if it goes on the defensive. That which can be done before deployment is completed makes a valuable framework for resistance. Part of this position may already be secured by concrete emplacements in peacetime. It is desirable for the position to be close to the railheads so that they can continue to operate uninterrupted after the enemy approaches the position. Work on fortifications should be organized on the basis of the "always ready" principle so that covering forces would be able to rely on them at any minute.

Work details can successfully build fortifications only if the cover posts a guard a certain distance in front of them. Initially, when the covering forces are small, a large percentage of them will be involved in providing this security to positions constructed in the most important sectors.

In general, as fortifications are built up and positions gradually get wider and new units arrive, covering will constantly change and the mission and design of the cover should be thought out day by day in the form of an album of tactical decisions for the entire period of mobilization and deployment.

Covering missions may be handled not only by defensive tactics but offensively; raids should be aimed against the nearest road junction or important man-made structures. If military operations are conducted in an atmosphere of an acute class struggle, we must ponder whether the appearance of our forces and their departure will place our sympathizers abroad in a difficult situation by abandoning the inhabitants who have expressed their sympathy and rendered assistance to our forces to the mercy of their political enemies. In a situation of acute national antagonism, raids of this kind often have negative consequences. Gurko's raid in 1877 in the Balkans led to massive Turkish reprisals against the Bulgarian population, who were inspired by his arrival. The two halfhearted French invasions of Alsace in August 1914 also compromised the Alsatians, who were French sympathizers.

In light of these considerations and also diplomatic considerations, the breaking of diplomatic relations and incidents of cross-border fire should not be taken by covering units as authorization to cross a border. Even cross-border cavalry and air raids should be made only after the high command has sent a telegraph announcing the beginning of hostilities; this order may not come at the same time as the declaration of war, and often it is disadvantageous to take the odium of crossing a border on oneself.

Covering commanders must be oriented to the procedure and place of arrival of reinforcements, the expectation of which often makes it possible for them to fight very fiercely. They also need to know the roads, bridges and structures they will have to be prepared to blow up, when they must refrain from blowing up roads and what roads must be spoiled. These instructions are part of a single overall demolitions preparation plan which must be devised in every district.

If a strong enemy attack makes it impossible to rely on the successful completion of deployment in a chosen sector, a front commander must not hesitate to issue an order to avoid decisive battles in this sector and move the deployment to another area. All the components of a withdrawal version of a cover plan should take this maneuver into account.

The Ideological Preparation of the Army

The implementation of an operational plan requires appropriate training for the army and its commanders. The German general staff, in trying to break through the ring of fortresses that were obstacles on the Germans' path in France, Belgium and Russia, did not limit themselves to bringing up their heavy artillery and reinforcing their technical units; they also issued a manual on attacking fortresses that extensively publicized the ideas of a quick attack and contradicted the age-old traditions of military engineers and organized exercises on attacking fortresses (e.g., the major fortress maneuvers at Poznan in 1907). The high command and the general staff made a great many field trips to fortresses in order to gain information on attacking and defending fortresses on a large scale.

The reports of corps and districts are an obligatory phase of training for every operational plan. The overall mission following from an operational plan is broken up into a number of operational and tactical problems for the front, the armies and the corps; if possible, these problems should be solved by the same echelons who will have to solve them in real life. At a district headquarters, perhaps by employing group discussion, these problems are checked, discussed and summarized, and the summary is then transmitted to the high command in a report. An operational plan constitutes a series of assignments; the high command uses the reports to get a clear idea of how fronts, armies and corps interpret the solution of these assignments, and the reports shed light on differences in the understanding of an operation and make it possible for the high command to consciously shift the operational training of their subordinates in a desired direction. Reports make it possible for subordinate commanders to get acquainted with their forthcoming activities. For example, a corps commander of a border district will have to become familiar with the idea of covering, the movement of forces from their stations to other points for getting into battle formation, quartering the troops and meeting their needs, organizing logistics and so forth. It is obvious that a district headquarters that has already answered these questions theoretically will be much more capable of handling the same questions in practice.

Assignments for field trips and war games create different situations that are possible variations of an operational plan. These bilateral exercises are also important for clarifying the weak aspects of our operational proposals. The side representing the enemy provides a practical criticism of your plan with its actions. Hence field trips of the general staff are often devoted to playing out situations that could provide guidelines for new and beneficial fundamental changes in the operational plan.

A typical error of the Russian leadership in games and trips is the desire to avoid slippery situations and play out only calm versions primarily involving a parallel clash of two fronts of equal strength. Incidentally, it is highly desirable to hone the thinking of commanders by discussing difficult situations which require clear solutions. It is absolutely necessary to select as subjects for these discussions not only situations that follow from the smooth course of proposed operations but situations that are close to catastrophe and involve a collapse in any particularly threatening sector. Strategic and operational thinking should become accustomed to working out situations such as the encirclement of Sheffer-Boiadel's forces at Lodz or the center of the 10th Russian army at Augustow. We must be prepared for operational storms as well as calm clear weather.

The Supply Plan

Regardless of the economic mobilization plan, a plan devised on a national scale, the military authorities must have their own plan for solving problems of supplying the armed forces in the event of a war. This plan must try to calculate all the different needs of the troops for supplies beforehand and indicate the ways they can be met. Regardless of economic programs, the operational plan must always be tied to existing material capabilities. The latter ultimately determine the number of men that can be intelligently employed and the possible activity of a front. Unwillingness to consider existing material capabilities leads to the construction of operational castles in the air or mobilization houses of cards and takes hundreds of thousands of citizens away from peacetime work and compels them to flutter about in reserve units without receiving any training. The number of mouths to be fed may be increased, but not the number of fighters.

In the winter of 1916-1917 the size of the Russian army increased by one-third and two-day fasts were extended to three-day fasts. It is probable that the army would have been stronger without this swelling if all the meat days were kept in the week. General Francois, the former brave commander of a Prussian corps, who was affected by the catastrophe Germany suffered in 1918 on account of the hunger blockade, was even inclined to analyze all phenomena in military history from the vantage point of the stomach and used the example of 1812 to try to prove this, which is, of course, a digression.

The plan must calculate existing material capabilities in the terms of existing peacetime stockpiles, orders given to industry, goods on the market and orders which could be filled by industry during a diplomatic crisis and during the first days of a war. The overall supply plan will obviously be broken up into sections in terms of different specialities, but these sections must be harmoniously interrelated; there are certain necessary internal relationships between the needs for yards of cloth, pairs of boots, rifles, ammunition and shells which are highly dependent on the nature of a future war and must be understood as much as possible. For example, before the World War it was believed that one shell would be expended for every 500 cartridges, but reality quickly forced a switch from a 1:500 ratio to a 1:100 ratio.

People who are sufficiently competent in handling goods on domestic markets could foresee the possibilities for procurements and the time needed to make them on the basis of the harvest and predictions of the upheavals in the markets produced by a war. Persons familiar with industry involved in making up economic mobilization plans could evaluate existing industrial capacity, namely the number of orders and the time needed to fill them. It is obvious that, given the current rate of Soviet economic growth, the supply plan must be carefully reviewed and revised every year.

An accounting of the material available to supply the armed forces will be expressed in a table indicating the supplies on hand and the rate of arrival of new supplies; and it would be useful to put the amount of supplies one can firmly count on and the amount of supplies whose procurements would require a certain amount of time in a single graph.

Of course, a supply plan must be coordinated in detail not only with procurement capabilities but also with transportation conditions. Supplies will have to travel a long way from the factory that makes them to the front that devours them. In a country with such great distances and such a weak transportation system as the USSR, supply presents major difficulties. We would be able to avoid breakdowns in supplies only by organizing larger stores than those which characterize small countries with good rail systems. If we determine the daily supply expenditures for all branches of service then we will have to store a larger number of daily rations in our stores to make up for the distance from the factory to a unit on the front. Of course, the amount of this liquid capital will differ for different types of items.There are seasonal supplies and different kinds of supplies, such as food, which are devoured on all fronts equally and depend on the number of combatants and the wealth of the theater; there are battle supplies, whose expenditure is highly dependent on the activity of the front; and there are positional supplies, where a halt in the action may immediately mean major requirements for wire, shovels, axes, saws and positional fortifications (cement, iron beams, shields, bricks, iron stove, lamps and so forth). Besides the different nature of supplies there are different requirements for echeloning them, centralizing or decentralizing them, and so forth.

Analysis of all these issues will reveal the kind of network of stores that will be required to meet the needs of planned operations, what kind of supplies and what proportions should be on hand in every store, the extent to which peacetime stockpiles should be minimized and the extent to which a planned mobilization and operational plan will strain our material resources.

The supply plan should try to minimize the burden on transportation, particularly in the critical days of mobilization and concentration, for which stores should be configured in peacetime where they must be in wartime, and mobilization stockpiles should be moved as close as possible to the place where they will be used (if a second-line regiment is mobilized at certain barracks, then the unit occupying these barracks in peacetime should store the supplies for this regiment also); the base of operation should be provided with the supplies it needs for the period of concentration movements.

If sufficient attention is not paid to the timely preparation of stockpiles, concentration movements will be very inefficient, because the railroads will provide a smaller percentage of the total number of trains they can handle for troop movements. Approximately 600,000 tons of oats alone are required to feed a million horses for a month[15]; while general calculations of transportation for

---

[15] In 1912 in our border districts we were supposed to keep in base stores primarily along the line of the western Dvina and the Dnepr, but also in forward-based intermediate and disbursement stores, 30 days worth of provisions, 20 days worth of oats and 15 days worth of hay.

supplies needed in the first two months of a war in the deployment area would probably yield a figure greatly in excess of 1,100 freight trains, whose place could be taken by the same number of troop trains; the reception and unloading of troop trains at railheads is a much less difficult operation than unloading trains containing quartermaster, engineer and artillery supplies. Savings could be effected in maintaining base stores only if there is a major improvement in the rail system. It is obvious that some freight would have to be transported after a war begins no matter what the situation is.

In subsequent operations, if the rail system is functioning properly, it would be better to avoid base and intermediate stores completely and have limited supplies on wheels and trains which could be sent directly to disbursement stores.

Toward the beginning of the World War our system involved transporting food supplies from the interior of the country to base depots and sending two series of trains to the theater of war between base and intermediate depots and between imtermediate and disbursement depots. For example, in 1914 the Russian command planned to send seven trains from base stores to intermediate stores and ten trains from the intermediate stores to the disbursement stores on a daily basis on the southwestern front. It is impossible to deny the soundness of this scheme, but it led to an increase in the number of noncombatants and two extra loadings and unloadings of trains, which could have been avoided if there were greater confidence in the deep rear and less of a desire on the part of the fronts to run their own completely specialized economies. The latter system made it possible for both France and Germany to greatly reduce the number of noncombatants in the World War.

The importance of the supply plan requires the participation of the persons directing the writing of the operational plan in devising it; the high command and its responsible employees must be familiarized with the possibilities and impossibilities of the supply plan. They should play a very active role in drawing up the supply plan. In fact, all the initial information for the supply plan depends on the nature of the planned operations. The planned operations determine the timing and extent of supply needs and the conditions in which they are transported from a base to active armed forces.

Supply and Regulated Military Operations.

The nature and extent of military operations should be suited to the existing economic base. Any offensive undertaking involves a certain expenditure of materiel; the ambition of a strategy must be harmonized with the availability of military supplies, especially munition, and the possibility of replenishing them. The calm on the French front which began in November 1914 can largely be explained by the fact that both the Germans and the Anglo-French forces had expended their available supply of shells. Falkenhayn's attack on Verdun in 1916 indicated prosperity in German depots, which had filled up in the course of a calm winter. Ludendorff always looked at his depots as a barometer by which he regulated his initiative. The misfortune of the Russian army in the summer of 1915 can be explained by the failure of Russian commanders to coordinate their actions on the front with the capabilities of their rear.

We should expect that a future war will change radically after the sides have completed their economic mobilization and the rear is ready to meet the army's military supply needs more fully and this war, if it does not end quickly, will probably, like the World War, produce two different kinds of strategies and tactics. Initially there will be a great deal of maneuvering, materiel will be expended more cautiously and the troops will be more energetic; the second phase will be marked by technical massiveness, the extensive use of new inventions, the materialization of the art of war, a loss of offensive spirit and disintegrating movements beginning in the rear and shaking the cohesiveness of the front.

The economy will be able to subordinate the nature of military operations and leave a mark on them. But anarchy may have catastrophic consequences in this case, and it would undoubtedly be beneficial if adaptation to economic conditions follows directives from the top. From this perspective we must not allow anarchic materialization of tactics. The question that arises when we differentiate between a theoretical infantry and a real infantry is the first warning.

This question deserves more attention because of the fact that, if economic forces are uneven, tactics of materially competing with the enemy threaten not only the exhaustion and disintegration of the rear but the collapse of the morale of the front. The Civil War offers a number of examples of maneuvers that are particularly valuable in that they often posed quite interesting maneuver solutions to problems with minimal expenditure of material resources.

Materiel expenditure rates, which people sometimes try to formalize and bureaucratize, are in fact extremely flexible and allow for major fluctuations. There was only one step from the seven rounds per rifle fired by the Prussian infantry in the entire war of 1866 to the 300 rounds per man fired in several units in one day in the Russo-Japanese War, but the effectiveness of rifle fire was approximately the same in both wars. The appetites of automatic weapons can be reduced more than the appetites of the human stomach. An automatic weapon is a machine which can fall silent, while the second is a living being which cannot come to a standstill for even one day. In wartime an incomparably greater percentage of equipment is lost and intentionally abandoned at positions and is expended needlessly in battle than is used intelligently when needed. The discipline and conscientiousness of cadres and intelligent leadership can work miracles with respect to reducing equipment expenditures.

Our most important task is to get over the ideology of extravagance and the idea that victory is won by the person who is most lavish in expending materiel. A lack of will to victory is primarily expressed in the excessive material requirements of the troops. For example, in the summer of 1915, as the German infantry was resting during its offensive into Russia, it demanded an ever-increasing number of rounds to attack the Russian positions although it knew that it was moving further and further away from the railroads and that it was increasingly difficult to deliver rounds. We believe that the supply crisis the Russian army suffered in 1915 was primarily a political crisis; references to a shortage of supply often conceal a crisis in consciousness.

COMBINING OPERATIONS
FOR ACHIEVING THE ULTIMATE
GOAL OF THE WAR

1. THE FORMS OF CONDUCTING
MILITARY OPERATIONS

Basic Principles

If one sees only a chaotic jumble of events in war, one should reject strategic art altogether. Strategic thinking begins when one in the course of military operation begins to see a certain path that must be travelled in order to achieve the goals of the war. The study of strategy was built around this path for a hundred years; its beginning was marked by Lloyd's treatise, and its end was marked by G. A. Leer's treatise. However, this path was interpreted as a geometric line representing an abstraction of the most important dirt roads along which an army moves. Leer saw in this operational line the basic idea of an operation in terms of its goal and direction; the section of this line which had been covered represented the territorial routes linking an armed force to its base (line of communication), while the section which had not been covered represented the idea and plan of the operation. The individual points on this line characterized stages (intermediate goals) on the way to achieving the ultimate goal. Leer's operational line encompassed the entire meaning of military operations, the head and tail of the phenomenon, because for Leer an operation was practically synonymous with war.

We cannot agree with these teaching even with regard to operation art, which was what Leer primarily had in mind. Intermediate goals were expressed by a geometric point, which made it possible to combine them into one operational line, a line of goals, because all of them, from Leer's point of view, were identical: namely destroy the enemy at a given point. However, this geometric method can in no way explain the proportioning of efforts. It completely ignores defensive goals, and it is impossible to say that a defense does not pursue goals. In addition, the offensives of modern fronts, which are a thousand kilometers wide, and battles in major operations dispersed over a vast area are very poorly expressed by a geometric line, which has no dimension of width, or by a point, which has no dimensions at all. We get no clarity whatsoever.

Military operations may take different forms: destruction, the war of attrition, the defensive, the offensive, war of maneuver and positional warfare. Each form has a significant effect on the strategic line of conduct. Therefore we shall begin our discussion with an analysis of these forms. Subsequently we shall get acquainted with the major effect of communications on the strategic form of operations. Then we shall make a cursory examination of what is represented by modern operations with limited goals whose combination is the responsibility of the strategist. Finally, we shall examine the questions included in the concept of a strategic line of conduct.

Destruction

In discussing the political goal of a war, we arrived at the conclusion that the political leadership is responsible for orienting the operations of the armed front toward destruction or attrition after attentive discussions with strategists. The contradiction between these forms is much deeper, more important and fraught with more significant consequences than the contradiction between the defensive and the offensive.

The task of strategy is greatly simplified if we or the enemy, following Napoleon and Moltke's examples try to end a war with a destructive strike. Treatises on strategy that were exclusively concerned with a strategy of destruction in essence turned into tracts on operational art, and G. A. Leer was completely right to put a subtitle, *The Tactics of a Theater of Military Operations*, under the title *Strategy* on the covers of his books. The passion of strategists of the old school to analyze Napoleon's campaigns was natural: Napoleon reduced an entire campaign to a single operation in a main theater; questions of strategy presented no difficulties and merely involved determining the main theater; the allocation of forces between the main and secondary theaters followed the principle of an overwhelming preference for the main theater,[1] and the statement of a goal for a single operation in a main theater could not summon any doubt, since in a strategy of destruction it comes down to destroying the personnel deployed by the enemy in this theater. In most cases the study of Napoleon's campaigns was reduced to a study of operational rather than strategic art. It was natural for Jomini to consider questions of strategy simpler than questions of tactics. This in no way meant to imply that we do not consider Napoleon a strategic giant, but given the prevailing techniques of waging war his strategic stature was swallowed up in politics: in a single sweeping perspective we can consider the wars of 1805, 1806, 1807 and 1809 as separate gigantic operations against enemies sponsored by England on the European continent; then we are impressed by the proper formulation of the goal of each war, the correct timing of the start of military operations and the extremely skillful conclusion of every campaign at the right moment. But there is no doubt that in Napoleon's era a destruction operation did not always lead immediately to the denouement; for example, in the wars of 1796-1797, 1812 and 1813 Napoleon had to resolve strategic problems. However, Napoleon's military historians are still historians of his individual operations and only political history has given us somewhat of a perspective for examining his strategic art.

The three basic elements of an operation, strength, time and space, are always combined in a strategy of destruction so that gaining time and space is a means

---

[1] The idea of destruction encourages actors in the secondary theater to be passive; this is true in both strategy and politics.

and defeating the mass of the enemy's army is the end. Everything is subordinated to the interests of the general operation, and in the general operation everything depends on a decisive point. For strategy this decisive point is a kind of magnetic needle in a compass that determines all maneuvering. There is only one pure line of destruction and there is only one correct decision; in essence a military leader is deprived of freedom of choice because his duty is to understand the decisions dictated by the situation. The idea of destruction forces him to consider all secondary interests, directions, and geographical objectives meaningless. Pauses in the development of military operations contradict the idea of destruction. If we look at the pause of six weeks between the battles at Aspern and Wagram it is clear that it was the result of Napoleon's thoughtlessness in preparing the first crossing of the Danube and his subsequent failure. A strategy of destruction is characterized by a unity of purpose, time, place and action. Examples of a strategy of destruction are truly classical in terms of their style, simplicity and consistency. Destruction theoreticians ridiculed the subtle fencing of 17th-century strategy. In fact, by comparison with the game of strategic jabs and defenses of Turenne, Napoleon and Moltke's assaults remind one of a shaft which shatter skulls with one blow.

A strategy of destruction requires yet another premise, namely the extraordinary victory. A geographic objective may be the goal of a destruction offensive only when the enemy's men become phantoms. Until then a destruction offensive must aim at the complete disorganization of the enemy's manpower and its complete destruction, splitting every link between his intact fragments and capturing the communications that are most important for the armed forces rather than the country as a whole.

A destruction campaign puts attacking armies in a very unfavorable material situation because they are weakened by the securing of the flanks and rear and because such a campaign requires such great efforts to supply these armies that one can only protect oneself from ultimate defeat by winning a series of outstanding operational victories. The success of destruction requires taking hundreds of thousands of prisoners, destroying entire armies and capturing thousands of guns, depots and carts. Only successes of this kind can prevent complete disaster in the final analysis. No such victories were won in Galicia, or in the "border battle" or in the Red Army offensive in 1920. In each case we were dealing with commonplace victories in which the enemy was pushed back with somewhat greater casualties than the attacking army suffered. This is totally insufficient.

The need for an extraordinary victory in destruction poses special requirements for the choice of the form of an operation. The enemy's main forces must be encircled or trapped by the sea or at a neutral border. Of course, this kind of goal is risky. If the resources at our disposal are inappropriate, we must completely avoid a strategy of destruction. If Moltke had not succeeded in completely destroying Bazaine and de MacMahon's forces on the way to Paris in 1870, the Germans would have been in a desperate situation at Paris. We cannot agree with Moltke's first decision on August 25, 1870, in preparing for the Sedan operation (concentrating at Damvillier) when he pursued the modest goal of frontally blocking de MacMahon's route to Metz. A strategy of destruction must take advantage of every opportunity to destroy the enemy completely, and Moltke should have immediately dispatched his main forces to cut off de MacMahon's route of retreat to the west.

The operational leadership of General Alekseev in the Galician operation of 1914 was even more dubious; strategy had given this operation the majestic goal of encircling all the Austrian armies through a double envelopment by both Russian wings; but General Alekseev's sole concern was to lower his risk and he tried to close in on the center, keeping his wings as a rear echelon. Such tactics could only lead to commonplace victories and push the Austrians out of eastern Galicia but ruled out the possibility of a campaign against Berlin or Vienna.

Schlieffen was completely right in harmonizing the idea behind the Cannae operation, the complete destruction of the enemy in an armed clash, with a strategy of destruction. His destruction ideas were characterized by a maximum concentration of forces on the marching right flank of the German invasion of France. In 1912, in response to Austrian requests to strengthen the German forces to be deployed against Russia, Schlieffen devised a plan to leave only the Landwehr with no field or reserve divisions to stop the Russians. All the field units were to be sent to the west in order to achieve sufficient superiority at a decisive point. In his view, Austria-Hungary's fate would be decided on the Seine rather than the Bug.

However subsequently, neither Schlieffen nor the younger Moltke kept to their logic. They were interested in getting the Austrians to go on the offensive against the Russians and distracting the Russians from an invasion of Germany. Thus they told the Austrian command that there was no need to waste any effort on the Serbian front and that they should throw all their forces against Russia, because the fate of the Serbian army would be decided along with the fate of the Russian armies. This was how the German general staff suggested that Austria should adopt the same plan of fighting on two fronts against Russia and Serbia that the German general staff had adopted against France and Russia. But it would have been senseless to carry out two destruction plans at the same time. The offensive of 49 Austro-Hungarian divisions was to create a second decisive point on the Bug whose importance would be close to that of the decisive point of 80 German divisions on the Marne. The Austrians' requests for assistance from East Prussia acquired a certain amount of weight. But the younger Moltke should have reckoned with the greater importance of the Eastern front; he detached 14 field and reserve divisions for the Eastern front and then attempted to steal five divisions from this detachment by cheating the Austrians, but the battle of Gumbinen compelled them to return to the Eastern front. The Schlieffen Plan was a destruction plan only to the extent that Germany was waging war on two fronts by itself and in no way agreed with Austria-Hungary's participation in the war. The logic of destruction required keeping the Austrians from an offensive on the Russian front until France had been defeated, and perhaps even having a few Austro-Hungarian corps occupy the Lorraine front in order to strengthen the right wing of the German invasion.

In these conditions a destruction offensive constitutes a series of successive operations that are so closely interlinked nternally that they combine into one gigantic operation. The starting position for the next operation follows directly from the goal achieved by the operation just concluded.

Currently we classify a destruction offensive as a series of operations that have a constant direction and a series of goals that compose a single straight logical line. For example, in 1870 Moltke conducted his first operation aimed at destroying Bazaine's army and encircled it at Metz; then he immediately moved toward his ultimate goal, Paris; on the way he discovered de MacMahon's stupid maneuver between the triple forces of the Germans and the Belgian border and his second operation eliminated this army at Sedan; and his third maneuver led him to a hunger blockade of Paris. Bismarck was right to demand the bombardment and attack of Paris, because an assault on Paris would have truly been appropriate to the strategy of destruction which the political situation had indicated for the war.

After the victory over the Austrians in Galicia in 1914 a strategy of destruction would have required a direct Russian offensive into Moravia and Silesia. However, we did not have the superior forces required for this, and because of the threat of the 9th Army surrounding our right flank, we had to avoid pursuing the Austrians and begin a new deployment on the Vistula, from the mouth of the San to Warsaw, which in turn required the withdrawal of the 9th, 4th and 5th armies. The new deployment constituted a radical departure from destruction principles. It was the beginning of a fencing match; but destruction tries to avoid fencing and has only one means of accomplishing this, the constant and energetic development of an assault on the enemy's most vital center; the more concentrated and massive our striking force in this case, the sooner the enemy is forced to orient his actions according to ours, that is, in the old terms, "we shall dictate operational principles to the enemy."

A strategy of destruction characterized most of the Red Army's offensive from the banks of the Dvina to the Vistula in 1920. The concentration of a striking force on the right wing and forward movement of this force hundreds of kilometers in fact tied down all the Poles' operational countermeasures and disrupted all their attempts to hold favorable positions from the Berezina to the Bug; the fencing and attrition of the World War evaporated. Napoleon's shaft, which decided the war in a single blow, had seemingly been resurrected in red. However, on the way to the Vistula, the Red Army, like the German armies on the way to the Marne, were unable to win extraordinary victories; geographical considerations came to bear on the final part of the offensive, because in the Polish Corridor the Red armies put greater effort into attempting to cut off the vital artery of the entire Polish nation rather than the lines of communications of the Polish armies. As if ignoring the Poles' material strengths in the armed conflict, the Red Army went into battle against the Versailles Treaty. This was already mysticism, particularly for a strategy of destruction.

Destruction involves not only speed and linearity, it also involves massiveness. In approaching the Vistula the Red armies had become so numerically weak and so cut off from their sources of supply that they were more phantoms than reality. In 1829, Dibich, who had gotten close to Constantinople under approximately the same conditions, was able to conclude a peace in time. In 1797, Napoleon, who was in a somewhat better situation near Vienna, was also able to conclude a peace which was very desirable to revolutionary France by giving Venice to the defeated Austrians. We overestimated our achievements and continued our offensive, and beyond the Bialystok-Brest line the culmination point of our possible successes was far behind, and every step forward worsened our situation.

The importance a strategy of destruction gives to a general operation of destroying an enemy greatly narrows the perspective of strategic thinking. The day after we complete an operation we shall face a completely new situation, and the extraordinary events of the operation will radically alter the situation and lead to a reevaluation of all values. With a strategy of destruction, which assigns such unique and overriding importance to an armed clash with the enemy, the situation acquires the characteristics of a kaleidoscopic spectacle: one click of a decisive operation produces a completely new, unexpected picture which is wholly unpredictable. In a strategy of destruction the day after an operation is shrouded in thick fog. Only if he possesses such an overwhelming superiority of forces as Napoleon in 1806 or Moltke in 1870 will a destruction strategist be able to keep the ultimate goal in mind guided by the compass of a "decisive point." In general, the "decisive point" of an operation is almost overwhelmingly dominant in a strategy of destruction, and any violation of its dictates is considered a dangerous deviation or "preconception."

Modern times have placed major limitations on a strategy of destruction. The first of these, the short range of modern operations and the forcible return to a five-day-march system, will be discussed in the next chapter. An operation must be divided into parts, and the advance of a front must be temporarily halted in order to repair railroads in the rear. The resulting pauses are quite effective for turning the war into positional warfare. The second limitation lies in the fact that currently the beginning of a war does not now constitute the culmination of strategic intensity. Military and economic mobilization provide second and third echelons of mobilized and equipped manpower. In the face of the armies improvised by Gambetta the elder Moltke had to deal with a second echelon of the completely unprepared French mobilization as early as 1870. France's standing armies had been destroyed in a single month, but Moltke had to fight the second echelon for four months. As it appears to us, this is the experience on which Moltke's views of a future German war on two fronts as a war of attrition were based. The Marengo operation of 1800 alone gave all of Italy to Napoleon, while the Jena operation of 1806 made it possible to eliminate all of Prussia as far as the Vistula. In our conditions Napoleon would have had to conduct successive operations of increasing difficulty against new forces gathered by the state.

The Advisability of an Operation

The increased significance of the general operation in a strategy of destruction has led to a situation in which the operation is no longer pictured as one means of waging war but instead constitutes the ultimate goal of the war and is important in and of itself. The question of the advisability of an operation fades to the background. Operational and tactical considerations become paramount. It does not matter where or when the enemy has to be destroyed; the only important consideration is making the attack decisive. It is important that tactical operations follow the line of least resistance. Thus from the perspective of a strategy of destruction, we should not criticize Ludendorff for selecting Amiens, the strategically least important sector at the juncture of the French and English armies, for a decisive attack in March 1918. In a strategy of destruction the direction of an assault is less important than its scale. The error of the German command led in its desire to minimize its risk, maintain a solid front and avoid the most extensive mixing of its own and the enemy's forces into the layer cake which would have been baked if the Germans had advanced while ignoring sectors occupied by the enemy; the Germans should have attempted to maximize the area of the operation, keeping in mind that all the units and resources of both sides mixed up on it would ultimately fall to the victor. On the contrary, Ludendorff's subsequent attempts on new sectors, which were in part demonstrative, clearly contradicted a strategy of destruction. This was merely the fencing of attrition, fencing which tied down the enemy's will to a much lesser extent; in the same way that the situation in which Germany found itself in 1918 could have justified an offensive in the style of destruction, active operations in a war of attrition were inappropriate.

The need to draw a clear line between a strategy of destruction and a strategy of attrition is nowhere more evident than in the question of the advisability of an operation (previously referred to as a general battle). G. A. Leer, whose entire thinking was based on destruction, made a gross error of logic, in our opinion, in discussing the advisability of the battle crowning an operation; Napoleon, of course, had no doubts concerning this, because a general battle was the ideal and goal for which he strived. To support his ideas, which conflict with a strategy of destruction, Leer had to resort to the ideas of theoreticians of attrition such as Moritz of Saxony, for whom "battles were the everyday refuge of stupidity," and Frederick the Great, who stated that "the battle is a tool of dull-witted generals" and should be engaged in only when the expected gains are greater than what we risk. Leer[2] even cites the speech to the Count of Alba, a military leader of the mid-16th century, which aimed to cool the ardor of his deputies, who demanded a battle against the French, and appealed to their intelligence and composure: the entire kingdom must not be put on the map against only the embroidered caftan of a French military leader; the latter will withdraw and will risk losing only his cart in a battle. Victory may also be bloodless; battles should only be fought: 1) to save an important fortress; 2) if reinforcements that could give the enemy decisive superiority are on their way; 3) at the beginning of a war, or to make a political impression on allies and secret enemies; 4) if there is a complete loss of enemy morale rendering him incapable of further resistance; and 5) when we are so pinned down that the only choice is between conquering or dying.

The arguments of Moritz, Frederick the Great and Alba are quite interesting, but they are completely unrelated to a strategy of destruction. Strategic theory can give meaning to the question of the advisability between destruction and attrition.[3]

---

[2]   G. A. Leer, *Strategiia* [Strategy], 5th edition (1893), part 1, pp. 336-337; Appendix 7, pp. 156-157.

[3]   There are shortsighted criticisms that regard the passage of the World War onto the rails of strategic attrition as the legacy of the mistakes and lack of foresight of the general staff. Such criticism, of course, is devoid of any "objective consiousness." We regard attrition in the World War as a historic necessity.

Attrition

The term attrition is a very poor expression of all the diverse shades of different strategic methods outside the realm of destruction. Both the"Potato War" (War of the Bavarian Succession) and the campaign of 1757 (the second year of the Seven Years' War), the two products of Frederick the Great's creativity, belong to the category of attrition, because they did not involve a decisive movement toward the ultimate goal of the war; the idea of a campaign on Vienna was absent in them. But one campaign involved completely bloodless maneuvers, while the other involved four major battles, Prague, Kolin, Rossbach and Leuthen. Attrition is characterized by the diversity in which it is manifested.[4] One kind of attrition is very close to a strategy of destruction, which even made it possible for the Prussian general staff to state, albeit unjustifiably, that Frederick the Great invented Napoleon's destruction techniques; the opposite kind may involve the formula "neither war nor peace"—the mere avoidance of a peace treaty accompanied by a mere threat of military operations. There is an entire range of intermediate forms between these two extremes. A strategy of destruction is unified and allows for only one correct decision. In a strategy of attrition the intensity of armed conflict may vary, and thus each level of intensity may have its own correct decision. One can determine the level of intensity required by a given situation only through very careful study of economic and political conditions. A very broad range is opened up for politics, and strategy should be very flexible.

A strategy of attrition in no way renounces in principle the destruction of enemy personnel as a goal of an operation. But in this it sees only a part of the mission of the armed front rather than the entire mission. Geographical objectives and secondary operations become much more important when a strategy of destruction is rejected. The allocation of forces among primary and secondary operations becomes a very complicated strategic problem, because the "decisive point"—i.e., that compass needle which makes it possible to justify easily a decision in destruction every time—is missing in a strategy of attrition.[5] We must ponder not only the orientation of efforts but also their proportioning.

During the World War French strategists analyzed these issues very poorly. They remained under the illusion that the French front was as important and decisive after the Schlieffen Plan had been foiled as it was before and that everything should be oriented toward it, even though the war had become a war of attrition. The French maintained that Germany continued to be the most important enemy against which it was worth expending efforts. Although in terms of a strategy of destruction Austria-Hungary was a secondary enemy, in terms of attrition it was even more important than Germany. Whereas a strategy of destruction should have pursued the operational line of least resistance for defeating the main German forces, a strategy of attrition should have pursued the

---

[4]   We admit the validity of the criticism that our categories of destruction and attrition are not two opposites—they are not black and white, but white and nonwhite. However, in our opinion, in this case there is no philosophical or logical lapse. The varying intensity of armed conflict is characterized by a large number of gradations of attrition and reaches its limit in destruction. Only for this limit are certain principles of strategy absolute; for other gradations they are conditional and at times completely false.

[5]   However, as we shall indicate below, it would be mistaken to consider the transition from destruction to attrition to be a transition from the realm of necessity to the realm of freedom.

strategic line of least resistance in the Triple Alliance, a line which ran through Austria-Hungary after the defeats inflicted on it by the Russians. As soon as the center of gravity of German activity had shifted to the Russian front in 1915, Great Britain and France should have done everything possible permitted by their communications on the Balkan front to support Serbia; the deployment of a 500,000-man Anglo-French army on the Danube would have forced Bulgaria to stay neutral, encouraged Romania to act, cut off any German communications with Turkey, made it possible for the Italians to come out through the border mountains, would have relieved the strain on the Russian front, which could have held in Poland, and would have greatly accelerated the collapse of Austria-Hungary. The World War could have been shortened by at least two years.

We can see the change in relations between primary and secondary areas that accompanied the switch to a strategy of attrition in the fate of the Riga-Szawli area. Initially, because we were thinking in terms of destruction, we rightly assigned very little importance to this area and limited ourselves to surveillance of it by home guard units. But once our front died down in the winter of 1914-1915 without a doubt this area became more important. A whole series of misfortunes came from there: the envelopment of the right flank of the 10th Army, the gradual spread of the Germans in Courland and ultimately the Vilna-Sventsiany operation.

Like a strategy of destruction, a strategy of attrition constitutes a search for material superiority and the fight for it, but this search is not limited solely to the desire to deploy superior forces in a decisive sector. We must still create the conditions for a "decisive point" to exist. The weary path of a strategy of attrition, which leads to the expenditure of much greater resources than a short destructive strike aimed at the heart of the enemy, is in general chosen only when a war cannot be ended by a single blow. The operations of a strategy of attrition are not so much direct stages toward the achievement of an ultimate goal as they are stages in the deployment of material superiority, which would ultimately deprive the enemy of the means for successful resistance.

The French love to talk about the decisive blow they planned to inflict in Lorraine by November 14, 1918, but had to abandon because of the conclusion of the armistice. We are quite skeptical of the feasibility of this blow at the end of the World War.

Ludendorff failed to inflict this decisive blow in early 1918; he would have fallen to the French in late 1918, and the French and Foch were very fortunate that this blow never became anything more than a threat. It seems to us that the mission of German strategy in 1918 was to anticipate and repel this decisive blow in order to make the Entente more amenable to an armistice and peace.

In the final analysis, only French chauvinism would ascribe the victory of the Entente to the successes of Marshal Foch in the French theater of operations, because the Germans still had vast resources for resistance. Ultimate victory was guaranteed by the collapse of Austria-Hungary, which had deep historical roots; the straight, logical line of victory in the Would War starts with the victory of the Russians in Galicia and ends with the victory of the Balkan front of the Serbs and the Entente.

Forty advancing French divisions would have encountered sufficient forces at very well fortified positions; the material means of resistance of the Germans was sufficient, and even in a situation of incipient disintegration the French would not have been able to get past the Saar River. We do not think that there is any reason to consider the entire World War as a prologue to this pitiful attack which was never carried out.

In fact, in a strategy of attrition all operations are primarily characterized by the fact that they have limited goals; a war does not proceed as a decisive assault but as a struggle for positions on the armed, political and economic fronts from which it would ultimately become possible to make such an assault. However, during this struggle all values are completely reevaluated. The main theater, in which the war becomes a stalemate and vast forces and resources are expended gradually loses its overriding importance. The decisive point, this warhorse of the strategy of destruction, turns into an expensive but empty trinket. On the other hand, geographical objectives that embody political and economic interests become overwhelmingly important. In strategy operational and tactical issues become increasingly secondary and technical. Instead of the Paris-Berlin logic of destruction we get the Paris-Salonica-Vienna-Berlin logic of attrition. On November 14, 1918, the Entente would have occupied decisive positions not on the Lorraine Front, as Foch asserted, but on the Danube.

A boxer concentrates his efforts on protecting his lower jaw from a punch, because this punch could cause him to lose consciousness and fall; protection against a decisive blow is the first rule of any conflict. A strategy of destruction, which aims to knock out the enemy at any minute, ties down the enemy's actions and forces him to orient his actions to ours.[6] The limited blows inflicted by the strategy of attrition constrain the enemy to a much lesser degree. Certain operations are not directly related to the ultimate goal and are only stumps which poorly subordinate the enemy's will to them. Every stump requires a special operational deployment. The enemy has a full opportunity to pursue his own goals in this game of operational deployments.[7] Napoleon's operational line was the only axis along which the events of the war developed, and the operational desires of his enemies had to conform completely to the will of the great destruction artist. Discord is completely possible in a strategy of attrition: in 1915 one could have imagined such a course of events, if the German main forces were still tied down on the French front, in which Ludendorff would gradually build his forces up in the Baltic provinces, while the Russian armies would capture the outlets from the Carpathians to the Hungarian plain.

In a strategy of destruction the unity of actions seems completely necessary; if in the first weeks of the World War France became the theater of the Germans' destruction efforts, the Russians were certainly obligated to invade East Prussia without hesitation in order to relieve the strain on France. But if the idea of destruction fades, then this kind of operational coordination is permissible only on a quite relative basis. The pursuit of limited goals makes it possible for each

---

[6] The boxing term implies dealing such a smashing blow that the opponent cannot stand on his feet for a specified period.

[7] The younger Moltke after the border battle in August 1914, believed that he had already scored a knockout. But the French were not tied down by the Germans along the entire front and were able to proceed to a new operational deployment by moving corps from the right flank to the center and to the left flank. It is this opportunity for new operational deployments that rules out a strategy of destruction.

operational stump to preserve its independence to a certain extent. In order to make it difficult for the enemy to employ his reserves systematically and consistently, the periods of activity in different theaters should generally coincide. But there was no need at all to tie our March 1916 offensive at Lake Naroch to the defense of Verdun, or continue the Brusilov operation because the French were quite successfully continuing the Somme operation, which was designed for attrition. Instead of coordination, in a war of attrition it is necessary for every operation in and of itself to lead to certain tangible achievements.

In a war of attrition a general operation does not form an impermeable screen which completely clouds our thinking concerning the subsequent development of a war. Echelons of military and economic mobilization are totally appropriate for a strategy of attrition but are alien in spirit to a strategy of destruction. A war of attrition is guided by longer-range goals than preparations for a forthcoming major operation. The very conduct of this operation, which is incapable of producing decisive results in a war of attrition, must often be, in the case of attrition, preconceived— that is, its direction should be subordinated to and coordinated with subsequent problems that must be resolved. In a war of attrition strategic problems are to a great extent complicated by this widening and deepening. For the strategist to be able to make a good decision, it is not enough for him to evaluate the most important direction of an operation correctly; he must keep the overall perspective of the war in mind. An example of a decision that follows from this perspective is Kitchener's four-year program of organizing new British units and limited British assistance to the French in the first years of the war.

Only operational reserves play an important role in a strategy of destruction— i.e., reserves that can be dispatched at a decisive moment to the decisive sector of an operation. A strategy of destruction, which assigns the decisive role to a general operation, is incapable of acknowledging any strategic reserves which do not take part in accomplishing the mission within the framework of time and space represented by the operation. But a strategy of attrition can and should take into consideration strategic reserves (e.g., the Russian Asiatic corps in 1914, militia forces, subsequent echelons of mobilization, colonial contingents, the delayed entry of allies into the war) and coordinate its line of conduct with them.

A strategy of destruction completes operations by the achievement of the ultimate goal of the war, In a war of attrition we sometimes get a situation in which the attacking side has achieved its limited ultimate war aim but the war continues because a solution has not been reached on the political and economic fronts. This was the case in the Russo-Japanese War: the ultimate war aim of the Japanese was to destroy the Russian Pacific fleet, capture its base, Port Arthur, and expel Russian troops from southern Manchuria. This goal was achieved the moment the Russian armies were defeated at Mukden. However, the war continued for another six months. Russia's vital centers were invulnerable to Japanese attack, and the Japanese had to wait for a revolutionary movement to develop in Russia. A similar situation characterized the last six months of the Crimean War: Sevastopol was rid of Russian troops on September 9, 1855, and at this moment the allies achieved their ultimate war aim, the destruction of the Russian Black Sea fleet and its base, but the Congress of Paris only opened on February 13, 1856. These periods of a war, which are characterized by a high level of activity on the political and economic fronts, are distinguished by calm on the military front interrupted only by outbreaks of desperation (e.g.,Tsushima) or very minor undertakings (Kinburn's attack in 1855 and the Sakhalin expedition in the summer of 1905).

The Strategic Offensive and Defensive

Every operation is inevitably a combination of defensive and offensive moments. Despite this, we differentiate between offensive and defensive operations depending on whether the strategist poses positive or negative goals. The advancement of a series of positive goals characterizes a strategic offensive, while a series of negative goals characterizes a strategic defensive.

We do not agree with the statement that any delay on the military front must always be to the detriment of the side pursuing positive goals. An offensive political goal may be tied to a strategic defensive, the conflict will be under way simultaneously on the economic and political fronts, and if time is working in our favor—that is, if the balance of pluses and minuses is to our advantage—then the military front, even if it is at a standstill, may gradually achieve a favorable change in the balance of forces. If a war is a kind of blockade, such as the Russian blockade of Shamil in Dagestan or the English blockade of Napoleon's France or the Kaiser's Germany, the military front may gain a great deal from time working in its favor. In general, a strategic defensive consisting of a series of operations with negative goals may pursue a positive ultimate goal. Of course, July 1918, when the armed front was moving forward, cannot be considered the time when the Entente began to pursue a positive ultimate goal regarding Germany. This pursuit began with the start of military operations, even though for many years it involved no forward movement of the front lines. Even the five-month defensive operations conducted by the Russians in 1915 in their withdrawal from Poland, which compelled the Germans to expend their best time and forces that could have been used to achieve major results in France, constitute, in terms of a strategy of attrition, a major link in the chain of events that led to Germany's ultimate defeat.

In general, the pursuit of negative goals, that is, fighting for the complete or partial maintenance of the status quo, requires less expenditure of forces or resources than the pursuit of positive goals, namely fighting for conquest and forward movement. It is easier to keep what you have than get something new. The weaker side will naturally go on the defensive.

These principles are obvious in both politics and the art of war, but only on the condition that the sides have a certain amount of stability and defensive capability in the status quo. In the same way that ocean waves grind the rocks on the shore against one another, historical conflict rounds off amorphous political formations, erodes boundaries which are too sinuous and gives rise to the stability required for defensive capabilities.

However, sometimes this condition is absent. The Treaty of Versailles has filled the map of Europe with historical oddities. The class struggle has created a layer cake of different interests and factions on this map. In these conditions the pursuit of the negative goal of maintaining the status quo may be the weakest rather than the strongest form of waging war: sometimes a superiority of forces will be required for a defensive rather than for an offensive, depriving the defensive of any meaning. This was the situation in the war of 1866 in the German theater of operations. Moltke considered this theater of war secondary to the

Bohemian theater and left only three divisions there against Middle German forces three times their size. The fragmentation of the German states and the open-field system of the Prussian domains resulting from the peace treaties of Westphalia and Vienna made defense incomparably more difficult for the Prussians than offense. The Prussians were fully capable of going on the offensive despite the superiority of the enemy's forces.

The same conditions are often encountered in a civil war; civil war breaks out over a vast area and definite fronts form only gradually. But iven the intensity of the class struggle, these definite fronts do not express the entire heart of the matter: each side's rear contains oases that make ready-made bases for the enemy: in advancing from the Volga to the Urals the Red forces did not get separated from their base, which is usually a significant disadvantage of an offensive, but approached new and wealthier sources of food and class and economic energy. If the political situation is right, why even think of a defensive? To put down armed uprisings in one's rear? The downfall of the Paris Commune in 1871 can partially be explained by its failure to consider the need for an offensive in order to establish communications with the provinces; Paris alone against all of France was an indefensible position in any case.

For centuries, since the time of Cardinal Richelieu, French diplomatic thinking has been nurtured on the idea of creating conditions of fragmentation, open fields, and weakness in Europe. As a result of the work of French policy, whose ideas are expressed in the Versailles "Peace" Treaty, all of Central Europe—Germany, Poland, Czechoslovakia and so forth has been placed in a situation which completely rules out the possibility of defense and positional warfare. The French vassals have been skillfully placed in the position of a squirrel compelled to turn the treadmill of militarism. The art of French policy lies in the skillful creation of unstable situations. This is the reason for the impermanence of this creation. The idea behind the Versailles Treaty, putting Germany in an indefensible position, has made it physically necessary for Germany to prepare for offensive operations. Poland will still have the opportunity to ponder how it should thank France for the gift of the Polish Corridor, which has put Poland first in line for a German attack.

Defensive operations ordinarily involve certain territorial losses. They tend to put off decisions to the last possible moment. Consequently, for a defense to be successful we must have expendable territory and time must operate to our advantage. These conditions will most probably be met in a large country which can more easily afford to lose scores or even hundreds of thousands of square kilometers of territory temporarily and which, as time goes on, will get the opportunity to utilize new resources scattered over vast distances. In terms of defense small countries are not independent and can exist only to the extent that they can count on external help. But the size of a territory alone in no way guarantees the success of a defensive: a state needs a resolute government and a stable domestic situation to survive the material losses associated with an enemy offensive and make time work in its favor rather than the enemy's. The leaders of a war must be firm and avoid squandering the manpower needed for a moment of crisis on defending different geographical treasures.

A strategic offensive requires a major expenditure of forces, gets us farther away from our base and requires the allocation of major forces for organizing and securing communications with the base. A precondition for a prolonged offensive is a continuous influx of fresh forces. The inevitable expenditures of an offensive lead to a situation in which its development under normal conditions, when there is no forward base, weakens the offender. This means that while an offensive may theoretically be considered unlimited, we must admit that its success will reach a culmination point and then fade as a result of material difficulties. The most artful strategic offensive will lead to a disaster if we do not have enough resources to reach the ultimate goal which will secure the peace for us.

The basic strategic thinking of the defensive should also be based on this characteristic of the offensive: namely, where is the limit at which one could put an end to the successes of the development of an offensive? This idea dominates strategic, operational and tactical art. The enemy has crushed our forward lines and is penetrating into the depth of our battle dispositions, and the tactician, in order to avoid frittering away his forces, must immediately try to get an idea of where and when he will be able to deploy his reserves, stop the enemy and go on the counterattack. If the forward lines have not been broken but the deployment front is greatly threatened, this question is also fundamental for the leadership of an operation. If we must wage defensive warfare, then the thinking of a strategist should primarily dwell on the position in time and space at which one could count on changing the course of a war, causing a crisis and switching from negative goals to positive goals (Torres Vedras in 1810, Chatalja in 1912, the Marne in 1914 and the Vistula in 1920).

An offensive that has passed its culmination point very quickly becomes an adventure, and any further development merely lays the groundwork for the enemy's transition from the pursuit of negative goals to the pursuit of positive goals, which could become very sweeping. The Carpathian adventure of the Southwestern front provided very fertile ground in the spring of 1915 for a major Austro-German offensive on the Russian front which lasted five months: the last Russian reserves and weapons were used up and the rear and flank of the Southwestern front became ever more vulnerable to Mackensen's imminent attack. General Falkenhayn admitted that he could not have anticipated any better conditions, and on April 13, 1915, he wrote the chief of the Austrian general staff instructing him not to offer fierce resistance to the Russians in the Carpathians in anticipation of a German attack, but that a breakthrough on the Danube would be easier and the "harvest" would be even greater the further the Russians managed to penetrate the mountains south of the planned front of attack.[8] The Austrians' intelligent compliance with this request could have led to a completely disconcerting success. The Russian armies were rescued from this disaster only by the major obstacles that the Hungarians placed in the way of a withdrawal maneuver through their territory. If this had not happened, the fate of Kornilov's division, which did not succeed in getting out of the mountains and was destroyed there, would have been shared by entire Russian armies.

Of course, all of the splendor of Foch's offensive in July 1918 was prepared by Ludendorff's unsuccessful advance on the Marne toward Chateau-Thierry. The maneuver of the Western front in mid-August 1920, i.e., the offensive toward the lower Vistula, was an ideal preparation for the Polish counterattack.

---

[8] Falkenhayn, *Verkhovnoe komandovanie* [The High Command], p. 83.

This makes it obvious how important it is to make a timely evaluation of the limit beyond which an offensive turns into an adventure and begins to lay the groundwork for an enemy counterattack. This is a very broad issue whose resolution requires taking into account the enemy's political and economic immunity to setbacks; his ability to keep his army ready for battle after prolonged defensive operations and retreats; and the forces that will be provided to us and to the enemy as a result of further echelons of military and economic mobilization. In a war of destruction both the culminating point of an offensive and the final line of defense are primarily defined by a line in space: Napoleon's army perished after traveling 2,000 kilometers from the French border to Moscow. In a war of attrition this line in part becomes a time line: in the fourth year of the war the fighting capabilities of the armed forces of the Central Powers had weakened drastically.

An attacker should remember that simply moving forward merely weakens him and is only advantageous to the extent that it reduces the distance to a culminating point in the space of which he can reap the fruits of his successes. Every kilometer the Germans covered after the border battle in the direction of the Marne was an obvious loss because they did not achieve noticeable tactical successes.[9]

A strategic defense should carefully ration out its efforts prior to a critical moment; on one hand, we must limit our territorial loses as much as possible and keep the enemy from cakewalking by compelling him to conduct major operations, carry out regroupings, bring up thousands of tons of supplies to the forward lines and cross difficult obstacles; on the other hand, we must keep our army at a certain level of combat-readiness below which we will only have to consider how to avoid contact with the enemy; we must give ourselves the opportunity of effecting a radical change in the situation. Not avoiding battle or getting distracted by battle is a difficult task which can often be handled only by a highly trained army.

Positional Warfare and Maneuver Warfare
If both sides set positive goals for an operation, then they participate in maneuver operations which often involve meeting engagements. The Russian Civil War, which offered such advantages for the pursuit of positive goals, was an extreme case of maneuver warfare. If both sides emphasize negative goals, then military operations become positional. When war is waged by a coalition, negative goals are much more common, because the egotistic interests of each ally impel it to give the other allies the honor of attacking the enemy and give itself the honor of vigilantly guarding what it has and saving its strength for the last minute so as to force the warring parties to take its interests into account in concluding a peace. That is why coalitional wars are more positional in nature than single combat between two states. France and Britain had learned these simple truths by the fall of 1914, whereas Russia began to ponder them only in the fall of 1916, which was the reason for Russia's very unfavorable position.

As long as both sides pursue negative goals, positional calm prevails. Casualties and materiel expenditures on the front are reduced, which has a very favorable effect on subsequent echelons of mobilization. Thus if both sides are quite poorly prepared and are very short of materiel, it is quite probable to expect

---

9   The issue of expanding the base of a war is examined above.

positional warfare. Very significant positional tendencies characterized the American Civil War, for which the North and South were poorly prepared. In the fall of 1877 the Russo-Turkish War in the Bulgarian theater was highly positional because of the inability of the Turks to pursue positive goals and the insufficient forces with which the Russians invaded the Balkans. Subsequent dispatches of new Russian corps to the theater were similar to contemporary successive echelons of mobilization. In the Russo-Japanese War the positional front on the Sha Ho River took root as a result of logistical difficulties affecting both sides and the depletion of forces on hand, which compelled a temporary switch to the pursuit of negative goals. A positional front may also easily be set up when one hostile army is a sea landing force whose mobility is constricted (Sevastopol in 1844-1855, Arkhangelsk in 1919).

Small countries are ill-suited for positional warfare. In fact, the fronts they would have to occupy are reduced on a much smaller scale than the territory whose resources would have to feed their resistance; if two states have similar boundaries and the front of one state is eight times shorter, then its territory would be 64 times smaller, and one needs more than a thousand square kilometers of a smoothly functioning rear to maintain one linear kilometer of a positional front. All of these figures are very relative, because the economic conditions of a territory are very important, but there is no doubt that a Great China is required to build a Great Wall of China and that it is impossible to armor plate a ship that has the tonnage of a torpedo boat.

The seductive lure of withdrawal is quite evident in a war of maneuver, and commanders must be strong-willed and conscientious in order to keep their troops from dispersing into an area rid of the enemy. In positional warfare the front of each side strives to lean on the front of the enemy. It seems that reality does not tolerate an empty space between the vanguards of both sides, and the overestimation of the importance of the terrain, which results from the casualties that are the cost of advancing several hundred meters, forces the fronts closer together. In essence, positional warfare, which pursues a negative goal, is based on the two-sided illusion of preparing for an offensive; Therefore in most cases a positional front is tactically characterized as the starting point for an attack rather than the most favorable position for a defense. The best positions are abandoned if there is an opportunity to move several kilometers forward. For years troops will stand in waterlogged trenches under fire on low ground sometimes only two or three kilometers in front of healthy, dry, elevated terrain. Positional warfare, where there is a great deal of equipment, where command is rigidly centralized and where warfare takes on such material forms and is seemingly organized scientifically, in reality constitutes an open field for anarchy. An illusion-free and intelligent high command can master this anarchy and achieve great results by systematically posting its own troops in advantageous sectors so as to force the enemy to deploy his forces extremely disadvantageously over hundreds of kilometers.

In the event that maneuver is avoided, there is a tendency for the importance of different sectors to be overestimated and the geographical value of the protected area comes to the forefront. A wealthy industrial center, an important road junction and the proximity of a rail line suitable for lateral maneuvers compel one to occupy a sector more firmly; poor country deprived of any valuable geographic objectives will be covered to a lesser extent; but this difference will not be as significant as in a war of maneuver, because secondary sectors in general become more important. The sector along the English Channel became the most important sector of the positional front in France and Belgium in 1914, because holding the northern coast of France would have provided significant benefits to the Germans for organizing a submarine blockade of Britain. The front in Lorraine and the Vosges, which had been studied in such detail by the French general staff before the war, became secondary, because on this front there were no important lines of communication or industrial cities (with the exception of Nancy).

It is easy to get involved in positional warfare, even against one's will, but it is not so easy to get out of it; no one managed to do it in the World War. If a positional front is comparatively small in size, surrounding an open flank may yield extremely good results. In peacetime the French had made preparations to set up a positional front on the Franco-German border; bypassing this front through Belgium constituted the basic idea behind the Schlieffen Plan. In its invasion of East Prussia in 1915 the Russian 10th Army occupied a positional front by early 1915 but did not extend its right wing to the Baltic, which gave Ludendorff the opportunity to surround the Russian right wing, which led to the encirclement of the 10th Army in the Augustow Forest. The threat of a disaster posed by this kind of flanking maneuver for an entire positional front makes it necessary to extend a positional front over the entire width of a theater and attach its flanks to reliable obstacles such as the sea or a neutral county capable of securing its neutrality by arms.

This was the essence of the "flight to the sea" which took place in 1914 beyond Mariskaia. This maneuver did not constitute the pursuit of common goals by both sides—out flanking the enemy—but the pursuit of a negative goal a countermaneuver against such an outflanking maneuver. The "flight to the sea" was a strategic defensive maneuver rather than an offensive maneuver.

There can be two kinds of positive goals whose pursuit is prepared for in the process of positional warfare: either applying pressure on the enemy without getting away from positional warfare or a positional operation (such as the Verdun and Somme operations of 1916 and the Flanders operation of 1917); or operations conducted for the purpose of switching from positional warfare to maneuver warfare. When there is a positional front covering an entire theater the latter option may be conducted in three ways: a breakthrough (Brusilov's offensive in 1916 and Nivelle's offensive in 1917); a flanking movement, which may involve violating a country's neutrality or bringing a new ally into the war (Romania in August 1916); or a withdrawal to bring about a general shift. The latter is based on the seductive appeal of withdrawal. One may withdraw from several sectors to create a broken front that could not be defended by any country. Several sectors could be completely abandoned, while behind the sectors still held one could gather strong reserves for going on the offensive. The enemy's advance must lay the groundwork for this offensive. Similar proposals were made several

---

[10] Ludendorff's remarkable withdrawal in March 1917 to the Siegfried line pursued the opposite goal of strengthening the front and making it more positional. After command had been turned over to Falkenhayn, the younger Moltke considered switching to positional warfare in France to be unacceptable and suggested a withdrawal maneuver in order to attack the French once they went on the pursuit.

times during the course of the World War but were not approved by responsible strategists. Apparently on wealthy terrain with an abundance of railroads this idea is purely theoretical and completely impractical.[10] A withdrawal would lead to the sacrifice of too many vital economic and transportation interests. But it is impossible not to notice that very favorable prospects for such a maneuver are opening up in the Belorussian-Polish theater.

In future wars we must reckon with the fact that at least certain sectors of a positional front will be organized from the very beginning, during the period of operational deployment. If a border extends only several hundred kilometers and is based on solid geographical positions, then we could expect the development of a continuous positional front from the very beginning of a war. In a future conflict, for example, a future Franco-German conflict, the massive amounts of materiel required for waging war and the need to wait for the results of industrial mobilization and subsequent echelons of military mobilization will make the temporary renunciation of the pursuit of positive military goals quite possible. Of course, positional warfare may take on milder forms, such as on the Russian front in the winter of 1914-1915, which allowed for quite extensive maneuvering in the gaps between positional sectors, but the positional fronts did not coincide everywhere (for example, a great deal of space was left between the Narev and the Prussian border of the Prasnyshskii squadron). But we must prepare for positional warfare. We may have to lay the groundwork for extensive maneuvers by forestalling enemy attempts to set up a positional front.

2. COMMUNICATIONS

Strategy is the Study of Communications

Maintaining the combat-readiness of armed forces by reinforcing and supplying them will be possible only if operations are conducted so that the forces operating on a front are connected to the interior regions of the country by satisfactory lines of communication. Lines of communication are so important that Willisen even defined all of strategy as the study of communications the most important task of the strategist as maintaining the possibility of meeting the supply needs of one's own army and depriving the enemy army of supplies. In fact, it is possible to examine tactical issues outside of communications, but the strategic element only comes to play in connection with communications.

Analysis of the war of destruction and war of attrition, the defensive and the offensive and maneuver and positional warfare has led to a whole series of viewpoints on the goals we can set in conducting military operations. There turns out to be an entire bacchanalia of different plausible solutions; we can only move from the infinite wealth of fantasy to the firm ground of reality by analyzing the issue of communications.

It is not sufficient to have forces and resources, we must have them where and when we need them. If in economics commerce[1] gives a commodity the invaluable property of turning up where and when there is a demand for it, then during wartime this invaluable property is imparted to troops and materiel by intelligent strategic leadership in the form of communications.

In 1812 the disaster which befell Napoleon's army was not due to the Russian winter but rather to the impossibility of supplying a massive army which had penetrated hundreds of kilometers into a poor, sparsely populated territory on bad dirt roads.

The approach taken by several generations of historians to the campaign of 1813 is quite interesting. The first historians ascribed Napoleon's setback to the weakening of his operational talents. Then historians began to ascribe his failures to the fact that the masses with which Napoleon operated had overgrown the possibilities of successful operations on interior operational lines. The next generation referred to the youth of Napoleon's army of 1813, that is, the new recruits who had replaced the French veterans who had perished in the snows of Russia and the backwaters of Spain. Finally, on the 100th anniversary of the campaign historians analyzed Napoleon's communications: Saxony was a very wealthy country, but Napoleon had tramped over a very small patch of ground for ten weeks with 100,000 soldiers and ultimately conditions in Saxony came to resemble those in the empty spaces of Belorussia; and his line of communication, a dirt road from the Elbe to the Rhine, was of course incapable of supplying such a large army. In fact, by the decisive moment of the battle of Leipzig the strength

---

[1]   This comparison with commerce seems even more appropriate when we consider that Goethe discussed the triune concepts of war, commerce and banditry, and Clausewitz, in defining the art of war, classified it neither as an art nor a science but equated it to commerce.

of the French army must have been cut in half, and there must have been a severe shortage of artillery rounds.[2]

In the mid 17th century the five-day march system of supply based on animal drawn carts took root. This system allowed armies to go no farther than 125 kilometers away from the stores of their base of operations. The wealth of the theaters in which the French revolutionary and Napoleonic armies operated, the remarkable ease with which the revolutionary forces adapted to the use of local resources, the speed with which the operations developed and the low expenditures of ordnance fostered the illusion that strategic art was independent of communications in the early 19th century. It was an illusion because, as we can see from the examples of 1812 and 1813, the larger number of troops and greater resistance meant that communications had a decisive effect.

The issue of communications may be examined on different scales. We shall call a theater of military operations the portion of the territory encompassed by military operations characterized by the presence of an independent network of communications and the interior regions of the nation on which it is based. This chapter primarily focuses on the study of the effect of communications on the scale of an individual theater. But communications may also be considered on the scale of the entire military front, namely the greater or lesser possibility of moving reserves between different theaters. These issues arise in coalition wars (e.g., the Entente in the World War), In a war on two fronts (Germany and the Soviet Union), and even in the event of a war on a single front if it extends over a vast distance, is divided by a major obstacle and constitutes two separate theaters of operations (the Belorussian and Ukrainian theaters, north and south of Polese). We shall dwell on these issues in our chapter on the strategic line of conduct. Finally, communications may be examined on a national scale: the interruption of Russia's communications through the Dardanelles and the Arkhangelsk and Murmansk railroads as outlets to the Arctic in the World War, the blockade of Germany in the World War, the need for Britain to maintain sea lines of communications, the Polish Corridor for Poland and so forth. However, we classify communications on a national scale as issues of conflict on the economic front; economists, after discussing them, will set appropriate goals for the military front, whereas strategy is concerned with them only indirectly, trying to relate them, like other geographical objectives, to the conditions of conflict on the military front.

Communications in 20th-Century Strategy

The importance of communications has grown in proportion to the amount of resources used in a war. Given the comparatively short distances and the presence of a good network of dirt roads, Moltke was relatively independent of railroads in setting operational goals; 50 years ago only laying siege to a large fortress required the high command to tackle the problem of moving siege guns, which required several score wide-gauge trains. Communications conditions made

---

[2] Of course, all of these explanations can only claim to hold a grain of truth, and we shall advance a new explanation—the success of the agitation directed by Stein and based on exciting German national feelings; this agitation not only led to the desertion of many Germans from Napoleon's army but to the sabotage of entire units. While Napoleon had previously drawn his forces from expanding the base of the war, now, as the revolutionary movement faltered and nationalistic propaganda succeeded, the expansion of the base of the war turned against him.

Moltke postpone the bombardment of Paris for three months. Now war has become so massive that the preparations for any major operation require more work by lines of communications than was previously required by the siege of a major fortress.

In the World War illusions about the possibility of breaking away from rail lines of communications were shattered for once and for all: the five-day march system was resurrected, and in the new system only a stationary store at a base was replaced by a line of main rail stations opened in the rear for traffic.[3] To the question of why the Germans lost the Marne Operation, many investigators have given the reasonable answer that the French were provided splendid support by their railways, while the German right flank and center were separated by more than 100 kilometers from the main stations; and in addition, the French railways that the German restored could only handle light, uncontrolled traffic. In the same way that a truck can travel only a certain distance determined by its supply of fuel and cannot go any farther, modern armies are chained[4] to a line of main rail stations. Apparently in a future edition we may even mention only a three-day march system. In the Civil War communications again temporarily lost their importance because of the poverty of the interior, the small number of persons involved and the extensive use of local resources: combatants even fought with weapons they had taken from the enemy. But the campaign of 1920 once again demonstrated the fleeting nature of the successes of an army that could not count on reliable railroad communications with the rear.

The system of communications presents a completely concrete fact. In some directions tons of freight can only be moved with extreme difficulty, whereas in other directions we could count on the delivery of 60,000 tons per day (10 trunk trains). In preparing for a war a strategist must determine the important directions and develop the tracks appropriately. In conducting military operations he must direct the operations in accordance with transportation capabilities.

Communications that govern the extent of an operational leap pose major obstacles to switching to a strategy of destruction. A major operation must be skillfully divided up into two or three smaller operations on the basis of communications requirements. At the beginning of the World War the German armies should have stopped after they reached the Ain River and waited a week for their communications to catch up to them. They should have given their rear a breather, even though it meant giving the enemy a breather also. The Russian command had to give such a breather in early November 1914 after the Ivangorod-Warsaw operation, after traveling about five days march from their initial disposition on the Vistula. At least a week was needed to put the railroads and highways that had been damaged by the Germans into any kind of order. They were unable to renew their offensive because the initiative had gone over to the Germans (the Lodz operation). When there are forced pauses or interruptions in

---

[3] We can refer to V. Triandafillov's detailed article entitled "Razmakh operatsii sovremennykh armii" [The Scale of Operations of Modern Armies] in *Voina i revoliutsiia*, no. 3 (March 1926), pp. 40-61.

[4] This chain consists of carts and trucks which quickly become less efficient at distances of 80 kilometers. The volume of vehicles used, bad dirt roads and shortages of carts and trucks shorten this chain, while the presence of waterways, the ability to rapidly restore trailways and weak enemy resistance, which make it possible to get by with less vehicles, lengthens this chain.

operations, one must generally have very superior forces in order to continue an offensive in the same direction.

The growing importance of communications makes wars of attrition increasingly probable. By causing concern for the continuity of the front and the integrity of junctions and lateral lines and leading to temporary defensives, the increased importance of communications has also led to a trend toward positional warfare, and has made it extremely difficult to switch from positional warfare to maneuver warfare.

An analysis of communications yields a large number of extremely important guidelines for strategic art: strategic thinking should pay sufficient attention to logistics; the basic directions for an offensive should coincide with the most important available trunk lines of communications, and the pace of an offensive can only temporarily lag behind the pace of restoration of railroads demolished by the enemy; the strategist should keep communications in mind even when he departs from an analysis of his own logistics and looks ahead at the enemy; and only attacks on the enemy that will cause him to lose important junctions and lateral lines should be given serious consideration, and the only way to destroy an enemy army is to cut off all the arteries supplying it.

The Useful Work of the Armed Front

The useful work of military forces is to a great extent determined by the condition of their communications. Operational art should place the troops in the best possible tactical position. Strategic art must place our operations in the best possible communications conditions vis-a vis-the enemy's. These advantages are even more important than tactical advantages. If lines of communication are functioning poorly, then an operation will suffocate.

According to official German calculations, one day of the indecisive battle at Gumbinen against three corps of Rennenkampf's army cost the Germans 14,700 casualties, while seven days of the operation against five corps of Samsonov's army supposedly only cost them 9,000[5] and ended in the complete destruction of the Russian center and the total defeat of both wings of the army. Does the clue to the incomparably more useful work of Rennenkampf's troops lie in the superiority of the 1st Army over the 2nd and the superiority of Rennenkampf's talents over Samsonov's, or in the arrival of Hindenburg and Ludendorff at the Russian front? All these questions must be answered in the negative. The Germans fought worse against Samsonov's troops than they did against Rennenkampf's. The 17th corps, remembering its panic and defeat at Gumbinen and having encountered the 4th division of the 6th Russian corps, for a long time limited itself to artillery fire and requests for aid from its neighbors. At the end of the day the splendid 2nd Prussian division had still not overcome the Keksholm guards regiment and had apparently lost its offensive spirit. At the moment of victory the 41st Prussian division set off a terrible panic. Ludendorff acted like a man who had missed the bus and his will and skill were least evident in this operation. To a great extent the solution lies in the fact that Rennenkampf's lines

---

[5] The last figure seems to be somewhat low. Numerous volunteers joined the German forces during the operation and increased the number of units present and thus the German calculations apparently only covered some of the casualties. But the overall picture is still accurate.

of communication were better than those of the 2nd Army. The Werzbolow line, the Suwalki rail semicircle, a dense network of roads in the rear and the fact that the operations were conducted at the terminus of East Prussia, which left both of Rennenkampf's flanks free, all provided splendid lines of communication for him. Samsonov had only one weak railroad spur running from his extreme left flank, he had no roads in the rear, he was cut off from his base, his left flank was facing in the direction of the lower Vistula, from which a strong attack could always be anticipated, and his right flank was hanging, all of which put him in a very bad position. To this we must add a number of clashes which disturbed Samsonov's mental equilibrium and compelled him to move from Neidenburg to the north, thus allowing the last moment for saving his lines communication slip away.

Official Austrian sources (the Vienna Archives) cast the troops of the Kiev Military District who made up Ruzskii and Brusilov's armies in a better light than the 4th and 5th Russian armies, which were primarily made up of soldiers from interior districts. Without fundamentally denying this, we cannot help but point out that Ruzskii and Brusilov's armies had communications which were just as good as Rennenkampf's, while those of the 4th and 5th were worse, partially resembling Samsonov's.

General Kluck was not immediately able to inflict a total defeat on Manoury's army in the Marne operation, which can primarily be explained by the very favorable communications situation of Manoury's army, which was deployed in Paris, and the very dubious communications situation of Kluck's army.

In order to allow the development of the spring offensive of 1915 on the Russian front, Falkenhayn concentrated Mackensen's army opposite the Danube in a sector where the Austrian front had the best railroad communications, while the Russians had railroads which were still not linked up and from which was the shortest distance to the flank and rear of the Russian armies' communications in the Carpathians. In early 1916 Falkenhayn chose the Verdun sector for his attack, where the Germans had overwhelming superiority in communications over the French, because traffic on both of the trunk lines leading to Verdun had been cut off, and the French had only one narrow-gauge track.

The usefulness of troops is determined not only by the stubbornness with which they fight in a face-to-face engagement but by the pressure they put on enemy communications, which rapidly reduces the enemy's capacity for resistance. Only on rare occasions can both conditions be met, and then the outcome is almost predetermined. Usually pressure on enemy communications is applied only at the expense of one's own communications. The Turks' attempt to apply pressure to the communications of the Russian Caucasian army at Sarakamysh led to a long march in a harsh winter on icy mountain paths and to the massive surrender of weak, frozen Turks in the Russian rear. Thus in principle we cannot condemn the deployments of the Russian 2nd, 4th, and 5th armies in August 1914; despite the fact that due to their communications, they were unable to fight as persistently as the 1st, 3rd, and 8th armies, they did their work on communications in sectors which were sensitive for the enemy. The presence of the 2nd Army affected the outcome of the battle of Gumbinen by reducing the persistence of the Germans. The presence of the 4th and 5th armies (reinforced by the 9th) produced a final solution to the Galician operation. Operational success can be gained by units that have completely abandoned their units and gone into the enemy's rear and fight with a front which is backwards. The 1st Prussian corps, which was extended 40 kilometers along the Russian border in Samsonov's rear facing Prussia with its back to Russia, trapped Samsonov's army in its net. Two Prussian divisions, which had come out between the Augustow Forest and Grodno with their backs to Grodno, captured the core of the 10th Russian army. We must nurture commanders and men who can fight with what they take with them without any lines of communications.

When we study the combat actions of troops, we are accustomed to immediately considering the tactical advantages and disadvantages presented by local conditions for both sides. When we try to study the strategic actions of troops, we must primarily learn to focus our attention on communications and get a full idea of the consequences that follow from these conditions. We should judge the scale and purpose of operations by the enemy communications they are designed to capture. We consider the Schlieffen Plan magnificent because he planned the deep capture of all the communications of the French armies deployed in Lorraine at the border with Germany. The same scale was planned by Ludendorff in 1915 for a destruction operation on the Russian front in the direction of Kovno and Minsk, operations designed to capture the Northwest, Bologoe-Sedlets and Aleksandrov trunk lines, namely all the railroads running north from Polese. During the period positional warfare and all the way up to the end of the French front, the greatest danger for the Germans was posed by their communications converging at a sector on the Maas River between Verdun and Holland; the concentration of German forces in front of Verdun was dictated by caution. Alekseev's puny stature as a strategist is evident from the fact that he never attacked the enemy's communications even in the favorable moments of the end of the battle of Galicia. Several operations in the Civil War, such as the Kiev operation against the Poles in the first half of 1920 and the operation against Wrangel in the fall of the same year, are of great strategic interest in terms of their plans, which were aimed at the complete capture of enemy communications.

The depth to which the issue of communications permeates all of strategy is evident from the fact that all of a strategist's concern for-self preservation is focused on his own communications and all of his plans for destroying the enemy concentrate on his communications. We shall dwell on the nature of the contradictions that arise in regard to communications between the requirements for self-preservation and the requirements for destroying the enemy.

Alexander the Great's Logic

By its very nature an offensive will lead us away from our base and stretch our communications and put them under threat of attack; the enemy retreating deep into his own country puts himself in a very favorable communications situation. Because of this the purpose of planning an offensive is to minimize these disadvantages as much as possible and secure the offensive, whereas the purpose of planning a defense is to maximize the threat to the attacker (flanking positions and attacks, withdrawals in eccentric directions).

A basic precondition for any operation is to put our forces in the most favorable communications situation (convenience and safety) vis-a-vis the enemy. Thus if we try to avoid building a house of cards and instead try to move toward our ultimate goal by achieving a series of intermediate goals, this should primarily involve creating good conditions for the communications of subsequent operations. The ideology of communications is formed by the chain of logic that connects operations into a single whole, namely the strategic line of conduct.

Alexander the Great resolved the problem of a very deep invasion of Asia in an exemplary manner for his time in terms of communications. He initially secured Greece, his base, from within by suppressing his political opponents (Thebes). Then he secured it from without by suppressing the barbarian tribes in the Balkans. Free from danger in his rear, he then crossed the Dardanelles into Asia. But as long as the Greek cities in Asia Minor were refuges for his political enemies who had fled from Greece, he could not remain calm, because these emigres could have easily caused trouble in Greece. After putting an end to them, Alexander still refrained from his dream—a campaign inside Persia—because the Asian fleet was still dominant in his rear, in the Mediterranean. This fleet had to be eliminated, and there was only one way to accomplish this: capturing the entire Asian coast where the fleet was based. In doing this Alexander disrupted communications between Persia and its wealthy African province, Egypt, which he captured without any great effort.[6] Only then, after establishing a new Afro-Asian rear for himself, did Alexander move to the Tigris River and inflict a decisive defeat on the Persians. His dream passed through many stages of materialization before it became a reality.

In every war, albeit on a miniature scale, we must try to ground our creativity in reality and follow the logical path traced out by Alexander the Great.

The operation of Woyrsch's Landwehr corps, the offensive from Kalisz and Czestochowa to the Vistula above Ivangorod, was conducted for the purpose of covering a vital artery of Austro-Hungarian concentration, the Krakow-Lwow trunk line, from the north. The German operation against Rennenkampf (Gumbinen) was conducted to secure German communications from the east during the promised Austrian attack across the Narev River against the communications of the Russian 4th and 5th armies. It was unsuccessful. The attack on Samsonov was launched by the Germans with a certain amount of risk, but the German command, which had Rennenkampf in its rear, decided not to follow it up to the Narev River and the city of Sedlets and instead undertook an operation to push the Russians back to Neman and relieve the pressure on its communications. This operation succeeded, but by the time the Germans had achieved the communications conditions needed for an attack on the Narev, the Austrians had already been routed in eastern Galicia and the Narev operation became pointless. After they were sure of East Prussia, the Germans sent their main forces to handle the mission that Woyrsch carried out in August, namely covering the communications of the Austrians, who were launching a new offensive against the San River, from the north. After the failure of this operation the Germans took advantage of the risky situation of the Russians' communications to launch an attack on Lodz.

---

[6] We can also justify the time Alexander spent capturing Egypt. The Persian state lived on caravan trade between India and the Mediterranean. The loss of the Asian coast deprived the Persian monarchy of its economic means of existence, affected the interests of all its urban centers and could not help but lead Persia to collapse. Alexander sped up rather than retarded this process by capturing Egypt.

Our communications in Poland, surrounded by East Prussia and Galicia, were in a difficult situation. We not only had to forget about an immediate invasion of Germany, on which the French were insisting,[7] we also had to be extremely wary of any operation involving large forces on the left bank of the Vistula. This situation would have been truly threatening for the Germans, and our communications would have been covered on the right by the Baltic and on the left by the Carpathians. This would have made it possible to count on reaching the Oder line in two operational leaps.

Its somewhat exaggerated estimate of our own forces and the French entreaties impelled our general staff to conduct two operations at the same time, in Galicia and East Prussia. There is no doubt that it would have been better (if the French had given us any hope of holding out without our assistance) to conduct an offensive in Galicia with superior forces, which undoubtedly would have compelled the Prussians either to go on the offensive against the Narev or voluntarily abandon East Prussia to provide direct support to the Austrians.

After the failure of the first invasion of East Prussia in August 1914, communications conditions required a repeat of this operation. The end of the Ivangorod-Warsaw operation was the most suitable moment for this. Only the cavalry could pursue the 9th Army retreating into Silesia. In early 1914 no less than 50 Russian divisions would have to be dispatched in order to put an end to this "hornets' nest." If this operation, in terms of men and materiel, were impossible, we should have completely avoided any other operations and go into winter in a waiting posture.

The Lodz operation was a setback for the Russians because it was conducted on the right bank of the Vistula.[8] Samsonov and Rennenkampf's setbacks made the East Prussian campaign unpopular. Russian strategists decided to move on to the next operation without taking care of this business first. As a result, the Russian flank all the way from Bialystok to Lodz was subject to Prussian attacks. Russian communications were hanging in the balance. No matter what transpired, it is obvious that the Russian offensive could not succeed.

Burning One's Own Ships

As long as the conditions for a destructive strike are lacking and one must try to create them, the logic employed by Alexander the Great before his invasion of Asia is completely applicable. However, this logic is totally inappropriate for the period of the development of a destruction operation, and Jomini and Leer were incorrect when they made the principles of the safety and convenience of an operational line into an eternal and inviolable law. The applicable chapters in their treatises contradict the idea of destruction on which their doctrine is based. In

---

[7] It is obvious that French strategists had the same thoughtless attitude toward the consequences of their suggestions for the Russians as they did when they insisted on the Romanian action in 1916 and the "Kerensky action" in 1918. If French strategy has not fundamentally changed since then, French allies and vassals should be on the lookout.

[8] Already in the 18th century Lloyd stated that "no matter how much Russia wants to take part in German affairs, it can only intervene in them as an auxiliary force and operate in Germany for only several months out of the year. Russia is completely incapable of holding on to any conquest west of the Vistula." *Strategiia v trudakh voennykh klassikov*, vol. 1, p. 52. In the conditions of the 20th century this was justifiable as long as German armed forces in Eastern Prussia remained intact.

analyzing Napoleon's campaigns, they did not understand the enormous risk Napoleon took that is involved in any strategy of destruction. As Clausewitz wrote,

> Success and danger inevitably go hand in hand and this is a dynamic law of war. Consequently, if we try to magnify our success, our danger is magnified proportionally and the only important question is whether this increase is appropriate for the requirements and characteristics of our situation.[9]

We must not condemn risk in general, but we must study beforehand whether risk is appropriate in a given instance. Only if the risk is inappropriate can we talk about an adventurer. Yermak Timofeevich was a conqueror, not an adventurer.

In 1519, after he heard about Mexico's wealth of gold, Velasquez, the Spanish governor general of Cuba, gathered an expedition in Santiago de Cuba consisting of 11 ships with 10 guns, 508 soldiers with 16 horses and 110 sailors under the command of Ferdinand Cortez, one of his most courageous subordinates. However, Velasquez, knowing Cortez's willfulness, ordered him to give up command of the expedition and return to shore. After receiving the order, Cortez told the sailors to raise the anchor, sailed off to Mexico and landed at Vera Cruz harbor, where his soldiers, after they discovered that Cortez was commanding them without legal authorization, started to mutiny. Cortez calmed them down. After deciding to go into Mexico to its capital, Cortez could not count on securing his communications for many hundreds of kilometers. The ships in Vera Cruz harbor could not be guarded and merely reminded him of the base that had disparaged his authority and had introduced dissension in his ranks. Cortez gave the order to burn the ships and moved deep into the country of the Aztecs. A week after his arrival in the capital he captured the Emperor Montezuma and began to exploit the country. A year later Velasquez gathered a new expedition (18 ships with 12 guns, 900 infantrymen, 85 cavalrymen) and dispatched it to Mexico to depose and arrest Cortez. Leaving 140 men in the capital Cortez moved with his best men to meet the new expedition, and despite its overwhelming numerical superiority, attacked it, routed it and added the members who were still alive to his ranks. Despite all the uprisings caused by the cruelties of exploitation, Cortez remained in control of the situation, swore the allegiance of the conquered empire to the Spanish Crown and left as soon as he was called back to Spain.

In Spanish conquista means conquest and conquistador means a conqueror. Cortez's remarkable ability to take risks should be the hallmark of every strategist whom history calls upon to accomplish daunting feats which require a plan of destruction. Didn't Hannibal burn his ships and go from Spain across the Pyrenees, the Alps the mighty Rhone and countries inhabited by hostile barbarian tribes into Italy, which had been organized by powerful Rome? But there was no other way as long as the enemy fleet dominated the sea. Hannibal abandoned communications because he had the same tactical superiority over the Romans as Cortez did over the Aztecs. In 1706 Eugene of Savoy, who was in a very desperate situation and had abandoned his communications, leaped to Turin, bypassing the French on the right bank of the Po, engaged the enemy in battle and pushed the French completely out of Lombardy with a single blow. In no way should such desperate feats be attempted in every case. We condemn Charles XII's Ukrainian

---

[9]   Letter to K. Redar dated December 27, 1827.

campaign of the following year and call it an adventure not because the Swedes were defeated at Poltava, but because this risk-taking was completely unjustified by the situation, given that things had been going pretty well for him in the Northern War.

Napoleon undoubtedly had the heart of a conquistador rather than the desire to cushion himself against a fall, as Jomini and Leer depict.

In order to break the power of England, which had continued to fight with France at a time when the enemies of the revolution on the continent had already concluded peace, Napoleon decided to launch a campaign to India and attack this source of English economic power. Given the balance of naval forces, it would have been impossible to reach India by sea. Napoleon decided to leap across the Mediterranean, land in Egypt and then follow the path of Alexander the Great.

An army of 32,300 men was loaded onto 232 transport ships escorted by 13 battleships and 20 small warships at different ports, including Toulon, Marseilles, Chivita-Vecchia and Corsica. The expedition set sail on May 19, 1798, took Malta on June 12 and on the night of July 2 began to land near Alexandria in Egypt. Nelson's English squadron, which had been looking for the French expedition, had set sail from Alexandria only three days before and accidentally lost Napoleon's expedition in the Mediterranean. On August 12 Nelson returned and in a battle at Abukir destroyed Napoleon's ships. There was no way to transport the second echelon of the expedition (6,000 men from Toulon) by sea. Napoleon was in the same position on the African coast as Cortez was on the American coast. The army became despondent. But Napoleon's order indicated that he was Cortez's equal:

> We are compelled to perform great feats, and we shall, we
> must create a great country, and we will. Seas on which
> others are superior separate us from our fatherland, but there
> is no sea to separate us from Africa and Asia. There are a lot
> of us, and we have many men here to fill our ranks. We will
> not be lacking ammunition, we have a lot of it, but if we
> should fall short, Champy and Conte will make it for us.

Egypt was to play the role of an intermediate base, and the French army was to get up to strength, acquire the camels and horses for the campaign, establish its sovereignty on the Nile after destroying the feudal state of the Mamelukes and march to India in the course of 15 months. Hostilities with Turkey compelled Napoleon to launch a hasty campaign into Syria. The failures of this campaign and the evident need to replace the Directorate in France, and Suvorov's victories in Italy distracted Napoleon from following up the Egyptian expedition. But just think of the number of fortunate coincidences that had to occur for Napoleon to even land in Egypt!

Tippoo Sahib, an Indian patriot who had organized a rebellion in India against English exploitation, played a major role in Napoleon's plans. A key role in Hannibal's plans was played by the promises of the Gauls, who had just been conquered by Rome, to launch a friendly rebellion against the Romans and assist the Carthaginian leader. In the campaign of 1920 great faith was placed in the Polish proletariat. The validity of these hopes for a forward base determine the advisability of the risk at which one's communications are placed in the process. Historical revolutionary wars often involve such hopes and impel leaders to take strategic risks.

Communications Destruction

Risk on a somewhat smaller, operational scale, involving abandoning communications for a period of only several days, is closely tied to a strategy of destruction. Engaging in battle on an inverted front was a goal which Napoleon persistently pursued in his best campaigns (1800, 1805, 1806, 1807), when he was convinced of his own tactical superiority. If we are completely doubtful of the possibility of engaging in a battle in this way in which both sides would temporarily lose their communications and the vanquished would be totally at the mercy of the victor, we should avoid a strategy of destruction, which relies solely on extraordinary victories.

Destruction requires conditions that would make it possible to determine whether any portion of the enemy's forces which has attempted to make a turning maneuver can be considered cutoff. The error in Pful's plan in 1812 lay in the fact that he did not figure out the destruction nature of Napoleon's invasion of Russia in its initial phase and tried to stop this invasion with one Russian army at a fortified position at the Drissa while having the other Russian army attack Napoleon's communications. Napoleon had sufficient forces to encircle and destroy both Russian armies simultaneously.

The very development of a destruction attack will place our communications in a somewhat safer situation. If the enemy has been grabbed by the throat, it is less probable that he will attack us from behind. The exposed right flank of the German front in the invasion of France, from the period of the border battle to the beginning of the Marne operation, was a surprise. All the communications of the three right-flank German armies were hanging in the wind. A single French cavalry division made a raid on them. Why not more? And why did the concentration of Manoury's army move from Amiens to Paris toward the enemy's flank when Manoury was already practically hanging over the enemy's rear?

The clue lies in the German drive for destruction. As long as the powerful German attack wave was rolling and threatened to crush and envelop the French armies, separate them from the Lorraine fortified front and open up a direct line of communication to Metz south of Verdun, and as long as the French command was terrorized by the scale of the German assault, Kluck's right flank was in a good position. A charging cavalryman only needs to know how to hack people, he can not use fencing techniques, and the pressure he applies is the best protection he has from enemy attacks.

The dangerous position of the German right wing was evident immediately after the front's advance had been held up somewhat and Paris had gotten out of the envelopment; this was understood simultaneously by both the German and the French commands. Moltke tried to halt two of his right-flank armies, turn them so that they faced Paris and give them a defensive mission. Kluck, who until then had moved with rare boldness and crisp maneuvers against Manoury, shared this view of the threat on the right and even overestimated the danger to German communications. In France everyone immediately got to work on the Galliepi plan for an attack from Paris. The new logic[10] immediately took hold of

---

[10] Many critics (for example, Pierfe) are inclined to castigate Joffre's actions in preparing for the Marne operation, proceeding from the perspective that the logic of attrition that had taken root in the course of the Marne operation itself. To us this seems completely unjustified; the critics are simply revealing their own lack of understanding.

everyone's head as soon as destruction no longer seemed imminent, and the "flight to the sea" was a further illustration of this.

3. AN OPERATION WITH A LIMITED GOAL

The Evolution of an Operation

Studying the methods of conducting an operation is a job for operational art rather than strategy. In devoting several pages in our treatise to an outline of operations, we do so not to plug a sensitive gap in the theory of operational art; strategy, which defines its task in the conduct of military operations as combining operations for achieving the ultimate goal, is not only interested in stating the goal of an operation but also makes certain requirements of the methods of achieving it. All branches of the art of war are closely interrelated: tactics takes the steps that make up an operational leap, and strategy points the way.

In the art of war an operation[1] means a combination of different actions aimed at achieving a goal set forth by strategy. Several operations integrated in time and space form a campaign, and the total number of campaigns over the course of a year is called a yearly campaign. One or several yearly campaigns ultimately lead to a situation in which both sides admit the bankruptcy of their violence and establish a truce. Operational deployment is not a separate operation but an essential element of every operation.

Therefore, we shall avoid dividing operations into primary and preparatory operations. Mobilization was previously considered a preparatory operation, but the latter is not an act of direct conduct of military operations but of the operation of logistics, and it seems to us that it would be inconvenient to apply operational terminology to this act. We consider the term "march-maneuver" outdated and have discarded it.

Before the end of the 19th century an operation was clearly divided into two parts: the maneuver designed to put our forces in the most advantageous position at the time of a decisive clash, and the battle itself.

Of course, the usual theories based on the experience of the Napoleonic wars also included a third phase, pursuit. Just think of all the flowery words theoreticians have expended on this necessary act of following up a success. It would be difficult to adhere to the logic of destruction if we avoided the idea of pursuit, i.e.,the colossal widening of the successes we have achieved. However, from Napoleon up to and including the World War we do not encounter a single pursuit that would follow from narrow tactical considerations in military history. The wars of 1853-1856, 1859, 1861-1865, 1866, 1780, 1877-1878, 1899-1903, 1904-1905 and 1914-1918 do not yield a single example of a pursuit, and because we strive to use concepts that exist in reality, we shall exclude pursuit from our presentation. In the process we encounter a number of misunderstandings that stem from the fact that theoreticians have often preferred to dwell on the desirable rather than the real, and the notion of strategic pursuit has practically taken root in modern minds.

---

[1]   In Latin *opera* means "works" and *operari* means "to act"; philologically, then, the word *operatsiia* [operation] means action.

It is difficult for the idea of a limited pursuit to hack its way through the flowery phraseology left by the past.

If we were to attempt to find anything in the military history of the last decade that would look like pursuit, we would have to look at the last days of the Russo-Turkish war, i.e., the movement of the Russian army after the Turks capitulated at Sheinov, or the last days of the World War on the Bulgarian front, when Bulgaria almost intentionally exposed its front, or finally, the complete collapse of the White armies in the Civil War of 1918-1920. Pursuit is possible only in circumstances of the complete collapse of an enemy state and its total political bankruptcy and in the last minutes before the elimination of armed resistance. The power of the modern state, its vast resources, its new echelons of mobilization, railroad maneuvers and communications systems all make pursuit impossible today. One can reap a harvest on a military front as long as the enemy is still not politically disorganized only within an operation, and pursuit is not the hallmark of a political rather than a military victory.

In Napoleon's days maneuvers often took ten days of marching or more (1806). The scale of Napoleonic maneuvers led to a situation in which the French, who created their own terminology for studying Napoleon's campaigns, still call an operation a "maneuver."

With the advent of railroads, in Moltke's era maneuvers for initial operations began to be carried out by in part by means of railroads of as an initial operational deployment; both sides disembarked not far from another, and the marching maneuvers were somewhat abbreviated in the initial operation. Subsequent operations (such as the Sedan operation) followed the Napoleonic pattern.

Currently every operation is preceded by a special operational deployment that is highly dependent on railroads. In view of the difficulty of moving armies too far away from the railroads, it is important to carry out this operational deployment as close as possible to the areas where the goal of the operation may be achieved. Thus the initial phases of all modern operations are similiar to Moltke's initial operations. But in their final phases they are quite different from Moltke's operations, because today battles, which are a phenomenon of the historical past, do not exist, and if these terms are still used they are used only as expressions that reveal a preference for the vividness of a concept rather than the

---

[2]   "The battle of Galicia," "the battle of the Marne" and "the battle at Tannenberg" are literary figures of speech that the victor uses to publicize his success among the masses. We can totally understand the desperation of several young historians of the Civil War, who have looked for similar specific phenomena in the Civil War and have been unable to find them, because such phenomena belong to the historical past along with the 19th century. But victors should never ignore an effective name for a successful operation. Napoleon called the battle of Borodino "the battle on the Moscow," although the Moscow River ran by the Russian right flank, where no one was fighting; Ludendorff called the Samsonov operation "the battle of Tannenberg," after the name of a hamlet located several kilometers from the site of the battle which had no operational significance whatsoever but was known for a battle in 1410 in which the Slavic tribes stopped a German drive toward the east. In both cases they were guided by the same considerations that compelled French stockbrokers to insist on changing the name of the Bogulma Railroad Company to the Volga-Bogulma Railroad Company, because the average Frenchman has an idea of where the Volga is but has absolutely no idea where the Bogulma is. In the Civil War these important propaganda details were often ignored, and headquarters communiques placed too much reliance on the geographical knowledge of the common man.

accuracy of its formulation.[2] Now the general battle has become dispersed over a large part of an operation.

A 19th century battle consisted of a series of clashes taking place over a short period of time in a small area with the enemies in close proximity; the total duration of a battle was not too much greater than the duration of an individual clash. From a strategic point of view Clausewitz could consider a battle a point in time and space. Once the cannons started firing Clausewitzian strategy took a breather, turning over all leadership to the tacticians until the battle ended. Troops were not replaced, regrouped, or reinforced, and they did not rest during a battle; besides them, only tactical reserves had the opportunity to take part in deciding the outcome. All of this was still true in Moltke's day, but conditions began to change once the Russo-Japanese War began.

The battle front began to get larger, and the sites of battles became fragmented and were great distances apart from one another. Whereas in Napoleon's day an advance of two or three kilometers into the enemy's battle formation led to his complete disintegration, currently penetrations of 60 to 70 kilometers do not always produce the same results (witness the Galician operation in August 1914, the German offensive of March 1918 and so forth). We need a whole combination of battles, a sequence of battles, and several days of marching with successful fighting to break the enemy's resistance. The overall duration of these clashes is easured in weeks rather than hours. The duration of a general clash over time is in one way related to the duration of an individual tactical clash, which at times may exhaust all the energy of a military unit. Troops must be replaced, given rest and provided with reinforcements and materiel as the clash develops; it is now possible to regroup forces, bring up new reserves from far away and supplement and adjust the initial deployment with new railroad maneuvers. A single thrust has become fragmented into many thrusts, and a single armed clash is sometimes separated from another by whole days of marching because the modern arena of battle has gotten so large. Movement, fighting, rest, offense, defense, reconnaissance, security, supply and reinforcement—all these individual activities are interlinked and constitute the content of a modern operation. Previously we could make a clear distinction between a battle, rest and marching.

Quantity has turned into quality. A battle once had only barely noticeable cracks dividing it into individual clashes. The expansion of a battle over time and space has led to a situation in which a battle has disintegrated into separate pieces which are evident only in an entire operation.

Whereas previously operations were divided into maneuvers and battles, now we must establish other distinctions: now maneuvers are conducted partially on rails and partially in the maelstrom of the battlefield in an attempt to combine individual clashes to achieve the goal of an operation. Maneuvers have become partly an element of operational deployment and partly a link between individual battles.

We have the same circumstances that have made destruction extremely difficult in modern warfare in mind when we emphasize the limited goals of modern operations. Once again we will point out that an attacker usually has worse communications with his rear than a defender, who has his entire rail system at his disposal. In planning an operation one must keep in mind not only the enemy's initial forces at the time an operation begins but the probable buildup of his forces during a battle. The attacker must compare his own present with the defender's future, which has become particularly disadvantageous now, in the present era of permanent mobilization and the rapid formation of new armed echelons in the rear. In 1870 Moltke began his invasion of France with 500,000 soldiers against 250,000. Today even this 2:1 ratio of attackers to defenders, which is not often encountered, may prove to be insufficient; if Moltke's offensive had been repeated 50 years later, it would have been drowned in a month in the sea of French numerical superiority. From this we should conclude that an offensive operation that is planned to be brief and to last no more than two weeks may be carried out with a much smaller ratio of attackers to defenders than is required by a six-week operation. Our superiority in numbers on the Western front in July 1920 was sufficient to get to the Neman and the Bug, but at the Vistula the balance of forces had to change in favor of the Poles.

Surprise

The art of conducting an operation is primarily the art of achieving material superiority over the enemy. There is no need to achieve material superiority over the entire front on which an operation is conducted. Battles occurring in different sectors are of decisive importance at different moments. An attacker faced with a defender possessing approximately equal forces (meaning, of course, not only the quantity but the quality of the men, the officers and the equipment) cannot count on success, because he has to operate under more difficult tactical conditions. An offensive is advantageous only insofar as one is able to gather overwhelmingly superior forces in secret in a decisive sector and then attack an enemy who is unprepared to use all his forces in this sector. But as we mentioned above, an operation is not made up of one series of battles but a large number of successive series. The first real pressure applied will reveal our plans to the enemy, and the enemy will do everything possible to counter us in the decisive sectors of attack with sufficient material forces to repel us. Hence the successful development of an operation primarily requires that it be uninterrupted. If necessity compels us to await the arrival of reinforcements and the delivery of supplies and halt the operation, the operation should be considered completed at the positions we have gained. Any attempts to restart an operation after a pause will encounter increasingly stiff resistance and the chances for its success are greatly reduced if the enemy in general has the resources to resist.

A secretly prepared operation must unfold at top speed. While we may speak of the slow pace of a general strategic offensive, which depends on restoring and linking railroads even in the conditions of a minimal number of man-made fortifications, such as on the Russo-Polish front, and could hardly exceed ten kilometers per day, it would be completely mistaken to transfer these figures to the speed of movements during an operation itself; in an operation our troops should be ready to march up to 40 kilometers per day, and the intervals between marches will often be taken up by fighting rather than resting.

The art of war cannot avoid the requirements of surprise. Military cleverness and stratagems permeate all of operational art and are the same kind of essential element in it that the concept of strength and its organized and rational utilization in battle is in tactics. Only operational riddles that cannot be deciphered by the enemy in time will be successful. This requirement of the art of war remains in force even for the leisurely conditions of positional warfare and despite all the latest means of intelligence. Even in the so-called "material battles" of positional warfare, which are designed to last entire months and involve trampling over the same piece of ground in an organized way and in which therefore gaining ground is less important than inflicting greater losses on the enemy than the losses we bear, even in these exceptional cases surprise in concentrating all materiel and the resultant surprise in beginning an operation is of great importance for success (e.g., Verdun in early 1916). In 1915 and 1916 the French committed serious operational errors by believing that modern means of intelligence and reconnaissance (aerial photography, espionage, interrogating prisoners) would make it impossible to keep an operation secret whose preparations lasted several weeks and were revealed by trench work on the front and rail and road traffic in the rear as well as the need for an extensive range for a mass of batteries. The French proceeded down the path of subordinating operational art to tactics; their fall operation in Champagne in 1915 and their summer operation at the Somme were prepared completely openly and were known to the Germans many weeks before they began. Operational art was completely eliminated, while tactics grew to gigantic proportions and revealed its inability to achieve major results by tactical means alone. Russian thinking, particularly in preparing the Brusilov operation in the spring of 1916, took a different route, and the German operational methods in late 1917 and early 1918 followed our lead. The most essential characteristics of the German methods were to restore to operational art its rights; surprise had to be achieved in positional warfare, and tactics and techniques that did not meet these requirements were considered obsolete and had to be discarded. It is impossible to conceal trench approaches to an enemy position, so one should avoid them, even if an infantry attack must begin from 2,000 paces; the requirements of tactical surprise are less important than the requirements of operational surprise; it is impossible to conceal an artillery range so to hell with it; we need to develop techniques by which massive artillery fire can be conducted without a range. We need to counter aerial surveillance with improved camouflage techniques no matter how many resources they require or how much they complicate logistics by requiring night movements on dirt roads. Switching to an appropriate way of thinking immediately changed the course of events on the front.

The Operation and Local Battles

Thinkers who still live by the remnants of the Napoleonic era are inclined to write operation with a capital O. Ludendorff dreamed of such an Operation in the World War: he would have called the attack of Vilna and Minsk in the middle of the summer of 1915 an Operation; however, Ludendorff did not call the Tarnopol breakthrough in 1917 in response to the "Kerensky offensive" an Operation, because for this breakthrough to grow into an Operation, according to Ludendorff it would have had to continue to the Black Sea and in the process cut off and take prisoner most of the Southwestern front and all of the Romanian front. The French have thought in the same vein: they are prepared to use the term Operation for the Lorraine attack, which was planned for November 14, 1918, but was never carried out because of the armistice, and in their fantasies was supposed to, cut off and encircle major German forces in Belgium.

In accordance with our notions of modern reality, do not spell operation with a capital O and have emphasized, in the title of this section, the limited goals of an operation; nevertheless we consider it necessary to make a definite distinction between operations that achieve an intermediate goal on the way to the end of military operations and local battles.

An operation does not go beyond the general combination of efforts for achieving the ultimate goal of a war because the results of one operation are the conditions in which strategy plans the next phase of the armed conflict, while actions that have no effect on the subsequent course of the war are purely local. If they acquire a large enough scale (such as the Japanese expedition to Sakhalin in the summer of 1905 the English colonial conquests in the World War and so forth), we are amenable to calling them local operations. Such actions often pursue the goal of occupying favorable diplomatic and economic positions in concluding a peace.

Any kind of operation has its costs, and the organizer of an operation seeks to cut these costs. Local battles are two-sided costs of an armed conflict; the more disorganized the front is, the higher the costs will be. Partisian warfare, although it is the embodiment of a lack of organization, is capable of greatly raising the cost of war for the enemy. Of course, higher costs are capable of defeating any undertaking; we have made this remark to avoid the accusation that we have a low regard for partisan warfare.

Insofar as we try to achieve positive goals, an operation is an incomparably more economical way of expending military force than local battles. Soldiers are very capable of seeing the difference between operational rationalism and operational shoddiness and are much more eager to sacrifice themselves when they feel that they are on the way to achieving the ultimate goal of a war. Commanders who abuse local battles (which the Russian command frequently did in the World War) themselves give evidence of the poverty of their operational talents. What may be completely impossible on a local scale or will require incommensurate sacrifices may be achieved incidentally and much less expensively on an operational scale.

Of course, well-prepared local battles may somewhat reduce the benefits derived by an enemy from positional calm. Our fire may make it somewhat more difficult for the enemy to dig trenches or lay mines in a forward zone. Separate attacks may take important—particularly as observation posts—sectors of his trenches away from the enemy and force him to occupy his front more densely. Night raids and sniper fire may add up to significant loses for the enemy and make it extremely difficult for him in the forward trenches. However, this kind of organization of positional activity in general is more of an issue for positional tactics than operational art or strategy.

The Material Battle

A material battle is made up of local battles that grow to gigantic proportions and are sustained not so much by human casualties[3] as by the expenditure of equipment and ordnance; deployment for a material battle should ensure us significant material superiority because of the surprise of the start of our operation

---

[3]   Foch waged the battle on the Somme in summer 1916 with an economical budget—2,000 men a day.

and our superiority in lines of communication leading to a given sector of a front or our overall superiority in equipment. In view of the massive nature of the resources used, the question of communications plays a very important role in a material battle. The lack of a trunk line leading to the French front at Verdun prior to 1916 made it possible for the Germans to maintain their initial material superiority for the three months the French took to build it.

In order to keep the enemy from jumping away from our material preparations for a battle, as Ludendorff did in 1917 by withdrawing from the Somme to the Siegfried line, it is important that the enemy be tied down by a valuable geographical objective behind the sector of the battlefront which would compel him to engage in battle under unfavorable conditions.

Such geographical objectives could include fortresses or cities which are valuable in terms of their legends and traditions (e.g., Verdun); important railroad junctions or lateral lines; important industrial centers; ports which are naval bases (Sevastopol in 1854-1855, the submarine bases on the coast of Flanders in 1917); or large stockpiles behind the enemy's front (the tens of thousands of freight trains belonging to the Germans in 1918). Such objectives can be considered chains that tie down a front. A material battle is ordinarily waged on a narrow front in order to maximize technical superiority and conserve our manpower to keep the battle going for a long time.

The goal of such a material operation is quite narrow— inflicting the maximum possible losses on the enemy while minimizing our own casualties and forcing the enemy to exhaust his reserves and material resources in an unfavorable situation. In the World War operations of this kind (e.g., Verdun, the battle of Flanders in 1917) were a very important part of military operations in 1916 and 1917 and swallowed up to 300,000 to 500,000 combatants from each side in four to six months. This is typical positional exhaustion of enemy forces. Only the initial phase of a material battle in which surprise is employed is operational. Subsequently there are halts which may last several weeks for the purpose of accumulating new material supplies, because a material battle is not conducted by morale alone. Thus it soon loses its operational character and becomes a derivative of tactics and economics, and maneuvers, tricks, cleverness, concealment and speed are superseded by industry, transportation and new manpower on the front. Operations become extremely material and the automatic delivery of material resources and reserves to the front comes to resemble the mechanical operation of a noria.[4] Any major operation on a positional front that does not pursue the goal of shifting from positional warfare to maneuver warfare soon becomes similar to a material battle.

---

[4] A *noria*—from the Arabic—is a wheel with an endless chain with buckets which brings up water for irrigation. Now a *noria* is used as a term for a device on an endless chain for delivering material to a machine; *norias* are also used in dredging operations for pulling up buckets of earth from the bottom and dumping them in a barge, as well as in turrets for delivering rounds and ammunition from a powder magazine. In a material battle divisions are moved to the front and then back to the rear for rest and recuperation as if they were attached to an invisible, automatic endless chain.

Economy of Forces

Within its leap an operation closely links all battles into a single entity. Battles are the components of an operation that tactically accomplish a number of missions into which the goal of the operation is divided.

The requirements of economy of force will be better met the closer the relationship between the individual battles of an operation, is the faster one series of battles follows another and the greater the pressure applied. Forces will always be expended uneconomically if the mission assigned to them is too hard to handle and leads to a breakdown. The requirements of economy will also be violated if forces are not utilized energetically enough to achieve the goal of an operation, because a reduction in the energy of utilization is equivalent to a reduction in manpower. And, of course, the very plan of an operation should be as economical as possible and preclude any excess casualties or efforts. Economy is particularly necessary in assigning roops to secondary sectors of the front, because only economy will make it possible to be strong enough in decisive sectors.

Operational Defense and Offense

Our pursuit of a positive goal in an operation and the desire to use surprise to achieve it leads us to the extensive deployment of men and resources. On the other hand, the pursuit of a negative goal compels us to delay the end of a deployment in order to retain the capability to concentrate efforts on the axes which, in the course of events, turn out to be the most important. In the first instance a formation is moved up to the front; in the second—it is more echeloned in depth. Offensive and defensive operations are not characterized by any greater or lesser percentage of offensive or defensive battles, but by forestalling an enemy in deployment (an offensive) or by delaying a deployment (defense). The first fully armed on the battle field is the attacker. Complete deployment demands immediate use; in the opposite case we must expect the enemy to direct his strikes on the most vulnerable points of our grouping (for example, on our flanks). An indecisive, wavering offensive, stoppable at its most critical points, gives an opponent the best chance. Such was the incursion of Samsonov's army into East Prussia. We forestalled the Germans in deployment but, in essence, both the supply conditions of the Russian corps and the necessity to wait for Rennenkampf's advance, as well as the reinforcement of the 1st army corps in the immediate region to the north of Mlava, required a temporary shift to the pursuit of a negative goal. and the adoption of a corresponding formation echeloned in depth. This was not realized, and therefore the Samsonov operation can be characterized as defense in an offensive formation, although such a defense should be avoided at all costs. The Lodz operation represents an analogous example: we pursued the positive goal of invading Silesia and Poznan, were the first to deploy, but the necessity to resupply forced our offensive at a certain point to be halted for a week; yet the formation remained offensive. Thus Ludendorff had a perfect chance to attack our flank and create a kind of Leiten[5] on an operational scale, The first defeat of Ludendorff himself in July 1918 is also explained by the fact that the German armies, having halted their unsuccessful offensive on the Marne, continued to remain in an offensive formation.

---

[5] The victory of Frederick II in 1757 over the Austrians, whose forces were 50 percent stronger, was achieved purely by a flanking strike by all the Prussian forces.

Thus we establish the necessity—despite the fact that an operation in the most whimsical way fuses tactical defense and offense—of drawing the sharpest line between operational defense and operational offense and not mixing the military logic of one or the other. One should not take an offensive position when there is no offensive, since it does not correspond to the elementary demands of defense, and since one may pay a severe penalty for doing so. From this follows the conclusion that in a period of rest between operations, and at a time of preparing for an operation, it is necessary to adhere to a defensive logic and to group one's forces accordingly. The entire offensive deployment, up until the moment of developing the operation, should correspond to the requirements of defense. The gradualness of transition from the existing troop formation to the deployment required by the operation should be thought through in all details. The possibility of a quick, secret and successful—and minimal risk-execution of an operational deployment must be deeply pondered in our decision-making: our thoughts on covering the deployment, which we expressed in the chapter on the war plan, relate not only to the initial deployment, but also apply to the preparatory period of every operation.

In order to judge the changes in the defensive capacity of a front during the preparatory period and select an appropriate moment for beginning an operation, a strategist must have a table of the gradual accumulation of forces and material in the area of operational deployment called for by the plan. It is desirable to express the readiness of the troops and logistics of an operation in percentage points. Previously this preparatory work was primarily done in the initial operational deployment plan, but now the preparation of this deployment must be extended to other kinds of deployment.

A tactical interpretation of defense leads us to passivity and the notion of repelling an enemy at an occupied position. The activity of a defense in tactics marks a transition to offensive operations, i.e., to a situation in which defense loses its most characteristic attributes. These tactical notions of defense and offense should in no way be extended to operational art.

An operational offensive means deploying first, and it is planned to launch and carry out an attack designed to overcome any resistance in a certain direction. A defense with a delayed deployment would operate very uneconomically, piling up troops in front of the head of the attacking side or occupying a series of successive positions in the direction of the attack. These defensive maneuvers, which expend armed forces in bundles in conditions for which the enemy is best prepared, are pitiful. Every offensive has a flank, and the grouping of defensive forces, the engineering of a defense, the combination of strong and weak sectors or provoking an encirclement or breakthrough in certain directions give the offender more cause for alarm; only on rare occasions will an offender be able to cover his flanks with completely reliable positions. Defensive maneuvers should primarily be based on flank counterattacks because the efforts applied, even if they do not accomplish their goal, will adversely affect the conditions for the development of the enemy's offensive, and the offensive will either have to stop or turn to another undesirable and unprepared direction; only the total destruction of the defensive forces on a flank will make it possible to continue the offensive as planned. Ludendorff responded to the threat of a Russian offensive in Silesia with an attack from Torun-Kalisz on Lodz. After going on the defensive the Russians were able to respond with an attack, albeit weak, on Warsaw and Lodz (Brzeziny); this was also a flank attack, and it put the Germans in a difficult situation.

If conditions have temporarily deprived the defense of the opportunity to respond with a countermaneuver, then the most economical way of stopping an offensive without exhausting our last forces will be backward leaps designed for the heaviness and massiveness of modern tactics. Backward leaps can be conducted on a tactical and operational scale. The tactical preparations for an attack, reconnaissance of our deployment and approaches and the organization of artillery and logistics require a lot of time. By moving away a half day's march we can gain a certain amount of time by forcing the enemy to make his tactical preparations all over again. But operational preparations for an attack on a fortified front need even more time by requiring the development of communications and concentrating a stockpile of munitions in the immediate rear contained in scores of trains. If we jump back two or three days' march, we can compel the enemy to repeat his operational preparations, repair the roads we have ruined and haul tens and hundreds of thousands of tons of supplies on them by cart and truck. Of course, operational and tactical backward leaps will achieve their goals only when they are made before the enemy is able to carry out his material preparation for a battle.

The Plan of an Operation

Significant superiority in numbers makes it easier to draw up a plan, and this kind of superiority also makes it easier to detail the plan. A plan in which the goal of an operation is explained, its form is determined and the occupation of a starting position for an operation is carefully thought out should also incorporate, in a certain perspective, the phases of its development without regard to the calendar. The approach is particularly necessary for drawing up individual plans for different services; rational organization of logistics requires at least the approximate determination of certain standards pertaining to time, space, and intensity that define the lines of communication needed, supplies and reinforcements, evacuation of wounded, the administration of occupied territory and so forth. If the development of an operation requires special equipment (such as equipment for crossing a large river or taking permanent fortifications), special troop equipment (packs for convoys that will have to be hauled across mountains), a large number of specialists (skiers in winter, political officers for organizing major centers) or special supplies (if a large starving, city is captured), the plan should take all these requirements into account ahead of time and prepare to meet them to the extent possible.

It is easier to foresee the first steps of an operation before major clashes than its subsequent development. However, we must refrain from the temptation of getting bogged down in the details of these initial preparatory operations. Even methodicalness can only be recommended to a certain extent, because if one is overly methodical, one will delay both the preparations for and development of an operation, curb initiative and have a difficult time taking advantage of favorable circumstances. Experience has demonstrated that excessively detailed preparations are ordinarily equivalent to the slow development of an operation. Seas of ink were not spilled in planning the Brusilov offensive in 1916 or the July offensive of the Western front in 1920. Our reaction to the carelessness of preparations and logistics that characterized the Red Army's Warsaw operation should not impel us to the opposite extreme. A plan will be sound when it does not leave too much to chance but also does not get bogged down in details and or delve too deeply into the various scenarios that may be encountered in carrying out the plan. In part a plan will consist of very accurate calculations of forces and resources, an analysis of the conditions for concentrating them, calculations of the number of pontoons needed and so forth, and in part it will consist of very hazy and approximate predictions.

We just cannot stand "perhaps," but there is no doubt that luck will affect the course of events. Even a splendid plan cannot always be carried out successfully. A plan must be flexible and avoid the idea of adhering to certain schedules. In carrying out a plan we must be ready to take advantage of all the favorable opportunities presented to us and the enemy's mistakes at any moment. If we are not ready for this, there is no way we can think of achieving extraordinary results.[6] Operational art does not allow for rigid decisions. In the Ulm operation of 1805 Napoleon made major revisions in his initial plan every day or two, and Moltke did the same in the Sedan operation of 1870. We must not hesitate to discard even the initial form of an operation we have chosen if the situation indicates another shorter way to the goal or makes it possible to achieve even better results than we have planned. On August 15, 1914, Ludendorff was only thinking of encircling the 13th corps, but in reality by the evening of the same day he managed to encircle three corps of the center of Samsonov's army in another perimeter. It is this understanding of the true role of command in an operation and a certain amount of modesty in evaluating the human capacity for prediction that should restrain the writer of a plan and safeguard him from inclinations towards long, wordy, detailed proposals that predict everything except the events that will actually occur. Work on military history and the art of war can improve our capabilities of drawing up good plans.

A plan should establish a first phase for getting close to the goal of an operation and divide the general mission of achieving this phase into a number of particular missions for the main elements of the front (or army) conducting an operation. In an offensive, a plan should clearly indicate the ecisive directions in which most of our efforts should be concentrated. In a defensive, if the operation is not merely conducted to gain time but also involves bringing the battle to a critical point, the basic task of the plan is to indicate the line at which decisive resistance should be offered to the enemy and where the plan anticipates a change in the overall development of an operation in our favor.

The basic topics of a plan to achieve the goal set for an operation concern the form an operation must try to take and the occupation of a starting position—the operational deployment of armed forces and materiel, which is the purpose of the material preparations for an operation.

---

[6] Long ago it was observed that of the two Roman counsels the wise Paul Emilius was killed at the battle of Cannae, while Terrentius, who was responsible for the defeat and saved himself by fleeing from the battlefield, subsequently recovered and left behind numerous progeny. Any leader who intelligently leads an operation can count on finding one of the ideological heirs of Terrentius in the person of his partner. T h e breed of such sorry military leaders is ineradicable.

The Forms of an Operation

We do not choose the forms of an operation—operational encirclement, breakthrough, envelopment or flank attack—arbitrarily. The forms of an operation are dictated by the balance of forces and resources, their existing deployments, the capacities of different trunk lines and the configuration of a theater and its most important positions. Given the current trend toward fronts that extend over an entire theater, a breakthrough will often be merely a secondary technique for achieving another form. For example, a breakthrough on the right flank of the 1st Army corps combined with the frontal success of the Germans against the 6th Army corps made it possible for the Germans to cut the center of Samsonov's army off from both its wings and encircle it. The Germans tried to develop the Tarnopol breakthrough in the summer of 1917 into a flank attack which was supposed to wipe out the entire Southwest and Romanian fronts and make it possible to pin the remnants of the Russian and Romanian forces against the Black Sea, but the railroad demolition carried out by the Russians as they withdrew and the Austrians' many troubles compelled the German command to reduce the scale of this flank attack.

The form of an operation must be coordinated with the qualities of command; one can rely on the separate actions of individual groups only to the extent that one can rely on the possibility of coordinating the work of their commanders (Zhilinskii, Samsonov and Rennenkampf in their invasion of East Prussia employing two armies from different directions). The form of an operation must also be appropriate for the characteristics of the forces used: if the main strength of an army lies in the massive nature of the equipment it employs (the French army, for example), it would be bad if the form of an operation required long marches and put the decisive points far away from the main railroad stations; if an army is purely positional (the English Army in 1916-1918) and is only capable of launching short, direct attacks, it would be bad if an operation were based on complex maneuvering with a predominance of encounter battles; or if our superiority lies in artillery and cavalry, it would be bad if an operation had to be carried out in wooded areas and so forth.

The form of an operation should put our forces in the best possible tactical situation; if the enemy has a system of prepared positions and strong lines,[7] then it would be good if an operation did not lead to a frontal attack but to a turning maneuver which would compel the enemy to regroup, deploy on a new, unprepared front and engage in battle in an unfavorable tactical situation.

At the same time the form of an operation should be as simple as possible. Piling up layer upon layer of battles and maneuvers in an operation is unacceptable not only because it makes command more difficult but because any excess maneuver or any battle which is not unavoidably necessary for achieving the goal of an operation holds the grave danger of distracting us from the goal. Large vanguards, battles at forward positions, feints and local battles can do us a great deal of harm even when they are successful. Nothing should be superfluous in an operation because it should be the embodiment of purposefulness. In terms of its

---

[7] In following up the Lutsk breakthrough in the summer of 1916 elements of the 2nd Finnish and 101st divisions made several successful assault crossings of a river which turned out to be the same old Styr'. This is not the best way of conducting an operation.

precision, clarity and symmetry the form of an operation should remind us of the straight lines of a Grecian temple rather than the swirls and whirls of Rococo.

From this perspective, a defense will be greatly improved if the final position planned for achieving decisive results coincides with our forward line, making it possible for us to avoid a number of rearguard battles, which could completely distract us from our goal. An ideal operational defensive is awaiting the approach of the enemy solely for the purpose of attacking him (e.g., Austerlitz). Sometimes it is possible to predetermine the direction of an enemy attack and concentrate sufficient forces in the flank ahead of time (Germans prior to the Lodz attack in early November 1914, and the deployment of the French in mid-July 1918). However, this requires delving into the enemy's attentions to the point of prejudging them and figuring them out in advance. The French Plan 17 also prepared for an Austerlitz but underestimated the forces and scale of the attack through Belgium. In most cases this line will have to be moved in depth in order to gain time for organizing a counterattack and create a favorable situation for launching one—a pocket in which enemy units that have broken through will end up. Alternative lines and positions should make it possible to organize a flank attack and distract the enemy's attention from his goal.

Operational Deployment

Operational deployment should correspond to the goals and form of an operation. If an operation pursues an offensive goal, forces should be grouped in accordance with the roads that will be used in the offensive. Sectors of a front should be prepared to turn into columns. The short range of modern operations compels us to occupy a starting position as close as possible to the enemy, and thus in preparing an offensive operation defensive considerations come to the forefront. If an operation is defensive, then forces should be grouped so as to enable the quickest possible concentration of efforts for repelling the enemy in crucial sectors with the least possible loss of ground; at the same time secondary sectors should be secured to the extent that events there will not affect the most important sectors. With certain exceptions, defenses need several days to carry out a deployment, which is not completed initially, because the choice of sectors does not depend on the defense. Careful observation of the enemy, the extensive use of fortifications, deeply echeloned deployments, solid operational reserves (partly on trains) and a great deal of concern for lateral lines of communication characterize an operational defensive, which, as we have seen, also permeates the preparatory phase of an offensive. The organization of a counterattack should be the main idea behind operational defensive deployment and preparations. Sometimes it will be advantageous to organize two or more compact groups connected only by a weak screen and flanking one another (on a small scale Staliupepen in August 1914). A well-developed system of lateral tracks will constitute the best guarantee of a timely flank counterattack.

Operational deployment concentrations may differ greatly. In 1914 the initial deployment of the Germans varied from approximately 2,000 to 3,000 troops per kilometer in Lorraine and got as high as 20,000 per kilometer on the right flank. This figure is clearly abnormal and indicates that the configuration of the theater (the salient of the Dutch border) made it impossible to complete the deployment before the beginning of an operation. Even in attack sectors of the front, given the weaponry employed in the World War, one-fourth this density (5,000) was sufficient if the development of an operation did not require a fan-like widening of the sector. On the Russian front in the World War the density of deployment in 1914 was as high as 2,000 to 4,000 soldiers per kilometer. In positional operations, because of the need for a successive wave of infantry in developing an operational deployment density became as high as one division every one to one and a half kilometers (up to 6,000 to 8,000 soldiers per kilometer, artillery included). In the Civil War in secondary sectors deployment density dropped to 50 men per kilometer whereas in the "battering ram" sectors density was approximately 1,000 men per kilometer.

Of course, concentrating our forces on the most important sectors, particularly where we plan to achieve positive results, is extremely desirable, but we must not forget that there are certain preconditions. The presence of strong local obstacles and fortifications on a sector for a front makes it easier to spread troops thinner here. The enemy's weakness and passivity also makes it easier to put a battering ram together. At the beginning of the summer of 1915 Ludendorff had 39.5 infantry and 8.5 cavalry divisions on this front; however, because the front was not sufficiently fortified everywhere and because the Russians had 20 percent more men than the Germans, although they had inadequate equipment and their ordnance was low, Ludendorff considered 37.5 of his divisions tied down to the sectors where they were and only two divisions free to concentrate in the sector chosen for an offensive. Ludendorff could maneuver only five percent of his forces.[8]

Offensives are primarily conducted on parallel routes. If possible, it is desirable for the operational front to be wider than the front on which the enemy will be fought, which allows the march to be somewhat concentric, to use a larger number of railroads, dirt roads and settlements and arrange logistics better. Despite the shortness of marches from the starting position to the battle that characterizes the modern operation and the overall parallel location of the fronts, one will often be able to gain such advantages for an attack sector by employing oblique demarcation lines so that the front of the attack units gets narrower as the front gets closer to the enemy, and gets wider in secondary sectors. Thus an attack sector will have a maximum number of routes at its disposal and, moreover, it will be more difficult for the enemy to guess the direction of our route in advance.

The Beginning of Preparations for an Operation
The days of halts between operations required by modern conditions are in no way a period of inactivity. At this time preparations for the next operation are made and the starting position for it is occupied. As we complete one operation, we should think about the next one. A strategist must look at the advance of our forces after a successful operation and their retreat after an unsuccessful operation from the perspective of grouping forces for a new attack. Of course, the goal of a new operation must agree with the results of a completed operation. No matter whether we are pursuing the enemy or he is pursuing us, these actions, insofar as

---

[8] Falkenhayn, *Verkhovnoe komandovanie*, p. 10. It is quite possible that Ludendorff somewhat understated this figure because he did not wish to go against the requirements of the high command, but he could not have understated it too much, because Falkenhayn did not protest.

the resistance of neither side has been finally broken, are merely elements of a new operational deployment and its covering. Hence a new operational plan begins to be implemented in orders that call for pursuing the enemy, stopping the offensive or retreating. Quite often the plan of a future operation will be indicated only in very general terms at this time, but we should not to postpone the development of a plan for the next operation for a long time in order to avoid useless troop movements and disorganization in the rear. The retreat of the French armies in 1914 after the border battle, which left the right wing at the Lorraine fortified front and sent the left wing east of Paris, already included a great many elements of the Marne operation. The starting position for the next operation is also the line of assembly for the troops who have completed one operation; it orients all actions, and a strategist should above all keep this in mind.

If we avoid the pursuit of positive goals, we must immediately proceed to prepare a defensive operation: we should immediately assign elements to deeply echeloned tactical and operational reserves and construct a system of fortified positions and material preparations for a countermaneuver.

An operation is characterized by the rapid expenditure of forces, whereas the period of pause and reparation should be a time for accumulation. One must not only replenish the soldiers and materiel that have been lost, one must also make every effort to conserve the troops' energy. Marches should be extremely short and vehicles should be used not only to gain time for moving troops but also to provide them the maximum possible comforts. In order to improve their living conditions it will often be necessary to build camps of barracks or improved dugouts.

Concern for the creature comforts of the troops is also concern for their morale and the authority of the commanders. An army judges the organization and forethought of its commanders by the creature comforts provided to the troops and the order and solicitousness of its logistical system. A warrior who has been lying on the ground for several days or has spent a week in a damp trench reacts to any material trifle like a man who is recovering from a severe illness.

4. THE STRATEGIC LINE OF CONDUCT

The Ultimate Goal of a War And the Goals of Operations

From the political goal of a war established by the agency leading the war the ultimate military goal for operations on the armed front toward which the efforts of the armies and the navy should be directed. If the war has entered such exceptional conditions that the ultimate goal of the war can be achieved in a single leap; the strategist has very little work to do: because making this leap, which is called an operation, is a matter for operational art. Strategy plays a much more important role when the goal cannot be achieved by a single operation and we must plan several steps on the way to the goal; when the boundaries encompassed by the war are vast and form several theaters of operations, separate operations will have to be conducted in these theaters. These simultaneous operations must be coordinated so that the particular goals they achieve form steps on the shortest path to achieving the ultimate goal of the war. Strategic guidelines are landmarks that indicate the goals towards which operations strive.[1] As the situation changes, some landmarks must be replaced by others; if an operation achieves one goal, it should be followed by another goal that initially orients operational preparation and then the operational assault.

Of course, we should not be deceived by the apparent simplicity of this work of a strategist. In wartime we must deal with the contrary will of the enemy, with different kinds of frictions and with the anarchic development of powerful processes at the base and on the front. It is extremely difficult to find the shortest, most convenient, truest and logical path to the ultimate goal of the war in these conditions. The advantage and intelligence of a certain goal depends on very complex interlinked conditions. The deployment of the armed forces of both sides in a theater of war only constitutes part of the considerations that must guide the strategist. He must be able to grasp the future of the war at least in part and predict the missions of the near future in order to lead the present mission. A strategist's thought should be divorced from the details of an operation and grasp the most important processes occurring at home and in the enemy's deep rear; only by grasping the nature of the evolution of the lives of the hostile states as a whole will a strategist be able to lift the veil of the future somewhat and assign missions to fronts and armies with relative confidence. The position in which the Russian high command was placed in 1914, completely isolated from the deep rear and the base, seems to us to be a particularly grave error. We wonder if perhaps the minister of war in Petrograd, who only had fragmentary information on the events at the front but had a better feel of the pulse of the rear than the supreme commander in chief in Baranovichi, might have been in a better position to set operational goals.

A comparison of the successes of the mobilization of our industry and German capabilities would have made it possible to make an appropriate decision concern-

---

[1] Operational art often deals with feints, which have a completely legitimate place in it; but the concept of a strategic feint lead to a mistake on an absolutely gigantic scale.

ing the permissible extent of our activity at the end of October 1914. The incorrect formulation of goals for operations began to lay the groundwork for the disaster of May 1915 a half year later. Ludendorff with his strategy of beating down the Russians in 1917, was either right or wrong, depending on the success of the Hindenburg program in German industry, depending on the strength of the German rear and its response to the slogans of the Russian Revolution, depending on whether the revolutionary movement among the French forces, which began in May 1917, would die down or spread, depending on the success of submarine warfare and the formation of the U.S. Army and depending on the energy left in Austria-Hungary, Bulgaria and Turkey. One can be a splendid operator but a poor strategist: Ludendorff was outstanding in organizing and leading an operation but he was unable to set goals for them and could not handle the orientation of operational activity.

In setting any particular goal, a strategist must take into account all the consequences of its achievement and the constraining effect it will have on the subsequent course of events. Falkenhayn tried to limit German operations on the Russian front as much as possible, which was correct, but in the spring of 1915 he authorized Ludendorff to carry out a demonstration in Courland; the German gentry could not greet the German troops unkindly, which tied the fate of the Baltic barons to the German armies. The withdrawal of the Germans would have sounded the death knell for all of German culture in Courland. Naturally Ludendorff began to tie his subsequent goals to the capture of Riga and an offensive into Russia. The situation of the Germans in Russia greatly deteriorated. The tsarist government, playing on national contradictions, got the opportunity to form Latvian units. Falkenhayn had to pay for his cheap fame in Courland with a persistent struggle against a new direction of strategy stemming from the occupation of Courland that was hostile to him, and was headed by Ludendorff. The conflict between these strategic currents in 1915 made it impossible for the German forces to achieve major successes on the Russian front.

Jomini[2] cites the following instructive example concerning the actions of the coalition in 1799. The Russians dispatched three force groups, including Suvorov's army to Italy and Rimskii-Korsakov's corps to Switzerland, and conducted a joint expedition with the English into Holland. Important English interests in Holland inspired this expedition, but next to Holland was Belgium, which before the revolution had belonged to Austria and was of great interest to the Austrians. The fact that Russian troops appeared in Holland, where it is true that they were extremely unsuccessful, compelled the Austrian army to move to the borders of Belgium. In fact, Viscount Carl's army was drawn from Switzerland to Mannheim; Rimskii-Korsakov, who was left stranded, was routed at Zurich; while Suvorov, instead of victories in Italy, discovered in Switzerland that there are no desperate situations from which it is impossible to get out with honor. Of course, the isolation of Rimskii-Korsakov and Suvorov had to follow from the diversion in Holland.

The Sequence of Operations

During the first year of the World War Germany carried out no less then nine operational deployments: 1) against Rennenkampf and Samsonov in East Prussia;

---

[2] Jomini, *Précis de l'art de guerre*, p. 179.

2) in Silesia for the Ivangorod-Warsaw operation; 3) between Kalisz and Torun for the Lodz operation; 4) a new deployment after Lodz involving major movements of troops from France to Poland with the direct support of the Austro-Hungarians; 5) for the August attack on the 10th Russian army involving preparations for the third echelon of German mobilization; 6) for the offensive in Courland; 7) for Mackensen's breakthrough; 8) a new change in deployment after the Germans took Lvov; (Mackensen changed the direction of the attack to the north, while Galwitz broke the Narev line); 9) deployment for the Kovno-Sventsiany-Minsk attack. In September 1915, when they occupied a positional front, the Germans carried out, on a smaller scale, a tenth deployment. These figures do not include regroupings, which, although they involved major railroad maneuvers, did not go beyond a single area; for example, the first deployment in East Prussia included three groupings: 1) against Rennenkampf at Gumbinen; 2) against Samsonov at Tannenberg, involving the movement of the 1st Prussian corps, the 3rd reserve division, the fortress reserves and Landwehr brigades on rails; and 3) against Rennenkampf in the battle at the Masurian Lakes, which involved the movement of two corps and one cavalry division from France.

Nine times in one year the Germans shifted the center of gravity of their operational deployment to different sectors of the extensive Memel-Kalisz-Czestochowa-Carpathian Ridge arc. It was obvious that no single one of these deployments was sufficient to achieve the ultimate goal of the German armed forces on the Russian front. The separate partial goals which lay en route to this ultimate goal had to be achieved successively by separate operations, each of which required its own deployment and were therefore not direct, geometrical continuations of one another in space.

Destruction is characterized by the belief that one operational starting position is enough to achieve the ultimate aim. Destruction operations that are continuous in space almost coalesce in their striving for the ultimate goal. Communications are protected by the very real danger of destruction of every enemy detachment that turned up behind our flanks. The enemy's goals are subordinate to the goals pursued by the side inflicting a destructive strike. The logic and sequence are completely clear.

But the nine different operational deployments carried out by the Germans on the Russian front in the first year of the World War did not constitute an arbitrary chaotic jumble. Despite the fact that they followed the logic of attrition,[3] these inner relationships can be fully clarified only by comparing the goals pursued in the first year in operations against the Russians. Operations are also sequential in pursuing the limited goals of attrition. In examining strategy from the perspective of its definition as a doctrine of communications, we have already pointed out that delving into the study of the communications of our own and the enemy's armies puts us on the firm ground of reality and makes it possible to introduce order, clarity and consistency in the pursuit of different goals.

The more profoundly we analyze the situation as a whole, even under conditions of attrition, the narrower the boundless field of fantasy before us becomes; our choice of goals from a large number of possible goals for operations

---

[3]   We should not be deceived by Ludendorff's extreme energy; Frederick the Great developed the same fierce intensity of warfare but nevertheless remained rooted in attrition.

will ultimately narrow down to one goal, which will seem a necessity to us; and our thinking will expose the preconditions for the next operation that will be engendered by the first operation and constitute its goal. An evenly running line of the front that yields complete freedom in choosing the sector in which the next operation can be conducted will not present itself to the strategist; his ultimate goal, completely overturning the structure of the enemy's a military front, compels him to establish a sequence in his actions and at any given moment undermine a particular pillar of this front. Here is where all his thoughts are concentrated, and all of his personality is expressed in the momentum provided for this work.

The Curve of Strategic Intensity

In establishing a sequence in operations and selecting and determing the scale of the next goal of an operation the modern strategist cannot be guided by the simple balance of our forces and those of the enemy on the armed front; he must also keep in mind the prospects for this balance to change and take reinforcement and supply capabilities, new echelons for mobilization and movements from other fronts into consideration. Previously strategists proceeded solely from the numbers of the first mobilization and the time required for concentration, but now we must keep in mind the probable curve of the subsequent growth of our own and the enemy's forces which is related to the possibilities of economic mobilization or outside support.

In the first year of the war operations on the Russian military front primarily had to be oriented toward the fact that we were catching up with the Austro-Germans in the strategic deployment of our forces.

We make a distinction between operational deployment, i.e., the occupation of a starting position by available forces, and strategic deployment, which is the achievement of the culminating point of the power of a military front. Operational deployment takes several days, whereas strategic deployment takes months.

At the beginning of the World War France tied down 80 percent of Germany's armed forces. We knew of Schlieffen and the younger Moltke hopes that they would be able to transfer the corps that had defeated France to the Russian front by the 40th day of the war. We ascribed excessive importance to these mistaken calculations of the German general staff. However, it seemed that the unsuccessful start of the war for the French confirmed them. For Russia it would be extremely desirable to encounter the pressure of the forces moved by Germany in a good defensive position after taking the San and the Vistula from Przemysl to Gdansk by the 40th day. This gave rise to the need to speed up an invasion of East Prussia and Galicia. In fact, we managed to complete the Galician operation successfully by the 43rd day of our mobilization, but we were completely unsuccessful in occupying the right bank of the Vistula in Prussia.

However, major movements of German forces from France to our front took place only by the 120th day of mobilization (cavalry and five corps in late November 1914). The Germans had to conduct the Ivangorod-Warsaw operation without a significant influx of forces and at an unfavorable time when the second Russian echelon, the Siberian corps, was arriving. The casualties of the first three weeks of the operations practically evened out: the Russians lost 500,000, the Austrians lost 350,000 and the Germans lost 50,000. Our second echelons, the Asian corps, got to the front more quickly than the second German echelon, which was made up of newly organized corps. This was the reason for the inappropriateness of the Ivangorod-Warsaw operation and its ultimate failure.

The mass movement of German corps from the west to the Russian front, on which the commands of both sides had counted, was partially replaced by subsequent echelons of German mobilization which continued into 1917. The third echelon of German mobilization had a painful impact on us in February 1915 (the Augustow Forest). The extravagance of the Russian command and the superiority of the organization of German industry soon became evident. Our activity did not reckon with the fact that the culminating point of our numerical and technical superiority was past, and that the curve of enemy forces on the Russian front had risen rapidly. The obligation of strategy in 1914 was to foresee 1915; if we had stopped after the Ivangorod-Warsaw operation or limited ourselves to directing our efforts toward the occupation of East Prussia, by the spring of 1916 we would have had 20 extra divisions, our entire army would have been in order and we would have had some kind of supplies.

At the end of the first month of the war 90 Russian divisions opposed 70 Austro-German divisions, and the latter included only 13 first-class German divisions. In the summer of 1915 130 understrength Russian divisions with empty depots opposed 135 Austro-German divisions, which included a large number of the best German infantry divisions and the entire German cavalry; and all of the German reserve units and reinforcements dispatched for the summer campaign, as high as 150 percent of the normal strength of the German divisions, were working against our front.

Operations on a front lead to a two-way expenditure of forces. In the American Civil War the commander in chief of the Northerners, General Grant observed after one of his not overly successful offensives that while the Northerners lost 15,000 men and the Southerners only 5,000, success was on the side of the Northerners, because they could make up for their losses, whereas the Southerners could not. In fact we cannot evaluate the advisability of force expenditure if we do not make an objective accounting of the reinforcement capabilities of both sides. Expenditures should be commensurate with income. In the same way that an extravagant nobleman yells that his administrator is stealing his money, Russian strategists tried to justify their own nearsightedness and extravagance by complaining about a lack of support from the rear the alliance between Russian headquarters and powerful bourgeois factions, which were interested in military orders and got the government to capitulate to their greed, even had a major success...

Shifts in the balance of forces such as those which caused Russia to drop out of the war and the United States to enter the war could not help but affect the line of strategic conduct. It is obvious that France had to try to put an end to Germany before the revolution enfeebled the Russian front (the Nivelle offensive), and if this were impossible, they had to hold out for 14 months until the United States had armed itself (Pétain and Foch's plan). Germany should not have wasted this time to fight the Russian Revolution and instead should have tried to break the French front early in the summer of 1917. But in this case Ludendorff committed a very grave error.

In a civil war, when a military organization is created during the course of military actions rather than before them, we see a gradual rise in the curve of strategic tension. But similar phenomena also characterize wars that have been prepared for many years, and for this reason we cannot put civil wars in a special category.

Only by correctly realising the breaks in the curve of the development of the forces of both sides and the moments at which each side is moving up and reaching a culminating point can a strategist quite validly select an offensive or defensive style of operation, proportion the energy of his fronts and set forth the goals of intermediate operations.

The Initial Moment of an Operation

Issues of fighting a battle constitute the content of tactical art, but operational art handles the issues of the moments of engagement and disengagement. Discussions of conducting an operation are matters for operational art, but determining the initial moment of an operation and its end point are strategic matters. In the same way the timing of going to war or getting out of it is a matter for politicians, not strategists.

It stands to reason that the initial moment of an operation must be coordinated with political requirements. Russia had been preparing for the Bosporus operation by the spring of 1917, but the February revolution completely ruled out the possibility of this kind of attack by sea. The end of the World War, with its subsequent revolutionary movements and upheavals, was the most inconvenient possible time for the bourgeois armies of the West to intervene in Russian affairs. At the end of the summer in 1919 the Poles had overwhelming superiority over the weak Soviet western front; the main forces of the Red armies were tied down by fighting the White armies of the Russian counterrevolution in the south and east. A Polish offensive could have been launched under more favorable conditions in 1919 than in 1920, when Denikin, Kolchak and Yudenich had already been eliminated. However, such an offensive would have amounted to rendering aid to Denikin, and there was a wide gap between the national interests of the Polish and Russian bourgeoisie. The Poles, who were guided exclusively by their national interests and underestimated the strengths of the Soviet system and the Red armies, preferred to sit by and watch as the Soviet Union struggled and was exhausted in order to engage in single combat with the Red front the next year. It is obvious that Wrangel also should not have become active at the time the Red armies were marching on Warsaw. If the Red armies had taken Warsaw, this would have made the conflict between the proletariat and bourgeois fronts a global one, which would have raised the stock of the White Guards in the Crimea, who would then be able to count on major support from their patrons. On the other hand, the withdrawal of the Red armies from the Vistula to the Berezina made Wrangel's army less necessary to the temporarily stabilized bourgeois structure of Europe, which had been spared a direct threat for the next few years. If Wrangel's operations had developed at a faster pace in the Soviet-Polish War, it is obvious that a truce would have been concluded more quickly on the Soviet Polish front and that Wrangel's rule in the Crimea would have ended in the next few months. Apparently Wrangel was mindful of these considerations, but an order from France, which was interested in Polish affairs, compelled this vassal to begin his operations at a personally unfavorable moment.

The initial moment of an operation must be coordinated with the overall military situation. Romania's entry into the war in August 1916 and the beginning of its offensive in Transylvania was two months late, because it coincided with the exhaustion of the Russian front and a reduction in energy on the Anglo-French front. The Sventsiany breakthrough, or the General Operation, of which Ludendorff dreamed was a month late, because the Russian forces had managed to scramble out of Poland, the German armies were already tired and the French were completing their preparations for the fall offensive of 1915 in Champagne.

The initial moment of an operation must be coordinated with the completion of our deployment. An operation will acquire a certain firmness, will be conducted with lightning speed and will lead to major results with few sacrifices if all the resources it requires are at hand, if all the necessary regroupings have been completed before it begins and if lines of communications are relieved of preparatory transports during the operation itself. In these conditions the work of soldiers may be done under the same conditions as factory work, which also requires preliminary concentration of raw materials and manpower and the preparation of manpower and factory equipment so that the factory can operate without interruptions and engage in mass production with minimal production costs.

However, this moment must also be coordinated with the moment when the balance of forces is favorable. If waiting for the tail of our operational deployment gives the enemy time to reinforce to a greater extent than we or if the overall military situation requires, operations will have to begin before deployment is completed.

Rennenkampf and Samsonov's offensive in East Prussia was begun with half the forces that should have been deployed against Germany as a result of the situation on the French front. Konrad put the Austro-Hungarian armies on a decisive offensive between the Vistula and the Bug with only 33 out of the 49.5 divisions he had by the end of the Galician operation. This decision was partially due to his calculations that by the 20th day of mobilization the Russians would be able to deploy 35 infantry divisions, and 10 days later this force would increase to 60 infantry divisions;[4] in reality the Russians had about 34 divisions by the 20th day, but by the end of the operation (the 43rd day of mobilization) they only had 51 infantry divisions. In fact, during the entire Galician operation there was a balance in the number of infantry divisions (823.5 Russian battalions as opposed to 801.5 Austrian battalions, but 3,060 good Russian guns against 2,140 bad Austrian guns, and 690 Russian squadrons and *sotnias*[5] against 398 Austrian) as a result of the fact that the Russians had a five-day advantage in mobilization and some Austrian corps were traveling toward the Danube. But the thinking of the Austrian general staff was nurtured on the idea that they had a ten-day advantage over the Russians in concentrating and that they must hurry with an attack before vast Russian forces could concentrate, and Konrad began the operation, but only

---

[4]   Even from the perspective of the Austrian plan this buildup cannot be considered equal to 70 percent, because all the cavalry and most of the field infantry divisions were included in the first figure, and the subsequent increase was primarily due to second-line divisions. In addition, the Austrians would have gotten many first line divisions from the Danube.

[5]   A *sotnia* is a cossack squadron—Editor.

completed the concentration of two left flank armies, which in reality had a significant superiority in forces over the 4th and 5th Russian armies.

The failures of the Russian offensive in East Prussia and the Austro-Hungarian offensive from Galicia compel us to be quite exacting in checking the reasons for beginning an operation prior to the completion of deployment. The illegitimacy of the latter makes the conduct of an operation weak and indecisive and forces one to look over one's shoulder and await the tail of reinforcements. A sense of the illegitimacy of deployment, in truth, strategic deployment, hung over all the Russian operations in Manchuria in 1904. Endless delays in operational deployment and the trickling in of new forces were typical of the Russian operations in the World War.

On the other hand, the Germans provide an example of the clear division of an operation into preparation and execution. Ludendorff broke this rule on only one occasion and, in our opinion, made a grave mistake. We have the beginning of the Lodz operation in mind. The moment of greatest operational intensity must coincide with the risis of an operation and not be delayed. The beginning of the Lodz operation coincided with the Germans' avoidance of a subsequent offensive on the Anglo-French front and the end of the Flanders operation. Seven infantry and two cavalry division could be transferred to the Russian front in the first line. A flank attack was launched November 11-22, 1914, using 11 infantry divisions; on November 23 the German forces that had broken into the rear of Lodz had to move north; and in late November the German front was subject to very heavy pressure. At this time reinforcements began to arrive from the west, and they had to be dispersed along the entire shaky German front. There is no doubt that if the attack had been made with 18 German divisions rather than 11, the entire 2nd Russian army and most of the 5th would have been destroyed, and the German front would not have been forced to undergo a series of major crises.[6]

Why didn't the German reserves go to the crisis of the operation? Falkenhayn and Ludendorff had not argued about moving them earlier. Of course it would have been good to move them two weeks earlier from the west to the east, and there were no objective reasons that would have prevented this movement. But if the reserves were two weeks late, why wasn't the beginning of the operation postponed for two weeks? The Austrians and German Landwehr left facing the Russian front had demonstrated their inability to attack energetically in the Lodz operation. But they would have been more successful on the defensive. The Russians proposed starting their offensive only four days later, while a week could have been given for the Russian operation to develop: the situation for a flank attack would have changed only for the better. Only a negligible portion of Silesia was threatened, and only for a very short time. It seems to us that Ludendorff's mistake was based on false notions of activity. He wanted to attack first, even if it was not the right time. But against Samsonov the Germans had begun their operational deployment only after they had completely figured out Samsonov's offensive, and they only gained from this. The desire to beat the enemy and excessive haste are to blame for the failures of many poorly prepared operations.

We have the same opinion of the May offensive of the Western front in 1920.

---

[6] We stated these views in 1919 in "Itogi germanskoi strategii" [A Summary of German Strategy], *Voennoe delo*, no. 20 (15 July 1919).

We have spoken of the desirability of beginning an operation only after deployment is complete. But we would be misunderstood if the reader believed that we meant the concentration of all the forces of the state; it is obvious that in this case we only have the forces designed for a particular operation and the completion of a certain echelon of mobilization rather than mobilization as a whole. Of course, there is no need to expect that all forces and resources will be unloaded from the cars. Some forces may be left on the rails as an operational reserve for a railroad maneuver. In accounting for the enemy forces that have to be dealt with, we also must not limit ourselves to counting what the enemy has at the front right now, we must also take into consideration what the railroads will bring him during the course of an operation. The war plan of the Austrian general staff contained a major error: the Russians will have 35 divisions on the 20th day and 60 divisions on the 30th day; therefore Austria should attack on the 20th day. After all, the Austrians could not dream of completing this extensive operation in less than ten day; therefore they should have figured: if we attack on the 20th day we will encounter everything the Russians bring by the 30th day, that is 60 divisions, whereas if we began to attack on the 30th day we would encounter a stronger Russian front and weaker reserves, because the vast majority of Russian transports will be completed in the first month.

However, the technical possibility of beginning an operation at a given time after completing all our deployment should in no way be interpreted as an obligation to begin it immediately. That France could complete its operational deployment by the 15th day should not have led the French general staff to conclude that they were obliged to go on the offensive against Germany on the 16th day. Despite the evidence indicating that the first German attack would be directed against France, the French did not make the slightest attempt to insert a clause in the military convention binding Russia and France to attack Germany stating that an offensive is obligatory only for the side against which Germany leaves fewer forces and that the other side could go on the defensive and use all means possible to gain time and delay the outcome. The thinking of the French strategists of the 20th century seems to be on a lower level than the thinking behind the Trachtenberg Plan for the fall campaign of 1813; this plan envisioned a forced offensive against Napoleon from three sides, the defense and even retreat of the armies of the allies, against which Napoleon himself was moving with the core of his forces, and a systematic offensive in other directions against the French screens.

The probability of suffering a decisive defeat increased when the French armies went on the offensive in the World War; in addition, from the point of view of strategy, the French offensive not only made the outcome more decisive but also accelerated it. Allied interests required a delay if possible. The French offensive led to a situation in which the Russians could expect the return of German corps from France to the Vistula by the 40th day. It would have been extremely desirable to include prolonging operations of the French front for at least two months in the plan. The extra three weeks at the disposal of the Russian strategists would have made it possible for them to organize an unhurried, systematic invasion of East Prussia and even extend their operations to Pomerania and Western Galicia, which undoubtedly would have immediately relieved the burden on the French front. In general, we could say that if the German destruction attack in France did not succeed in the first month, it would never have been completed, because the Russian front would have tied down too many German forces.

From the point of view of allied strategy, the fact that the French did not fight the border battle to the end and moved the action to the Marne was extremely good. This postponed the outcome for 15 days and cost the Germans two corps and one cavalry division that had to be transferred to East Prussia.

Awaiting a favorable moment for beginning an offensive means maintaining a defensive formation. Operational deployment for an offensive should be completed only at the last minute.

The decision to begin an operation is particularly important if the operation is a major break in our line of conduct and if, for example, it marks a transition from a strategic defense to offense. Foch foresaw such a break in 1918 but was unable to establish its date precisely: he first planned it for the beginning of May, and then for June; German activity confused the Anglo-French preparations and forced them to postpone their counteroffensive to July. The following idea of Lenin's is frequently cited :

> An uprising should be based on a turning point in the history
> of a rising revolution when the vanguard of the people is
> most active and the wavering in the ranks of enemies and the
> ranks of weak, half-hearted, indecisive friends of the revolu-
> tion is greatest.[7]

This statement contains the idea of awaiting the completion of the deployment of revolutionary forces and the need to coordinate this moment with the overall situation as portrayed by enemies and fence sitters.

The Breakthrough of an Operation

Operational plans must be carried out in an atmosphere of energetic counter-action and many obstacles and frictions. Rigid, implacable striving for a preformalized goal is inappropriate in strategy. The conduct of an operation is always a kind of compromise. New information may lead to a completely new interpretation of the goal of an operation. In the Samsonov operation Ludendorff originally planned only to encircle the 13th Russian corps on the closest sector south of Allenstein, but this goal was not achieved because the 13th corps had slipped away behind the 15th. But the Germans did manage to close a much wider ring than was initially planned. A half year later in February 1915, Ludendorff set the goal of defeating the 10th Russian army, which was extended in East Prussia by a cordon, with an open right flank, and on its shoulders make a breakthrough through the upper Bobr to the Grodno-Bialystok sector employing four news corps, the next echelon of mobilization. This would have been a great help to the Austro-Hungarians, who were expending all their efforts on saving Przemysl Fortress. However, this goal exceeded the means available. The plan was too broad and luxurious for this moment of the war, and Ludendorff could have been satisfied with less. Despite the favorable course of events for the Germans, the several Russian divisions of the center surrounded in the Augustow Forest cost the Germans ten days. The Russians had concentrated sufficient reserves; the Bobr marshes had begun to thaw; the German forces, who were concentrated in an unpopulated area at a bad time of year, suffered; logistics were poor; and

---

[7]   Lenin, *Sochineniia* [Works], vol. 14, part 2, p. 136.

counteroperations begun on the Narev by the Russians achieved a number of successes and swallowed up all the German reinforcements. In these conditions Ludendorff renounced his broad goal, and because the disadvantages of his positions in front of the Bobr and the Neman, where the operational readiness of the Russians had improved because of the presence of long-term theater operations, he pulled his front back to the Augustow-Suwalki line.

We should note an extremely negative aspect of this kind of forcible reduction in the extent of an operation: not only is an important intermediate goal not achieved, but the failure of the first attempt makes it extremely difficult to repeat it. The fatigued German troops saw the Osowiec-Grodno line as an inaccessible obstacle, while on the entire Bobr line the Germans were faced with concrete fortifications. In July 1915, five months later, an attack on the Bialystok-Grodno line was extremely important because of the development of Mackensen's offensive in Galicia. However, the Germans avoided it because Ludendorff had called it tactically impossible. In exactly the same way the failure of the Germans to break through the Lorraine front at the time of the Marne operation in 1914 secured this front for the entire World War. The failure of the first Russian offensive in East Prussia placed the mark of futility on all subsequent attempts to repeat it.

Every well-prepared operation is an attack begun under favorable conditions and designed to achieve major successes in its first steps. Insofar as the enemy is still capable of resisting, he concentrates new forces and resources after a certain amount of time; the advantages of surprise and preparation are gradually lost by the attacker; his initial forward advance makes his communications more difficult; the operation becomes slower and advancing becomes increasingly difficult; the losses suffered by the defender are increasingly outweighed by the losses suffered by the attacker. Simple frontal clashes between equal forces are a very poor way to operate, and if an operation is not stopped in time, an offender may wind up in a completely helpless situation, and a defensive counterattack could lead to catastrophic results (e.g., our offensive in the Carpathians in April, 1915; the last month of the Verdun offensive).

The duty of strategy is to keep offensive operations from getting drawn out to the last gasp; great leadership ability is required to stop an offensive in time without getting distracted by minor partial successes which could still be achieved. As soon as our forces lose their tactical advantages, the strategist must reexamine the issue of continuing an operation and end it at an appropriate line and sometimes even abandon some of the territory that has been captured. It stands to reason that the importance of a goal and the possibility of achieving it, albeit at the cost of major casualties, may compel us to continue an operation under unfavorable tactical conditions. We shall mention that persistence and doggedness, which may turn into obstinacy, are not unconditional benefactors in the art of war; one needs flexibility to avoid banging one's head against the wall. The Russian high command was inflexible during the World War: it drove the troops to exhaustion, and thus its fate was to lead exhausted troops. Hence Russian operations were conducted at a slow trot, while German troops, who were better taken care of, operated at a gallop and with flair.

If the enemy has managed to deploy superior forces and we are forced to go on the defensive in a crisis situation, the job of strategy is to determine the impossibility of a favorable outcome in time and stop it as soon as possible before the crisis comes. Obstinacy is also inappropriate in this case. One of Ludendorff's best decisions was halting the Ivangorod-Warsaw operation in time: if the German troops had begun their withdrawal to Silesia two or three days later instead of on October 17, 1914, the Lodz operation of November 11 would have been impossible, the German army would have been truly licked and its combat-readiness would have been greatly diminished for a long time.

In this instance abandoning an operation that had taken a bad turn for the Germans was justified by the fact that Ludendorff could not expect a break in his favor and could only expect everything to get much worse over time. A strategist must weigh the entire future of an operation before giving the order to abandon it. Of course the flexibility we need has nothing in common with a fundamental avoidance of crises and risky situations. The same wisdom that requires one to walk away from a hopeless situation finds risk that holds the promise of gain completely acceptable.

Whereas in the past pursuit ensued after the end of the clashes that made up a battle and began outside the field on which the battle was fought, now pursuit is incorporated within the operation. Troops who have managed to avoid encirclement and destruction for the entire operation slip away, partly by means of railroads, regroup rapidly and are reinforced; therefore we do not need pursuit, we need to prepare a new operation.

The end of an offensive operation is marked by a transition to defense. By causing the operation to stop, the defender has already achieved a great deal. In early summer 1915 the Russian armies succeeded in halting the development of German operations several times—that is, they achieved the goals of operational defense. However, our critical weapons and ordnance supply situation and the enemy's overwhelming material superiority negated the efforts that had been made: it was easier for the enemy to make up for his losses and get new supplies and begin an operation again without any particular difficulty, while our modus operandi led to the increasing exhaustion of our armed forces. It would have been better for us to resort to more economical methods of gaining time—recoil.

Operations on Interior Lines

In operational art operations on interior lines mean actions by which we successively shift the center of gravity of our efforts against enemy forces attacking in different sectors and beat them separately. Because a side that uses this technique must put itself in an interior position, that is, subject itself to the possibility of attacks from different sides, these operations are very hazardous. The area available for deploying rears is extremely limited. As rears have gotten larger and communications have been improved and now make it possible to coordinate the actions of armies attacking in different operational sectors, operating on interior lines has become extremely difficult and may easily lead to operational encirclement. It is successful only when the enemy command is uncoordinated (Samsonov, Rennenkampf and Zhilinskii). In the late fall of 1916, Romania, which had been subjected to an attack on Wallachia by Falkenhayn from the northwest and Mackensen from the south, experienced all the inconveniences of operating on internal lines. Wrangel, who had emerged from the Crimea, successfully practiced this only until the semi-circle of Red forces around him was organized, and then his armies faced disaster.

Operations on interior lines considered on a strategic scale involve successive movement of the center of gravity from one theater to another. One condition for the success of these operations is the presence of railroad lines connecting these theaters. The conditions for such operations arise when fighting is under way on several fronts. In the World War the Central Powers were in these conditions and were able to concentrate successive attacks on France, Russia, Serbia and Italy. A favorable condition for strategic operations on interior lines is the formation of positional fronts, which make it possible to limit oneself to a minimum of forces for the defense and organize a powerful strategic reserve whose guest appearances in each theater of the war lead to a favorable break in the situation.

In the Civil War Soviet Russia was in a favorable interior position. Moscow is a powerful railroad junction. Our enemies were attacking from all corners of the earth. There were either no lateral lines of communication between them (Kolchak, Denikin and the Arkhangelsk front of the Whites) or these communications were not used to coordinate operations (the Poles and Denikin, the Poles and Yudenich). This made it possible for the Reds to concentrate superior forces successively on every front.

Operations on interior lines on a strategic scale do not cramp operational logistics or threaten to lead to a loss of communication and operational encirclement; at the same time they maintain favorable conditions for operational interior lines.[8] Sometimes when the boundary affected by the art of war is very long and there are two theaters on it, strategic operations on interior lines may be employed in fighting a single enemy. For example, in 1920 the Poles, who initially directed the center of gravity of their efforts to the south from Polese were then compelled to move troops to the north because of the initiative we had seized north of Polese. The Warsaw operation was characterized by a new influx of Polish forces from the south which made it possible to organize an attack from the direction of Lublin.

Strategic work on interior lines raises the issue of the order of attacking different enemies—a question that is extremely hard for strategists. Political requirements, which are not always properly taken into account are particularly important for resolving it. All we have to do is remember the completely contradictory answers to the question of the initial direction of a German attack in a simultaneous war against Russia and France which the elder Moltke and Schlieffen gave. The same problem was important for the German command in 1915-1917, and, in our opinion, neither Falkenhayn nor Ludendorff in particulay resolved it satisfactorily.

Sometimes resolving the question of the sequence of operations on different fronts is more a matter of politics than strategy. That was the case in selecting Kolchak or Denikin as the object for the first offensive of the Red Army in 1919. Which of them could constitute a greater political threat: Kolchak, who possessed

---

[8] The elder Moltke proposal to make strategic use of interior lines in a war by Prussia against Austria and France. See A. Svechin, *Istoriia voennogo iskusstva*, vol. 3, pp. 135-142.

[9] It seems to us that Kolchak was politically stronger and that the disintegration of his rear occurred as a result of excessive mobilizations and defeats at the front, whereas in Krasnov and Denikin's cases this disintegration preceded military setbacks. But we are not sufficiently competent to resolve this question. In practice the first attack on Denikin was inspired by economic requirements and the desire to seize the Ukraine after the German withdrawal more quickly.

a great deal of authority but relied on the very sparsely populated territory of Siberia, or Denikin, who was in the wealthy grain-growing South with its Cossacks but with the hatred for the gentry which grows so abundantly on black earth and its characteristic national, autonomic, antistate and anarchist tendencies.[9]

But strategy requires the achievement of intermediate goals. Incidentally other operations of 1918 in the east were not taken to the Urals and the operations in the south were not taken to the Kuban when the government began sending all resources to the east. And apparently there was a great danger that the summer operation against Kolchak in 1919 would not lead to the complete capture of the Urals, because the military command tried to begin weakening the Eastern front in favor of the Southern front, where Denikin's offensive had covered a vast territory. We believe that the Red Army had nothing to gain by beginning a decisive offensive against Denikin two months earlier and would probably have encountered more serious resistance. The situation on the class front of the conflict was such that territorial expansion weakened Denikin rather than strengthened him.

If we are surrounded and fighting on several fronts, a strategy of destruction requires that we turn against the most important enemy at the root of the coalition. A strategy of attrition demands that we first secure our rear and flanks and thus create favorable conditions for an offensive in the main theater.

That is why Konrad wanted to put an end to Serbia before beginning major operations on the Russian front, although he was able to do this because of energetic German opposition. In 1920 Poland was a more formidable enemy than Wrangel. From the perspective of destruction, it would have been correct to direct most of our efforts against Warsaw. In fact, wouldn't the sovietization of Poland and the expansion of the revolution on a European scale have put an end to Wrangel by itself without any effort on the part of the Red Army? The decisive point—Warsaw—would have decided the fate of the Crimea. But all this reasoning would have been completely faulty if the conditions for destruction did not exist and the decisive point was a phantom. We had to defeat Wrangel and even the most important centers of banditry to secure our communications before launching a major European offensive. Strategy cannot examine the Warsaw operation in isolation. In the final analysis, Wrangel won the Warsaw operation, not Pilsudski; the Poles' Lublin attack was made possible by the divided attention of the Southern front and the fact that the latter was pursuing local goals in Poland rather than an energetic offensive to the Vistula. As goals of operations Warsaw and the Crimea were set in an order opposite the one they should have, which had unpleasant consequences.

The Simultaneous Pursuit of Several Positive Goals

Two simultaneous offensive operations are very seldom successful. At the beginning of the World War the Central Powers sent approximately 55 percent of their troops to attack France; left 40 percent against Russia, primarily for an offensive operation from Galicia between the Bug and the Vistula; and 5 percent tried to operate offensively against Serbia. They did not succeed in achieving positive goals in any theater.

Concentrating all one's resources on a single major operation is undoubtedly capable of yielding a major economy of force. An enemy front capable of withstanding scores of minor assaults can be broken by one strong blow. In certain conditions, an operation must be massive enough in order to achieve at least minimal results, otherwise the elasticity of fronts and the inertia of resistance compel everything to return to its initial position. One must strive for the ultimate goal in steps which are as long as possible; it is always desirable to take advantage of superiority in numbers in the most decisive way possible. Excessive modesty is no benefactor in tactics, operational art or strategy.

However, at times the simultaneous pursuit of two positive goals is dictated by political conditions. The military convention with France required the Russian armies to invade East Prussia in 1914; at the same time the forces of our deployment surrounding Galicia could only have been used if our armies went on the offensive, because only an offensive operation would make it possible to use the masses of the 3rd and 8th Russian armies against the Austrians. These masses could only be deployed in the Kiev Military District because of logistical considerations. The Russian forces paid for their offensive in East Prussia (30 divisions suffered severe setbacks), while 50 Russian divisions won an ordinary victory in Galicia. In the fall of 1919 favorable political conditions required the Red Army to go on the offensive against Denikin and develop the Siberian offensive successfully. Both undertakings were crowned with success. In 1866 Moltke concentrated 19 divisions in the main Bohemian theater against the Austrians and left only three divisions (reinforced by Landwehr) in the German theater against the minor German states; however, quite extensive positive goals were pursued at the same time in both theaters, which we have already ascribed to the carved up nature of the secondary theater and the resultant lack of defensive capability in the situation which had been created there.

Sometimes one major operation is practically impossible because there are either no communications between different theaters (Russia, Serbia and France in the World War and the White fronts in the Civil War) or the lateral lines are so weak that the masses of troops deployed in one theater are quite firmly bound to it (France and Italy; the Soviet theaters in Belorussia and the Ukraine). In a coalition war, however, integration of all resources for a single operation is often prevented not by the weakness of lines of communication but the fact that each ally is pursuing his own special political goal; this was the reason for the difference in the conduct of operations by Germany and Austria-Hungary in August 1914; Romanian forces conducted a Rumanian operation in Transylvania in 1916, while in 1917 the British conducted a British operation in Flanders.

If one side has the opportunities for strategic work on interior lines, the other side is forced to operate on exterior lines. The wider the ring of strategic encirclement, the less good it does for the encircling side, because the chances of turning a strategic encirclement into an operational encirclement disappear. If in 1911 any Frenchman or Russian imagined that Russian and French troops invading Germany would shake hands somewhere between the Elbe and the Rhine, this was simply a childish daydream.

These disadvantages of encirclement on the military front are compensated by the advantages the encircling side extracts on the economic and political fronts. In these conditions destruction attempts from different fronts are condemned to a lack of coordination and disorganization; the side in the interior position will concentrate the center of gravity of his efforts against the most threatening operation and thus will be able to stop the development of this operation. One must take advantage of the fact that the encircled side will be more quickly politically and economically exhausted and war on all borders will lead to the more rapid achievement of the culminating point of strategic intensity. When strategic intensity begins to diminish, when the enemy's front is deprived of major reserves, rendered punchless, when it becomes quite incapable of launching major counterattacks and is only able to offer passive—in these conditions strategic work on exterior lines is even advantageous and a decisive offensive will be dictated by the situation.

Small separate attacks may be even more economical than a single major operation. They make it possible to avoid the loss of time and efforts, which are always the excess costs of a major concentration, and to a large extent it becomes unnecessary to build additional roads, depots or even barracks for the troops, and less work has to be done in concentration and concealing this concentration. Months of time and millions of workdays are saved and one can take more advantage of surprise. Every offensive operation is beneficial in its first half as long as the enemy has not managed to make up for the fact that the attacker was the first to deploy. Small operations have more periods that are favorable for surprise but, it is true, are not as beneficial. If the enemy's reserves have been exhausted and small operations are undertaken simultaneously, the latter have the opportunity to maintain the initiative that has been seized almost as long as major operations. Foch's offensive in the second half of 1918 had this kind of divided nature. It is completely acceptable for operations to get smaller as the enemy is exhausted. Whereas strategic work on interior lines is superior on the ascending part of the curve of strategic intensity, operations on exterior lines are preferable on the descending part.

If a strategic encirclement or envelopment takes place on a moderate diameter (the Russian forward theater in 1914, namely the area of Poland between East Prussia and Galicia on a meridian of only 300 kilometers) and there is the hope of going from a strategic encirclement to an operational encirclement, and if one theater of operations is operationally too cramped for the mobilized masses, then the division of one operation into two may be justified, because it makes it possible to achieve more extensive results.

It is obvious that Mackensen's operation in the summer of 1915 directed from Galicia in the south to Cholm should have encountered much fewer difficulties and produced much greater results when Galwitz's operation began to develop from the north, from East Prussia across the Narev; but the delay of Galwitz's operation and the overly slow pace of its development made it difficult to catch the Russian armies withdrawing from the left bank of the Vistula in a pincer. In the same way the German front in France formed a wide convex arc; the greatest success was promised by the development of two operations at the base of this arc, on the left wing in the area of Verdun running to the north.

In general, encirclement on a broad scale requires, if the configuration of a neutral border or coastlines does not offer special advantages, two or more coordinated operations.[10] This encirclement may be the goal of a destruction or attrition strategy. The elder Moltke in putting together a plan for a war on two fronts, planned an attack with a limited goal on the Russian front; however this attack on the Narev and subsequently on Sedlets, together with the operations of the Austrians from Galicia on Sedlets, was to encircle immediately and eliminate all Russian forces on the Vistula. Falkenhayn implemented this idea in 1915, while the strategy of destruction, in the person of Ludendorff, dreamed of an encirclement on a much wider scale; on Minsk.

As we know, by the time of the Marne operation the younger Moltke had significantly altered the Schlieffen plan: instead of the Marne operation alone he wanted to have a second operation,[11] the Lorraine operation; if it had succeeded, this operation would have resembled the Samsonov massacre transformed from an operational to a strategic scale (the capture of not a few corps, but of a few armies). As we know, the inadequately prepared and unenergetically led Lorraine operation was never carried out, and the assets expended on it were lacking at the Marne; the implementation of Moltke's idea proved to be fatal for the German invasion. However, in essence we cannot object to the form of Moltke's operation. The second part of the Schlieffen plan, encircling the French forces somewhere at the Swiss border, became vaguer and more dubious as the plan grew broader and as the right enveloping wing of the Germans got larger and larger; without an extraordinary victory in carrying out the first half of the plan the second part, in our view, was completely unfeasible. After the semi-success of the border battle Schlieffen himself would probably have rejected the second half of the plan. With the vast fronts of today, one wing must march five hundred or more kilometers to effect an encirclement, which is operationally impractical. Two simultaneous operations putting all or art of an enemy front in a vise significantly reduce the extent of required operational leaps and make them practical. The thoughts of the destruction strategists of today are drawn to this kind of operation. However, we should not forget the extraordinary difficulties involved.

Proportioning Operations

While we may not always have to pursue two positive goals simultaneously, we will practically always have to expend assets on achieving one or several negative goals along with our efforts to achieve a single positive goal. From this follows an extremely critical task for the strategist, allocating assets and the possibilities of replacing them among different operations. A strategist must act as a national or even alliance-wide quartermaster who plays the role of an allocator.

---

[10] We write operation with a small "o" and cannot consider actions on different fronts whose goals are only coordinated on a strategic scale to be a single operation. An ultimate operational encirclement may be the result of two different operations conducted sequentially or simultaneously. The Samsonov catastrophe was the result of one operation, but the capture of all the lines of communication of half a dozen Russian armies would more probably be achieved by two operations. Auxiliary operations, such as the operations of the Austrians against the 3rd and 8th Russian armies in August 1914 to secure the flank and rear of the Austrian attack on Lublin-Cholm, were in essence part of a very important operation and, in our view, the analysis of these operations should be a task for operational art.

[11] It seems to us that this decision by the younger Moltke was based on unreliable information on the situation in Lorraine just as the decision to send a corps from France to East Prussia was due to unreliable information on the results of the border war.

The technique of a strategy of destruction—cheating secondary theaters as much as possible in favor of the main theater—sometimes leads only to negative results in a strategy of attrition, namely increasing the number of idle troops at the expense of active troops. The Russian high command, proceeding from the belief that the way to Petrograd and Moscow runs north from Polese, called the theater north of Polese the main theater and thus grouped the bulk of the Russian forces here: in March of 1915 there were 1,220,000 Russian bayonets and swords facing 620,000 Germans, a 2:1 superiority, while south of Polese there were 512,000 Russians facing 441,000 Austro-Germans, a superiority of only 16 percent. Our most important operation in 1916 was the Brusilov offensive, which we had to conduct practically without taking any advantage of our numerical superiority. Even in August 1916, when the Brusilov offensive was already under way, the forces operating south of Polese were only comparable to the forces idle to the north of it: 863,000 and 853,000. In general whereas in a strategy of destruction the division of theaters into main and secondary theaters introduces clarity, in a strategy of attrition it is only vague and confusing.[12]

Every operation including a defensive operation must be provided with assets appropriate for its goal. A strategy of attrition is characterized by the fact that the strategist, without taking his eye off the ultimate goal, selects a positive intermediate goal on the basis of the free assets at his disposal to pursue negative goals. That is how Ludendorff acted on the Russian front in 1914 and 1915; this should in no way be interpreted as preference for defensive missions over offensive missions; for example, in 1914 Ludendorff tightly gripped the negative goal of defending East Prussia: in order to take elements of the 8th Army for the Lodz operation he gave this army the mission of not defending East Prussian territory to the fullest extent and, if necessary, withdrawing in the east to the line of the Masurian Lakes and the Angerap River. However, all the assets available were deployed for this modest negative goal. That was how the groundwork was set for the second Russian invasion of East Prussia.

---

[12] It seems to me that this incorrect division has also kept us from making a good assessment of the Soviet-Polish War. In May 1920 the Poles had put half of their forces on the defensive north of Polese and dispatched half to the right bank of the Ukraine. Strategic criticism based on a division into main and secondary theaters condemned this deployment of the Polish forces and attempted to confirm its conclusion by references to Foch. However, because the Poles had rejected the idea of destruction, a campaign on Moscow was ridiculous to them because their positive goals were in the Ukraine, which was also the most important theater for them.

As we know, the Red forces south of Polese were supported only by Budennyi's cavalry army, and all the other reserves and replacements were sent north of Polese. Our criticism has emphasized the correct assessment by our command of the significance of the main and secondary theaters and, as its reward, the fact that the Polish maneuver was completely unreflected in our deployments. To us the situation seems different. The Southwestern front, despite the fact that it was considered secondary and received corresponding forces, was able to encircle a large part of the Polish forces in June, but the latter was able to break out of this weak ring. If the interests of the Eastern front had not predominated over the interests of the Southwestern front in the consciousness of our strategy and the Southwestern front had been appropriately reinforced, we could have counted on surrounding and capturing the best Polish forces at Kiev. This Sedan could have truly been the starting point for putting our strategy on a destruction track and for a campaign on the Vistula, quite possibly through Lvov.

The proper solution of a difficult problem, i.e., providing the necessary assets for every operation, requires a strategist to be a master of operational art; if he were merely a dilettante he would hardly be able to match the goals with the available resources. Mastery of the subtleties of operational art is particularly important for a strategist compelled to follow a line of attrition.

The Strategic Reserve

A strategist allocates forces and resources among operations in both space and time. Any operation, even a successful one, particularly if one must operate under conditions of poor communications, irrecoverably swallows up some of the forces and resources deployed for it and entails a certain expenditure of time and energy. This liability of one operation is reflected in subsequent operations. The loss of 40,000 German infantrymen in the Ivangorod-Warsaw operation required extraordinary replacements because of the activity of the Russian front. This deprived the German high command of the opportunity to bring Buelow's 2nd Army up to strength[13] and make an energetic attack on the Somme with its assistance. The latter was needed because, given the calm of the entire German front in France, an isolated German offensive in Flanders was obviously incapable of succeeding because the Anglo-French had concentrated reserves from all their armies against it. These 40,000 trained infantry replacements undoubtedly constituted a reserve element, and sending them to the east rather than the west meant the failure of the Battle of Flanders, positional calm in France and an increase in the burden on the Russian armies. This reserve, which was the result of the work of the rear and was maintained in the rear, could have been more justifiably considered a national reserve rather than a strategic reserve.

A national reserve will always consist of units that have not yet completely formed or achieved full combat-readiness, as well as trained replacements and stockpiles. The exhaustion of the national reserve will quickly compel the contraction of a military front and accelerate the denouement; for example, in 1917 Germany had exhausted its national reserve of manpower, which also determined the events of the last months of the war.

However, in addition to national reserves, modern warfare also leaves room for strategic reserves, that is, fully trained and mobilized units that are not tied to an operational goal. An operational reserve is what we call any division that is counted on to achieve an operational goal we set but has still not deployed and is still not tied down to any sector. Operational reserves will maneuver primarily on rails. A strategic reserve is formed when we set operational goals that are more modest than the forces we have. A strategic reserve is strategic wealth, which is naturally put aside if the front is not fighting at full pitch. It may take the form of corps in the remote rear and observation armies at neutral borders, but may also consist of units used to fill our positions in secondary sectors to give them the necessary battle sectors but which may be removed and employed in another direction.

Of course, the concept of a strategic reserve radically contradicts the ideas of destruction, which require extreme intensity to achieve success at a decisive point. But this concept logically fits within the framework of a war of attrition. A prolonged conflict is generally impossible without a strategic reserve. The lack of

---

[13] Falkenhayn, *Verkhovnoe Komandovanie*, pp. 40-41.

a strategic reserve indicates maximum operational stress, which of course cannot be permanent.

Up to the moment of general maximum intensity of the forces of the state, which is characterized by the completion of economic mobilization and subsequent echelons of mobilization, we can consider the operations of the armed front from the perspective of covering this prolonged mobilization in our country and interfering with the enemy's mobilization. Periods of gathering forces in which the interests of this accumulation will supersede the interests of achieving certain secondary intermediate goals may be completely legitimate during the course of a war. If we sacrifice our interests in gathering forces to carrying out secondary operations, we will gradually expend everything the state has given us for the war drop by drop and will have to renounce the opportunity of achieving major results.

Of course, at times maintaining a strategic reserve is a gross error. At the beginning of the World War the Russian command had the opportunity to beat the German-Austrians in strategic deployment and achieve major intermediate goals. Keeping the 6th and 7th armies on the Baltic and Black Sea coasts constituted the temporary maintenance of a strategic reserve which only retarded our deployment and was the reason for the Russians' insufficient superiority of forces in East Prussia and Galicia. But subsequently the Russian command took the dangerous course of setting the maximum possible intermediate goals: from the Lodz operation to the positional calm that came in 1915 the Russian military front operated without any strategic reserve and at the peak of intensity; as the result of this every setback had grave consequences and was irreparable.[14]

A strategic reserve that would not be used at the proper moment would only be a symptom of cowardice, inaction and passivity, indicating excess baggage borne by the nation on the military front, and would testify to the modesty of the creative abilities of a military leader, the excessive prolongation of a war and favorable moments which had been allowed to slip away. A strategic reserve inserted in a war at the proper moment indicates that a strategist has solved a very difficult problem successfully and that he dominates events and does not get carried away by eddies and currents he does not understand.

The establishment of a positional front, which makes it possible to achieve negative goals with smaller forces, greatly facilitates the organization of a strategic reserve. In fact, we had a very large one, approximately 30 percent of the entire strength of the military front, by the spring of 1916. We were not able to put it into the war all at the same time, but it was largely responsible for the difficulties faced by the German command in the summer of 1916.

---

[14] The author of these lines, starting in late 1914, spoke out sharply at Russian headquarters about the need to avoid the pursuit of positive goals and accumulate a strategic reserve.

[15] The organization of this strategic reserve was caused by the high command's renunciation of "any participation in a drive for military undertakings of dubious stability and for vague military missions," which followed from the idea that "Germany will win the war if it succeeds in avoiding putting extraordinary strain on its domestic and foreign forces." (Falkenhayn, *Verkhovnoe komandovanie*, p. 143). Falkenhayn's rejection of Ludendorff's plan for launching a destruction attack on Minsk in the summer of 1915 was very intelligent, because it led to the creation of a strategic reserve in conditions in which this was extremely desirable.

In November 1914, when a positional front had been established in France, Germany was able to make major savings on the front; however, they were immediately transferred to the operational reserve of the Russian front where they were expended. This was the fate of the first echelons of mobilization. Germany was able to create a strategic reserve only after a positional front had been established in Russia. The Serbian campaign in the fall of 1915 and the beginning of the Verdun operation in 1916 were characteristic of German conduct of military operations involving the maintenance of a strategic reserve.[15] The events of the summer of 1916 greatly exhausted Germany's strategic reserve. Ludendorff squandered it once and for all when he joined the high command organizing the Romanian campaign. Despite all the success achieved in Romania, the depletion of this reserve delayed the German preparations for the spring campaign of 1917 and caused them to avoid the pursuit of any positive goals on the French front; a convenient opportunity for inflicting a major blow on the French in May of 1917 created by the reduction in the fighting ability of the Russian army and the revolutionary movement in the French army had to be missed.

In early 1918 Russia's withdrawal from the war gave Ludendorff the opportunity to create a solid strategic reserve and provided the diplomats with the opportunity to start negotiations behind a completely solid German front. However, Ludendorff's decision was to use the assets freed by the withdrawal to maximize the goal pursued in France—to destroy the French before the arrival of American reinforcements. Ludendorff immediately transferred these divisions to an operational reserve on the Anglo-French front. We could say that Ludendorff was completely ignorant of the concept of a strategic reserve. In the reality of a war of attrition these kinds of operations had to lead to disaster.

Strategic reserves are particularly important for a coalition against which an enemy can operate on interior lines. France and Britain had learned this well by the fall of 1914. While encouraging the Russians to be active, they built up their own armies qualitatively and quantitatively by pursuing only modest active goals on the front. Concern for a strategic reserve is especially characteristic of British strategy. The Kitchener program was above all a program of accumulating forces and forming a strong strategic reserve. The British energetically developed operations in theaters outside Europe because they considered them short-term expeditions (in East Africa they were mistaken) where they could temporarily send some of their excess forces for a guest performance, but in France itself they were interested in occcupying the shortest possible front and maintaining the largest possible strategic reserve. The weight of every member of a coalition in negotiations primarily depends not so much on the efforts it has made on the front as on its free surplus of forces.

Neither Kolchak nor Denikin possessed the slightest strategic reserve in the Civil War; their offensive undertakings not only relied on all the forces at their disposal but even exceeded them. This made the catastrophes they suffered even worse.

---

[16]   The first duty of the general staff is to select a way of operating which in accordance with the quality of the armed forces trained for war, could affect a hostile nation in a desirable way in the shortest time possible. *Angliiskii polevoi ustav*, part 2, chapter 2, section 4, paragraph 6.

The Strategic Line of Conduct

We have dwelled on several of the most important issues of strategic logic. A strategist who knows the requirements of the evolution of the military profession, understands the resources needed at a given moment and has an idea of the strengths and capabilities of both sides and the nature of a future war dwells on a certain way of resolving strategic questions that should lead him to the ultimate goal of the operations of a military front,[16] plans a series of intermediate goals and the sequence in which they are achieved; regulates strategic intensity and at every moment tries, if not to subordinate, to tie the interests of the present to the interests of the strategic "tomorrow" of the future. He is not independent in his decisions but must coordinate the solution of the problems of the war on the military front with the course of events on the political and economic fronts. Every question the strategist must resolve is extremely simple, but a correct answer requires a great depth of understanding of the situation of the war as a whole; theory can only emphasize the diversity of possible solutions as a function of different conditions. But a strategist cannot limit himself to correct answers for each question individually. The answer to one strategic question will only be correct when it is in harmony with the answers to other strategic questions. We have put harmony in the preparations of a nation for war at the forefront, but it is no less important in the leadership of a war, only the characteristics of harmony in this case are immeasurably more subtle. This coordination, this achievement of harmony,[17] is the essence of strategy and it forces us to classify practical work on strategy as an art.

In terms of strategic leadership of a military front, which is understood as combining operations for achieving the ultimate goal of the war, a very important task for art is selecting a line of strategic conduct that would represent the harmony of the required coordination; in this line should lie the key to the interpretation of the requirements of the constantly changing situation; it cannot yield a prediction of the actual course of events on the military front, but at any given moment it should make it possible for us to react to military events in accordance with the logic to which everything should be subordinated for achieving victory in a given war.

We have placed particular emphasis on the impossibility of predicting the actual course of events in a war because among the masses brilliance is always regarded as the ability to make accurate predictions. The more brilliant a leader, the more the masses consider him to be a prophet. These notions are quite common and are often held by ignorant critics. In essence, they require a military leader to guess the future and go beyond the bounds of human mental capacities. Napoleon and everyone posturing as a genius have at times been inclined to support this error. However, real life does not encourage prophecy or clairvoyancy. In strategy prophecy may only be charlatanism, and even a genius is incapable of seeing how a war will unfold. But he must put together a perspective in which he will evaluate the phenomena of war. A military leader needs a working hypothesis. Of course, not every military leader will take the trouble or have the opportunity to think about the nature of a future war. Strategic mediocrity perhaps prefers to proceed from stereotypes and recipes. Reality will be a cruel

---

[17] This basic task of the strategist, in Falkenhayn's words, lies in tirelessly reducing particulars into a single entity. Falkenhayn, *Verkhovnoe Komandovanie*, p. 124.

disappointment for such a poor excuse for a leader; the theory of strategic art cannot have him in mind.

Our statements will perhaps seem abstract and suspended in a vacuum, because the students of war are often reluctant to devote even a few pages in their weighty treatises to a discussion of the strategic line of conduct in a given war. But the strategic line of conduct is a reality, and even an unwise but somewhat consistent and honest strategist has his own line of conduct and his own approach to evaluating a situation. Contemporary military history, which tries to proceed from a single, absolute, uniquely correct line of strategic conduct, is incapable of clarifying the meaning and relationships in the jumble of military events that it considers some sort of chaos. The titles "strategic essays" on some campaign or another sound like crude boasting, a cruel imitation and "fools' gold." Military history is still only an operational protocol.

The line of political conduct is a generally accepted concept. Everyone understands that War Communism or the New Economic Policy has its own special logic of coordination. Finding a logical line that is most appropriate for the conditions of the economic base at a given moment is the most important task of the art of politics. In strategy every military front has its own base, and operations on the military front are only derivatives of the bases of both sides. The clue to the choice of an appropriate line of strategic conduct lies in a profound analysis of these bases. Strategy is a part of politics, a foreshortening of politics, and it is constructed on the same base. From this, in the final analysis, follows the subordination of strategy to politics. A strategic line of conduct should be the projection of the general political line of conduct on a military front.

In essence all our work is devoted to issues associated with the strategic line of conduct. We have tried to outline it theoretically from different vantage points. We could make our presentation more specific in nature only in the form of a strategic analysis of some campaign.

COMMAND

1. STRATEGIC LEADERSHIP

The General Staff.

In the organization of military command over the last century the Prussian system has predominated. In this system highly respected persons in the Junker feudal system were appointed to high command posts in the army; primarily they were members of German ruling dynasties, sometimes quite young and sometimes generals with a great deal of seniority. These persons were very important in society but their talents as specialists in strategic or operational art were negligible. In essence these Prussian commanders merely chaperoned the chiefs of staff, who did all the important work.

In the four and a half years of the World War Hindenburg agreed with all of Ludendorff's reports and never made a single revision in any of Ludendorff's plans.

The advantages of the German system lay in the fact that while it maintained the appearance of feudal seniority, it made it possible to assign critical work to talented specialists regardless of their age or rank. The armies were entrusted to a young general or even a colonel who officially was only a "chief" (chief of staff) and who had a proper representative of the idea of feudal seniority with him. It stands to reason that the benefits of this system disappear in an army that has finally rid itself of feudal prejudice and accepts the command of young leaders with satisfaction, regardless of any line of seniority.

However, this does not mean that the general staff is a remnant of feudalism. As seniority is abolished, the relationships between a commander and a chief of staff are becoming more normal. However, in modern warfare a commander must rely on an entire team of select assistants who understand one another well, are cohesive, suited for any kind of critical work and deserve complete confidence.

This kind of team is already required to bring order to the gigantic task of preparing for war. Only a general staff, a collection of persons who have forged and tested their military views under the same conditions and under the same leadership, who have been carefully selected and are bound to one another by mutual responsibility and concerted efforts to achieve fundamental improvements in building the army, is capable of coordinating and harmonizing preparations which are so extensive, so diverse and run in so many different directions, A variety of specialists are required in the military profession; the specialty of the general staff should be to combine individual efforts into a single entity, eliminate friction and achieve a high level of organization.

War requires this harmonizing specialty; at a watchworks there are special masters of the highest qualifications who do not make anything but merely assemble the individual wheels and springs of the watch mechanism into a single working entity; war has an even more complex mechanism and it takes even greater art to put it together. The contemporary forms of an operation, into which the battle has developed, make it impossible for one man to lead it; in order to employ modern operational forms we need tens and hundreds of trusted agents, each of whom would be a conscientious representative of the military high command rather than a mere bureaucrat. No number of telegrams will be capable of providing communications if there is no general staff: the telegrams will mean one thing to the writer and another thing to the reader.

Armed conflict as it is currently understood requires a general staff; this is not an organizational whim and will of course arise in any army: a decree cannot abolish it, but it can regulate it and give the general staff the most intelligent organizational configuration. This configuration should correspond to all the characteristics of an army.

In defending the need for a general staff, we in no way intend to say that it does not make mistakes. The sins of any general staff, including the Russian, were many, but they have to be combatted, but in order to do this the general staff has to be given legal recognition.

Dragomirov, who in 1866 was a military agent attached to the Prussian army, idealized in the persons of the Austrian general staff negative characteristics and vices of the staff and indicated the most important dangers.

The corps of the Austrian general staff is distinguished by scholarly pedantry and a complete lack of practicality. They know how to act but they do not know how to set goals. The dispositions and instructions are extremely long and claim to be written so that in practice a commander doesn't have to think so much as remember what paragraph he should carry out at any given minute.

The reason for this tendency can be explained as follows: as representatives of theoretical knowledge in an army in which officers are not inclined to acquire this knowledge, general staff officers by necessity are placed in an isolated position, and as a consequence, there are probably many general staff officers who believe in their invariable superiority over line officers only because they know, let us say, military history by heart. In turn, line officers cannot help be disturbed by this pomposity, moreover, because it is completely unjustified in practice and leads to the most ridiculous errors when we are talking about the life of the army. Thus they consider themselves worth more than they are, and the others avoid them more than they deserve, and these forces, instead of walking hand in hand, drown one another out without having sufficient points of contact between them or mutual understanding.[1]

Count Czernin, a very intelligent Austrian politician of the World War, has stated that much of what Dragomirov said was still true 50 years later:

> Some of our general staff was very bad. There were exceptions, but they only proved the rule. First of all, the general staff had practically no contact with the troops. The gentlemen of the general staff sat in the rear and wrote orders. They practically never met with the soldiers where the bullets were flying. During the war the troops learned to hate the general staff. The situation was different in the German army. The German officers of the general staff demanded a lot, gave a lot themselves and most important went out on the battlefield and set an example.[2]

In fact, an employee of the general staff must always be ready to break bread with the troops and should not make his desk a barricade separating him from the battlefield. Ludendorff, one of the inspirers of the idea of the assault on Lige on the fourth day of mobilization, maintained his authority in the army only because at a time when the assault had ground to a halt he took command of a handful of soldiers and broke through the perimeter of the fortress.

Among other things, a tested general staff makes it possible to get by with brief orders. When workers meet for the first time it takes a large number of lines to get operational ideas across; in addition to the characteristics of a given decision, a number of general ideas must be discussed; but once the general views of one echelon become known to another echelon, operational ideas may be expressed laconically, and despite this brevity, there will be less room for misinterpretation. In the same way that two Hughes type printers on different ends of a telegraph wire must be first adjusted by a mechanic in order to print out a telegraph accurately and quickly, the general staff of both sides reaching an understanding must be first adjusted by a master experienced in strategy and operational art.

A general staff should always speak the same language and use certain expressions for the same thoughts.

Of course, it is impossible to get all the members of a general staff to hold the same views, particularly in our era of the rapid development of the art of war. Complete unity of doctrine and the lack of differences in the interpretation of operational and tactical issues could be achieved only at the cost of stopping efforts for further development. This unity of doctrine was apparently achieved in the Prussian general staff before the World War, but only for insufficiently attentive observers. The Germans themselves denied any such unity. The course of the war indicated how different were the conclusions drawn from the same military situation by different leaders (Moltke, Falkenhayn, Ludendorff). In any event, an exchange of opinions made discussions over the course of many years before the war helps a general staff to keep discussions brief during operations and reduce the unproductive expenses of directing military operations.

---

[1]   M. Dragomirov, *Ocherki avstro-prusskoi voiny v 1866 g.* [Essays on the Austro-Prussian War of 1866] (St. Petersburg: 1867), pp. 69-78.

[2]   Czernin, *Im Weltkriege*, p. 28.

Views on the unity of military doctrine are extremely distorted in France. During the preparations for the war the persecution of dissidents greatly retarded the transition to new strategic and operational ideas and was the reason for the generally reactionary nature of the French art of war. During the World War Nivelle was an extreme representative of the idea of the unity of doctrine as the most reliable guarantee of the success of an operation. After planning to carry out a decisive breakthrough, he first of all demanded faith in the success of the operation and dismissed any chiefs who expressed the slightest doubts. A corps artillery chief who tried to tell him that there were only unimportant observation posts in his attack sector was driven out. Officially this operation was greatly approved and everyone glorified the successes that would be achieved but then wrote confidential letters to influential politicians asking them to keep the army from launching an operation that had absolutely no chance of success. However, they did not have civic courage to repeat these doubts in front of Nivelle at a special meeting called by Minister Painlevé.

The role of the general staff in overcoming parochial interests is particularly important. In war these interests are sometimes particularly sensitive. Two regiments, corps or fronts next to one another sometimes are not a single entity but rather a kind of federation. The egoism of senior commanders and their separatist tendencies have been striking in all eras and under all regimes. It is much harder to discipline the high command than the Red Army man. The general staff consists of agents of a single entity who are not tied to the local interests of a given unit or to certain traditions but to the idea of victory on the military front as a whole. The duty of the general staff is to set these overall goals and combat parochial deviations.

The Location of Headquarters

In the 17th and 18th centuries wars were usually led from the capital rather than the active army. Army commanders were strategically subordinate to the center. Despite the lack of a telegraph system, questions concerning engagement in a general battle and the direction of development of operations were quite frequently dispatched by courier for resolution in the capital. This kind of command met the requirements of a war of attrition; in fact, operations only pursued limited goals; the significance of the overall political leadership of the war was great, and the resources of the state also had to be coordinated with the intensity of the war. In the last years of the Seven Years' War Austria-Hungary began to reduce its army for economic reasons. The capital had a better idea of the limits of intensity, the possibility of replenishing the stores, paying the troops and recruiting new replacements.

In the 19th century, when Napoleon and Moltke were around, there were several wars of destruction in which the entire leadership of the war was handed over to the active army. The rear operated only in the preparatory period, and when military operations began the life and work of the rear faded into the background. War was primarily waged with forces and resources stockpiled beforehand. A decisive point was created in a theater, and the outcome at this decisive point decided the fate of a state. In these conditions the entire center of gravity of the leadership of a short destruction campaign passed to the active army and even to the most important sector of the battlefield. Foch criticized Moltke for the fact that during the Battle of Gravelot-Saint-Privat he stayed 12 kilometers away from the decisive point of the battle, which was on the left flank. In 1870 the Prussian minister of war accompanied the staff of the commander in chief, personifying the subordinate position of the rear.

In many respects, including command, the 20th century is closer to the 17th than the 19th. We mainly wage the limited operations of a strategy of attrition; the rear and its work are much more important, and the political and economic fronts of the conflict are frightfully intense. It seems to us that now strategic leadership must be concentrated in the capital. Only then will it be possible to coordinate activities on the military front and other fronts and avoid many misunderstandings. It is obvious that we should try to provide the same opportunity for strategists to concentrate on their work and remain apart from the interests of day-to-day routine and the same opportunity to maintain secrecy as are provided by locating headquarters in a remote area (such as Baranovichi in 1914). During the World War Falkenhayn debated the question of whether the minister of war belongs in the rear or at headquarters. Our answer is that headquarters belong in the rear. This does not keep headquarters from applying pressure on the leadership of an operation if necessary and sending out a temporary operational post in a vital direction, perhaps where front headquarters is located or even further forward, in a train that gets as close to the front line as the range of vehicle or aerial reconnaissance.

Orienting the Actions of One's Forces

The strength of command lies in its orientation. The one who knows is the one who commands.

Headquarters must try to make direct contact with the front line despite the hierarchical ladder of staffs. In addition to the quantitative, chronological and geometric information provided by staffs, we must also get a clear idea of what is really happening in armed clashes, what their nature is, what are the merits of the troops of both sides, what their tactics and morale are like and how to look at the information that is coming in. But this contact with the front could be best made by observers rather than moving headquarters itself forward. The study of new forms of warfare is a necessary part of the activity of the high command; the new course of events in warfare can be understood and evaluated only if the events are measured by a new yardstick.

A correct and sober evaluation of one's own forces is a necessary precondition for a good decision because we must know what the troops can provide in order to make reasonable requirements of them. A leader should not try to hide any shortcomings of his men or exaggerate their virtues. Only then will he be able to lead them confidently. Because the virtues of his men will constantly change in wartime, a leader must maintain close contact with them and in particular make accurate observations of their actions in battle, where the pulse beats faster and their virtues and shortcomings are more evident.

Napoleon ordinarily had information on the points his corps had reached at nightfall by around midnight and could give orders for the next day. Night time when the troops were resting, was enough time for all reports to get to headquarters and for subsequent orders from the commander to reach the troops. It is true that sometimes Napoleon had to give orders hurriedly with his eyes closed (for example, in 1809 the attack by main forces from Abensberg to Landshut was directed not at the main forces of Viscount Karl but rather his left covering detachment). Now, despite the telephone and telegraph, one night is not enough time for the increasingly complex command structure to make reports and decisions.

The results of major battles do not become clear so quickly. The significance of the victory at Koeniggraetz was clear to Moltke and the Prussians only on the third day, and the Elbe River beyond which the Austrians retreated concealed the condition of the losers from the Prussians. The evening after the battle Moltke sent a telegram to Berlin in which he mentioned 20 captured guns; the next day he increased this figure to 50, but in fact 174 guns had been captured from the Austrians but it took a great deal of time to count them. Our military agent Dragomirov, who was on the Prussian side, mentioned that on the evening after the battle some of the winners were asking, who won, our side or theirs? "Such battles are no less confusing for the winners as they are for the losers."[3]

In the World War the semi-victory of the Russians at Gumbinen posed a difficult problem for both Russian and German headquarters. The German army's withdrawal began on the evening of August 20, and on the morning of August 22 neither the German nor the Russian high command had a clear understanding of the results of this clash. German headquarters, in order to clarify the situation, entered into direct talks with the corps commanders. Only on the evening of August 21 did the Germans locate their 1st Prussian cavalry corps, which had gone far into the Russian rear[4], whereas not all of the Russian cavalry had been located by August 22. On this day, when the enemy was no longer facing Rennenkampf's army, it was reinforced with the 2nd Army corps at the expense of Samsonov's army due to "strong enemy resistance."

Moltke's most glaring errors in leading the war were due to the fact that he was hesitant to establish his own intelligence system made up of selected general staff officers dispatched to army headquarters to provide independent reports on the results achieved. He responded to the entreaties of his assistants by saying that neither the German army commanders nor their chiefs of staff deserved this mistrust. As a result, in evaluating the results of the border battle, he was completely under the power of the official optimism of the hierarchical echelons.

Moltke got such a clear idea of the decisive importance of the operation on the French front that upon receiving a panicky report concerning the setback at Gumbinen he refused to dispatch reinforcements to East Prussia from the west immediately; his thinking from August 21 to August 23 was characterized by the fact that he ordered the 9th Reserve Corps, which had been left in Germany to guard the coastline, to go to France, while the 33rd and 34th Landwehr brigades were kept on the coast in order to follow the 9th reserve corps if necessary. But when on August 21 he began to receive reports of thousands of prisoners, masses of captured guns and enormous French casualties from all the armies, he made the *fundamental* mistake of believing them and deciding to move six corps to East Prussia, two each from the right wing, center and left wing. According to orders issued early in the morning on August 25, the guards reserve and 11th corps

---

[3] M. Dragomirov, *Ocherki austro-prusskoi; voiny v 1866 g.*, pp. 189-190.

[4] Reichsarchiv, *Der Weltkrieg*, vol 2, pp. 102-108.

actually began to move, weakening the Germans' vital right wing. The other movements were delayed and then cancelled.[5]

In the Civil War the truth about many events never made it to headquarters. Not all the staffs were objective enough. On August 18, 1920, the Western front tried to maintain an optimistic view of the development of the Polish attack from the south. On the evening of August 16 the commander of the 8th division reported that "elements of the Mozyr group have evidently completely disintegrated," and on the following morning reported that "my division as a battle-ready unit has already disappeared." But as late as August 18 the front reported that "elements of the 8th division attacked Garwolin, but haphazardly, and have withdrawn to Novo-Minsk," and "the withdrawal of the 16th Army and the Mozyr group can be ascribed to exhaustion and the overexhaustion of the latter." The high command was operating with units that no longer existed. As late as August 23, when the operation was completely over, headquarters wrote:

> now the enemy himself is getting involved in a risky operation and now this risk is increasing with every step forward. This had given us the complete possibility of seizing the initiative from the enemy with comparatively small forces and without difficulty.

This directive had absolutely no basis in reality.[6]

The quickness of the orientation of the high command to a great extent determines the methods of leading operations. In maneuver warfare it takes approximately 18 to 24 hours for the high command to get a very rough idea of the events on the front, and the delay is particularly great at critical moments when many important lines of communication cease to operate.[7] In positional warfare one can get a fairly accurate idea after 12 hours; by means of telegraph and telephone conversations that bypassed several hieracchial echelons Ludendorff in 1918 was able to find out about enemy breakthroughs six to seven hours after they began.

From this information we must conclude that in maneuver warfare the high command will ordinarily be able to react to events on the front only on the third day after they happen, whereas in positional warfare they will be able to react on the very same day, and divisions in reserve near railroad stations where rolling stock is kept could begin moving to a new destination 10 to 12 hours after events begin on the front. Thus command may be centralized to a much greater extent in positional warfare than in maneuver warfare. If important decisions must come from the top in maneuver warfare, they will invariably be very late and inappro-

---

[5] Ibid., vol. 1, pp. 433-440.

[6] B. Shaposhnikov, *Na Visle* [On the Visla] (Moscow: Gosvoenizdat, 1924), pp. 101, 183, 190.

[7] Since before the World War insufficient attention was given to the questions of the organization of communications in Germany, and the possibility of using radiotelegraphs was exaggerated, in the Marne operation. The German headquarters was oriented very badly, and totally haphazardly; the fourth volume of the official history of the World War (Reichsarchiv, *Der Weltkrieg*, vol. 4) sets forth the dramatic position of the German headquarters, which had no wire connections with three armies during the Marne crisis. But the German headquarters simultaneously fulfilled the function of the staff of the front...

priate for the rapidly developing situation. If three or four days elapse between the time an event occurs on the front and the time the orders of headquarters are actually carried out, it will be very important, of course, for headquarters to try to limit itself to issuing orders of a long-term and basic nature; everything of a more immediate nature should be left to the discretion of subordinate echelons.

The orienting and goal-setting work of headquarters should naturally proceed at a calm, even, moderate pace. Nervousness indicates organizational or leadership flaws which are transmitted to all subordinate echelons.

Analyzing the Enemy's Intentions

Whereas information on the actions of one's own troops reaches the high command with a great deal of delay and inaccuracy, even greater difficulties must be overcome in order to get a timely idea of the enemy.

Above all one must get an idea of the deployment of enemy forces and the reserves he has at his disposal for communications with the rear and lateral movements; familiarity with the enemy's political and economic conditions and the personalities of his leaders should help us grasp the most important factors on which the logic of his decisions will be based. It would be mistaken to assume that the enemy will employ textbook methods and counter our maneuvers with the most natural, from our point of view, countermeasures. The enemy will be guided by his own logic based on motives rather than by our logic, and it is extremely important to penetrate the dialectics of the enemy's thinking. Analyzing an enemy army primarily means clarifying what it will do at a critical moment. One must be a psychologist, one must know the ethnographic characteristics of the enemy nation and all of his social factions and tendencies, and one must make an acute evaluation of the finest details without losing a broad perspective—only then will one be able to fully match one's decision with the behavior of the enemy. After all, we will have to conduct an operation against a moving enemy rather than a stationary, frozen one. Benedek's army in 1866 was still at Olmutz when Moltke planned to attack it from two sides in the area of Gitschin and Josephstadt. The Sedan maneuver of de MacMahon's army was a very clear departure from academic logic, but two people, Podbleski, the quartermaster general of Moltke's army, and Friedrich Engels, both figured it out in embryo. For practically his entire military career Napoleon solved his problems offensively, but in the fall campaign of 1813, one could have guessed that he would have gone on a strategic defensive on the Elbe after studying the makeup of the French Army, which had an overwhelming majority of new recruits. If units have just been formed and do not have an organized rear (Gambetta's armies in 1870 and the Civil War armies of 1918), one could predict that they will be tied down to the railroad and maneuver only along the tracks. At the very beginning of the World War one could have predicted that the British would manage to create a positional army, but not an army of maneuver.

It is quite important for all intelligence to be coordinated by one person relieved of any other duties. One should not hesitate to put the most talented member of the leadership staff in charge. Only an outstanding mind would be capable of deciphering enemy strategy. The professional work of intelligence agencies lags far behind the level required to draw the necessary strategic conclusions from intelligence work and thus organize intelligence itself appropriately.

We must be able to work with the information we have on the enemy, which will practically never be complete or reliable. Strategic intelligence provides information that is insufficient and late. The most important information is based more on omens and hunches than on hard facts. One plays out an operation in the dark. The advice given by the systems analysts that one should only take completely reliable information into account merely caused Clausewitz to laugh at this misunderstanding of the heart of the matter. This reliable information is available only on rare occasions, and then operational work becomes extremely simple.

Making a Decision

A strategic decision, for the most part, involves setting an intermediate goal that would be the shortest logical link on the way to the ultimate goal and at the same time would be appropriate for the resources available to achieve the goal. Military operations are not conducted with lyrics or declamations or reminiscences but with certain material resources. If the goal is not appropriate for the available material resources, the idea in our plan will turn into a "phrase" and will be expressed in the form of a futile shaking of fists, but we will not get an attack capable of hurting the enemy and leading us to an operational victory. For example, the offensive idea of the French Plan 17 in August 1914 was such a "phrase"; in the border battle of August 19-23 French strategy only shook its fists and placed the French armies in very grave danger.

A true strategist not only stands on the ground of reality but also puts down roots in it; this reality feeds his fantasy; and his creativity is only armed with material that actually exists. His desires and hopes are not suspended in a fourth dimension but grow from this reality.

The purpose of a planned operation should be completely clear; unclear formulations of the goal limited to an indication of direction and allowing for several interpretations should not be allowed because they will inevitably lead to hesitation in decisions during an operation with all the negative consequences of hesitant, infirm command.

The correct decision may be made only after mature reflection on the situation. Antole France once observed that he envied two professions that were free of the tortures of doubt—priests and soldiers. This view of the art of war as something which is straightforward and only requires decisiveness and certainty and an inborn temperament and perhaps a certain amount of cleverness but not the higher manifestations of the judgement capacities of a human being is an old hallowed tradition of delusion. The prevalent ideology in the recruit armies of the 18th Century did not permit any hesitation among military men. A military man had to give a quick answer to any question. Scharnhorst, who entered the Prussian service at the beginning of the 19th Century, complained that he could not get

---

[8] We will not be too cruel in our judgments of Frederick's military men or the Suvorov school: as late as the eve of the World War Bergson's philosophy, which glorified intuition and was quite skeptical of human reasoning capacity, prevailed in Paris, the universal center of civilization, at the Sorbonne: "reason dries out everything it touches with its icy touch; the real, the concrete and the living slip away from it; reason can only freeze it and impoverish it under the pretext of analysis."

thoughtful, conscientious answers from officers because everyone tried to answer as quickly as possible without delving into the heart of the matter. This was the result of the "I don't know which we had idealized in the person of Suvorov"[8] and which led to jesters' maxims. Viazemskii, in defending the work of Orlov, who was close to the Decembrists, stated that in general one cannot ask for higher achievements from a pen sharpened by a sword.[9] It has been claimed that any profound theoretician (such as Clausewitz) will prove to be weak in practice because he will not have enough information to make a decision and he will foresee all the possible negative consequences of any decision. People proclaimed the merits of blindness: Izmail could be taken by storm only at night, and at dawn our warriors, from the height of its walls, could only be surprised at how they had decided to clamber up such steep slopes.

In continuing this discussion we could have said that several of the most risky operations of the Civil War were successful thanks to the chiefs' ignorance of operational art, which permitted them to operate as if they were in the dark and did not notice the risk at which they had placed their troops. Of course this is not true. Before storming Izmail Suvorov set up training walls with the same profile and exercised his troops on them in the daytime before moving them out as night for the attack. The military knowledge acquired after the Civil War by commanders who had distinguished themselves in it will make it difficult for them to achieve new successes, but of course will require the expenditure of a great deal of moral efforts for completely conscientious decisions. In essence, excessive caution and a profound understanding of a matter requiring risk have nothing in common.

Dialectics acknowledges the radically contradictory requirements of the art of war.

Of course, being a theoretician is not enough to hold to a good decision. A philosopher may be a child in life, but one cannot approach strategic problems with childish thinking. Unshakable will is expressed not in holding to a direction that has been taken but in always keeping the ultimate goal in mind.

It is particularly dangerous when people of weak character want to seem dogged. Above we described how Moltke, under the influence of exaggerated information about the results of the border battle, decided to move troops from the French front to East Prussia early in the morning on August 25, 1914. On August 27 the corps in question, the guards reserve and 11th and 5th corps, were just assembling at the border stations. But information obtained on August 26 and 27 did not confirm the first news of a major victory in the border battle. From East Prussia came Ludendorff's first reports of success in the operation against Samsonov and that two or three Russian corps had already been routed and that a major victory was expected on the next day. Domes and Tapen, the general staff officers closest to Moltke, reported that it would be both desirable and possible to cancel the movement. But Moltke feared the bad impression that withdrawing the corps from the front and returning them would make and agreed only to cancel the movement of the 5th corps. In justifying his refusal, Moltke repeated certain

9   Gershenzon, *Istoriia molodoi Rossii* [The History of Young Russia], p. 22.

10   Reichsarchiv, *Der Weltkrieg*, vol. 1, pp. 604-609.

words: *ordre, contre-ordre, désorde* (order, countermand, disorder)[10]. The fate of the Marne had been decided.

Dialectics cannot be driven out of the realm of strategic thought because it is the essence of strategic thought. In order to avoid getting bogged down in details one must return as frequently as possible to the broadest points of view. A strategist must be prepared to cultivate his decisions in a fierce battle with doubt. The greatest danger is presented by a switch from boldness to halfheartedness, which is always characteristic of quick and energetic but immature decisions. Making impressions at meetings and impulsiveness are of no value to strategy at all.

Activity

Broad plans, like any castle in the air, do not require any material resources. However, a human cannot create anything, he is only capable of organizing and disciplining; therefore in order to achieve great results he must have a sufficient base and resources appropriate for the goal he has set. However, strategic thinking has not always been disciplined enough to agree with these modest claims. Professor Foch preached the absolute necessity of going on the offensive: the weaker we are, the more we need to go on the offensive; it is true that after he became the commander in chief of the Entente in 1918, in the first half of that year, when he had no superiority in numbers, he went on the defensive, and only in the second half, when he had great superiority in numbers, did he go on the offensive.

Quite often the mistakes observed in setting a goal that is inappropriate for the resources available to achieve it can be ascribed to false notions of activity. Defense was given the disrespectful epithet of "base" [*podlyi*]. All academic courses before the war glorified the merits of offense, activity and seizing the initiative.[11] However, true activity primarily lies in a sober look at the conditions of a war; one must see everything as it is and not construct a deceptive future for oneself. Initiative may be interpreted as a narrow concept defined solely by time; beating the enemy to the punch and seizing the initiative. In this case, we must agree with Clausewitz that all the advantages of initiative are limited to the gain provided by surprise, because surprise will follow from seizing the initiative; but

---

[11] The French were the most wholehearted proponents of this. In the thinking of Grandmaison, which lay at the heart of the castles in the air of French Deployment Plan 17, all these misconceptions were excessive, and the concepts got a different meaning. The human race is inclined to do this. Here is an observation that applies to the Peloponnesian War, which preceded the World War by 2,344 years, written by a contemporary: "Even words came to be used in a different sense than before and acquired a different meaning. Senseless courage came to be called martial ardor, reasonableness came to be called latent cowardice, and intelligence came to be called a cover for inaction, and a person who always tried to think before he acted was called a simpleton. Mad movements at full speed were understood as courage, while moderation was merely understood as noble pretext for inaction. People who cursed loudly were considered the most reliable and positive people and contradicting them made one a suspicious citizen. People who insisted on acting in an uncompromising manner were called traitors and scaremongers." *Fukidid* [Thucydides], vol. 3, p. 82; Meshchenko-Zhebelev's translation (Izd. Sabashnikovykh, 1915), p. 225, corrected by Ed. Schwarz, *Thucydides und sein Werk*. Hans Delbrueck, *Weltgeschichte*, vol. 1 (1924), p. 283. Only in a situation of this kind of psychology can we understand why General Michel, who had proposed preparing for a German turning maneuver through Belgium, was dismissed and replaced by Joffre.

in other respects initiative is just as unimportant in strategy as it is in a game. However, we can also make a more profound interpretation of preserving the initiative as the art of carrying out one's will in a struggle with the enemy. True initiative may involve compelling the enemy to attack in conditions that are unfavorable for him. Who truly has the initiative, the troops laying siege to a fortress or a garrison making a sortie? Tactical initiative undoubtedly belongs to the garrison, but operational initiative remains in the hands of the besiegers who have forced the garrison to make a sortie which could lead to a defeat and has no operational prospects whatsoever. In essence, Ludendorff's offensives on the Western front in 1918, which were compelled by the exhaustion of blockaded Germany and the anticipated arrival of American reinforcements, were these kinds of sorties.

Very prominent military men have committed grave errors in the name of preserving the initiative they have seized. The younger Moltke, in order to keep the initiative, did not stop the German armies by early September 1914 at the Ain River, no matter how desirable this seemed for many reasons, and kept them moving to the Marne River in operational conditions that had already been evaluated as poor, After his first two semisuccessful offensives in early 1918, Ludendorff did not stop and go on the defensive but started a "second Marne" in July 1918 in very poor strategic and operational conditions again in order "to preserve the initiative." However, neither the first nor the second Marne helped preserve it, the desire of the German command to retain the initiative led to a situation in which the French got all the advantages of a second hand and were able to demonstrate their activity in the most favorable possible conditions on both occasions. The mirage of destroying the enemy distorts all perspective and makes us forget about quite real disadvantages and stick our heads in a noose if only to preserve the initiative.

Not every movement forward is in essence a strategic offensive. Willisen and von der Goltz consider only an offensive that would threaten the capture of enemy communications (a wide turning maneuver or very deep breakthrough) a strategic offensive. On September 28, 1914, the 9th German army went on the offensive north of the Vistula from Upper Silesia in order to envelop the right flank of the Russian armies that had invaded Galicia. However, by October 4 Ludendorff had gotten the impression that the Russians were preparing to counter his envelopment with superior forces on the middle Vistula and would go on the offensive on the entire front from Warsaw to the mouth of the San River. The 9th German army continued to move forward even more quickly and on a wider front; however the purpose of this movement was not to attack the Russians but to occupy a good defensive position along the Vistula.

This kind of capture of a geographical position good for a defensive may rightly be considered an operational offensive. But from a strategic point of view, Ludendorff had already gone on the defensive by continuing to move forward to the Vistula because he had changed from the pursuit of a positive goal—attacking the Russians' right wing, to a negative goal—holding up the Russians' right wing as the Austrian offensive against the San River developed.

An offensive at any and all costs, as an a priori method of operation, leads to a situation in which our forces are dispersed where the enemy permits, activity degenerates into weakness, into an offensive "phrase", into a very dubious location of the front somewhere ahead and a return to the "starting position."

The High Command and Tactics

The nature of tactics is determined by the conditions that unfold in a battle. Regulations and instructions during a battle are laws only insofar as they meet the requirements of battle. However, it would be mistaken to conclude from this that the high command can just fold its arms and let tactics develop anarchically during a war.

The high command should above all be clearly conscious of the enemy's and its own tactics and their strong and weak points; this is necessary to understand the results of armed clashes and clarify the enemy's intentions and logic and understand the techniques of operational art; one of the basic tasks of command on the military front is to put our forces in a better tactical position, which is impossible without this. For example, in the Russo-Turkish War of 1877 a strong point of the Turks was their ability to build fortifications quickly and their dogged defense, while their weak point was their inability to maneuver or go on the offensive beyond a partial counterattack. From this strategists should have obviously concluded that instead of a frontal attack on the Plevna fortifications of Osman Pasha we should have made a daring maneuver against his communications, which would have forced the Turkish general to come out in the open and attack and maneuver.

But the high command cannot remain slavishly subordinate to the tactical reality that unfolds on the battlefield. The training and indoctrination of troops and their commanders, differences in equipment and different innovations and inventions also constitute an important art of military reality. If one is oriented to what is transpiring on the battlefield and tactical evolution, one can attempt to influence it. New divisions are organized and trained in the rear and a network of military schools operates to train junior commanders and improve the technical skills of men who have already served on the front lines. Every month the front receives 5 to 20 percent new replacements. Materiel burns up as quickly as people do on the front. The experience of the most artful tacticians must be evaluated and publicized for all the armed forces. Good, valuable conclusions are the work of a few minds, but everyone can take advantage of them. These tactical conclusions are only a part of the art of conducting military operations and should therefore be coordinated with strategic and operational requirements. In the World War this tactical work was not done independently by the Russian army: we used reworked and direct translations of French tactical experience, which came from a completely different operational situation, and these foreign translations confused the troops more than helped them.

Certain strategic requirements—the need to prepare for maneuver warfare or for defense in positional warfare, for a breakthrough or for a landing, the need for a firm defense in certain sectors without conceding any territory to the enemy, or the need to save manpower, conduct prolonged battles, particularly on extended fronts, and so forth—are the directives from which tactical training and the guidelines that regulate it should proceed. In peacetime the situation is not so clear, but French tactics proceed from very definite operational views which are apparently quite inapplicable to Russian conditions. In wartime tactics should completely reject encyclopedias and teach only those tactics required by strategy. Only the high command can judge the latter.

However, no matter how important the tactical requirements made by the high command are, we must refrain from putting tactical specialists in high positions because the basic activity of the high command is of a completely different nature.

Secrecy

Surprise, which is the backbone of offense, is, according to Clausewitz, an eagle that has two wings,—concealment and speed. Operational art and its preparations should guarantee the speed of the development of an operation, but neither the most careful operational concealment nor the extreme efforts of the troops will do any good if the enemy has managed to discover our intentions.

It is easiest of all to fathom the most important strategic secrets of countries where no distinction is made between truly secret information and secrets, which by their very nature, are common knowledge (such as two-kilometer topographical maps or service life or tactical information). In Austria before the World War everything was considered a secret, and all military secrets were sold for three rubles or a bit more. The Austrian general Krauss (the commandant of the military academy and chief of staff of a front during the war) said that in 1910, during a crisis in Austro-Serbian relations, he found out about a strategic deployment planned against Serbia from the conversations of officers in a Vienna street cafe. During the war even operational orders and reports did not mention the name of the town from which they were sent but simply said "halting point." Even now it is still difficult to understand the Austrian war archives! Major headquarters were given code names: the code name of the headquarters of the Balkan front was "Center-Prince," but what was the purpose of this secret, which was written on all the houses in the Serbian-populated city of Valievo, and how long would it take to figure it out? In order to avoid attracting attention they prohibited a commander and his chief of staff from coming to headquarters to clarify important misunderstandings, even though he had been ordered to prepare for a critical mission. All this gave rise to major frictions. At the same time, in making secret preparations for the spring attack of 1916 from the Tyrol, the Austrians changed the name of the "Territorial Defense Headquarters," the headquarters of a separate corps which was stationed in the Tyrol, to "11th Army Headquarters." And because this headquarters corresponded with many government agencies in Austria-Hungary, everyone's attention was immediately drawn to the forthcoming operation.[12]

The use of code names, such as the "Alberich works," "Siegfried line" or the "Mikhailovskii attack," as the German staffs did in preparing operation, is undoubtedly beneficial. However, these words should be chosen from words not used in ordinary military language (it would be best of all to use the names of Greek philosophers or mythical characters) to avoid causing misunderstandings. In no case should we allow our intentions to be encoded in smart-aleck in operational correspondence, because this can only lead to friction. An example is a directive to the Southwestern front dated July 23, 1920, in which a cavalry army

---

[12] Alfred Krauss, *Die Ursachen unserer Niederlage*, pp. 122, 141, 186.

[13] B. Shaposhnikov, *Na Visle*, pp. 92-93. Apparently Shaposhnikov's explanation cannot be considered exhaustive, therefore this fact requires further attentive study.

was instructed to protect itself from Lvov, concentrate its forces on a narrow front and operate in a certain direction without dispersing or blunting the force of the attack. According to B. Shaposhnikov's explanation,[13] the words "in a certain direction" meant "in the direction of Lublin," which the commanders of the front knew and which was encoding the intentions of our headquarters. As we know, the cavalry army did not go to Lublin on time, and if the order to send it there had not been given in such a tricky form but had been spelled out in black and white, it would have probably have had a somewhat greater effect.

Modern communications equipment is highly insecure. Documents dispatched by motor vehicles will fall into enemy hands much more frequently than documents carried by horsemen. A motor vehicle is limited to the roads, does not challenge the persons it encounters, can easily fall into an ambush and can get from our zone into the enemy's zone in a matter of minutes. Everyone knows how the Novogeorgievsk engineers carrying the plans of the fortress drove into the positions of the Germans who had come to attack the fortress. There were quite a few cases in which important orders dispatched by motor vehicle fell into enemy hands during the maneuver phase of the World War.

On August 24, 1914, the division cavalry of the 6th French corps captured a German vehicle with documents that revealed that on August 25 the 16th Prussian corps would attack the 6th French corps from a front at Otain, and that the attack would be supported by the 33rd Prussian reserve division, which after leaving Metz, would attack the 6th corps on its right flank. The commander of the 6th French corps, General Manoury, who had gotten such a detailed idea of the enemy's situations, prepared an echelon that would itself attack the flank of the 33rd Prussian Division as it maneuvered. This was a complete success: the Germans were repelled everywhere with heavy losses, and Manoury was appointed commander of the 6th Army for this victory.[14]

The radiotelegraph presents incomparably greater hazards. A nation that has spent the money to set up an institute with a staff of 100 can crack any code in 24 hours if there are enough lines in a message. This is where the Russians failed in 1914 and built up the reputations of the German generals.

On the morning of August 31, 1914, the Eiffel Tower received and decoded a German radio message: German cavalry would cross the Oise River at Bali and move to the railroad from Laon to Soissons in the direction of Vauxalon. This message was passed on to the commander of the 5th Army, General Lanrezac, who moved one brigade of the 38th division from the closest Valabreg group to the Vauxalon by rail, reinforced it with an artillery battalion, and sent Abono's cavalry division from the right flank of the army to help it through Cran-Vali.[15] Obviously the German cavalry did not succeed in its raid. As for the Russians, for the first six months of the war they fought in conditions that were known to the Germans.

We could cite several examples of the carelessness of German radiotelegraph. It almost destroyed the German operation of encircling the center of the 10th Russian army in the Augustow Forest by transmitting the German deployment, which was twice encoded but immediately picked up by the Eiffel Tower and

[14] Grouard, *La conduite de la guerre jusqu'à la bataille de la Marne*, p. 54.

[15] Lanrezac, *La plan de campagne française*, p. 252.

transmitted to Russian headquarters and the staff of the 10th Russian army. Only the total confusion of the command of this army got the Germans out of trouble. But the Russian radiotelegraph broke all the records in the World War. Careless, lazy staff officers are more dangerous than spies and turncoats: they eagerly turn to the radiotelegraph and blurt out very important secrets, sometimes without even encoding them. Our radiotelegraph made the Germans look brilliant. Our radiotelegraph gave the Germans not only all the positions of Samsonov's corps and their subsequent routes but also told them that Rennenkampf would not come to Samsonov's aid and that their hands were untied.[16]

Strategic information is often given out by the bad habit of junior officers of duplicating all the information contained in the instructions of higher echelons in their own orders. In the battle of Groitsa on October 9, 1914, the Germans captured an order from a Russian officer that described a maneuver to deploy 30 Russian corps on the Vistula from Warsaw to the mouth of the San. This information should not even been given in an order to an army and should never have been on a line officer going into battle. Suvorov's idea that every warrior should understand his maneuver has been distorted. Corps commanders may still be orally informed of general missions in a theater, but these missions should not be publicized more widely. A soldier's maneuver includes only a very small part of an operation and should be explained within its framework.

The Poles made the same mistake in an order for the 3rd Polish army dated August 8, 1920, in which they indicated that they planned to complete the concentration of a new Polish army in the area of Lublin for the purpose of eliminating the Russians in the north nine days later, on August 17. These very important principles of the operation planned for the Vistula were publicized in the army order in order to explain the mission assigned to the 3rd Army: delay the Russians advancing toward the Weprz River in order to provide security for this new army's concentration. This order was captured in Wlodaw by the 12th Army and was known to our headquarters on August 10,[17] and if there had not been so much friction in command, we would have been able to prepare to counter the Polish attack or simply avoid it before it started.

Communiques for the Press

One important function of strategic leadership is to provide daily press communiques concerning events in the theater of operations. Given the great interest of the public involved in a war, attempts to keep silent about important events that have transpired leads to the spread of rumors and wild suggestions. One aspect of keeping the rear functioning smoothly is to provide it with correct information. The Austrians, who did not provide any information to the press in the first days on the war, soon felt all the inconveniences of the situation they had created.

---

[16] An order for the 1st Army that was transmitted unencoded to the 4th Russian corps on the morning of August 25. Reichsarchiv, *Der Weltkrieg, 1914-1918*, vol. 2, pp. 136, 170. After receiving this telegram, Hindenburg renounced his original intention of leaving the 17th Prussian corps to face Rennenkampf and moved it against Samsonov's right wing. Only the 1st cavalry division was left to face Rennenkampf.

[17] B. Shaposhnikov, *Na Visle*, pp. 80, 81, 96, 101.

Press communiques should be absolutely believable; the rear has many ties to the front and will soon get an idea of distortions of the truth in bulletins, and the confidence placed in the high command which it needs to accomplish its difficult mission will primarily suffer.

Distorting war events in our favor also poses the great danger of concealing from the public the difficulties that must be overcome and lowering the intensity of the efforts which must be made to achieve the aims of the war. In addition, the events reported by headquarters do have a future. Events must have a logic, and if our troops are winning everywhere, but as a result the front stays in the same place or even moves backward, we can only arrive at conclusions that are unfortunate for the high command.

But of course communiques should not spread panic or despair and should never mention our proposals or publicize the preparations for new operations.

The communiques of the warring sides are reprinted and commented on by the press all over the world. The high command must keep this in mind, because communiques play an important role on the political and economic fronts; in the "current moment" of agitation in speeches and articles this information is at the forefront. Nevertheless, we must refrain from crude propaganda in the text of communiques.

Communiques play an important role in keeping the public interested in the war and should therefore be written in a good literary style and provide interesting subjects for the military commentators of newspapers and magazines and not merely contain dry information on several remote settlements unknown to the public that have been lost or captured by us.

At the same time communiques must sometimes remove the veil of anonymity and secrecy covering the actions of troops and certain commanders. When an operation has already unfolded and is coming to an end, the enemy will manage to get an idea of most of the units operating against him. Describing the feats of certain divisions and regiments and mentioning the names of outstanding leaders is the best reward the high command can give to heroic units and their commanders, and this reward will also constitute a very important incentive for others to maximize their efforts.

In general, anonymity is inappropriate for battle. A feat must be recognized immediately as such rather than be the subject of subsequent evenings of reminiscences. Hence in addition to its evaluation the high command should organize the extensive publication of war correspondence, reports, photographs, etc. In many cases a description of a battle published two weeks later is no longer a military secret. Only the high command is competent to recognize the absence of a military secret in a description, and only it can break through the obstacles of military censorship. Military censorship is necessary, but a bureaucratic attitude toward it reduces the public's interest in the war and, by making the army's actions anonymous, makes the lazy more impudent and lowers the ardor of the best people.

Orienting the Operation of the Rear

The high command is the director of the colossal efforts that must be made to adapt to the requirements of a war, which are always new. It is most probable that even the best trained army will not always have the staff it needs. It is impossible to adjust the requirements of war to the existing staff and regulations, and the latter must be changed to fit the situation. In the process the activity of command should be aimed not only at new staff development, as was the case in the Russian army in the World War, but must immediately proceed to reduce agencies that have proven to be idle; otherwise the ratio of noncombatants to combatants will go through the ceiling. For example, positional warfare requires many new formations, but at the same time it makes it possible to reduce significantly the number of transports and agencies that are needed only for a deep offensive in enemy territory; if this reduction is not made, the war will become much more costly, and the rear will probably be hit by a food and manpower crisis.

Economic mobilization may be prepared in very general terms in peacetime, and the program for economic mobilization may concern only the first phase of the war. Only war will indicate what war needs. The high command must transmit the industrial quota program it wants and indicate the times at which these quotas must be met. This program must be coordinated with the command's strategic proposals. The ratio of heavy to light artillery, the attention given to tanks and the demand for wire to construct many fences between the Baltic and the Black Seas are to a great extent determined only by the offensive or defensive intentions of strategy. The number of yards of overcoat cloth follows from the number of age groups to be drafted, while delivery time is determined by the anticipated sequence of drafts. The percentage of urban buildings that must be turned into hospitals depends on whether the front is calm or stormy. The network of military schools that provide short-term and inadequate training must regulate their training plan in accordance with the number of replacement commanders required every month.

A great deal of effort is wasted even when the war is organized. This organization can be improved, extra mouths can be eliminated and all heads and muscles can be utilized only by establishing close contact between the conduct of military operations and the work of the entire nation. In regulating the course of military operations, the strategist must report to the supreme leadership of the base the efforts and equipment the situation on the military front requires as information which depends on the base. A strategist's work is the work of a customer who does not control production but orients it. The integral leadership of the war makes the final decision.

2. METHODS OF COMMAND

The Order and the Directive

A commander may indicate his decision to his subordinates either in the categorical form of a battle order, which indicates the situation in which it will be carried, out or in the form of a directive limited to a statement of the goals of operations for the next few days, which provides the executor with a great deal of freedom in choosing methods of achieving them.

Sometimes instead of *direktiva* [directive] the Russian word *nastavlenie* [direction] is used, but it has a different meaning. A *nastavlenie* consists of relatively binding guidelines and advice, which often goes into detail; depending on the situation, the executor of an order can and even should ignore this advice. A directive should not be confused with a *nastavlenie*. A directive's brief indications of a goal should never be semiobligatory. The use of directives as a means of command is possible only when the commander to whom the directive is given has been indoctrinated not to abuse this freedom of action and will actually pursue the goal indicated in it; command of directives cannot be used where it is possible to assume that a subordinate commander is merely looking for an excuse to pursue his own special private goals and get away from the common goal.

Command by directives offers great advantages but also poses great dangers if the commanders are unsuitable. We believe that the most important requirement that should be made in selecting high commanders, starting with a corps commander, is the appointment of persons who could be commanded by indicating goals and not regulating all their actions with hard and fast orders. From the perspective of strategy, the most important test would be a judgment as to whether a given person is capable of pursuing a certain goal or is only capable of carrying out separate orders.

As we know, Napoleon preferred to command by orders, whereas Moltke preferred to command by directives. The conditions of the time and place at which an order is given have a decisive effect on preferences for one or the other. There is a wide gap between Napoleon's command in the battle at Jena in 1806 and Moltke's command in the battle of Gravelot and St.-Privat in 1870. Napoleon spent the night before the battle with his troops; his tent was pitched inside the carré of a regiment to which he wanted to give special attention; Napoleon could give orders at the last minute after taking into account all reconnaissance data received by dawn. The main quarters of the Prussian king and Moltke at Metz were located at Pont-à-Mousson, 30 kilometers from the battlefield. On August 16 the battle at Mars-la-Tour took place. On the morning of August 17 the Prussian king and Moltke arrived at an observation post on a height near Flavini. The troops were just assembling. The battle would take place on the next day. At 2:00 P.M. on August 17 Moltke issued a disposition for August 18, and then he and the Prussian king went back 30 kilometers. They had to rest and prepare for a difficult day ahead. Moltke gave exemplary orders, but 12 hours before Napoleon did. Of course he was less informed and his order were less exact; there were variations, no matter how undesirable they were: if the enemy stays at Metz, do one thing, and if he tries to withdraw along the Belgian border, do another thing.[1]

Of course today, despite the telegraph, orders have to be given even earlier than in Moltke's time. However, we must do everything we can to combat the development of variations in operational orders. One should not pile up operational plans on staffs. It is extremely important to choose the right minute to give an order: not too early when it cannot be accurate enough, and not too late when even the best ideas are condemned to futility. One cannot overestimate the importance of choosing the right moment to give an order; Napoleon was the master of this art: he always pondered several variations, but never shared his ideas with anyone, and at the appropriate minute with lightning speed he proceeded to carry out one of them.

Directives decentralize commands to a great extent; this will do no harm if there are no centrifugal tendencies in a high command and if there is a general staff which has been indoctrinated to understand the art of war in the same way and is prepared to do battle against parochial interests everywhere.

Like his uncle, the younger Moltke commanded by directives, and his setback on the Marne did a great deal to discredit this method of command. However, Moltke's mistake did not lie in the fact that his guidelines were too general for the army commanders but in the fact that he refrained from stating his opinion on a very important issue that had led to sharp disagreements among the army commanders, particularly Kluck and Buelow. A military leader cannot hold back in a crisis on the front; a directive should in no way be a form of silence or avoiding responsibility.

Positional warfare allows for much greater centralization of command than does maneuver warfare. Hence it is not surprising that as a result of the four-year *sitzkrieg* there was a definite trend in favor of command by order, which before the war seemed to be a completely obsolete method of strategic or even operational leadership. This trend is most vividly evident in Ludendorff's style of command. An order involves intervening in the work of a subordinate commander and correcting any errors he makes in execution. In the morning Ludendorff loved to talk on the telephone to the fronts and all the chiefs of staff of the armies. This style of command expands the competence of headquarters and undermines the authority and importance of subordinate commanders. It is remarkable that not one German general distinguished himself on the French front in 1917 and 1918 because Ludendorff simply made all of them his flunkies.

The situation was different on the Russian front. Russian headquarters was too delicate with the authority of subordinate commanders and did not want to undermine it by acting like a school teacher correcting the errors of her pupils. The mistaken direction of Rennenkampf's movement to Koenigsberg was observed by headquarters for two days and led to perplexity, but Quartermaster General Yu. Danilov, who was in charge of Russian strategy, was hesitant to correct him; "the one on the spot knows better," Suvorov said; but when headquarters spoke out it was too late, and Samsonov's army had perished. Given the egotistical centrifugal interests of the Southwestern and Northwestern fronts, one of which was waging an Austrian war, the other, a German war, while no one was waging the World

---

[1] There is a splendid analysis of this issue in Fritz Hoenig, *24 Stunden Moltkescher Strategie am 18 August 1870*, 3rd edition (Leipzig: 1897).

War, the excessively mild[2] directives from headquarters encouraged the development of anarchic leaders who recognized no one's authority rather than strong and independent leaders.

Of course, there are times when the intervention of the high command in operational and tactical details is absolutely necessary. In August 1870 in the movement of the 1st and and 2nd Prussian armies in a very narrow front (two corps on one road) toward the Saar River, and given the numerous frictions at the junction of these two armies, Moltke himself had to interfere in the organizaiton of the march of both armies. In the World War, in August 1914 the entire vast 1st German army had only three roads at its disposal which converged at the city of Aachen. Troop traffic had to be controlled on the narrow streets of this city, and a special traffic officer had to be appointed so that troop traffic could keep moving for four days and nights, so troops could receive their supplies, which had been cut off by the city's cramped conditions, and so forth. Of course, the army staff had to interfere in questions ordinarily handled by a division or corps commander.[3]

When confronted with disobedience on the front the elder Moltke immediately switched to orders which began, "I hereby order..," and were signed by the Prussian king. When we look at the history of the wars of 1866 and 1870 and encounter such rare orders, we can be sure that Moltke had to overcome some kind of internal enemy who had ignored the authority of his directives (e.g., Vogel von Falkenstein, Steinmetz).

As a result the feverish manifestation of private initiative and the lack of authority on the part of headquarters, the Civil War of 1918-1920 had the same tendency toward centralization of command and orders as the positional period of the World War. The lack of authority was evident in the fact that as late as 1920 headquarters had to send rough drafts of its directives to the fronts, and only after agreements had been made with the fronts could the directives be finalized. Specialists consulted and gave advice in their directives, which lost the will they needed, and the subordination of one directive began only when the will of another came to the forefront.[4]

Station-to-station calls became quite common in the command of the Russian headquarters in both the World War and the Civil War. Telegrams between staffs to correct misunderstandings are a normal occurrence. But conversations between military leaders and senior operational commanders are completely different. Debates between chiefs and subordinates and the desire of a senior officer to persuade his junior or vice versa seem completely inappropriate. Any explana-

---

[2] This mildness was due to an organizational defect. The supreme commander in chief, Nikolai Nikolaevich, had never studied strategy at all, just like his chief of staff General Yanushkevich. Regarding Yu. Danilov's strategic efforts, he affected a posture of neutrality, which for the most part was approving. But the authority of Danilov, who had much less seniority than the chiefs of staff of the fronts, was insufficient. If an argument started and had to be settled from up top, Nikolai Nikolaevich systematically avoided doing this and suggested making compromises with the fronts.

[3] Hans Kuhl, *Germanskii general'nyi shtab* [The German General Staff], pp. 201-202.

[4] A very important and wise directive from the commander in chief dated August 11 (No. 4738) concerning the movement of the Southwestern front in the direction of Lublin (which had to begin immediately) ended with the sentence: "I request your conclusion concerning the above." This gave no hint of will at all. Quoted from B. Shaposhnikov, *Na Visle*, pp. 96, 97, 101, 102.

tions, cautions, advice, ideas or requests can only undermine the effectiveness of a directive or order. Only a very authoritative commander can attempt to focus the energy and courage of a subordinate by a conversation. In general, the authority of command will gain if a subordinate sends his reports by telegraph and if his superior transmits his agreement or disagreement and satisfaction or dissatisfaction in a reply written up in the imperative form of an order. It does not take much time to edit a telegraph reply accurately, carefully and firmly.

However, in the final analysis, circumstances dictate that command is a matter for tact and an understanding of human psychology. Some subordinates need and deserve freedom, while others need to be led on a tight leash, while still others, who may be great and necessary people, will fly off the handle and have to be persuaded. True organization begins when there are no expendable people, and true command begins when one can take care of any rebellion in two or three hours when there are no sympathizers but there is discipline.

People are very obstinate, but among the most obstinate are great military leaders. The authoritativeness of the high command makes it much easier to employ them. The younger Moltke and Falkenhayn in particular were not authoritative enough in the German army, and Germany had to pay a high price for this.

In organizing the Red Army the authority of different echelons is determined by the choice of both commanders and political officers. Great damage will be done to the authority of a higher echelon if a high authoritative political officer is assigned to a subordinate revolutionary military council of a front or army.

As we know, people sometimes write orders to relieve themselves of responsibility. This terrible form of command reduces any authority the person signing the order may have, and it gives evidence of the disintegration of command, civic cowardice and the betrayal of national interests to save one's own skin. We know of such orders from the experience of imperialist warfare.

Excessive orders and directives undermine the attention they command and their force. Three directives were sent to the Southwestern command on August 11 and 12, 1920 (Nos. 4738, 4752 and 4766[5]). The last directive arrived first, and none of them were carried out. In command a strategist must avoid rhetorical repetition. The ability to issue a directive many days in advance without immediately having to change or supplement it is a hallmark of strategic maturity.

Orders have to be considered detonators of the energy available on a military front; as we know, a slab of gun cotton lit by a match will burn calmly, but a slab of gun cotton ignited by a capsule of mercury fulminate will produce an energetic explosion; the ability to be detonated in different ways is as characteristic of troops as it is of all explosives. One kind of order will lead to indifferent execution, while another kind will lead to an energetic burst of enthusiasm. We cannot establish general rules because conditions and personalities require a particular kind of detonation in every case.

Private Initiative
It is clear that partisan tendencies, which still had not died down in 1920, had to have led to a tendency toward categorical battle orders in the Red Army as a reaction. However, medicine sometimes does more harm to the body than the

---

[5]   Ibid., p. 97.

disease it is designed to cure. Halfhearted, bureaucratic execution of orders, which minimizes the useful work of the army on a military front, is the most dangerous of all. In many respects the Red Army owes its success in the Civil War to a powerful and fierce burst of private initiative; the problem lies in disciplining private initiative rather than uprooting the conditions for its manifestation.

When a revolution starts, there is no need to worry about private initiative because it is everywhere. But in normal conditions, when there is no particular revolutionary enthusiasm, initiative is a very fragile phenomenon which must be carefully cultivated. The great bureaucratic toy soldier of all time, Prussia in 1806, was so easily defeated by the Jena operation alone simply because it was incapable of demonstrating any initiative; Stein's reform was aimed at encouraging initiative in the country. His circular of 1807 proclaimed:

> Officials must no longer be dumb mechanical tools in the hands of the monarch or machines which simply carry out orders and never put their will or own point of view into their work. I demand that from now on they should solve problems on their own and take personal initiative in the matter. I will not give them detailed instruction and forbid them to appeal to the central government for advice. I will punish the incapable and halfhearted and I will award the courageous and artful.

Initiative in the army can only exist on the basis of extensive initiative in civilian society. It requires a patient and forgiving attitude toward certain unsuccessful manifestations; field service regulations must be concerned with it,[6] and it requires that all command be adapted to the possibilities of manifesting it, and it requires directives rather than orders.

Discord in the means of achieving a goal does not harm the cause. But a terrible evil is done by attacking the goal set by a superior; we must comprehensively combat this phenomenon, which leads to the most evil anarchy in command. Because the old theory always gave the choice of means to the commander assigned the mission, then "the right of suggestion" that appeared under the flag of a liberal conclusion from the experience of the World War has apparently led to the right of subordinates to suggest a common goal of action to the superior; this inference could only have been the fruit an amazing deception. All goals can only be set from above, since they must stem from a comparatively broader political and military view. Suggesting goals on the basis of private initiative defeats any kind of organization; the very idea of such an order could turn any thinking military man into an enemy of any initiative or directive.

---

[6] Field regulations are often more reminiscent of the Joker than Stein. The regulations of the Bourbon restoration provide an example of the desire to suppress initiative. n order introducing the French field service regulations in 1818 announced that "His Majesty, confident that his service will gain if his troops are subject to a uniform discipline and regime established in regulations, that regulations should foresee and govern all details and make it impossible for anything to be decided arbitrarily or remain uncertain, and that officers who have been transferred from one unit to another should not find any difference in unit administration, confirms these regulations." The ideology that tries to keep anything from being decided arbitrarily or remaining uncertain is still with us today.

Tact and psychology are also required for initiative; dilettantes, people striving for personal success rather than the success of the common cause, people who lack an understanding of their moral responsibility and adventurers should usually be reined in; reliable and dedicated people whose thinking and behavior are well known to the strategist should be given all possible opportunities to develop.

Measures of Real Influence

The high command has several ways of affecting the course of military events besides the orders it sends to its subordinates.

Strategic and operational reserves are the basic means of affecting military events. The possibility of adding new forces in the hands of a high command makes its orders much more authoritative. Russian headquarters experienced such improvements in the authority of command when it had the divisions left on the Baltic and Black Sea coasts at its disposal or when the Asiatic corps became available. German headquarters gained new strategic capital with new echelons of mobilization. The twilight of the gods begins when the rear ceases to bear reserves. We must know how to scavenge troops from the fronts and the armies—not excess troops, but troops without which we could get by temporarily. This involves major frictions. Field service regulations which have prepared our thinking by establishing broad normal fronts for a defense may make this difficult task easier for the high command.

In Russia the superiority of local interests over national interests often made regroupings insignificant during the World War; it is clear that the high command, in trying to get troops for their reserves, primarily turned to units in the reserves of a front or army so that the front could recreate its own reserve by withdrawing some of the divisions in contact with the enemy to the rear. Hence several commanders who were fond of their own best corps tried to keep them by having them occupy sectors of a positional front, while the weakest units were kept behind where they were accessible to the high command. Whereas the Germans classified their divisions as positional (not so good) and assault (better) and concentrated them in the rear, we acted in the opposite way and often conducted regroupings using the least combat-ready units, to whom even the most critical missions were assigned.

In addition to reserves in the form of organized military units, there are other national reserves in the thousands of graduates of accelerated course of command, the hundreds of thousands of reservists for replacements and stockpiles of weapons, food, clothing and vehicles. Regulating the allocation of materiel and replacements also increases the authority of the high command, and at the same time only the high command is capable of making the most rational use of the nation's limited material resources in accordance with the goal pursued. All of this was very poorly understood at the beginning of the World War; with respect to field command in 1914 Russian headquarters was completely divorced from handling replacements and materiel, and every front had its own independent rear and asked the minister of war for everything it needed on its own. The strategic leadership of the Russian headquarters had no material base, which made it quite weak. On the other hand, two fronts were consumers and competitors, and were not so much interested in the economical expenditure of national resources at the front as they were in getting the most valuable and rare items of supply from the ministry of war to their own depots as quickly as possible. The first ordnance crisis in the second month of the war was apparently the result of this unhealthy competition.

Of course, the high command needs to have full disposal of the materiel provided by the rear not only to emphasize the dependence of the fronts on it. The high command must hold the point of view that military actions on the front are only a derivative of the condition of the two bases on which the armed forces of both sides operate, and that consequently the leadership of military actions above all should be based on full competence in the disposal of the resources provided by the base without which the representation of its interests is impossible.

We also classify changing the boundaries between fronts and armies as another means. In fact, sometimes it is almost impossible to remove troops from one echelon. But this may be achieved by reducing the sector of the neighbor and assigning responsibility for a broader sector to a front or army which has hidden sources of strength. The weak command of Russian headquarters was often compelled to resort to this method of command. In October 1914 headquarters was unable to get a reserve from the fronts to defend Warsaw and attack the Germans there but after transferring Warsaw to the responsibility of one front and then another, headquarters forced them to move all the free forces at their disposal in the direction of Warsaw. The disadvantages of this method include the radical change in the established network of communications and the disruption of operational relations and the radical change in the stress and direction of the activities of the rear. This is how a weakwilled command with few reserves commands; it results in a reduction in the useful work of the military system and should be avoided unless absolutely necessary.

Ultimately we need control. A commander who has given an order is obligated to monitor its execution; observation of execution makes an order specific and gives it true force. Although high command posts are occupied by the most responsible and deserving men, an order there should not become a word cast into the wind; one must make sure that an order has reached its destination, has been understood and has been carried out. Replacing a directive with an order indicating what must be done in the next day or two is only one constrictive kind of control. Requiring copies of all the most important operational orders of subordinate echelons is a normal kind of strategic control. Interesting information is often provided by official enemy communiques on the war because they invariably mention the enemy's capture of prisoners, guns and trophies, whereas our reports often try to keep enemy events quiet. Interrogations and investigations are now permissible only in exceptional cases (e.g., the interrogation of General Panteleev after the Samsonov disaster) because the invasion of formal legalism into strategic and operational issues reduces the love for responsibility which is extremely valuable for all participants in a war. Forms of control should not disrupt the atmosphere of trust that is necessary for successful strategic work.

The Harmony of Organization

The division of land forces operating in a single theater into partial armies which were previously encountered only in coalition wars was successfully applied by Moltke in 1866 and has since become quite common. In the strategic deployment of 1914 an even newer echelon of operational leadership apeared in the Russian forces—the front. The absence of this echelon when the Germans invaded France led to significant command difficulties. During the World War front command as an organized echelon became quite common. We also encountered it throughout the entire Civil War.

The reality of the front over six years (1914-1920) raises some doubts; its short history is not fraught with organizational achievements. In Russia the first year of maneuver warfare involved endless frictions between two fronts, while in the positional war we had three fronts whose actions we simply could not coordinate. Ludendorff also complained about the difficulties of command this organizational innovation created for him in France in 1917 and 1918. Fronts were undoubtedly appropriate in the Civil War as long as each combined its efforts in a separate theater against a separate enemy (the Northern, Eastern and Southern fronts). But when it came time to coordinate the operations of two fronts against a common enemy (the Poles), we were unsuccessful.[7] Every front had more weight and inertia than the high command could overcome; tying their efforts to a single operational goal was a difficult task, that was better avoided after having attempted at the last minute to transfer two armies of the Southwestern front, which had operated against the Poles, to the Western front, which was weighted down with its own five armies (including the Mozyr group). Incidentally, the Red Army had no corps echelon in the Civil War because it was considered an extra echelon of operational command.

Every extra echelon is an unconditional evil. The development of the front echelon can be ascribed to the impossibility of organizing separate rears for the large numbers of armies. When armies are no larger than a million soldiers and there is a only one enemy, all we need is one front. Its headquarters will in essence exercise operational command over all active forces subordinate to the commander in chief, who stays in the capital and simultaneously functions as the minister of war. And if there are secondary enemies in addition to the main enemy, it would be better to organize separate armies against them and do without a front echelon.

Clausewitz observed that every echelon should have at least three organizational units subordinate to it; when there are two subordinate echelons tactical and operational leadership get extremely complicated. Russian headquarters fully experienced this in 1914. Division into two fronts was unacceptable, because it constituted a very severe attack on the authority of the high command. If there was a persistent need to divide into fronts, then we should have had three, because two halves would have naturally fallen apart, since Vienna, Berlin, Lvov and

---

[7]   Strictly speaking, there were not two fronts operating against the Poles in 1920 but one and a half, because the Southwestern front was operating simultaneously in Volynia against the Poles and against Wrangel, who had left the Crimea. The Southwestern front had to operate in a situation in which it was chasing two rabbits at the same time. Of course, one front command cannot handle two theaters, or in this case, two wars. This is the job of the high command. We should have created completely different echelons and divided the Southwestern front into two parts. Given the small numbers involved in 1920, it would probably have been better to get by with no front organization and have two separate armies. But in 1920 we probably should have called these organizations fronts in order to give them authority. In terms of numbers, the armies of the Civil War era were essentially corps.

Warsaw as goals for the fronts were too diverse. The German offensive against the Russians in the spring of 1915 was begun by Mackensen's group (the 11th German and 4th Austrian armies) and the Hindenburg-Ludendorff front (the 8th, 9th, 10th and Neman armies, the Galwitz group and then the 12th army). The Woyrsch group and the Southern army were subordinate to Austro-Hungarian command. Thus Falkenhayn had settled up with the Austrian command and had two subordinate echelons, namely Mackensen and Hindenburg and Ludendorff; the latter included five armies; in these conditions command had to suffer the same desperate debate as the command of two fronts of the Russian headquarter, because Hindenburg's popularity and the aura of his achievements made it possible for Ludendorff to be as stubborn as possible. As a result, Falkenhayn was forced to form a third front to engender better conditions by taking away the 9th Army from Ludendorff, which was on the left bank of the Vistula opposite Warsaw, and attaching it to the Woyrsch group. In order to be manageable, a part should be in a certain proportion to the whole. Otherwise there will be too many strong jolts. Ludendorff's operational competence had to be reduced in order to dictate one's will to him. The nature of Falkenhayn's action is clearly evident from the fact that the new front of Leopold of Bavaria Front, was dependent on Ludendorff for supplies.[8]

In order to lighten fronts and make them easier to command from above, their rear borders should not be made too wide and one must avoid creating satrapies. The German-occupied general-governorship of Warsaw was taken out of the hands of the front; as the Germans on our front said, Ludendorff had been deprived of the kingdom of Poland and had to be satisfied with the grand principality of Lithuania.

Friction

Any organizational shortcoming increases friction in the conduct of military operations, that is, the amount of efforts unproductively expended by the troops and the command on overcoming internal rough spots. To reduce these unproductive expenses, commanders are above all obligated to study their subordinate commanders and their views on the art of war, their temperaments and the troops subordinate to them and their skills. A report indicating a difficult situation should be understood in completely different ways, depending on whether it was signed by a man who military men would characterize as a "panic monger," a stable warrior dedicated to the common cause or an experienced, brave, but cautious commander who has only local interests at heart and is egotistically trying to obtain part of the common reserve. All of these commanders must be talked to in a particular language. Individuality in command lies in the fact that every word has it weight. When the command has stabilized and people have become familiar with one another, problems of command will be resolved more smoothly and many rough spots will completely disappear. On the other hand, a change in command will lead to a new painful period of adjustment. Now high military commanders are killed not by bullets, as was the case in the 17th century, but by defeats, which makes it necessary to relieve them; every commander who achieves the relief of an enemy commander by his successes can take credit for it. This is a trophy of victory.

---

[8]   Ludendorff, *Moi vospominaniia o voine 1914-1918 gg.*, vol. 1, p. 124.

At the beginning of a war, friction is particularly great: the troops are in an unfamiliar campaign situation; commanders have not fully grasped their roles; hastily organized staffs have not yet coordinated the division of labor; logistical commands have only begun to look around; and the entire military machine is squeaky, expending a great deal of effort internally to smooth out the rough spots. The war began in an atmosphere of this friction and the Samsonov disaster struck like lightning. A month after the war began, despite the weakening of the cadre due to casualties, this disaster would have been practically impossible or would have required a great deal of additional effort from the enemy and an extra week of time: the commanders and troops would have had the skills they needed.

Frictions among territorial units in the difficult conditions of maneuver warfare will be great and require more time to disappear, but the frictions among subsequent echelons of mobilization will be particularly hazardous if a sufficient number of select commanders from the active forces is not appointed to the new formations and pass on a valuable part of their experience to them. But friction is both a child's and an old man's disease.

Friction grows with a reduction in the authority of the high command, and setbacks undermine this authority; one could imagine an unfortunate course of events when everyone in an army begins to argue with the orders they have been given, and a change in command, no matter how undesirable it is, is the only way of saving the command from disintegration. But at the root of insufficient authority is not only battlefield luck or misfortune: Authority is connected with personality, the degree of respect for it, its past, the complete agreement between words and deeds, heroic feats of petty careerism, and respect for firmness of will, the profundity of knowledge, and integrity.

To overcome friction the high command must be carefully selected; it should be well organized and have its own intelligence agency and not solely rely on the intelligence of subordinate echelons. Finally, it must be on top of tactical and technical requirements and know how to make contact with the troops.

Local interests, which oppose egotistical requirements to the needs of the whole, are a particularly malignant source of friction. Strategic particularism can be uprooted only with an extremely high level of national enthusiasm and a very authoritative command.

APPENDIX 1

Editor's note: The following review appeared in the main journal of the Red Army's General Staff, *Voina i revoliutsiia* [War and Revolution], no. 5 (May 1927), pp. 182-186.

CRITIQUE AND BIBLIOGRAPHY
by A. Vol'pe
A. Svechin, *Strategiia* [Strategy], 2nd edition
(Moscow: Voennyi vestnik, 1927), 263 pp. 5,000 copies printed.

The mere fact that a second edition of this book became a necessity one year after the first one appeared in print is, under the existing conditions of the overproduction of books, vivid testimony to its high acclaim on the part of its readers, both military and civilian. Indeed, this came as no surprise.

However, it was Nietzsche who said that any book may be either good or bad depending on who reads it, when and how. And for many people *Strategy* by Professor Svechin, despite its obvious merits, might as well be dangerous, imbued as it is with grains of bitter skepticism.

Recent military experience is vast and complex, contradictory and unexplored. Conclusions based upon it may be incomplete and erroneous. At the same time Professor Svechin is unwilling to be bound by any ready-made conclusions or conventional rules. Breaking down old principles, he does not come up with new ones. All he provides is food for thought, while in military matters one has to deal with decisions which are always related to specific issues.

Strategy by A. Svechin is dangerous because it is abstract. But no one is in a position to dictate the form of a written work to a man of letters who is free in his artistic endeavor, is loaded with facts, possesses an exquisite style and has a wonderful command of words. But Professor Svechin could not maintain his approach throughout the book, and its new edition shows that the author has come a long way since the times when he vehemently denied the possibility of creating a positive course of strategy, which in fact he did himself as all the issues raised in his book are begging for conclusions.

Lack of an established system of views is a specific feature of our military-related writings as we find ourselves in the process of continuous growth. Many authors writing about tactics and strategy as the main areas of military art discard their own old ideas quite easily in subsequent editions of their books. If one compares the latest editions of *Taktika* [Tactics] by Verkhovskii and Morozov, *Pekhota* [Infantry] by Lignau, *Istoriia voennogo iskusstva* [The History of Military Art] by Svechin with the first editions of the same books, the difference in terms of both form and content would be striking. There are two main reasons for this:

first, authors are driven by the desire to widen the scope of their books and to update them with fresh information, and second, public opinion and critics compel them to revise their works according to the needs of students in the field and the reading public. *Strategy* by Svechin seems to have taken a similar direction.

The book is not replete with amendments as compared to its first edition. However, they relate to major issues that change the very concept of the book dramatically. The time has come for Professor Svechin to make concessions.

We shall begin with the main issue—the strategies of "attrition" and "destruction."

Professor Svechin considers these notions as categories underlying the very essence of military art. In his theory he gives the same treatment to the notions of "positional warfare" and "maneuver warfare," "offense" and "defense."

In his work Professor Svechin provided a positive description of the strategy of "attrition," while the definition of "destruction" is given in a very superfluous manner, as if only for the sake of argument and comparison. In this respect his work appears to be a precise and finished piece. However, this is achieved mainly by artificial means.

It was comrade Toporkov who first drew attention to the lack of "polarity" between the definitions of destruction and attrition. Indeed, in the first edition of *Strategy* destruction is described as a brutal and straightforward attempt to destroy the enemy by a "knock-out blow," while attrition is not viewed as a strategy opposed to destruction. The first edition contains the following very important passage:

> However, we deem it necessary not to throw the theory of destruction into the dustbin of history; we refer to it in this book not only for the sake of dialectically describing the opposing theory of attrition. We admit the possibility of using under modern conditions the strategy of destruction; indeed, the enemy whose territory can be traversed by foot from one border to another within a week should be destroyed by such a strategy; but even with regard to a larger country which is in a state of political disarray destruction is the most viable form of strategy.[1]

In the second edition this paragraph has been omitted. The opposing elements of the two strategies seems to have emerged more clearly, but there remains a suggestion that the strategy of attrition encompasses the whole range of strategic methods other than destruction.

> One kind of attrition is very close to a strategy of destruction, which even made it possible for the Prussian general staff to state, albeit unjustifiably, that Frederick the Great invented Napoleon's destruction techniques; the opposite kind may involve the formula "neither war nor peace"—the mere avoidance of a peace treaty accompanied by a mere threat military operations.[2]

---

[1]   A. Svechin, *Strategiia* [Strategy], 1st edition (Moscow: Gosvoenizdat, 1926), p. 259.

[2]   A. Svechin, *Strategiia* [Strategy], 2nd edition (Moscow: Voennyi vestnik, 1927), p. 179.

This only goes to show that opposing elements can be found not only in the relationship between attrition and destruction, but also within attrition itself.

According to Svechin, attrition does not negate the destruction of the enemy's manpower and the possibility of inflicting heavy blows upon him.

Besides, attrition does not hamper the achievement of the final and decisive goals of war. Professor Svechin rejects the definition of attrition as a strategy of limited objectives.

Furthermore, attrition may require the mobilization of all forces of a state in a military effort.

In sum, we are faced with a very strange type of attrition that somehow has replaced destruction and is now represented by a single strategic system which is very broad and flexible, while Professor Svechin is struggling against a nonexistent strategy of destruction. This type of destruction is studied from a theoretical, abstract point of view and is brought to a limit that could hardly have been achieved by Napoleon in his strategic endeavors; it is rather an idealistic concept, as Professor Svechin himself points out in the preface to the book. In short, taking for granted that theory is flexible enough to allow any extremes, Professor Svechin invented an enemy for himself and is fighting him successfully.

But real life tends to smooth over extreme views and may demand that the enemy be defeated by all means available, whether political or strategic.

Professor Svechin makes a vain attempt to refer to Lenin as a follower of the strategy of attrition in politics. The experience of the Russian Revolution shows that Lenin was a strategist who was capable of combining destruction and attrition depending on the progress of the revolutionary events.

The October Revolution was fought and won under the slogans of utter destruction—to dissolve the interim government of Kerensky, to seize power, to immediately confiscate the lands belonging to major landowners, to suppress the armed opposition of the counterrevolutionary forces ... in short, Lenin led the first stage of the Revolution as a strategist of destruction proceeding from the existing balance of forces in the country. But as soon as the Revolution came into direct contact with the external capitalist world, Lenin's policies turned into extremely flexible and; compromise-seeking maneuvering—the Brest peace agreement, armistice with Poland, the buffer Far Eastern Republic, etc. When the development of the Revolution reached the point that put into question the continued existence of the union between workers and peasants, Lenin turned to "attrition" in internal policy as well. In fact, the proclaimed New Economic Policy was described as the transitional stage "from assault to protracted siege."

In the final analysis, strategy is the science that studies the military balance of forces. When this balance is favorable it is unwise to renounce a bold strategy of destruction; when the balance of forces precludes a direct strike, a strategy of limited objectives and even defense is needed.

The argument over the concepts of "destruction" and "attrition" has been going on for quite some time, so we may attempt to draw some conclusions.

The parties to the argument agree that:

1) modern warfare between large states cannot be finished in one major battle or even in a number of successive operations pursuing the same objective;

2) the outcome of a war results not only from the clash between the armed forces, but also from conflicting political and economic factors;

3) due to the use of large masses of military personnel and materiel, modern warfare may become protracted and bring about heavy casualties;

4) military preparations include not only the deployment of armed forces, but also the overall national economic effort;

5) mobilization has acquired a repeated, "permanent" nature and draws on human as well as all other resources of the country;

6) battle has ceased to be the only means of achieving the objectives of war;

7) neither the strategy of Napoleon nor the strategy of Moltke is sufficient for victory; the latest world and civil wars enriched military theory with a number of important new facts that have not yet been thoroughly studied.

What, then, are the points on which the parties to the argument disagree?

Primarily, it is the pace of operations and the nature of initial engagements with the enemy. Professor Svechin believes that armed struggle reaches its climax not in the beginning of the war but at the next stage when economic mobilization takes place and large masses of trained and equipped personnel start moving to the front. For this reason at the beginning of the war one should not pursue goals that are not commensurate with time and resources available. In fact, realistic planning is something that anyone would support.

As a counterpoint to these ideas it is argued that military preparations are likely to take years to carry out, that the first operation may be thoroughly planned in advance, that a country may be capable of ensuring military superiority over the enemy to such an extent that it would make it possible either to destroy the enemy completely or at least to create the most advantageous strategic situation at the frontline for carrying out further military operations, etc.

The argument over this particular point cannot be settled as an abstract, theoretical issue. In real-life situations both sides may be right under specific conditions. In this respect it is interesting to note the opinion of Culman, who, while believing that the main goal of strategy is the destruction of the enemy's forces, advocates delaying the decisive strategic effort.

Among various aspects in the first part of the book dealing with the relationship between politics and strategy one cannot fail to notice that Professor Svechin gives priority to politics over strategy rather reluctantly, though he is quite right when he corrects Clausewitz, saying that war is not a continuation but a part of politics carried out by different means. We should refer our readers to a critical review by A. Shifres of the book by comrade Shaposhnikov[3] in which the author disagrees with Professor Svechin, stressing the points on which the latter is obviously mistaken; and here we completely agree with A. Shifres.

The chapter on "The Economic Plan of War" is of paramount importance in Professor Svechin's book. The fact that the ideas put forward by the author are not new does not belittle their significance. In connection with problems of transportation the special role of railroads is highlighted, and is reiterated further on. In a less developed country the contradiction between the mechanized nature of modern warfare and insufficient means of transportation has to be overcome, and this often creates conditions for the development of railroad, horse-drawn and automotive transportation.

---

[3] *Voina i revoliutsiia*, no. 2 (February 1927), pp. 179-183.

With regard to economic mobilization the author explains that it cannot be executed in a single exercise even if it takes a long time since the economic potential of a country increases gradually, step by step.

In this connection Professor Svechin proposes setting up an economic general staff. We are against the idea of having two headquarters instead of one: if one functions effectively no one needs an extra planning body which only creates additional problems.

In this country the most important task is to rivet the attention of public opinion and the party to military-related economic preparations and then to find the right balance between the peaceful construction of socialist and military buildup.

The chapter on the "Building the Armed Forces" is the most substantive and captivating part of Professor Svechin's book from the military point of view. Neither in the basic provisions nor in the subsequent statements did we find indications that the armed forces should be organized in accordance with the chosen strategy of attrition or destruction. The author seems to be somewhat inconsistent on this point. Irrespective of his strategic doctrine, Professor Svechin in a simple and convincing manner proves that a country should have a strong army and provides much valuable and practical advice pertaining to any military strategy.

We would like to stress a number of specific points here.

Morale of an army is a necessary prerequisite for its combat capability. Paying tribute to the realities of our times, Professor Svechin casually mentions that the source of a soldier's moral strength lies in his class consciousness without stressing its high priority in the current system of training in the Soviet army. This is an obvious and glaring omission. However, Professor Svechin finds convincing words when he expresses his point of view on the relationship between military equipment and human resources. The argument between the proponents of the "human factor" and those advocating reliance on military technology seems to be over in this day and age. Professor Svechin quotes the following remarkable statement by Le Bon:

> We should not think that the significance of the human being and everything directly associated with him has diminished as a result of massive technological development... The multiplicity of human material, human physical capacity for work and training, human morale, organization, discipline and leadership are all factors that cannot be replaced by any technical equipment, whether it be machinery in industry or battleships and guns in war. The sense of technology lies in enhancing and multiplying the effectiveness of these factors rather than in eliminating them.[4]

Professor Svechin's opposition to the improper balance between combat troops and logistical units is something that can be effectively borrowed by those who are responsible for building the Red Army. In fact, comrade Voroshilov has been struggling against it since he occupied the post of People's Commissar for Defense.

---

[4] Svechin, *Strategiia*, 2nd edition, p. 113, nn.

During the Civil War the ratio between combat and noncombat personnel was 10-12 to one, a catastrophic situation in itself. In 1914 the tsar's army had two noncombat servicemen for each combatant; later this ratio changed and became three (and even more) to one.

In Germany in October 1916 the ratio between combat personnel and noncombat, or logistic, units was only one to 0.86.

To overcome this flaw Professor Svechin recommends bringing together all logistical units under a unified command that would control them from the deep rear. We do not believe this would be a wise step in the Red Army where logistical services have long been neglected. But Professor Svechin goes even further and recommends transferin divisional support services to the command of the corps as the main logistical unit in order to substantially increase the railroad mobility of the army.

Professor Svechin's description of the relationships between various branches and services is conspicuously abstract. Organizational matters cannot be solved in such a manner, and the mention of local geographic conditions, the nature of war and the state of military equipment and human resources does not sound convincing.

Specific measures to organize hundreds of thousands and even millions of people require great efficiency, clarity and rules to go by. Regarding organizational matters, Professor Svechin has become the victim of his own disrespect for specific action. Organizational matters require very specific action, despite the contradictory, complex and questionable experience of recent wars.

Action on organizational matters should be taken long before the war starts. Millions of people and horses must be distributed by military branches and formations, and they cannot wait for speculations that would result in the most "improved" form of their organization.

Mistakes do occur here, and Professor Svechin provides little help to the Red Army in this complex and practical area of military development efforts.

The chapter on "Military Mobilization" is both brilliant and innovative. One can safely assume that the term "permanent mobilization" will find its place in our military-related literature and in everyday usage. The demand that mobilization plans be separated from the plans of operational deployment for the forward echelon is hardly feasible, though it is justified and possible with regard to subsequent echelons. The flexibility of the mobilization plan allowing for separate mobilizations is of great interest and deserves close scrutiny.

The flexibility of the mobilization plan is closely related to the flexibility of the operational plan[5] inasmuch as there must be several scenarios for the latter which could be implemented in the course of transportation depending on the prevailing situation during the initial stage of war. Thus the mobile flexibility of mobilization and operational deployment could be achieved by employing railroad transportation and echeloned mobilization in various combinations. These ideas put forward by Professor Svechin are of great practical (as opposed to purely academic or abstract) value to the General Staff.

In fact, Professor Svechin pays a great deal of attention to the problems of mobilization, and it comes as no surprise that his outstanding book is imbued with this mood. For him mobilization is no longer detailed, precise and tedious work

---

[5]   Ibid., pp. 152-156.

carried out according to certain patterns; nor does it require the involvement of highly qualified experts from the General Staff. While this view holds true with regard to the development of the mobilization plan for the first military echelon, one should not forget about the subsequent echelons, the mobilization of various sectors of the national economy and of public opinion, etc. The mobilization activities in their entirety go well beyond purely mechanical exercise, and we do not agree with comrade Shaposhnikov, who in his book *Mozg armii* [The Brain of the Army], considers the issues of mobilization to be of secondary importance and unworthy of the attention of the General Staff.[6]

In the chapter on "Preparing Border Theaters" it is interesting to note the rebuke given to Professor Svechin by Professor Velichko.[7] This indisputable and longstanding authority on military engineering attacked Svechin for alleged disrespect with regard to eminent experts as well as old fortresses that had been destroyed rather quickly by the fire of German heavy artillery. We are not in a position to judge whether Professor Svechin commits a crime by not recommending reconstructing defunct fortresses. However, we cannot afford to follow Professor Velichko's suggestion that border theaters should be reinforced by building a lasting defensive line, i.e., a system of frontier posts and fortresses. For quite a number of years to come the government of the USSR will hardly be able to spend more than 1-2 percent (mentioned by Professor Svechin) of its military budget on such fortifications.

In conclusion we would like to dwell on the method of argument employed by Professor Svechin. It is common knowledge that dialectical materialism seeks not only to cognize the world but also to transform it. But Professor Svechin's dialectic does not pursue any positive goals, and he seems content merely to observe changing phenomena and look for contradictions that make possible the transition from quantity to quality and negation of negation.

At the same time Professor Svechin stops short of "transforming the world," leaving this for his readers. All these features—"objectivity," the composure of a detached observer, lack of personal feelings with regard to specific issues—make this book look like a translated work.

We have to stop here since the last two chapters of Professor Svechin's *Strategy* are not easy to discuss within the framework of a short critical review. One can only note that the author covers almost the whole range of issues related to campaign tactics as part of the broader strategy. It is understandable that there are not many controversial points in those chapters.

Taken as a whole, Professor Svechin's book still remains the only fundamental work on strategy. We are convinced that its second edition will be out of print very soon and an additional one will be necessary.

The book is a specimen of quality publishing.

---

[6] B. Shaposhnikov. *Mozg armii* [The Brain of the Army] (Moscow: Voennyi vestnik, 1927), vol. 1, pp. 67-68.

[7] *Voina i revoliutsiia*, no. 4 (April 1926), pp. 152-155.

\

APPENDIX 2

Editor's note: The following review appeared in the main journal of the Red Army's General Staff, *Voina i revoliutsiia* [War and Revolution], no. 1 (January 1928), pp. 152-158.

CRITIQUE AND BIBLIOGRAPHY
by V. Novitskii
A. Svechin. *Strategiia* [Strategy]. 2nd edition.
Moscow: Voennyi vestnik, 1927. 263 pp.

"In essence, all of strategy," writes the author of the present work, "is basically a contemplation of military history."[1] There can be no doubt that the study and analysis of military history is useful for the strategist. But in our meditation on the past, can we overlook such a fact as the general unpreparedness for the form of armed struggle which the World War assumed within just several weeks of its initiation? Can one fail to consider the decisive significance that the hypnosis of the Franco-Prussian War had on that basic lack of readiness—a lack of readiness which never would have been, it would seem, if, according to the claim of the author, the World War had assumed the form of a war of attrition as a result of historical necessity? Finally, is it possible—considering such a basic mistake on the part of the General Staffs (the quintessence of military specialists)—to deny that military history is not always a reliable basis for determining the character of a future war; and that, in general, great caution and discretion are necessary in examining this question? In our opinion, a truly useful examination of military history should not exclude the application of a more direct way of determining the character of a future war—namely, the immediate consideration of a currently relevant assessment of the future often is useful in overcoming the hypnosis of the past.

Overcoming the hypnosis of the past, in part, the hypnosis of the World War—no simple task for the modern man—and the author of the present work, entitled *Strategy*, clearly shows the difficulty of solving this problem. "We are looking at modern war with all its possibilities," the author writes in the preface. But we do not see the objective author of the preface when he considers the substance of strategy per se. In his analysis, the author distinctly and decisively departs from the perspective of protracted war, war of attrition, permanent mobilization and so on.

For example, where the issue concerns a protracted future war, the author does not dwell on such arguments:

---

[1] A. Svechin, *Strategiia* [Strategy], 2nd edition (Moscow: Voennyi vestnik, 1927), p. 23.

In the historical period we are now entering, we must anticipate a return to the prolonged preparations for war... [T]he desire to use the resources of one's dominions (England) and the black African colonies (France), the need to arm (Germany) and the low level of peacetime readiness (the United States) have convinced us of this.[2]

Is it really possible to formulate such a question? Is it really admissible for a strategist to fail to take into account, that in the conditions of war, that which will be advantageous and provide solutions for the interests of one side—will to an even greater extent be disadvantageous and inadmissible for the other side? And even allowing—in the most extreme case—that England's dominions or the blacks of the French Empire are of considerable and serious military significance for these great powers, and that the very character of an armed struggle for them should be determined independently from the exploitation of these elements for their military might, are there not reasons to suggest that the enemy of these powers in a future war would not be disposed to wait for the mass of these soldiers from the other continents to appear on the continent of Europe under the banners of these powers? It seems to us that such a calculation would be too naive in the best of circumstances. But if such a naivete is not permitted, and assuming, on the contrary, that the enemies of the stated powers would be interested in finding a solution through a strategy of destruction—then could one consider that the war nonetheless would take on a protracted character? This is precisely what the author has done by formulating the question in the following manner: "If destruction is feasible and s attempted by one side, the opposing side is compelled to organize his counteractions in accordance with the logic of destruction."[3]

If such is the case, the author should naturally recognize that, however advantageous it would be in his opinion for France to wait for its colonial blacks and for England to wait for its dominions and so forth—this could nevertheless not alter the protracted character of a future war. To take a concrete example, could one acknowledge that in the case of an armed conflict between France and Germany both sides would conduct a struggle of attrition according to the argument presented by the author; and that both sides would exclude the possibility of the French or German commands calculating their own good by finding a resolution in the strategy of destruction? Furthermore, in favor of this solution, it is possible to find arguments at least as serious as the author's, that (for the German command) although there would be an attempt to utilize the brilliant maneuver and battle qualities of their troops; for the French there would be a policy not to permit the Germans to deploy all their forces to that end.

Regarding the issue of the difficulties of the strategy of destruction, the author makes the following argument:

Modern times have placed major limitations on a strategy of destruction. The first of these [is] the short range of modern operations... The second limitation lies in the fact that currently the beginning of a war does not now constitute the culmination of strategic intensity. Military and economic

---

2   Ibid., p. 135.

3   Ibid., p. 40

mobilization provide the second and third echelons of mobilized and equipped manpower.[4]

(Question: is the equipping of the troops included in the concept of mobilized
manpower or not?) If it is included, then what is the difference between
"mobilized" and "equipped" forces? We doubt that after the march on Paris, or
after the Battle of Warsaw, or after the mighty attack of the Russian army and so
forth, that it would be possible to acknowledge that modern operations are short-
ranged. But even if we take the author's perspective in this matter, we cannot in
any way share his point of view or acknowledge the admissibility of his second
argument. The author writes about the difficulties of a policy of destruction, and
at the same time says that these difficulties are caused by an echeloning of
mobilization. And continuing in his own words: "Echelons of military and
economic mobilization are totally appropriate for a strategy of attrition but are
alien in spirit to a strategy of destruction."[5] Of course, if echeloned mobilization
were the only type of mobilization, the author would have grounds for justifing
the difficulty of the policy of destruction on the basis of the peculiarities of
echeloned mobilization. But the fact of the matter is a bit different. Nobody who
is in full possession of his faculties and in his right mind, and who is preparing for
a struggle based on a policy of destruction, would base his operation on an
echeloned mobilization. And if this is so, why do we find here distinctive
attributes and properties of echeloned mobilization? The contrary is the case. It
should be completely evident to any muser on the history of the World War that
it is precisely the underestimation of the meaning of the complete and final arming
of forces (which actually is echeloning), and not the massed mobilization by the
Germans in significant measure which brought about the situation at the Marne.
Actually, if the Germans would have mobilized five extra corps immediately—
and this, undoubtedly, they would have been able to do—the outcome of the
Marne would have been different; and we can postulate that even the strategy of
our respected author would not have been founded on the basis of the permanence of mobilization, at least to a certain degree at this time.

But in those circumstances when the author talks of the strategy of destruction,
and not of permanent mobilization and so forth—he not only does not concern
himself with serious argumentation from his own point of view, but he will not,
for anything, respect even the facts should they not correspond to his theories.
What can be clearer and more evident than this inconsistency—even within the
author's own claims—than a conflict with the historical examples brought forward on the very same page?

Let us look at what the author maintains:

> Quite recently mobilization seemed to be a moment; mobili-
> zation agencies mined the peacetime structure of the state in
> order to set off a one-time explosion and gather the human
> masses and materiel with which the war would begin to be
> waged, and be concluded in the course of two to three
> weeks.[6]

---

[4] Ibid., p. 177.

[5] Ibid., p. 182

Now let us see what experience says:

> In peacetime only 70 percent of the physically strongest
> segment of the German population was liable for military
> service; only a portion of this 70 percent was mobilized
> immediately when war was declared while the other portion
> was to be reinforcements for them.[7]

Where here is the war to be "waged" and "concluded"?

In general when it comes to mobilization, the author in our view is too exacting and severe. Let us take, for example, one of his requirements:

> An army should be able to mobilize any number of any
> divisions without disrupting the mobilization readiness of
> the other divisions in the process. The mobilization of an
> entire army should be merely the sum of the mobilizations of
> all its units and not constitute a self-contained entity.[8]

Just what kind of notion underlies this requirement? Of course, if this is necessary then the techniques of mobilization would be capable of solving such a problem. First of all, however, we are supposing that the operation of mobilization planning is not far off and that it is something that cannot take care of itself. In order to make such a demand on mobilization, it is completely necessary that strategy either have "N" number of variants of strategic plans (if not excluding the possibility, then at least making the preparations of the respective mobilization plans pointless), or that strategy be required to have no plans at all. In this case, a study would calculate that the art of the mobilizer would cover its strategic weakness. But for the present, for the reader acquainted with *Strategy*, we assume that the second situation is far more likely; in the long run we have to explain precisely why.

However, the possibility of a solution to the problem from the standpoint of mobilization alone in no way proves that its problems can be solved on the basic levels, especially in the area of transport support for mobilization. "Railroads," the author writes,

> have a very difficult task in mobilization. They themselves
> have to be mobilized, that is, prepared for concentration
> transports. But at the same time they have to do a great deal
> of work on mobilization transports: that is, moving hun-
> dreds of thousands called-up reserves and requisitioned
> horses, delivering military freight quickly and at the same
> time providing covering transports, i.e., transports for the
> purpose of strengthening important sectors in border areas.[9]

It is completely obvious that in such conditions the development of a whole series of variants (including variants which allow an unimpeded transfer from one variant to another) is a problem which scarcely has any solutions. Further-more, in the event that this work was done correctly in the strategic and

---

6   Ibid., p. 132.

7   Ibid.

8   Ibid., p. 134.

9   Ibid., p. 143.

operational- planning activities, there is no necessity whatsoever to even posit such a possibility.

But it is a question whether or not these basic ideas, which *Strategy* provides, are correct for these kinds of operations. We will let the reader judge.

> By their very essence the war plan and the campaign plan should not merely call for the absolute growth of the armed forces but should prepare them for the missions the army and navy will have to carry out once a war begins.[10]

One intensely correct idea of the author in the given situation is completely out of agreement with his very own claim that, "a war plan is primarily a program for the development of the armed forces and resources of a state over several years."[11] It is quite impossible to agree that this last assertion is correct. Thus the question automatically arises regarding similar contradictions which demand a more profound method of approach and a more thorough analysis. We shall attempt to go deeper into the ideas and formulations of the author when it comes to his ideas on the essence of systematic preparations.

Let us take, for example, his entirely plausible requirement for a plan of operations:

> [A]n operational plan must be flexible and have several versions, which would make it possible to choose between a war of destruction and a war of attrition, between the defensive and the offensive and between attacking one nation or another state in a hostile alliance, depending on political guidelines.[12]

What purpose or value is there to such a plan suitable to all situations of life, but in this matter is not worth anything? Can someone with elementary competence in strategy really recommend a simultaneous preparation for a struggle based on destruction and one based on attrition? Can one really without the greatest risk spread thinly one's attention and resources both for the preparation of a destructive blow and also for the mobilization of industry? Can one really, while preparing for a destructive blow accept an echeloned mobilization which, as the author himself acknowledges, is alien to the spirit of the strategy of destruction?

Where can one find the proper approach to the solution of these questions? Once again, our author has the answers. "A strategist will be implacable," writes the author

> in pursuing destruction. If a destructive strike is planned, then his concern for the overall base should recede far into the background. Schlieffen was completely logical in assigning only negligible forces to defend major German economic interests in Lorraine, Alsace and East Prussia.[13]

---

[10] Ibid., p. 108.

[11] Ibid., p. 105.

[12] Ibid., p. 152.

[13] Ibid., p. 97.

[14] Ibid., p. 43.

Or here:

> What is the point of preparing for a ten-year war if the preparations are so detrimental to our initial military efforts that an enemy employing destruction techniques is able to achieve his political aims in two to three months?[14]

It is difficult to put all these contradictions together; difficult to understand how there is such a significant abundance of them in this work, which, after all, is appearing in its second edition. These contradictions are numerous even in other sections—for example, where the author treats the issue regarding the cooperation of politics, economics and strategy.

Here are examples of these contradictions:

"War is waged," writes the author, "not only on an armed front; it is also waged on the class and economic fronts. Operations on all fronts must be coordinated by politics."[15] Just several pages later he says: "The political goal should be appropriate to one's war-waging capabilities."[16] If the first assertion about the three fronts is really not in error, then why should the political objective not respond to the combined possibilities of all these fronts, but only to the military one? If all the remaining fronts do not merit attention, then why in the world talk about them? And if they are to be recognized as truly significant, then why not consider their possibility with the arrangement of the political objective?

Or another example no less indicative: "Domestic politics should strive to maximize the use of a state's strengths to achieve the aims of the war."[17] "Strategy decides issues associated with the employment of the armed forces and all the resources of a country for achieving ultimate war aims."[18] Therefore there can be no doubt that strategy should be understood as the "art of military leaders."[19]

In this example there is a contradiction analogous to the one cited above. On the one hand, there is the thoroughly correct idea regarding the utilization of the armed forces and the resources of the country. To some extent this is the correct notion that politics utilizes all the forces of the country for the achievement of its war aims. On the other hand, it is a narrowly bureaucratic approach, where it is the military leader who solves the questions regarding the use of all the country's resources for attaining the war objective.

If we delve deeper into this question, we come to new contradictions, perhaps more considerable ones.

The author puts forward the idea of an Economic General Staff. "The Economic General Staff," writes the author,

> is a reflection of the current broader notion of the leadership of a war. If war invloves armed, class and economic fronts, military agencies responsible for directing preparations and preparing themselves to lead these fronts must be organized ahead of time. The organization of a military economic staff is an urgent measure.

---

[15] Ibid., p. 30.

[16] Ibid., p. 37.

[17] Ibid., p. 84.

[18] Ibid., p. 15.

[19] Ibid., p. 19.

The experience of the past has demonstrated that without a special military agency the activity of different extradepartmental agencies involved in overall preparations for war may die (the National Defense Council organized in France 20 years ago) or be concentrated exclusively on resolving current problems of peacetime (the Council of Labor and Defense in past years in the Soviet Union).[20]

Having adduced the actual direction of the author regarding operations on all fronts (the military, the class and the economic) should there be agreement between politics[21] and the idea of an Economic Staff? Is it not necessary to understand that the author submits—regardless of how minor this is for him—to the fashionable idea of an Economic General Staff, recognizing in theory that the formation of such a thing should be in the hands of policymakers? And in maintaining this idea with an immediate urgency, the author continues as follows:

> A policy that would renounce the retention of its authority over the leadership of a war, and acknowledge the primacy of military specialists and silently conform to their requirements, would itself acknowledge its own bankruptcy. In the eyes of a politician even strategy should be military technology, and the technical leadership of a war should be subordinate to the political leadership, because war is a part of politics. Strategy may be understood as coordinating military operations with the requirements of politics.[22]

But then what is the meaning and purpose of those political staffs which the author mentions on that very same page of his work? Does it really mean that the political staff is subordinate to those who consolidate the economic staff? And if it is subordinate, then how can one coordinate such an organizational structure with the politician's leadership role? What a glorious history is this against the background of the poverty of strategy!

In formulating this issue we allow ourselves to express our own opinion. This consolidation should not be produced at the ministerial level, but rather by a superior organ. This organ need not be economic or political or just any other kind of bureaucracy; rather it should be a State General Staff. We have already written about this in a 1923 issue of the journal *Voennoe khoziaistvo* [Military Economy], in which there appeared an article on the notion of an economic general staff. Now, however, after a thorough acquaintance with Svechin's *Strategy*, we are strengthened to an even greater extent in our certainty in having been correct with our earlier expressed point of view.

But if the author, as we have seen in many situations, allows inconsistency and contradictions in an area strictly set aside for strategic issues, then when it comes to mobilization he expressly expounds a theory of permanent mobilization which he, however, sometimes calls "echeloned". In our opinion, there is clearly a difference between the concepts of permanent and echeloned mobilization; but in

---

[20] Ibid., p. 70.

[21] Ibid., p. 30.

[22] Ibid., p. 84.

Strategy we take them as equivalent concepts. Hence, let us consider what permanent mobilization really is.

The author has already written the following in the first edition:

> We can refer to a series of new material factors which force us to accept a new point of view about strategic art. Let us point out, for example, the concept of permanent military mobilization which sets back the moment of the maximum strategic effort now from twenty days of war to several months.[23]

Here is yet another contradiction characteristic of this author. In fact, on page 43 he writes:

> Inasmuch as military budgets, despite their growth, have lagged behind economic growth... maximum strategic intensity is feasible only half a year after the end of economic mobilization, that is, no earlier than the second year of the war.[24]

Several months and the second year of the war is a slight difference.

In this way, permanence of mobilization is placed in a series of new material factors which determine this author-strategist's perspective on strategic art. In this way, strategy depends on mobilization. Is this approach correct? In our opinion, it is diametrically opposed to what is correct. Strategy—its interests and efforts—should have priority. Mobilization, on the other hand, should adapt its technique to the requirements of strategy. The author himself admits this: "Echelons of military and economic mobilization are totally appropriate for a strategy of attrition but are alien in spirit to a strategy of destruction."[25] If this is so, then permanent mobilization should predetermine the character of a future war; for with permanent mobilization it is impossible to conduct a war based on a strategy of destruction. But the author himself, a proponent of the concept of war of attrition, nevertheless cannot exclude the possibility of a policy of destruction. But there is no doubt that war based on destruction requires a different type of mobilization than permanent mobilization. Is it possible that there are other types of mobilization other than the permanent type? (It is the echeloned type—according to the terminology of the author). It seems to us that anyone who has been involved with mobilization could give an affirmative answer to this question without any wavering or doubt. But if this is so, you strategists, do not give assent to mobilization; do not hint that it is bound to the freedom of your decisions, but decide freely, and state what you need from mobilization. We think that with the current techniques of mobilization it will prove to be a proposition that will satisfy any of your serious requirements. In any case, without having asked us, do not let your perspective on mobilization be predetermined by the possibility or expediency of any one thing or another.

How was the theory of permanent mobilization created? Evidently, the first cause was the experience of a poor analysis of the World War. The World War demonstrated that the mobiliziation possibilities of the contemporary state are

---

[23] A. Svechin. *Strategiia* [Strategy]. 1st edition. Moscow: Gosvoenizdat, 1926, p. 7.

[24] A. Svechin. *Strategiia*, 2nd edition, p. 43.

[25] Ibid., p. 182.

significantly greater than was stated in the beginning. Due to the incorrect estimation of these possibilities, mobilization was prolonged and acquired a look of permanence. What kind of conclusion was made from this? The conclusion was that contemporary mobilization was one of permanence. It seems to us that a different conclusion would have been more correct, in particular that the calculation for mobilization options ought to be done more carefully, and that their underestimate allowed during the World War ought not to be permitted again. The error in calculation brought about a shortage of reserves of arms, supplies and so on. Indeed it was necessary to resort to the mobilization of industry. As a result, the following conclusion was made: "You mobilize industry" instead of concluding there is a necessity to accumulate reserves. Owing to this underestimate and underuse of mobilization options, and owing to the shortage of reserves and the necessity to mobilize industry—the World War took on a prolonged character. From this, the conclusion was made that "wars of the future will probably be prolonged."[26] And if the the wars are long, then you must surely rely on a mobilization of industry; and you will then begin to wage war seriously during the second year of hostilities.

In the meantime, is it really possible to accept the theory of permanent mobilization in general? Isn't this view of permanence of mobilization, a view acquired during the World War, deceptive? It seems to us that this question deserves a serious consideration.

First of all, what is mobilization? According to the popular and widely accepted meaning, mobilization is the period of transition from a status of peace until the outbreak of hostilities. What particular characteristics are there during this period? Even though one is always preparing for this event, the exact moment of transition is always sudden, to a significant extent, and the first day is established merely by the mobilization telegram. The transition itself proceeds according to a plan that has been worked out in detail. In the course of the fulfillment of this transition, it becomes the first plan in the life of the state. All remaining interests are subordinated to the mobilization interests. In so far as the enemy also mobilizes, the effort to prevent his readiness plays a very obvious role in the considerations of mobilization. Not only the days, but also the hours are taken into account in the considerations of mobilization. There arises a tendency to seek speed records in mobilization, and there is indeed a tendency to work for faster mobilizations than what is actually necessary. We completely agree with the author's acknowledgement regarding what is intolerable in this very effort to set speed records. But can one consider the rejection of record-making to be equivalent to the acceptance of the idea of permanence (echeloning) of mobilization? Are the subsequent echelons of an echeloned mobilization in fact a mobilization?

First of all, the basic preliminary outline of the timeframes of subsequent mobilizations (to use the author's terminology) is determined also at the beginning of a war. The exact time is fixed long before the implementation. With the designation of this time period, absent are those moments which, along with the actual mobilization, prompt us to designate the beginning of this moment, if possibile, at the nearest midnight. Due to this, in order to fulfill such a type of subsequent mobilization there are left significant periods of time for the immedi-

---

[26] Ibid., p. 43.

ate preparation, and the fulfillment of such a type of mobilization is drawn out in time. On the one hand, the significance of the planned preparation lies in the presence of a preparatory period of time, along with a prolonging of mobilization. On the other hand, it falls out along with the comparison with the first echelon of mobilization (the author's expression). Finally, all the subsequent echelons are, to a significant degree, mere particulars and do not involve the comprehensiveness of all the elements of state life, as does the first echelon.

To summarize, in general one should recognize that in the mobilization of all subsequent echelons (of permanent mobilization), there is significantly more than a mere similarity to an annual call-up than with mobilization itself. And insofar as a correct designation is equivalent to a correct understanding, adapting these subsequent echeleons to the concept of mobilization in our opinion is impossible to justify. In essence, permanent mobilization ceases to be mobilization, having become permanent. Morover, we definitely consider the theory of permanent mobilization to be a consequence of a misunderstanding of the World War experience, of the unfortunate conclusions of this experience, and most of all, of a misunderstanding of the essence of mobilization.

Ultimately, however, in considering this work in both the sphere of strategy and the sphere of mobilization, we conclude that it lacks a clarity and precision which this critic expected to find. Moreover, the words of the author ring out with a particular kind of wicked irony when the work (to use his own evaluation) "has been written for a rather modest purpose, namely... to make it possible for strategic thinking to get out of the back alleys and dead ends and onto the main road."[27] It seems to us that the entire mass of contradictions, inconsistancies and poorly argued propositions creates the diametrically opposite result from what the author intended. In any case, he fails to help us get back "onto the main road."

Regarding the author's basic propositions, it seems to us that his exultation of a strategy of attrition is dangerous. When trying to justify the advantage of a struggle based on a strategy of attrition for all the great powers, the author does not even mention the USSR. After all, is such a strategy really acceptable to us?

To begin with, can our mobilized industry really compete with the mobilized industry of our enemies? Aren't our industries totally lacking in a serious infrastructure to the extent that we can declare—in both the ability to rapidly mobilize industry and expand such productive capabilities—that we find ourselves in far less favorable conditions? And in drawing a conclusion from this— would not one have to say that the transition to a struggle based on attrition does not meet our interests?

But we admit that even a rivalry in this sphere would be something that is possibile. Even in this latter case, would we have the right to exclude the possibility of the enemy's transition to a strategy of destruction, if we were compelled toward that transition to a strategy of destruction? And in this case, until that moment when our industry could expand, we would be forced to have our foundation exclusively in reserves at that time, as our enemy would undoubtedly be able to count on the world market. And could we allow in such a situation that we would be able to count on success? And even if we could not, there would be the possibility to prolong the struggle until that point in time when we would have the opportunity to make use of our mobilized industry.

---

[27] Ibid., p. 23.

No. Neither a strategy of attrition nor a strategy of destruction predicated on the initiative of the enemy—forced and therefore unprepared and lacking the major advantages—are promising or offering us of success. So where is the exit? Where is our strategy?

Our strategy undoubtedly is a strategy of destruction. Our strategy is a strategy of rapid and decisive attack, the reckoning of which is based on our very first successes to demonstrate to the world market the nature of the risk inherent in subsidizing the enemy. Only in such a way would such aid be withheld, aid which in other conditions hampers the conduct of armed struggle. And of course, our strategy is a strategy of striving for decisive results.

If this is so, then should not we all turn our attention to securing the maximum development, accumulating the best means for a swift and rapid strike and securing the best economic resources in everything to the end that they would be set aside for that attack?

If this is so, then should not we also cultivate our personnel in the spirit of action and strategy of destruction?

"von der Goltz sharply distinguishes himself from the other classics," writes A. Svechin in the introduction to the first volume of *Strategy in the Works of the Military Classics*,

> by the absence of a one-sided line of thinking; but this is because he, as a professor of strategy at the Turkish academy of the general staff, naturally should have vividly felt the dependence of strategy on the audience for whom he reads, on the theater of war in which it will be fought and the army that will apply it, and this necessity of a national-geographical approach he depicts with his own breadth, color and conviction.[28]

What a pity that the author of our *Strategy* did not remain a Professor of Strategy at the Turkish Academy of the General Staff.

---

[28] A. Svechin (ed.). *Strategiia v trudakh voennykh klassikov* [Strategy in the Works of the Military Classics] (Moscow: Vysshei voennyi redaktsionnyi sovet, 1924), Vol. 1, p. 13.

APPENDIX

APPENDIX 3

Editor's note: The following review appeared in the main journal of the Red Army's General Staff, *Voina i revoliutsiia* [War and Revolution], no. 1 (January 1928), pp. 158-160.

WHAT IS MOBILIZATION AND IS IT REALLY PERMANENT?
I. Modlin
Review of A. Svechin's *Strategiia* [Strategy]. 2nd edition
(Moscow: Voennyi vestnik, 1927).

Our special interest in this book by A. Svechin is kindled by an unconventional assertion we find among its other theoretical generalizations based on the study of past, primarily recent wars that modern mobilization in general and military (or army) mobilization in particular is essentially a permanent process.

The novelty of this approach adopted by a recognized authority on the subject, the enthusiastic acclaim for it by comrade Vol'pe who is convinced that the term "permanent mobilization" will gain currency in literature on military matters and in common parlance,[1] its growing, albeit implicit and uncritical acceptance compel us to take a very close look at this aspect of comrade Svechin's work in an effort to analyze it as best we can. We believe we should undertake this analysis not only out of purely academic curiosity and that it will have important practical implications.

To this day we have understood mobilization as the passage of the army (and the country) from a peace to a war footing, a process carried out in accordance with a preestablished timetable and prior plans. Now comrade Svechin, by claiming that it is a permanent process, brings into focus a new feature of mobilization, which, as he puts it, highlights its temporal dimension.

Given comrade Svechin's unorthodox views, a new definition of mobilization in terms of his theory would appear to be in order. However, asserting that mobilization is permanent and speaking about new related phenomena, comrade Svechin, for some reason, did not think he had to supply a new term for a concept to describe the process that transforms the army in the time of peace (when it is a school of war) into the army in the time of war (when it is a tool of war). Nor did he find it necessary to provide a new definition, reflecting his views on mobilization, to justify his peculiar use of the term which he had not coined.

Let us address all the main arguments comrade Svechin employs to support his theory.

---

[1] See: *Voina i revoliutsiia*, no. 5 (May 1927), p. 186.

"It was undoubtedly a mistake," he writes, "that preparations for the World War were in essence preparations for a small war and had essentially small mobilizations in mind." (p. 132) To make the point, he refers to a number of specific instances where new units, which he himself describes as "improvised," had to be deployed, when the war was already in progress, to compensate for the mistakes made in the preparations. Consequently, he concludes, mobilization continued throughout the war. In other words, modern mobilization is a permanent process.

This is, generally speaking, the line of reasoning comrade Svechin follows. Let us first of all note that his logic is clearly flawed. Indeed, even if, for argument's sake, we were to accept his claim that preparations "for the World War were in essence preparations for a small war" which resulted in a number of mistakes that subsequently had to be corrected, does this necessarily entail "permanency" of mobilization? Would this not amount to opposing mistakes to principles, something comrade Svechin objects to elsewhere in his book?

Let us put aside comrade Svechin's conclusions for a moment, and see whether he was right in assessing the preparations "for the world war as for essentially a small-scale war with mainly small-scale mobilizations in mind."

Let us first compare this statement by comrade Svechin with another opinion on that issue by an equally respected authority.

> Everybody was aware that a *general* war was inevitable. This followed from the imperialist policies of the great powers. Moreover, grand objectives perceived throughout the *entire universe*, inflamed passions and the desire to enjoy the spoils of victory for a long time to come *made it necessary to anticipate the scale and nature of the coming war*... That nature of the coming war was a natural consequence of the existing political situation. Preparations had to be made, and *Europe was hard at work getting ready for it mainly in two ways*—through the coalition and the *unbridled buildup of armaments in which the states vied with each other.*[2] [Emphasis added—I. M.]

Countries	Army strength in time of peace	Army strength when deployed	Increase in army size
Russia	1,500,000	5,000,000	Over 3 times
Belgium	58,000	231,000	4 times
France	884,000	4,584,000	Over 5 times
Austria-Hungary	450,000	2,450,000	Almost 5.5 times
Germany	840,000	5,340,000	Over 6 times

---

[2] See: A. Zaionchkovskii, *Mirovaia voina 1914-1918 gg. Obshchii strategicheskii ocherk* [The World War 1914-1918. A General Strategic Outline] (Moscow: Gosudarstvennoe voennoe izdatel'stvo, 1924), pp. 10-11.

Secondly, we believe that the following table convincingly demonstrates the fallacy of comrade Svechin's assumption.

As can be seen from this table, the Russian army was not as fully deployed as others. However, if we take note of the fact that to deploy its army Russia called up all its trained reserve forces (3,114,000 low-rank reservists and 400,000 servicemen of the first class, drafted from reserve to active duty), we have to admit that the Russian army was also mobilized to its capacity.

Let us also recall here an opinion by Field Marshal Moltke, a source of inspiration for military thought before the World War, who believed that an army could be deployed to only twice its size, compared to its strength in the time of peace, without undermining its combat readiness.

Finally, to conclude our discussion of comrade Svechin's claim, let us also point out that his idea is in fact far from being original and was first formulated much earlier by a French general, Sérigny, who wrote in his *Thoughts on Military Art*: "Preparing for a small-scale war, it [the General Staff] carried out a tiny mobilization."[3]

We can thus see that both writers express essentially the same idea which is, moreover, couched in very similar terms.

However, there is one important distinction to be made here. Sérigny's reference is not to the military mobilization or inadequate preparation for the deployment of the French armed forces, but to the preparedness for war of the country as a whole and, above all, its economy. This can be clearly seen in the sentence immediately following the above-quoted passage from his book: "Due to a lack of general knowledge, most of its officers [of the French General Staff] could not understand the economic problems generated by modern warfare."[4]

Unlike Sérigny, comrade Svechin attributes his identical statement to the military mobilization and thus clearly makes a mistake.[5]

By deciding not to give a new definition to the concept "mobilization," comrade Svechin in fact left us guessing about the essential meaning of permanent mobilization. As we see it, what comrade Svechin means is that, because mobilization is now a permanent process, the deployment of the armed forces continues without interruption throughout the whole war. This probably signifies that the armed forces can and must be deployed to their maximum capacity only toward the very end of the war. But what are we then to make of the statement comrade Svechin makes on page seven that "permanent military mobilization" now moves "the moment of greatest strategic intensity from the twentieth day of a war *to several months ahead*?" Comrade Svechin can hardly answer this question himself because already on page 43 he shifts his ground and states exactly this: "maximum strategic intensity is feasible only half a year after the end of economic mobilization, that is, *no earlier than the second year of the war*." [Emphasis added in both sentences—I.M.]

The confused comrade Svechin is clearly hard put to clarify this issue for us and we have to dig out an answer ourselves. Furthermore, nowhere in comrade Svechin's book could we find as much as a hint regarding what, in his view,

3   Sérigny, *Razmyshleniia o voennom iskusstve* [Thoughts on Military Art], Russian translation by M. Kamenskii (Moscow: Gosudarstvennoe voennoe izdatel'stvo, 1924), p. 39.

4   Ibid.

5   Ibid.

defines "the moment of greatest strategic intensity," another question we have to decide ourselves. We assume that the peak is reached when a country's last resources are engaged in the war effort and there is nothing left to replace them if they are expended—the defeated country is forced to its knees.

In other words, according to our reading, this point must coincide with the end but not the beginning or middle of the war.

On the basis of this interpretation of the "strategic peak" and considering comrade Svechin's dogged determination to prove that troop levels continue to increase on a permanent basis throughout the war, we would be justified in expecting to see a far greater number of troops engaged in the "final and decisive battle" of a modern war than the army combat strength in the beginning or middle of the war. The actual experience of the World War, however, belies this general conclusion.

Most of the resources infused into the army in the course of the war are used to compensate for the losses sustained in it. This is borne out by a vast expansion of the rear while troop levels at the front generally remain stable. (By the end of the war, the overall strength of the French army stood at 8,000,000 compared to the initial figure of 4,584,000. While the size of the army almost doubled, the number of servicemen at the front remained at 1,700,000-1,800,000.) The actual increase in the number of combat forces is not that significant; however, it is something to be expected in any war.

In view of the above, comrade Svechin cannot, of course, invoke the experience of the United States to make out his case, especially since, if war were to break out on that continent, the mobilization of its armed forces would not even be perceived as a permanent process.

A concluding remark: We believe that science and art, in one way or another, must serve a practical purpose. Consequently, the theory of permanent mobilization must also be viewed in the context of the practical objectives it is intended to achieve.

We know, however, that all subsequent drafts, supplies of horses and transports, and other support actions taken in the course of the war to maintain existing army units or to deploy new ones, cannot be carried out in ways this is done during the mobilization period, as we understand it. Therefore, it makes no sense and is in fact inadvisable to use the same term to describe phenomena, totally different in form and substance, no matter how many common features an outside and unsophisticated observer may perceive in them. This same consideration annuls any real and practical value of comrade Svechin's theory.

BIBLIOGRAPHY

of publications by and about Aleksandr A. Svechin

Books written by Svechin:

Evoliutsiia voennogo iskusstva [The Evolution of Military Art]. Volume 1. Moscow: Gosvoenizdat, 1927. 383 pp. 4200 copies published.

Evoliutsiia voennogo iskusstva [The Evolution of Military Art]. Volume 2. Moscow: Gosvoenizdat, 1928. 619 pp. 4000 copies published.

Iskusstvo vozhdeniia polka po opytu voiny 1914-1918 gg. [The Art of Leading a Regiment accroding to the Experience of the War, 1914-1918]. Volume 1. Moscow-Leningrad: Gosizdat, 1930. 216 pp. 5000 copies published.

Iskusstvo vozhdeniia polka po opytu voiny 1914-1918 gg. [The Art of Leading a Regiment accroding to the Experience of the War, 1914-1918]. Volume 2. Moscow-Leningrad: Gosizdat, 1930.

Istoriia voennogo iskusstva. Ch. 1. Klassicheskii mir i srednie veka [History of military art. Part 1: The Classical World and the Middle Ages]. Moscow: Vysshei voennyi redatsionnyi sovet, 1922. 136 pp. 2000 copies published.

Istoriia voennogo iskusstva. Ch. 2. Novye veka [History of military art. Part 2: The New Eras]. Moscow: Vysshei voennyi redatsionnyi sovet, 1922. 153 pp. 2000 copies published.

Istoriia voennogo iskusstva. Ch. 3. Noveishee vremia [History of military art. Part 3: Moderns Times]. Moscow: Vysshei voennyi redatsionnyi sovet, 1923. 215 pp. 5000 copies published.

Istoriia voennogo iskusstva. Letskii, chitannye na uskorennom kurse Akademii General'nogo staba RKKA v 1918/19 uchebnom godu [The History of Military Art: Lectures Read at the Accelerated Course of the RKKA Academy of the General Staff in the 1918-1919 Academic Year]. Volume 1. Moscow: Izdanie Akademii general'nogo shtaba RKKA, 1920. 240 pp.

Klauzevits [Clausewitz]. Moscow: Zhurnal'no-gazetnoe ob'edinenie, 1935. 288 pp. 40,000 copies published.

Predrazsudki i boevaia deistvitel'nost' [Prejudices and Combat Reality]. St. Petersburg: Komissioner Voenno-uchebnykh zavedeniia, 1907. 136 pp.

Strategiia [Strategy]. 1st edition. Moscow: Gosvoenizdat, 1926. 396 pp. 5000 copies published.

Strategiia [Strategy]. 2nd edition. Moscow: Voennyi Vestnik, 1927. 263 pp. 5000 copies published.

Strategiia XX veka v pervom etape [Strategy of the 20th Century at the First Stage]. Moscow: Akademiia General'nogo shtaba, 1937. 140 pp. 1000 copies published.

Takticheskie uroki russko-iaposnskoi voiny [Tactical Lessons of the Russo-Japanese War]. St. Petersburg : Officer's Rifle School, 1912. 216 pp. plus 1 map.

V vostochnom otriade: Ot liaoiana k Tiurenchenu i obratno. Marshi, vtrechi, boi, nabliudeniia [In an Eastern Detachment: From Liaoyuan to Turenchen and Back. Marches, Meetings, Battles, Observations]. Warsaw: 1908. 261 pp.

Voina v gorakh. Takticheskoe issledovanie po opytu russko-iaponskoi voiny. [War in the Mountains. A Tactical Study Based on the Experience of the Russo-Japanese War]. Part 1. St. Petersburg: V. A. Berezovskii Publishing House, 1907. 140 pp.

Voina v gorakh. Takticheskoe issledovanie po opytu russko-iaponskoi voiny. [War in the Mountains. A Tactical Study Based on the Experience of the Russo-Japanese War]. Part 2. St. Petersburg: V. A. Berezovskii Publishing House, 1907. 64 pp.

Vozdukhoplavanie v Germanii [Airships in Germany]. St. Petersburg: V. A. Berezovskii Publishing House, 1910. 40 pp.

Books edited and/or translated by Svechin:

Gilchevskii, K. *Boevye deistviia vttoorocherednykh chastei v mirovuiu voinu* [Combat Actions of Secondary Units in the World War]. Moscow: Gosizdat, 1928. 136 pp. 3000 copies published.

Klausevitz, K. *Osnovy strategicheskogo resheniia* [Principles of Strategic Decision]. Translated from t he German. Moscow: Gosizdat, 1924. 31 pp. 5000 copies published.

Ludendorf, E. *Moi vospominaniia o voine 1914-1918 gg.* [My Memoirs on the War, 1914-1918]. Translated f rom the 5th German edition. Volume 1. Moscow: Vysshei voennyi redatsionnyi sovet, 1923. 326 pp. 7000 copies published.

Ludendorf, E. *Moi vospominaniia o voine 1914-1918 gg.* [My Memoirs on the War, 1914-1918]. Translated f rom the 5th German edition. Volume 2. Moscow: Vysshei voennyi redatsionnyi sovet, 1924. 316 pp. 7000 copies published.

von Schlieffen, A. *Kanny* [Cannae]. Translated from the German. Moscow: Vysshei voennyi redaktsionnyi sovet, 1923. 215 pp. 2000 copies published.

Strategiia v trudakh voennykh klassikov [Strategy in the Works of the Military Classics]. Volume 1. Moscow: Vysshei voennyi redaktsionnyi sovet, 1924. 367 pp. 5000 copies published.

Strategiia v trudakh voennykh klassikov [Strategy in the Works of the Military Classics]. Volume 2. Moscow: Gosvoenizdat, 1926. 288 pp. 5000 copies published.

Voenno-istoricheskii sbornik. Trudy Komissii po issledovaniiu i ispol'zovaniiu opyta voiny 1914-1918 gg [Military-History Collection. Works of the Commission on the Study and Use of the Experience of the War of 1914-1918]. Volume 1. Moscow: Tipografiia I. D. Sytina, 1919. 179 pp., plus 16 maps.

Voenno-istoricheskii sbornik. Trudy Komissii po issledovaniiu i ispol'zovaniiu opyta voiny 1914-1918 gg [Military-History Collection. Works of the Commission on the Study and Use of the Experience of the War of 1914-1918]. Volume 2. Moscow: Tipografiia I. D. Sytina, 1919. 224 pp., plus 10 maps.

Voenno-istoricheskii sbornik. Trudy Komissii po issledovaniiu i ispol'zovaniiu opyta voiny 1914-1918 gg [Military-History Collection. Works of the Commission on the Study and Use of the Experience of the War of 1914-1918]. Volume 3. Moscow: Tipografiia I. D. Sytina, 1920. 191 pp., plus 21 maps.

Voenno-istoricheskii sbornik. Trudy Komissii po issledovaniiu i ispol'zovaniiu opyta voiny 1914-1918 gg [Military-History Collection. Works of the Commission on the Study and Use of the Experience of the War of 1914-1918]. Volume 3. Moscow: Tipografiia I. D. Sytina, 1921. 192 pp., plus 16 maps.

Zhadnov, N. *Russkie voennoplennye v mirovoi voine 1914-1918 gg* [Russian Prisoners of War in the War of 1914-1918. Parts 1, 2 and 3. Moscow: Voennaia tipografiia Vseroglavshtaba, 1920. 376 pp.

Books in co-authorship:
(with Iu. D. Romanovskii). *Russko-iaponskaia voina, 1904-1905 gg.* [The Russo-Japanese War, 1904-1905] (Oranienbaum: Izdanie Ofitserskoi Strelkovoi Shkoly, 1910). 387 pp., plus 5 maps.

Articles by Svechin:
"Analiz odnoi oshibki" [Analysis of a mistake], *Voennyi vestnik*, no. 16 (1926), pp. 20-23.

"Aviatsiia i massy" [Aviation and masses], *Vestnik vozdushnogo flota*, no. 2 (1930), pp. 3-7.

"Bezmolvnyi front" [The silent front], *Voennyi vestnik*, no. 6 (1924), pp. 10-19.

"Bol'shaia voennaia programma" [The Grand War Program], *Russkaia mysl'*, god 34, kn. 8 (August 1913), pp. 19-20.

"Chernyi krest" [The Iron Cross], *Voennyi vestnik*, no. 1 (January 1924), pp. 22-26.

"Edinaia voennaia doktrina" [A unified military doctrine], *Voennoe delo*, no. 8 (26 April 1920), pp. 225-233.

"Evoliutsiia operativnogo razvertyvania" [The evolution of operational deployment], *Voina i revoliutsii* a, no. 5 (May 1926), pp. 3-26.

"Evoliutsiia strategicheskikh teorii" [The evolution of strategic theory], in: B. Gorev, ed., *Voina i voennoe iskusstvo v svete istoricheskogo materializma* [War and Military Art in the Light of Historical Materialism] (Moscow: Gosizdat, Otdel voenlit, 1927), pp. 88-100.

"General Ludendorf" [General Ludendorff], *Voennaia mysl' i revoliutsiia*, no. 1 (January-February 1924), pp. 471-475.

"Geroizm ili predatel'stvo?" [Heroism or betrayal?], *Voennaia mysl' i revoliutsiia*, no. 2 (June 1923), pp. 90-97.

"Gosudarstvennyi i frontovoi tyl" [The state and front rear], *Voina i revoliutsiia*, no. 11 (November 1928), pp. 94-108.

"Iaponskaia armiia v 1904 g. i na soremennom etape" [The Japanese Army in 1904 and at present], *Voina i revoliutsiia*, no. 3-4 (March-April 1934), pp. 86-101.

"Inspektorskaia bolezn' i militsiia" [The inspector's illness and the militia], *Vestnik militsionnoi armii*, no. 18 (1920), pp. 21-22.

"Itogi germanskoi strategii" [The results of German strategy], *Voennoe delo*, no. 20 (15 July 1919), pp. 657-662.

"Izuchenie voennoi istorii" [The study of military history], *Voina i revolutsiia*, no. 4 (April 1927), pp . 49-66.

"Kapitalizm v voennom iskusstce" [Capitalism in military art], *Vestnik militsionnoi armii*, no. 4-5 (1921), pp. 17-22.

"Kultur'no-klassovye tipy armii" [Cultural-class types of armies], parts 1-2, *Voennoe delo*, nos. 5-6 (23 February 1919). pp. 225-230.

"Kultur'no-klassovye tipy armii," part 3, Voennoe delo, no. 7-8 (22 March 1919). pp. 307-311.

"Kultur'no-klassovye tipy armii," part 4, *Voennoe delo*, no. 9-10 (31 March 1919). pp. 378-381.

"Kultur'no-klassovye tipy armii," part 5, *Voennoe delo*, no. 13-14 (18 April 1919). pp. 479-482.

"Kultur'no-klassovye tipy armii," part 6, *Voennoe delo*, no. 15-16 (2 May 1919). pp. 541-546.

"Kultur'no-klassovye tipy armii," part 7, *Voennoe delo*, no. 17-18 (15 May 1919). pp. 602-606.

"Kultur'no-klassovye tipy armii," part 8, *Voennoe delo*, no. 19 (30 June 1919). pp. 641-644.

"Kultur'no-klassovye tipy armii," part 9, *Voennoe delo*, no. 21-22 (31 July 1919). pp. 696-701.

"Manevr tekhniki" [Maneuver of technology], *Front nauki i tekhniki*, no. 7 (1934), pp. 35-41.

"Militsiia, kak ideal. Kritika tezisov L. Trotskogo" [The Militia as an ideal. A Critique of L. Trotskii's theses], *Voennoe delo*, no. 11-12 (7 April 1919), pp. 436-438.

"Moshchinnyi vek" [A powerful era], *Vestnik militsionnoi armii*, no. 14 (1921).

"Nemnogo otkrovennosti" [A bit of candor], *Voennyi vestnik*, no. 40 (1925), pp. 26-30.

"Opasnye illiuzii" [Dangerous illusions], *Voennaia mysl' i revoliutsiia*, no. 2 (March 1924), pp. 44-55.

"Osnovy sovremennoi iaponskoi strategii i taktiki" [Principles of modern Japanese strategy and tactics], *Voennaia mysl'*, No. 1 (1937), pp. 141-165.

"Osnovy voennoi doktriny" [Principles of military doctrine], *Voennoe delo*, no. 2 (8 March 1920), pp. 38-41.

"Otvet tov. Kvesinu" [Response to com. Khvesin], *Voennyi vestnik*, no. 44 (24 November 1928), pp. 54-61.

"Otvetstvennost' i takticheskie zadachi" [Responsibility and tactical missions], *Voennaia nauka i revoliutsiia*, no. 2 (December 1921), pp. 177-180.

"Perina, detina, latyna..." [A featherbed, a young fellow, a Philistine], *Voennoe delo*, no. 23-24 (15 August 1919), pp. 751-752.

"Pis'mo v redaktsiiu" [Letter to the editor], *Voennyi vestnik*, no. 48 (December 1928), p. 62.

"Pochemu my ne uspevaem v taktike?" [Why aren't we successful in tactics?], *Voennyi vestnik*, no. 4 (1926), pp. 4-6.

"Russkaia, frantsuzskaia i angliiskaia armii v 1916 godu" [The Russian, French and British Armies in 191 6], *Voennoe delo*, no. 32-33 (10 November 1919), pp. 984-987.

"Strategicheskii ocherk Russko-iaponskoi voiny ot nachala kampanii do srazheniia pod Liaoianom vkliuchitel'no" [A strategic outline of the Russo-Japanese War from beginning of the campaign to the engagement at Liaoyuan inclusively], *Voennyi sbornik*, no. 3 (March 1907), pp. 47-69; no. 4 (April 1907), pp. 47-63; and no. 5 (May 1907), pp. 47-69.

"Strategicheskie i operativnye etiudy" [Strategic and operational studies] in the book *Sbornik Voennoi akademii RKKA im. M. V. Frunze* [Collection of the M. V. Frunze Military Academy of the RKKA]. Volume 1. Moscow: Izdanie Voennoi akademii RKKA im. M.V. Frunze, 1928, pp. 30-49.

"Takticheskii fakt" [A tactical fact], *Voina i revoliutsiia*, no. 7-8 (July-August 1934), pp. 42-53.

"Teoriia i prikladnoi metod v izuchenii strategii" [Theory and the applied method in the study of strategy], *Pod znamenom Il'icha*, no. 7 (August 1925), pp. 39-41.

"U istochnikov operativnoi mysli" [The sources of operational thought], *Krasnaia zvezda*, nos. 57, 59 and 60 (1929)

untitled, *Krasnye zori*, no. 11 (November 1924).

untitled, *Krasnaia zvezda*, no. 135 (1929).

"Voennaia igra" [The war game], *Voennaia mysl' i revoliutsiia*, no. 3 (July 1923), pp. 76-80.

"Voennaia igra" [The war game], reprinted in *Voennaia mysl*, no. 10 (October 1988), pp. 54-57.

"Voennoe iskusstvo" [Military Art], *Bol'shaia sovetskaia entsiklopediia*, 1st edition, vol. 12 (Moscow: 1928), pp. 218-229.

"Voennoe iskusstvo v budushchei voine" [Military art in war of the future], *Pravda*, no. 97 (1927).

"Vtoraia chast' mirovoi voiny" [The second part of the World War], *Voennaia mysl' i revoliutsiia*, no. 5 (September-October 1923), pp. 23-37.

"Zadachi voenno-istoricheskoi komissii" [Tasks of the military-history commission], *Voennoe delo*, no. 1 (11 January 1919), pp. 48-49.

Works about Svechin:

Ageev, A. "Voennyi teoretik i voennyi istorik A. A. Svechin" [The military theorist and military historian A. A. Svechin], *Voenno-istoricheskii zhurnal*, no. 8 (August 1978), pp. 126-128.

Bukhartsev. "Problema voin i dialecticheskie" potugi prof. Svechina" [The problem of wars and the vain "dialectical" attempts of Professor Svechin]. *Bol'shevik*, no. 1 (January 1931).

Khvesin, T. "O pervom tome knigi A. Svechina 'Evoliutsiia voennogo iskusstva'" [On the first volume of A. Svechin's book *The Evolution of Military Art*], *Voennyi vestnik*, no. 43 (17 November 1928), pp. 57-64.

Khvesin, T. "Dlinno, no neubeditel'no" [Long, but unconvincing], *Voennyi vestnik*, no. 46 (8 December 1928), pp. 57-61.

Kokoshin, A. A. "A. A. Svechin. O voine i politike" [A. A. Svechin. On War and Politics]. *Mezhdunaro dnaia zhizn'*, no. 10 (October 1988), pp. 133-142.

Kokoshin, Andrei A. "A. A. Svechin: On War and Politics. *International Afairs*, no. 11 (November 1988), pp. 118-126.

Kokoshin, A. A. and V. N. Lobov, "Predvidenie (General Svechin ob evoliutsii voennogo iskusstva)" [Foresight (General Svechin on the evolution of military art)], *Znamia*, no. 2 (February 1990), pp. 170-182.

"Po povodu polemini tt. Svechina i Khesina" [Regarding the polemic between comrades Svechin and Khesin], *Voennyi vestnik*, no. 2 (12 January 1929), pp. 61-62.

Protiv reaktsionnykh teorii na voenno-nauchnom fronte. Kritika strategicheskikh i voenno-istoricheskikh vzgliadov prof. Svechina [Against Reactionary Theories on the Military-Scientific Front. A critique of the strategic and military-history views of Professor Svechin.]. Moscow: Gosvoenizdat, 1931. 104 pp. 10,000 copies published.

Tukhachevskii, M. "Protiv reaktsionnykh teorii na voenno-nauchnom fronte. (Kritika strategicheskikh i voenno-istoricheskikh vzgliadov prof. Svechina)," *Problemy marskizma*, no. 8-9 (1931), pp. 187-209.

INDEX